Prokofiev

From Russia to the West

1891–1935

Prokofiev

From Russia to the West
1891–1935

David Nice

Yale University Press
New Haven and London

For information about this and other Yale University Press publications, please contact
U.S. Office: sales.press@yale.edu yalebooks.com
Europe Office: sales@yaleup.co.uk www.yaleup.co.uk

Set in Columbus MT by Northern Phototypesetting Co. Ltd, Bolton
Printed in Great Britain by Biddles Ltd, Guildford and Kings Lynn
ISBN 0–300–09914–2 (hbk.)

A catalogue record for this book is available from the Library of Congress and the British Library

2 4 6 8 10 9 7 5 3 1

For Jeremy

Contents

Illustrations

Preface

One fine day in Moscow in the summer of 1993, I returned to my lodgings flourishing a mint condition, two-volume full score of Prokofiev's Soviet opera *Semyon Kotko*, purchased in a music shop for next to nothing. The schoolteacher taking tea with my landlady looked at me sternly. 'That's bad propaganda from our shameful past', she remarked, 'and no-one will ever perform it.' Although I knew there was much good music in the work, I could hardly contradict her prophecy. Only a few years later the conductor Valery Gergiev proved us wrong by initiating a full-scale production at the Maryinsky Theatre in St Petersburg; this was the most spectacular in a series of rehabilitations of Prokofiev's Soviet-era works which had begun in 1991, the centenary of the composer's birth, and which looks set to continue throughout 2003, the fiftieth anniversary of his death.

Access to the whole range of Prokofiev's music has increased dramatically over the past decade. The wider public now knows there is much more to his multifaceted musical personality than the striding Montagues and Capulets from *Romeo and Juliet*, the slightly off-kilter tunefulness of *Peter and the Wolf* and the mock-military manoeuvres of *Lieutenant Kijé*. British choral sopranos happily cry 'Stalin' on a top C in airings of the ambiguous 1939 'birthday toast' *Zdravitsa* and concert-goers thrill to live performances of the *Cantata for the 20th Anniversary of the Soviet Revolution*; the recording industry's obsession with 'the complete' has given us nearly all the songs – good and bad, personal and party-line – on CD. Little remains unavailable in printed form, and the work of the Prokofiev Association in tandem with the publisher Boosey & Hawkes is quickly filling in the gaps.

A seemingly insatiable appetite for what Russian composers would or would not do in Stalin's Soviet Union still overshadows our acquaintance with the middle-period works Prokofiev composed while he was based in Paris. Perhaps the relative complexity or lack of surface glitter in these pieces will never attract the music-loving public at large. As I prepared this first volume of Prokofiev's life and music, I came to know better such underrated scores as the Fourth and Fifth Piano

Concertos, the ballet *Sur le Borysthène* and the transitional *Symphonic Song*, which came as revelations. Not only could one understand the composer's observation from the perspective of his later years that after a second or third play-through the 'outlines of a real face' emerge in the shape of unorthodox and irregular melodic lines; it was also abundantly clear that no creative crisis loomed for Prokofiev before the heads-or-tails return to Russia in 1936. This is as evident in his writings of the time as it is in the music; he believed totally in what he created and was simply trying to find new means of clothing the essentially lyrical self-expression which remains a constant throughout his composing life. In this, as in so much else, the ideological cold war waged between Soviet critics readily dismissive of their leading composer's decadent time in the West and American critics who were liable to doubt the validity of Prokofiev's Soviet-era music still leaves its mark. Bland references to the 'triumph of the human spirit' in the later works and drying-up of inspiration in the music of the early 1930s continue to ape the party line. There is a simple corrective: if one studies and listens to the music, a greater complexity, if not the instant truth about 'what the composer wanted', will make itself felt. There are the usual dangers of over-interpretation, in the absence of Prokofiev's own subjective commentary on his works; but the journey from his utterly characteristic early fantasies to the monuments of the later years provides plenty of clues to a consistent, self-renewing personality.

Less straightforward is the relationship between the artist's life and works. No composer, on the face of it, is less representative than Prokofiev of the Dostoyevskian chaos, contradictions and darkness the romantic Westerner expects from a Russian creative artist. Prokofiev's punctuality, love of chess-like stratagems and suspicion of the chance element in games as in life are at odds with the fantasy of his music. Perhaps there is a clue in the prose style of his autobiographical writings and diaries; clarity is the essence, but sudden whimsical turns of phrase can round off a perfectly ordinary sentence with a flourish. Otherwise, very little in the immense body of work that confronts the biographer gives the game away. It is easy enough to find Prokofiev's love of the fantastical in *The Giant*, the opera he wrote as a nine-year-old, and to follow the line through to *The Love for Three Oranges*; but nothing accounts for the much deeper vein of diablerie – 'subcutaneous' music, as the late Christopher Palmer perfectly described it – in *The Fiery Angel*. No dabbler in ouija boards or visitor to fortune-tellers, Prokofiev drew the spiritual line at an attachment to Christian Science which began in the early 1920s; but even this was to try and give meaning to his ambition and achievements. It is one of the many terrible ironies of his life that his Christian Science teacher in the mid-1930s advised Prokofiev not to be afraid of 'too much success', driving him back, at what turned out to be the worst possible time, to live in the Soviet Union where that success seemed most readily to hand.

The many character-traits that emerge clearly from his letters and writings warn against a one-dimensional portrait. Thumbnail sketches of Prokofiev tend to emphasize his arrogance and solipsism. The adored only child who found himself, through anomalies in the Russian education system at the beginning of the nineteenth century, much the youngest in his class at the St Petersburg Conservatory, may have behaved at times like a spoilt brat; the talented young composer at large in the Paris of the 1920s could be outrageously rude to unwelcome acquaintances. Yet these are only facets of a complex personality. The individual who springs to life from the 40 boxes of letters and papers at the Prokofiev Archive in Goldsmiths College, London, has many faces. He is intemperate and undiplomatic to agents and performers who he feels are lacking in their duty to his reputation, but infinitely kind and patient to young music-lovers who seek advice or autographs (as the typically candid reply reproduced on page xviii vividly illustrates). He can be negligent of colleagues who believe themselves to be his intimate friends, and his friendship is not readily given; but he is touchingly loyal to people with whom he formed relationships in his youth, and an astonishingly tender series of letters to his mother's sister, his aunt Katya, reveals his concern for relatives suffering in the Soviet Russia he left behind. It is a concern that extends to painstaking arrangements for their financial well-being and it reveals, too, that he was far from naive about the regime's power to dominate and imprison the innocent.

Delicate questions concerning the breakdown of Prokofiev's first marriage, and the legality of his second, are not the subject of the present volume. His dynamic and volatile relationship with his first wife Lina, however, embodied much more than the tears and quarrels which an outsider like Nicolas Nabokov emphasizes at the expense of so much else. The charming, cultured and gently humorous character of Prokofiev's sons, Sviatoslav and Oleg, remains the strongest tribute to a firm, perhaps occasionally remote but always loving father. The family's continuing devotion to the deeper understanding of Sergey Sergeyevich Prokofiev speaks more eloquently than this biography possibly could of a man whose greatest gift remains, as his otherwise evasive colleague Igor Stravinsky so vividly described it, his force of personality.

The Prokofiev family leaves me with a final quandary over crucial material which I have only touched upon: just as my edited manuscript went to print, Sviatoslav's decoding of Prokofiev's full diaries from 1907 to 1933, written in the composer's characteristic shorthand with the vowels missing, appeared in a Russian edition ('sprkfv') beautifully presented in two volumes by Sviatoslav's son Serge. Running to nearly 1600 pages, the diaries call out for a full translation. They will provide a rich autobiographical complement to the new source material used here and will enhance our understanding of Prokofiev's complex personality. The year 2003 sees a disembargo, after 50 years, on further papers in Russian archives. It is possible that this new material will shed further light on the composer's years in the Soviet Union, a period on which this otherwise prolific correspondent and diarist has left little private commentary other than his works (a minefield of speculation). With or without fresh sources, I hope that my next volume, *The Soviet Years*, will be the better for the time spent pondering the final legacy.

The present volume is the result of chance conversations, meetings with remarkable people and incidental acquaintances without which it would not have taken the present form. Its roots were put down during a trip to Leningrad, as St Petersburg was then, in early 1991, to prepare British audiences for a new production of *War and Peace* conducted by Valery Gergiev. Talking to the director of the television transmission, Peter Maniura, about some of Prokofiev's later works, I found he was as baffled as I was by the bland face value at which they were usually taken. The notes he asked me to write for the London Symphony Orchestra's Prokofiev centenary series made me think longer and harder about the music.

Some years later I felt ready to embark on a lengthier project than short biographies and journalism. I am indebted to Barry Millington, who was then reviews editor of the *BBC Music Magazine*, for encouraging my thoughts about Prokofiev and putting me in touch with, among others, Robert Baldock at Yale University Press. His tactful prompting and willingness to let the work take a natural course beyond its initial deadline were reflected in the patient encouragement of his colleague at Yale, Malcolm Gerratt. My first task was to take a rudimentary knowledge of Russian to proficient reading level, and I am delighted to have spent several years as the pupil of the translator Joan Pemberton Smith. Our treasured reading of Pushkin and Chekhov will, I hope, soon be resumed. I acquired my teacher at the same time as I made the acquaintance of Noëlle Mann, curator of the Serge Prokofiev Archive at Goldsmiths College; Joan and I were fellow members of the Kalina Choir, specializing in Russian music, which Noëlle was running and conducting. After many months spent poring over documents, and so much help and support in difficult times, it is hardly surprising that our challenging acquaintance has developed into a valued friendship. It continues through a shared teaching engagement at Goldsmiths College, our work on the invaluable *Three Oranges* journal – a publication way beyond the usual standards of the enthusiasts' newsletter – and plans for 2003.

I had already encountered the charm and enthusiasm of Oleg, the younger of Prokofiev's two sons, at several round-table discussions; it was a privilege to come to know him better in the company of his initially more reserved but no less gracious brother Sviatoslav. One sunny afternoon in the summer of 1998 we parted company with plans to talk again after his return from a family holiday. The list of 'questions for Oleg' with which I had finally decided to burden him, when I could be sure not to retread familiar ground, remained unanswered with his sudden death in Alderney at the age of sixty-nine. Oleg's widow Frances, who gave so unforgettable and accepting a speech at his memorial service, later wrote in the inaugural issue of *Three Oranges*: 'it strikes me now that as he got older, his momentum speeded up somewhat and that his welcome of innovation and change, not necessarily the hallmark of later years, was a characteristic'. This was as true of the man as it was of his work as a highly original painter and sculptor; I remember the benign surprise with which he told me of hearing an experimental piece of music by his son Gabriel, and especially the expression with which he declared it 'quite good, actually'. In this context I must also mention the deaths of Christopher Palmer, a good friend of Oleg and Frances whose unrealized Prokofiev biography would have been graced by a unique and thought-provoking style, and more recently of Sviatoslav's wife Nadezhda, who greeted me so warmly in their Paris flat. The detailed advice of Sviatoslav on the later chapters of this first volume has been of incalculable value, and I am honoured to have come to know him better. His son Serge has been tirelessly involved with many aspects of the Serge Prokofiev Association; I thank him especially for his generous help with family photographs and permissions.

Much Russian warmth and generosity greeted me on my visits to Moscow and St Petersburg and it is impossible to list everyone responsible. In Moscow I thank especially Natalya Savkina and Viktor Varunts, who helped me negotiate the daunting unapproachability of RGALI, the State Archive of Literature and Art; Marina Rakhmanova and the delightful staff at the Glinka State Central Museum of Musical Culture; Marina Sokolinskaya; Yulya and Andrey Kunin and their extended family; and Sasha Dugdale at the British Council, generous donor of a small grant which helped with an all-too-brief visit. In St Petersburg my thanks go to Sima Romashova and her family, Katya Novikova during her time at the Maryinsky Theatre, and the proffered assistance of Elizabeth White – not taken but much appreciated.

A more general thanks goes to all the American organizations and archives which responded so promptly and helpfully to my inquiries, especially Lee Grady at the State Historical Society of Wisconsin, Marc Mandel at the Boston Symphony Orchestra and Frank Vilella at the Chicago Symphony Orchestra. My thanks are due to Jon Baxendale for setting the music examples and to Margot Levy for compiling the index. Other home thoughts go to Carl and Sally Attwood, Fiona Bantock, Simon Bell, Colin Dunn in the hire library of Boosey and Hawkes, David Fanning, Marina Frolova Walker, Marianna Hazeldine, Stephen Johnson and Kate Jones, Charles Kerry for his advice on the manuscript, the Peakes of Westhill, Ledbury, for two idyllic August fortnights, Jane Rosen of the Society for Co-operation in Russian and Soviet Studies for the long-term loan of several essential Russian texts, and Gerald Stonehill for his advice on Prokofiev's Duo-Art piano rolls. Above all, I thank Jeremy O'Sullivan for his patience and his tireless help, especially in the uphill struggle of the past few months.

David Nice
London, January 2003

Acknowledgments

Shorter extracts from published works are fully credited in the notes and bibliography. Special thanks for permissions are due to RGALI, the Russian State Archive of Literature and Art, for permission to make extensive translations, and for the use of several music examples, from the volume of Prokofiev-Myaskovsky letters (*S. S. Prokofiev I N. Ya. Myaskovsky: Perepiska*; Moscow: Sovietsky Kompozitor, Moscow); to Harlow Robinson for several lines reproduced from his translations of the early, unpublished correspondence between Prokofiev and Eleonora Damskaya (*Selected Letters of Sergei Prokofiev*; Boston: Northeastern University Press, 1998); and to Yelena Poldyaeva for her selection from the Prokofiev-Souvchinsky correspondence (in *Pyotr Souvchinsky I yevo vremya*; tor, Moscow: Kompozitor, 1999).

The Prokofiev family is to be thanked for its kind permission to use so many of the photographs and the quotations from Prokofiev's juvenilia (in music examples 2a, 3, 4, 5, 6, 7a, 8). Copyright and permissions for other music examples are as follows: exx 2b and 71 © Copyright 1936 by Hawkes & Son (London) Ltd.; exx.9 and 10 © Copyright 1917 by Hawkes & Son (London) Ltd.; ex.13 © Copyright by Anton J Benjamin GmbH; exx. 14, 19 , 22 and 23 by kind permission of Robert Forberg Musikverlag GmbH; ex.15 © Copyright 1947 Hawkes & Son (London) Ltd.; ex.16 © Copyright 1998 by Boosey & Hawkes Music Publishers Ltd.; ex.17 © Copyright 1998 by Boosey & Hawkes Music Publishers Ltd.; ex.18 © Copyright 1978 by Hawkes & Son (London) Ltd.; exx.20a and 21 © Copyright 1980 by Boosey & Hawkes Music Publishers Ltd.; ex.20b © Copyright 1905 by Adolph Furstner. U.S. Copyright renewed. Copyright assigned 1943 to Hawkes & Son (London) Ltd (A Boosey & Hawkes Company) for the World ex Germany, Italy, Portugal, and the former territories of the USSR (ex Estonia, Latvia and Lithuania); exx. 24 and 25 © Copyright 1925 by Hawkes & Son (London) Ltd.; exx.26b and 27 © Copyright 1923 by Hawkes & Son (London) Ltd.; exx. 28 and 48a © Copyright 1931 by Hawkes & Son (London) Ltd.; ex.29 © Copyright 1922, 1932 by Hawkes & Son (London) Ltd.; exx.30, 31 and 32 © Copyright 1931 by Hawkes

& Son (London) Ltd.; ex.33a © Copyright 1926 by Hawkes & Son (London) Ltd.; ex.34 © Copyright 1933 by Hawkes & Son (London) Ltd.; ex.35 © Copyright 1922 by Hawkes & Son (London) Ltd.; ex.36 © Copyright 1921 by Hawkes & Son (London) Ltd.; exx.37 and 38 © Copyright 1922 by Hawkes & Son (London) Ltd.; ex.39 © Copyright 1922 by Hawkes & Son (London) Ltd.; ex.41 © Copyright 1921 by Hawkes & Son (London) Ltd.; ex.42 © Copyright 1923 by Hawkes & Son (London) Ltd.; exx. 43a, 51, 52 and 53 © Copyright 1957, 1977 by Hawkes & Son (London) Ltd.; ex.43b © Copyright 1923 by Hawkes & Son (London) Ltd.; exx.44 and 45 © Copyright 1925 by Hawkes & Son (London) Ltd.; ex.46 © Copyright 1927 by Hawkes & Son (London) Ltd.; ex.47 © Copyright 1929 by Hawkes & Son (London) Ltd.; exx.48b and 49 © Copyright 1928 by Hawkes & Son (London) Ltd.; ex.50 © Copyright 1948 by Hawkes & Son (London) Ltd.; exx.54 and 55 © Copyright 1929 by Hawkes & Son (London) Ltd., © Copyright in the USA by Boosey & Hawkes, Inc.; ex.56 © Copyright 1930 by Hawkes & Son (London) Ltd.; ex.57 © Copyright 1931 by Hawkes & Son (London) Ltd.; exx.58a and 59 © Copyright 1937 by Hawkes & Son (London) Ltd.; ex.58b © Copyright Boosey & Hawkes Music Publishers Ltd for the UK, British Commonwealth (ex Canada), Eire and South Africa; exx.60 and 61 © Copyright 1932 by Hawkes & Son (London) Ltd.; ex.62 © Copyright Boosey & Hawkes Music Publishers Ltd for the UK, British Commonwealth (ex Canada), Eire and South Africa; ex.63 and 64 © Copyright 1936 by Hawkes & Son (London) Ltd.; ex.65 © Copyright 1933 by Hawkes & Son (London) Ltd.; ex.66 © 1935 by Hawkes and Son (London) Ltd.; ex.67 © Copyright 1938 by Hawkes & Son (London) Ltd.; ex.68a and 69a © Copyright Boosey & Hawkes Music Publishers Ltd for the UK, British Commonwealth (ex Canada), Eire and South Africa); ex.70 © Copyright Boosey & Hawkes Music Publishers Ltd for the UK, British Commonwealth (ex Canada), Eire and South Africa; ex.72 © Copyright 1937 by Hawkes & Son (London) Ltd. All examples listed other than exx.14, 19, 22 and 23 by permission of Boosey & Hawkes Music Publishers Ltd.

Every effort has been made to trace copyright holders; any mistakes or omissions will be corrected in the second volume.

A note on transliteration and dates

There is a certain idiosyncrasy in my transliteration of Russian names and titles but I have endeavoured to tread as fine a line as possible between how the Russian sounds and the spellings well established in the West. Prokofiev was caught between several versions of his name: to the French he was Serge Prokofieff, and he frequently signed himself as such (because he had a French governess, 'Serge' was a familiar form from his youth); his English publishers Boosey & Hawkes, who inherited the Paris-based Éditions Russes de Musique which issued most of his works, use 'Prokofieff' to this day. 'Prokofiev' remains the English standard, though strictly speaking it should be 'Prokofyev'. Western familiarity leaves us with Diaghilev and Chaliapin rather than Dyagilev and Shalyapin; but 'Rakhmaninov' and 'Skryabin' have become familiar through more recent usage. The cyrillic 'e' becomes 'ye' at the beginning of names and after vowels or hard/soft signs; the prime that usually represents the soft sign has been omitted.

In Russia before 1 February 1918 the Julian calendar was used, according to which dates in the nineteenth century were 12 days behind the Gregorian calendar, used in western Europe, and 13 days behind in the early twentieth century. Throughout the first part of this book, I have used these 'Old Style' dates as Prokofiev, his correspondents and his critics used them. On the few occasions when Prokofiev wrote home from England or France during his early travels, both dates are given.

MANGER HOTELS · NEW YORK CITY

HOTELS
UNDER SAME
MANAGEMENT
WOLCOTT
ENDICOTT
HERMITAGE
WOODSTOCK
CUMBERLAND
GRAND
TIMES SQUARE
YORK
MANGER
BELL APARTMENT
MARTHA WASHINGTON
ALSO
PLAZA HOTEL
CHICAGO.

GREAT NORTHERN HOTEL
109-121 W. 56TH STREET
MAIN ENTRANCE
118 W. 57TH STREET
TELEPHONE CIRCLE 1900

March 28
1930

S. Halpern, Richmond Hill
N.Y.

Dear Mr. Halpern,

Your question is too big to be answered in a few words – and for ~~more~~ many I have no time, as I am sailing to Europe in a few hours.

Anyhow, I think that ~~a~~ quite an important point of my success in music is the fact that I always worked for the sake of music itself, and not for ~~a~~ the sake of personal success.

In March 1930, just before the end of his latest American tour, Prokofiev received a letter from Seymour Halpern, a 16-year-old New York high school student. Halpern requested an answer to the question 'What do you attribute your success in life to?' The part of his reply reproduced here is characteristic both of Prokofiev's attitude to helping young people, whether he knew them personally or not, and of his simple, utterly sincere philosophy of work.

Part One

Russia: Childhood and Youth

1891–1918

Prologue
Speak, memory

Two great creative artists, exhausted by years of war and Soviet rule, meet in the Kremlin Hospital. The convalescent is the film director Sergey Eisenstein, felled by a heart attack in February of the year in question, 1946. He tells his visitor, Sergey Prokofiev, that 'when life is finished, all that remains is a postscript'. Prokofiev's prescription for the most useful of postscripts is the assemblage and publication of Eisenstein's memoirs.

Such advice is typical of Prokofiev and his belief in the salvation of work. He had followed it himself long before the postscript era of his own life. (At the time of the hospital conversation the worst was yet to come for both men, first with the party's attacks on Part Two of Eisenstein's *Ivan the Terrible*, then with Zhdanov's accusations of 'formalism' in Prokofiev's music.) The long autobiography of Prokofiev's early years, surely the most detailed ever written by a composer and the equal of Carl Nielsen's childhood memoirs in bringing the past alive, was begun in July 1937. This was at the height of Stalin's purges and at a time when, according to his elder son Sviatoslav, Prokofiev kept his thoughts about the disappearance of friends and relatives to himself; life could be over with a knock on the door. Composition was an essential way of staying sane, though an increasingly constricted one; recreating the Russia to which Prokofiev was still so deeply attached may have been more important. His own creed could have been that when life is uncertain and you doubt the validity of your experience, you should revisit the past and assemble your memories as thoroughly and precisely as you can. Later, in the grim first months after the Soviet Union found itself propelled into the Second World War, Prokofiev wrote a shorter biography which went beyond the early days at the St Petersburg Conservatory, now neatly summarized, to the watershed year of 1936 (it is referred to throughout this book as the 'short autobiography'). The attempt to put into a Soviet context his experiences in America, France and Germany was a brave venture involving few compromises. In 1949 Prokofiev wrote to a colleague asking for further archive material which would have enabled him to extend the longer work; but for the remaining three years of his life, when he was still composing so much, his postscript remained no more than a dream.

It helped that Prokofiev was a disciplined literary stylist and that he had hoarded and organized so much material from his past (perhaps because his doting governess and aunts had helped to give permanent form to each of his youthful musical utterances). His skill was to outline an event with exemplary clarity and then, in a blunt or witty one-liner, to give his present, often highly idiosyncratic and invariably self-critical view of it. Unfortunately much of the fuller memoir remains unappreciated by non-Russian admirers of his music. The American edition of 1979 is well presented and illustrated, but among the many passages it omits are several crucial impressions of childhood and Prokofiev's colourful descriptions of his forays into the world of chess, giving the false impression that the musical sphere was the only one in which he moved assuredly. The English edition, edited by Francis King, is shorter still. I am indebted to the Russian publication for a fuller portrait of the artist as a child and young man than I had thought it possible to create. Having the composer's sane and gently ironic voice as a guide through his early years, however honed and polished, is a fine substitute for knowing him. Later, when the multiple personalities in the correspondence take over – and so many of the letters have been preserved by Prokofiev, the most meticulous of self-archivists – one gets closer still to the composer and his character.

I
Of giants and battleships
1891–1904

All happy families resemble one another, Tolstoy tells us; and well-to-do happy families in the Russian countryside before the Revolution, so countless émigré accounts would have us believe, were no exception. Prokofiev may have spent his childhood on a country estate, like so many other members of the Russian intelligentsia, but his circumstances were relatively unusual. He was brought up by his parents and his maternal grandmother in a squat, one-storey building shaded on one side by a chestnut tree and with a lilac beneath one of the bedroom windows. Around it spread an orchard which ran down to the confluence of two streams; beyond that lay the infinite Ukrainian steppe, broken by black-earth fields, the occasional ancient burial mound and a fast-developing network of railways and stations which would eventually render the landscape unrecognizable. This was Sontsovka in the Bakhmut district of the Ukraine, then still part of Russia, two and a half days' train journey from Moscow and 25 kilometres from the nearest railway station. Seryozhenka, as his mother called him, shared the luxury of privileged country children in joining the rituals and tasks of the peasants, but his father was no *barin* or country squire: he merely ran the estate for the landowner.

Sergey Alexeyevich Prokofiev, a Muscovite by birth, had chosen agronomy over chemistry by going on from commercial high school to the Petrovsko-Razumovskaya Agricultural Academy, where he had steered clear of the occasional student riot but refused to betray his colleagues. On reflection the composer thought that his father's dislike of the startlingly violent, even bleak, ending to his precocious only child's first opera stemmed from a fear of clashing with authority: 'it was not for his nine-year-old son to play at being a revolutionary so thoughtlessly'.[1] Yet Sergey Alexeyevich remained essentially a typical liberal of the 1860s, and the woman he was to marry shared his enlightened views. In the eyes of her old schoolfriend, Olya Filimonova, Marya Grigoryevna Zhitkova was hardly pretty but possessed a good figure as well as wit and liveliness; Filimonova believed 'her future husband was attracted to her intellectually'.[2] They were both, their future son was to note with pride, the cleverest members of their respective families.

Marya Grigoryevna was a friend of the Smirnov girls, daughters of Sergey Alexeyevich's older sister Nadezhda and her husband Mikhail, with whom the serious-minded agriculture student happened to be living in Moscow. Originally serfs from the region in which the Tolstoy family held the now famous estate of Yasnaya Polyana, the Zhitkovs had done well by the emancipation of 1861, but the business affairs of Marya's father did not prosper and the Smirnovs seem to have regarded the Zhitkov girls as poor relations who were nevertheless lively, cultured company for their daughters. Once Marya had overcome her fear of the bearded, bespectacled student and fallen in love with him, Nadezhda and Mikhail made it clear that a dowryless girl would not be welcome in the family. Moved by a written testament by his mother as a young girl in love, Prokofiev quotes in his autobiography from a dignified letter she sent his father, dated 10 November 1876, in which she tells him 'Apart from myself, with bitter regrets, I can offer you nothing, and I wish no more from you'.[3]

The young agronomist, in turn, could offer her only a life of enterprising struggle. With a relatively small sum left to him by his parents, he had bought a small estate, Nikolayevka in the Smolensk district, where they lived following their wedding in the summer of 1877. Yet it was a costly enterprise: if Sergey Alexeyevich was to put his progressive ideas into practice he would need to invest in new machinery he could ill afford. The solution to their problems came from a wealthier, former fellow-student at the Agricultural Academy, Dmitry Sontsov. He lived on one of his family estates near Kursk but needed an educated soil engineer to help with the other, a less appealing prospect in the remote Ukrainian steppes. It must, the composer conjectures, have been a wilderness when his parents arrived a year after their marriage, and it was a risk: although the basic salary was acceptable, it would take years to bring a welcome profit from Sontsov's incentive of 20 per cent commission on the annual yield. Yet Sontsov clearly meant well, and his promise not to interfere was an added attraction. The Prokofievs remained in Sontsovka for the rest of their married life.

The year of Seryozhenka's birth, 1891, was disastrous for rural Russia. The harvest failed and famine followed; the only benefit was the brief increase of power for the *zemstva*, or local communes, in the last years of Alexander III's reign. The affliction of 1891 was one the Prokofievs were able to weather. Their real concern must have been for the survival of their new son, born on 15 April (27 April new style) and fed by a robust wet-nurse to avoid the complications which had brought about the deaths of two daughters born before him, nurtured on their mother's milk. The first, Marya, had lived only to the age of two, while her sister Lyubov died at nine months. The losses were a further blow to the unfortunate mother's already faltering religious faith, but she did not make her 'Sergushchenka' aware of the circumstances beyond dressing him in girl's clothes until the age of three and devoting herself to him wholeheartedly and understandably.

Social life in rural Ukraine was more stultifying than it might have been on estates nearer to Moscow or St Petersburg, and the only firm friends the Prokofievs were to make in all their time there were the doctor and the veterinary surgeon, who was to become one of Seryozhenka's many older companions. There were visits from his mother's vivacious sister Tatyana (doting Aunt Tanya), and a significant excursion to their elder sister's estate at Pokrovskoye was to bring the young Prokofiev closer to the more conventional jollity of a large, well-to-do family in the country. (This sister, Katya, had married Alexander Dmitrievich Rayevsky, descendant of the famous general in the 1812 campaign; his post in the bureaucratic, snobbery-ridden civil service was equivalent to that of a colonel in the army.) Prokofiev's only playmates of a similar age in Sontsovka were the children of the household staff and the peasants who lived in the nearby village – an admirably democratic upbringing, we might imagine, until Prokofiev tells us that they all had to call him *barchuk* ('little master'), address him with the formal Russian second person 'vy', never the intimate 'ty', and be sure not to annoy him. A certain sternness in his character, he fancifully believed, may have come from the milk of the sturdy wet-nurse, but there was also a residual arrogance to be traced, surely, to his little friends carefully guarding their tongues in front of the adored only child.

Prokofiev's parents differed in their attitude to the folk in their charge. Sergey Alexeyevich made a point of calling every peasant on the estate *bratyets* ('little brother'); to him, Prokofiev wrote, 'matters of culture and humanity were basic qualities',[4] while Marya Grigoryevna's view of intellect and talent, attained in her case in the face of considerable hardship, led her to be altogether more aloof to the peasants; nevertheless her philanthropy towards the local population was not distant. Whether his parents set up the local school Prokofiev was unable to remember, but his mother certainly took up the role of practical leader among the peasants. Teaching soon exhausted her patience but she zealously carried out the duties of the school's sponsor for the next 25 years and was awarded a gold medal for her pains.

While Sergey Alexeyevich respected music with a certain philosophical detachment, his wife loved it with all her heart. Looking back, Prokofiev made no attempt to sentimentalize her musicianship, or claim that she had pianistic skills which might have flourished in a different environment, but he accorded her the virtues of persistence, love and taste. The embryonic composer was treated to six hours of piano music a day, and from the cradle onwards Beethoven's earlier piano sonatas were constant companions (there is, surely, a homage to the brilliant C major passage of op.27 no.1, a work well within Marya Grigoryevna's grasp, in the Ninth Sonata's slow movement). The young Seryozha fell asleep to the sounds of Beethoven, Schubert or Chopin below, just as his second son Oleg would remember dozing to the strains of his father practising the Third Piano Concerto three and a half decades later. Marya Grigoryevna's judgment of contemporary Russian music proved less sound: she found the solid, foursquare virtues of Anton Rubinstein, founder of the St Petersburg Conservatory, superior to the genius he and his brother Nikolay had helped to nurture, Pyotr Ilyich Tchaikovsky. In a few years' time, she would have her son to enlighten her as she accompanied him to the concert halls of the two great cities.

Prokofiev began to manifest signs of musical talent at the age of four. Sitting alongside his mother as she practised middle-range *études*, he was allowed to improvise in the top two octaves – the first of her many wise indulgences. He wanted to claim the music he heard as his own, but already he had original ideas which bore no correspondence to the ornamental, more or less musical doodlings he committed to paper. Finally his mother explained some fundamental rules of notation and, with all the care of a novice, wrote down the five-and-a-half-year-old's first piece. Entitled *Indian Galop*, for the charmingly absurd reason that the boy had half-heard talk of the famine then rife on the subcontinent, it otherwise claims our interest only in that it was originally in F major but without a B flat – which, Prokofiev wryly notes, 'does not betoken a sympathy with the Lydian mode';[5] he was merely forgivably shy of the black notes. Several bars survive in the catalogue of early works the list-crazy young composer undertook in 1902, this time with the B flat inserted, as Prokofiev's mother had insisted.[6]

Three exercises in forms that would last Prokofiev a lifetime, a waltz and two marches, were joined by a rondo (again, the main themes survive in the few bars of the catalogue), and this time he managed, with difficulty, to write them down himself on staves ruled by his father's steward Vanka. He even wrote his first score, a third march for four hands in 1898, inspired by his mother's duets with her friend Yekaterina Lyashchenko. Devoted Aunt Tanya had the works copied out and bound in St Petersburg. Unlike her future labours over her nephew's first opera, the lavish end result seems to have disappeared, but three more pieces from the same year (a polka, another waltz and a second march) survive on yellowed paper, covered with ink blots and proudly entitled 'My Piano Pieces, Aged Seven, S. Prokofiev'.[7] Shostakovich's stricture over childhood pieces – 'all those preludes are the same, and the reader hurries on to the fugue'[8] – may apply here, but in Prokofiev's next step a sense of fantasy runs way ahead of technical accomplishment and already reveals a riotous imagination at work.

In the meantime, Marya Grigoryevna tried to instil some discipline into her eager son, starting with 20-minute piano lessons for the seven-year-old which increased to an hour by the time he was nine. Prokofiev weighs up the good and the bad in her method with characteristic objectivity:

> Her main aim was to maintain my interest in music and not to alienate me . . . So she spent as little time as possible on exercise and as much as possible on acquaintance with the musical literature. This is an excellent example which all mamas should bear in mind[9] . . . There was another side of the coin. I didn't learn any piece properly, so carelessness in execution was the result. Another carelessness resulted – an imprecise positioning of the fingers on the keys . . . This inattentiveness to detail and impurity of technique was my bane for the whole of the ensuing period I spent at the conservatory.[10]

Her charming side is reinforced by her 'liberalism' in the face of an impossibility in Seryozhenka's first opera. Towards the end, the piano line flew higher and higher until it disappeared off the keyboard (perhaps this is the source of the helium-filled, strip-cartoon way the 'big tune' behaves in the peroration of the First Piano Concerto). The final F was outside the keyboard's range, but Marya Grigoryevna decided it should remain, because such practicalities 'must not stifle the fantasy of a young composer'.[11] But he certainly needed more discipline at the piano. His first tutor at Sontsovka, Reinhold Glière, was to echo Prokofiev's own observation – 'his manner of playing was careless and he did not hold his hands properly on the keyboard'[12] – and supported his comment by reporting the desperate cry of Anna Yesipova, Prokofiev's most distinguished piano teacher at the St Petersburg Conservatory: 'either you will place your hands properly on the keyboard or leave my class'.[13] The 20-year-old Prokofiev was to decide on the former course.

Glière's musical influence at Sontsovka was preceded, several years earlier, by the arrival of Prokofiev's first governess. Stravinsky recounts a childhood accompanied by successive governesses of all nations, unmemorable and horrible in turn; but Prokofiev was luckier, like Tchaikovsky before him, to fall under the influence of a Frenchwoman he could love. Finding the right young woman, as far as Marya Grigoryevna was concerned, deserved a great deal of trouble, and having considered all the candidates 'repulsive' on a trip to St Petersburg, she dealt with a Warsaw agency that boasted a direct line to Paris, with 'good pronunciation guaranteed 100 per cent'.[14] The appointee was Louise Roblin, genteel offspring of a father who had died from wounds incurred in the 1871 siege of Paris. She had a way with pianos and horses, though when she arrived at Sontsovka the imperious Serguschenka lost no time in setting to rights her ignorance of the Russian language and of the nature of caviar – duly mocked in the first of his many literary creations, *The Adventures of Mademoiselle.* Louise did not instil in Prokofiev a love for so lofty a French icon as Joan of Arc, the brightest vision of Tchaikovsky's youthful days; sentimental French novels were more her mark, among them *Les Malheurs de Sophie* (also cited by Vladimir Nabokov as a favourite of his own childhood 'Mademoiselle'). She might have been a little deficient in expressing her feelings: Prokofiev remained puzzled by her complacent remark, 'that's fine weather for burying your grandmother',[15] following the old lady's death in 1900. She certainly had a neater hand than Marya Grigoryevna for notating Prokofiev's early inspirations, and the first of many such fair copies, another March for four hands, dates from 1899.[16]

Clean-enunciating 'Mademoiselle' was useful in many ways but the boy's education was, for the most part, rigorously supervised by his parents: his father for Russian, mathematics, geography and history, his mother for foreign languages and the study of the Old and New Testaments then so essential for admittance to secondary schools. Again, his parents' attitudes to religion differed. Following the deaths of her two daughters, his mother found herself increasingly removed from the simple faith of her sisters, and her fatalism can be summed up by her declaration 'the worse it gets, the more natural that is; the better, the more surprising it is'.[17] His father had the usual atheism of a Russian scientist of his class but felt that the church might be more effective than the slow process of education in combating the drunkenness and violence rife in a village like Sontsovka. He observed holy days for propriety's sake and, like all families in their position, the Prokofievs had pride of place in church for the Easter service, which remained in Prokofiev's memory as a mêlée of foul smells and flaming torches. Yet this was as much part of the country calendar as the *molitba* ('threshing'), which was the climax of the season and, thanks to Sergey Alexeyevich's good husbandry, more mechanized than the one vividly described by Tolstoy in *Anna Karenina*. Whether the Sontsovka peasants rioted after a bad harvest, like so many others who went on the rampage known as *ravnenie* ('levelling'), is not recorded but there was always the threat of violence, which was to become manifest in the momentous year of 1905. Sergey Alexeyevich always slept with a revolver under his pillow because, says Prokofiev with typical understatement, 'the district was very wild, and precautions were not superfluous'.[18] The young Seryozha sometimes accompanied the two watchmen, Gavrila and Mikhaila, enthusiastically flailing their wooden rattle as he went.

What was Prokofiev's attitude to the local music-making? Peasant song plays a vital and original part in Russian music from Glinka's memorable 5/4 wedding chorus in *A Life for the Tsar* onwards and lies behind the extraordinary experiments in metre and rhythm of Stravinsky's *The Rite of Spring* and *Les Noces*. When he returned to the Soviet Union in 1936, Prokofiev's natural attitude to original melody helped him create his own brand of Russian song; and had he been more inclined to flatter the bureaucrats, he could have cited passages from his full autobiography to stress in standard ideological language the native influences of his childhood. Glière must have thought he was helping his younger colleague by doing just that with his own account of the child's 'sensitivity' to folk music:

> In the evenings there often reached our ears the strains of lovely Ukrainian melodies sung by the peasants coming home from their work in the fields. I believe that these early childhood impressions must have had their impact on the soul of the boy who was so sensitive to every sort of beauty. They undoubtedly contributed to his artistic development and gave the future composer that deep feeling for folk music so vividly manifested in many of his own compositions.[19]

Compare that with Prokofiev's own, far more circumspect, account:

> In the village the girls 'sang' but it may have been because in the Sontsovka district the songs were poor, or because I was irritated by the reedy delivery of the village maidens that I never listened to them or remembered a single one of them. It is possible that subconsciously these songs filtered through to me. At least, when, 24 years later, I first tried to make my music Russian, the material, my own but in the Russian mould, flowed easily and naturally.[20]

Unvarnished folkloric style, with its own earthy rules of delivery, could not have been further removed from the salon pieces and opera excerpts Seryozha and his mother were playing through at the same time on the 700-rouble Shreder piano newly delivered to Sontsovka (the cultured local doctor bought the old one). At the beginning of the new century, on his first visit to Moscow with his parents, Prokofiev saw his first operas, starting with *Faust* at the Solodovnikov Theatre in that politely evergreen version by Gounod (who had already won the lifelong – and unexpected – devotion of Stravinsky). Prokofiev's reactions to the reality of the opera as it measured up to his mother's prefatory remarks were those of any intelligent child: how boring it was before the devil turned up, and why should he be dressed in red? The Kermesse waltz and the soldiers' chorus were familiar from the piano versions played at Sontsovka; the duel with Valentin made a predictable impression. Borodin's *Prince Igor* at the same theatre must have been something of an ordeal for an eight-year-old, though Prokofiev felt sorry for the prince's final flight back to Putivl. Of *The Sleeping Beauty* at the Bolshoy he was to recall above all the floating effect of the 'Panorama', in which the Lilac Fairy leads the prince to Aurora's castle on an enchanted boat. This was still the era of the aristocratic artist-impresario Ivan Vsevolozhsky, director of the Imperial Theatres and arbiter of 'imperial style', who had presented Tchaikovsky's last two ballets with an opulence even the composer felt to be excessive.

The immediate results, on the family's return to Sontsovka, were the first stirrings of Prokofiev's own opera. Like *The Love for Three Oranges*, this had its origins in *commedia dell'arte*-style improvisatory drama in which Prokofiev assumed the role of a little Diaghilev among the local children, among them Stenya, the housekeeper's daughter, and Yegorka, the overseer's son. The autobiographer's charming account of their dramatic discussions – inexplicably absent from both English-language translations – itself reads like the scenario for a film, and a 1991 television documentary did indeed recreate a tableau from the opera that resulted, *Velikan* ('The Giant'). Prokofiev provides plenty of childish dialogue:

> 'Stenya, let's say you're sitting and reading a book. Suddenly the Giant goes past. Scared, you exclaim: "who goes there?" and he replies: "I, it is I", after which he enters and wants to capture you. At this point Yegorka and I are passing by and we hear you crying out. Then Yegorka exclaims. "What's that, shall we shoot?" And I say, "no, wait, the circumstances aren't right". "Will you pull out a knife?" interjects Yegorka. And I say, "Now fire". At that moment the Giant sees us and quickly steps back.'
>
> 'Ah, I fall in a faint,' concludes Stenya.
>
> 'And after this we go out,' says Yegorka.
>
> 'How am I to know who's my rescuer?' says Stenya. A moment of reflection. We all arrive at a general conclusion:
>
> 'Going out, we unexpectedly drop our visiting card. At first you cry, because you're alone and so unhappy, but then you come across our card and decide to write us a letter.'[21]

On this hopeful note the first scene closes. The rest developed apace, with music to give it the status of an opera. It cheered up Aunt Tanya, more in need of consolation than her sisters following the death of Grandmother Zhitkova, and she promptly had the score, neatly copied by 'Mademoiselle', placed in a handsome red folder with a gold inscription, '*Velikan*: Opera in Three Acts. Composition of Seryozhenka Prokofiev'. When in 1901 the Prokofievs visited the country estate of Aunt Katya and her family, Aunt Tanya was rewarded for her interest: she played the Giant, while Cousin Katya, one of the Rayevskys' daughters, and their son Shurik replaced the housekeeper's daughter with the 'common' name and Yegorka. Cousin Andryusha, Shurik's brother, conjured up an orchestra at the piano.

Aunt Tanya's presentation survives in the Moscow archives, missing 14 of the 27 pages.[22] Between it and Prokofiev's own reconstruction in his autobiography we can piece together a fair picture of this early fantasy. In Act I the dynamics are perhaps more remarkable than the simple tonic–dominant music. Like Tchaikovsky or Verdi before him, Seryozhenka the composer likes extremes: *pppp* (at the end of the overture) and *ffff* (for the Giant's threatening aria in Act I scene 2).The Giant's ranting is fun to behold, of course, but the theme that Prokofiev later came to regard as 'probably the best I composed during this entire time'[23] remained, by the 1940s, in his memory alone; again it is moving to see it in his own, mature hand (Ex.1).[24]

Ex.1 *The Giant*

Act II begins with fierce runs, evidence that Prokofiev, as he put it, had come to 'discover the sweetness of the chromatic scale'.[25] Birds chirrup grace-noted song (like the bird in *Peter and the Wolf*, over-generously notes Prokofiev's Soviet biographer Israel Nestyev) before both Sergeyev, the more or less eponymous hero, and the Giant have their ariosos. When, in scene 2, the Giant becomes a threat to the King, troops must be amassed, and in scene 3 they strut to battle, like Gounod's soldiers, to a tune that was also influenced by the examples in Meyerbeer's *Le Prophète* and Verdi's *Aida*. After the obligatory operatic march, there has to be a waltz for Ustinya's party in Act III (after all, Tchaikovsky composed one for Tatyana's name-day in *Eugene Onegin*, as Prokofiev was by now aware). Since it breaks off in mid-flow in the manuscript, and there are no words for Act III, only the autobiographer can inform us of the horrifying dénouement: 'the King suddenly appears . . . he sings that he can no longer combat the Giant, that he curses everyone – and he stabs himself with his dagger. Everyone is shaken, but then they sing "Long live our Giant"'.[26] It was this seemingly nihilistic ending that so disturbed the peace-loving Sergey Alexeyevich. Uncle Sasha Rayevsky had no such reservations during the 1901 'production' and Prokofiev proudly records his prophetic words: 'well, Seryozha, when they put you on in the Imperial Theatres, remember your opera was first performed in my home!'[27]

There was now no stopping the enthusiastic young opera composer. He began a second work, *Na pustynnykh ostrovakh* ('On Desert Islands'), with a long overture and plenty of opportunity for the elements to rage in the manner of Chopin's 12th *étude*; as a result, the 'innovations' included diminished 7ths, which the young Prokofiev would have absorbed aurally from the great operatic models, and double sharps. It was at once more pretentious than *The Giant* and less memorable for the older composer – perhaps because only a few bars survive. At any rate, when he came to have his photograph taken in front of a pasteboard piano at the end of 1901, 'The Giant' was inscribed on the score beside him in some copies, 'On Desert Islands' in rather fewer.

Prokofiev also continued his flow of shorter pieces, most of them absorbed into the world of his latest opera. There were eccentricities in his first inscriptions 'for Papa's nameday' (his own, too, of course), neither of which has survived in full: one was in 12/8, for no good reason, while the other is 'scored' for four hands at one piano and zither. This was not the only new music-producing item in the Prokofiev household; it was followed by an Ariston, a mechanical reproducing instrument, and an early phonograph which played quickly worn-down cylinders of marches, heard through rubber earphones. Naturally, the eager infant prodigy wanted to write music for both. As a participant in the short-lived history of the reproducing piano in the early 1920s, in a way he was granted his wish.

Our real interest in the juvenilia begins with one of the few pieces from the long gestation period of *On Desert Islands* that was not swallowed up in the bigger project: a Tarantella, last of three more pieces for the next paternal nameday still in the archives[28] and the very first piece in Nestyev's published selection of 'juvenilia'. Perhaps Prokofiev woke to the form's potential on his visit to the Rayevskys' estate, for this vigorous Sicilian dance seems to have been a liberating influence for well-bred young ladies in the country, and Cousin Katya is more likely to have demonstrated it than Ustinya on her best behaviour back in Sontsovka. The tarantella was to serve Prokofiev as a basis for several 6/8 inspirations in his early sonatas; he returned to it for the finale of the Eighth Sonata, where it has a similar manic intensity to its role in the last movement of Schubert's C minor Sonata D958. The later piece with which this first Tarantella (Ex.2*a*) has most in common, though, is its corresponding number in the *Music for Children* of 1935, which achieves greater effect through even simpler means (Ex.2*b*). In both cases, the single right-hand line does exactly what one expects of a good tarantella. Yet while the bright, major-key

Ex.2*a* Tarantella (1901)

Ex.2*b* Tarantella (*Music for Children*, 1935)

coda of the 1935 Tarantella is neater, the unexpected chromatic runs at the end of the 1901 example point towards the devilish audacity of bolder works only a few years in the future.

Prokofiev's parents continued his operatic education by taking him to St Petersburg for the first time, in December 1901. The works he saw were representative of the Maryinsky Theatre's repertory: Glinka's *A Life for the Tsar*, Dargomyzhsky's *Rusalka*, Anton Rubinstein's *The Demon* (performed regularly, Rimsky-Korsakov believed, merely because of the huge popularity of the great bass Fyodor Chaliapin), *La traviata* and *Carmen*. Prokofiev does not remark on the Maryinsky's handsome auditorium; if, for him as for Stravinsky, 'to enter the blue-and-gold interior of that heavily perfumed hall was . . . like entering the most sacred of temples',[29] he does not say so. Nor does he expound, as Stravinsky does, on the beauties of several generations of Italian architecture in St Petersburg: Rastrelli's Baroque fantasies for the Empress Elizabeth, Rossi's neo-classical buildings for Alexander I and Nicholas I. He could hardly be expected to pay them much attention at the age of nine, but his subsequent years at the conservatory seem to have heightened his visual sense very little. He was more interested in chess, for ever-indulgent Aunt Tanya had found the budding young player an opponent from a real chess club – a mere fifth-grader, admittedly, but still an impressive victim. The gift of this sporting gentleman, one Solovyev, was an old chess journal which Prokofiev devoured avidly, little thinking that in a few years' time he would meet one of the players whose games were featured, the world champion Emanuel Lasker.

St Petersburg may have catered for the pursuits Prokofiev held dearest, but Moscow remained his mecca, if only because the family's journey there marked a new stage in his development: 'I became acquainted with the world of professional composers'.[30] The family's entrée was achieved through a friend of a friend, the 20-year-old Yury (Shura or Shurochek) Pomerantsev, soon to be a silver medallist at the Moscow Conservatory and, following his studies in Leipzig with the St Petersburg favourite Arthur Nikisch, a conductor of modest abilities. His brief test of the precocious nine-year-old revealed perfect pitch and prompted a recommendation to Sergey Taneyev, professor at the conservatory. It was a great honour and a line back to Tchaikovsky, who had noted his one-time protégé's immersion in counterpoint, an anathema, with bewildered admiration. In the world of inspired amateurism that was 19th-century Russian music, Taneyev stood apart. As Prokofiev was shortly to do, he had undertaken his conservatory training at a tender age and was the first student there to win a gold medal in both composition and performance (he introduced Moscow audiences to Tchaikovsky's First Piano Concerto). His academic training was even more rigorous than Rimsky-Korsakov's belated attempts to keep one step ahead of his students at the St Petersburg Conservatory, and the results were more impressive: the choral writing of his official op.1, *John of Damascus*, is superbly crafted; and when Prokofiev met him his complex masterpiece, *At the Reading of a Psalm*, lay 13 years in the future. Taneyev's real genius, though, was for chamber music and he created an utterly individual series of string quartets and quintets which are only now beginning to be reassessed.

Taneyev's personality proved more whimsical than his music at that fateful audition but he was severe on the indulgent aunt's presentation of *The Giant* – 'Seryozhenka' should be replaced by the adult 'Sergey' – and insisted on the correct instruction of harmony, 'otherwise the young composer would acquire bad habits from which he would find it difficult to extricate himself later on'.[31] Perhaps he thought Seryozha was older: his diary records meeting 'a young boy of 12'; but in any case he noted 'outstanding talent . . . he played his compositions – absolute pitch, he recognizes intervals, chords'.[32] He recommended further lessons with Pomerantsev while the family was in Moscow, during which the friendly young man was sometimes angered by the wilful child's deliberate mistakes, and he also invited the unwitting young talent to some private rehearsals in select company. From the diary we can piece together the programmes, which included preparations for the premiere of Taneyev's mature Symphony in C minor and, in early March, two sessions devoted to Tchaikovsky's Second Symphony, the 'Little Russian', so-called because of the Ukrainian folk song which is the basis for the finale that had so dazzled Rimsky-Korsakov and friends. Tchaikovsky had thoroughly revised the work in 1879–80, providing a virtually new and more concise first movement, and it was this relatively unfamiliar version which Prokofiev was privileged to hear. Taneyev's final act of patronage was to recommend another young student to visit Sontsovka in the summer for a longer-term course of musical tuition. Prokofiev later found out he was lucky not to fall under the iron rod of Taneyev's first choice, Alexander Goldenweiser. He was to be taught instead by the more straightforward

Reinhold Glière. Goldenweiser went to Yasnaya Polyana, where Taneyev had already caused the pathologically jealous Tolstoy groundless distress because of his innocent friendship with the writer's long-suffering wife.

Glière was no doubt subject to happier, if less illustrious, influences in Sontsovka during the summer of 1902. Decades later it would not be difficult for him to find kind things to say about the enlightened adults he met there: the 'outwardly morose'[33] father who could be so tender and loving towards his only son, the tall mother 'with beautiful, intelligent eyes'[34] and the vivacious Aunt Tanya 'with a gift for all sorts of pastimes and interesting amusements'.[35] 'Mademoiselle' Louise, who had returned to Sontsovka following a succession of unsatisfactory German governesses, does not merit a mention; she may have had a soft spot for the young tutor, but his heart was already another's. Seryozha struck Glière as 'gentle' – which seems hard to believe – 'warm-hearted',[36] proud of his own achievements and stubborn in his studies (he was more persistent with a new craze, marbles). Prokofiev's first impressions were of 'a pleasant chap, comfortable to be with and not taking up a lot of space'.[37] The summer routine was not especially arduous: a swim in the river before breakfast, music with the new master from 10 until 11, other subjects first with his father and then his mother, plenty of fun and games after dinner – described with great spirit in the diary Prokofiev began to keep the following year.

The non-musical lessons left Glière free to practise his violin and to compose, which he was already doing prolifically. He had completed his First Symphony on graduating from the Moscow Conservatory in 1900, and the Second would eventually be based on an octet composed during his second summer at Sontsovka. Both works continue the attractively scored, solidly tuneful work of the post-Tchaikovskian Russian symphony alongside Glazunov's regular offerings in the genre; the heyday of Glière's late Romantic style was to come with the Third Symphony (*Ilya Muromets*), a gargantuan and often startlingly imaginative epic. His job now was to nurture the obvious talent of a much younger composer, and Marya Grigoryevna bowed out, the sharp-eyed youth noticed, not without a certain jealousy manifest in her critical observations. The advances her son made in his piano studies had another alarming effect: she stopped playing altogether.

Glière's first step was to explain the nature of song form to his charge – the need to compose in four-bar phrases (instinctively grasped in the Tarantella of 1901) and to follow them with a central trio section in a related key before returning to the opening idea with new figurations if possible. The pupil's correct, concise responses had to be called something: they became *pesenki* ('little songs'), for want of anything better. At the end of a week there were already six 'little songs'; in six years' time there would be almost 70, grouped into sets and neatly labelled. These first essays in academic correctness are less interesting than the works either side of them, tempting though it may be for Nestyev to see the future composer of *The Love for Three Oranges* in a march that fanfares, with a certain rhythmic vitality, on a single note against the fundamental progressions on which Glière insisted. The fifth 'song', *Maestoso,* at least proved popular at a Moscow soirée in 1903, when the young composer had to play it five times.

In piano lessons Glière could afford to be more original. He encouraged his pupil to hear a Beethoven sonata in orchestral terms by deciding what instruments would suit the themes he played on the keyboard (a technique later advocated by that great mentor of many Russian pianists Heinrich Neuhaus, as his one-time pupil, the conductor Yevgeny Svetlanov, has emphasized). It helped not only to develop Prokofiev's surprisingly selective knowledge of the orchestra but inspired him to orchestrate the storm music from *On Desert Islands* and set him thinking that it was time to compose a symphony. Glière's suggestion that a single-movement piece would be a more suitable starting-point was swept aside; it had to be a four-movement creation. This time the talented youngster's unsupervised work on a first subject yielded an irregular (19-bar) theme; what Glière had to explain were the rules of sonata form – the notion of a development was completely new to the would-be symphonist – of modulation and of key relations between movements. By the end of the summer, with more than a little help from Glière, the orchestration was well under way. All that survives are the few themes that Prokofiev was able to recall for his autobiography, and his memory failed him on the later stages of the work. It is probably no loss; how could the young composer manage anything genuinely *allegro con brio* when he still had to learn to walk, *andante*-style?

Prokofiev the autobiographer looks back on Glière's influence with the same objective balance that he had applied to his parents. Apart from vital knowledge, he also acquired the firm conviction that music was more than a mere game. The inspired lover of lopsided themes, however, could never quite pardon the careful craftsman for advocating 'square structure' without the proviso 'that it should be learnt so it could be forgotten later'.[38] But Glière can hardly be blamed for sticking to basic modulations. The child Prokofiev was running way ahead of himself in his symphonic ambitions, and the mature composer seemed to forget all too easily why the young music teacher had come to him in the first place. At this stage, firm rules were vital, as Taneyev had realized.

The working relationship with Glière proceeded by post, though Seryozha continued his cavalier attitude to regular exercises from Anton Arensky's harmony book; he was much more interested in making a four-hand piano version of the symphony, copied out by the faithful Louise. It seemed to Marya Grigoryevna that her son's symphony was the talk of the musical circles they frequented on their visit to Moscow in November 1902, when Glière was happy enough once more to present his protégé to Taneyev – even to the extent of passing off some of the counterpoint he had supplied in the symphony as his pupil's work. The Moscow master was as kindhearted as before, if a little bantering; he recommended more tuition from Glière, especially in harmony, and his chuckling criticism of so many basic progressions in the symphony turned out to be something of a watershed in the career of the *enfant terrible* in waiting. Prokofiev the autobiographer is unusually expansive in his image: 'the microbe had penetrated the organism and required a long incubation period. Only four years later my harmonic inventions were attracting attention'.[39] Later, Taneyev, noting with surprise the wealth of 'false notes' in Prokofiev's dazzling op.2 piano pieces, would be reminded, to his surprise, that it was he who nudged the boy 'on to such a slippery path'.[40]

The concert scene had its share of delights, though a Chaliapin recital passes without comment and the boy who was soon to become an enthusiastic Wagnerite told his father that *Die Walküre* at the Bolshoy was 'a dreadfully boring opera without motifs, without action but making a great deal of noise'.[41] The budding critic's verdict on a concert conducted by the visiting Arthur Nikisch is more temperate and contains what is his first recorded comparison: 'I felt that the overture [to Glinka's *Ruslan and Lyudmila*] came out generally smoother and better than with [Vasily] Safonov [director of the Moscow Conservatory since Taneyev's sideways step to mere professor and conductor-in-chief of the Russian Musical Society in Moscow]'.[42] The programme also included Grieg's *Peer Gynt* Suite no.1 and Tchaikovsky's First Piano Concerto with Nikolay Medtner, Rakhmaninov's equal as both virtuoso and (some would argue) composer, as the soloist.

Returning to Sontsovka via St Petersburg, Prokofiev set to work on the Violin Sonata Glière had suggested he compose alongside several new *pesenki* to launch a second set of 12. A lifetime's habit of never wasting a good melody begins with the opening theme of the sonata, which was to become the basis of the *Ballade* op.15 for cello and piano (1912); thus it has the distinction of being his first inspiration not to come under the heading of 'juvenilia'. Newly absorbed influences emerge in the *pesenki*: the Brahms–Liszt style in the C minor no.1, and Chopin, previously rejected for all his mother's pleading, in the *Mélodie*, no.7. Here Prokofiev followed Goldenweiser's advice in having the lower octave of the theme interlaced with the left-hand arpeggios. There is an economical, Beethovenian touch in the one-bar excursion of the admirable melody from E flat major into C major (Ex.3).

After much soul-searching, which turned out to be connected with a fiancée in Moscow, Glière returned to Sontsovka for a second summer, in 1903, and once more had to yield to the young composer's imperative. This time he let him work on a third opera, though the master chose the subject: thumbing through Sergey Alexeyevich's complete edition of Alexander Pushkin, Russian literature's greatest and most influential figure, he lit on one of the four 'little tragedies', *Pir vo vremya chumy* ('A Feast in Time of Plague'). Two of these concise masterpieces had already been set, to the highest standards, by Dargomyzhsky (who had adhered very strictly to the demands of the text in *The Stone Guest*, Pushkin's slant on the Don Juan legend) and Rimsky-Korsakov (an equally verse-faithful setting of *Mozart and Salieri*; Pushkin's dramatization of the conflict between divine genius and plodding craftsmanship has been further explored by Peter Shaffer in his play *Amadeus*, 1979). Rakhmaninov was

Ex.3 *Mélodie* in E flat major

shortly to prove worthy of their company in his imaginative operatic treatment of *The Miserly Knight.* There had been a musical version of *A Feast in Time of Plague* by the least inspired of the 'mighty little handful' (also known as the Five), César Cui. It may not stand comparison with any of the other Pushkin one-act operas, but it could hardly avoid being more accomplished than Prokofiev's first attempt, with its tentative steps in writing for the leading tenor, baritone and bass. Needless to say, the arrogant youth did not think so when Glière sent him a copy of Cui's score, which he played 'belligerently'[43] and confidently denounced as 'a bad opera'.[44] What he reveals of his own fledgling attempt hardly inspires confidence, though the plague theme first heard in the lengthy, technically competent overture is apt enough in its chromatic triplet patterns and abundance of diminished 7ths.

It was at this time that Prokofiev began his first diary, which gives us a more vivid picture of the summer's pleasures than of the workings of the creative mind (though his compositional activity is drily chronicled). He tells us of the French novels Mademoiselle encouraged him to read, the vicissitudes of an infected ear undergone by his beloved puppy Shango and numerous games which seem to have been another form of theatre over which he could hold sway. In addition to horse-riding and croquet, a massive battle of tin soldiers had Aunt Tanya, both tutors and the local children assuming responsibility for various Latin American countries; and a diary entry for Sunday 3 August charts the standard Russian officer's method of resolving differences. The square brackets are Prokofiev's own:

> Got up late. Hot day. Before lunch Reinhold Moritsevich and I quarrelled, and he challenged me to a duel. His second was Mlle and mine was Nikita. We hit each other with 'automatics' loaded with rubber balls, taking it in turns to fire. Reinhold Moritsevich hit me in the stomach and lightly brushed my shoulder and arm a few times. I struck him in the left shoulder [the duel, which had begun correctly, then degenerated into a general entertainment. Then M-lle and Nikita shot at each other. Mlle hit Nikita on the leg with her fourth shot; but he hit her on each of his shots – once on the forehead, once in the stomach and once in the head. There were other less interesting duels].[45]

As in the previous year, the 1903 compositions did not come to a halt when Glière left. Marya Grigoryevna's regular departure to the warmer climes of Sukhumi in the Crimea, where her friend Olya was now living on the lush Black Sea estate of her husband Nikolay Smetsky, launched two more *pesenki* ready for her return and his first *romance,* a setting of a poem by Lermontov, *Skazhi mne, vetka Palestina* ('Tell me, twig of Palestine'). He was reading Pushkin for pleasure now, and there were other interests. A statistical view of history surfaces for the first time in his lists of the kings of Portugal and England, soon joined by the other rulers of Europe. The diary also brings with it the first reference to contemporary events: on 19 November he hears that 'war with Japan is inevitable, that a whole corps of

600,000 soldiers has been sent from Moscow to Manchuria'.[46] The source was a well-informed citizen of Moscow, to which the Prokofievs had again travelled to tap culture at its source. His parents went to the theatre more often than he did but he was allowed to sample Shakespeare, well done at Vladimir Nemirovich-Danchenko's Moscow Arts Theatre. The play was *Julius Caesar*, about which all he has to say is 'very good, but too long – from 7.30 to 12.30'.[47] No doubt his father managed to see one of the house specialities, a play by Anton Chekhov, news of whose death the following year brought an astonishing change to Sergey Alexeyevich's face which his son could not understand.

Seryozha's diary, childlike in general things and altogether more advanced in matters musical, reveals two parallel imaginative worlds. Lists of purchases – toy cannon, toy pistol, stamp album – are interwoven with records of musical events. A chamber recital including Schubert's String Quintet at the conservatory left him unmoved: 'I was looking for opulence and dramatic moments'.[48] Yet he liked Massenet's *Werther* enough to write out the horn theme accompanying the hero's suicidal thoughts, and he did the same with the opening bars of Tchaikovsky's Grand Sonata for piano, played by the master's virtuoso pupil Alexander Ziloti. Kindly Taneyev showed genuine enthusiasm for *A Feast in Time of Plague*: 'you could write it out in score and have it performed, it's so smoothly written'.[49] He delighted the boy by lending him his score of Tchaikovsky's *Eugene Onegin* to study back in Sontsovka – no insignificant gesture from someone who had famously dissented with the older composer over Tchaikovsky's Fourth Symphony, written at roughly the same time as the opera. A less glorious foretaste of professional life came in Prokofiev's battle with a nauseatingly correct girl pupil of Safonov, competing with him in the interpretation of the stormy finale from Beethoven's Fifth Sonata in C minor. The result: 'inspiration without mastery had collided with mastery without inspiration'.[50]

The next step on that road to mastery was taken in St Petersburg at the beginning of 1904. Unavoidable plans for their son's secondary-level education had already ruffled the placid surface of the Prokofievs' domestic existence. If he were to attend a high school, it would have to be a high-quality one in Moscow and not a provincial 'Dotheboys Hall' which would put the delicate child at risk. This in turn would give Marya Grigoryevna the escape route to the city life she craved, since she would have to live with beloved Seryozha. 'In that case, all that remains for me is to shoot myself', Prokofiev heard his father say behind a closed door, and there were tears all round[51] – the only record of serious marital strife in the autobiography. The obstacles of long-term separation must have been resolved, because at the start of 1904 St Petersburg was looking like a more attractive proposition: after all, the well-to-do Rayevskys might open up a new social world for Marya Grigoryevna, and Tanya wanted her there. The solution came unexpectedly when the young Prokofiev had another entrée to a figure who was to St Petersburg musical life what Taneyev was to Muscovite musicians, Alexander Glazunov.

As precociously assured as Taneyev, the 16-year-old Glazunov had dazzled St Petersburg society in 1882 with his First Symphony, by which stage he was already, as Stravinsky drily noted, 'a cut and dried academician'.[52] By 1904, with six more well-made and attractive symphonies to his credit, he already held a high position in the St Petersburg Conservatory and, following the upheavals of 1905, was to become its director, very much with his predecessor Rimsky-Korsakov's blessing. He struck Seryozha at their first meeting as less welcoming than Taneyev, and Marya Grigoryevna was already drawing unfavourable comparisons with the warm-hearted Moscow set when he arrived unexpectedly at their lodging and announced: 'I have come to try and persuade you to send your son to the conservatory'.[53] His mother's doubts were reasonable enough: better a first-rate professional in some other sphere, free to pursue his real love as a hobby, than a second-rate musician. But again, Glazunov spoke with blunt assurance: 'if a child with abilities like your son's shouldn't be sent to the conservatory, then who should?'[54] His persuasive speech reassured Marya Grigoryevna that her son would receive a thorough training in non-musical subjects alongside composition classes, and the matter was settled.

If Glazunov had seemed more remote than Taneyev, the acolyte he recommended for Prokofiev's interim training, Mikhail Mikhailovich Chernov, was no Glière, and his dry little lessons in counterpoint failed to inspire the boy. The greatest musician of them all, Nikolay Rimsky-Korsakov, remained offstage, learning of the prodigy through Glière's enthusiastic descriptions. Prokofiev did see his first Rimsky-Korsakov opera in St Petersburg: *The Snow Maiden*, Rimsky-Korsakov's third opera, which remained his own 'favourite child' until his death. Based on a charming drama by the founding father of Russian theatre, Nikolay Ostrovsky, it was an ideally fresh and piquant example for a budding composer, and Prokofiev was to come to love it, quoting the heroine's entrance aria with affection in his *Classical* Symphony. He did not, in 1904, grasp the musical language immediately, and probably for that reason preferred the last two acts to their equally inspired predecessors.

An unearthly maiden was to become the subject of Prokofiev's next opera, thanks to a meeting with a lady of literary pretensions in St Petersburg. Marya Grigoryevna Kilschtedt, a well-to-do friend of the Rayevskys, was charmed by Seryozha and presumably flattered him into thinking he was the ideal composer to set her libretto to music. The subject she proposed already existed in liquid Russian verse, for Pushkin's romantic mentor Vasily Zhukovsky had translated Friedrich de la Motte Fouqué's tale of a lovesick water-nymph, *Undine* (1811), into hexameters. There had been one unsuccessful operatic adaptation in 1848; another, which the self-critical Tchaikovsky destroyed in 1875, may have been more inspired, on the evidence of the few pieces saved from the flames and the love-duet which he reworked as the well-known *pas d'action* between Odette and the Prince in *Swan Lake*. Prokofiev must have known of Tchaikovsky's ill-fated project. The two Prokofiev acts to have survived in manuscript, the third and fourth, were composed in 1907, three years after he took up Madame Kilschtedt's suggestion, but assuming that Undine's leitmotif had been in existence from the start, two of several variants in the later acts surely reflect the work's Tchaikovskian origins. This Undine is the descendant of Odette via the tragic 'forbidden question' theme in Wagner's *Lohengrin* (Ex.4).[55]

Ex.4 *Undine*

Just how well Prokofiev knew his Tchaikovsky operas is documented in the best testament to his wide-ranging imagination on the eve of his entry into the St Petersburg Conservatory. In the cardboard-covered 50-page book his mother gave him to note all his observations,[56] there is a list of all the operas from which he had played excerpts, with the timings precisely given; here we find mention of Tchaikovsky's early *Oprichnik* and the revision of his comic opera *Vakula the Smith*, *Cherevichki* ('The Slippers'), as well as *Eugene Onegin* (heading the list, and much the most played) and *The Queen of Spades*. The French repertory comes next in favour – Meyerbeer's *Les Huguenots*, Bizet's *Carmen* and Delibes' *Lakmé* as well as the ubiquitous Gounod – closely followed by the Italians (Verdi, Puccini's *Tosca* and Boito's *Nerone*).

Otherwise, non-musical amusements have the upper hand. The book begins in February 1904 with a code that turns out to be Prokofiev's way of trying to stop his parents reading his diary, but normal script is soon resumed. The chief rondo theme is Russia's ill-fated war with Japan, newly launched at the beginning of the year. Aunt Katya may have wrung her hands and walked about the St Petersburg apartment muttering 'What a disaster', but for Seryozha it was a merry jape and he noted the battleships of the various fleets with an interest that borders on the obsessive. As the war developed, there are long observations on 'the coefficiency of our cruisers and battleships' and – much more entertaining – vivid sketches of sea-battles. In a little fable Japan becomes a flea, England a bulldog and Russia, not surprisingly, a lion. Readings of La Fontaine may have been the inspiration, as they were more directly for an accomplished little French poem called 'Le Loup et l'agneau'. Literary pastimes include charades, the art of the rebus – riddling a name by breaking it up into syllables or letters ('mon premier est le nom de mon dernier et mon tout est un capitale') – in Russian and French and a drama, *Nord-Express*. Towering over these is Prokofiev's first sustained attempt at narrative, the poem *Graf* ('The Count'), whose querulous protagonist was destined for a miserable end but not before he had continued to dominate his creator's imagination throughout his first St Petersburg term.

The flowers that bloomed in the Ukrainian spring are neatly illustrated in Prokofiev's notebook alongside various doodles. With the constant reminders of croquet and summer pastimes (the latest was stilt-walking), it creates the image of a happy time in Sontsovka. But the objective autobiographer abruptly banishes sentiment with his description of his August departure for St Petersburg: 'I was not particularly unhappy about leaving Sontsovka. It was a place I didn't like very much . . . I had a feeling that many interesting things were in store for me, and Papa had promised to come to St Petersburg in a month'.[57] The vivid image of an unsentimental child, facing each new challenge with the assurance born of his parents' devotion, persists to the last.

2
Prokosha in St Petersburg 1904–6

The city that was the young Prokofiev's goal in 1904 had more to offer than just the balls and receptions for the nobility of a hundred years earlier. True, the extravagant glitter of court life continued as before – an astonishing photograph taken the previous year shows hundreds of guests in the Winter Palace lavishly dressed as fairy-tale courtiers to celebrate the city's bicentenary – and remained as remote as ever from the 11½-hour working day which was the lot of most factory employees. That at least was an improvement on the 15 hours most workers had known at the start of Nicholas II's reign, though owing to the weak-willed vacillations of their tsar, one step forward in social conditions was invariably followed by two steps back.

Yet thanks to the legacy of the mid-19th-century intelligentsia, there were now infinite possibilities for creative artists in every field; even the usually terse septuagenarian Stravinsky could look back on St Petersburg in 'the two decades before *The Firebird* [1910]' as 'a very exciting place to be'.[1] When Prokofiev first went to St Petersburg, Sergey Diaghilev, the future perpetrator of the Ballets Russes' 'shock of the new', gave the impression of being tied to the relatively short apron-strings of the city's past. He was organizing a major exhibition of historic Russian portraiture in the yellow and white neo-classical building of the Tauride Palace, first occupied by Catherine the Great's lover Prince Potemkin. The style of Catherine's St Petersburg dominated Diaghilev's imagination as well as those of the artists formerly gathered round him under the banner of *Mir iskusstva* ('World of Art'), among them Alexandre Benois, Konstantin Somov, Yevgeny Lanceray and Valentin Serov (described by Stravinsky as 'the conscience of *Mir iskusstva*',[2] and technically the finest painter of them all). Despite the exhibition's retrospective quality, it was to be noted even by Soviet art critics as an 'event of epoch-making significance' opening 'a new era in the study of Russian and European art of the 18th century and the first half of the 19th century'.[3] The upheavals of 1905 were to give younger *mir iskusstniki* such as Mstislav Dobuzhinsky contemporary subject matter to enrich the scope of St Petersburg art.

One turn-of-the-century craze the *Mir iskusstva* painters for the most part avoided was the shadow-world of symbolism. In poetry and the theatre, it was still the rage and Prokofiev was to cling on to it in the first song settings of his maturity, well behind the times. It was soon under siege from the self-styled Acmeists, who launched their counter-attack with a new cult of the primitive, while the crystalline poetry of Anna Akhmatova and Marina Tsvetayeva would deal the true death-blow to decadence. In the novel, Andrey Bely was already leavening symbolism with scathing satire in his extraordinary portrait of a city *Petersburg*, featuring a central figure worthy of Gogol; and the hard-hitting prose of an author with real concern for social deprivation, Maxim Gorky, was in the ascendant. In the theatre the hazy, perfumed abstractions of the Belgian Maurice Maeterlinck, warmly welcomed by Anton Chekhov shortly before his death, would dominate the stage for years. Here the breath of fresh air was to come from the audacious young theatre director Vsevolod Meyerhold, about to make his name at Komissarzhevskaya's Theatre in St Petersburg with productions that included Maeterlinck's *Soeur Béatrice* and *Pelléas et Mélisande*, but better known to posterity for breaking down theatrical barriers with his various stagings of Alexander Blok's *The Showbooth* and his faith in the improvisatory skills of the Italian *commedia dell'arte*.

Opera productions at the Maryinsky Theatre now presented a splendid match of the visual with the musical. Many of the great artists who lent their skills to set and costume design had begun to do so for the wealthy merchant Savva Mamontov's private opera company in the 1880s. A tentative attempt to apply those bracing lessons to the conservative institution of the Maryinsky came in 1901 when Diaghilev, as 'Official for Special Commissions', invited his artistic colleagues Lev Bakst, Alexandre Benois, Konstantin Korovin, Yevgeny Lanceray and Valentin Serov to work together on the sets and costumes of Delibes' *Sylvia*. Conflict with the Ministry of the Court resulted in Diaghilev's dismissal before the project reached fruition, and he had to wait for the warmer cooperation of the Parisians to realize a similar ambition. Meanwhile Alexander Golovin, who designed the gorgeous blue and gold curtain that still hangs in front of the stage of the Maryinsky Theatre, brought to swirling, brilliant visual life the theatre's productions of Anton Rubinstein's *The Demon*, Glinka's *Ruslan and Lyudmila*, Wagner's *Das Rheingold* and Rimsky-Korsakov's *The Maid of Pskov*. The establishment now accepted what only a few decades earlier had been regarded as experimental.

Rimsky-Korsakov, the grand old man of Russian music since Tchaikovsky's death in 1893, had recently celebrated his 60th birthday; Stravinsky, leader of the 'young Korsakovs' and a private pupil of the master, composed a chorus to mark the occasion. Although Rimsky-Korsakov was intolerant of Richard Strauss's domination of 'progressive' Western music and found the scores of Russia's most radical new voice, Alexander Skryabin, sick and disturbed, he still sought out new and interesting harmonic progressions alongside ever more rich and rare orchestration in each of his operas. Unusual compound time-signatures were a feature too, though these harked back to the flexible folk metres first reflected in Glinka's *A Life for the Tsar*. In an amusing scene from the autobiography introducing the new Sontsovka veterinary surgeon Vasily Morolev, Prokofiev describes his initiation into the rhythmic wonders of a chorus in 11/4 time from the first scene of Rimsky-Korsakov's *Sadko*. Waiting to remove his thermometer from the rear end of a horse in the Sontsovka stables, Morolev sings the elders' chorus from Act I and Prokofiev discovers that it fits the legendary phrase 'Rimsky-*Kor*sakov has gone com*plete*ly mad!' ('Rimsky-*Kor*sakov sovsem s u*ma* soshol').[4]

As Morolev, an enthusiastic music-lover, realized, *Sadko* is stocked with memorable set pieces, tirelessly inventive variations on authentic Russian declamation and liquid orchestral effects for the scene when the minstrel descends to the sea-king's realms, many of them dating back to the tone-poem on the subject Rimsky-Korsakov completed as a young man. Prokofiev was to hear it several years after his arrival in St Petersburg. Ready and waiting in the autumn of 1904, however, and destined to become Prokofiev's first headlong musical infatuation was Rimsky-Korsakov's true operatic masterpiece. *The Legend of the Invisible City of Kitezh and the Maiden Fevroniya*, profound in its nature worship and its holy, Orthodox choruses, strikes a rare note of concern for the future of Russian culture. For the first time in Rimsky-Korsakov's music, a fable acquires contemporary significance, to play an even stronger part in the more detached comedy of his swansong, *The Golden Cockerel*. Like most other leading figures, he was about to be implicated in the first revolutionary upheavals of 1905, when his liberal principles and unshakable humanity placed him firmly on the side of his students at the conservatory.

That, however, was some months in the future when the 13-year-old Prokofiev, still in short trousers, undertook his examinations for what his parents hoped would be a secure schooling at Russia's finest musical institution. He was not, as it turned out, required to take the first of them (elementary theory), but his attitude on the eve is revealing. As his mother wrote to Sergey Alexeyevich back in Sontsovka, it was one of indifference. 'This is partly a good thing', she added, 'and it's probably in his nature.'[5] He faced all the questions on academic subjects a week later with equanimity, though he should probably have been given a '5' (grade A) in French rather than the '4' he received. Confidence was now running high in Marya Grigoryevna, praising to her husband 'our eternal trinity – your, mine and Sergusha's toil' and certain in her happiness that they had done the right thing not to expose their tender son to the harsh world of a secondary school.[6]

Finally there came the most auspicious examination of the three, in theory of composition, before a panel of 12 professors led by Rimsky-Korsakov and Glazunov. Marya Grigoryevna, having shaken the hand of Professor Rimsky-Korsakov, withdrew, 'not wishing to foist myself on these local gods'.[7] The great man then threw up his hands in horror at the number of candidates, but it can hardly have been difficult to separate the wheat from the chaff. One forlorn creature produced a solitary song, admitting that it lacked accompaniment; young

Prokofiev produced two folios which included a bound copybook of his 24 *pesenki.* He was asked to play a Mozart sonata he already knew, followed by one with which he was unfamiliar. After confirming his perfect pitch, his knowledge of harmony (good) and his ability to sing in tune (slightly flawed), Rimsky-Korsakov turned to his compositions. Glazunov was surprised to find he had written the first act of *Undine* since they had last met, but Rimsky-Korsakov stopped the composer after a few pages. He must have been more impressed by the 'little song' chosen for performance; it was the eighth from series 3, a *Vivo* in G minor dedicated to 'Papochka' back in July, 'my best piano piece which Chernov had approved'.[8] With the exception of the ending to the early Tarantella, none of the piano pieces reveals so clearly that sense of the fantastical or the diabolical which was to take audacious shape in Prokofiev's first numbered compositions. At the same time, the heritage is clear. This is a piquant offspring of the wicked fairy Carabosse's entourage in *The Sleeping Beauty* and the trolls of his beloved Grieg (Ex.5). A songlike central section in total contrast to the surrounding impishness also reflects Tchaikovsky, this time the composer of the Grand Sonata or the Concert Fantasia, in the powerful climax to a simple romantic melody.

Ex.5 *Vivo* in G minor

The professors were in no doubt of the young composer's promise, though the clashing timetables of musical and other academic studies remained a stumbling-block for some time. The continuation of Prokofiev's general education now brought him into contact with other students of various ages. He was not sexually precocious. His friendship with the Sontsovka doctor's three daughters had been 'comradely, and without a hint of flirtation',[9] and now he remained naively indifferent to the female sex. A year later, older students would mock him when their ribald conversation about a soprano who 'made an effort' for a valuable male contact so that he would 'make an effort' for her went over his head: 'Prokosha's a good boy, he doesn't know about such things'.[10] His naivety might have brought him into contact, or so his elders thought, with the kind of unnamed horrors hinted at so often by Henry James. He quickly made friends with a boy three years his senior, one Potemkin, 'pleasant in his manner but somewhat undisciplined',[11] only to have his mother advised against the friendship by the conservatory's deputy inspector. Prokofiev, who heard dark, adult mutterings along the lines of 'undesirable company . . . bad record . . . a very dissolute youth',[12] never found out anything 'bad' about his supposedly depraved friend, but there are hints that rejected, waddling Potemkin may have been homosexual.

The students of the harmony class were all male and Prokofiev was in the curious situation of being much the youngest. Vasily Shpis, nearly two decades his senior, viewed him with understandable suspicion and the reaction of his other classmates was cautiously comrade-like at best; but among them were two students soon to be of much assistance in his early career: Boris Asafyev, sickly, stooping, wearing a threadbare, double-breasted jacket, and Anatoly Kankarovich, ' a thin brunette with a pale face and a retreating forehead, as if the front part of his cranium had been lopped off'.[13]

Taking the class was a venerable name and a rather less venerable human being who, in Prokofiev's eyes, was guiltier of a worse crime than the animosity of the older students: indifference. Anatoly Lyadov's laziness was legendary since his expulsion from composition classes at the conservatory as a 19-year-old in 1876. His teacher at the time, Rimsky-Korsakov, later stated the root of the problem lay in a boyhood passed 'without supervision and without system'.[14] That most influential of 19th-century critics Vladimir Stasov had looked forward in vain to 'large-scale symphonic works from one so richly endowed with musical ideas and a sense of form'.[15] Inspirations for a barely begun opera, *Zoryushka*, would live on in *Kikimora* and *The Enchanted Lake*, two of his three miniature orchestral masterpieces; by 1904 only the first, depicting the flight of the Russian witch, Baba Yaga, in a deft three minutes, had appeared. Lyadov's sluggishness later gave the young Stravinsky his first major break: Diaghilev, who regarded Lyadov as Russia's 'leading composer' after the death of Rimsky-Korsakov, commissioned him to write the score for *The Firebird*, which then passed from Lyadov to Stravinsky via Nikolay Tcherepnin, Diaghilev's second choice. It was the mature Stravinsky's belief that such a 'short-winded, *pianissimo* composer' could never have written a 'long and noisy ballet'. Stravinsky liked Lyadov as a person, describing him as 'sweet and charming' with a love of 'tender, fantastical things';[16] but his private teacher Rimsky-Korsakov's curt dismissal of whatever thoughts he might have had of studying at the conservatory shielded him from any experience of Lyadov as a mentor.

Prokofiev much enjoyed his teacher's arrangements of eight Russian folksongs when they were first performed in 1906, but he had no words of praise for Lyadov the man. It was bad enough that the harmony lessons were so dry, with their pedantic insistence on mastering the first, fourth and fifth degrees of the scale and punishments for parallel 5ths and octaves; it says more about Prokofiev's character than his teacher's, however, that the impetuous young pupil with his unhelpful disregard for mastering the basics 'never linked Lyadov's classes with my own plans for composition'.[17] He is amusing at first about Lyadov's physiognomy, and especially his bald head – 'big, very smooth, gleaming, and from it came a smell like the card table on which we used to play *vingt* in Sontsovka'.[18] But it soon came to be associated with the lack of interest that Lyadov, ever anxious to finish the lessons before time, gave out to his students, and Prokofiev's usually objective prose becomes incontinent with the language of loathing: 'I can still see his fat figure with his swollen little eyes, his bloated fat face, the short arms with the hands stuffed deep in the trouser pockets, swaying on the tips of his prunella shoes, hoping that the student would go away and leave him in peace'.[19] It was not entirely fair, for in the upheavals that followed Lyadov was to show a decency that Prokofiev the autobiographer admits but seems unwilling to acknowledge with good grace.

Fortunately there was a counterweight to offset this disillusioning acquaintance. Alexander Winkler, whose advanced class for obligatory piano Prokofiev entered later in his first term, proved as attentive and conscientious as Lyadov was peevish and aloof. It cannot have been easy for the impetuous Prokofiev to submit to the iron discipline of good piano technique, but it was thanks only to Winkler that he began to acquire it over the next few years. As so often, the candid autobiographer corrects an alternative view which gilds with hindsight. The memoirs of Morolev, the enthusiastic Sontsovka veterinary surgeon whose backwoods existence was to be enlivened by the return of the young native in the summer of 1905, speak of a pianistic 'clarity, purity, expressiveness – and at the same time you felt that no passages were giving him trouble, that he played the instrument easily and freely'.[20] Prokofiev quotes Morolev to make a tart correction: 'there was, certainly, expressiveness; but as for clarity and purity, there was no clarity, and the purity was only illusory'.[21] Perhaps, he tries to suggest by way of reconciliation, Morolev was confusing the fledgling pianist in his mind with the more disciplined young man of five years later, 'by which time I had rid myself of many bad habits'.

With Winkler, Prokofiev now undertook a more detailed study of the early Beethoven sonatas he had begun to know in Sontsovka alongside Bach preludes and fugues. He heard little music of any significance that autumn. A great pianist,

Alexander Ziloti, whose infamous cut-down version of Tchaikovsky's Second Piano Concerto replaced the original in the repertoire until very recently, had turned conductor and launched his own season of concerts to outstrip in popularity the more patrician and conservatively planned events of the Russian Musical Society (RMO). Conservatory students, so long as their exercises were in order, had access to the rehearsals of both organizations, and in marked contrast to a predictably dull Anton Rubinstein programme at the RMO, Prokofiev heard a perplexing novelty item at one of the Ziloti rehearsals. There the German actor and impresario Ernst von Possart, for whom Richard Strauss had composed his Tennyson curiosity *Enoch Arden*, so 'shouted, howled and was beside himself' in melodramatic recitation to a piece by the now-forgotten composer Max von Schillings that the adolescent Prokofiev 'in embarrassment looked to one side in bewilderment as to why this was necessary'[22] (the mature voice of a newspaper critic was altogether more impressed). Giants of the Russian repertory and Western classics prevailed, then as now, at the Maryinsky Theatre, where Chaliapin was singing Musorgsky's *Boris Godunov* in the second of Rimsky-Korsakov's two performing versions. The astonished autobiographer has to admit no memory of the event, though a letter to his father harshly criticizes the production of Tchaikovsky's *Queen of Spades* he saw there: 'it's a good opera, but the singing, playing and designs were abominable'.[23]

The resourceful only child found plenty of amusement at home. His mother and Aunt Tanya had moved from their temporary dwelling in a lodging vacated by the Rayevskys to a reasonably central apartment on Sadovaya Ulitsa, between the Yekaterinsky Canal and the Fontanka, within close earshot of the bells of the Pokrov Church. It was a small flat with five main rooms divided by a corridor; the boy's was much the smallest, and adjacent to his aunt's. 'Seryozha is very pleased with his room', Marya Grigoryevna wrote to her husband, 'He spends all his time sitting in it'[24] – at a desk, the autobiographer adds, which inspired in him the lifelong habit of solitary study. Here he played chess with the few boys who visited the little household, resumed his general studies at home when the clash with musical subjects at the conservatory became a problem, concluded his long narrative poem 'The Count' and devised ever more elaborate commentaries on the Russian battleships participating in the war against Japan – with not the slightest inkling that it would end in disaster.

Simultaneous with the wasteful war came the first big upheaval in the history of 20th-century Russia, one of many that would affect Prokofiev's musical plans. On Sunday 9 January 1905 thousands of working-class petitioners arriving at the Winter Palace to ask the tsar for a constitution were fired on by cossacks; hundreds died in the chaos. A personal testimony handed down to a Russian of a later generation, who reported on it with firm conviction to the author, claimed that the catastrophe was launched when troops fired into the nearby trees, hoping the noise would disperse the crowds. Unfortunately, children were perched there seeking a better view, and they fell dying to the ground. With this tragic accident, apparently, the panic began. Prokofiev and his mother arrived in St Petersburg three days later, having spent Christmas in Sontsovka and the previous few days in Moscow. In a letter to his father, Seryozha merely mentions their relative freedom of movement, 'although you often meet cossack patrols of two to five men',[25] and the boarded-up shops before turning to a characteristically detailed account of his latest meeting with the indulgent Taneyev. The autobiographer points out, reasonably enough, that what little reflectiveness his younger self showed about the political events rapidly unfolding before his eyes was derived from 'those around me and above all my mother'.[26] Marya Grigoryevna took fright at the strikes and uprisings of early 1905; for her any kind of revolution should evolve as a liberal, reasoned process and not as what Prokofiev calls 'an unintellectual action'[27] – though her reactions were less conservative than those of Aunt Tanya, who worked in the 'department of the Empress Marya', or Aunt Katya, naturally expected to toe the imperial line as wife of the high-ranking Rayevsky.

The city continued, Prokofiev tells us, to quake from 'underground explosions'.[28] But for a while musical life continued with few interruptions, giving Prokofiev a chance to play several of his *pesenki* to admiring classmates in Lyadov's absence. His operatic heroine Undine came under the scrutiny of her literary guardian Madame Kilschtedt, now much diminished by the recent upheavals, and his fictional count breathed his last:

> The sharp knife went straight to his heart
> And thus the poor count died – so that's that.[29]

Then the unexpected happened: the Revolution struck to the heart of Prokofiev's musical world-within-a-world. 'Just imagine', he wrote to his father on 5 February, 'a strike began at the conservatory today.'[30] Kankarovich, the political conscience of the Lyadov class, went to a meeting at which objections were raised to a student who, as a soldier, had fired on the workers, and to the capricious behaviour of the celebrated Leopold Auer, dedicatee of Tchaikovsky's Violin Concerto and now an old reactionary who acted according to caprice (not least in hitting his students over the head with his bow). At the premiere of Glazunov's sweet, succinct and tuneful Violin Concerto later that month, the composer was cheered, but Auer as soloist was loudly hissed (Prokofiev went to the concert: it also featured Mozart's C minor Mass which, in his early quest for piquant harmonies and dramatic sensation, he found 'boring and lengthy').[31]

Marya Grigoryevna, initially dismissive, found some of the students' demands sensible: it was reasonable, for example, that they should reclaim the conservatory's theatre, usually rented out, for their own regular performances. But soon the trouble spread. The conservatory was closed, but only temporarily; on 9 March students occupied the building, broke some windows and made a chemical protest referred to as the 'stinking obstruction'. There were over a hundred arrests, and now it was time for the institution's senior figure to show his solidarity with his students. 'Rimsky-Korsakov has had published in one of the Moscow newspapers an interesting letter about the St Petersburg Conservatory', Prokofiev informed his father on 19 March 1905.[32] Rimsky-Korsakov's letter declared the building closed until 1 September, against the wishes of the Imperial Music Society's Petersburg branch which, in turn, contravened the decision of the artistic leadership. He concluded:

> Is any progress in the field of music possible at an institution where the resolutions of the Art Council have no meaning, where, under its charter, the musical artists are subordinate to the Directorate – that is, to a group of amateurs and dilettantes . . . at an institution totally indifferent to the fate of its students in questions of education?
>
> All the above regulations of the Charter and the actions of the administration of the Conservatory I find inexpedient, anti-artistic, and callous from the moral point of view, and I consider it my duty to express my protest.[33]

Four days later Rimsky-Korsakov registered his protest at a meeting. The rapid development of events is neatly recorded in Prokofiev's letters to his father:

> *March 23* As a result of the letter (the one which I wrote to you about when you were in Moscow), Rimsky-Korsakov was informed by the directors of the Musical Society (under the chairmanship of Grand Duke Konstantin Konstantinovich) that he was dismissed from his post as professor. [Among the other major figures at the conservatory, Glazunov, Lyadov, Yesipova and Benois supported him; Auer was on the side of the reactionaries.][34]

> *March 27* Everyone sympathizes with Rimsky-Korsakov. 130 professors sent him a letter of solidarity; the Moscow musicians have made a protest on the occasion of his dismissal from office. Even the high-school students have sent him a letter of support.[35]

> *March 30* The theory students are sending a statement to the Board of Directors saying that since Rimsky-Korsakov, Glazunov and Lyadov have left they no longer want to remain at the conservatory, and requesting that their papers be returned. They asked me to sign it and with mother's consent I did. ['Very important', Prokofiev adds as comment on the letter, 'my first political statement.'][36]

Prokofiev's father, remembering his own turbulent student days, was horrified at the thought that the removal of the papers might jeopardize his son's chances of further education. In fact the protest was never sent; but that academic year had come effectively to an abrupt and enigmatic end, with talk of private classes beginning the following September. There was one spectacular finale in the shape of a performance given by conservatory students in Komissarzhevskaya's Theatre. Its second half never took place; as with a similar event for which Prokofiev and his classmate Kankarovich had led the fund-raising to present a congratulatory wreath to their teacher Lyadov – in itself a semi-political statement, for the other wreaths were to be presented to Rimsky-Korsakov and Glazunov – officials cancelled it to avoid further disruption. But in this case the point had already been made at the main event, which was the premiere of Rimsky-Korsakov's imaginative (and purely escapist) one-act opera *Kashchey the Immortal*, conducted by Glazunov.

The opera was followed by what Rimsky-Korsakov's close friend and chronicler Vasily Yastrebtsev described as 'an enormous political demonstration, the like of which I never saw before or since'.[37] Countless speeches and tributes were brought to an end only by the shaken, embarrassed composer, who according to Yastrebtsev 'did not want this festive occasion in his honour to be linked in the public's mind with the memory of the "iron curtain" which was lowered, obviously on the orders of the police, even as the reading of the address was beginning'.[38] Prokofiev missed this momentous occasion but he did attend a few of the *Kashchey* rehearsals; he especially liked the characterization of the ogre's daughter Kashcheyevna, ultimately transfigured by pity but darkly encircled for much of the opera by seductive chains of 3rds.

'Now is such an unexpected time in Russian life that every day brings new things as if it were another year', wrote Marya Grigoryevna to her husband on 31 March 1905. 'In the autumn we sent our son to the conservatory, and in the spring we're taking him back . . . we have found out to our cost that one cannot swim against the tide.'[39] Even back in Sontsovka there was no escape from the catalogue of upheavals and disasters. A loud-mouthed engineer horrified Prokofiev with his guffawing assertion that he had placed a whip-or-be-whipped bet on the outcome of the Russo-Japanese War and was confident of thrashing his rival when Russia lost. 'The thought that we could lose never entered my head', recounts the composer, 'and I looked with amazement at this man who had voluntarily agreed to be whipped – and publicly, at that.'[40] Yet on 27 May the impossible happened: Russia's Baltic fleet was conclusively routed off Tsushima. The end to what interior minister Plehve had called 'a little victorious war to stop the revolutionary tide'[41] signified to many that Russian imperial might had gone for ever. At the news of his beloved battleships' demise, Prokofiev felt like 'a man who had lost his entire family'[42] – but his notebook obsessions with naval 'coefficiency' continued all the same. Closer to home were the rural disturbances which had begun before the events of January 1905 but which now spread to Sontsovka just as Prokofiev returned home. Sergey Alexeyevich tried to keep the peace but he was powerless to prevent the waves of burning haystacks on neighbouring farms. Prokofiev describes this unexpected threat to his childhood sense of stability with his usual vividness:

> They would wake me up at the sounding of the alarm, and in the dark southern night the bright light of flames could be seen on the horizon. I felt inconsolable and disturbed, and my parents sent me back to bed, where for a long time I would turn from side to side, in no state to go back to sleep.[43]

The leaden clanging of the *nabat* (alarm bell) was especially upsetting. It had already played a memorable part in Russian opera, dominating for example the Act I finale of Borodin's *Prince Igor*, but Prokofiev was able to endow it with special significance at the opening of the Third Symphony – a hair-raising introduction to the ostinato theme of *The Fiery Angel* – and the 'fire' sequence that brings panic into the Ukrainian village setting of *Semyon Kotko*.

Still, that summer brought its blessings. There was the new friendship with Morolev, a competent pianist, willing audience for Prokofiev's recitals of Beethoven sonatas as well as the piquant new note of Skryabin's op.3 Mazurkas and (best of all) a merry but careless chess partner. An old Sontsovka pleasure, tournaments on stilts, resumed with Prokofiev spontaneously granted leadership by the local children, and it was joined by a new pastime: learning to ride the bicycle chosen with care in St Petersburg and ridden rather more recklessly until a potentially serious accident prompted greater caution. A camera from doting Aunt Tanya prompted some boring documentation from Prokofiev the train-spotter, though its real benefit was to yield delightfully impromptu photographs of fun and games, and (in 1908) the celebrated picture of Prokofiev full-length front and back which was pasted together to form a cardboard cut-out. Moving on to 'adult' literature, the statistician again applied his own marking system to register his enthusiasm. He began with Turgenev's *Nest of Gentlefolk*, meriting the top mark of 5 (an 'A'), while Gogol's *Dead Souls*, which one might have thought closer to his own future brand of wayward comedy, only reached '5–'. Later in the year *War and Peace* was awarded a 5, though the critical reader noted, for the first and certainly not the last time, that it could have been compressed; two of the plays of Ostrovsky were considered 'boring'[44] and only received a 2 and a 3 (the following summer's ratings show impeccable taste: Turgenev's *Rudin*, 3+; Gogol's *Evenings on a Farm near Dikanka*, 4+; Lermontov's *A Hero of our Time*, 5).

This and the following summer at Sontsovka also saw further work on the *pesenki*, destined to die a natural death early in the conservatory academic year of 1907–8. For the time being, many of them were written to order, to celebrate a family name-day or birthday, but the process of refinement continued towards what Asafyev the sympathetic critic was to define as 'true Prokofiev genre'.[45] Throughout 1905 there was a divergence, as Prokofiev pointed out, between two types of piano work. The newcomers were 'big, sweeping pieces conceived on a broad scale, and they always came out rather awkwardly and unfinished'.[46] Among these are the seventh piece of the fifth series, his fourth *romance*, *Allegro con fuoco*, with an overlong introduction (all that the examiners allowed him to play at the autumn entrance examination) and what both the composer and Asafyev described as 'Schumannesque agitations'[47] in the central sequence, and its predecessor in the final listing, actually composed later. This A flat major Allegro aims high with its syncopated left-hand octaves and its loose, fantasia-like construction, while its bullish declaration of independence features one harmonic progression which would have made Lyadov blanch (Ex.6).

Ex.6 Allegro in A flat major

'Along with these pieces', the autobiographer adds, 'there were pieces that were shorter and at the same time more intimate in cast, and these *pesenki* were better constructed and finer in terms of form.'[48] The increasing harmonic piquancy helps us to hear the real Prokofiev here. In the D minor Allegro (no.4 of series 5), the staccato exchanges between left and right hand still owe much to Schumann and Tchaikovsky (and especially the latter's 'August' from *The Seasons*), but the daring leaps and unsettled harmonies of Prokofiev's first minuet, the 11th piece in the same series, composed at the end of the year, makes it sound more like a *Valse grotesque* until we reach the trio section. A scherzo 'for dear Mama' from the end of January 1906 is more remarkable for the bright sonorities of its tarantella-like 3rds in the right hand and disappointingly placid in its central melody; but the daring line continues in a D minor *Allegro non troppo*. Its sudden surprising climb in an initially stable, ostinato-like bass, mirrored by Straussian harmonic caprice in the treble, is also the starting-point of a G minor Waltz, a mere 40 bars long and playable in nearly as many seconds. Prokofiev's individual homages to the basic genres are beginning to take shape, and in the *Tempo di marcia* which follows in series 5 there is at last a prototype for an authentic miniature masterpiece, the March that launches op.12. In that revision Prokofiev would spice up the progressions and the inner lines, make more of the piano's extreme upper register and replace the rather heavy central sequence with two new ideas of complementary impishness; but the idea is unmistakably here in outline (Exx.7*a* and *b*).

Ex.7*a* March in F minor (1906)

Ex.7*b* March, op.12, no.1

In the last completed numbers of the fifth series, Prokofiev is completely himself. Asafyev sees in the startling final chords of the *Prestissimo* a premonition of the surprising cadence at the end of the March in *The Love for Three Oranges*, while the 'Study Scherzo' posits a different blueprint for the pieces to come, its wayward excursions into distant keys swiftly brought to book by witty reiteration of the C major home key. There is already a hint here of the effervescent comedy favoured by the French composers of the 1920s. The 'morbid' harmonies of Skryabin which Rimsky-Korsakov so detested are never allowed to settle, but the celebration of the tonic is just as brittle; the *pesenka* is already snapping at the heels of well-dressed convention like the *sobachki* ('doggies') which were about to take its place.

With these last *pesenki* Glière's legacy to his precocious pupil officially came to an end. Prokofiev the autobiographer continues his relentless fire on Lyadov with yet another reminder that the creative mainspring of his first important teacher outlasted the dead hand of the reluctant conservatory professor. Lyadov also comes off badly once more in comparison with the diligent Winkler, who now took Prokofiev into his special piano class. Yet when civic unrest throughout the autumn term of 1905 led to the conservatory's closure again the following January, Lyadov was diligent enough to take on Prokofiev as a private pupil free of charge. Admittedly his parents preferred to pay for better results; but Lyadov's comments are not those of an apathetic teacher. His insistence on pure voice-leading was merely one way of applying the bridle to the undisciplined teenager, comparable to Winkler's endless finger-strengthening exercises, and his criticisms were by no means without foundation. '(Lyadov) says that Seryozha has a very flippant attitude to everything', wrote Marya Grigoryevna to her husband on 3 February. 'He has to work more seriously. He knows the rules, but he makes mistakes, he does not criticize himself enough.'[49]

Prokofiev admits that these one-to-one occasions were an improvement on earlier classes. There was discussion of good examples in counterpoint, and – curiously, though rather admirably – Lyadov recommended Tchaikovsky's *The Sleeping Beauty*, lending the pupil his score with a personal inscription from the master; the future composer of *Ala and Lolly* and *Chout* was unimpressed by 'all those ballet numbers'.[50] Yet when Lyadov showed curiosity enough to discover his pupil's favourite composers, Tchaikovsky was one of the three choices, even though Prokofiev by then knew only the second of his six symphonies. Grieg, probably the most sincerely chosen candidate because Prokofiev knew many of the *Lyric Pieces* well, was rated harmful, a dilettante who lacked technique; but Wagner, like Tchaikovsky, was good.

At this stage, the composer concedes, there might have been an element of snobbery in his declaration of Wagnerian affinities, but there was prophecy too. In early 1906 he rated *Tannhäuser* more for the Pilgrims' Chorus than anything else, and '*Meistersinger* interested me, but I can't say that the wondrous beauty of this opera, which I came to love so much later, revealed itself to me at first'.[51] Yet epiphany was just round the corner. Prokofiev ascribed his first acquaintance with *Der Ring des Nibelungen* to the season of 1907–8, but it must have been at least a year earlier, for he writes of it as an unprecedented occasion; the *Ring* as a Russian creation launched itself on a voracious St Petersburg public the previous season, while the Maryinsky production of *Das Rheingold* which Prokofiev describes so vividly as part of the complete cycle was given its premiere at the end of 1905. Prokofiev stepped boldly into rehearsals, with a full score under his arm generously lent him by Glazunov – only to be told by Rimsky-Korsakov that a piano score would distract him less from understanding what was happening on stage. He witnessed a group of singers in everyday clothes, and between them 'an actor . . . turning and wriggling, lively as quicksilver'.[52]

This was the Loge of Ivan Yershov, 'a singer possessed of a very powerful though rather constricted voice and a fine acting talent',[53] whose assumption of the roles of Loge, Siegmund and Siegfried, as well as his brilliant creation of the rogue Grishka Kuterma in the premiere of Rimsky-Korsakov's *The Legend of the Invisible City of Kitezh*, was the talk of the season; he now eclipsed the glory years of Nikolay Figner's performances as Radames. According to a contemporary, his commitment was such that he 'would actually blanch when stabbed by Hagen each time and involuntarily blush upon discovering Brünnhilde to be a woman'.[54] Critical consensus held that Yershov and the conductor, that Czech-born grand old man of Russian music Eduard Nápravník, were beacons in the general gloom of an uninspiring production, but for the Prokofievs this was no obstacle; they obtained a subscription for a series that season and over the next two years with difficulty. From each cycle the enthusiastic teenager took away something new, and in the synthesis of his impressions he noted especially the forging scene in *Siegfried* and the 'dashing, tousled whirlwind'[55] of 'Siegfried's Journey down the Rhine' in *Götterdämmerung*. Of the four operas, he reflected most musicians' preferences in favouring *Die Walküre* and *Götterdämmerung*.

The effect on a new generation of Russian musicians was comparable to the unveiling of the *Ring* cycle by a visiting German company in February 1889 – an event that had profoundly affected the orchestral soundworld of Rimsky-Korsakov's operas. The young Prokofiev, though, was too strong a personality to let the Wagnerian ethos take hold. *Undine* continued to make slow progress and was finally abandoned in the summer of 1908; it would be another four years before he began another opera. More successful were his first steps in composing fully fledged piano sonatas. The first one of his conservatory years, begun in St Petersburg in early 1906, was composed that summer. This was the F minor 'Grand Sonata', 'no.2', the first movement of which he was to take over with few changes in 1909 as his official Sonata no.1 op.1. Yet the pianist Frederic Chiu, an outstanding Prokofiev interpreter, is right to find this selfconscious exercise in the vein of Rakhmaninov or early Skryabin 'agreeably musical and pianistically comfortable, but lacking the piquant imagery that peppers his other works'.[56] More original is the first *pesenek* of the fifth series, composed at the beginning of the year; the opening gesture quoted in the autobiography is much more significant in terms of the 'real' Prokofiev. This C sharp minor piece originally began with the right-hand melody doubled in the bass for the third and fourth beats – a method against conservatory rules which, Prokofiev even then felt, 'accentuated and strengthened the expressiveness of the melody'[57] (Ex.8). He was persuaded to alter it, but points out that the doubling was later to become a hallmark of his maturity: in orchestral terms, the first bassoon often holds the melody along with the first flute, as in the well-known opening of the Fifth Symphony. This was a rare stroke of originality in a work which was dominated, in Asafyev's words, by 'romantic pathos with

Ex.8 *Pesenka* in C sharp minor

inevitable triplets'.[58] Between more summer chess matches, Morolev found time to admire these diligent efforts on a larger scale. Yet Prokofiev was about to find another friend better qualified to help him along an individual path. With approval from a fellow student who was to play a major role in his life, he was about to allow his more audacious side free rein.

3
A friend for life
1906–9

With life at the St Petersburg Conservatory back to normal, the academic year of 1906–7 turned out to be a watershed in Prokofiev's life. The reason lay not in his first orchestration classes with Rimsky-Korsakov, too overcrowded to be of much benefit, or his initial meetings with Nikolay Tcherepnin, an unusually animated figure among the professors he had encountered so far. The most fertile source of inspiration was a new fellow-student, Nikolay Myaskovsky. Prokofiev recalled his arrival with customary clarity:

> Myaskovsky arrived at the conservatory in the army uniform of a lieutenant in an engineers' battalion, carrying a big yellow portfolio under one arm. He sported a moustache and beard. He was always reserved, polite and quiet. His reserve attracted one to him, and at the same time he held people at a distance. He was 25 years old.[1]

Almost exactly ten years Prokofiev's senior – their birthdays were only a week apart – Myaskovsky could hardly have been more different in temperament, and the circumstances of his life had much to do with his outwardly phlegmatic character. Born into a military family, he had an innate love of music and drama much like Prokofiev's; as a child, he devised tunes for solitary puppet-shows which he intoned with comb and paper. But in place of his mother, who died young, came an aunt who combined strict musical skills with a religious nature bordering on the fanatical; weekends in the Myaskovsky household were occasions of solemn gloom. His father, of course, expected him to do his soldierly duty; but if he was no rebel scion of a military family like Henry James's Owen Wingrave, he soon decided with quiet tenacity that a soldier's life was not to be his goal. An 1896 performance of Tchaikovsky's Sixth Symphony conducted by Arthur Nikisch, idol of Marya Grigoryevna and her son, came as a blinding revelation. After squeezing in musical studies at the two cadet colleges where he received the greater part of his education, Myaskovsky graduated in 1899 – marked out, as he wrote in his autobiographical notes, for 'a military career for which I had nothing but the strongest distaste, and to which I had been doomed by family and social tradition alone'.[2]

Just how far removed the sensitive Myaskovsky must have been from the roistering life of arrogant St Petersburg officers, which had changed very little since the descriptions given in *Anna Karenina*, can be gleaned from Prokofiev's hostile relations with his cousin Katyechka's fiancé, Paul Ignatyev. Boorishly intruding on the teenage Prokofiev's sleep, this all-too-typical specimen of a St Petersburg officer railed against his new friend, whom he knew as a fellow engineering officer, declaring that Myaskovsky 'used to be a comely lad, but now he's let himself go, conducts himself sluggishly, like a drowsy fly in autumn'.[3] It speaks volumes about Ignatyev's character that following an unreasonable quarrel with a cabby, he lodged a complaint which had the unfortunate worker drummed out of St Petersburg. His refusal to listen to the pleas of the man's desperate wife distressed all three Prokofievs beyond measure. The liberal father is depicted by his son in a towering rage, shouting: 'oh, it goes without saying, his lordship officer must be especially respected, he mustn't be touched, and he must do what he likes',[4] before rushing out of the room and slamming the door behind him. Unsurprisingly, Ignatyev was to remain true to officer type by making married life a misery for Katyechka.

Family honour and arms would return to haunt Myaskovsky in the First World War but his prospects as a young man rapidly improved. He associated with more liberal, widely educated contemporaries at the School of Military Engineering in St Petersburg, and though he was soon drummed into a succession of Reserve Sappers' Battalions, his musical education continued with Glière – less than a year after the young tutor's second summer at Sontsovka – and another composer–teacher, Ivan Kryzhanovsky. He also spent many evenings with literary friends, and would certainly have been the first to introduce Prokofiev to three symbolist poets who already meant so much to him by 1906: Konstantin Balmont, Zinayda Gippius and Dmitry Merezhkovsky. His musical knowledge was no less up to the minute; Rimsky-Korsakov could not help sneering at the would-be student's tastes at the entrance examination to the conservatory, gibing that 'he no doubt enjoys the famous passage from *Salome*'[5] (a reference, apparently, to the chaotic bitonal passage in Strauss's 1903 opera before John the Baptist's execution). Whether or not Myaskovsky knew it then, he commended Strauss's score to Prokofiev at the end of 1907 – only to have it returned with the observation that the younger fellow-student 'didn't take any pleasure in all those scratchings'.[6]

When he arrived at the conservatory, Myaskovsky had already gained access through his teacher Kryzhanovsky to those Evenings of Contemporary Music which were to launch Prokofiev's reputation as a composer (several of Myaskovsky's songs to poems by Gippius had already been performed there). Yet he smarted at the thought of his dilettantism and determined to struggle for his musical independence. Only release from battalion life, in the spring of 1907, brought with it any real sense of possibility for creative freedom. He made his mark from the start, though, calmly distinguishable from two of the other newcomers to Lyadov's classes: the unruly Lazar Saminsky, his polar opposite who turned out to have resented the young whippersnapper Prokofiev, and the 'neurasthenic' Boris Chefranov. The outsider's affectation of lassitude is nicely represented by one of Prokofiev's many dramatized dialogues in his autobiography:

> 'I live with my father.' 'That's pleasant.' 'Or not', he added indifferently through his moustache.
>
> That indifference annoyed me a little, and I retorted by way of an argument: 'Look, if you get married, then you'll discover straight away that to live separately is more pleasant.'
>
> 'I have no matrimonial inclinations', Myaskovsky avowed through his moustache.
>
> 'Matrimonial?' I asked, hearing this word for the first time.
>
> 'The inclination to enter into marriage', explained Myaskovsky, and with this the conversation came to an end.[7]

For all his assumed reserve, Myaskovsky soon forged alliances with Prokofiev, Asafyev, Kankarovich and the regular-featured Boris Zakharov, who joined the class that November. Myaskovsky was to look back on Lyadov's influence with greater generosity than Prokofiev: of course, neither would ever show any of their serious, out-of-lessons work to so discouraging a mentor, and 'the help . . . of such an experienced pedagogue and so outstanding a composer would have saved a great expenditure of energy [on our parts]'. But, he continues,

> I can't completely deny that the unusual strictness of [Lyadov's] demands – nagging, even – his exceptional methodical clarity, unusual taste and extremely sharp critical flair thoroughly strengthened our technique and developed our sense of style. I remember Lyadov with admiration and gratitude, but also with terror.[8]

Lyadov had now taken over Rimsky-Korsakov's teaching of counterpoint, which those students already at the conservatory embarked on without the customary examination, and fugue, the next step. Orchestration classes with the master of the orchestra himself should have been enlightening but there were too many students clustered round the piano, the hours were long and the arduous exercises in arranging piano classics (beginning with Schubert's Marches for four hands) not to the taste of the impatient Prokofiev.

Rimsky-Korsakov explained the role of each instrument, singing the individual parts – 'a composer needs a seven-octave voice'[9] – but, in Prokofiev's opinion, his views on the 'right' instrument used in the scoring exercises were dogmatic; the pupil felt decidedly harassed when the master impatiently dismissed the solo oboe he had found suitable for a passage in a Beethoven sonata in favour of the clarinet – the woodwind instrument he preferred for its mellower tones. Prokofiev found a more patient paragon of teaching in Nikolay Tcherepnin, soon to achieve limited fame as the composer of the first score commissioned for Diaghilev's Ballets Russes,

Le Pavillon d'Armide. In his score-reading classes, Tcherepnin encouraged students to extract the essence from orchestral scores on the piano, and at sight. Clearly Prokofiev impressed him, for Tcherepnin asked if he would like to join his conducting class, the first of its kind in Russia since its instigation in 1903; however, the diffident youth's reply – 'to be honest, I don't know'[10] – postponed the opportunity for another year.

Many of Prokofiev's more exciting discoveries in contemporary music were made through the enthusiasms of his fellow students. Shortly after Max Reger, the German champion of pure music, had conducted his new Serenade at a Ziloti concert on 2 December 1906, Myaskovsky arrived at the next Lyadov class with a four-hand piano arrangement of it in his yellow folder, and they played it through together. This customary way for good sightreaders to become acquainted with the orchestral repertory in the days before recordings became more widely available gave Myaskovsky and Prokofiev a joint voyage of discovery through works that were either old but unfamiliar to them, including Beethoven's Seventh and Ninth Symphonies, or newly minted, like each of Glazunov's latest symphonies and Dukas' *L'Apprenti sorcier*, which greatly impressed the two students. Within two years, under the ever-increasing impact of Skryabin, they would draw a line under the more conservative of living composers. But for now their academic masters were still included in the vanguard – not least Rimsky-Korsakov who, resistant as he may have been to innovations in music, continued to experiment with fresh harmonic techniques within the relatively safe orbit of his operas.

Tcherepnin encouraged within his classes a love of Rimsky-Korsakov's earlier operas such as *May Night* and *Christmas Eve*, backing them up with anecdote, but in 1907 such enlightenment was overshadowed by the February premiere of *The Legend of the Invisible City of Kitezh*. If indeed Prokofiev attended the first Maryinsky *Ring* cycle in the year of its inception, as he implies, and not in 1909, the date he gives, then this must have been quite a season; and if the Prokofiev family were to return for their annual *Ring* experience, the enthusiastic student made sure that he saw this new wonder thrice more that season in the company of his family – the fourth time on one of his father's few visits, sitting for once in a better seat than the wealthy Zakharov instead of the usual 36-kopeck gallery place where 'the heat and stuffiness . . . were frightful'[11] (Myaskovsky recommended a cool, silk shirt for such occasions). Breathless hearsay from fellow students had not exaggerated the marvels of *The Invisible City*. Prokofiev cites the metrical and orchestral complexities of the choruses, the radiant depiction of the forest flowers in the first act and in the most profoundly moving of all Rimsky-Korsakov's apotheoses, the muted menace of the Tartar horns and – best of all, he thought – the orchestral interlude depicting the battle between the unfortunate Russians and their enemy.

The examinations at the end of that academic year brought no distinguished results from Lyadov's class. Only Asafyev, strictly speaking, passed all round; but leniency remained the order of the day, and Prokofiev and his colleagues could look forward to the next stage. He returned to Sontsovka with the most important yield of the year: the works he had written in his free time. Eight new short pieces in one notebook continued the tradition of the *pesenki*, but they were no longer being written for family namedays. In fact Prokofiev dedicated them all to 'respected Vasily Mitrofanovich' (Morolev), and it was the Sontsovka veterinary surgeon, now living in a district on the Dnieper river, who came up with a new sobriquet. These were all 'rather savage "doggies" whose bite was exceptionally painful'[12] (the Russian word 'sobachek' has sometimes been mistranslated as 'puppy'; strictly it means 'little dog', but 'doggy' better conveys what Prokofiev regarded as the absurdity of the title). There was one exception to the prevailing snappiness in the first piece, *Upryok* ('Reproach'), which Prokofiev instructed Morolev to play 'very *piano*, tenderly and rather peacefully'[13] – an A minor 6/8 reverie which, like its colleagues in the bright-green music book, has not survived other than in the handful of bars Prokofiev quotes in his autobiography. This was not the only example of a lyricism that was to surprise Prokofiev's critics every time it surfaced. When the young opera composer at last laid *Undine* to rest that summer, the watery death of the hero Hildebrand turned out quietly and with an unresolved cadence which shocked Morolev; and further gentle tunefulness was just round the corner at the start of *Skazka* ('Fairy Tale'), heading the first collection of his short pieces to be published.

Yet the impression of the capricious little monster-composer prevailed. Even Myaskovsky, who had seen the pieces before their dedicatee had a chance to play them through, returned them in amazement at 'what a snake we've been cherishing in our bosom'.[14] He was less impressed with the second sonata, though he copied it out because 'it is very important for me to see how fledgling composers work as they begin to compose seriously'[15] and was amused at Prokofiev's numbering system, but his prophecy that it would be scratched out in favour of the true 'number one' turned out to be not an entirely accurate prophecy. As we know, Prokofiev did submit the first movement of his original second sonata for the official status 'no.1, op.1', and felt he deserved the reproach of friends for doing so; he was to have fewer doubts about brushing up the third sonata, on which he now embarked in early 1907, with Myaskovsky's encouragement, as his op.28 in 1917. We do not know precisely what changes he made, but the unusual structure remained the same; for the first time in 1907, revelling in a newfound mastery of sonata form, he abbreviated the reappearance of the exposition material in his recapitulation.[16] This is not merely a stylistic device: the first of his simple 'white-note' melodies, the lyrical countersubject, probably supported by a new, more chromatic, left-hand inner line in 1917 (Ex.9), simply gets caught up in the now unstoppable excitement of its predecessor and, with no time to dream second time round, joins in the tempestuous dance (Ex.10). 12/8 metre, implied within the 4/4 time-signature, is all that links this clear-headed whirlwind with op.1; the chromatic textures are leaner and harder-hitting, the rhythms leap and spring, and – even assuming that Prokofiev made radical changes to the development in 1917 – the

Ex.9 Piano Sonata no.3, op.28

anticipation of the grimmer whirlwinds set in motion by the Sixth Sonata remains astonishing. Above all, for the first time in a larger-scale piece, Prokofiev stops worrying about the conventions of sonata form and knits together the sharply defined characteristics of the last *pesenki* and the first *sobachki*.

The correspondence of a liftetime between Prokofiev and Myaskovsky began in the summer of 1907 with the first of some 450 letters. As the autobiographer notes, he had 'reached the age where correspondence becomes an important event in life – almost a religious rite'.[17] In those first seven letters which passed between Sontsovka and the Myaskovskys' summer residence in Oranienbaum, there is already a Russian love of endearments. Prokofiev ridicules pompous modes of address – 'Respected Nikolay Yakovlevich! (Beloved Kolyechka!)';[18] 'Infinitely excellent Nikolai Yakovlevich! Dear one! Fearfully dear one!'[19] – while Myaskovsky responds with extravagant affection that looks odd only in translation: 'beloved of my heart',[20] 'light of my eyes'.[21] The full range of tender diminutives was to be exploited over the next few years. Prokofiev becomes Serge (in a premonition of his Parisian years), Sergunchik, Sergusha, Seryozha, Seryozhenka and Serzhinka, while Myaskovsky is addressed with even greater ingenuity as Lieber Kola, Kolo, Kukulechka, Kolyunya, Kolyusha, Kolyunechka, Kolyunichek, Myaskusya, Nyamusya, Nyamulenka, Nyamushenochek and Nyamochka (these last four derived from his first name and patronymic; later Prokofiev came to like 'Nick Yak').

In 1907, apart from a long-running exchange over Myaskovsky's fanciful turn of phrase and his near-illegible handwriting, the correspondence was limited to a detailed and supportive mutual commentary on each composer's new works. This,

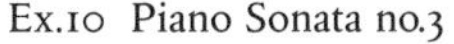

Ex.10 Piano Sonata no.3

as Myaskovsky noted in retrospect, was the first summer in which he came close to professional-composer status. He complained to Prokofiev of 'idleness and inertia'[22] as obstacles to an orchestral composition, but in spite of his habitual lack of self-confidence, this was a prolific time for him in the field of chamber and instrumental music. Prokofiev's first steps in criticism were bluntly laid at the service of his friend's music. He went through the 12 short piano pieces (some a mere eight bars long) that Myaskovsky was to gather under the collective title *Flofion*, and his examination bears out Myaskovsky's warning that there were risky things only in a few places. He rejected the chance to look over his friend's new *romances* to texts by Yevgeny Baratynsky, and though his thoughts on the string quartet Myaskovsky finished that year are not on record, he must have been dismissive of the genre, for the following year he expresses his hope that Myaskovsky will get round to the symphony he has promised, 'but not a filthy quartet'.[23]

Prokofiev's most useful criticism is reserved for the two piano sonatas, the third and fourth of his conservatory years, which Myaskovsky eventually entrusted to the printer's hands: the D minor Sonata published in 1910 as his op.6, when two movements were added to the opening three-part fugue and its developmental sequel, and the four-movement work Myaskovsky thought of calling *Sonate-Fantaisie*, revised as the Fifth Sonata in B major op.64 no.1. His colleague may have been scornful of the way the consoling, songlike melody at the heart of the slow movement is repeated in full four times,[24] but in the midst of so much often fascinating diversity of style, this is the real Myaskovsky – a true successor to the Tchaikovsky of the Sixth Symphony in the easing of oppressive melancholy by the power of song.

With his own two sonatas ready and waiting by the beginning of the summer, their worth merely reinforced by Myaskovsky's selective but fundamentally approving comments, Prokofiev was less industrious. We learn of a sonatina, which has not survived but which would surely have stayed close to the classical tonic–dominant style Myaskovsky defines as his own ideal in this form. With his first letter, Prokofiev also included two 'doggies'. The second and more ambitious is tantalizingly described as the whinings of Wagner's scheming dwarf Mime cooled by the tempo of this C minor *Furioso ma lento*, and Myaskovsky expended much energy on finding a suitably lugubrious name for this 'quasi-Kashcheyevshchina';[25] but this, too, has vanished, and we know more about its 'carnival-like' predecessor simply because Prokofiev the autobiographer tells us what its main theme was – none other than the Puck-like tarantella which replaces the opening pretensions of the First Piano Concerto (Ex.11). The values of the two friends emphasize brevity and clarity, but Myaskovsky clearly felt a gulf not just between the more audacious freshness of Prokofiev's sonatas and his own, where 'everything's Germanically thick and firmly stitched', but also between 'the diversity and sometimes the inscrutable extremity of my tastes' and what he so aptly named as Prokofiev's defining quality of 'causticity' (*kolkost*).[26] The fact remains that with one jaunty tune Prokofiev, in the long term, was to eclipse all his friend's labours that summer.

Ex.11 *Sobachek* in D flat major (1907)

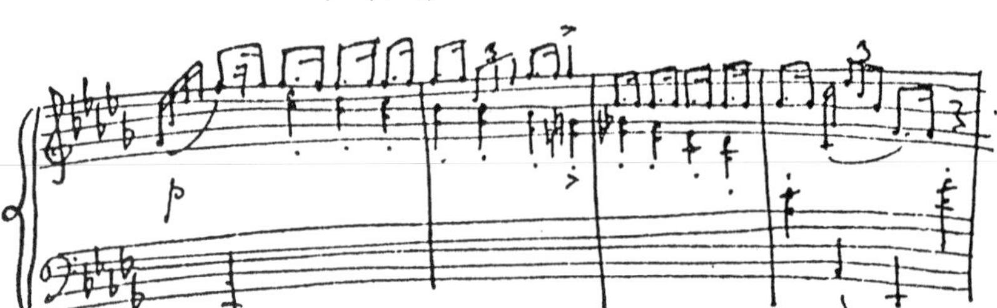

Still, they were racing ahead of their classmates. Asafyev was pitied for his dabbling in children's operas and the necessary naivety of style required. 'I'd never write that sort of thing', scoffs Prokofiev;[27] but in the very different climate of Soviet Russia he was to make a virtue of necessity and become the supreme master of 'children's music' (*detskaya muzyka*). Zakharov merited more respect: he was capable, Myaskovsky decided, of the occasional unexpected harmony and fine turn of phrase. Here, too, a strong correspondence might have developed, but after one exchange Zakharov replied no more – and this, as it turned out, was typical of his character: 'to throw out a line with an enchanting smile and then, when one had bitten on it, to vanish into thin air together with that beautiful smile'.[28] Morolev was a more faithful correspondent. In one of his letters on his return to the Dnieper from Sontsovka, he paid Prokofiev a fine compliment by comparing the fast-improving pianist's delivery of Wagner's *Liebestod* favourably with Nikisch's relatively dragged-out conducting of the same piece. Morolev also kept Prokofiev updated on new developments in the world of chess, a passion which by now had put stilt-walking and toy-pistol tournaments in the shade. It was, in any case, another summer of hard work; the assured young composer would have written much more had he not been firmly recommended the value of a grounding in other academic subjects.

The classes at the conservatory, which he at last rejoined in September 1907 after a long period of private tuition, had something new to teach him: a lesson in flirtation, if not in love. With 17 girls and only three boys in the group, Seryozha was 'like a monk who found himself in a nunnery instead of a monastery'.[29] There was an element of danger in his silent observations of 'the Bessonova girl',[30] whom he nicknamed 'coquette' for her rolling eyes and whose chatty attempts to establish a more intimate relationship with a dozing Seryozha at the conservatory ball of January 1908 are amusingly described. A more durable, if in some respects no less uneasy friendship was with Vera Alpers, 'a girl with a fine figure, but a colourless face, "pale as from birth"',[31] who took the female lead opposite Prokofiev in some short-lived amateur dramatics (the play was *Summer Picture* by Tatyana Shchepkina-Kupernik). Alpers's first impressions, as recounted in later years, were of 'a tall, animated boy, decidedly blond, with lively eyes, a nicely creamy complexion and pronounced, full lips, very neatly dressed and combed. He held himself with dignity'.[32] The strength of Vera's fast-growing infatuation was not to be reciprocated. At this stage Prokofiev was too engrossed in his romantic friendship with Myaskovsky and was not embarrassed to recall a spiteful act of jealousy against a mutual friend who had taken what he considered his own rightful seat next to Myaskovsky in a rehearsal: 'in my fury, I seized hold of my rival with my nails', and the offending hand had to be 'unscrewed' by the howling unfortunate.[33] Myaskovsky candidly confirmed this incident to Mira Mendelson, Prokofiev's second wife, some 40 years later.

The boy from Sontsovka, who had now started to shave, took his first steps as a debutant composer on the evening of 17 December. The event had been coordinated by a graduate of the conservatory, Yekaterina Ranushevich, who is likely to go down in history for her address to the aspiring musician: 'you know, there's a legend about you: that Prokofiev can't bear to hear two true notes in succession. That's because his piano at home is out of tune and he's accustomed to it!'[34] In his diary Prokofiev noted that the pieces he played that evening prompted 'lively talk', and they would lead to a far more impressive and influential recital showcase the following season. The lyrical *Reproach* was joined by *Fairy Tale* – equally smooth, quintessentially diatonic Prokofiev to begin with, holding a few chromatic surprises up its sleeve – and the daring *Prizrak* ('Phantom'), based on a 5/8 ostinato in the bass maintained for 43 of the piece's 49 bars. On sober advice Prokofiev decided not to play the even more evanescent *Shutka* ('Jest'), but in 1907 it was to provide an elusive interlude between *Fairy Tale* and the two fiercer pieces of op.3 – a March based on the characteristic descent of a chromatic scale as well as *Phantom*.

The tamer binary-form exercises for Lyadov's class did not go entirely to waste. Three turn up in op.12, and the malevolent inspiration for the Scherzo of the Second Sonata is also a spectre of the classroom though, as Prokofiev points out, 'these pieces were expanded and made considerably more complex than those I took to the class'.[35] He also composed the fourth of the conservatory-era sonatas, of which he could later remember hardly anything except a fierce exchange of left- and right-hand chords and the fact that it was similar to Skryabin's *Satanic Poem* (which suggests that the loss is regrettable). Then he launched a joint composition Violin Sonata with a sonata Allegro from which he later salvaged a theme for the opera *Maddalena* (Kankarovich composed a central minuet and Myaskovsky rounded off the work with a finale).

Clearly Prokofiev was improving as a pianist. For pleasure he took up one of Medtner's two *Fairy Tales* op.8, admiring the way 'all the notes he wrote were right there under one's fingers',[36] though he would have to wait until his American years to master the piece at the correct tempo. Out of duty in Winkler's class, he practised the fierce discipline of scales in double 3rds, which needed to be good enough to open the gates to the advanced piano class. The examination pieces for the spring of 1908 were a Kessler *Étude*, Bach's Fugue in C minor and Schumann's *Traumes Wirren*; a theme from Handel's *Messiah* became the subject of a four-part fugue. Winkler's report on the technical examination – 'very capable, but doesn't work very painstakingly' – was eclipsed by Glazunov's less discriminating enthusiasm: 'brilliant technique and very beautiful tone'.[37] For the orchestration examination in May, Rimsky-Korsakov gave out 4s all round and the usual adjectives of a report; 'capable', the highest accolade, was reserved for Prokofiev and Zakharov. The task here was Grieg's *Humoreske* in D which in spite of Kankarovich's help Prokofiev 'dragged . . . behind me, like a cart up a hill'.[38] Although he passed, he was to look back with circumspection: 'it wasn't until five or six years later, when I was composing one orchestral piece a year, that I learnt to score decently . . . In spite of my love for Rimsky-Korsakov, I was not then able to take advantage of the brilliant knowledge which he exuded'.[39]

This was unfortunate, since although Prokofiev had just completed a fifth sonata, portions of which he was to rework for the outer movements of the official Fourth Piano Sonata op.29, his heart and soul were set on a symphony, possibly spurred on by Myaskovsky who had decided that in this field lay the greatest freedom of expression. Myaskovsky had a head start; Prokofiev thought up his first theme in flight from the last examination at the end of May 1908, on the train that would take him to the steamer for the resort of Sukhumi in the Crimea. This prelude to a lifelong love of travel to foreign climes came about as a result of his mother's friendship with Olya Smetskaya née Filimonova. In 1902 Olya's wealthy philanthropist husband had set up a sanatorium for tuberculosis sufferers in the balmy subtropical Black Sea climate. Along with what Prokofiev describes as a 'coquettish' house,[40] the Smetskys also had permission to cut down a forest and build a botanic garden (and although they were officially class enemies after the Revolution, they were allowed to keep their property as a reward for having beautified the region and opened their estate to the people). Marya Grigoryevna had visited once before, during that summer of 1903 when she left father and son behind in Sontsovka for a fortnight; now Seryozha joined her and was entranced by 'the south, June, the dark sea, the delicious scent of the southern trees, the lively port'[41] (though he points out that his love of nature only evolved when he was in his mid-30s).

It was not an environment conducive to creative work, though Prokofiev spent up to two hours a day engaged in the pleasurable study of Rimsky-Korsakov's compact and charming piano concerto, the work that would have such an effect on his first experiment in the genre. The problem, he told Myaskovsky, was the 'splendid' Bechstein on which he practised: 'good for playing Wagner on, but for composing impossible – heaven knows why'.[42] For that reason he postponed work on the symphony until he was back in Sontsovka towards the end of June. The 120 pages of score Myaskovsky sent him of his own C minor Symphony may have encouraged him to do otherwise: reacting to it, he lays down a creed that was to serve him well for the next three decades:

> Your *longueurs*, as you put it, make me very wretched. For what can be worse than a long symphony? To me, the ideal of a perfect size for a symphony is one that runs for 20, maximum 30, minutes and I am trying to write mine as compressed as possible. I'm crossing out with a pencil, in the most ruthless fashion, anything that seems in the least bit pompous.[43]

He was not to achieve lightness of touch in his own first movement: by July he was finding its themes 'heavy, inflexible and in no way well organized in the development'.[44] Foreshadowed by bass clarinet and first bassoon in a short introduction, the main theme which Prokofiev defined as slithering begins promisingly with wide-leaping intervals but lapses into conventional sequences, while the second subject, unusually loud and confident, verges on the banal. Prokofiev gives indications for scoring and a fair number of links in the correspondence, while a surviving manuscript of a first-violin part in the State Archive fleshes out a sense of the overall structure and shows some modifications to the original idea (that second subject is now *mf espressivo*, for example, rather than a bald *forte*).[45] He was clearly proud of carrying out his plan in the finale, which he completed in August and which he described to Myaskovsky as 'amazingly laconic: main subject 13 bars; bridge passage 10 bars; second subject 20 bars';[46] Myaskovsky at last turned tail in his C minor work and emulated his friend's brevity in a corresponding movement that also verges on the elliptical.

It is exciting to see Prokofiev's letters accompanied by such elaborate musical examples, but there is a special frisson when we come to the gist of the central Andante, 'not at all cold, although a little solemn in character' as Prokofiev first defined it.[47] The theme, the autobiographer assures us, was the one conceived on the train to Sukhumi (Ex.12). This admirable serpent was to be the sole survivor of the apprentice symphony – selected for four-hand arrangement by Myaskovsky, preserved in the same key and the same lugubrious register for the Fourth Piano Sonata's slow movement and finally returned to its original clothing in the arrangement

Ex.12 Symphony in E minor – Andante

Prokofiev made of that very different movement for orchestra in 1934 (here, too, a bass clarinet takes the solo). It is touching, if somewhat bizarre, to find Myaskovsky still harping on the merits of his friend's 'delightful, fascinating E minor offspring'[48] as late as the end of 1915, just before the premiere of the *Scythian Suite* (which may have made him nostalgic for an orchestral work with its feet on firm symphonic ground). But then Prokofiev, who was too busy with other projects to revise the orchestration which Myaskovsky considered the only problem with the piece, probably had better judgment than his less inspired colleague, who allowed his own C minor Symphony to be published in 1929; it remains grim testimony to the very failing he bewailed in Prokofiev's work.

'Poorly orchestrated'[49] was Prokofiev's own verdict too when Glazunov, a suspicious but nevertheless pragmatic benefactor, won him a private hearing of his symphony the following February. The premiere took place at the hands of the Court Orchestra and its conductor Hugo Wahrlich in an under-rehearsed performance that merely emphasized the gaucheries of scoring. Apart from Tcherepnin, whose conducting classes were proving uncommonly enlightening, Glazunov was the young composer's only ally among the older generation of creative pedagogues though, as the autobiographer notes, 'his interest in the boy whose parents he had persuaded to send their son to the conservatory was giving way to the irritating impression produced by this teenager who was becoming a young man and beginning to compose utterly disagreeable things'.[50] Lyadov, considered beneath contempt in the matter of independent composition, never had the chance to champion the symphony; nor did Rimsky-Korsakov, who might in time have come to nurture the clever teenager as he had the 26-year-old Stravinsky up to his death, on 21 June 1908. Prokofiev pays sincere tribute to the loss – 'it made me very sad; my heart ached'[51] – and tells us that he planned a funeral tribute with a slow introduction and a quotation from Rimsky-Korsakov's orchestral fantasy *Fairy Tale*, based on Pushkin's magical preface to his *Ruslan and Lyudmila*. Stravinsky's homage, a *Chant funèbre* for wind instruments, did achieve a performance, more than a year after his own hyper-romantic and unashamedly derivative (first) Symphony in E flat. Its premiere had taken place under the same circumstances as Prokofiev's orchestral debut as symphonist, with Wahrlich and the Court Orchestra, but the event – and all awareness of the older musician at this time – must have escaped Prokofiev's notice.

Glazunov was probably less dismayed by the fledgling symphony than Prokofiev cared to think. It was still, for all the occasional dissonance, close to his own well-made models, though Prokofiev was now beginning to reject them. He continued to play them through in four-hand arrangements with Myaskovsky; at the beginning of January his postcards to his friend make reference to reductions of Glazunov's Fifth, Sixth, Seventh and Eighth symphonies. Yet when he criticized Myaskovsky's piling-up of counterpoint towards the end of his symphony that summer he took a swipe at the elaborate finale of Glazunov's Seventh Symphony

– one of his best – and, unlike Myaskovsky, he was beginning to find the academic mastery and the ceremonials of Glazunov's triumphant parades decidedly old-fashioned. Rakhmaninov's lyrical style, though there were 'amazingly beautiful things'[52] in some of his narrow-compassed themes – which we now treasure the more for their affinity to Russian Orthodox chant – was, he thought, too often trotted out as a placid formula to provide an alternative. 'We wanted something new, something that took flight and was unexpected'[53] – and that winged quality could only be found in the mysteries of Skryabin.

Prokofiev had grown up alongside Skryabin's ever more adventurous, if ultimately self-restricting, path towards a special kind of light. He had introduced the Chopin-inspired Mazurkas of Skryabin's op.3 to Morolev in Sontsovka during the summer of 1905, delighted to find something 'new and piquant';[54] but early the following year found himself baffled, if intrigued, by the voluptuously orchestrated and harmonized *écroulements formidables* of the Third Symphony, *The Divine Poem*, with its vaguely theosophical struggle towards what Skryabin described in the printed introduction to the score as the spirit's 'joyful and exhilarating affirmation of . . . its unity with the universe'.[55] Passionate enlightenment came with a second performance of Skryabin's most popular orchestral work, the *Poem of Ecstasy*, after a private audition at the Manege in January 1909 which initially produced only headaches; and from now on Prokofiev and Myaskovsky eagerly sought out Skryabin's new piano sonatas (from no.5 onwards) hot off the press. The opinion reached in maturity was ultimately to reflect that of Rimsky-Korsakov, who had lived long enough to play *Ecstasy* (as Prokofiev would call it) on the piano and who was to agree with his friend Vasily Yastrebtsev that such consonance-free music, with its endless enharmonic modulations, might be very good but could ultimately result only in monotony. Prokofiev the autobiographer gives a balanced criticism:

> Basically Skryabin was trying to find a new basis for harmony. The principles he found were very interesting, but in proportion to their complexity they were like a stone round Skryabin's neck, making it difficult for invention in the realm of melody and, chiefly, the movement of the voices.[56]

There was something of a stone round his own neck at the time, to be removed at will. It was the boulder of decadent art, veering towards the darkly expressionist, which he now reflected in two of the piano pieces incorporated into his op.4. One, *Navazhdenie* (*Suggestion diabolique*), was merely a pounding, heavily chordal intensification of his innate impish streak; the other, *Otchayanie* ('Despair') followed on the heels of *Phantom* with another ostinato, this time carrying to extreme the keening chromaticism of his latest pieces (Ex.13). This is a long piece, too, calling into question the sincerity of Prokofiev's expression. One wonders what, apart from the burning manor houses on the Sontsovka horizon, gave him cause for such gloom; was Myaskovsky's melancholy infectious? Whereas only the first of the op.3 pieces lasts longer than 45 seconds, the bracing *Poryv* ('Elan') of op.4 alone carries the short, sharp bite of the quintessential Prokofiev 'doggy'.

Ex.13 *Despair*, op.4 no.3

There is something selfconscious in this, an attempt to impress with a fashionable outpouring of black bile, and it comes as no surprise to discover that Prokofiev worked on *Suggestion diabolique* and *Despair* alongside the symphony in the summer of 1908 with a crucial concert engagement in mind. Earlier that year he had made the acquaintance of three influential men in the St Petersburg musical world, the guiding lights behind the Evenings of Contemporary Music held on Thursdays in the Reform School on the Moika Canal. These enterprising events were by no means confined to native talent; according to Stravinsky, whose music was first performed there in 1909, they also introduced Russian audiences to the chamber masterpieces of Debussy and Ravel and interlaced the new with the old. 'This was important and rare', wrote Stravinsky, 'for so many organizations are dedicated to new music, and so few to the centuries before Bach. I heard Monteverdi there for the first time, in an arrangement by d'Indy, I think, and Couperin and Montéclair; and Bach was performed in quantity.'[57] The leading *sovremennitsi* ('contemporaryites') were the bibliophile and music-lover Alfred Nurok – 'the liveliest and most energetic, with a bald and knobbly head'[58] – the physically unappealing Vyacheslav Karatygin, who as St Petersburg's most eloquent and level-headed music critic was to be a wise friend to both Prokofiev and Myaskovsky, and the short, 'exceptionally venomous'[59] aesthete Walter Nouvel, perhaps the most familiar name to us owing to his long-term friendship with Diaghilev and his chronicling of the early history of the Ballets Russes.

At his first audition, Prokofiev played them three of the pieces later placed in the op.3 collection, the two already prepared for the next set – they must have been *Elan* and *Remembrance*, a tougher lyrical proposition than the winsome *Fairy Tale* – and *Snezhok*, a gentle snow-scene composed alongside Myaskovsky's own, much more stinging impression of the same phenomenon. This uncharacteristically delicate piece of impressionism, with its soft parallel 2nds, never found its way into any of the official oeuvre because Prokofiev thought it too insubstantial; but he did recall it, four years before his death, on the back of an excerpt from *War and Peace* dealing with Prince Andrey's delirium.[60]

The spontaneous enthusiasm displayed by the *sovremennitsi* took the young pianist–composer by surprise. Karatygin, detecting a fusion of Reger, Musorgsky and Grieg, welcomed this new style as 'the antithesis of Skryabin – and thank God such an antithesis has arrived'.[61] During the following autumn, 18 December was the date finally fixed for the 'contemporary evening' at which Prokofiev was to impress the musical world (the jury also had a preview of the symphony, but rightly found it less original than the piano pieces). His contribution introduced the chromatic strain by degrees with lyrical pieces – *Fairy Tale*, *Snezhok* ('Snow') and *Reminiscence* – before sidling into the audacities of *Elan*, *Despair* and *Suggestion diabolique* together with a piece Prokofiev later claimed to have forgotten entirely, *Molby* ('Entreaties'). 'I can say that I played much better than at home, so that both the sovremennitsi and Winkler liked my performance', Prokofiev wrote to Myaskovsky the following day, after informing him about three of his own songs to verses by Zinayda Gippius performed in the same evening (objectively reporting the soprano's judgment that 'your *romances* were composed as if for a machine, not a singer'). He continues about himself:

> When I stepped out on to the stage, they applauded me; they applauded after each piece (except for *Snow*), and especially well at the end. The most successful pieces were *Reminiscence*, *Despair* and *Suggestion diabolique*. In a word, we'll now hear the abuse of the critics, of whom, it seems, there were six present.[62]

The four influential reviews that appeared were far from abusive, and Prokofiev would hardly have expected harsh words from Winkler, still his piano tutor, who gave a balanced teacher's report in the German-language *St Petersburg Zeitung*. Defining Prokofiev as 'still in his *Sturm und Drang* period . . . under the strong influence of the decadent movement in art', Winkler looked prophetically beyond adolescence for 'the finest fruits of his unique talent'.[63] He found *Suggestion diabolique* eminently pianistic (which, incidentally, has not prevented the conductor Gennady Rozhdestvensky from making a colourful transcription including parts for four accordions) but 'very decadent', a label the mature Prokofiev rejects for this 'clear and purposeful piece'.[64] Even in St Petersburg's relatively incestuous musical world, which permitted Winkler to write about his pupil, Karatygin could hardly have lent his eloquence to the evening, for he had accompanied Sofya Demidova in the Myaskovsky songs. His soapbox in the newspaper *Rech* was taken instead by one Timofeyev, who could give the young composer cause to rejoice that his 'strange' harmonies were deemed 'mannered' and went 'beyond the bounds of beauty'.[65] The longest review, and the first to be printed two days after the concert, was in *Slovo* under the pseudonym 'N. Sem'. Its orotund phrases clothe plenty of common sense:

> This young composer, who has not yet finished his musical education, belongs to that extreme tendency of modernists, and in his daring and originality he goes much further than contemporary French composers . . . It is a talent still not in perfect equilibrium, still yielding to every impulse and given to extravagant combinations of sounds, but one that finds with great adroitness a logical basis for all the most daring modulations . . . This composer's enormous strength of fantasy and his inventiveness give him an excess of creative material.[66]

One final, much more succinct critical footnote comes from a composer who claimed to be there that evening (though Prokofiev cites Pavel Chesnokov, devotee of striking religious music, as the sole representative of the profession; maybe he was simply not introduced to his near-contemporary at the time): Stravinsky ascribes the event to two years earlier, and wonders whether Rimsky-Korsakov could have been present (he had already been dead for six months). But what he does say gives us the key to his lifelong opinion of Prokofiev: 'his performance was remarkable – but I have always liked his music hearing him play it – and the music had personality'.[67]

Personality is certainly strongly felt in all these pieces, as in so many of their unpublished predecessors. It was present in other fields, too. The young man's assurance in chess now led him to be pitted against distinguished seniors, just as his music had done. His partners included a minister, an eminent translator who knew Goethe's *Faust* from first line to last and, best of all, the man who dominated the chess world for several decades, the great Emanuel Lasker. As proof that he, too, could have taken the path of professional player, the 18-year-old Prokofiev drew at the end of a five-hour game with the master and left the room proudly to congratulations on all sides. He refers to it with justifiable but slightly mocking pride in a letter alongside his latest chess game by correspondence with the ever-willing Morolev, advising him to perceive in his moves 'a well-formed figure of note roughly equal to the strength of Lasker'.[68]

Dignified and aloof from classroom smart-aleckry, Prokofiev had also won the admiration of several girls in the academic classes, though few took the flirtations as seriously as the pale-faced Vera Alpers. Her diary reveals her growing admiration, from objective curiosity to a Tatyana-like infatuation. At the beginning of December 1908 she wondered 'why I feel sympathetic towards him – in the first place, he's a terrible egotist; in the second, there are many unsympathetic things about him, and yet . . . '. One of the 'and yets' was the inner man she saw revealed through his piano studies: 'he plays so attentively and with so much thoughtfulness, and somehow becomes one with the piano and the music. He's definitely talented. I should like Mama to see how he behaves with me'. By January she was in love, writing after an evening in his company, 'I was very happy, why – I don't know, I don't wish to know'.[69]

Her feelings were not reciprocated. Prokofiev reserved his prose for the girls ('Verochka is not very pretty, but she looks quite good from behind'[70]) and his poetry for male friendships. As far as he was concerned, there was nothing in the air but comradeship with Vera, although a series of letters he wrote to her in the summer of 1909 have a specific tone of badinage running through them. He bewails the 'god-forsaken corner'[71] of Sontsovka and recalls his escape from the clutches of Doctor Reberg's daughters to Morolev's new base of Nikopol, where he 'played [chess and music] to the point of stupefaction, swam in the Dnieper, went on bicycle rides and picnics, went to the circus – in short I've put on three pounds, though now I'm home again I'm taking hematogen'[72] (to try and lose them again; later the health-conscious youth tells Vera he has succeeded). The countryside was not always as quiet as he had hoped, as this passage, in which Prokofiev drops his bantering tone in favour of a directness fit for a Chekhov short story, reveals:

> Recently civilization penetrated our backwoods in the shape of a gramophone which one of the peasants went and bought. And now towards evening this devilish invention stands in the open air outside his hut and begins to wheeze its frightful song. The gathering crowd expresses its pleasure in uproar and attempts to sing along, the dogs bark and howl, the cows returning from the fields bellow and run in every direction and to cap all this torture, someone in a neighbouring hut starts to play the harmonica out of tune! At first I shut all the windows, then I sit down to play the piano, but finally I lose my temper and go riding off on my bicycle into the fields to rescue myself from this fearful cacophony.[73]

An excursion southwards was more to his liking, giving us one of the few glimpses in his writings of the Caucasian resort where he was to spend so much time with his mother over the next few years. He describes Kislovodsk to Vera as 'one of the liveliest health resorts in Russia' and goes on to describe the 'magnificent circumstances' he finds there: 'a Shreder concert grand, an enchanting view from the balcony, 16-foot-high ceilings, baths filled with Narzan mineral water, a female companion (a pupil of Rubinstein) to play four-hand arrangements with, and more'.[74] After such a description he falls back on insult, telling Vera he has torn up the 'disgusting' photograph she has sent of herself and that her last letter so reeked of boredom that he has buried it in a drawer.

Perhaps Vera still hoped that Prokofiev might be playing Benedict to her Beatrice, but her common sense must have told her that they were to be no more than good friends. From her perspective the real spanner in the works was Maximilian Anatolyevich Schmidthof, a young man of Prokofiev's age who caught his eye as a page-turner for a student recital. 'The youth interested me in his appearance', he later recalled. 'He had a huge, rectangular forehead, quite a handsome though rather flattish face and a completely independent manner.'[75] Schmidthof was amused by Prokofiev's flirtatious remark after the concert: 'you turned pages most artistically'.[76] They were to become close friends. Many years later Prokofiev's wife Lina touched somewhat testily on this romantic friendship when, in conversation with the writer Harvey Sachs, she spoke of the chess club to which her husband had belonged as a youth. The club, she told Sachs, 'gave one the possibility of having multi-tastes, you know, different tastes'. And the conversation continues obliquely:

> LP: . . . He had a close chum, a pianist, he dedicated some things to him, but he would never talk about it . . .
> HS: Was the pianist homosexual?
> LP: Well, he belonged to the club.
> HS: Did Prokofiev ever speak about it?
> LP: No, he never talked about it. He changed the subject.
> HS: But he never admitted such a thing to you?
> LP: No. But perhaps he had such tendencies, but I don't think he had an affair with a man, although he had such tendencies . . . You understand me, well if you don't . . . And those are things I would never refer to.[77]

Nor, it seemed, could Prokofiev. Lina goes on to recall a conversation in which someone remarked '"do you know that students of the literary institute are reputed to be very perverse?" He blushed, he blushed, so I left the room. I was sorry for him'.[78]

Whatever the truth, in the spring of 1909 Schmidthof now made a triangle of the Alpers–Prokofiev relationship. Vera's diary for mid-April suggests a souring: 'I'm displeased that he became acquainted with Max, because Max evidently wants us to quarrel'.[79] Schmidthof introduced Seryozha to the 'cold bath of pessimism'[80] in Schopenhauer's philosophy. There were already shadows on the horizon: Schmidthof's inclination to depression, which was to send him into retreat for most of the next summer, is underlined by one of the letters to Alpers. For now, though, they walked and talked. It was a happy time that Prokofiev remembered with obvious nostalgia: 'in such a fashion, roughly but rather cheerfully as happens when one is 17, we took our walks through the streets and quays of St Petersburg in the early spring of 1909'.[81] The autobiography takes us only a few months further, perhaps significantly stopping short of the darker events – one of them Schmidthof's suicide – which within a few years would bring about the death of innocence.

4
Classical, symbolical
1909–13

'When you're marching towards your goal, don't look at the corpses you have to walk over.'[1] The giver of this harsh advice was the mild-tempered Myaskovsky, who, like Prokofiev but unlike several of their contemporaries, was never to act on it when times were hardest, in the 1930s and late 1940s. He was merely trying to apply pressure to Prokofiev the pianist to move on from Winkler's diligent but hardly inspirational tuition to the more prestigious classes of Anna Nikolayevna Yesipova, Zakharov's guiding light. Yesipova, otherwise known to Prokofiev and others as 'Madame Annette Essipoff' and defined to Morolev as 'a very well-known professor, if not in Europe, then certainly in Russia',[2] had studied under the great Theodor Leschetizky and was hardly inferior to him in transcendental technique. A piano roll she made in 1906 of Liszt's flowery *Paraphrase de concert* on themes from Verdi's *Rigoletto* demonstrates the high style she could still muster long after her retirement from the concert platform. She had been holding her classes at the conservatory since 1893.

The recipient of Myaskovsky's maxim has been labelled ruthless, but the events that followed are less often noted. One was that when Prokofiev quoted Myaskovsky in a letter to his father, he drily responded with due liberal scruple, 'the trouble is, the corpses sometimes stand up and strike you on the back of the head'.[3] The other was the conscientious youth's way of easing the transition to Yesipova. One of the last pieces on which he had worked intensively with Winkler was the taxing, staccato C major *Étude* of Anton Rubinstein, featured in a student recital alongside a more familiar example of the genre by Chopin and a Brahms rhapsody. It was on the strength of his playing of the Rubinstein *Étude* that Yesipova agreed to admit Prokofiev into her class, so long as he had the permission of his current teacher. Prokofiev then left a monument to his first, unruly steps in pianistic discipline by composing four *études* of his own and dedicating them to Winkler.

There is no concession in any of them to the mannerly, technical finger-flexing of Chopin, Czerny or Rubinstein. They are studies only in the ferocious demands of the rapid figurations and closer to fantasias in their play of ideas; this is especially true of no.3, where harmonically rootless Andante sequences anticipating the experiments of the late 1920s give way to gradually accelerating chromatic whirlwinds. The vein of devilishness in the numbers that had already gone into opp.3 and 4 is intensified. While the *Suggestion diabolique* conveys its incessant terror through pounding chords in 3rds, the perpetual motion of the first (and still the most striking) of these *études* is conveyed by a hail of semiquavers through which a buoyant staccato tune fitfully peers and is tugged downwards into the neighbouring minor key. Its impressive transformation into calmer playfulness in the middle section is capped by the sleight-of-hand return of the witches' sabbath (Ex.14). Prokofiev adds to the terror in his first flirtation with that Russian stock-in-trade of the supernatural, the whole-tone scale, which also appears in the fourth *étude*; the difficulties merely intensify for the end of the piece, when the pianist is asked to rage in the depths (a slightly more playable alternative is provided for four bars).

The titanic strength unleashed here and the spreading on to three staves in the third *étude* were to find more intense expression in the Second Piano Concerto. We must take Prokofiev's word for it that complexity and dissonance also played a part in one of the two works (now lost) that he submitted for the spring examinations of 1909. It was a setting of the final scene in Pushkin's *A Feast in Time of Plague*

Ex.14 *Étude*, op.2 no.1

(Allegro) ***tranquillo***

(which he had set in its entirety as a pupil of Glière in 1903). His new anti-clerical stance would have won him points in Soviet times: Pushkin's priest was 'no easy-going churchman but a middle-aged prelate who foamed at the mouth as he railed'.[4] The teeth-gnashing idiom would no doubt strike us as an interesting precursor to the angular audacities in the second and third parts of his first 'mature' opera, *Maddalena*, and much of *The Gambler*. Also sunk, leaving traces only in the autobiography, is the last of the conservatory sonatas, the 'unofficial' sixth, too 'diversely styled'[5] to be reworked, with a 'Regerish'[6] first movement, another attempt at the diatonic, 'white-note' writing first seen in *Fairy Tale* and a finale fashioned from the second of these fledgling sonatas.

Lyadov bewailed this would-be Skryabin's contempt for the rules but gave Prokofiev sufficiently good marks to earn him the title of 'Free Artist', the expected plaudit for the end of his first conservatory period. The student was to remember him, at least, which could hardly be said of the time he had spent over the previous six months studying composition with the the Latvian-born composer Yosif Wihtol (Jazeps Vitols). Amenable as he may have been to innovation, Wihtol comes an indifferent bottom of Prokofiev's teacher-ratings; he had taught 'with passive indifference'.[7] The continuing inspiration of Nikolay Tcherepnin, however, who had by now taken Prokofiev into his conducting class, bore fruit that summer. Tcherepnin's aesthetics, at least in the realm of teaching, corresponded with the taste for the 18th century held by his colleagues in the *Mir iskusstva* movement; while the artists Somov, Serov and Benois celebrated the graceful aspects of Catherine the Great's court, Tcherepnin preached the values of Mozart and Haydn. He may not have embedded them in his own music; the fragment he composed for *The Firebird* before the task passed to Stravinsky called for impressionistic tone-painting, and the Watteauesque setting of his ballet *Le Pavillon d'Armide* is hardly reflected in the music. Yet he transmitted his enthusiasm for the rococo masters to Prokofiev, and the result was a work that might be described as the first Russian neo-classical score after Tchaikovsky, the Sinfonietta.

Its title was the same as Rimsky-Korsakov's light-hearted exercise in the genre, but its classical themes, if not the sometimes unwieldy structures used to contain them, originate in Tcherepnin's teachings. Myaskovsky was not impressed that June when Prokofiev sent him the middle of his projected five movements, the Intermezzo. That was hardly surprising since he was in sombre mood, too tense to compose or to contemplate the four-hand piano arrangement he had promised of his friend's symphony; and an intermezzo, as Prokofiev was bound to remind him, was by definition 'a fragment for relaxation, because it has to be in the first place simple, and in the second place not long or gaudy (over-colourful), so as not to compel the listener to strain the attention, so he can rest – especially when an intermezzo falls between such movements as I intend [to make] of my Scherzo and my Andante'.[8] The Andante, as it turned out, was to present a surprising austerity between the warm-hearted *giocoso* of the opening movement and the delicate *vivace* of the Intermezzo, while the Scherzo offered several striking ideas, starting with the initial pizzicato (restricted in the later revision to violins only).

Myaskovsky had certainly been highly critical of the Intermezzo, which seems to be derived from the work's winsome opening theme but, in the compositional chronology, must have given birth to it: he found it 'poverty-stricken' instead of merely simple, with 'neither invention nor fantasy in it'.[9] As Prokofiev revealed later that summer, such negativity nearly derailed him from the course of 'jolly little' music.[10] The revelation shows us a rare chink of vulnerability in the usually confident young composer's armour, and Myaskovsky's reply, in its idiosyncratic way, is a moving testament to a mostly altruistic working friendship:

> after I'd quarrelled with your Intermezzo (which, however, in certain places was entirely justifiable), you wrote to me that it had affected you like water off a duck's back, but now you've gone and told me of a certain despair. This last remark depressed me a great deal – is it possible that you are such a feeble, unbalanced musician and so little talented (in your own opinion) that one can't say anything disapproving to you, but instead has to praise you indiscriminately? . . . knowing as you do my opinion concerning your muse, you could react with less distress to my assaults on you, because at the bottom of them lies neither empty criticism nor even (surprise, surprise!) professional envy, but solely the desire to see in you, at least, the Russian Wagner (in his general significance).[11]

As more of the Sinfonietta arrived through the post, Myaskovsky rallied to its support and especially to the first movement, which he found 'well-proportioned, cheerful and gracious'[12] – even if it lacked a shapely climax. But he held to his preference for the kind of complicated vein he had enjoyed in the setting of the scene from *A Feast in Time of Plague* 'because not only your fiery temperament but also your purely external technical merits are evident, without which for me music has only half its value'.[13] And he harps incessantly on the Intermezzo sequence, oscillating between the keys of A major and C major, of which only a trace remains at the very end of the revised movement we hear today and to which Myaskovsky refers as S–A–S–A, 'an incredibly bad melody and very monotonously orchestrated',[14] 'nothing more than a blot in the style of the very indecent banalities of the terrible Richard'.[15] The mention of Strauss, an inescapable force of those years, is curiously apt, for although the master's first so-called 'neo-classical' experiment, *Ariadne auf Naxos*, was then several years in the future, the one score Prokofiev truly brings to mind is *Till Eulenspiegel*, if only briefly in the quirky woodwind phrases of the first-movement codetta (Ex.15). Another negative influence, as far as Myaskovsky was concerned, was Sibelius. He can have been thinking only of the intriguingly taut, predominantly cheerful and concise Third Symphony, which Prokofiev had heard Sibelius conduct in a rehearsal for one of the Ziloti concerts in November 1907 and in which traces of early neo-classicism can also be detected.

Ex.15 Sinfonietta, op.5/48–I. Allegro giocoso

Fl. I, II
Ob. I, II
Cl. I, II
Fag. I, II
Tbn. I, II
Cor. I, II
Cor. III, IV
V. I
V. II
Vla.
Vc.
Cb.

a 2
unis.
arco
pizz.
cresc.

Ex.15 *cont.*

We should be wary of judging the Sinfonietta familiar from recordings and concert performances as the inspiration of 1909. It is unfortunate that Kankarovich's plans to give its premiere in his concerts at Voronezh that summer came to nothing because the parts might have survived and given us a chance of assessing the original. Prokofiev tells us that the two revisions he made, in 1914–15 and 1929, essentially polished up the orchestration rather than adding anything new. Yet the 1929 version tellingly boasts a different opus number, 48, and the work's most impressive characteristic, the transparency which is offset by occasional flourishes of a more acerbic style, belongs to the world of the European years.

Nevertheless, the Sinfonietta was as startling a departure from the gloomy, symbolist-drenched inspirations of those years as the spikier, more exhilarating of the earlier piano pieces. Intriguingly, too, Prokofiev and Myaskovsky could not have been further removed in their aims than they were in the summer of 1909. When Myaskovsky finally roused himself from self-disgust and apathy it was to compose a baggy monster of a tone-poem called *Silence*, a compendium of howls, laments, rushing waters and fugal thunderstorms based on a cosmic melodrama by Edgar Allan Poe.[16] Myaskovsky had proposed the subject as a suitable theme for his friend, but Prokofiev found it simply bad. The Russian craze for Poe had been disseminated through the translations of his greatest champion, Konstantin Balmont, the most varied and richest of the so-called symbolists, whose version of Poe's *The Bells* was to yield one of Russian music's greatest choral masterpieces in 1915, Rakhmaninov's choral symphony of the same name. One Russian literary critic has described Balmont's evolution during the first decade of the 20th century as a move 'from sentimentalism and aestheticism-made-music to an intellectually aggressive, in part Nietzschean decadent emotionalism',[17] but it certainly took his poetry out of the shadows and into the radiant light of the sun, aligning him with the more earthy, primitive verse of other movements opposed to the hazy dream of the symbolists.

Nearly 24 years Prokofiev's senior, Balmont did not to get to know this 'thin-as-a-rake blonde youth',[18] as he was to describe him in a memoir written much later, until 1916, when Prokofiev was among distinguished visitors to the poet's house on Vasilyevsky Island in Petrograd (the former Petersburg). In the unpublished memoir of 1927, Balmont contrasts his 'manly strength' with the feminine, pre-Raphaelite demeanour and excessive refinement of his own son, who died in Moscow in 1917. He was impressed that Prokofiev took from the 'dangerous delights' of his poetry 'only its most basic elements, the force of its pantheistic rapture and the clear expressiveness of its lyric components . . . he did not become intoxicated by the flowery and overwhelming fragrance of Balmontian nature-worship'.[19]

This was to apply to all Prokofiev's settings of Balmont verses, and when he first set the poet to music in the 1909–10 conservatory year, following in the footsteps of Myaskovsky and his one-time teacher Glière, he focussed on the brighter, if still limpid, side of Balmont's output. The first of the settings for female chorus and orchestra, *Bely lebed* ('The White Swan'), is rooted in a clear D major, its atmospheric water music as much indebted to Wagner's nature poetry as many of Rimsky-Korsakov's later operatic tableaux. The harmonic side-slips of the choral writing look forward more than anything in Prokofiev's early music to the flavourings he was to add when he composed essentially diatonic Russian themes for Soviet ceremonials (Ex.16). Only the 'decadent' text, or a failure to look at these pieces properly, could have blinded Prokofiev's Soviet biographer Nestyev to the

Ex.16 Two Poems, op.7 – *Bely lebed*

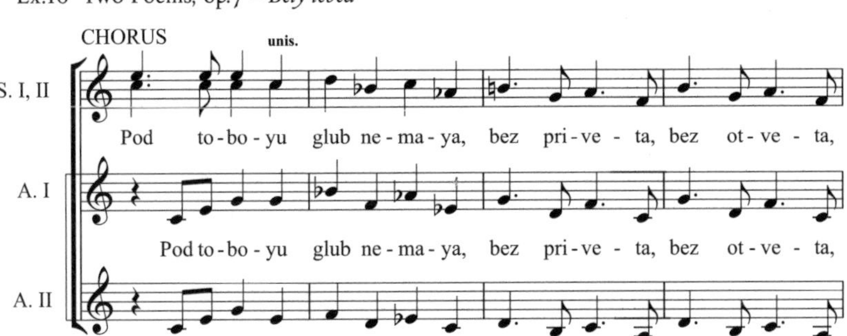

Ex.16 *cont.*

obvious connection. He asserted that the songs were 'too unusual and difficult' and that 'for a long time, simple and natural choral writing did not come easily to Prokofiev'.[20] Yet nothing could be simpler than the resolutely tonal passages for four-part women's chorus. Only occasionally, when Prokofiev wants to underline the perfumed magic of the second poem, a seascape, is there a greater burden placed on the singers, as at the point following an orchestral passage of static E major luminosity. Here, as the poet declares 'I'm happy. I sleep', the inner parts unfurl a special kind of enchantment before returning to base (Ex.17). The whole-tone exoticism inevitably suggests the influence of Debussy, but his was not an example that Prokofiev at this time would have been proud to acknowledge. In a letter to Myaskovsky of March 1909 he tells him of hearing a four-hand arrangement of 'Lyamer' at Zakharov's: 'it's rubbish'.[21] In a footnote Myaskovsky expresses astonishment that this looks like a reference to Debussy's 'three symphonic sketches' (*La Mer*).

Prokofiev's four other bows in the direction of symbolism were to be fashionably murky rather than lucid. He chose another Balmont poem as one of his first two opus-numbered songs for solo voice, *Yest drugiye planety* ('There are other planets'), of which he was to remain unduly proud, though its rather clichéd, chromatic monotony seems almost as studied as the deliberate repetitions of *Despair*. The choice of poet for the second setting, Tchaikovsky's friend and putative lover Alexey Apukhtin, is perhaps surprising but the melancholy sentiments foreshadow the symbolism that was just round the corner. The setting for this song, *Otchalila lodka*

Ex.17 Two Poems – *Volna*

('The boat pushed off'), is a telling Andantino nebbioso, and it shares with the tone-poem *Osenneye* ('Autumnal') the oppressive atmosphere of Rakhmaninov's Böcklin-inspired tone-poem *The Isle of the Dead.* Ultimately, the melodic line, if not declamatory as Nestyev claims, is hardly distinctive, and Myaskovsky did not hesitate to say so in the magazine *Muzyka* several years after op.9 had been written.

Another related pair of hothouse plants, though not devised as such, were the two orchestral works composed in the summer of 1910. There are compelling, non-musical reasons why Prokofiev was always to prefer the second, the title of which, *Autumnal,* the same as a now-vanished piano piece he had written at the same time as *Snow,* was an afterthought. In the first place, it was bound to win Myaskovsky's approval, close as it is to the oppressive gloom of his own *Silence,* and on receipt of it that September he defines it in terms of his own piece when he declares that 'a hopeless, doleful-cold colour is maintained amazingly well'.[22] Second, *Autumnal* followed the loss of Prokofiev's father, who died after a long illness from liver cancer on 23 July, aged 64. The son could only have felt the deepest grief for the father he had seen relatively little in recent years but whom there can be no doubt he loved as well as respected. He simply chose not to express that grief in correspondence even with close friends, relating the sad fact to Myaskovsky in a letter of 5 August only to move on to practicalities of musical performance. Myaskovsky did the same by way of response, but his letter suggests the terse emotional code on which both had clearly agreed: 'you know that I love you with all my soul, which is why there's no sense in my talking of my sympathy for you in your sorrow, you must simply be assured of it'.[23]

If *Autumnal* was wrung from the soul, the result is not noticeably different from the other symbolist-inspired pieces: it is all shuddering atmosphere, with a lusher if more conventional central section possibly inspired by the nostalgia at the heart of Rakhmaninov's *The Isle of the Dead*, which Prokofiev later cited as a model. *Sni* ('Dreams'), the other orchestral work of 1910, has perhaps more to offer. Prokofiev admits that the dedication to Skryabin, evoked at the head of the manuscript in the reference to 'the composer who began with *Reverie*', shows more resolve to follow in the footsteps of his fast-fading idol than the music itself. More light breaks through the D minor opening than might be expected, and the theme that floats across the dreamscape on clarinet and oboe is more apt to haunt our unconscious than anything in *Autumnal*. When it slips from its lilting 6/8 into a more tenacious 2/4, the flecks of muted trumpets heightening the chromatic support provide the first orchestral anticipation of the mature composer (Ex.18). The shaping of the material is a miracle of concision alongside Myaskovsky's meandering *Silence*. There are two lush climaxes, restrained in comparison to the overheated orgasms of Skryabin; after the first, earlier dreams resurface in their original form and after the second, the music returns to its hypnotic starting-point. Taken on its own impressionistic terms, the orchestration, which includes triple woodwind, six horns and two harps, is accomplished, and it is the only purely orchestral score of the period which Prokofiev never revised. He had a chance to hear it again on his visit to the Soviet Union in 1927, when he described it in his diary as 'sweet, gentle, rather soporific', reflecting that 'if my style has changed now, so much the better: everyone will see what I represented in the past and what I have now become'.[24]

The progressive improvement in the fortunes of the choral songs, the Sinfonietta, *Autumnal* and *Dreams*, all composed in just over a year, helps to chart the battle for recognition of the recently designated 'free artist'. From the fate of the Sinfonietta, which remained unperformed until Prokofiev first revised it in 1914–15, to the premiere of *Autumnal* in the summer of 1911 marked a big step forward, and the fact that Prokofiev had learnt to conduct in the interim ensured the modest

Ex.18 *Dreams*, op.6

launch of two of the four works. It was, again, the encouragement of Tcherepnin that set Prokofiev on his third musical career. Lively as discussions with the amiable Tcherepnin may have been, his teaching methods were distinctly unorthodox – 'get a cat and box its ears, making sure your blows are sharp and rhythmic'[25] – and Prokofiev bewailed his lack of technique, turning to his classmate Kankarovich to learn how to deal with such complex metres as 12/8 and 6/4. He may, however, have been refracting his own inadequacies, for in his short autobiography he is honest enough to quote (or recreate, after his own laconic style) Tcherepnin's judgment when he did finally stand timidly before the conservatory's second orchestra: 'you have no facility for conducting, but since I believe in you as a composer and I know that you will more than once have to conduct your own works, I'm going to teach you how to conduct'.[26] He was never to become a natural like Rakhmaninov, the only Russian equal of Strauss and Mahler as a composer-conductor. Yet at least he had the advantage of an early start, unlike Tchaikovsky, who did not overcome his nerves to become a sufficiently accomplished conductor of his own music until he was in his 40s.

Tcherepnin had guided Prokofiev's appearances with care, making sure that he was not overburdened when he did finally take up his baton, timidly at first, in front of his fellow students. Prokofiev advertised the occasion to Myaskovsky in November 1909. He conducted the first movement only of Schubert's 'Unfinished' Symphony; another student took over for the second movement, and Kankarovich conducted

Weber's *Oberon* overture, followed by a Chorus of Enchanted Maidens from César Cui's uncompleted opera *Rogdana.* A significant event, sidestepped by Nestyev and other Soviet critics, was the conservatory concert in early 1910 when Prokofiev's music featured there for the first time; even though only the first of the two Balmont choruses was performed, and though the composer took up his now-familiar role as conductor of the choral students in public, he had only a piano and not an orchestra to lend support. The event has been overshadowed by another conservatory 'first': his appearance that November as composer, conductor (of *Dreams*) and solo pianist (in his official First Sonata op.1). 'Isn't that truly splendid?'[27] he wrote engagingly to Morolev of his threefold success, adding that most of the critics had gone to a Skryabin concert on the same evening.

The real breakthrough, for both *Dreams* and *Autumnal,* came the following summer. Prokofiev's hopes for a professional airing had rested with the St Petersburg-based conductor Emil Cooper; but they came to nothing, and it was the pioneer of an innovatory fringe institution in Moscow, Konstantin Saradzhev, who provided his first opportunity. Saradzhev had strong links with the forward-looking magazine *Muzyka,* founded in 1910 by the enterprising Vladimir Derzhanovsky. Between them, Saradzhev and Derzhanovsky could obviously do more for young composers of large-scale orchestral works than those St Petersburg *sovremenniks* who were limited to the promotion of chamber music. As had been the case in St Petersburg, the influential figure who provided the introduction was Myaskovsky's one-time teacher Kryzhanovsky, though this time it was Prokofiev's selfless friend, cast out into the world now that his conservatory training was over, who turned potential into action. Prokofiev had sent Saradzhev three of his scores, but it was not until Myaskovsky arrived in Moscow in June 1911 for the premiere of *Silence* that events gathered pace. Prokofiev charmingly relates Myaskovsky's reception there to their mutual friend Boris Zakharov:

> They greeted him there like a prophet from another country, they were astonished by his *Silence,* they expected new pieces for performance, they sought the collaboration of the journals, they proposed to publish scores and they paid attention to every word without question. 'Mimosa-ish Koko', to be sure, knit his brow and dodged and only had a brainwave on the last point: he publicized my pieces so successfully that *Dreams* will be played on 29 (June), *Autumnal* a little later, and my concerto, which I haven't finished yet, next season. I'm moved to tears.[28]

Clearly he meant it. In one of those rare moments in the Prokofiev–Myaskovsky correspondence where more than the usual good-natured banter makes itself felt, Prokofiev expresses his gratitude for his friend's concern – 'not only moving but completely amazing' – adding, with his usual flippancy, that if Saradzhev could make out *Silence,* 'then he'll be able to conduct my simple little pieces with one finger'.[29]

The concerts took place out of doors, in Sokolniki Park in Moscow: not as auspicious as a performance in the season proper because many of the city's influential musicians had left for their dachas. St Petersburg boasted a similar if less ambitious programme in an open wooden building in the beautiful park of Pavlovsk Palace (it was here in 1865 that Tchaikovsky's *Characteristic Dances*, his first music to have a public airing, had been given its premiere under the baton of Johann Strauss II). Kankarovich made amends in Pavlovsk for having fled from Voronezh before he could conduct the Sinfonietta there by giving *Dreams* its third performance on 9 July, between the two Sokolniki events. *Dreams* in Sokolniki Park had not gone well, Prokofiev told his mother, because there had been only one rehearsal and Saradzhev 'dragged out the tempos'[30] – an accusation he was to level at Kankarovich, too ('towards the end it began to be boring').[31] In Pavlovsk things were much worse, partly because again there was only one rehearsal and Kankarovich could do nothing about it. The orchestra constantly played out of tune and the audience's attitude was anything but serious. It was a Saturday night crowd; *Dreams* would have gone down better with Tuesday's Russian music enthusiasts. Yet Kankarovich had no charge of that series, and he could hardly have slotted *Dreams* into the non-Russian Friday evening concerts.

Compensation came with the premiere of *Autumnal*, which Prokofiev felt was 'a much easier piece than *Dreams* for both the orchestra and the conductor'.[32] Saradzhev was laid up with an injured knee and his replacement was Alexander Medtner, 'brother of the composer. He's a less experienced conductor than Saradzhev, but he likes *Autumnal* very much and he's settled down to the business very seriously'.[33] The performance went well, and Prokofiev reported his satisfaction. The reviews did not agree, and their patronizing tone reached its apogee in *Golos Moskvy* ('The Voice of Moscow'), where the critic thought it 'a mistake to give so much attention to this callow youth, this musical fledgling, twice in one season'[34] and compared the limited scope of Prokofiev's talent to the pastel charms of the minor 19th-century symphonist Vasily Kalinnikov. The sabre-rattling was ominous: the chief music critic of *Golos Moskvy*, Leonid Sabaneyev, was to become Prokofiev's deadliest opponent until he made himself look ridiculous, as critics still do from time to time, by writing a review of an event that never took place.

Enjoying the long-term support of Saradzhev and Derzhanovsky, Prokofiev and Myaskovsky were not too bothered. This was a testing time for both young men; Prokofiev was still a graduate student at the conservatory, but the death of his father had placed financial constraints on mother and son, and in his letters to Marya Grigoryevna he dutifully reports his expenditures. It was vital that he should find willing publishers; the struggle for recognition in print was harder than the drive for live performances. His first port of call in 1910 was the new Russian Music Publishing House, founded by the enterprising double-bass virtuoso turned conductor Sergey (later Serge) Koussevitzky with financial underpinning from his millionairess wife Natalya. Koussevitzky, who had written a powerful polemic against the drudgery of the jobbing musician based on his galley years in the Bolshoy Orchestra, should have been sympathetic to a struggling young composer trying to do something new, and eventually he would become one of Prokofiev's staunchest supporters in the West. Now, however, his hands were tied by the presence among his consultant-composers of Rakhmaninov and Medtner who were already showing their arch-reactionary colours and, according to Prokofiev, 'turned down with extraordinary unanimity everything that had the slightest suspicion of novelty'.[35] It says much for the rather more open-minded young composer that he retained his respect for their music throughout the years to come.

The rejection must have been all the more surprising since Prokofiev had withheld his modernist poison and proffered a hothouse plant that showed little 'suspicion of novelty': the First Sonata reworked from the first movement of his early conservatory experiment in the genre. He had been canny enough to suggest the sonata to Glière for the recital he had arranged for him in Moscow, as part of the series run by the dramatic soprano Marya Deisha-Sionitskaya, on 21 February 1910. Writing to Glière about the programme, Prokofiev begs to sidestep the earlier eccentricities of the pieces first performed at the St Petersburg Evenings of Contemporary Music. The sonata, which Prokofiev regarded as an olive branch to his backwoods friend Morolev and his even more conservative teacher Lyadov, was offered instead as a new work, along with the *Études* which marked his ferocious new maturity. The offer was accepted, and eight months after his Moscow debut Prokofiev was writing to another leading light of his early days, Taneyev, begging him to send a letter of recommendation to the Moscow publisher Pyotr Jurgenson, in the hope that he might print the sonata and 'a couple of *études*'.[36] Taneyev could have done more for Prokofiev than merely to commend him as 'a young and talented composer' whose works 'ought to be published';[37] towards the end of November Prokofiev reported that Jurgenson had written back saying he had 'no time to examine the works of new composers, and returned my MSS'.[38]

A second, much more emphatic plea to Jurgenson came from the St Petersburg musicologist Alexander Ossovsky. Although he played less of a role in Prokofiev's life than Taneyev, Ossovsky offered the kind of energetic assistance a struggling musician often seeks. Giving Prokofiev's conservatory credentials and stating baldly that 'it would be a sin not to assist his first steps along the thorny path of art', Ossovsky continues:

> You have it in your power to give courage to Mr Prokofiev as a composer, and to encourage him to continue composing by publishing the works he sets before you. Besides excellent technique, they show a clear compositional gift and a delightfully youthful determination to go his own way, and not to follow the well-trodden path. There's boldness and fantasy there.
>
> People who cherish the development of talented young Russians and who appreciate new paths in art have already begun to pay attention to Prokofiev

> among us here in St Petersburg. His compositions are beginning to be performed at our concerts and the press is discussing them. In one of the recent issues of *Apollon*, in an article by V. Karatygin about contemporary Russian music, the name of Prokofiev is cited as the 'hope' of our music [paraphrasing Karatygin's greeting at the audition for Prokofiev's debut with the St Petersburg *sovremenniks*].
>
> By publishing Prokofiev's music your firm will not only be adhering to its finest traditions of support to our musical culture, but will suffer no loss on the commercial front, for Prokofiev's compositions ought to make their own way and find a market. I shall be very happy if these lines will induce you to favour our fledgling composer with your attention. After all, there are not so many recognized composers of talent among our young people. We must foster them.[39]

This time Jurgenson swallowed the elaborate bait and offered Prokofiev 100 roubles for the sonata and 12 of the early pieces, though only the sonata and the four numbers of op.3 were published that year. The fees steadily increased until the end of the association in 1916.

Prokofiev could hardly have imagined that within several years Jurgenson would be willing to run to the expense of an orchestral score, but that is what happened with his First Piano Concerto in 1913. The work had a practical basis, but it was with the prospect of performance rather than publication that the composer finally began to realize a project with which he toyed in the summer of 1911. He must have had a fleeting regret when Derzhanovsky invited him to be soloist in a concerto in place of a violinist who had fallen out with Alexander Medtner. Prokofiev had to refuse, he told his mother, 'since my Grieg, Saint-Saëns and R[imsky]-Korsakov concertos were in too much disarray for me to play them in concert, least of all with an orchestra'.[40] He turned down the alternative of playing his First Sonata owing to the cost of travel between Moscow and St Petersburg the extra engagement would have involved (clearly the pay was not the enticement of these summer events). The opportunity of making his debut as a concert soloist was not, however, lost for long. A year later he would have his own concerto ready to offer Derzhanovsky and Saradzhev.

Prokofiev had a useful working acquaintance with the concerto repertory from the many four-hand arrangements. Writing to Morolev in November 1909 he recommends Rakhmaninov's Second Concerto (which 'begins with chords, then there's a broad theme on Do–Re–Do. It's a very beautiful and well-known concerto')[41] and the Saint-Saëns concerto he had presumably studied well enough to consider playing at Sokolniki, the 'pleasant and elegant'[42] Second. This must have been at the command of Yesipova, who gave him a varied diet for the summer of 1912 as he prepared the performance of his own concerto: Beethoven's 'Emperor', Rubinstein's Fourth, Rakhmaninov's First and Second again, still being urged on the reluctant Morolev with the typically brusque commendation 'fascinating . . . if I'm not mistaken, you didn't get to the heart of the latter; try it again so as not to be a fool'.[43]

If Prokofiev made any alliances as a concerto composer, though, they were with the first work of its kind he ever studied, Rimsky-Korsakov's accomplished and genial miniature (for its quarter-hour scope rather than its format, which is essentially a series of Lisztian variations on a Russian folksong supplied by Balakirev) and Richard Strauss's early *Burleske*, which he had examined in a four-hand arrangement in December 1909 and found lacking in flavour. In fact its witty gestures, so prescient of *Till Eulenspiegel*, have much in common with the playful wit of Prokofiev's own First Concerto, though he rejected the cumbersome repetitions of the sonata form Strauss had determined to follow. Admirers have detected a Scythian wildness about the opening, but it is surely a satirical attempt at the grand gesture in the manner, if not the melodic style, of the famous introduction to Tchaikovsky's First Concerto (they share the key of D flat major).

Unlike Tchaikovsky's tune, though, Prokofiev's tongue-in-cheek grandeur reappears twice more, at the centrepoint of the concerto, with the piano now providing assertive accompaniment, and in the tintinnabulant conclusion. After the first expectant pause, however, Prokofiev cocks a snook at all that and plunges us into a heady cadenza before taking us on a whistlestop tour round his kennel of 'doggies'. His already established and lifelong habit of sidestepping into neighbouring keys is established by the piano's catch-me-if-you-can cadenza-like excursion in C major, with a quick trip into D minor, before D flat major reappears very much on the pianist's terms for his own, insouciant tune. In fact this latest in his long line of tarantella numbers is one of those two *sobachki* enclosed in the first letter to Myaskovsky back in the summer of 1907; though we would never have known it if the autobiographer had not cared to tell us.

It is tempting to find traces of that second piece from 1907 (described by Myaskovsky as lugubriously like Mime's whinings) in the concerto's abrupt plunge into creeping E minor shadowlands, for the first violins' keening minor-2nd figure is very much the musical wail that characterizes Wagner's dwarf (and Musorgsky's *Yurodivy* or Holy Fool in *Boris Godunov*). This brief spate of slightly satirical turn-of-the-century weeping is brushed aside by peals of chromatic laughter before the introductory music returns. But the slow movement that follows after a pause is surely more in earnest. Here, at the work's core, is a late Romantic cry from the heart that moves from muted strings and drifting woodwind solos in the manner of *Dreams* to full-blown lament, the piano pounding heavy threefold chords in *Petrushka*-like despair – a pointer to the more tragic vein of the Second Piano Concerto, as those seduced by the flanking high spirits tend to forget (Ex.19). It was to counter charges of superficial brilliance and 'footballishness', the autobiographer tells us, that he strove for greater depth in the Second Concerto. His outline of the First Concerto would lead us to believe that the Andante is merely the briefest of interludes before the development; but it stands very much at the centre, and the 'development' is merely an elaborated parade of all the material between the first and second statements of the introductory music, which makes a final reappearance, doubled by shrill trumpets and horns, and abruptly implodes as it rockets skywards to cascades of double octaves from the soloist.

Installed for a month and a half from early June 1912 in Yessentuki, one of several summer resorts in the northern Caucasus currently favoured by his mother, Prokofiev was fully conscious of the important premiere ahead. 'I intend to study my concerto', he wrote to Morolev, 'which, by the way, isn't an easy thing, but I have to play it well – in Moscow, they say, the hall [the *narodny dom* or People's House, once referred to by Prokofiev as *maison publique*] is [always] crammed with the public and there's going to be anything up to 6000 listeners, it's the first time I'll have played with an orchestra, I have to know it by heart to play it confidently.'[44] The piano in Yessentuki was not ideal for study: he told Myaskovsky, whose First Symphony was at last due to be heard in Moscow earlier in July, that it wasn't 'up

Ex.19 Piano Concerto no.1, op.10 – Andante assai

Ex.19 *cont.*

to'[45] the notes B flat, B and C. His confidence undented, and irritated only by the theft en route to Moscow of his grey suit and the tailcoat trousers he needed for the concert, he was able to tell Max Schmidthof of his 'total success'[46] as pianist in the first rehearsal on 24 July, the eve of the performance. He complained, though, of the orchestra, which improved only towards the end of the session, bewailed the mediocre instrument he had been given and lamented the fact that he had had to spend five hours late into the sweltering July night rewriting the horn parts because the players refused to read them as written in C. This was in fact the first time he had followed Liszt's example in writing out a whole score with all the parts, horns and clarinets included, in C, a habit he would pursue for the rest of his life (though he would have to make sure that the copyist for the individual parts transposed them into the keys most familiar to the players in question).

Everything went well enough on the day. Accustomed to a florid style in addressing the literary Schmidthof, Prokofiev fell back on the more laconic vein of narrative he usually adopted with Myaskovsky to tell Schmidthof about his success:

> The concerto went well. Saradzhev realized splendidly all the tempos. The music was in my fingers. The orchestra was on a slightly lower level than us, and contributed some rubbish of its own. In terms of instrumentation, they say, the concerto sounded well, and the orchestra never once obscured the piano part. The outward success was considerable; there were a lot of summonses to the platform and three encores: I played the Gavotte [soon to be incorporated into op.12] and the fourth *Étude* (twice); I didn't have anything else to hand. I'm satisfied. To play with an orchestra was not difficult, and exceptionally pleasant.[47]

The reviews for this and the Pavlovsk performance in mid-August, conducted by Alexander Aslanov, were acceptably mixed. Angry with the 'idiot' Sabaneyev's damning verdict on the performance of Myaskovsky's symphony earlier in July, Prokofiev had looked forward exuberantly to his 'twitterings',[48] and he was not disappointed. 'This energetic, rhythmic, harsh, coarse, primitive cacophony hardly deserves to be called music', raged the enemy, adding with strange logic that a 'real talent' would not have overstepped the mark in this way.[49] This and other, paler echoes of it hardly mattered when the *sovremennitsy* Karatygin in St Petersburg and Derzhanovsky, writing as 'Florestan' in *Utro Rossy*, managed to express their opinions in print; both were right to counter claims of musical muddiness by insisting on the piece's pulsating brilliance. Perhaps even more flattering was the relatively independent voice of the critic for the *Peterburgsky listok* who linked Prokofiev with Skryabin – Sabaneyev's god – as a joint figurehead of a fourth stage in 'the development of Russian music',[50] following Glinka and Rubinstein, Tchaikovsky and Rimsky-Korsakov, Glazunov and Arensky. The generalization was fair enough, even if we would now be inclined to leave out the third stage altogether.

It was an extraordinarily busy summer, and four-hour tennis sessions in Yessentuki were very much part of Prokofiev's schedule, perhaps to make amends for a winter during which influenza had been followed by three weeks in bed with pleurisy in early April, the composer working all the while on a new piano piece, the Toccata, and revisions to *Dreams*. Now he faced what he described to Tcherepnin as an '*embarras de richesse*'[51] on the performing front which was getting in the way of his work; he even felt he would have to turn down one of two promised performances of the Sinfonietta in order to have some composing time in August (neither, as it happened, took place). Tcherepnin was also the recipient of news that he was finishing an opera, *Maddalena*. The conducting classes were shortly to propel Prokofiev towards the opera repertoire and he had hopes of his own work being performed (his first collaboration with the conservatory's opera class did not take place until the end of the following year, when he conducted the Amneris–Aida scene and the magnificent final act of *Aida* to commemorate the centenary of Verdi's birth).

Perhaps unsurprisingly, with no performance in prospect and all the other demands of 1912 looming, Prokofiev orchestrated only the first scene of *Maddalena* that summer before devoting himself to studying his concerto. He was to progress no further, though all four scenes of his opera had been completed in piano score the previous August. Myaskovsky had been privy to his friend's first thoughts in June 1911, when he had spent as long each day on the score as he was to do a year later on tennis. The subject was a play by 'Baron Lieven', the *nom de plume* of Magda Gustavovna Lieven Orlova, dismissed in a line of the autobiography as 'a young lady of fashion, more pleasant in her social manner than talented in her dramaturgy'.[52] We know nothing of her relationship with Prokofiev, working or otherwise, though there was little collaboration since the play *Maddalena* had appeared in 1905. In his diary for 1911 Prokofiev noted the idea of beautiful evil in the shape of the protagonist – part madonna, part demon, like so many women depicted in turn-of-the-century symbolist literature – as attractive in itself and commended the cinematographic speed of the action, which would certainly keep boredom at bay. (The reference to cinema is interesting in itself; Gorky made his famous definition of the new form as a kingdom of shadows in 1896, but it was not until a decade later that short silent films began to be seen in St Petersburg, starting with scenes from *Boris Godunov* and followed in 1910 by Pyotr Chardynin's representation of *The Queen of Spades*.)

As a musical dramatist with a good eye for a racy libretto, Prokofiev was certainly right, though Lieven's poetic imagination never goes beyond the clichés of symbolism: a blood-red sunset, lovers floating along a Venetian canal 'like the fragrant petals of some gigantic rose', a storm as poetic fallacy. Her drama, drawn in part from Boccaccio's *Decameron*, is an original variation on the love triangle of Oscar Wilde's unfinished verse drama *A Florentine Tragedy* (1908), with a different outcome: while Wilde's brutish husband kills the handsome lover, providing the only possible aphrodisiac for his jaded young wife, Lieven has the two rivals kill each other, leaving Maddalena to enjoy her freedom without a twinge of conscience. In her declaration 'both good and evil have made my soul their dwelling' – the good belonging to her husband, the evil to her tortured relationship with the reclusive alchemist Stenio – Maddalena is the first of three divided Prokofiev heroines, closely followed by the archetypal Dostoyevskian female lead Polina in *The Gambler* and the schizophrenic Renata in *The Fiery Angel*, anticipated musically in Maddalena's final cries for help.

It is only in the first scene, and those elements of the last that repeat it, that Prokofiev succumbs to the hazy musical symbolism which had governed the Balmont settings as well as *Dreams* and *Autumnal*, and only because the character in question, at that point in the action, requires it. As in *Dreams*, he comes up with an especially memorable theme for Maddalena's fascinating madonna aspect. Its violin chromatics look back to another heroine taking in the sultry air, Strauss's Salome (which had still not reached the Russian stage, though *Elektra* was to arrive at the Maryinsky in 1913).

While Prokofiev's upper strings drift in 6ths against a watery backdrop (Ex.20*a*), Strauss's princess slips into waltz time with seductive 3rds and 6ths supported by the additional glitter of the celesta (Ex.20*b*). Just as Strauss's silvery music for his heroine becomes horribly distorted through her obsession with John the Baptist, so this principal theme of Maddalena, already a dabbler in the darker side of human nature, soon hints at depravity in cloudier instrumentation; there is also an unresolved pair of chords given out by three muted trumpets to hint at the heart of darkness.

With the very different characterizations of husband and lover, though, Prokofiev comes out of the symbolist wood. Stenio's soundworld, from what we can glean from the original piano score at this point, is suitably miasmic; ostinatos take over from sensuous atmosphere. And Gennaro, the only extrovert, pours out his ardour in the first of Prokofiev's characteristically athletic, wide-leaping love

Ex.20*a* *Maddalena*, op.13

Ex.20*b* Strauss, *Salome*

themes. Whether this reflects first experience of sexual love, and whether Prokofiev's relationship with a new girlfriend was more involved than he dared to be with the seductive Bessonova, can only be left to the reader's imagination (Ex.21). In a letter to Derzhanovsky in the autumn of 1911 Myaskovsky declared that 'in its intensity of style the opera resembles the works of Richard Strauss'[53] – a judgment that may suit its opening but hardly fits these racy scenes of conflict between husband, wife and lover. Myaskovsky goes too far, revealing only his blind-spot, in adding that the piece 'lacks the banality of Strauss':[54] Prokofiev's use of intense chromaticism by fits and starts never approaches the dramatic fluidity with which Strauss turns the screw in *Salome* or *Elektra*, exciting though it is to re-encounter some of the furious semiquaver activities of the more diabolical piano pieces.

Ex.21 *Maddalena*

The older composer, however, was right in his final qualification: 'the work can hardly be staged in our country despite its theatrical effectiveness. I have not encountered a more difficult vocal score, and there is no chance of the "worthies" approving it'.[55] The orchestration Prokofiev planned for all four scenes does not go beyond triple wind and brass, and in the first (admittedly calmest) scene, the only one in which the composer's intentions were carried out, it never threatens to drown the voices. Yet even if the soprano singing Maddalena and the tenor singing Gennaro take alternatives to their respective single high Cs, the high-lying tessitura and the difficulties of pitching the wayward vocal lines make these roles unusually taxing; and the forceful, often declamatory baritone part of Stenio would surely be beyond the fledgling maturity of a conservatory student. So Tcherepnin left well alone. In the first of the countless cases of unlucky timing which were to dog Prokofiev's operatic career, the enterprising new Free Theatre (of the former Arts Theatre eminence Konstantin Mardzhanov), which had apparently undertaken to give the premiere in its one and only season (1913–14), went bankrupt before the production could take place. Why this was not in the inaugural season as promised remains unclear; had all gone well for the next theatrical year, *Maddalena* could well have found itself sharing the bill with Stravinsky's *The Nightingale*, completed on the basis that it, too, would launch the composer's stage career in Russia at the Free Theatre. Derzhanovsky, the two composers' benefactor, however, sounded warning bells for the tricky *Maddalena*'s wellbeing in Free Theatre hands when he warned Stravinsky that the troupe assembled there were 'yet on the level of students, and students with very dubious *musical* training at that'.[56]

Other attempts failed, including Myaskovsky's in a surprising overture to the Association of Contemporary Music in 1924, and as the manuscript was lodged with Koussevitzky's Russian Music Publishing House in Paris (subsequently taken over by Boosey & Hawkes), Prokofiev would have been unable to gain access to the score even if he had wanted to during his later years in the Soviet Union. In the early 1970s the composer's first wife Lina and their second son Oleg, newly settled in England, discussed with the conductor Edward Downes the possibility of completing the orchestration. Downes' task, as he describes it in the preface to the vocal score, was 'similar to what Deryck Cooke did for Mahler's Tenth Symphony – to present a version which, while not pretending to be the final thoughts of the composer, has been orchestrated in the light of a long experience of conducting his other works; it will enable the public to hear a wonderful opera that would otherwise be unavailable to them'.[57] Even if at times the selective scoring for wind and brass in the later scenes looks forward to the Prokofiev of the late 1920s and early 30s, it is remarkably close to what the composer would no doubt have achieved in revision, and Downes's labour of love has given the work a generous lease of life since its BBC Radio 3 premiere, recorded in December 1978 and first broadcast the following March. The maverick champion of the first studio recording, Gennady Rozhdestvensky, saw fit to spice the orchestration further with xylophone and celesta, and his concert performance at the Royal Festival Hall in London on 3 December 1997 set the seal of distinction with a first-rate cast, less than a month after a rather unclear production from Moscow's Helikon Opera had visited the smaller Queen Elizabeth Hall. Maddalena has perhaps had an even more glorious renaissance than she deserves.

Out of a number of possible double-bill companions for Prokofiev's one-acter, Schoenberg's 'monodrama' *Erwartung* would be the most extreme. Composed two years before Lieven's symbolist drama cast its spell on Prokofiev, *Erwartung*, with its unrelieved nightmare drenched in atonalism, shows us just how far Prokofiev still had to go in terms of operatic modernism; that he was by no means oblivious to the real music of the future, however, is demonstrated by his championship of Schoenberg's Three Piano Pieces op.11, which he played at one of the Evenings of Contemporary Music in 1911. This, the first performance of Schoenberg's music in Russia, was plunging in at the deep end, as Karatygin noted when he reviewed the first performance of Schoenberg's lush, early tone-poem *Pelleas und Melisande*, conducted by the composer in the Russian capital, over a year later. 'St Petersburg is getting acquainted with Schoenberg in reverse order', Karatygin wrote, noting the recent performance of the 'wonderful' op.10 Quartet and marvelling at the mildness of the symphony-concert audience in comparison to the Homeric laughter which had broken out in the hall at Prokofiev's performance.[58]

What his piano teacher might have made of this is hard to imagine. Yesipova was intent on limiting her pupils to the Classical–Romantic repertoire of her youth. As usual, such autocratic behaviour only fostered rebellion in Prokofiev. He resented her attempts, as he saw it, to 'make everyone fit a standard pattern';[59] she expressed her dissatisfaction that he had 'assimilated little of my method' at the examinations concluding their first year together, adding that he was 'very talented but rather unpolished'.[60] Although he still scoffed at Chopin, he was far from rejecting the music of earlier centuries; it simply needed a patient enthusiast like Tcherepnin to encourage him rather than a dictatorial mentor.

When Prokofiev could lead the way and develop his teacher's taste he was happy. On Taneyev's recommendation he had arranged the A minor Organ Fugue of the late 17th-century Danish composer Dietrich Buxtehude, much admired by Bach, for his first piano examinations with Yesipova, and proudly told Taneyev that 'Anna Nikolayevna was much interested in Buxtehude's fugues. I happen to know that she later took a whole volume of them to Glazunov'.[61] The Buxtehude piece in question was not the one he later arranged as a novelty for the classical tastes of his American audiences, but the memory acted as a prompt in 1918. An early Romantic role model, Schumann's Toccata, which he had been studying for Winkler the season before he changed teachers, provided a mere pretext for his own thoroughly modern exercise in the genre. It has little in common with Schumann's genial drawing of melodic lines out of the perpetual motion, but takes up at more sustained length and with even greater chromatic density where the *Études* left off; if the pianist has the physical stamina, it could be played in recital as a fifth study, the crowning glory of the early 'toccata line' Prokofiev described in his short autobiography.

He was still careful to preserve a balancing act between his own, newfound version of classicism and modernism. The ten pieces he assembled for his op.12 were the most diverse collection to date and had to be put in order from an assortment of the blotchiest manuscripts. The earliest dated back to his first music for Morolev and two of the simple binary and ternary form pieces he had written for Lyadov – much altered, of course, as op.12's March, Gavotte and Scherzo. The latter suggests an interesting link with a major event of 1906, when Oskar Fried conducted Mahler's Second Symphony in St Petersburg, for it starts in the same 3/8 metre with slithery, right-hand semiquavers as Mahler's witty-grotesque 'Sermon of St Anthony to the fishes' from the folk settings of *Des Knaben Wunderhorn*, also the third movement of the symphony. Prokofiev was not, apparently, there to share in Stravinsky's wonderment when Mahler conducted his Fifth Symphony in the city a year later, but the Scherzo suggests that he took a passing interest in the earlier performance, if only by looking at the score.

Next to be composed was the Mazurka, in the summer of 1909, as another guilt-offering alongside the *Études* for Winkler. Its acerbity comes from the succession of 4ths in both hands which Myaskovsky, admitting that the piece might be technically beyond him, had dismissed as 'not novel . . . I know of a waltz in the same vein by the Kievian Yankovsky'.[62] He received the dedication in op.12, so perhaps he mastered it after all. The 4ths still irked Asafyev enough in 1915 for him to label the piece as 'the prank of a spoilt youth'.[63] Otherwise none of the pieces so far mentioned contains more than a few dissonant passages, becoming obstreperous only in the reprises. Cleverly, Prokofiev used them to provide the glossy outer coating to the more bitter pills of the wayward Caprice, the bass-clef croakings of the *Humoresque Scherzo*, subsequently arranged for four bassoons, and the fierce dissection of classical form in the aggressive Allemande. Its dedication to Maximilian Schmidthof is the first reminder of that regrettably under-documented romantic friendship, to be abruptly terminated by Schmidthof's suicide in the spring of 1913. The assumption made by the pianist Alexander Toradze that the Second Piano Concerto is a tragic memorial to Schmidthof deserves some consideration in its rightful place; but the *Legenda* of op.12, which Prokofiev himself thought the finest of the set, seems the more likely candidate. Curiously, it is the only one of the pieces without a dedication.

It begins by anticipating the shifting hues of the *Visions fugitives* in its contrast of nostalgic Andantino and malign, *pianissimo* Adagio before embarking on an Andante religioso of greater emotional depth than anything Prokofiev had composed to date. Why 'religioso' from this least godly of young composers remains an enigma. In his only written mention of the terrible event beyond his letters to Schmidthof's sister, he tells us that 'when I was 19, my father died; my attitude to his death was atheistic. And it was the same at 22 when I lost a close friend who had written before his death "farewell". I took this "good-bye" especially bitterly as coming from a human consciousness which had departed conclusively and for ever'.[64] Perhaps the answer is that a dark and lugubrious tribute would have been to play Schmidthof at his own macabre, even fashionable game. 'Suicides were very much in vogue in St Petersburg early in the century', writes the musicologist Nicolas Slonimsky, who got as far as putting the noose round his neck as a 19-year-old in 1913; 'there was a romantic aura in the act'.[65] Prokofiev may not have had any pretensions to spirituality, but he repeatedly rose above the morbid current of the times, never more unexpectedly than here.

After the vision of the *Legenda* fades, there is something strangely moving about the rippling, C major radiance of the Prelude that follows. It stands for life, not death, and especially for the evidently delightful character of its dedicatee, Eleonora Damskaya, a harpist at the conservatory to whom Prokofiev wrote a precious sequence of witty and capricious, if hardly amorous, letters. Her name figures prominently in Prokofiev's collection of programmes for recitals given by conservatory students at about this time, alongside a few other stars of the future including Jascha Heifetz (soloist in the first movement of Raff's Violin Concerto on 24 January 1913).[66] It is for Damskaya's instrument that the Prelude was written, though it also provides the sensitive pianist with ample opportunity to conjure a silvery, harp-like effect. Prokofiev later chose it to join the March, Gavotte, Rigaudon and Scherzo for his first Duo-Art piano rolls in America, gauging accurately what the public might like best of op.12 but avoiding the more sombre portions of a diverse collection. Op.12 reflects on its own terms the 'friends pictured within' Elgar's 'Enigma' Variations, with Schmidthof playing Nimrod to Damskaya's Dorabella. But there is nothing in Elgar's idealized catalogue of women friends to match the musical portrait (if portrait it be) of Talya Meshcherskaya, the dedicatee of the Caprice, which interlaces innocuous D major with disorienting chromatics in a freewheeling form that threatens to veer out of control. The Meshcherskys were a wealthy St Petersburg family who had first welcomed the eccentrically dressed 19-year-old composer to their musical evenings as a contrast to the correct young men in military uniforms who frequented their salon. Prokofiev's interest soon homed in on one of the daughters – not Talya but her sister Nina, 14 at the time of their first meeting, with whom he was to enjoy his first romance. Nina, in fact, is the 'Fiake' to whom the Rigaudon is dedicated, and she was not pleased with Prokofiev's mischievous use of a family nickname.

The much more unified character of the sonata which bears the next opus number in Prokofiev's output despite its diverse origins is unmistakably lean and pugnacious. These were not qualities which the 'well-balanced, healthy'[67] young man, observed by his fellow student Yury Tyulin about this time, shared with many of his conservatory acquaintances, though Tyulin thought they surfaced in his much more defiant attitude towards his mentors and critics. The Second Piano Sonata is a bracing slap in the face for them, and his sworn enemy Sabaneyev was not to disappoint in declaring it a true offspring of 'the modern "football" generation . . . stupid, inane and blockheaded'.[68] It was composed in Kislovodsk in the summer of 1912, on a piano at the back of a pharmacy, and Prokofiev exuberantly announced its completion date, 28 August, to Myaskovsky, ready as ever to spread the good news among musical circles. (Myaskovsky's analysis, with musical quotations, observing the sonata form which Prokofiev uses to better effect in the characteristically abbreviated recapitulations than in developments, eventually appeared in *Muzyka* in January 1914.) The first movement was expanded from a short sonatina – a form both Prokofiev and Myaskovsky had long reserved for simple textures, which is how the sonata appears on the printed page – and the the spiky Scherzo, with its sharply undulating chromatic lines on the inside and central sequence of chords skipping between repeated notes in octaves, is another unlikely offshoot from Lyadov's class of 1908.

Yet apart from the string of memorable short inventions, which would be enough to keep the sonata in the repertory, there is an overall firmness of purpose that goes beyond the finale's fatigued reminiscence of the first movement's briefly lachrymose, Skryabinesque second subject just when the dance seems to have run out of steam. The leanness of the opening, a Rakhmaninov theme and accompaniment cut down to the bare bones and swiftly mocked by throbbing semitonal clashes, takes its peculiar tension from the interplay of the single left-hand line's 6/8 flow and the urgently climbing 2/4 melody in the right (Ex.22). The finale, beginning with explicit treatment of Prokofiev's beloved tarantella form and moving by way of a lively transition to a second, creepier idea in 2/4, goes on to combine the two metres unobtrusively by superimposing the tarantella's 'link music' over the second subject's ostinato in the bass (Ex.23). (Eventually the two main ideas will be much more obviously presented simultaneously.) The Andante, Prokofiev's great slow movement before the

Ex.22 Piano Sonata no.2, op.14 – I. Allegro, ma non troppo

Ex.23 Piano Sonata no.2 – IV. Vivace

Legenda of op.12, begins with the sonata's characteristic spareness of texture, this time to reiterate something of the keening oppressiveness of op.4's *Despair* in a daring G sharp minor, quickly melting into the diatonic lucidity familiar from the beginning of *Fairy Tale.* A belated midnight visitor in 7/8, haunted by another of those now-familiar chromatic inner lines of which Prokofiev is so fond in his piano music, anticipates the intangible phantoms of the *Visions fugitives.* Indeed, the Andante as a whole looks even further forward to the slow movements of the great Sixth and Seventh sonatas, which merely add a patina of nostalgia to the sense of hopeless suffering so protractedly observed and, for the first time in Prokofiev's music, seemingly felt here.

This is the beginning of what Russian critics, in a more favourable version of the Soviet line, describe as the newfound profundity of 'psychological motifs'[69] in Prokofiev's music. In his short autobiography Prokofiev provides a coda to the works of these years in his famous identification of the 'four lines' now apparent in his music: the classical, the modern, the toccata or 'motor' line and the lyrical.[70] He might have added another, possibly as a subheading under 'the modern': that tragic mode which expresses itself with genuine intensity in the Second Sonata's slow movement and runs in torrents through the Second Piano Concerto. There it happily coincided with a primitive-monumental vein which now exploded with full force as Russian artists, in their latest bid for modernism, decided to return to their prehistoric roots.

5
Sun worship
1913–16

1913 has gone down in musical history as the year that gave noisy and painful birth to Stravinsky's *The Rite of Spring*, narrowly missed by Prokofiev when he travelled to London and Paris as a cultural tourist for the first time that summer. Other, no less momentous, events epitomized the accelerated pace at which all the Russian arts were hurtling towards the future. Painting, as usual, led the way, though its cue came from the works of the revolutionary French artists so discriminatingly bought by two wealthy Moscow collectors, Ivan Morosov, who set standards with his Cézannes, Monets, Gauguins and Renoirs, and Sergey Shchukin, whose more adventurous tastes embraced Matisse and Picasso. Two of the 'big four' in 20th-century Russian art, Mikhail Larionov and his pupil Natalya Goncharova, had wrought their own kind of primitivism as early as 1909, using native peasant arts as their basis but finding the same kind of novel displacement in every area the ever-perceptive Karatygin was to hear in *The Rite of Spring*. Now, in 1913, they embraced the shortest-lived of the '-isms', Rayonnism, unleashed in Larionov's exhibition 'The Target' in March, when he defined its style, if not its machine-led content, as 'concerned with spatial forms which are obtained through the crossing of reflected rays from various objects'.[1]

Two more far-reaching artistic movements were born at the end of the year. The Ukrainian Vladimir Tatlin went to Paris and was inspired by his meeting with Picasso to create his first three-dimensional abstracts, the basis of Constructivism. And Kasimir Malevich freed himself from Goncharova's apron-strings with his first exercise in the supernatural geometrical style he was to call 'Suprematism', a white and black square painted as a backcloth for Alexey Kruchonykh's futurist 'opera' *Victory over the Sun*. Its style was very much part of that desire to shock which surfaced in the antics of its proponents, who painted their faces and wore radishes in their buttonholes; among them was the 20-year-old poet Vladimir Mayakovsky, who joined the artists in a chaotic film made the same year, *Drama in Cabaret no.13*, and whose first play *Vladimir Mayakovsky: A Tragedy* played on alternate nights with *Victory over the Sun* in the Luna Park Theatre in Moscow that December.

The theme of *Victory over the Sun*, however, points to the confusion in the literary arts: these futurists want to bury the sun, too much a property of the old-brigade symbolists like Balmont and Merezhkovsky to rule over their brave new world.[2] But for others equally committed to progress, the sun was part of that vitality which also embraced a return to primitive values. The Acmeists, led by the vibrant Sergey Gorodetsky towards their greatest triumphs in 1913 and including Anna Akhmatova and Osip Mandelstam, needed it as part of their 'resounding and colourful world',[3] while Goncharova and Larionov were to crown their first successes for Diaghilev with sun-drenched vibrancy. Prokofiev, who continued to revere the heliotropic tendencies of the symbolists as initiated by Balmont at the beginning of the century, embraced the sun in his own, freewheeling philosophy. His musical depiction of it at the end of the *Scythian Suite* was to be typically ambivalent, both analogous to that concept of reaching out to the divine self which ends Skryabin's later orchestral works in a blaze of light and independently modernistic enough to be invoked, along with many of Skryabin's symphonic journeys, as a portent of the joyous revolution to come. The source of light remained a preoccupation for the young Prokofiev: for nearly two years from October 1916 he used the still-vital question 'What do you think about the sun?' as a means of getting the famous names among his acquaintance to grace his autograph book with an observation as well as a signature. Among those represented are Balmont, Chaliapin and Mikhail Fokine, Goncharova and Larionov, Koussevitzky, Mayakovsky and Artur Rubinstein, who noted: 'Le roi soleil a dit: L'état, c'est moi. Vous, mon cher Prokofiev, pourriez dire: Le soleil, c'est moi'.[4]

The atmosphere in both major Russian cities in 1913 remained Janus-headed. The 300th anniversary of the Romanov dynasty, which unwittingly inspired so-called avant-garde art with the revelatory icons displayed as part of the 'Ancient Russian Painting' exhibition, gave rise to a string of lavish fancy-dress festivities. At one of these the ambassador Anatoly Nekludov commented to Count Witte that it was a little like Pushkin's *A Feast in Time of Plague*, 'or rather "before the plague"', to which the Count replied: 'We are going God knows where; God alone knows to what abyss! It is impossible to go on like this'.[5] On the brink of change, Diaghilev's all-Russian venture in Paris, the Ballets Russes, was not about to jettison the recent as it shocked with the new. The success of the early enterprises, such as Fokine's 1910 choreography for Rimsky-Korsakov's *Sheherazade* with sumptuous designs by Bakst, was revised for continuity (the third movement of Rimsky-Korsakov's 'symphonic suite', cut at the first production, was even restored in 1914 to provide an extended *pas de deux*). There were rich patrons to please, and since 19th-century Russian opera was still by no means familiar in the West, Diaghilev knew that Londoners especially would be glad to make the acquaintance of past sacred monsters, especially if there was a star like Chaliapin involved.

Stravinsky, though, was following his own line of progress which had nothing to do with those pretty, well-mannered ballets furnished by Prokofiev's beloved Tcherepnin (*Le Pavillon d'Armide* had been followed in 1911 by music for *Narcisse*, with the latest dance sensation Vaslav Nijinsky in the title role and the now familiar visual extravaganza of Bakst). It is curious to think of such successes as *The Firebird*, *Petrushka* and *The Rite of Spring* unfolding in Paris while Prokofiev cultivated his own magic garden back in St Petersburg. In fact Russia knew a little more of at least the first two ballets than we might suppose, thanks partly to the balanced criticism of Myaskovsky; and it was Prokofiev's bad luck if he had heard nothing of either before he arrived in Paris in July 1913 (though he had probably looked at the scores). Several years earlier, Myaskovsky had unintentionally anticipated the overriding quality of Prokofiev's own first attempt at ballet music when he complained to him of the 'clamorous trifles'[6] set down by Alexander Ziloti for the autumn of 1910. The 'Infernal Dance' included among them is surely the enchanted whirl of *The Firebird*'s fairytale ogre Kashchey and his entourage, which concluded the five-movement suite conducted by Ziloti on 23 October 1910 (and published in 1912 by Jurgenson, the firm which was then favouring Prokofiev). In an article for *Muzyka* that month, Myaskovsky praised Stravinsky's freshness of invention and temperament, especially his unusual cheerfulness, and hailed him as the heir apparent to Rimsky-Korsakov while ultimately questioning the originality of this brilliant synthesis.

Myaskovsky's considered verdict stands in marked contrast to Prokofiev's callow assessment of the prelude to *The Firebird* when Stravinsky played it through to him. (Though Prokofiev gives only a rough timescale for this event, recorded in his autobiography, it must have taken place in the late summer or autumn of 1913.) He merely invited Stravinsky's hostility by telling him 'there was no music in this introduction, and if there was any it came from *Sadko*'[7] – meaning the slow, oscillating introduction both to Rimsky-Korsakov's early tone-poem and to his opera on the same subject, which begins with the same three notes as Stravinsky's shadowy prelude. He failed to point out the originality in the turn Stravinsky's music then takes which, as Myaskovsky had noted, lies in the succession of major and minor 3rds dominating Kashchey's music throughout much of the ballet. Prokofiev's other criticism – 'no music'[8] – is aired at length in his Parisian acquaintanceship with *Petrushka*. This, too, had been enthusiastically acclaimed as 'life itself'[9] by Myaskovsky in the January 1913 edition of *Muzyka*, this time coinciding with a performance of three sequences conducted by Koussevitzky, the fast-risen star who was far from Myaskovsky's or Stravinsky's ideal. Myaskovsky berates Prokofiev for having 'rushed off impetuously' and missed the premiere, adding that the music 'turned out to be altogether more entrancing than in the score'.[10]

With all the brash confidence of youth, Prokofiev again fired off a less detailed verdict later that year, though this time his opinion was based on a proper hearing of the complete score with Fokine's choreography and Nijinsky's dancing to complement its illustrative qualities. And those elements were what he objected to most, in letters that June first to Myaskovsky and later to Tcherepnin, who had just left Paris when Prokofiev arrived at the beginning of the month. He praises the dynamism of Stravinsky's approach and the often witty orchestration; but he bewails to Tcherepnin 'the low level of the composer's attitude to music as music',[11] enlarging on this to Myaskovsky: 'in the most interesting moments and the liveliest parts of the scenario he writes not music but something which more brilliantly illustrates the moment'.[12]

This attitude (which he would have occasion to change over the next few years) is, however, a good deal more positive than his feelings about *Daphnis et Chloé*, of which the illustrative action music is dismissed as plain wretched or, worse, laughable and in which even the poetic approach he commends to the well-connected Tcherepnin becomes, in less guarded comments to Myaskovsky, merely 'soporific'.[13] Unfortunately Prokofiev slips up when he most needs to impress his professor, castigating Debussy as the composer of this 'watery' music.[14] Ravel's *Daphnis et Chloé* was in its second year, while Debussy's most enigmatic score, *Jeux*, which Prokofiev perhaps fortunately did not see, had been a relative flop at its Paris premiere in May and caused amusement as *Playtime* in London later that season. The other ballets he describes are Florent Schmitt's *La Tragédie de Salomé* ('simply tasteless'[15]), the still-abbreviated *Sheherazade* ('luxuriantly staged and in perfect harmony with the music'[16]), Fokine's exciting choreography for the Polovtsian Dances from Borodin's *Prince Igor* and *Carnaval*, for which Tcherepnin had provided several of the arrangements of Schumann's score (he was solely responsible for the orchestration of Fokine's Schumannesque sequel, *Papillons*, given its premiere in St Petersburg in March 1912, when Prokofiev had been too ill to go and see it). The young spectator's critical faculties are especially sharp here. 'I was charmed by many of the numbers', he tells Tcherepnin, 'but disappointed by others which were specifically designed for the piano. And the production? Is it possible that Schumann's illustrations, so graphic and aromatic, give so little food for a fantastic *mise en scène*?'[17]

Prokofiev was also an enthusiastic tourist, charmingly aware in his correspondence of the broadening of his outlook. 'The liveliness of the French, the tempo at which life is conducted and the general level of culture have fascinated me',[18] he told Tcherepnin, outlining qualities that he would come to view a little more ambivalently when Paris eventually became his base. He enjoyed an exhibition of sculpture, found the Louvre instructive but labyrinthine and climbed the Eiffel Tower 'with great animation',[19] not forgetting to write Eleonora Damskaya a postcard at the top. In his Paris pension he met up with Anna Zherebtsova-Andreyeva and her husband Nikolay Andreyev, a Maryinsky Theatre tenor who was taking part in Diaghilev's especially ambitious operatic season. In London the Russians stunned the best society – and eclipsed the British unveiling of *The Rite of Spring* – with a first glimpse of Musorgsky's *Boris Godunov* and *Khovanshchina* (both in Rimsky-Korsakov's arrangements, of course, further adapted by Diaghilev) along with Rimsky-Korsakov's *The Maid of Pskov*, which Diaghilev promoted as *Ivan the Terrible*. Making a vital four-day diversion to London Prokofiev was there at the 'glittering opening night of the Russian opera'[20] on 11 June, and in his diary he writes reverently about the caged-animal magnificence of Chaliapin's Boris

(Andreyev was playing Prince Shuisky opposite the great bass). He suffered from his inability to speak English, presumably making a mental note to study the language in the near future, found Oxford and Regent Streets inferior to the Paris boulevards, and took an excursion to Windsor with a fellow student from the conservatory, Mikhail Shteiman.

'Now I'm stuck in Royat', he wrote to Tcherepnin from the Auvergne at the end of June, 'where Mama intends to drink the waters and take the baths. This is a quiet resort for elderly people. To rescue myself from boredom, I study literally all day: I'm learning my new concerto, which has turned out to be disgracefully difficult and mercilessly tiring.'[21] The serious study which he had sacrificed to the pursuit of pleasure in the two capitals could be postponed no longer: he was due to give the premiere of his Second Piano Concerto at Pavlovsk. The original date of 2 August was soon moved to 24 August, giving him the opportunity of several blissful weeks in the summer heat at Gurzuf in the Crimea shortly after he returned to Russia via Switzerland. At Gurzuf he was the guest of the well-to-do Meshcherskys, who had retreated there for the summer. He shared musical soirées with his idol, the tenor Ivan Yershov, playing Schumann's *Carnaval* as well as Wagner overtures to entertain the musical family, and strenuously enjoyed his usual range of physical exercise, on this occasion extended to include races in chariots drawn by tartar horses. Through Nina's eyes, it was 'a fairy-tale summer of flowers and cypresses, with moonlit walks to the sea at night'.[22] But Prokofiev the ambitious performer-composer was not quite ready to lose his head over a girl, and despite their flirtation Nina's first romance was with another man 15 years her senior. Prokofiev continued to work on the concerto for a couple of hours a day and even managed to make some corrections to *Maddalena*, the renewed prospect of which he had taken up with Derzhanovsky as he passed through Moscow on his way to the south. Another spell of summer enchantment was to follow the concerto premiere, when he went to stay with Zakharov and his family at the fashionable resort of Terioki, north of St Petersburg on the Gulf of Finland. There he also made the acquaintance of two sisters, Zoya and Lidya Karneyeva who, like Zakharov, were to become lifelong friends.

Prokofiev had established the future of the Second Piano Concerto in a meeting with the powers of Pavlovsk just before leaving for the West, when he scornfully wrote to Myaskovsky of hearing 'fat Shurenok'[23] Glazunov conduct two movements of his incidental music to Wilde's *Salome* and the Sixth Symphony. He also played Glazunov his First Concerto along with the first and third movements from the newly completed Second. The arch-romantic, so widely mocked for voting against the competition performance of the First Concerto the following year and for walking out of the *Scythian Suite*'s premiere, was by no means actively hostile to the young man's most provocative score to date, though he might have done more to champion its cause with the committee of the Belyayev concerts ('a Mitrofanish graveyard',[24] Prokofiev whimsically declared that decaying concert scene, playing on the first name of its late founder). Myaskovsky learnt that the Pavlovsk panel 'appreciated those somewhat old-fashioned qualities of logic and technique, as well as that which they didn't possess themselves ("liveliness of temperament"), but the frightful dissonance of the music remained as unthinkable to them as ever'[25] – though not so unthinkable as to blight the concerto's chances of performance.

Even for Myaskovsky the pleasure of looking through the concerto must have been mixed. With his own predilection for dark, sombre scoring, he had always preferred his friend's more weightily complex pieces, and this was the heaviest yet. But he was on the retreat from his balanced support of Stravinsky with a far less positive assessment of *The Rite of Spring* just round the corner – and Stravinsky's high-handedness that summer in expecting Myaskovsky to be his copyist can hardly have helped – while his admiration for *Petrushka* had been eclipsed, at least in the letter to Prokofiev, by his love of the senior romantic Medtner's Second Piano Sonata. His praise of the Second Concerto as he helped prepare the parts at the beginning of August seems to highlight the 'old-fashioned qualities' admired by the Pavlovsk set, and is a little at odds with his claim that he could not sleep at night for sheer excitement: 'this is a classical concerto composed with lucidity of form, concision of thought and a definition and prominence of outline'.[26] He praises the melodies rather than the colossal and dissonant climaxes, singling out the gravely beautiful theme which crawls out of the finale's tempest (Ex.24). No doubt its simple diatonic cast made it the only suitable candidate for Myaskovsky's own limited pianistic skills, but he was surely right to love its 'elusive voice';[27] and Prokofiev's sense of theatre in allowing this most wistful of his themes to surface very late in the work is pure genius.

Ex.24 Piano Concerto no.2, op.16 – IV. Allegro tempestoso (Meno mosso)

The Second Piano Concerto that we hear today is not the one that was to shock the Pavlovsk audience at its 1913 premiere. Left behind in Petrograd when Prokofiev moved in 1918, the manuscript was lost in a fire during the difficult years following the Revolution; and Prokofiev had a new version, by his own avowal 'less foursquare' and 'slightly more complex in its contrapuntal fabric' but with the thematic material entirely preserved,[28] ready by 1924 for a Paris performance conducted by Koussevitzky, by which time his Third Concerto was already doing the rounds. Yet by then he had played the solo role sufficiently often to remember most of the details, and the likelihood is that many of the refinements belong to the orchestration, the chasteness of which belies the work's wild reputation. The magical writing for divided violins and violas near the start (which would surely have been beyond the wiry strings of the orchestra at Pavlovsk), the haunting woodwind echoes of the soloist's opening theme and the coup of holding back the heavier brass for the massive climax of the first movement have the stamp of the composer's economical maturity.

Only in the ironically named Intermezzo does Prokofiev let the orchestra hold centre stage, with the soloist nimbly cavorting between the bass-heavy monsters of a lumbering parade. The near-impossible execution of the solo part, which might have been made for the big-boned offspring of the Russian piano school in the second half of the 20th century, is surely the only reason why the Second has lagged behind the concertos either side of it. Prokofiev would seem to have two precedents for letting a cadenza do the development's work in the first movement: Tchaikovsky's Concert Fantasia, where the piano plays uninterrupted by the orchestra for some seven minutes; and the longer of the two first-movement cadenzas in Rakhmaninov's Third Concerto, which he may have despised for its subject matter but the manner of which undoubtedly influenced his own heaviest work (from the Rakhmaninov, too, comes the telescoped reprise once the battle is over). Much of this – how much we shall never know – was the work of the 1923–4 revision. In writing which spreads on to three staves in the manner of the *Études*, the expansive opening theme reaches its apogee in double-octave exchanges between the extremes of the instrument with the all-important 12/8 of its support pounding away in heavy chords in the middle staff (Ex.25). The striding movement of the juggernaut is then subjected to even more vertiginous treatment, while the simple, dying falls of the concerto's opening return to deliver a series of fatal blows as the colossal climax of the cadenza drags in the full orchestra.

Alexander Toradze, most unorthodox of the concerto's more recent champions, hears a tragic heartbeat in those falling 3rds, a frame to a programmatic reliving of the Schmidthof affair, claiming that 'it was the shock of Schmidthof's death that shaped this piece in its agonizing final form'.[29] He is, however, misleading in his implication that Prokofiev had merely 'sketched some ideas for a future concerto, and shared them with Maximilian'.[30] 'I composed this piece during the winter', Prokofiev told Schmidthof's sister Katya shortly after Schmidthof's suicide. 'Max was always interested in it, and was the first to whom I played excerpts of what I'd written. That's why, after his death, I dedicated it "to the memory of Maximilian Anatolievich Schmidthof"'.[31] There is also the simple explanation given in the short autobiography of how 'the charges of showy brilliance and certain "acrobatic" tendencies in the First Concerto induced me to strive for greater depth in the Second',[32] though this does not entirely explain how the depth was achieved. Toradze's written programme is very subjective. If it helps to intensify his own performance, so

Ex.25 Piano Concerto no.2 – I. Andantino (Poco meno mosso)

much the better. But there is plenty of high-spirited fun here which cannot simply be explained as fond reminiscence of times past. Prokofiev cannot resist inserting into the first movement a gavotte-like Allegretto marked 'elegante' in the style of the *sobachki*: surely another quirky self-portrait rather than a sketch of the lugubrious Schmidthof. The toccata-scherzo is more dazzling good fun than menacing obsession (though Rakhmaninov seems to have benefited from its acquaintance in the undeniably demonic context of his much later *Rhapsody on a Theme of Paganini*) and not, perhaps, persistently chromatic in its semiquaver runs for long enough to qualify as a successor to the queasy finale of Chopin's Second Sonata. There is too much fashionable, 'Scythian' uproar and too many picturesque episodes in the intermezzo to tie it exclusively to a personal tragedy.

Besides, descriptions of Prokofiev's early performances suggest a buoyant approach, full of elan and revelling in the piece's confrontational quality. 'Prokofiev plays with a triumphant air at the RMO', Asafyev wrote about his friend's first successful breach of the prestigious concert series in January 1915, 'and his lovable smiling mug looks on indifferently as the audience giggles and hisses, etc.'[33] We are indebted to an extra-musical journalist of the *Peterburgskaya gazeta* for the most vivid description of the Pavlovsk premiere:

> A youth with the face of a high-school student appears on the platform. It is Sergey Prokofiev. He seats himself at the piano and starts either wiping the keyboard or testing the keys. All this is done with a dry, sharp touch. The audience is bewildered. Some people are indignant. One couple gets up and moves towards the exit [exclaiming] 'Such music is enough to drive you mad'. Others: 'What is he doing, trying to make fun of us?' More listeners follow the first couple from various parts of the hall. Prokofiev plays the second movement of his concerto . . . The more daring members of the audience hiss . . . Finally the young artist concludes his concerto with a mercilessly dissonant combination of brasses. The scandal in the audience is now full-blown. The majority hisses. Prokofiev bows defiantly and plays an encore. The audience rushes away. On all sides there are exclamations: 'The devil take all this Futurist music! We want to hear something pleasant! [They heard Rimsky-Korsakov's *Sheherazade* in the second half.] We can hear music like this from our cats at home'. Another group – the progressive critics – are in raptures: 'A work of genius! How original! What spirit and invention!'[34]

Russia's most intelligent critic, Karatygin, was of course among them, and his voice was heard in no fewer than three important publications. Against the ravings of such anti-modernists as the predictably hostile Bernstein, who had already attacked the First Piano Concerto as well as Myaskovsky's Second Symphony earlier in the Pavlovsk season and who decided that the cadenzas might as well have been 'created by capriciously emptying an inkwell on a piece of paper',[35] Karatygin's chapter and verse were infinitely more civilized and ultimately more influential. His conclusion, as ever, was apt: 'the public hissed. This is meaningless. In ten years' time it will make amends for last night's jeering by unanimously applauding a composer with a European reputation'.[36]

Several figures in the musical establishment whose opinions really mattered still kept their doors closed to him. Ziloti returned the score the following April, suggesting the young composer had yet to 'find himself'.[37] By way of counter-attack, Myaskovsky vented his spleen in *Muzyka* under the signature 'Misanthrope', the title of his new song sequence, with a powerful polemic against the bastions of tradition. This had some impact on Ziloti. In the meantime, Prokofiev's suspicion that the grand conductor was too saturated with 'idle-sounding French spices'[38] to respond proved correct: in private Ziloti liked to contrast the fragrance of Debussy with the stench of Prokofiev's concerto. Derzhanovsky remained a firm supporter. His negotiations with the Mardzhanov Free Theatre over *Maddalena* were doomed to failure, but he did provide Prokofiev with just about the only performing opportunities he could manage in the scramble towards the final examinations of the 1913–14 conservatory year. 'I'm prepared to perform the following items', Prokofiev told him in October 1913, listing the Sonata op.14, the third *Étude* of op.2, *Fairy Tale* from op.3, the Prelude, Rigaudon and *Legenda* from op.12 and finally *Despair* and *Suggestion diabolique* from op.4. 'I don't have time to prepare more than these pieces on account of the great quantity of conservatory work, but I beg to perform without fail the Ballade, for I'd be very interested to hear it played.'[39]

Perhaps he was most intrigued at the thought of partnering the renowned cellist Yevsey Belousov, for the piece itself was the most conventional in his half of the programme. It could hardly be otherwise when the introduction and the first five bars of the leading theme are the earliest of his inspirations to have found a place in a later work; they come, as Prokofiev proudly announces in his childhood autobiography, from the violin sonata he had composed for Glière at the age of 11. The piece then takes an altogether more complex turn, though the unusual indecisiveness Prokofiev showed over the coda – he rewrote it altogether in April 1914 but tore off the altered manuscript when Myaskovsky declared it tedious – perhaps suggests a lack of urgency. At any rate it came in useful as a graduation piece to please the more conservative professors at the conservatory.

No doubt the Ballade complemented Myaskovsky's own First Cello Sonata rather well at the Moscow Evening of Contemporary Music on 22 January. Myaskovsky's other contributions, song settings of Gippius and Ivanov sung by Derzhanovsky's wife Yekaterina Koposova, offered hints for Prokofiev's next vocal works. Koposova also gave the first Russian performance of Stravinsky's *Japanese Lyrics* and his Balmont settings from 1911. Stravinsky's native land at last seemed to be catching up with his latest trains of thought, for Koussevitzky's Moscow and St Petersburg performances of *The Rite of Spring* followed in February – only to be discreetly rejected even by such an intelligence as Karatygin. It must have been the Petersburg performance which put Prokofiev, according to Stravinsky, under the spell of *The Rite of Spring.* The detractors, of course, had a field day. Sabaneyev was there for the Contemporary Evening, and his abuse of Prokofiev's Second Piano Sonata was flattering in comparison to the mean-minded dissection of the *Japanese Lyrics* – a sign that Prokofiev was clearly in good company.

The sonata was undoubtedly the quirky star of the show, both here and in St Petersburg. The lovably conservative Morolev, still treating animals in Nikopol, might have enjoyed the Ballade but clearly found the latest evidence of Prokofiev's progressive streak too much. Prokofiev upbraided his 'Nikopolian porker' in the highest of spirits that Easter: 'it's a great pity you didn't understand my Second Sonata – it's enjoyed great success here, they think it's a hundred times better than the first and it's often enlarged upon in all lectures on new music'.[40] His examinations had all been 'crowned with crosses in the shapes of "5s", he told Morolev, and his conducting duties were coming to an end. He had just taken charge of a student performance of Mozart's *Le nozze di Figaro,* his first complete opera at the conservatory. Tcherepnin's mark was among the '5s', but his final report was not without criticism: 'Has acquired a rather sound technique in conducting, which will prove useful when conducting his own works. Has a terribly thankless and heavy hand. Capacity for work is exceptional'.[41]

One big trial lay ahead, and Prokofiev told Morolev about it: 'medals have been abolished with us, but there is a prize – a Shreder grand piano – for the best pupil. On the 22nd there's going to be a competition between the five best students. I'm playing my concerto, three others are playing the Liszt [First Concerto] and the only girl's performing the Saint-Saëns [Second] Concerto'.[42] Yesipova would have done her best to discourage Prokofiev's decision but she had been ill that winter and Prokofiev took advantage of her absence to go his own way as usual. There would be no recurrence of a previous situation where he had entered a competition in complete disregard of her instructions, found himself compelled to play her the pieces as he had decided to interpret them and, when 'Madame Annette' disapproved, had to withdraw as there was no time to relearn them. The prospect this time was clearly one to be relished not feared, even though it was to be a public competition in front of the assembled members of the conservatory.

Prokofiev bewailed to Morolev his lack of free time but there was an enticing distraction that he had no intention of sacrificing: 'a grandiose chess tournament beginning here . . . The whole chess world is assembling with king Lasker at the head and all the pretenders to his throne'.[43] Lasker, who had dominated the chess world for the past two decades and took a fee of 4000 roubles for his participation, was nearly toppled by the man who would turn out to be his rightful heir, the assured 26-year-old Cuban José Capablanca. Angered by the form of Capablanca's previous challenge after his precocious victory in San Sebastián in 1911, Lasker viewed him with hostility. Prokofiev saw things more poetically in an article he wrote for *Dyen*: 'I would like to compare these two pillars of the chess world to two geniuses of the music world, Mozart and Bach. And while I see the complex, deep

Lasker as the majestic Bach, the lively and impetuous Capablanca is the eternally young Mozart who created with the same ease, and sometimes the same lovable carefree quality as Capablanca'.[44] There was another analogy which Prokofiev could not afford to make, at least in print. Capablanca's unshakable self-confidence and virtues of precision and simplicity were essentially his own. The difference, in 1914 at least, was in the last steps necessary to victory. Capablanca, as Prokofiev observed in his article, gained the audience's sympathy with his gracious victories in the first few days. But in the seventh of the ten final rounds, he lost his one and a half point lead to Lasker. Deathly pale, Capablanca left the table without shaking hands. The following day he lost to Siegbert Tarrasch (commended in Prokofiev's article for his fine piano playing). Lasker took the crown.

Prokofiev's relations with the strongest rival in his own contest, the Lyapunov pupil Nadezhda Golubovskaya, were altogether more courteous: 'on the evening before the examination we asked after the condition of each other's fingers, and in the long hours during which the judges had retired to make their decision we played chess'.[45] He won the battle of the pianos, though not before a heated debate between those in his favour – progressives and former pupils of Yesipova – and those against, chiefly Glazunov, who then read the announcement 'flaccidly and indistinctly'.[46] Among the papers in the Glinka Museum's Prokofiev archive, a programme written in faded ink for that momentous day, 22 April, tells a slightly different story both from the one Prokofiev predicted to Morolev and the one he recounted in his autobiography.[47] Here we learn that two of the other competitors played the Saint-Saëns; Prokofiev, the last to appear, played not only his own First Concerto but also Liszt's majestically awkward transcription of Wagner's *Tannhäuser* Overture as well, which suggests that the cards were already stacked in his favour. The fact that Jurgenson had printed copies of the score, even though it was only because the judges had insisted they needed to study it before the performance, must also have helped. What we do know is that he had sterling support for the concerto on a second piano from his fellow student and conductor of promise Vladimir Dranishnikov, who had been 'worn out by the awkward accompaniment',[48] though he liked the music itself; Prokofiev's confidence in him was not misplaced. On 11 May, two days after his exuberant report on the chess tournament, he played the concerto again at the conservatory, this time with full orchestra conducted by his 'father and benefactor'[49] Tcherepnin. Prokofiev himself conducted *Processional*, a new work by his contemporary Andrey Shcherbachev.

Two more glittering prizes followed. As a present for winning, his mother sent him, with modest resources, on a second visit to London; this was to have significant consequences. And before he left St Petersburg, he capped the exhilaration of his 1909 draw with Lasker by challenging Capablanca to three games as part of a simultaneous display, winning the third; an incredulous Myaskovsky had to ask, tongue in cheek, whether he needed to cheat. After his triumph Prokofiev took tea with Capablanca. He was a little dismayed, when he played through the Liszt transcription of the

Tannhäuser Overture, that Capablanca displayed 'total ignorance, saying that he'd heard the piece somewhere but didn't know what it was',[50] but this was no obstacle to their talking and walking round St Petersburg until three in the morning. He was still musing on 'adorable Capablanchik'[51] to Eleonora Damskaya as he travelled third-class from Newcastle to London in mid-June. His journey, this time without his mother, had taken him via Stockholm through Norway, where he found he liked 'Grieg's homeland and his compatriots too',[52] followed by a 24-hour crossing to England.

Characteristically, Prokofiev managed to establish a useful routine in London after a week. Tcherepnin had provided him with an introduction to the English representative of Breitkopf & Härtel, Otto Kling, who provided a studio in the company's central London offices. There Prokofiev worked on corrections to the Sinfonietta, which he was at last to perform for the first time in one of Ziloti's concerts that October. The afternoons were frequently devoted to vital meetings with famous musicians, the evenings to absorbing miracles old and new in Diaghilev's most opulent and unforgettable season at Drury Lane. If Prokofiev undertook any edifying sightseeing, he makes no mention of it in his letters home. His favourite pastimes were shopping for brightly coloured socks, playing bridge with Andreyev (again an invaluable guide), watching prize-fighters knock each other unconscious at a boxing match (which he conjured up for his mother with a relish only a little short of the detailed description he also gave to Damskaya) and spying on lovers in Hyde Park on a free evening. It is curious that he gives such an uninhibited account of his voyeurism to Damskaya – one of several indications that her role was more that of confidante than girlfriend.

Apart from a second trip to Windsor, his only excursion was a three-day visit to Birmingham to stay with another Tcherepnin connection, the composer Granville Bantock, Principal of the Midland School of Music in Birmingham and currently Professor of Music at the university. A staunch colleague of Elgar, 'Gran' had not always been held in the highest esteem by him as a composer, though it was Elgar's publishing friend A.J. Jaeger ('Nimrod') who made the rudest remarks in their correspondence about such characteristic exotica as the *Russian Scenes* ('very weak twaddle, nicely scored of course'[53]). Bantock's greater value was as a sympathetic promoter of deserving new music. He had championed Sibelius, who dedicated his Third Symphony to him, and now, according to Prokofiev, was 'in great raptures over my compositions',[54] intending to put on a performance of the Second Piano Concerto in the autumn (in fact it had to wait many years for its British premiere). Staying with this kindest of hosts in a 'comfortable house surrounded by a green garden'[55] seems to have been a pleasant experience for the young composer. Bantock's cursory house diary for the period does at least tell us that late in the evening of 4 July he 'played chess with Prokofiew and was beaten' – not, presumably, the reason why he felt 'rather seedy'[56] the following day, which led him to palm off his guest on family and friends.

Prokofiev had to work harder for the mightier powers of the day. Walter Nouvel, who was in London, invited him to lunch with Diaghilev at the Savoy Hotel the day before his Birmingham sojourn. He played his Second Piano Concerto, Second Piano Sonata and *Maddalena*. Diaghilev, Prokofiev told his mother,

> didn't like the subject of *Maddalena* very much, but on the other hand he did very much like the music of my Second Concerto, and he announced that he wants to put it on in the coming year. That's to say, the concerto will be performed as a concerto, but along with it there'll be a mimetic scene which will be danced by ballet artists. In a word, a new Diaghilevish stunt. This idea isn't completely to my taste, but perhaps it will come out curiously. Alongside this discussions proceed about the commissioning from me of an independent ballet.[57]

A further meeting with the 'society of other organizers of the Russian spectacle'[58] followed on the afternoon of his return from Birmingham. It was at this meeting that the Spanish artist José-Maria Sert exclaimed 'mais c'est une bête féroce',[59] linking the brilliant young composer-pianist with those progressive French painters who favoured wild, extreme use of colours. He was a fauve with attitude to boot. Perhaps it was the youthful bluntness with which Prokofiev expressed his doubts about the 'new Diaghilevish stunt' which created the initial impression of arrogance noted by the impresario in a letter to Stravinsky the following year.

The ballets Prokofiev saw in London that season reinforced the impression of a company wrapped in vintage gold leaf. The best was the already historic *Firebird*, in which he warmed to Fokine's quaint choreography for Kashchey's myrmidons but once again raised the question of Stravinsky's score as pure music and especially of what he felt was the failure to achieve the appropriate solemnity for the final apotheosis. *Midas*, with 'worthy'[60] music by Rimsky-Korsakov's son-in-law and supporter Maximilian Steinberg, he judged 'boring'[61] to Tcherepnin and nice but ephemeral to Myaskovsky. *The Legend of Joseph* must have come as a bitter disappointment to an admirer, however ambivalent, of Richard Strauss; no-one since has been able to disagree with Prokofiev's verdict on the score's 'total lack of any happy inspirations and a great amount of clichés and cheap effects',[62] which the excessive opulence of Bakst's Veronese-inspired costumes and Sert's set designs hardly concealed. Still, Prokofiev saw Strauss, 'a tall, handsome grey-haired gentleman',[63] who conducted three of the six performances, and noted of Léonide Massine, whose other-worldliness made him a suitably godly substitute for the newly married *persona non grata* Nijinsky, that he was 'a quiet, even taciturn youth who has fallen only by chance into this hurly-burly'.[64]

Diaghilev's novel staging of Rimsky-Korsakov's *The Golden Cockerel* should have been in marked contrast to the overkill of *The Legend of Joseph*, especially since it introduced to Western audiences Goncharova's first, brilliant designs for Diaghilev. Unfortunately his decision to place the singers at the side of the stage and to present the work as a ballet punctured the fairy-tale illusion. Not even the ballerina Tamara Karsavina, working hard for her money by appearing throughout in several of the triple bills, could bring vitality to the Queen of Shemakhan's lengthy seduction of the ridiculous Tsar Dodon, which Prokofiev must have been hearing for the first time when he described it as 'extremely boring, cold and unimaginative'.[65] Stravinsky's *The Nightingale*, a casualty like *Maddalena* of the Mardzhanov Free Theatre's premature closure, was luckier in finding a home with Diaghilev, but Prokofiev disliked the score's 'deliberate and unnecessary scratching' as well as its 'pallid humour and lack of liveliness'.[66] Again, dance was paramount; both operas appeared alongside ballets in full programmes, as *Maddalena* and the opera Prokofiev tentatively told Diaghilev he wanted to write based on Dostoyevsky's *The Gambler* never could, and never would. *The Nightingale*, perhaps, turned Prokofiev's attention to the Hans Christian Andersen source, which would prompt him in several months' time to take up his own original idea for a setting of *The Ugly Duckling*.

Of the more traditional operas of the season – if indeed he saw them – Prokofiev says nothing. This time Diaghilev added Rimsky-Korsakov's *May Night* and a complete *Prince Igor* to the repertory. He was able to dare so much thanks to the ever more lavish sponsorship of the millionaire pill-manufacturer Joseph Beecham, who had supported the London seasons since 1911 with royal approval. Prokofiev explains his role in the proceedings, and the prestige he could expect to draw from his generous financial underpinning, in detail to his mother, adding that 'to meet and be on good terms with Beecham is extremely essential, all the more because his son is an excellent musician and fiercely loves Russian music'.[67] A scheduled meeting with Thomas Beecham, who had played a small role conducting Balakirev's *Thamar* and one performance of *Petrushka*, failed to take place; Beecham never did include Prokofiev's works among his principal Russian loves. There was one last encounter which should have borne substantial fruit. On 1 July Prokofiev played his compositions to 'the chief conductor of Diaghilev, [Pierre] Monteux, who is arranging a series of subscription concerts in the manner of the Ziloti ones. He was completely enraptured by both my concertos and invited me to appear in Paris in the winter with my Second Concerto, and if it appears in scenic form under Diaghilev's aegis then with the First. We haven't yet spoken about the financial arrangements'.[68] His pragmatic approach to securing a decent contract with Diaghilev was not entirely self-motivated; his widowed mother had spent a miserable summer at home so that her son could further his career in the West, and the money would have allowed them to return to Paris and London together the following year.

All these dreams had to be suspended. A month after the assassination of Archduke Ferdinand of Austria in Sarajevo on 28 June, Austria declared war on Serbia and Tsar Nicholas II ordered immediate mobilization. Returning to Russia via Germany, Prokofiev arrived in St Petersburg to find a letter from Myaskovsky dated 6 August, telling him that he was 'beyond reach – in the city of Borovichi in the Novgorod district, serving in the military field-engineers' half company, where I occupy the rank of lieutenant'.[69] Prokofiev was exempt from military service as a widow's only son (and remained so, despite the threat of second-division drafts to replenish the Russian army's dwindling resources later that year), so the two friends' lives now took very different turns. In Borovichi, Myaskovsky found himself all too busy doing nothing, observing the military routine which gave him no time to 'read a paper, write a letter or other such diversions; I've already stopped thinking about music'.[70] Prokofiev made an uncomfortable journey to comfortable Kislovodsk, where he joined his mother for the next month and a half. His routine continued much as usual: walking, sunbathing for a tan which made him 'look like a copper basin',[71] games of chess and bridge, the novel study of English ('60 new words for each lesson'[72]) and more work on revising the Sinfonietta for the Ziloti premiere; it now had '67% new material'.[73]

The presence of the Meshcherskys at Kislovodsk had a special significance. In the spring Prokofiev had begun giving piano lessons to Nina and a romance developed sufficiently for him 'jokingly' to dub her the Clara Wieck to his Schumann[74] and to talk to her on the telephone in the evenings. The flames of an 'all-consuming love'[75] were fanned that summer when the lessons were replaced by Mozart sonatas in which Prokofiev added improvisatory flourishes to his left-hand accompaniment. 'I think', recalled Nina in later life, 'that Mozart would have liked it.'[76] Since there is no mention of the romance in Prokofiev's autobiography, we would only have Nina's word for it were it not for references in his recently published diaries and a coy confession to Eleonora Damskaya that he had 'landed in a bitter war. I'm fighting like a madman. The war, by the way, is successful, although part of a lousy town in my territory has been occupied. The name of that little town is My Heart'.[77] At this stage the real war was food only for jolly analogy. Like most Russians, Prokofiev had no inkling of the bloody turn it would soon take and gave 'Nyamusya' Myaskovsky a characteristically brittle slap on the back: 'I sympathize very much with you in your hardship, the more since, devil take it, you're not cut out to be a warrior, but I see an advantage in it since, in the first place, to straighten one's back in the fresh air far away is good for your health and in the second place such violent abstinence will goad you to work and, having become a little out of the habit of composing, and being half starved, you'll certainly write something exceptionally fresh'.[78]

With Myaskovsky's move to a new military base in Kapitolovo, close to Petrograd, the patriotically renamed Petersburg, the autumn brought the two friends geographically closer; but a long-planned car journey Prokofiev intended to make with their mutual friend Boris Zakharov came to a halt with early snows, and their lives continued worlds apart. Myaskovsky now found it hard to believe he had ever composed any symphonies, let alone that his latest, the Third, was due for a distinguished premiere. Prokofiev, on the other hand, had now got the bit between his teeth with the Diaghilev project. The negotiations with St Petersburg writers, which he had told his mother he was expecting on his return, had brought him into contact with Sergey Gorodetsky, two of whose poems Stravinsky had set to music and accompanied in his debut as composer-pianist at one of the Evenings of Contemporary Music back in December 1907.

In the Soviet era Gorodetsky was to be lambasted by Shostakovich as a 'miserable poet and great scoundrel'[79] for, among other things, his dutiful reversification of the libretto to Glinka's *A Life for the Tsar* (as *Ivan Susanin*). But in *Yar*, the 1906 collection from which Stravinsky drew his texts, he acquired a reputation for driving the vanguard of an increasingly fashionable return to Russian paganism. The untranslatable word 'Yar' itself has pagan connotations of spring and Yarilo, its sun-god representative in the pantheon, is hailed by all in the final 11/4 chorus of Rimsky-Korsakov's *The Snow Maiden*. Some of the poems in the collection indeed bear the stamp of what Prince Mirsky described as 'mystical anarchism';[80] three of them could even have prompted the dream of pagan sacrifice which led Stravinsky to the subject of *The Rite of Spring*. Diaghilev's injunction to Prokofiev had been sufficiently vague to allow him to hope that his latest protégé might do something completely different from *The Rite*, and with hindsight we can see that the impresario rarely succeeded on the occasions when old atmosphere was resuscitated. Yet with Gorodetsky (one of several possibilities) now involved, there could only be a repetition, and a somewhat confused one at that.

The symbolic cue for an exhilarating indulgence in orchestral noise for noise's sake was the Scythian people, whose savage deeds are recounted in the *Histories* of that likable Greek pioneer Herodotus. Driven out of Asia by the Medes, they settled in what is now southern Russia before moving to the Crimea, holding sway in one region or another from the end of the 7th century BC to the 2nd century AD and leaving a beautifully crafted treasury of gold objects, the best of which can be seen in the Hermitage Museum. That 'Scythian' become a byword for savagery and gave birth to a special noun, 'skifstvo' ('Scythianism'), was partly a result of the fuss about Prokofiev's ballet music when it was eventually presented to the Russian public as the *Scythian Suite* at the beginning of 1916; but as early as 1912 there had been a crude tone-poem on the subject, *Skify* ('Scythians'), by Vladimir Senilov, a now-forgotten disciple of Rimsky-Korsakov.

Gorodetsky's vague mythologizing of history allowed the few beliefs the Scythians were known to hold – in the elements, a Great Goddess and the tombs of their ancestors – to be bolstered by the pantheon of their successors, the early Slavs. Prokofiev's first announcement of the outline Gorodetsky had at last sent him in early October hinted to Myaskovsky only of '9th-century[!], idols, bulls in the sky'[81] and in the original scenario the Slavic god Perun presides over the dazzling triumph of light at the end of the ballet. Its title, *Ala and Lolly*, bore a curious resemblance to *Aleyla and Leyla*, the ballet on a quite different subject on which Lyadov had been working up to his death that August, and it hints at the abduction scenario of *Daphnis et Chloé*, the 'watery' Ravel ballet Prokofiev had attributed to Debussy. Many years later, in 1932, Prokofiev's secretary forwarded to a Viennese musical organization the most detailed scenario to survive:

> The chief [sun] god, Veles, had a daughter Ala, a wooden idol, revered by the people. The enemy god [Chuzhbog] – a strange, shadowy, nocturnal deity – carried off Ala. In his nocturnal kingdom, the enemy god tried to take possession of her, but each time he approached Ala, there fell upon her a moonbeam, down which came the daughters of the moon, who defended her and consoled her – and the god of darkness, powerless before the light, was forced to recoil. Lolly, popular hero, in love with Ala, sets out on a campaign against the enemy god, to free her. In the course of unequal combat against the god, the mortal was about to succumb, but the sun rises on the horizon and with his rays kills the dark god.[82]

Prokofiev proceeded much further that autumn than the mere sketches about which he writes in his autobiography, and he even hoped his 'frenzied'[83] efforts would result in all five scenes being ready in five weeks. By the end of October the Moscow ballet master Boris Romanov, who had choreographed Schmitt's *La Tragédie de Salomé* and Stravinsky's *The Nightingale* for Diaghilev, was there to help focus his thoughts. The deadline passed, and in December, with the piano score unfinished, Prokofiev took the unusual step of indulging his mood for 'orchestral tone-painting' by turning to the orchestration and 'taking pleasure in every kind of instrumental combination'.[84] There could be an enchanted nocturne for the only point of repose, the visit of the moon-daughters, to parallel the anticipatory prelude to the second part of Stravinsky's *The Rite of Spring*, and the blinding intervention of the sun at the end would mark a new sonic departure – no sacrificial dance or *Daphnis* bacchanal but a magnesium flare of the brightest light. As Prokofiev had suspected, the verdict was already a thumbs-down from Nurok and Nouvel, who talked only of the score's 'embellishments and impetuousness'[85] and wrote to Diaghilev behind the composer's back that his new great hope had written 'something absurd to an absurd plot'.[86]

They were more complimentary about the Scherzo from op.12 which he performed with six of its companions, the Toccata – so long withheld, now heard for the first time – and the Second Piano Sonata at an Evening of Contemporary Music on 29 November. The Evenings, he told Myaskovsky, continued in lively fashion to play their part in what he described as the 'modest jog-trot'[87] of Petrograd's musical life, though Ziloti's performance of the Sinfonietta had not taken place because his venue, the Hall of the Nobility, had been requisitioned as a hospital. Myaskovsky was in the curious position of being popular favourite *in absentia* when Koussevitzky gave the premiere of his Third Symphony. The performance, witnessed by Prokofiev and reported with the usual candid reservations, took place as Myaskovsky prepared to dice with death close to the front line near the city of Lvov. At first this reluctant traveller found himself enchanted by what he portrayed as the picture-postcard mix of Poles and Jews, local girls and soldiers in Lvov and the neighbouring villages, and by the snowy pine forests around Kapitolovo, but soon he was experiencing at first hand the horrors that had already claimed 50,000

Russian lives in the first month of war. Myaskovsky's vivid description of his experience of uninterrupted artillery fire at the front line with 'a sort of queasy feeling in my heart and an awareness of total helplessness'[88] occasioned an unusually thoughtful response from the usually brusque Prokofiev: 'I sympathize with your misfortunes with all my soul – taking them into account, it seems even shameful to write to you about our peaceful trivialities here'.[89] Not even when curtly dismissing the news of his father's death had Prokofiev stopped to apologize for the ensuing details of those 'peaceful trivialities'.

He was, all the same, prepared to venture beyond Petrograd's ivory tower to further the musical relationship on which more hopes were pinned than any other. Before he left on an adventurous journey to see Diaghilev in Rome, he gave another performance of his Second Piano Concerto at the RMO, conducted by Nikolay Malko, a former fellow-student in Tcherepnin's classes and the one pupil who would truly pass the flame on to the next generation. He also nearly succeeded in taking a wife with him to Italy, if the memoirs of Nina Meshcherskaya, under her married name of Krivosheina, are to be trusted. She talks of a tour to Italy in the autumn of 1914 and places the time of the intended marriage round a second visit; but as Prokofiev crossed war-torn Europe only once, and as the dates coincide with the immediate aftermath of Meshcherskaya's successful collaboration with Prokofiev over the song-narrative *The Ugly Duckling*, early 1915 seems more likely.

Matters came to a head when Prokofiev visited the Meshcherskys who were living in Tsarskoye Selo, just outside Petrograd, and asked Nina to marry him. For Nina there were grave obstacles, and the prospect of travelling in time of war was almost less horrifying than finally telling her parents about her relationship with the composer; but Prokofiev, as Krivosheina recalls, 'declared with his characteristic abruptness and authority, almost commanded: today, tomorrow, soonest – that I was to proclaim everything to my parents and leave for Italy!'[90] Immediately a scandal broke, with Nina's father both astonished by the revelation and adamant that marriage to an 'artist' could not be taken seriously. Two strong-willed men of different generations met, a heated argument ensued and stalemate left elopement as the only answer. Nina, it seemed, would have to leave home alone, and as she tried to do so by the main entrance, apprehension by the family steward was inevitable. Many years later did Prokofiev imagine Nina, as she described herself so vividly, hoarse with emotion and denouncing her sister, when he gave full orchestral vent to Natasha's despair after the failed elopement in *War and Peace*? The breadth of the wide-ranging and daringly extended passage for violins suggests deep personal experience. At any rate, it was the end of the affair; Nina was moved to Yekaterinoslav, and though she spoke to Prokofiev over the telephone back in Petrograd they never met again.

If indeed early 1915 was the date of the catastrophe – and some kind of break is hinted at in his diaries – Prokofiev revealed nothing of it in his postcards to Eleonora Damskaya on the road to Rome, braving the hazards of wartime Europe and telling his fellow student about the unfolding perils of his roundabout journey. Apparently in high spirits but with a heavy cold, he parried with spirit the advice of a fellow passenger on the train from Kiev not to marry young, dodged cholera in Romania and mines across the Danube, enjoyed Bulgarian newspapers and Serbian friendliness and finally boarded a boat from Salonika to Brindisi via Athens. His path was smoothed by a consular fellow-traveller who assisted with border formalities. Even so, the centre of Diaghilev's activities in Rome must have seemed like another world. Having met Prokofiev's 1000-franc bill for travel as promised, the impresario helped him, as the composer put it in one of several letters to his mother, to work off the weight he had accumulated en route in a dazzling round of rehearsals, interviews with the press, dinners with rich and influential 'pomposities'[91] and photographic sessions. Sadly, there is nothing like Tchaikovsky's record of what especially impressed him in the eternal city.

Prokofiev had a great deal to say about the futurist noise-making of Filippo Marinetti and his circle, writing about it for *Muzyka* as a cultural phenomenon, but without enthusiasm. The sentiment is implicitly the same as a perceptive *Tatler* article of the previous London season which had compared Marinetti's extravaganza *A Meeting of Motorcars and Aeroplanes* unfavourably with the Diaghilev enterprise: 'without the Russians to cause a draught through the over-stuffy atmosphere of our minds, we should have to fall back on Signor Marinetti and his foolish futurism of noises'.[92] According to a much later interview in an American paper, Prokofiev joined Stravinsky in a four-hand performance of *The Rite of Spring* for the benefit of Marinetti and his circle and came to appreciate a score he had not understood in the theatre: 'with Stravinsky sitting by me, it was an astonishing experience. I read music quite quickly and well and Stravinsky was there to poke me with his elbow and help me with his remarks'.[93]

Prokofiev's European debut with his usual calling-card, the Second Piano Concerto, took place in neither of the expected cities – Paris or London – but in Rome with the Augusteo Orchestra, on 7 March, only two weeks after Stravinsky had appeared there. The orchestra and conductor, Bernardino Molinari, described by Prokofiev to his mother as 'excellent',[94] organized an ovation for him during the rehearsals, but the audience, which was a large one thanks to the usual Diaghilev publicity drive, gave the concerto only a modest reception, though the absence of encores was merely in accordance with Italian tradition. (Prokofiev also played, as advertised, one of the *Études* and the Prelude, Rigaudon and March from op.12.) 'All the critics praised me as a pianist', he told his mother. 'A few were content with the music, others had reservations and a third group were abusive. Especially of the latter opinion were those papers with a German bias.'[95] *Il messaggero*, which had stoked up hopes of a second Stravinsky, found itself disappointed and bewailed 'an artist still lacking individuality and wandering between the old and the new'.[96]

Diaghilev had a more bitter pill in store, though he tried with his usual cultural diplomacy to sugar it with a trip to Naples in the company of Massine. Over the question of *Ala and Lolly*, which was Diaghilev's real reason for summoning Prokofiev to Italy, the obedient son was even more dutiful towards this latest surrogate father. 'There will be a lot of fundamental changes to the subject; he hasn't yet heard the music',[97] he told his mother before his departure for Naples. 'The ballet needs essential changes, with which I agree'[98] came the news on 10 March, and four days later, 'as far as the ballet's concerned, there have been a lot of changes'.[99] There certainly had: Diaghilev was sending Prokofiev back to the drawing-board with a new subject. Myaskovsky was not alone in finding it 'interesting how you carelessly and completely cut up your new offspring at Diaghilev's command'.[100] But at least he would be able to chew the cud with Stravinsky, 'who is going to make available a lot of important material from Russian antiquity'.[101] And although the 'committee' did not travel on to Palermo as planned, sunny days, interesting walks and Diaghilev-supervised museum visits in Naples, as well as trips to Pompeii and Capri, made Prokofiev powerless to protest in the face of so much kindness – which is just what the cunning Diaghilev had planned. Prokofiev, for his part, behaved with unusual dignity, changing Diaghilev's previous opinion of him, and Massine found 'his unique blend of boyish high spirits and Russian intensity very appealing'.[102]

Prokofiev caught up with Stravinsky not on his new home territory in Switzerland, as had originally been planned, with another concert engagement thrown in for good measure, but in Milan. There was excitement in steering towards a new project to replace *Ala and Lolly*, for Diaghilev and Stravinsky were moving closer to authentic and historic Russian sources, the long-term result of which was to be Stravinsky's masterpiece of Russian folk stylization *Svadebka* ('The Wedding', best known in the West under its French title *Les Noces*). Prokofiev must have been privy to Stravinsky's thoughts on the subject, for on his return to Russia, he told Stravinsky, Derzhanovsky had 'knocked up'[103] an article on *Les Noces* from the small amount of information the travelling young composer had given him. It was this report which was rehashed, not entirely to Stravinsky's displeasure but according to Prokofiev in mangled form, in another publication.

Of greater value to Prokofiev than the folk songs Stravinsky had collected on his last trip to Russia was his reference to the ultimate Russian fairy-tale compendium, Alexander Afanasyev's three-volume *Narodniya Russkiya skazki*. Stravinsky was to draw on its strands of animal and soldier fables for his other two stage works of the war years, the burlesque we know as *Renard* and *The Soldier's Tale*. It was surely his canny knack for synthesis that gave Prokofiev the outline for *Skazka pro shuta* ('The Tale of the Buffoon'), known as *Chout*. Afanasyev's mania for tale-collecting furnishes three variants on the savage story of the Russian buffoon, though only the first, from the Perm district, really concerned Stravinsky, Diaghilev and Prokofiev. From the series of practical jokes played by the protagonist on a priest, a merchant and seven other buffoons in turn, full of macabre ingredients and culminating in more deaths than *Hamlet*, a shapely and grotesquely funny scenario resulted. The 'magic' whip which the buffoon uses to extract money from the gullible seven is supposed to restore a victim knifed to death rather than simply beaten, as the seven wives are in the ballet; and from the earlier saga with the priest comes the episode of the buffoon extricating himself from his awkward disguise as a merchant's chosen bride by the substitution of a goat which the merchant believes to be his sweetheart enchanted. There are no gruesome drownings as in the Afanasyev version, only the clever money-making of the ever-resourceful buffoon and a happy ending with the marriage of the other buffoons' seven daughters with the seven soldiers who belatedly appear on the scene.

This is all a long way from the cod mythology of *Ala and Lolly*, but Prokofiev remained adamant that much of the rejected score deserved salvaging. So his task, once safely back in Petrograd, was twofold: to please Diaghilev with the new commission which, war permitting, would be ready for a projected 1916 Paris season, and to find a concert-hall home for *Ala and Lolly*. It is a measure of how high his stock had risen with that conservative francophile Ziloti that he was able to press his case with the influential conductor. Ziloti's concert series had now found a new home in the no less splendid surroundings of the Maryinsky Theatre. In July Prokofiev told him that the suite put together from his 'winter sketches' and already three-quarters orchestrated 'consists of four movements, written for quadruple [woodwind], runs for about 17 minutes, and preserves for itself the proposed title of the ballet *Ala and Lolly*'.[104] Prokofiev hoped this more radical offering might supersede the relatively straightforwardly orchestrated Sinfonietta in Ziloti's new season, but the grand old man surprised him by accepting both, assigning the *Scythian Suite*, as it was subtitled, to a later date. The only sour note was Ziloti's refusal, for a variety of reasons, to include Myaskovsky's Third Symphony in his series; the fact that Prokofiev was prepared to drive home his enthusiasm for the work and his patent displeasure with Ziloti every time he spoke to him proved again what a loyal friend he was.

In his letter to Stravinsky earlier that summer Prokofiev announced that *Chout*, 'which sets itself to music easily, cheerfully and jaggedly',[105] was to remain his own affair; he had not shown sketches to Diaghilev's emissaries Nouvel and Nurok and did not intend to do so. He was still smarting over their premature and unfavourable report on *Ala and Lolly* to the impresario, and with some justice: Nouvel was to eat his words when he heard the suite, as Prokofiev lost no time in telling Diaghilev in 1918. It remains impossible to glean a fair impression of *Ala and Lolly* from the piano score, which is all that Nouvel had seen. Prokofiev had stuck his neck out in the instrumentation of the Second Piano Concerto, especially in the first orchestral Scythianisms of the juggernaut Intermezzo, but he had never before allowed himself to be so intoxicated by the possibilities of a large orchestra. The late Romantic complement of woodwind includes the added glamour of alto flute and bass oboe, as used in the biggest scores of Stravinsky and Strauss, and a rare E flat trumpet shrills away at the top of an (ideally) 18-strong brass section. Two harps, celesta and piano play an important, often seductive role, and nine percussion instruments add what seems like an indiscriminate glitter (though the manuscript of the original score shows that Prokofiev pruned back the clatter of the xylophone halfway through the fourth movement[106]).

Garish sonorities clamour for the audience's attention at the start and end of the suite. In the opening 'Adoration of Veles and Ala', the panic could be either what one Russian critic hears as 'savage yells, ominous incantations, the clatter of horses' hooves'[107] or the 'nightmarish' 'cannons, aeroplanes, machine-guns, exploding bullets, sleepless nights'[108] and constant movement which Myaskovsky evoked to haunt his friend with ever more grim news of life at the front. If so, it is a no less plausible intrusion of world events than the dying fall at the end of Strauss's *Eine Alpensinfonie*, a similarly disturbing passage from another, older composer who simply got on with his business when war struck. What follows, though, is almost quaintly Scythian, blunter in outline than the additive rhythms of Senilov's 'Theme of the Scyths' (Ex.26*a*) but following in its heavy footsteps (Ex.26*b*). Harmonized in bare 4ths, this is the first of three incantatory passages. The others are the chant of the eight horns and upper strings (first and second violins again a 4th apart) in the straightforward wild rumpus of Chuzhbog and the dark spirits – 'seven reptiles which crawl around him', according to the most detailed scenario[109] – which proceeds in the manner of Kashchey's Infernal Dance in *The Firebird*, and the more elusively pitched brass choruses which wail against the woodwind flurries and the high resounding B flats of the indescribably brilliant final sunrise. The 'adoration' theme, though, is the only one to infiltrate the more reflective moments of the score. The horns, now muted, apply it at a late stage and against indeterminate pitches to the hypnotic portrayal of Ala's essence in the opening movement's second half. The recurrence provides a link with the louder music when we least expect it, but it also adds a much-needed melody to the steadily accumulating atmospherics of the three flutes, nebulous *divisi* violins and slithering viola chromatics.

Ex.26a Senilov, *Skify*

Ex.26b *Scythian Suite*, op.20 – I. Adoration of Veles and Ala

The other passage of eerie calm, the third movement's night picture, begins with a simple diatonic theme for piccolo, harps and piano quite unlike anything else in the score, characterizing the lunar assistance given to Ala in her hour of need, and ends with a ten-part string discord that is Prokofiev's only explicit homage to *The Rite of Spring* (rarely, incidentally, does he so much as nod at the metrical quick-change act for which *The Rite* is most often celebrated). But not even the paring away of some 20 bars of mood music from the original manuscript and the brief frothing which represents the terrors assailing Ala can disguise the fact that stronger thematic material needs to come to the rescue here. Prokofiev's fascination with impressionistic effects for their own sake is similar to Bartók's in his roughly contemporary score for *The Wooden Prince*, and it is a measure of both composers' fledgling individuality that a master-refiner among today's conductors, Pierre Boulez, can find wonders in the raw material.

Ala and Lolly was at least a good training-ground for the play of sonorities which Prokofiev went on to wrap round themes of real substance in *Chout*. There is, though, one jolly little tune that points to the future and it comes when we might least expect it – as Lolly seems to be gaining the upper hand over Chuzhbog before the sun-god has to come to his rescue (Ex.27). Its jauntiness is unmistakably similar to the second theme of *Chout*'s somersaulting finale, though the two are not as close in terms of composition as one might imagine, for this other cheerful song was added to a revised finale only when Diaghilev finally managed to put on *Chout* in 1921 (Ex.28).

With the sinking of the *Lusitania* in May 1915, the prospect of a journey to western Europe changed from adventure to nightmare, and Marya Grigoryevna must have added special pressure in the face of losing her only child. So Prokofiev did not

Ex.27 *Scythian Suite* – IV. Glorious departure of Lolly and cortège of the sun

Ex.28 *Chout*, op.21 – Final dance

see Diaghilev and Stravinsky as he had hoped and *Chout* remained in the black-and-white of short score until after the war. Much of what we hear in the ballet is the work of an orchestrator with six crucial years' more experience behind him. And yet it remains the broadly comic sequel to *Ala and Lolly*, a more successful answer to *Petrushka* than the Scythian ballet had been to *The Firebird* and *The Rite of Spring*; so this is surely the right place to contemplate its folksy fantastics. The rewritten 1920 finale is, admittedly, its most beguiling single number (an imaginative encore alternative, surely, to the ubiquitous 'Death of Tybalt' from *Romeo and Juliet* which is so many Russian orchestras' calling-card) but there are earlier, spirited echoes of the fairground puppets' performance in the 'Danse du rire' of the buffoon and his wife. How much of Diaghilev's original brief to 'write music that is genuinely Russian'[110] remains? Prokofiev thought he was digging up native melodies even without conscious childhood memories of local colour, but the opening sequence as the curtain rises, with sinuous woodwind solos against a seething chromatic backdrop, and the revolutions of the seven buffoons' ill-fated wives have more of an oriental flavour, perhaps to reflect the tale's Perm provenance. The closest Prokofiev comes to Russian folk style is in the processional of the merchant who ignores the seven buffoons' daughters and chooses the mischief-maker *en travesti* to be his bride. The other buffoons burst upon the action in scene 1 in lurid, Scythian attire, and the violence that the trickster supposedly inflicts upon his wife, and which they duly imitate, abounds in semitonal trumpet clashes.

Admirable human qualities are either artificial or spring from fake sources. The 'white-note' demureness of the disguised buffoon is a curious starting-point for the gallery of fresh young Prokofiev heroines: Juliet, Natasha and Tatyana (in the incidental music to *Eugene Onegin*) will share the flute and string colourings of the prospective bride, but the way in which the diatonic writing soon becomes embroiled in more complex textures is much more prophetic of Renata's music in *The Fiery Angel* (and all this is duly indicated across five staves, with pointers to the instrumentation, in the 1915 short score). Cellos ooze crocodile tears as the seven buffoons brutally prod and poke the 'girl', good preparation for the lachrymose prince in *The Love for Three Oranges*, while the smooth serenade of the merchant on his wedding night is oddly counterpointed by pecking cor anglais and muted trumpets in the weirdest of love duets. There is a parody of Scythian chanting as the servants shake the possessed creature this way and that, and an oblique mockery of Stravinsky's 'ritual of the ancestors' in the 'Lento con tristezza' of the goat's burial. *Petrushka* is pointedly evoked immediately before this in the wistful clarinet solo above high, muted, tremolo strings – the pathetic elegiac treatment of the buffoon's theme exactly parallels the death of Stravinsky's puppet – and earlier in the chuntering bassoons of the whip-wielding seven buffoons; having killed their wives they, like Stravinsky's magician before the ghost of Petrushka shrieks at him, are not as smart as they think.

The invention in each of the six scenes is of an unflaggingly high quality, if of a more lurid cut and format than the more sophisticated *Petrushka.* Nothing in the Stravinsky ballet, though, quite accounts for Prokofiev's utterly original opening gestures, spread with seeming haphazardness across different orchestral groups like the much slower-moving *Klangfarben* in the third of Schoenberg's Five Orchestral Pieces. This 'whistling and rattling which sounded as if dust were being wiped off the orchestra at the beginning of the performance'[111] remained unchanged between 1915 and 1920, though its slightly varied reprises between the earlier scenes (*Chout*'s equivalent of the fairground drumming between tableaux in *Petrushka*), belongs to the excess baggage of the revision. Intriguingly, the opening whistle is also the concluding gesture of the original version, which will certainly come as a surprise to anyone familiar with the final hammering of the ballet as we know it. As with *The Gambler*, Prokofiev's first closing gesture was the more audacious; but no doubt Diaghilev, who had been unhappy with the *pianissimo* close of *Petrushka*, brought pressure to bear for a glittering, applause-winning curtain.

Prokofiev would remain in the shadow of Stravinsky, nine years his senior, for a while to come. Even a responsible Russian critic like Karatygin, who proceeded to distance himself from the direction Stravinsky was taking, could not help commenting on his superiority over Prokofiev as an orchestrator. His review of the *Scythian Suite*'s first performance, conducted by the composer in the Ziloti series on 16 January 1916, did however praise its impressionistic vein and its 'neo-heterophony', which he defined as 'the superimposition of one pattern on another without any particular relation between the two':[112] this was a good thing. Among the other articles, only Prokofiev's old classmate Asafyev echoed Karatygin's view in *Muzyka*, though his line was more traditional as he argued the case for an honourable successor to Borodin's Polovtsian Dances.

For many other listeners and musicians, *Ala and Lolly* was sheer chaos. In his short autobiography Prokofiev presents an exuberant picture of the premiere, with Glazunov famously storming out eight bars before the end of the magnesium-flare sunrise and Ziloti quite unexpectedly walking up and down in delight and quoting Mayakovsky's famous maxim 'A slap in the face!'[113] Outwardly, Prokofiev preserved his natural buoyancy, telling a friend while dressing for the first rehearsal that 'the price of rotten eggs and apples has gone up in St Petersburg'.[114] Yet it could not have been so easy to confront the wrath of high society in the Maryinsky Theatre, stronghold of Russian culture, and without the prop of brilliant pianism to soften the blow. His old conservatory friend Yury Tyulin, passing down that spirited remark, shows more concern for the effect so many bad feelings must have had on the developing composer. The orchestra, according to Tyulin, tormented Prokofiev by 'openly demonstrating its hostility':

> There was no room for the two harpists in the orchestra pit, so they sat on the stage and kept asking him questions in an irritated tone. During their pauses they

covered their ears with the wide collars (then fashionable) of their dresses. But Prokofiev continued his work with the orchestra with patience and concentration, as if nothing had happened, and came out after the rehearsal, serious but satisfied.

'Everything is all right', he replied to my anxious question.

You could not help but marvel at his self-possession.[115]

For Tyulin, that self-possession amounted to the same kind of heroism the pianist Claudio Arrau describes at length in a sympathetic article, supported by his understanding of psychoanalysis, in which he compares the tribulations of a young man making his way in the world to the trials of Tamino in Mozart's *Die Zauberflöte.* Prokofiev may not have had to deal with the stress that was now beginning to tell on his sensitive, melancholic friend at the front – by enrolling in Professor Gandshin's organ class at the conservatory he sidestepped the next wave of conscriptions – but the pressures he did have to face could easily have broken his spirit. The spotlight has always been turned on what he endured, two decades later, in Stalin's Soviet Russia; but the events of the next two years were, in their way, to be just as taxing. Only Prokofiev's peculiar brand of youthful resilience could turn them into an adventure.

6
A game of chance
1915–18

When Diaghilev exclaimed, as Prokofiev later recalled, that 'there in that putrid St Petersburg of yours they've forgotten how to compose in the Russian style',[1] his definition was limited by the only kind of Russian music on his mind – the sort he had used, with Stravinsky's help, to reflect a new wave of folk and fairy-tale nationalism. The younger composer was about to prove him wrong in a quite different fashion; indeed, he might have done so much sooner if at that first meeting in June 1914 Diaghilev's distaste for opera had not led him to reject outright what Prokofiev really wanted: to adapt Dostoyevsky's *The Gambler* for the operatic stage. As Prokofiev was shortly to explain to his public, Stravinsky and Diaghilev had predicted 'the degeneration of the operatic form' only because of 'the recent decline of the composer's interest in the stage aspect, resulting in a lack of dramatic fluidity and a mass of boring conventions'.[2] But what if the singers were allowed to present their roles dramatically, without being weighed down by those conventions, in a series of fast-moving dialogues, if every word were to be heard above a transparent orchestra, and if the prose of the original were to be followed as closely as possible, discarding the 'absurd convention' of 'writing operas on rhymed texts'?[3]

Prokofiev's enthusiasm for a Dostoyevsky work as an operatic subject stands out in bold relief against the lamentable interregnum of Russian opera at that time, when the state theatres were following any one of three courses: consolidating the native classics of the previous century, Wagnermania (abruptly terminated in 1914 with the outbreak of war) and braving a handful of contemporary Western masterpieces such as Strauss's *Elektra*. Tackling one of Dostoyevsky's major novels like *The Possessed*, which Prokofiev claimed to Vera Alpers to have read over two evenings in 1909 and to have enjoyed more than most of the writer's works, would probably have ended in failure, as had Myaskovsky's ambition to write an opera based on *The Idiot* (though it was the increasing mental strain of his military duties on Myaskovsky that halted that project). The 150-page novella *Igrok* ('The Gambler'), though it brought its own problems, was an excellent choice. When Prokofiev rather bizarrely described it as the least Dostoyevskian of the master's works, he could have been referring only to its locale; Dostoyevsky's fictional town of Roulettenburg was modelled on the Baden-Baden the author had known well as a one-time gambler.

The Gambler's supporting cast of laconic Englishmen, shady French adventurers and preposterous Germans must have tickled Prokofiev's fancy as he embarked on his first European travels. The principal characters, though, were Russians abroad as he himself had recently become, and in the obsessive behaviour of the protagonist Alexey, a lowly schoolmaster derided by good society, his beloved Polina – hysterical, capricious, fundamentally good-hearted (an archetypal Dostoyevsky heroine) – the ridiculous General and unpredictable Grandmama, lie the seeds of a characteristic Dostoyevskian chaos. To bring order to this narrative of a gambler who seems to be improvising the story as he goes along was the honourable task of a composer more enticed by the logical world of chess and the occasional game of bridge than the roulette wheel. He had learnt his lesson in Royat in 1913, when he visited the casino and played *petits chevaux* – 'much worse than roulette, as the odds are totally unfair'.[4] After a predictable pattern of some gain and even greater loss, he gambled small amounts over the next few days, lost and 'ceased to go to this unprofitable establishment'.[5]

Prokofiev had every intention of preserving the feverish quality of Dostoyevsky's prose dialogues. In this, at least, he had a precedent. Knowing nothing of the Czech composer Janáček's claims to be a pioneer of operatic prose with his first masterpiece *Jenůfa* (1904), he would at least have been able to add to Janáček's citing of the French composer Alfred Bruneau as a solitary model a much more distinguished name: Modest Musorgsky. *Boris Godunov*, it is true, contains only one prose scene to the original three of its Pushkin source, and Musorgsky could hardly have bypassed the disorderly comedy in the hut on the Lithuanian border. But Prokofiev certainly knew about the second of two St Petersburg performances, in 1906 and 1909, of *Marriage*, Musorgsky's unfinished adaptation of a Gogol comedy.

Marriage had been composed in the late 1860s when the realistic principles of the 'mighty handful' were at their height. *Boris Godunov* was just round the corner, and comparison of its two versions shows us how far Musorgsky moved away from 'artistic reproduction of human speech'[6] to something altogether more operatic in the melodramatic sense. But in 1868 his aims were much the same as Prokofiev's in 1915. 'Here's what I would like', Musorgsky wrote to Glinka's sister Lyudmila Shestakova. 'That my characters speak on stage as living people speak, but so that the character and force of their intonation, supported by the orchestra which is the musical background for their speech, hit the target head on.'[7] The principle was no less vividly realized, with the support of a piano rather than full orchestra, in the extraordinarily individual songs Musorgsky began to compose at this time, to his own free-flowing texts. They include the idiot's serenade *Savishna*, several lampoons on contemporary critics and artistic life – the short *Klassik* and the lengthy *Rayok*

– and *With Nurse*, the first of the pioneering *Nursery* cycle realistically rendering in song a child's chatter. Although Prokofiev's comments on Musorgsky throughout his correspondence are frustratingly sparse, these are the only possible models for several voice and piano works, utterly different in tone and style from the earlier songs, which he composed en route to *The Gambler*.

The trail begins with a little gem from October 1913, a letter to the lovable if unreliable Boris Zakharov in Vienna, couched in the whimsical prose Prokofiev reserved for his closest friends and set to music along lines also followed by Rakhmaninov in his 1908 tribute to Stanislavsky.[8] Its harmonic language is straightforwardly diatonic for the most part but changes key as Prokofiev touches on different subjects. His hyperbolic apologies for not having written for so long tremble on the dominant of C minor, but as he moves on to thank Zakharov for his Viennese card the music settles in C major: the composer as sincere friend. Myaskovsky is depicted in suitably sombre flat keys – D flat minor and E flat minor (as Prokofiev mentions his setting of a Gippius poem). When he turns to the theme of female friends there is a typically quirky modulation via B major to A major, which sinks to the relative minor as he explains how he has fallen out with their friends Teríokì and Zoya and Lidya, 'all because of Zoya's intelligence. She said "How intelligent I am" [a bright D major trill on the word 'intelligent'] and I replied [in a truculent G minor reminiscent of Musorgsky] "Your intelligence is perfectly suited to a hen-house of small size"'. The affable C major returns as Prokofiev ends, his florid signature 'Sergusya' trailing off into the ether (and the singer's falsetto, if the setting is to be sung by a baritone).

That Prokofiev was no enemy of the right sort of female intelligence is underlined by a major project with Nina Meshcherskaya, swiftly completed in the happy autumn days between their summer idyll and the failed elopement early the following year. According to Nina, the choice of Hans Christian Andersen's 'fairy tale' *The Ugly Duckling* for this voice-and-piano hybrid – titled *skazka* rather than 'song' or 'romance' – was hers. Its essential simplicity, especially in the clarity of the piano part, reflects the musical language of the 'Letter to Zakharov', though the tale, of course, is more universal and, since Nina's adaptation includes most of Andersen's details, it runs at much greater length. Too great a length, thought Karatygin, who defined *Gadky utyonok* ('The Ugly Duckling') as 'something close to a symphonic poem for voice and piano'.[9] He was generally favourable about the January 1915 premiere, for which Prokofiev accompanied his old travelling-companion Anna Zherebtsova-Andreyeva, and was not slow to point out that 'in the realm of witty musically illustrative devices Prokofiev reveals something of a kinship with Musorgsky'.[10]

Karatygin's only other criticism, that the duckling's blossoming into a swan 'might have been more poetic and plastic',[11] seems hard to defend: the joyful diatonic cantilena as the bird discovers its true identity, majestically anticipated by the arrival of the three fellow swans, is perfectly in proportion to the rest of the tale. In the early stages there is just enough pathos to offset the neutral watercolour sketches of the summer sun, the bored mother duckling and her sprightly young. The ugly duckling's distress is gently outlined at first, anticipating in the sad simplicity of one refrain the musical portrait of Natasha in *War and Peace* (Ex.29). And the fairy-tale lightness of touch in the piano is only intensified in the darkest part of the tale, the outcast's life in autumn and winter.

Ex.29 *The Ugly Duckling*, op18

This briefly dissonant strain is much more pervasive, and aptly so for the surprising subject of urban poverty, throughout the next character-study, *Pod kryshey* ('Under the Roof'), which Prokofiev composed in 1915, apparently in the hope that Derzhanovsky would include it in one of his Moscow Evenings of Contemporary Music. Unlike *The Ugly Duckling*, which Prokofiev insisted on allowing to 'waddle along *solo*',[12] *Under the Roof* eventually took pride of place in the disparate op.23 set of songs, a group that shows how wide-ranging Prokofiev continued to be in his choice of authors. Only two of the five were to remain acceptable in the Soviet era, when Nestyev noted that both Vyacheslav Goryansky, author of *Under the Roof*, and Nikolay Agnivtsev, giving rise with *Kudesnik* ('The Wizard') to what Nestyev called 'a type of satirical song neglected since Musorgsky's day',[13] contributed to 'the most anti-government humorous magazine of that period',[14] *Novy satyrikon*. (It is a pity that Prokofiev did not make the acquaintance of another more distinguished contributor, Vladimir Mayakovsky, until some time later.) Social criticism may lie at the heart of Goryansky's verses, but Prokofiev's elaborate accompaniment and the highly nuanced vocal line reject realism in favour of the slum dweller's poetic response to nature in the city. Beginning with the wistful theme that disappears bars into the piano introduction, what little melody there is remains tenuous, a series of 'fugitive visions' dimly sensed by the protagonist. It seems to cry out for symphonic treatment and has been imaginatively orchestrated by the conductor Gennady Rozhdestvensky. The tone of *The Wizard* is altogether blunter but harmonically no less elusive; only the ballad-like 'once-upon-a-time' refrain sets us down on firm ground at a distance from the gnarly gait of the misanthropic inventor and his fatally insubstantial creation of an ideal, subservient woman.

The other three songs of op.23 set poets from an older school, confirming to Nestyev in 1957 'an open concession to the vogue of decadence'.[15] Boris Verin, author of *Doversya mne* ('Trust me'), was the pen name of Boris Bashkirov, now a close friend Prokofiev had in common with the Meshcherskys and with whom he was to spend the summer of 1916. He was perhaps more deserving of Nestyev's scorn and merely aped the aestheticism of the previous generation. They are represented here by Balmont, whose poetry Prokofiev had no intention of jettisoning simply because it was now fashionable to do so, and Zinayda Gippius, who was a firm favourite with both Myaskovsky and the *sovremenniks*, and whose *Seroye platitse* ('The Grey Dress') Prokofiev set to music specifically for Derzhanovsky in July 1915 (at which point he mentions a single song as op.23, presumably *Under the Roof*). None of the settings, however, are as predictable as the verses perhaps deserve. The music for Gippius's strange inquisition of the symbolical blind child in the grey dress sidesteps most of the musical repeats the dialogue might suggest. The relatively songlike legato lines of *Trust me* float in a void close to atonality, and the chromatic phrases of remembered passion which disrupt the garden imagery of Balmont's poem are poised halfway between the heroine's outcry at the end of *Maddalena* and the hysterics of those operatic heroines to come, Polina and Renata.

These are not easy songs to like, but they do at least show Prokofiev trying to respond in a new and unexpected way to each poet. There is no reason why they should be performed as a set, and only four of the five were scattered throughout the first chamber concert to be devoted entirely to Prokofiev, on 27 November 1916. By then the vocal portions served to draw attention to *The Gambler*'s imminent staging, and fell respectively to Yevgenya Popova, the soprano intended for Polina, and Ivan Alchevsky, the tenor due to share the role of Alexey with the great Ivan Yershov. Prokofiev wrote of Alchevsky in the same glowing terms he had reserved for the revelation of seeing Yershov in the *Ring* nearly a decade earlier, describing 'that Alchevsky who enraptures me so much' as 'an extremely wonderful singer, whose intonation has the freedom and accuracy of a keyboard instrument'.[16] He sang *The Ugly Duckling* as well as *The Wizard* and *V moyem sadu* ('In my Garden'), while Popova leavened the more experimental *Trust me* and *The Grey Dress* with the softer edges of op.9.

These were distinguished singers, and they were due to create their operatic roles within the hallowed portals of Russia's leading opera house. Prokofiev had not lost hope of taking up *The Gambler* even when his Diaghilev projects needed the lion's share of his attention. In January 1915 he had written to Derzhanovsky that 'the idea about *The Gambler* never went off the boil for me and is now fresher than ever, but I first need to complete the ballet [*Ala and Lolly*]. When I've finished it, then I'll start on my beloved 'Gambler', if I don't need to rest from the big project to dash off smaller things'.[17] Yet even as he found himself basking in newfound popularity, Prokofiev must have been especially delighted to find a friend in the highest of places later that year when Ziloti introduced him to Albert Coates, a St Petersburg-born Englishman. The successor to the grand old septuagenarian Eduard Nápravník as chief conductor of the Maryinsky Theatre, Coates 'had no fear of new music', as Prokofiev noted laconically in his short autobiography, 'and said: "Write your *Gambler*, we'll stage it." It would be hard to imagine a more favourable opportunity. I reread *The Gambler*, wrote the libretto and in the autumn of 1915 began to compose the music'.[18]

Myaskovsky resentfully noted that his friend's 'Dostoyevshchina'[19] must be partly responsible for Prokofiev's long silence as correspondent. By the following February he had reached the work's first real cornerstone, having moved swiftly, if at times drily, in outlining the complex and shadowy relationships between the main characters. 'Babulenka has arrived safely in Roulettenburg', he wrote in one of his vivacious letters to his family friend Tatyana Ruzskaya, 'has penetrated the entourage not without a certain liveliness and has disappeared into the depths of the hotel, and at the present moment she's already losing at roulette, she's keeping the General waiting in anguish [*avec angoisse*] on stage to babble and shout incoherently. You understand: I have finished the Second Act and I'm writing the Third.'[20] In March 1916, poised to write both libretto and music for the difficult last act, he was pleased with his work so far: 'Quite a few musicians to whom I played this [third] act have found – and I agree – that I've succeeded with Babulenka best of all'.[21] This opinion was reinforced in the second of the two 'interviews' he gave to *Birzhevie vedomost* that May.

Prokofiev was probably right. When he came to make a thorough revision of *The Gambler* in 1927, Babulenka's scenes were among the few to survive more or less intact. (Most performances use this edition, although in 2000 Gennady Rozhdestvensky made history – followed by a very quick exit from a tangled administrative web at Moscow's Bolshoy Theatre – by giving the world premiere of the original version; the fact that Prokofiev's manuscripts of both full scores survive makes it possible to describe, at least in outline, the respects in which they differ.[22]) A greater, more human creation than that other petulant old woman, the Countess in Tchaikovsky's (and Pushkin's) *The Queen of Spades*, Babulenka goes straight to the point in her impetuous analysis of the assembled company. She represents the purest breath of Russia in the work; but the doom of her native character is to send her to the gaming tables despite her shrewd understanding of human nature. To her essentially tragic figure belongs the brief refrain of one of the opera's outstanding 'white-note' melodies. The first, signalling Alexey's infatuation with Polina, begins the opera in C major, only briefly sidestepping into a neighbouring D flat major (Ex.30), while the incipient tragedy of Babulenka's journey to Roulettenburg, and the disaster it brings to the General, is suggested in the piquant harmonies of the opera's second most memorable theme (Ex.31).

Ex.30 *The Gambler*, op.24 – Act I

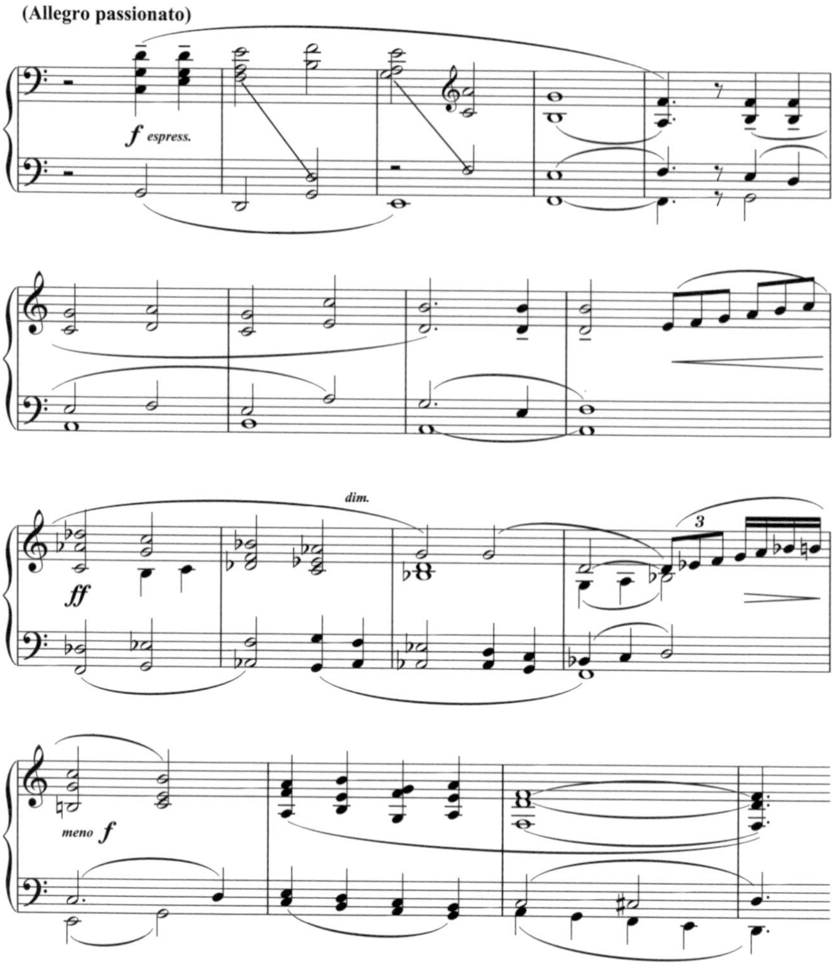

A third vein, the grotesque, is powerfully underlined by the increasing dissonances added to the conversational style in Act III, as matters reach a head. It must surely have been this turning of the psychological screw that even the tolerant Marya Grigoryevna found too much to bear as her son pounded out his new invention on the piano. Once Babulenka has made her sad exit, the stage is left to the wretched General, whose shattered nerves are superbly represented by a miserable bitonal idea with second violins and muted violas oscillating in wan 6ths between A flat major and F major while a grim pedal C throbs in the bass (Ex.32). Its tension is magnificently sustained in the General's final crisis – much expanded, like so many of the comic gestures, in the revision.

Act IV hurtles to the event we have all been waiting for, Alexey's madcap success in the casino, and here Prokofiev the librettist ran into deep waters in the spring of

Ex.31 *The Gambler* – Act III

Ex.32 *The Gambler* – Act III

1916; on the first of several occasions a literary friend, Boris Demchinsky, came to his aid. Dostoyevsky's gambling scenes are described with the passion and precision that can come only from first-hand experience, and they punctuate the narrative from the early chapters onwards. In delaying this singular action until a late stage, Prokofiev sacrificed one of the novelist's best scenes, Babulenka's bewildered attempts to find a pattern for success with Alexey helpless by her side; but by concentrating on a single orgy of roulette, he was able to create an ensemble of the utmost brilliance and complexity. What we hear today is not all the work of 1916. The whirling ostinato of the game above reiterations of the love music in the preceding interlude mostly comes from the revision, replacing frenetic but directionless 12/8 babble; and the first part of the scene, when Alexey bankrupts a roulette game before our very eyes, was later fleshed out with more individuals such as the 'dame comme-ci-comme-ça' for the 1929 Brussels premiere, though the unforgettable fluttering of the ball round the roulette wheel, on flutes, oboes and piano, belongs to 1916.

The second part of the roulette game, when various louche characters comment on Alexey's progress at another table, is more or less the same in both versions, but the second interlude is again very different, the shorter original containing no role for the full chorus (and in 1916 no ghostly echoes of the gaming table returned to haunt Alexey in the final scene, at least not until the very end). Although so much of the revision is undoubtedly for the better, especially in the earlier stages when characters referred to in the many dialogues interrupt the action to give greater variety, there is a good case for hearing the original final scene, a more detailed, vocally taxing confrontation between Alexey and Polina with a longer and less conventional love-making 'interlude'. The ending is astonishingly daring for 1916; instead of the crashing brass chords which conclusively bring down the curtain in the revised *Gambler*, the open-ended story of Alexey's obsession is eerily suggested by a final phantom roulette game which evaporates with the *pianissimo* sound of the lone celesta. This, of course, is a far more fitting question mark for a story which continues, in Dostoyevsky's tale, in Paris with Alexey as the pathetic and terminally bored puppet of the adventuress Blanche.

The roulette scene would have been a gift for the 'cinematic' theatre of a director who was striding towards the peak of his career. Vsevolod Meyerhold was now in the enviable position of having an experimental 'studio', where he could further his radical new ideas on dramatic art, and running theatre and opera productions to the highest possible standards at both the Alexandrinsky and Maryinsky theatres. Prokofiev had clearly hoped that his *Gambler*, like the Maryinsky productions of *Boris Godunov* and *Elektra*, would be graced with Meyerhold's innovatory touch and the opulence of Alexander Golovin's designs. In the event, he was told that Golovin would hold up the project too long, and although a first meeting with Meyerhold in October 1916 was positive, the director soon handed over the production to a colleague as he was too busy with other schemes, not least a lavish production of Lermontov's *Maskarade*. He was, however, to recommend an operatic subject from a sphere very dear to him, the world of *commedia dell'arte*, which was to bear a very different sort of fruit. In the meantime that other disciple of the new, Albert Coates, having successfully fought against the reactionary wing of the Imperial Theatres' board of directors, would soon find himself facing the incomprehension of singers and musicians, and a far more powerful adversary: the winds of change that swept Russia in 1917, the year *The Gambler* should have been born on stage.

Prokofiev, at any rate, kept his part of the bargain. He orchestrated the first three acts at a furious rate over the summer of 1916 between tennis tournaments at Kuokkala, on the Gulf of Finland outside Petrograd. It was not all intense hard work: between Kuokkala labours, there was time for a July trip down the Volga to Astrakhan in the company of the now ubiquitous Boris Bashkirov, with plenty of chess games along the way, and a further detour to Georgia; in a playful poem, 'Sergunya' relates how the indolent chatterbox 'Borunya' was so prostrated by the river journey that he overslept, leaving his composer friend to complete the even more exotic homeward stage of the journey alone.[23]

The piano score of *The Gambler* was lithographed at the Imperial Theatres' expense. The full score of the third act bears the date '22 January 1917', just under a week before the first orchestral rehearsals at the Maryinsky. Then, with the upheavals of February 1917, began the chain of events that would propel both *The Gambler* and its composer into long-term absence from Russia. *The Gambler* followed *Maddalena* in the line of chance casualties that bedevilled Prokofiev's music throughout his life. But he was not short of realizable performances. Interrupted lines of communication with Diaghilev made a premiere for *Chout*, too, seem ever more unlikely. His concertos were still in demand, however, while the *Scythian Suite* had created another rumpus in one of Koussevitzky's concerts and his eminence in chamber music was confirmed by the Ziloti Evening.

There was even an unexpected premiere in England. 'What an odd way the Russians have of coming to us!' wrote M. (for Montagu) Montagu-Nathan in the October 1916 issue of *The Musical Times*:

> Prokofiev the Rubinstein prize-winner, the triumphant virtuoso, composer and performer of two fine Pianoforte Concertos and two ambitious Sonatas, the symphonist, the trump card of Siloti, Diaghilef's 'latest find', whose 'Scythian Suite' drove Glazounov from the hall in which it was being performed, this 'raging futurist', 'barbarian', '*enfant terrible*', is introduced to a 'Promenade' audience as the composer of an inoffensive and entirely insignificant Scherzo for four bassoons.[24]

This was an arrangement Prokofiev had made the previous year of the *Humoresque Scherzo* from the op.12 set of piano pieces; Montagu-Nathan, who described the original as 'a small pianoforte piece imitating the play of four bassoons',[25] knew and appreciated it from having studied the score along with the other works he mentions. The Russian premiere of the bassoon transcription lagged behind the Philharmonia performance at the Proms by several months; on that occasion, the Ziloti chamber evening cited in connection with the op.23 songs, it must have been overshadowed by another work-in-waiting, the *Sarcasms*.

Here Prokofiev is happier to play Dostoyevsky's Alexey, not to mention Gorodetsky's 'dark god', than wistful Babulenka, though the capricious free rein he gives to bad humour predates all those musical portraits. According to Nestyev the first of the five *Sarcasms* was composed in 1912, the second and third in 1913, the last two in early 1914, all of them stored up, like the Toccata, for the right occasion. Prokofiev told Myaskovsky at the end of May 1915 that he had been tentatively introducing these more venomous offspring to people, who 'clutch at their heads: one so as to cover the ears, another to express delight, a third so as to pity the poor author, once so very promising'.[26] Yet with the death of Skryabin the previous month, Prokofiev's music for piano was the freshest to be heard in Russia, and he knew it. The competition, Rakhmaninov and Medtner, were from an older generation, and with the characteristically abrupt if not downright gauche style which never deserted him, he managed to offend both men. Rakhmaninov he braved at a Skryabin memorial concert: Prokofiev tried gauchely to smooth over controversy about Rakhmaninov's 'earthbound' performance of Skryabin's Fifth Sonata by saying after the concert, 'after all, Sergey Vasilyevich, you did play it extremely well'; to which the master wryly replied, 'and you, I daresay, expected me to play it badly?' before turning away.[27] Medtner was ruffled by Prokofiev's judgment that a sonata he had chosen for performance was 'properly for domestic use only'[28] (Prokofiev had wanted to hear Medtner's altogether more complicated A minor example).

Decidedly not 'for domestic use', the *Sarcasms* confounded an outraged Medtner and a stony Rakhmaninov when Prokofiev played them in Moscow. An intensification of the more dissonant early pieces, they traffic in clashing chords and loud extremes – the *ff* bass at the start of the first piece, which opposes an even louder treble (and wins) in the fourth – and deliberately evoke the infernal juggernaut of the *Suggestion diabolique* (in the Allegro precipitato of no.3). The now familiar diatonic limpidity does break through the first two pieces, but by the fifth and last, a moral stance on the harmful grimaces and flourishes emerges. The music traces it by beginning with something like a parody of *The Rite of Spring*'s metrical freedom and pounding chords, which quickly fizzles out into *Petrushka*-like irresolution. Unlike Stravinsky's puppet, though, this malcontent does not rally to insult the public but simply sinks into lugubrious introspection. Could this be a mirror held up to the pre-Revolutionary malaise Prokofiev had witnessed in so many of his contemporaries? The epigraph he added certainly points up the objective view of bad behaviour: 'sometimes we laugh maliciously at someone or something, but when we take a closer look, we see how pitiful and unhappy is the object of our ridicule, and then we begin to feel uncomfortable – the laughter rings in our ears, but now someone else is laughing at us'.[29]

Asafyev could only marvel at the way his old friend got away with such audacity before the polite society which would have booed the iconoclast poet Vladimir Mayakovsky off the stage. And yet, he added in his memoirs, 'Prokofiev's *Sarcasms* are more taunting, more trenchant than the verses of the early Mayakovsky, and the horror of them is more terrifying and powerful'.[30] A more reactionary critic used the Mayakovsky tag as an insult after the official first performance in November 1916.

The poet himself was soon to become an admirer. So, too, was Maxim Gorky, that tenacious chronicler of squalid living conditions and the need for change in pre-Revolutionary Russia, who heard the *Sarcasms* at a literary and musical evening arranged to coincide with an exhibition of paintings the following February. Gorky was there to read excerpts from his autobiographical masterpiece *Childhood* and Jascha Heifetz also participated. In a radio speech honouring the writer after his death in 1934, Prokofiev recalled how 'Gorky, to whom I was introduced after the performance, talked to me about these pieces very seriously and attentively, showing himself to be a person with an acute and profound feeling for music'.[31]

Many years later, under very different circumstances, Gorky wisely countered Prokofiev's desire to write 'cheerful and energetic music' to suit the official Soviet mood with the retort, 'we also need a sincere and tender music'.[32] In the early 1930s Prokofiev was able to provide that for a series of staged Russian classics. There were also more rose-like works, perhaps surprisingly, among the thorns in the years leading up to the Revolution, evident as always when the subject demanded. At the first Moscow event devoted exclusively to Prokofiev's music (shortly before Prokofiev's meeting with Gorky), alongside the *Sarcasms*, the ubiquitous Ballade and a selection of now-familiar songs, Prokofiev accompanied the soprano Zinaida Artimyeva in the premiere of his *Five Poems of Anna Akhmatova* op.27. He had completed these lucid counterparts to *The Gambler* and the songs of op.23 while working on the opera the previous autumn, in homage to the woman who saw herself as the poet chosen by fate to fill the vacuum following the decline of symbolism. Anna Akhmatova was born Anna Gorenko two years before Prokofiev and spent much of her childhood in the regal surroundings of Tsarskoye Selo (the village outside St Petersburg where the tsar's summer palace was situated) from which she was considered to derive her air of melancholy aristocracy. She arrived in St Petersburg in 1911 at a crucial moment for Russian poetry. That year, her husband Nikolay Gumilyov joined colleagues including Sergey Gorodetsky, the librettist of *Ala and Lolly*, to form the Poets' Guild, a counterblast to symbolism which defined its aims as 'Acmeist' or 'Adamist'. Gumilyov was soon able to clarify the tag: 'Acmeism in Greek means the point of highest achievement, the time of blossoming; Adamism means a virile, firm and clear outlook on life'.[33]

Each of the poets in the group interpreted this differently. Akhmatova responded to it, and to Mikhail Kuzmin's call for clarity, with poetry that used lucid, bright language but embodied much pain and suffering. In her first collection, *Evening* (1912), and in *Rosary* (1913) the tone is introspective and personal; it was not until *White Flock* (1917) that her steely brand of prophetic pessimism became bound up with the destiny of the homeland she felt it her duty never to desert. Many of the poems in *White Flock* date from the years leading up to the Revolution, when the worsening effects of the war made it impossible to turn inwards. Prokofiev's choice of five in 1916, however, was necessarily restricted to the theme of love and hope fulfilled or betrayed, much of it relating to Akhmatova's unhappy relationship with

Gumilyov, in the first two volumes. We do not know whether Prokofiev ever met Akhmatova about that time; in his autobiography he would not even be able to refer to the long-disgraced poet by name. It seems, however, that she was present when he participated in one of the concerts given on the splendid Bechstein owned by the editor of *Apollon*, Sergey Makovsky, and Karatygin's connections with that magazine would no doubt have pointed Prokofiev towards Ahkmatova's contributions. In any case, by 1916 Akhmatova was already perceived as one of St Petersburg's leading poets.

Even given the lyricism of which Prokofiev had already proved himself capable, the mature restraint and refinement of the *Five Poems of Anna Akhmatova* come as a surprise. The spare settings, with their generally soft dynamics, uncluttered piano part and often ethereally high-lying soprano line capture perfectly Vasily Gippius's definition of *Evening* as 'restrained pain, compressed lips, and eyes just about to cry';[34] and in fact there is only one explicit *fortissimo* outburst, in *Nastoyashchuyu nezhnost* ('True Tenderness'). Even the happiness of the first and fourth songs seems evanescent in its fragile transparency. Again, Prokofiev uses clear diatonic language, this time whittled away to the leanest piano writing, to represent the treasured things lost: the 'yellow transparent haze of the sun' which lives on as a faint memory in the winter of the third song, the singer's definition of 'true tenderness' – a quiet miracle of the simplest musical means – and the symbolic ideal of the grey-eyed king of the fifth song, briefly represented by a portion of a simple descending scale which is conjured again to underline the father of the child with 'eyes of grey' woken by its quietly distraught mother. Veiled dissonances characterize the obstacles to happiness, with a stalking tritone to suggest the unhappy marriage of the third song (*Pamyat o solntse*, 'Memory of the Sun') and the insensitive husband of the fifth (*Seroglazy korol*, 'The Grey-Eyed King').

One of Moscow's leading critics, Yury Engel, was at the premiere. Welcoming the 25-year-old artist 'so quickly risen to prominence in Petrograd' but 'less well known in Moscow', Engel described at length the 'slap in the face' of Prokofiev's *Sarcasms* before changing his tune to welcome the Akhmatova settings in a brief lyrical interlude: 'Having said all this it is hard to expect from Prokofiev's music tenderness, warmth, depth of feeling – in a word, lyrical charm. Some say that there is none of this in the music of the young composer but, having listened to his romances to words by Akhmatova, it's difficult to agree with this'.[35] The exception, for Engel, only proved the rule, and he ends with the same opinion he might have voiced several years earlier:

> the strength of the bright, effervescent art of Prokofiev in every case is not in lyricism, but in energy, immediacy, not in Adagio but in Allegro, not in Appassionato but in Scherzando, Strepitoso. And there is one important circumstance: we do not apply to the art of Prokofiev the words so often applied to contemporary art – 'sickly', 'brittle' and so on. This is something of a wild brawny fellow – a mustang grazing on pastures.[36]

Engel, of course, had only the Akhmatova settings as the opposite side of the coin. Leaving aside the songlike numbers in the early piano pieces, he could not have known the singing themes Prokofiev already had in waiting for the First Violin Concerto and what would eventually become the Third Piano Concerto, though he might have taken a look at Babulenka's music in the lithographed piano score of *The Gambler*.

It was not long before his even more perceptive fellow-critic Karatygin had another opus with which to take up the gauntlet for a new, sensitive Prokofiev, and much of this, too, was ready and waiting in February 1917. 'Prokofiev and tenderness – you don't believe it?' he wrote in *Nash vek*. 'You will see for yourself when this charming suite is published.'[37] The 'suite' was *Visions fugitives*, a group of pieces sketched in 1915 (nos.5, 6, 10, 16 and 17), 1916 (nos.2, 3, 7, 12, 13 and 20) and 1917 (nos.1, 4, 8, 9, 11, 14, 15, 18 and 19). Its title was drawn from a 1903 collection by Balmont, a poet whose words had already featured extensively in Prokofiev's pre-Akhmatova songs and whose status as a symbolist of an earlier generation left few points of contact with Akhmatova. In his poem 'I do not know wisdom' he coins his own, virtually untranslatable plural, *mimolyotnosti* (literally 'transiences'), the word translated as 'visions fugitives'. Three lines are usually quoted, but the whole of this short poem is worth bringing to life:

I do not know wisdom – leave that to others –
I only turn fugitive visions into verse.
In each fugitive vision I see worlds,
Full of the changing play of rainbows.
Don't curse me, you wise ones. What are you to me?
The fact is I'm only a cloudlet, full of fire.
The fact is I'm only a cloudlet. Look: I'm floating.
And I summon dreamers . . . You I summon not.[38]

So much for the motto; the idiom of the *Visions fugitives* is far removed from the hazy symbolism of the earlier Balmont settings. Its closest equivalent, if anything, is Akhmatova's *White Flock*, which includes poems from as far back as 1912. Starting with the wistful treble of no.1, the *Visions fugitives* share with Prokofiev's Akhmatova settings the same blend of 'white-note' melodies and chromatic mysteries in refined dynamics (*pp* and *ppp* are even more common here). But although the piano writing remains similarly clear and uncluttered throughout, there is also a new and more disturbing vein of the dynamic malice found in the early piano pieces as well as a more elusive sadness. In this respect, parts of the *Visions fugitives* could be compared to Akhmatova's melancholic city poetry as well as her laments for the war at the front and Revolutionary upheaval at home, all of them new dimensions in her third collection.

The dates of Prokofiev's individual pieces belie a pre-ordained sequence and were rarely presented as such by the composer-pianist, but there is a musical logic to the set. The first numbers play with his usual harmonic evasiveness round A minor or C major, with the fifth and the sixth as a scherzo and tarantella from a more innocent time; the clouds of the 'picturesque' harp-like seventh are dispersed as Prokofiev's most winsome vein of new melody re-emerges in its successor – another 'white-note' melody regardless of whether it is being heard in A major or C major. The simple theme that interrupts the lopsided playfulness of no.11 was to provide the 19-year-old David Oistrakh with his first inkling that the 'tempestuous, defiant' Prokofiev could be 'as touching as a child' when he heard the composer play it at his 1927 Odessa recital.[39]

After the midpoint, the *Visions* seem to pass through the crucible of the *Sarcasms*, and the later stages palpably darken. The happy, 'white-note' vein tries to ride the turbulent chromatic wave in no.15 but is immersed, and the lulls between the storms have an intangible sadness about them. Although the 'epilogue' of no.20 was not among the last pieces to be composed, its spectral question mark is the perfect end to the series. More often commented upon, though, is the last of the upheavals, no.19, which seems to be the cause of its successor's irresolute torpor. In this Presto agitatissimo, a simplified reflection of his earlier piano-piece terrors and the Toccata, Prokofiev claimed to have invested his immediate impressions of the February Revolution, an event which the autobiographer of the Soviet era declares he and his friends 'hailed gladly'.[40] He was at least honest enough to categorize the mood of the piano piece as depicting 'the agitation of the crowd rather than the inner essence of the Revolution'.[41]

Seething resentment against the tsarist regime and its refusal to end a protracted war, of whose grim reality Prokofiev would at least have been aware from the battle-fatigued Myaskovsky feeding on his disillusionment in Tallinn, had finally overflowed. The trouble in Petrograd, which began with the protests of thousands of women on Women's Day and escalated in a series of food riots and fires, ended in the tsar's abdication. Prokofiev was there, 'taking refuge from time to time behind projecting walls when the shooting became too intense',[42] but still enjoying, like thousands of middle-class citizens, the unstoppable cultural life of the city, which culminated in Meyerhold's famous production of Lermontov's *Maskarade* at the Alexandrinsky Theatre. The play, with its message of retribution for heedless merrymakers, was mirrored in the gorgeous decadence of Alexander Golovin's numerous elaborate designs and in the cream of Petrograd society who paid a fortune to see it; again, the analogy of Pushkin's *A Feast in Time of Plague* was on everyone's lips. The dress rehearsal took place during the February troubles, and the production lived on as one of Meyerhold's greatest triumphs in Soviet Russia. Plans for another potential hit of the season, even without Meyerhold in charge, foundered with a new administration at the Maryinsky as *The Gambler* was rescheduled for what would turn out to be an even more turbulent autumn. The establishment of the only hope for democracy, Alexander Kerensky's bourgeois Provisional Government, and the burning question of how it would handle the war – its answer, as it turned out, being to prolong it –

mattered less to Prokofiev than whether he could push for *The Gambler* at the Bolshoy in Moscow now that unstable Petrograd had failed him. This was a pattern he would, with frustration, try to repeat during the Soviet era. After his February collision with danger, which he must have reckoned just as transient as the disturbances he and his mother had met on their return to St Petersburg in January 1905, the fate of *The Gambler* was the only source of anxiety, as his letters to Derzhanovsky in April and May indicate.

'How could it have happened that he did not hear the true music of the Revolution, that his works bear no trace even of the fiery rhythms of the Revolutionary songs which filled the air of Russian cities at that time?' asks Nestyev.[43] It happened because, apart from the usual concert appearances, Prokofiev spent little time in the cities that spring and summer. Lenin's return, massive strikes and the first of the Bolsheviks' attempts to seize power in July came and went during what was certainly the most diverse, if not the most productive, of all his composing years: the northern landscapes outside Petrograd assisted in the realization of the First Symphony, the *Classical*, and the reworking of the Third Piano Sonata (discussed in the context of its original version) and the limpid purity of Russia's eastern rivers found its way into the orchestration of the First Violin Concerto.

If the precedent for a symphony written by a latterday Haydn had already been established through Tcherepnin's teachings and their first fruits in the Sinfonietta, the circumstances of the *Classical* Symphony were unique. Leaving behind in Petrograd the Shreder grand, his Rubinstein prize, Prokofiev survived with no substitute in the country and made the discovery that 'thematic material composed without a piano was often of better quality'.[44] In fact most of the symphony's thematic material was already waiting in the earlier sketches. The ideas for the Gavotte came first. Since that first, precocious exercise in neo-classicism, the Sinfonietta, Prokofiev had gone further in spicing 18th-century forms with the harmonies of the present in the op.12 piano pieces. So, too, had Richard Strauss, who in his 1913 incidental music to Hugo von Hofmannsthal's adaptation of Molière's *Le Bourgeois Gentilhomme* had featured a gavotte with equally acidulous harmonic sideslips softened by the glow of a limpid chamber orchestra. The Gavotte was to be the quirkiest of the *Classical* Symphony's four movements, constantly modulating from the first to the last bar of the gavotte proper. Eccentricity is kept in check by perfect brevity and varied dynamics – the quiet reprise fades to *pianissimo* – both of which would be lost when the Gavotte served as choreographic padding for the exit of the guests in *Romeo and Juliet* 18 years later.

There is one other similarly wayward theme in the opening Allegro, the elegant second subject for first violins supported only by bassoon and pizzicato basses which skips down the octave on each progression and unleashes a more-than-classical forcefulness in the development. Yet the intention remains purer elsewhere in the *Classical* Symphony. It is, however, never merely the placid evocation of 'the "good old days" of hoop skirts and powdered wigs'[45] mentioned in the programme for the first performance. Prokofiev had no wish to ally himself so totally with the

18th-century evocations of Diaghilev's circle at the turn of the century or with the present-day reactionaries of old St Petersburg society. The sheer freshness of the themes is vital, with relatively few twists or dissonances to sully their purity, and it is especially effective in the finale. It was there that Prokofiev did most of his reworking that spring, further refining his new material to eliminate minor chords. The exposition's wealth of invention is rounded off by a melody that sounds oddly familiar (Ex.33*a*). Prokofiev's peaceful Russian idyll in May and early June 1917 might well have prompted him to think of the 'refrains of Springtime songs' so dreamily imagined by Rimsky-Korsakov's wistful Snow Maiden (Ex.33*b*). Whether the reference was conscious, the composer surely acknowledged it as such shortly before his death, referring to (and ending with) the astrologer's music in *The Golden Cockerel* in his last symphony, the Seventh. Taken together, these two evocations of a fresh, spontaneous early Rimsky-Korsakov opera and his last, satiric essay in the form suggest a play on tradition typical of Russian music.

In his short autobiography, Prokofiev was careful to suggest that both the completion of the *Classical* Symphony and the orchestration of the First Violin

Ex.33a *Classical* Symphony, op.25 – IV. Finale

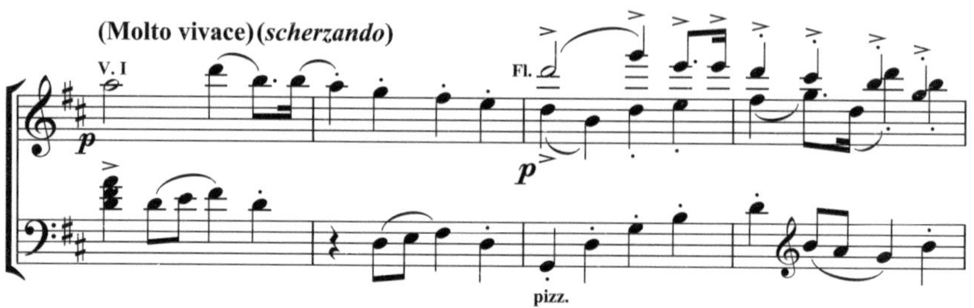

Ex.33b Rimsky-Korsakov, *The Snow Maiden* – Prologue

Concerto had been achieved in creative isolation but close enough to the nerve-centre of Revolutionary activity to keep in touch with momentous events. In fact this was true only of the earlier stages; more inspiration came to him on another river trip. It would not have gone down well in the Soviet era to emphasize touristic pleasures experienced at the same time as Myaskovsky, shell-shocked in Tallinn, received news of the uprising in nearby Kronstadt and found his social conscience deeply stirred (or so he later wrote). 'Nobody is slaughtering anybody yet',[46] Prokofiev wrote in high spirits to Eleonora Damskaya on 21 May, slipping in a request for rationed chocolate, as he travelled south-west to pick up the boat to Kazan. There, apparently spontaneously, he 'decided to betray the Volga and to take a look at the Kama',[47] parting company with his travelling companion, Alexander Aslanov. His detour took him along another mighty river as far east as the foot of the mighty Ural mountains and the beginnings of Siberia.

Telling Myaskovsky of his progress with the 'symphoshka' which his friend had apparently dubbed 'gutter music',[48] he allowed for Myaskovsky's 'rudimentary' geographic knowledge by giving a description of the Kama at Cherdin – 'wild, virginal and exceptionally beautiful, with its red mountainous shores covered in dark Siberian pines'.[49] The virginal and beautiful aspects could certainly be applied to the opening theme of the Violin Concerto he was now orchestrating, sketched as the beginning of a concertino back in 1915[50] (hence the early opus number, which actually precedes the *Scythian Suite*). Here is yet another sign that gentle lyricism was in the ascendant and, unlike the Akhmatova settings and the *Visions fugitives*, it needs no special pleading with today's concert-goers. Pure song for the soloist at the beginning of a violin concerto was nothing new, though Prokofiev may have taken specific note of the shimmering string support for the violinist in the opening bars of the Sibelius concerto as well as the roving, seemingly improvised quality of Sibelius's melody.

His own melody, predominantly sweet and dreamy rather than dark and dramatic like Sibelius's, runs for some 44 bars before dissolving its profile in low, irresolute trills. At first the secondary material that follows, another gavotte of twisted reasoning, seems to come from a different world. But the magical negotiation back to the silk-spinning of the opening seems perfectly natural. This time the flute takes over the melody in all its pristine beauty while the harpist and soloist provide a gleaming reflection which surely owes something to the magic of that summer journey down the Kama; and the spell is cast even more wistfully at the end of the concerto. Between these fugitive visions Prokofiev entertains his listeners and the soloist with a scherzo that runs wild with every conceivable violinistic effect – pizzicato, harmonics, spiccato (staccato bowing) and *sul ponticello* (playing close to the instrument's bridge). The orchestration snaps back with the resourcefulness of rushing clarinet figurations, pulsing horns and the baleful rearing of the tuba. Although the finale soon gives the impression of treading water before the work's initial haven can be reached again, its opening sets up a curious tension between the violinist's cantabile melody and the dry, tick-tocking accompaniment, anticipating the ambiguous slow movement of the Second Violin Concerto by nearly two decades. The affecting elaborations of clarinet and flute in the final vision were added in 1924 after early performances, Prokofiev told Myaskovsky, 'because without some sort of divertissement like that it sounded dreadfully like the overture to *Lohengrin*'.[51]

As a work in which lyricism dominates exuberance, the concerto would soon have been widely noted as the greatest possible contrast to the First Piano Concerto, with which the composer obliged his newly eager public twice that summer. The Violin Concerto was due to be included in the Ziloti series in November 1917 though not with Heifetz, the obvious candidate for soloist, who had left Russia a few days after his appearance alongside Prokofiev at the soirée attended by Gorky. The violinist Paweł Kokhański, who was teaching at the Petrograd Conservatory and had advised Prokofiev on the limits of the possible in violin technique, should have given the premiere. In any case the October upheavals were to put a stop to that, and to Prokofiev's intended return to Petrograd from his mother's favoured retreat of Kislovodsk. He headed for the south shortly after dodging the latest disturbances and (again) the ever-widening circle of military call-ups, thanks only to Gorky's special pleading.[52] Though his letters brush aside the danger of the times, he took the precaution of lodging a suitcase of manuscripts with Koussevitzky, who as head of the publishing house which retained the name of its old owner, Gutheil, had taken over from Jurgenson the responsibility for publishing all new Prokofiev works from the end of 1916.

The only peril Prokofiev experienced on his roundabout journey southwards turned out to be tooth trouble, though even this was turned to good creative use. In the second of two short stories – 'an angry one', he promised Eleonora Damskaya, 'owing to my teeth'[53] – dental horror is invested in a ferocious English governess whose vulpine fangs, 'long and terrible', sit in a glass overnight and are thrown away by the pupil and heroine, Tanya, in revenge.[54] Tanya's earlier adventures in the mushroom kingdom parallel those of Alice in Wonderland, suggesting a strong vein of whimsy from the composer who was soon to embark on *The Love for Three Oranges*. The preceding story, *A Bad Dog*, begun in Petrograd and concluded in Yessentuki, just north-east of Kislovodsk, on 30 July,[55] also reveals a sense of fantasy foreshadowing Bulgakov: the 'bad dog' is a poodle who leaps through a window to devour the heroine's celebrated apricot pie. This is one ingredient that brings lightness to a Florentine love triangle; the other is the identity of the dog's owner, revealed at the end of the story as Arthur Schopenhauer, whose valuable papers the hero has destroyed in another act of revenge. It was certainly at the urging of his indolent philosophic friend Bashkirov that Prokofiev had taken up reading Schopenhauer and Kant in the summer of 1916; but he must also have remembered the philosophical leanings of his old friend Schmidthof. In any case, it was the anecdotal rather than the spiritual aspect of the solitary Schopenhauer's life which he used to enliven his story: in his later years, living in Frankfurt, the philosopher became a devoted poodle-owner and his favourite, Butz, who was encouraged to sit by the window when a military parade passed by, was known by local children as 'young Mr Schopenhauer'.

Work on the stories proceeded in Yessentuki alongside Kant studies and orchestration of the *Classical* Symphony: the full score begins with the inscription '5 August 1917 Yessentuki' and at the end of the finale we find the date '10 September'.[56] There were also meetings with Bashkirov and the soprano Nina Koshits (as she then was; it was Prokofiev who later advised her to become 'Koshetz' if she wanted to avoid mirth among American audiences). Described by Koussevitzky as a 'Chaliapin in petticoats', this already distinguished prima donna was not to replace Nina Meshcherskaya in Prokofiev's heart, as she clearly desired – if the somewhat flippant tone of Prokofiev's letter to Damskaya from Yessentuki is to be taken seriously – not to resume her previous summer's liaison with Rakhmaninov. 'Chaliapin in trousers' was in Kislovodsk, where he had just given a concert, and Prokofiev met him there. Russia's greatest bass, with his wider experience of life, was clearly more concerned about the national situation, writing to his daughter that she would have to join him if conditions further north became too severe and that 'things are all right here, at least as far as food is concerned . . . quite often we have white bread';[57] he would be in Petrograd singing King Philip in Verdi's *Don Carlo* on the evening of Wednesday 25 October when Lenin and Trotsky's Bolshevik forces seized power at a signal from the cruiser *Aurora*. As that earth-shaking October began, and accommodation with his mother in the Grand Hotel in Kislovodsk was still not ready, Prokofiev travelled not north but further south for another expedition which would have to be airbrushed out of the Soviet history books, ascending via Teberda to a dizzying Caucasian height of 9000 feet.

Settling into the relative comfort of Kislovodsk, Prokofiev had two clear objectives: another performance of the First Piano Concerto there and a surprising new compositional project. The third of his short stories, completed the following year under very different circumstances from the journey to the Caucasus, takes a leading Assyriologist as its hero, and now it was one of Balmont's poetic renderings of an obscure incantation from the time of the Akkadians, predecessors of the Babylonians, which he decided to set to music. Begun before the October Revolution, *Semero ikh* ('Seven, they are Seven') could hardly claim to parallel the most significant upheavals of 1917; but its apocalyptic, if oddly objective, sense of doom was clearly triggered by the catastrophic events of the protracted war – and presumably Myaskovsky's graphic descriptions of some of the consequences – as well as the unrest of the previous few months. The frenetic holocaust of *Semero ikh* also provides a natural sequel to an earlier setting of Balmont's most hauntingly mystical poem, *Zvezdoliky* ('The Star-Faced One'), made by Stravinsky in 1911 between *Petrushka* and *The Rite of Spring* and dedicated to Debussy. *Zvezdoliky* was narrowly to miss sharing a belated 1924 premiere with *Semero ikh*, and remain unperformed until 1939. Like Prokofiev's Balmont incantation, the brevity of Stravinsky's work has made it hard to place, though it is not as difficult to perform as Stravinsky liked to make out.

The only real problem is the pitching of the close harmony, a kind of expectant meditation which makes a perfect introduction to Prokofiev's frenetic action.

The style is well suited to the theme in both pieces. In *Semero ikh* Prokofiev added several lines of his own to the exhortation of Balmont's Assyrian, frenziedly trying to ward off the evil influence of seven infernal agents. The extra text (presumably made with the poet's cooperation) vividly reflects a world governed by the dogs of war:

They make the sky and the earth shrink.
They confine whole countries as if behind doors.
They grind nations as nations grind corn.

Even by the standards of the *Scythian Suite*, the rather selfconscious modernism of the score is unusual in Prokofiev's output. Joining a vast orchestra, with trombones playing riotous glissandos in the final bout of communal cursing, is a richly divided chorus and a *tenore drammatico* whose difficult task it is to lead the initial ritual from 'loud whispers' of 'seven, they are seven' to a loud declamation which lies uncomfortably in the upper register (Ex.34). The sense of strain in this tenor role is 'really frightful',[58] as the American critic Olin Downes was to report at the premiere seven years later, and presumably deliberate. Did Prokofiev really think that Alchevsky, Andreyev or Yershov would hazard their voices in his service? Choral sopranos also have a taxing time – a memorable one, too, when they join with altos to force the work's nearest approximation to a chanted melody through a tintinnabulation of high orchestral frequencies. As the incantation's later stages unleash a flurry of changing metres followed by a numbing thrash of ostinato curses, the blueprint for the much better-known convent mayhem of *The Fiery Angel*'s last act unmistakably emerges. Prokofiev may just have been having fun with his 'seven devils', offspring of the seven reptiles in the second movement of the *Scythian Suite*, but a performance of the right intensity can reveal something unnerving in this music, as in its operatic successor – and the very nature of the piece, freewheeling massively in its mere seven or so minutes (to the five of Stravinsky's *Zvezdoliky*), militates against that happening.[59]

Writing out the short score of so unpianistically conceived a piece must have been hard enough, but orchestrating it proved a nightmare – as revealed by Prokofiev's comments in his autobiography and the uncharacteristically messy state of the manuscript (dated 'Kislovodsk 13 December 1917').[60] More straightforward was the other task he had mapped out for his Kislovodsk stay: the Fourth Piano Sonata, built round a theme he had composed on his first, very different, journey southwards in 1908. Transposed note for note two tones higher, but in an even deeper register, than the serpentine candidate for the slow movement of the 1908 symphony, his favourite Andante theme still held as central a position in the sonata as it had in the symphony. Its long-delayed sequel, though, was now a white-note melody characteristic of his newfound lyricism, yoked to its chromatic companion in typical but more than usually sinister fashion towards the end of the movement

Ex.34 *Semero ikh*, op.30

(Ex.35). Flanking this seminal inspiration were a C minor first movement of similar introspection, but with clearer textures and a melodic flexibility which some critics have found evocative of Medtner's storytelling plasticity, and an extrovert finale with a hint of demonism lurking round another white-note theme of even more disarming innocence. It is difficult to know how much these two movements owe to the original sonata of 1908, which is lost. A fair amount, the dedication to Schmidthof seems to suggest; and the striking contrasts between the lugubrious meditation of the bass-clef *skazka* or fairy tale which begins the sonata, becoming explicitly tragic only in the big-boned development, and the final bullish euphoria may be another portrait of Schmidthof.

The Fourth Piano Sonata was the last project to keep Prokofiev busy in the northern Caucasus. By the end of 1917 time began to stretch before him. He had tried

Ex.35 Piano Sonata no. 4, op.29 – II. Andante assai

to return north by train three times in the later part of that cataclysmic October and again on 3 November. The Ziloti concert dates came and went unrealized. 'Could I ever have dreamt when we parted at the Nikolayevsky Station that I would greet the month of December in Kislovodsk?' he wrote to Damskaya at the beginning of that month. 'Actually, this is one of the few remote places where it is possible to live decently. People feel this and more and more of them keep arriving.'[61] Social distractions were pleasingly few; the round of comfortable middle-class treats, exercises at the local gymnasium and walks in the mountains continued, while yet another threat of military call-up seemed all too remote. What, in any case, could visiting Red Guards achieve in an area that was under the control of the Whites? 'The local Chechens would slaughter them in a moment on the stairs of the Grand Hotel, if they did not manage to do so right at the railway station', declared Prokofiev with a rare insight in to the real situation.[62] Marya Grigoryevna was less willing to indulge in displays of robust indifference; she keenly felt her status as a refugee, isolated from everything she loved and knew.

Her son required only pen and paper to feel rooted. With composition of the sonata and 'incantation' completed, his thoughts were turning to 'a Third [Piano] Concerto, in C major, in three movements'.[63] But he needed to return to 'the terrible city of Petrograd'.[64] By mid-January he was seriously considering it – 'but only after the re-establishment of order . . . on Petrograd's streets, and in Petrograd's stomachs'.[65] The cue finally came with the collapse of the anti-Bolshevik Kaledin Front on the River Don in March. Embarking on a nine-day train journey to the new capital of Moscow with the written protection of the now Soviet Kislovodsk authorities, he had little to fear from Lenin's regime; his contacts with it were small but select. Asafyev had helped to pave the way with an article promoting his colleague's music, 'The Road to Happiness', written under his new pseudonym of 'Igor Glebov' in the Bolshevik magazine *Novaya zhizn* ('New Life') in July 1917. *Novaya zhizn* had been used as the name for the first daily Bolshevik newspaper, co-founded in 1905 by Maxim Gorky along with Anatoly Lunacharsky, another senior figure shortly to play a godfather role. It resurfaced for the irrepressible Gorky's latest publishing venture, launched in April 1917. Asafyev was its chief musical contributor; on the poetic side the 24-year-old Mayakovsky had pledged his loyalty. These were the four distinguished names that would guide Prokofiev over the broken glass of the two cities in early 1918.

One of two snapshots of him at the time comes in a colourful, rather confused account by Mayakovsky's fellow futurist Vasily Kamensky. Its essence, as the ever-precise Prokofiev noted to Asafyev in 1931 on receiving a copy of the book in which it appears, was 'nice' but 'garbled'.[66] It does, at least, land us vividly in the Poets' Café of which Kamensky and Mayakovsky were frequent habitués during its six-month existence, that March evening in 1918 when Prokofiev approached the piano 'quivering with eagerness like a flame'[67] to play his *Suggestion diabolique* – not as recent a work as Kamensky supposed. His much-quoted image, though, persists in the mythology: 'the whole café seemed to be on fire; it was as if the very beams and rafters were in flames yellow as the composer's hair, and we stood there ready to be burnt alive in the fire of his astounding music'.[68] Mayakovsky needed no special persuasion. He had already confided to Asafyev his own enthusiasm for Prokofiev's music as a torrent of rain by which the listener was all too willing to be drenched. The picture Kamensky claims Mayakovsky sketched of Prokofiev on that occasion, with the inscription 'Sergey Sergeyevich playing on the tenderest nerves of Vladimir Vladimirovich',[69] is nowhere to be found. There are two other testaments: the inscription 'to the global president of the department of music, from the global president of the department of poetry'[70] on a copy of the revolutionary verses *War and the World* and the signature dated '22 March 1918' in Prokofiev's 'sun-questionnaire',[71] preceded by two lines from the fiery, torrential love poem *A Cloud in Trousers*. This early poetic dithyramb had been written in 1915 when

Mayakovsky was, as he wrote in it, 'handsome, 22 years old'; it has everything in common with Prokofiev's more audacious early music except a conscious mastery of form, which the composer had already discovered and which Gorky had hoped the impetuous poet would eventually adopt.

Two artists from an older world met to hear Prokofiev play passages from *Semero ikh*: Koussevitzky, at whose cultured establishment off the Arbat in Moscow the meeting took place, and Balmont, who touched on this encounter in the unpublished memoir his daughter was to hand over to Prokofiev in Moscow a decade later. Balmont compared Prokofiev on the eve of his departure to the brilliant pagan gods Perun and Yarilo:

> he intersperses passages of original music with sharp aphorisms. He jokes, he's cheerful, intoxicated with his own strength and enterprise . . . As soon as he has gone, Koussevitzky leafs through the score, stands up, strides up and down the room, sighs and, flushing with emotion, says, 'You know, in richness and originality of orchestration there's nothing in the world can match this for such outstanding musical imagination'.[72]

Koussevitzky would have to wait six years to put his admiration into practice.

What did take place in 1918 was the premiere of an altogether gentler masterpiece. Following two evenings in which Prokofiev played his latest sonatas and the *Visions fugitives*, he took the role of conductor of the very orchestra which had 'previewed' his youthful symphonic exercise in the first performance of the *Classical* Symphony. The programme for this auspicious event reveals Soviet steps towards adopting the Western calendar ('8th' follows '21st April' in brackets) as well as a still eclectic programme. The new symphony must have seemed light and slim indeed after Skryabin's Third (*The Divine Poem*); it was followed by Stravinsky's *Faun and Shepherdess* and his earliest suite from *The Firebird*. All the other works in the programme were conducted by Nikolay Malko.

That such a heady mix could still be enjoyed was due largely to the most influential member of the audience. Anatoly Lunacharsky had always seemed the most humane of the intellectuals behind the Revolution. His philosophical curiosity verged on the mystical, bringing him into conflict on several occasions with the infinitely more pragmatic Lenin. Yet he had showed his devotion to the party by the stoicism with which he bore his long-term solitary confinement and deportation in the late 1890s, and he had been imprisoned again by Kerensky's government in July 1917. His role in the events of that year was beyond reproach, as Isaac Deutscher eloquently outlines in his introduction to the first English edition of Lunacharsky's *Revolutionary Silhouettes* in 1923:

> The 'soft' 'God-seeker' with the air of the absent-minded professor surprised and astonished all who saw him by his indomitable militancy and energy. He was the great orator of Red Petrograd, second only to Trotsky, addressing every day, or

> even several times a day, huge, hungry and angry crowds of workers, soldiers and sailors, and breaking down almost effortlessly, by his sheer sincerity and sensitivity, all barriers of social origin and education that might have separated him from them. The crowds were spellbound by him and loved him.[73]

This was a person who might have been hard pressed to make the choice Dostoyevsky's fledgling revolutionaries in *The Possessed* had posited between Raphael and a pair of boots. As the man Lenin had cannily appointed as Commissar for Education – which was essentially the same as a minister for culture – Lunacharsky soon made his views on the continuity of civilization apparent. Culture was to be preserved and made meaningful to the masses by means of an adult education scheme which, if not entirely successful, has never been followed through so thoughtfully or systematically by any latter-day government bandying the buzzword 'accessibility'. In November 1917 he attempted to overcome the hostility of the Union of Artists to 'new forms of artistic life and artistic enlightenment';[74] Mayakovsky supported him to the hilt.

Prokofiev would have been of infinite value in Lunacharsky's wide-ranging scheme, and had he been undecided over his future by the time of his meeting with him, this most persuasive of speakers might well have won him over. During the previous summer, however, he had met an American businessman, Cyrus McCormick Junior, who held out the prospect of American fame and fortune. McCormick was the son of an even more famous Cyrus, inventor of the first commercially successful mechanical reaper, and he was visiting Russia as part of a special diplomatic mission to keep the Russians on the allies' side. A cultured man with links to the arts in Chicago, McCormick even offered to pay for a copy of the *Scythian Suite* so that he could keep abreast of new Russian music. On the day of his return journey by the Trans-Siberian Express, McCormick recorded in his diary, he was visited by the young composer who 'came to tell me he could have his symphonic suite copied for me'.[75] This Prokofiev did, enlisting the help of a Mr Barker for this special English edition, and left it at the American Embassy in Petrograd in mid-August 1917. Despite diligent efforts by McCormick to trace its whereabouts, the score was not retrieved at the time,[76] though Prokofiev did at least have his own copy to ensure the *Scythian Suite*'s American premiere the following year. As for McCormick, he returned to America with scores including many of Prokofiev's most recent piano pieces, the *Humoresque Scherzo* in its arrangement for four bassoons and the First Piano Concerto.

With the promise of new territory to conquer, Prokofiev wanted leave to set out for the USA by way of South America. Lunacharsky had the sensitivity not to try and bully this most tenacious of young men out of his decision. He must surely have been less naively confident than the composer of a quick return; instead of the half-year or so Prokofiev intended to tour abroad, nearly nine years were to pass before he would set foot on Soviet soil again. In a scene rich in potential for any film, Prokofiev was conducted to Lunacharsky's office in the Winter Palace by Gorky and Alexandre Benois, who was repairing the damage done there by the guns of the *Aurora*. The composer dramatizes the meeting with his usual neatness in his short autobiography, where Lunacharsky answers his request 'gaily' with the now-famous words 'You are a revolutionary in music, as we are in life – we should work together. But if you want to go to America I will not stand in your way.'[77] His written permission, serving as passport, gave 'the famous composer S.S. Prokofiev' leave to travel abroad 'owing to poor health and artistic necessity'.[78] A none-too-feeble Prokofiev left jauntily on the last Trans-Siberian Express to reach Vladivostok before war manoeuvres blocked this strategic route; he narrowly missed the assassination of the royal family, the bitterest of Soviet winters and the first great stage production of the Soviet era, Mayakovsky's *Mystère-Bouffe*, blessed by Lunacharsky and directed by Meyerhold. This revolutionary in theatre had one great gift to bestow on the revolutionary in music, which he told a friend he had delivered into Prokofiev's hands on the very eve of his departure.[79] It was the first, 1914 issue of his little blue-and-yellow-jacketed magazine *The Love for Three Oranges*, containing the full scenario of the story that would inspire Prokofiev's first masterpiece on Western soil.

Part Two

America, France and Germany

1918–35

7
In quest of three oranges
1918–19

'I pity the exile's lot', wrote a steely-eyed Anna Akhmatova from her Petrograd isolation in 1922.

> Like a convict, like an invalid,
> Dark is your road, wanderer,
> Your foreign bread reeks of wormwood.[1]

The condition Akhmatova's pungent image conveys was to start gnawing at Prokofiev shortly after that poem was written, fostered by re-established contact with friends left behind like Myaskovsky and Asafyev. Yet his quest for what he clearly expected to be short-term adventure abroad in May 1918 takes on the character of a cheerful intermezzo alongside the earlier defections of Stravinsky, Diaghilev and Rakhmaninov and the more urgent subsequent departures of other musical friends and colleagues. Among them were the Koussevitzkys, who followed him a year later, concealing, as Parisian legend had it, Madame's jewels in Monsieur's double-bass case.

Prokofiev was now experienced at travelling in times of war and upheaval. His journey along the Trans-Siberian route, on the last train to leave Moscow for some years, mirrored his earlier, high-risk return rail travel to central Europe in the spring of 1915 and to the Caucasus, where he had left his mother safe for now in Kislovodsk. It was only in retrospect that he appreciated the dangers of passing through the front held by the Czech army in Siberia. The letters and cards he sent throughout May 1918 reveal only exuberance and the thrill of seeing new places. Blizzards did little to disrupt the speed and comfort of the journey between Moscow and Krasnoyarsk. He was 'getting fat from lots of eating and the absence of exercise',[2] as he had on the journey to Rome. The direct route to Vladivostok via Harbin had been cut by a Cossack general, but the lengthier alternative allowed him to wax lyrical over the beauties of Lake Baikal and Khabarovsk, 'a charming little patriarchal place on the shore of the wide Amur'.[3] He also made what was to be his last direct contact with Myaskovsky for nearly five years with a drier observation on the less distinguished stopping-post of Arkhara, 'remarkable for the fact that all Arkharans were born there (and where doesn't fate take us on the road to America!)'.[4]

Prokofiev's usual ability to amuse himself found an outlet in the study of Spanish, in preparation for the concerts he expected to give in South America, reading up on the Babylonian culture he had evoked in *Semero ikh* and writing a surreal short story which links a fictional Assyriologist with the sudden, inexplicable disappearance of the Eiffel Tower from Paris. The iron giant's progress to Babylon, halted in Switzerland, makes *The Wandering Tower* a nightmarish fictional counterpoint to his own journey; other phantasmagoria connected with the private life of a railway engineer found their way into a rather more arcane second story, *Misunderstandings Sometimes Occur*.[5] Both tales continued to help occupy him as he boarded the *Khosan-Maru* from Vladivostok to Yokohama in Japan, his pockets jingling with worthless roubles but very few yen.

He found time to remind Stravinsky of his existence with a postcard from the Nara Hotel 'in the midst of Buddhist temples and sacred deer',[6] sent to Clarens and forwarded to Morges, in which he mentioned that he had already tried to contact Diaghilev via the Russian Embassy in Madrid. His benefactor in Japan was a wealthy and highly cultured patron of the arts, Motoo Ohtaguro, who had already written about him in a Japanese book on contemporary music. Ohtaguro now arranged two concerts for him in the prestigious venue of the Imperial Theatre as well as one in Yokohama and invited him to his summer home, an act of hospitality captured in a photograph of Prokofiev with Ohtaguro and his wife (dressed in a kimono). Prokofiev was not to forget his anglophile host when he heard of the devastating Tokyo earthquake in September 1923: he sent a letter of anxious inquiry, 'hoping your home and music library were spared',[7] and soon received an elegantly reassuring reply. The English-language programme for the Tokyo recitals billed him as 'The Gigantic Russian Composer and Pianistic Virtuoso', adding rather more enigmatically 'The Another Rubinstein Prizz Winner [*sic*]'.[8] Small audiences brought Prokofiev little profit but 'they listened attentively, sat amazingly still and applauded my technique'.[9]

Prokofiev stayed in Japan longer than he intended: the plan had been to board another boat from Japan to Valparaiso so as to take advantage of the South American concert season before finding fame and fortune in the USA. But he discovered that he had just missed one boat, and the next would not be departing for a month. Influenced by a Russian engineer who was travelling to Chicago to open a glue factory,[10] he plumped for a journey that would end in San Francisco later that summer. He had, in any case, prepared his path to America with a letter to Cyrus McCormick (the businessman who had asked for his compositions at the Winter Palace the previous summer), begging (in French) 'pardon for abusing your great kindness'.[11] He needed McCormick, as a well-known and influential American, to testify for him so that he could receive the necessary visa on his American passport. McCormick diligently set the wheels in motion while Prokofiev sailed towards America.

A tantalizing reference in the autobiography to 'a marvellous stop-over in Honolulu'[12] can now be reinforced by the enchanted impressions given in the recently published diaries, where the traveller forgets his penurious state surrounded by the brilliant light and the dazzling flowers of Waikiki Beach and lives, for a few brief hours, the dream of a lotus-eater. Then the voyage resumed, and with it work on themes for a wholly diatonic, 'white-note' string quartet he had started in Petrograd; one of them was eventually to play the leading thematic role in *The Fiery Angel*. So a crucial musical idea for his third full-length opera took shape before a note had been written of the second. Nevertheless, it was also in the south Pacific that he turned his attention to Meyerhold's gift and conceived a usable outline for *Lyubov k tryom apelsinam* ('The Love for Three Oranges').

It was an unexpected new direction for opera, but it had been in the air since September 1913, when Meyerhold had realized a dream and opened his own theatre studio in St Petersburg. One of the three branches of discipline was a thorough schooling in the history and technique of the *commedia dell'arte* in which the tutor, Vladimir Solovyov, took students through the stock-in-trade of this unique improvisational tradition. Central to his teaching were the *fiabe teatrali* of the 18th-century Venetian playwright Carlo Gozzi. Launched as a riposte to the acrimonious war between the flatulent, high-flown theatre of the Abbé Chiari, purveyor of the 12-syllable Martellian verses so mocked in *The Love for Three Oranges*, and Carlo Goldoni, the prosaic dramatist of everyday life, Gozzi's fables attempted to bring an older, now debased entertainment back into the arena and to give a new lease of life to one of its best exponents, the *commedia dell'arte* troupe of Antonio Sacchi. Since Sacchi's actors improvised, true to the basic character traits of Truffaldino, Brighella, Smeraldina, Pantalone and so on, Gozzi gave them only an outline for their first joint project, *The Love for Three Oranges*, based on a traditional nursery tale which first appeared in literary form in Giambattista Basile's *Pentamerone* of 1634. Interlacing the tale's naive magical ingredients with the antics of Sacchi's troupe, and larding it with references to Chiari and Goldoni, Gozzi's entertainment had its premiere in Venice at the end of January 1761. Nine more fully scripted *fiabe* followed at close intervals, among them the 'theatrical tragi-comic Chinese fable' *Turandot*, before Gozzi decided that the genre had run its course and turned to adapting Spanish drama.

Meyerhold and his company were not alone in generating renewed interest in the *commedia dell'arte* at a time when artists and audiences were beginning to weary of cultural over-inflation. Meyerhold may even have taken his cue from Richard Strauss, whom he had thought of asking to set *The Love for Three Oranges* to music in 1913; he had decided against it because of what he defined as Strauss's 'lack of taste'[13] after his production of *Elektra* at the Maryinsky Theatre. By then Strauss had already engaged his own poet, Hugo von Hofmannsthal, in the creation of an operatic clash between lofty mythology and *commedia dell'arte* inserted within Hofmannsthal's adaptation of Molière's *Le Bourgeois Gentilhomme* – the splendid hybrid

Ariadne auf Naxos. It is unlikely that Strauss would not have discussed its premiere, in October 1912, when he arrived in Moscow less than four months later. There is one especially curious correspondence with the Hofmannsthal/Strauss *Bürger als Edelmann* within the Meyerhold journal, and it is one of the few scenes that Prokofiev rejected wholesale: the third intermezzo set in the palace kitchens where the servants and the cooks dance, the latter performing a bergamasque. Meyerhold must have heard about Strauss and Hofmannsthal's dancing cooks who prance on with the *bourgeois gentilhomme*'s dinner, and the waiter who pops out of the *omelette surprise* to offer up a sensuous waltz. There was another crucial development on the way to Prokofiev's opera. In 1912 the German-Italian composer pianist Ferruccio Busoni saw a *commedia dell'arte* performance in Bologna and embarked on the path that eventually resulted in the 1917 double bill *Arlecchino* and *Turandot* (he had already adorned the play with incidental music in 1905). When Puccini took over the story in the early 1920s it lost much of its sprightly, Gozzian irony; but Busoni's *Turandot* is remarkably close in its *scherzando* spirit, if not its sequence of short set pieces, to much of the opera Prokofiev was about to write.

The booklet he studied on his journey to America contained the Meyerhold syndicate's thoughts on Gozzi's *L'amore delle tre melarance* in the shape of an overhauled scenario.[14] It was, in a sense, the vital manifesto for this first issue of their magazine, which took the same name as Gozzi's play and the Hoffmannesque subtitle 'Journal of Doctor Dapertutto'. Clearly, contemporary readers were not going to understand much, if anything, about the old Chiari–Goldoni squabble, cited at regular intervals in Gozzi's text and personified by the conflict between the ineffectual wizard Chelio and the strident witch Fata Morgana. It was a good idea, then, to establish the conflict of interests right at the start. Meyerhold's visual imagination provided a detailed synopsis of his *mise-en-scène*, followed by a prologue in which tragedians and comedians come into conflict. To the rival gangs, who battle with quills in Meyerhold and with umbrellas and riding whips in Prokofiev's adaptation, the libretto adds romantics bearing leafy boughs and philistine empty-heads who belabour the romantics with walking sticks. Pro-Gozzi eccentrics – three in Meyerhold, ten to suit Prokofiev's divided chorus – rush in to separate the squabblers. In the course of Meyerhold's action it is mostly the three jesters in the tower who comment on the action and remind us of the framework, but Prokofiev has all his factions not only observe but intervene at the direst moment.

As for the fairy story proper, the 'old grandmother's tale' adapted by Gozzi from familiar Italian sources, it follows a similar course for its first half in all three versions. A hypochondriac prince, stuffed with Chiari's gloomy Martellian verses, causes grief to his father (the King of Diamonds in Meyerhold and Gozzi, the King of Clubs in Prokofiev) and is controlled by the scheming Leandro, who changes suit and role from Knave of Diamonds in the literary sources to King of Spades in the opera libretto. Leandro and the king's bizarre niece Clarice, both in cahoots with the witch Fata Morgana, use the black Smeraldina as their willing tool (mentioned only briefly in the first part of Gozzi's story, but wisely introduced into the action at an early stage by Prokofiev). Common to all three versions are the comic Truffaldino's efforts to make the prince laugh both in private and in public with spectacular divertissements, Fata Morgana's Carabosse-like appearance at the festivities and the tumble she takes which finally breaks the spell, only to be followed by her curse that the prince should fall in love with three oranges.

Prokofiev then cuts to the chase, and with his lifelong love of the truly fantastical, focusses on one strange detail in the castle of the giant Creonta where the oranges are to be found. Gozzi and Meyerhold debunk the supernatural apparatus with none-too-terrifying obstacles requiring simple solutions, including a gate that needs oiling and a cook who has been left to clean out the oven with her vast dugs (Meyerhold coyly substitutes 'hands') when a broom will do. Prokofiev concentrates on the Cook, turns her into a monstrous bass and has Truffaldino divert her with a 'magic' ribbon. The princesses who step out of the oranges in the next scene could easily be saved by water from the nearby lake in the versions by Gozzi and Meyerhold; it takes the intervention of Prokofiev's Eccentrics with a bucket of water to preserve the last of them. Smeraldina then transforms the maiden into a white dove in Gozzi and Meyerhold, for which Prokofiev with bizarre aplomb substitutes a giant rat. This obviates the need for a scene in the royal kitchens when the dove tells Truffaldino what has happened; again Prokofiev has the extraneous action interfere, with the Eccentrics locking Fata Morgana up in a tower so that Chelio can be seen to triumph. The denouement in the libretto is both swifter and better geared to music when the villains bolt for it and disappear under the protection of their patroness.

Much of this, at least, Prokofiev had 'planned out a little'[15] by the time the *Grotius* docked in San Francisco Harbour on 21 August 1918.[16] As America was one of several countries actively supporting the war on Bolshevism from within Russia, funding the former tsarist generals and admirals now leading the 'Whites' in the civil war, Prokofiev was subject to interrogation on his political stance during three days' detention on Angel Island. The line of question and answer feature in an anecdotal snapshot from the autobiography: '"Have you ever spent time in prison?" "I have." "That's bad. Where?" "Here on your island." "So you want to joke about it!"'[17] 'The immigration officers would make good music critics', he later told a West Coast newspaper.[18] 'I know this because they promptly disbelieved all the statements I made about myself when I came to America.' But all ended well, he continued: 'the Russian consul declared that the only force I would use would be that of my digits on the piano keys, so finally I was allowed to enter your charming country'. What Prokofiev did next differs in his own accounts from what his future wife remembered. He writes that the 300 dollars that tided him over until his arrival in New York came from 'some fellow travellers who had become interested in me';[19] Lina recalled that cultured members of the Russian community in San Francisco, to whom he had been provided letters of introduction, bailed him out. We can trust her in outline when she remembers one 'Professor Kahl, art historian and musician' who offered Prokofiev the opportunity of giving a lecture-recital to repay the debt.[20]

One of the first people Prokofiev was glad to see shortly after his arrival in New York in early September was the ever-supportive McCormick, who had come from Chicago. McCormick had done his best to promote the piano pieces he had brought back from his Russian mission to the pianist, conductor and composer Ossip Gabrilovich at the Carnegie Hall. Yet Gabrilovich was true to form as a St Petersburg-born musician of the Glazunov generation (though only four years older than Stravinsky) when he returned them with the dry comment, 'that sort of music does not appeal to me'.[21] (He liked one of the Myaskovsky pieces McCormick had sent him, the early piano sonata, but reserved all his praise for Glière's massive and opulent *Ilya Muromets* Symphony, which Frederick Stock had already conducted in Chicago.)

By mid-September Prokofiev was installed at the flat of Adolph Bolm, Diaghilev's greatest male dancer before the rise of Nijinsky. It was Bolm who gave somewhat evasive information about Diaghilev's bewilderment over *Chout*, prompting Prokofiev to write the impresario a letter wanting to know 'the destiny of my poor *Buffoon* so traitorously buried in the secret folds of your briefcase'.[22] In Bolm's apartment at 15 East 59th Street he gave his first interview to the *New York Times*. The paper announced his arrival with the surprised subheading 'Serge Prokofieff Says Musicians Are Still Active In His Land', an important point to impress upon Americans suspicious of 'the land of the Bolsheviki'.[23] The 'big specimen of the fair-haired northern Russian race'[24] gave a brief account of his fraught journey on the Trans-Siberian Express and pointed out that 'Glazunoff, the head of the Petrograd Conservatory, had obtained 50,000 roubles for its work from the Bolsheviki'[25] (loyal propaganda to thank Lunacharsky for his support).

The humming, cosmopolitan city which was to be his base for the next year stood on the brink of the jazz age and the hits of George Gershwin, the first of them the song *Swanee* in 1920. At the time of Prokofiev's arrival, Gershwin might not have been a big name, but the interpreter of *Swanee* certainly was: Al Jolson, whose appearances in *Sinbad* at the Winter Gardens, leading a 150-strong company, ensured a successful run. Exactly what Prokofiev thought of the commercial song was to be revealed later in his friendship with his fellow-composer Vladimir Dukelsky, soon to become known as Vernon Duke; Lina recalled how irritated he was when the ubiquitous *Dardanella* dogged an early meeting of the couple in the Palm Court Hotel.[26] The American concert scene was better established than most Russians realized, with the New York Philharmonic being the third oldest orchestra in the world, Chicago and Boston already boasting distinguished pedigrees and the Philadelphia Orchestra rising from small-town status to greatness under Leopold Stokowski. With such figures as Stokowski, and Stock in Chicago, concert life was hardly moribund – even if, as Prokofiev lamented, the 'discussion of new music, tendencies and composers' which had played a 'not insignificant part' in the cultural life of Moscow and Petrograd was lacking in America.[27] In the world of opera, the Metropolitan company in New York had lost something of its vitality since the glory days of Gustav Mahler less than a decade earlier, but it could still boast stars who hit the headlines – Rosa Ponselle in Verdi's *La forza del destino*, Geraldine Farrar as Tosca, Caruso in *L'elisir d'amore*.

The Americans' hunger for stars was more of a bane than a blessing for serious musicians like Prokofiev who were trying to establish a reputation, though in the field of pianism the demand for accuracy and brilliance of execution was, as he noted, extremely high. The great names alongside whom he was to be measured had made their mark here much earlier – Skryabin in 1906, Rakhmaninov in the 1909–10 season, when he had created a sensation with his New York performance of the Third Piano Concerto under Mahler's baton. Other leading pianist-composers were the legendary Josef Hofmann and a name much on concert-goers' lips in late 1918, the Ukrainian-born American Leo Ornstein, 'experimenter in meta-pianistic sonorities' as Nicolas Slonimsky described him.[28] Despite that early flagging of his arrival by the *New York Times*, Prokofiev did not exactly burst on the New York scene. His first appearance was scheduled for a 'Liberty Loan Russian Concert' at Carnegie Hall on 19 October, for which he was advertised (as 'composer-pianist') fairly low down a billing led by Bolm and his Metropolitan Opera Ballet, Skryabin's great champion Modest Altschuler and his Russian Symphony Orchestra, and the sopranos Yevgenya Fonarova and Vera Janacopulos (soon to become a firm friend).[29]

In fact, Prokofiev cancelled the engagement because of illness. Incapable of idleness, he spent the next day working on a short story, *The Two Marquises*. His debut took place instead on 29 October in the less grand surroundings of the Brooklyn Museum, as part of an event to accompany 120 paintings by Boris Anisfeld, one of Diaghilev's most distinguished artists in the Bakst mould. Bolm performed his own choreography, as originally planned, to two of the *Visions fugitives*; the 'pianist-composer' had the limelight in pieces from op.12. The *Brooklyn Daily Eagle* was more perceptive than it realized in complaining that the revolutionary 'lion' of expectation 'roared as gently as the gentlest dove'.[30]

Sensation, however, was the tenor of the much more significant reviews that appeared after his official solo debut at the Aeolian Hall, the second-string venue for recitalists, on 20 November. Prokofiev had made a conscious effort to evoke his two great predecessors in New York by including two Rakhmaninov preludes and three of Skryabin's less acerbic pieces between his own *Études*, the Second Piano Sonata and four shorter pieces including his piano arrangement of the Gavotte from the *Classical* Symphony and the *Suggestion diabolique*. Nothing, it seems, had changed in the lurid, sweeping imagery of the New York press since the papers had described Rakhmaninov's first recital as making the listeners feel 'as if they were prisoners bound for Siberia'[31] and more than once dubbed Skryabin a 'cossack Chopin'. Richard Aldrich of the *New York Times*, at any rate, had not modified much about his colourful writing for a decade. On this occasion he visualized in the finale of the Second Piano Sonata 'a charge of mammoths on some vast immemorial Asiatic plateau' and declared of the composer that 'the instruments of percussion rule in his Scythian brains'. The 'blond, slender, modest' young man had surpassed that other 'musical anarch' Ornstein. 'His fingers are steel, his wrists steel, his biceps and triceps steel, his scapula steel'; only the almost obligatory 'Bolshevist' tag was missing. Objecting to his 'brutal' treatment of trifles, Aldrich compared him unfavourably with Hofmann in Rakhmaninov and Skryabin at some length and, while finding Prokofiev's own music essentially 'cerebral', managed to capture something of its essence: 'He is a psychologist of the uglier emotions – hate, contempt, rage – above all rage – disgust, despair, mockery, and defiance legitimately serve as models for moods. Occasionally there are moments of tenderness, exquisite jewels that briefly sparkle and then melt into seething undertow'.[32]

These were tough words, but not entirely unperceptive, and more worthy of attention than those of the *New York Herald*'s vaguer critic, who noted the 'personal magnetism' of Prokofiev's pianistic style while dismissing the music as 'formless and impressionistic vapourings . . . very modern without being very interesting'.[33] Fortunately it was the more positive response that lingered after the recital: 'a parterre of pianists'[34] including Rakhmaninov were there to take note, contracts from pianola firms and publishing companies followed and, in a neat vignette from the short autobiography, a black lift-attendant 'took my arm and exclaimed, not disrespectfully, "steel muscles"'.[35] The pressure was on, and little over three weeks later Prokofiev was back for two programmes with Altschuler's orchestra that could only evoke further comparisons with Skryabin's similar collaboration 13 years earlier. Altschuler certainly needed all the publicity he could get, with greater figures like Stokowski stealing all the Tchaikovskian thunder in the 25th anniversary year of the composer's death. The programmes, certainly, were as interesting as any symphony concerts in which Prokofiev's music had featured in Russia. On the first evening, 10 December, the *Humoresque Scherzo* in its arrangement for four bassoons and the First Piano Concerto found themselves in the company of Rakhmaninov's Second Symphony, Lyadov's *Baba Yaga*, two of Ippolitov-Ivanov's *Caucasian Sketches* and Altschuler's arrangement for strings of Skryabin's Nocturne. Links with the first programme were made the following afternoon, when in the first part of the concert Altschuler conducted Skryabin's First Symphony and Sergey Vasilenko's *Hircus nocturnus* – a witches' sabbath based on Merezhovsky in which the nocturnal goat of the title becomes Dionysus and flies away at the head of a witch-pack. The all-Prokofiev second half featured the composer as soloist in his Third Sonata, along with several shorter works, and as conductor in the *Classical* Symphony.

Again there were polarities in the critics' reviews. Among the relatively sympathetic, James Gibbons Huneker in the *New York Times* was no Karatygin, and his gauche and inaccurate attempt to describe the musical progress of the concerto reveals the lower standards of criticism Prokofiev frequently had to accept in America:

> The first piano concerto of Serge Batuishka [*sic*] was in one movement, but compounded of many rhythms and recondite noises. It took twelve minutes to play. It might fairly be called an Etude in Rhythms, for the lyric episode is like an amorous night in June sandwiched between two xylophones. The composer handled the keyboard – handled is the precise word – and the duel that ensued between his ten flail-like fingers was to the death – the death of euphony. The first descending figure, it is hardly a theme – is persistently affirmed in various nontonalities by the orchestra till the slow mood, the piano all the while shrieking, groaning, howling, fighting back, and in several instances it seemed to rear and bite the hand that chastised it.[36]

One searches in vain for the 'first descending figure' and the ensuing 'nontonalities'; after all, the concerto's opening signature-tune ascends in a rooted D flat major. Yet Huneker did at least come down emphatically on the side of the 'tall, calm young man' he dubbed 'Fortissimist' and, following the familiar Skryabin tag, 'the Cossack Chopin for the next generation'.[37] The second programme led him to realize that Prokofiev had 'many strings to his bow: a mastery of old forms not being the most inconspicuous'. This time he found that 'Fortissimist' could play with 'delicacy, charm, and a wide colour gamut. He is not yet to be compressed into a critical formula. We should like to hear him in a Chopin or Schumann recital'.[38]

The notorious Herbert Krehbiel of the *New York Tribune,* on the other hand, proved worthy of Sabaneyev. His scurrilous abuse might have been predicted from his earlier railings against Debussy's *La Mer* and Strauss's *Salome.* Here the piano pieces were held to 'die the death of abortions', the *Classical* Symphony was 'simply puerile' and did this Russian not realize that decadent German music had provided 'as much musical guano as civilized soil could bear'?[39] Krehbiel proved worthy of Sabaneyev, too, for mistakenly attributing the 'filthy orgy'[40] of Vasilenko's piece to Prokofiev, and had to eat humble pie the day after the review appeared by admitting that he had not been able to study his programme properly.

Huneker, thankfully, represented the reaction of the audience, which he described as 'too stunned to analyze its feelings' at the end of the concerto: 'It was completely overcome'.[41] Among those listeners was a 21-year-old woman fresh from college, determined to become a singer and acquainted with the latest musical events, thanks to her family and friends. Her name was Carolina Codina, and she had the kind of multinational ancestry which makes even the mixed parentage of an archetypal European sophisticate such as the writer Sybille Bedford look simple. The father of Lina, as she preferred to call herself, was Catalan; it was from his mother that she later took her stage name of Llubera. Born in Barcelona and a composer of national songs, Juan Codina was in Milan studying singing when he met Lina's mother, Olga. Daughter of Caroline Verlet of Montbéliard and Vladimir Nemyssky, a liberal but severe judge who spoke both Polish and Russian, Madame Codina had Huguenot blood, which marked her out in her husband's family as 'la heretica'.[42] Carolina, their only child, was born in Madrid on 21 October 1897, spent her early years in Cuba, visited her maternal grandfather in the Caucasus and began her education in Geneva. French, then, was her first language; she began to learn English only at the age of ten when the family moved to New York. Petite and dark, with flashing brown eyes, she took after her Spanish father; this, as much as her 'internationalism', appealed to Prokofiev, whose romantic interest in her retaining a Spanish passport was to have fatal consequences for her status in the Soviet Union.

Lina first heard about Prokofiev when her mother's biochemist friend invited them to the first of the Altschuler concerts to hear 'that . . . as they call him "decadent, modern, crazy" composer'.[43] Lina liked the rhythmic, virtuoso quality of his playing but she was equally struck by how thin he was – 'you would think he would break in half when he bowed'.[44] Bashfully, she at first declined to join the party of congratulation backstage; but curiosity overcame shyness as she approached his room:

> Slowly I opened the door, slipped my head in and looked. I saw them talking to him, and he saw me over their shoulders and smiled at me and laughed because I looked so funny. Then I laughed too, and my friends said, 'Oh, there she is', and they drew me in, and I could not run away because it was too late. And I felt a sort of attraction – he was tall, thin, with blond, slightly reddish, hair.[45]

Friends did what they could to set up Lina and Sergey as a couple, not least because they looked good together. They next met for Sunday lunch. Lina disliked the manner of this 'nasty young man',[46] whose idea of a friendly conversation was applied sarcasm and who did not like to be teased in return. This gave her mother a chance to put in a word about the general unseriousness of Russian musicians; but attraction overcame irritation, and Madame Codina's disapproval over her daughter going out with a man to whom she was 'not even engaged',[47] along with her attempt to thwart the outing on the grounds that Lina 'doesn't have the appropriate evening dress',[48] was no obstacle. They went together to a Rakhmaninov recital, to the movies and the theatre, and to a supper of self-styled 'Bohemians', where the Don Juanish Artur Rubinstein asked his young friend within Lina's earshot where he had found such a beauty. Not even Prokofiev's ungallant refusal on one occasion to see her home, bundling her into a taxi instead, cooled relations for long. The first kiss took place during a stay on Staten Island, where they were guests of Vera Janacopoulos and Alexey Stal. They drifted in flat-bottomed boats up creeks, and 'Linette' posed as a Valkyrie alongside a bonfire while Prokofiev, rake in hand, stood by laughing. Prokofiev said he preferred this timid girl 'after all those aggressive American women'.[49]

Their fledgling careers separated them for periods, but the piquancy of Prokofiev's first significant romance since the ill-fated affair with Nina Meshcherskaya must have added further flavour to the exciting early months of 1919. Everything was slowly falling into place, and the greatest gift of all was the commission he had secured from the Chicago Opera Company to compose *The Love for Three Oranges.* This hoped-for goal had been secured in December when he unleashed the *Scythian Suite,* the one major orchestral score he dared not entrust to the New Yorkers, on the rather more liberal Chicago audiences. McCormick, of course, was behind it, even though he had never received the copy of the *Scythian Suite* Prokofiev had diligently prepared for him; fortunately the work was one of the major scores Prokofiev had brought on his voyage. McCormick also had good contacts in the opera world: his brother Harold, partner in the McCormick Harvesting Machine Company, together with his wife was the driving (and funding) force behind the Chicago Grand Opera Association.

The two concerts took place not with its enterprising chief Frederick Stock, a former viola player in the 27-year-old orchestra who was to be the longest-running of its principal conductors, but with his second-in-command, Eric DeLamarter. Prokofiev appeared as soloist in the First Concerto in a first half that began with *The Star-Spangled Banner* and Haydn's Symphony no.7 (*Le Midi*) ; after the interval, the sledgehammer blow of the *Scythian Suite* was softened by d'Indy's *La Forêt enchantée* and Chabrier's *España.* The programme was more successful than the New York events with Altschuler's orchestra, though the presence of the *Scythian Suite* inevitably had critics reaching for every epithet other than the one suggested by the work itself, so 'Bolshevist' came most readily to hand. 'The red flag of musical anarchy raged tempestuously in staid old Orchestra Hall yesterday', declared the Chicago *Herald-Examiner*;[50] while *Current Opinion* detected a strain of 'new, brutally realistic psychology'[51] common to Russian politics and music. That would unquestionably have been the verdict on *The Gambler* if Prokofiev had brought the score with him, but it was in chaotic Petrograd. It was the prospect of tradition rather than innovation which so delighted the director of the Chicago Opera in *The Love for Three Oranges.* As an Italian who had come to America to take charge of the Metropolitan Opera, Cleofonte Campanini waxed sentimental over the choice of author who had reached Prokofiev via Meyerhold's tradition, nicely encapsulated by Prokofiev in his autobiography: '"Gozzi! Our beloved Gozzi! But that is wonderful!" cried the Italian'.[52] A contract was signed for the work to be completed for the beginning of the 1919–20 season.

Before bringing his operatic fairy tale to life, Prokofiev had a clutch of new piano pieces – his first since leaving Russian soil – to offer to publishers and to play in his next New York recitals. In his adaptation of Gozzi's prologue to *The Love for Three Oranges,* spoken by a small boy, Meyerhold retains the advice to the spectators to 'picture yourselves . . . sitting with your grandmothers round the fire'.[53] But the *Skazki staroy babushki* ('Tales of an Old Grandmother') op.31 are four yarns far removed from the clear-cut action and poster-paint naivety of *The Love for Three Oranges.* The epigraph dictates the mood: 'some memories have been half-erased in her mind, but others will never disappear'. This, along with the constant thought of how his own ageing mother must be faring back home, helps to explain why these leanly written sequels to the free forms of the *Sarcasms* and the more elliptical of the

Visions fugitives have much of the melodic Prokofiev about them, and why the themes are so elusive. A plausible refugee from the 'white-note quartet' discarded en route to America, the most familiar of them in no.2 needs only a few bars to reveal a whiff of homesickness for the Russia left behind (Ex.36). Its shadowy descent to the bass and an even quieter dynamic level (*pp*), as well as the faltering memory that intervenes, are typical of the set. Only once, in the chromatic progress of no.3's bogeyman, do the dynamics reach *forte* for a bar and a half.

Ex.36 *Tales of an Old Grandmother*, op.31 – II. Andantino

The old woman's memory finally sets a 12/8 dance in motion in the last piece. Dance is the starting-point of the next opus for piano, a suite of four dances, op.32, that merely continues the wayward harmonic progressions and spruce rhythms familiar from as far back as the early *pesenki*. There is nothing in the first three pieces quite as distinctive as the dances in op.12 – though the familiar engagement of a melody played by right and left hands two octaves apart in the middle of the Gavotte is vintage Prokofiev. The final Waltz, his first since the early days, opulently pits regretful experience against innocence in a way that looks back across the war years to Ravel's *Valses nobles et sentimentales* and forward to the more memorable third movement of the Sixth Piano Sonata; it is a surprisingly expansive conclusion to an otherwise unadventurous group.

Negotiations with the American publishing firms for whom opp.31 and 32 were written came to nothing, and the pieces went into print only three years later when relations with Koussevitzky had been resumed. In two other commercial ventures Prokofiev was more successful. He now had a New York agent, Fitzhugh Haensel, of the partnership Haensel & Jones, a practitioner of the old school with whom he struck up a gentleman's agreement to pass on 15 per cent of the takings (25 per cent was customary). Haensel, though, was no great promoter – according to Lina he baulked even at the necessary expense of advertising in *Musical America*[54] – so Prokofiev had to champion his own music, spending time and effort that would undoubtedly have been better given to composing. He would nevertheless remain loyal to Haensel, despite frequent plans to move elsewhere, throughout the rest of his time in the West. His best promotional coup came on 25 February, when he signed a contract with the Aeolian Company to make five piano rolls a year for their Duo-Art system.[55]

In 1913, nine years after the unveiling of the first reproducing piano from the Welte-Mignon company in Germany, Aeolian (USA) went into business in a bid to sell more instruments. The process of making paper rolls for the proud owner of the Aeolian Reproducing Piano has been defined[56] as 'an advanced digital system' (in the original sense of 'digital'): 'recordings' were made by a tracker bar connected to the piano via electric contacts, capable of reproducing not only the notes but also the pianist's interpretation (this was a considerable advance on the standard pianola, which merely registered the notes, speed and expression being determined by pedalling during the 'playback' of the roll). Busoni hailed it as 'the cinematograph of the piano';[57] Stravinsky, who would certainly have had time to communicate his enthusiasm to Prokofiev, discovered its potential in 1914 and even wrote a piece specifically for the 'player piano'. In 1921 he hoped to make rolls of all his works as 'a means of imposing some restriction on the notorious liberty, especially widespread today, which prevents the public from obtaining a correct idea of the author's intentions'.[58] He switched his allegiance to the phonograph seven years later, when the advent of electrical recording vastly improved sound quality; the doom of the Aeolian Duo-Art reproducing piano, having passed its heyday in 1925 with the manufacture of more than 192,000 instruments, was sealed.

Prokofiev made few contributions to this now undervalued genre after 1925. 'The Old Castle' with the preceding Promenade from Musorgsky's *Pictures at an Exhibition* ('Ballet of the Chicks in their Shells' and 'Bydlo' were recorded in 1923) and his one Duo-Art homage to his old friend Myaskovsky with two of the latter's op.25 in March 1930. His choice of repertoire from the signing of the contract in 1919, only partly dictated by the demands of the market, began with the simplest of his pieces, the C major piano/harp Prelude from op.12 that May, and the March from the same set in June; the Gavotte and the Rigaudon followed in 1920. His most adventurous strain was represented by two of the *Sarcasms* eight months after he had first performed them, along with a selection from Musorgsky's *Pictures at an Exhibition* in the Aeolian Hall on 30 March 1919 – 'Mr Prokofieff juggles with jangling combinations of notes with considerable skill', opined the *New York Times*[59] – and, most ambitiously, the Toccata (February 1921).

He gave Duo-Art a taste of Rakhmaninov (who made rolls for the rival company Ampico) in the shape of the G minor Prelude he had included in his Aeolian Hall debut, preserved for posterity his idiosyncratic view of Skryabin and gave a clue to two of his roots with a Gavotte by Glazunov and a whistle-stop tour of Rimsky-Korsakov's *Sheherazade* which is a disappointingly long way from the virtuoso transcription one might have expected – merely a routine potpourri. The character of other interpretations is not easily discerned owing to discrepancies in contemporary reproduction,[60] but, in the broadest terms, the touch is crisp and clear, the range of dynamics supposedly guaranteed by the Duo-Art system not as wide as one might expect (*pianissimos* are non-existent) and the rubato magisterially capricious (above all in Musorgsky's 'Ballet of the Chicks in their Shells' and the *Sarcasms*).

Between the signing of the Aeolian contract and his first recording for the company, Prokofiev succumbed to the gravest illness: 'scarlet fever, combined with diphtheria and an abscess in my throat which nearly suffocated me'.[61] Never one to dwell on the life-threatening, he records in his short autobiography an American lady who confessed that she had sent roses for his deathbed, 'slightly regretful that her bouquet had gone to waste'.[62] The long-term legacy of this setback was a weak heart, which still afflicted him in the summer of 1923, but the passing of the fever left him hungry for work. It is characteristic, too, that he relished the sickbed hypochondria of the prince in his latest operatic fairy tale, underlining it with a series of parodied musical groans – a neat extension to the mock weeping of the protagonist in *Chout*, where the cellos also wail in high register. With his usual punctuality, he had finished the piano score of *The Love for Three Oranges* by June and the orchestration by the beginning of October. He was well within the terms of Campanini's contract, which had kept him financially afloat during those crucial months. Two amusing details reflect the fun he must have had: Lina was touched that he changed the name of the first princess from Violetta to Linetta – without pausing, one presumes, to wonder why her character should be the first to die – and the trumpet which announces the herald was allocated to bass trombone.

The Love for Three Oranges is a leaner, more compact score than *The Gambler*, partly, Prokofiev admitted, to suit American tastes, but more because this was no intense psychological drama but a parade of fantastical characters, each distinguished by a handful of gestures. In terms of the *commedia dell'arte* tradition inherited from Gozzi and Meyerhold, it might even be characterized as an opera-ballet; the bright *scherzando* writing for piccolo, flute and glockenspiel which is shared by the ten 'Eccentrics' presenting the show and their representative in the drama, Truffaldino, suggests at least an acrobat double for the prince's comic sidekick (who makes an exquisitely deft ten-bar mime appearance in Act I scene 3 and is seen at the end of a 'probably very long' comic dance for the prince as the curtain rises on the hypochondriac's sick-room). Much of Meyerhold's text cues musical 'numbers', from the 'loud noise of trumpets and drums'[63] of the opening riot and the later court march which Prokofiev anticipates, first with a select offstage band and then as a brilliant full-orchestral *entr'acte* as the 'hit tune' of the score. The two divertissements with which Truffaldino tries to make the prince laugh are suitably adapted from Meyerhold and Gozzi to provide a monsters' combat in the vein of the dark god's stomp from the *Scythian Suite* and a grotesque guzzlers' number to follow the fountains of oil and wine (piccolo, flute and harp).

Prokofiev's model for the march may well have been Rimsky-Korsakov's number for the quaint King of the Berendeyans in *The Snow Maiden*. But the Russian fairy-tale world of Prokofiev's childhood and Rimsky's scores, hinted at in the airborne Scherzo of the travellers in search of the oranges, is perhaps less open to parody or imitation than the suggestions of Wagner's Siegfried, who has to wrestle his treasure from Fafner-as-dragon – a tuba – just as the prince needs to steal his oranges from the kitchen of Creonta's castle. Apart from the tuba's tritonal threat to accompany the bass-in-drag cook – easily seduced by a flimsy ribbon – Prokofiev steers clear of Wagnerisms, even when the magician Chelio appears, like Wotan as Wanderer, before the prince and Truffaldino in their hour of need. Indeed, much of the quest music in the second half of the opera shows Prokofiev's concern to keep the orchestra lean and clear beneath the text at its sharpest.

Yet the score does have the supernatural power to make the flesh creep in a way that is entirely Prokofiev's own. He takes Gozzi's absurd rivals, Chelio and Fata Morgana, seriously, even if that seriousness never lasts long. They share a fateful triplet figure most strikingly and frequently heard on muted trombones. Their card game, faithfully adapted from Meyerhold's first intermezzo, is surrounded by frenetic chromatic patterns and the comic-grotesque whirlwind dances of little devils; but their set pieces, Fata Morgana's curse at the end of the second act and Chelio's invocation of Farfarello at the beginning of the third, are skilfully scored – mostly for strings divided in anything up to 15 parts – so that the dramatic soprano and the blustering bass seem to be dominating much larger orchestral forces than those that are actually used. The final passage with a touch of the infernal, the pursuit of Fata Morgana's minions (spared Gozzi's and Meyerhold's sentence of death by being delivered to their mistress) is purely orchestral – a canny mix of the Scythian mode with the spangled 'eccentric' idiom.

There are as few purely vocally based themes as there are recurrent leitmotifs in the opera (in this respect one wonders whether Prokofiev studied Verdi's *Falstaff* for the master's ability to sum up an idea or a character in a few bars). One fits both the Russian and French texts like a leitmotif as the Eccentrics announce their drama (Ex.37). In the work's subtlest music-theatre moment, it appears on three muted trumpets as the prince steals the oranges from under the nose of the distracted cook. The other theme provides pause for lyrical pathos as the desperate refrain of the princesses (Ex.38). In each case it is for the voice alone, though a soulful violin echoes it to greater intensity as Ninetta begs her prince for a drink. The scene for the young prince and princess inevitably becomes the lyrical highpoint of the score, from the moment Ninetta declares 'I have loved you all my life', a unison woodwind phrase heard only once in the opera (twice in the subsequent suite) and the essence of French

Ex.37 *The Love for Three Oranges*, op.33 – Prologue

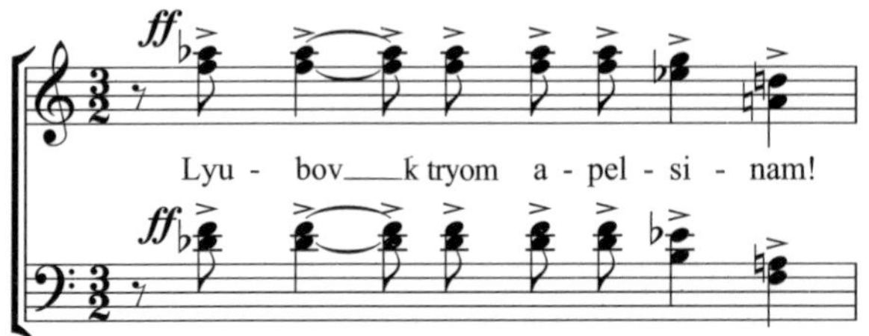

Ex.38 *The Love for Three Oranges* – Act III

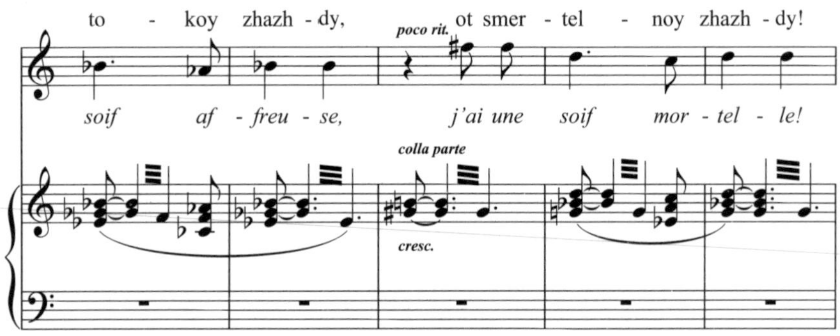

music, echoing the Debussy of *Pelléas et Mélisande* and the Ravel of *Daphnis et Chloé* and the song cycle *Shéhérazade*. Duly undercut here as the provenance of the swooning romantics, whom Prokofiev mockingly introduces as another faction, lyricism is restricted to the oboe theme of the bizarre Clarice and a curiously haunting, brief imitative lament for strings as the King and Pantalone chew over the miserable prince's predicament; curiously, it anticipates Natasha's anguish in *War and Peace* when her elopement with Anatol is curtailed. No single ingredient in the soufflé mixture is allowed to linger too long, not even the potent sourness of Fata Morgana's diablerie. Prokofiev might well have echoed Berlioz's remark that his comic opera *Béatrice et Bénédict* was a 'caprice written with the point of a needle'; its character can change, however, according to which of the two languages is used – the Russian text Prokofiev originally set, or the French translation for the premiere on which he collaborated with Vera Janacopulos, which inevitably lightens the mood.

With his part of the contract fulfilled, Prokofiev had only to wait and see his fantasy realized on the Chicago stage – as he had every reason, that autumn, to believe it would be. Campanini's sudden death in December 1920 and the theatre's cautious withdrawal of *The Love for Three Oranges* from that season's repertory came as another of those untimely blows which were to bedevil Prokofiev's operatic career. In the meantime he dashed off a commission from six compatriots newly arrived in America via the Far East; they were collectively known as the Zimro Ensemble and were touring the world under the auspices of the Russian Zionist Organization. Prokofiev later doubted the financial viability of their aims to fund a conservatory in Jerusalem when they hardly earned enough to feed themselves.[64] Their guiding light was the Moscow-trained clarinettist Simeon Bellison, appointed principal clarinettist of the Maryinsky Theatre in 1915 and soon to take up the same post in the New York Philharmonic Symphony Orchestra. The choice Prokofiev made from the 'notebook of Jewish themes'[65] they gave him has never been traced to any authentic sources; it seems most likely that Bellison composed them himself *in modo ebraico*. At any rate the first of the melodies in the resulting *Overture on Hebrew Themes*, which the clarinet emphatically declaims in D minor after an introductory C minor jaunt from strings and piano, unmistakably conjures the centuries-old *klezmer* tradition of Jewish community music with its alternation of low and high register and hairpin dynamics;[66] the second, introduced by the cello and echoed by the first violin, has romantic harmonies to suit its nostalgic song (Ex.39*a*).

Studying the score three years later, Prokofiev's old colleague Myaskovsky waxed lyrical about this second theme, to which Prokofiev dryly responded that 'from the musical point of view, the only worthwhile part, if you please, is the final section, and that, I think, is probably the result of my sweetness and diatonicism'.[67] He was referring in fact to the smoothing out of this theme in the coda (Ex.39*b*). Perhaps Prokofiev rated this passage more highly than the rest because it was his only real opportunity, as he saw it, to deal in his own fashion with alien material. He made

Ex.39a *Overture on Hebrew Themes*, op.34

Ex.39*a cont.*

it clear to Myaskovsky that he 'composed it in a day and a half',[68] carried out the instrumentation in just over a week and had not even wanted to give the work an opus number. In 1929 he confirmed his low opinion to Andrew Fraser, a Scots writer whose article he took the time to correct: Fraser described the Overture as 'a beautiful and pathetic work', to which he retorted 'its technique is conventional, its form is bad (4 + 4 + 4 + 4)'.[69] At least to Myaskovsky he praised the bold outlines of the piece – 'as if more than six musicians were playing'[70] – and its effect is undoubtedly more immediate in the original version, his first expansive piece of chamber music, than in the orchestration he made in 1934. The Zimro Ensemble gave a triumphant first performance in January 1920; the Soviet premiere took place in 1924, with the Beethoven Quartet providing the backbone of the instrumentalists, and the piece's subsequent fortunes varied according to the fluctuations of Russian anti-Semitism. Even in the 1970s, according to Yuly Turovsky, it could be performed only if the qualifying 'Hebrew' were left out of the title (as if any listener could have failed to guess the provenance of the themes); it is now a staple in the Russian chamber repertoire.

There is one interesting footnote to Prokofiev's temporary, reluctant and, at this stage in his career, unlikely flirtation with folk music. The following March the ethnomusicologist Alfred Swan sent him two Russian folk songs from the famous Istomin and Dyutch collection of 1886 and asked him to provide novel harmonies. He did, and Swan later reproduced one of them in his own study of the influences of the folk idiom on Russian music[71] (Ex.40). Prokofiev would have cause to return to these songs in connection with Lina's repertoire. Now, before carrying out the harmonization, he wrote a characteristically courteous letter to Swan telling him that he would perform the task 'as soon as I can tear myself away from the com-

Ex.39b *Overture on Hebrew Themes*

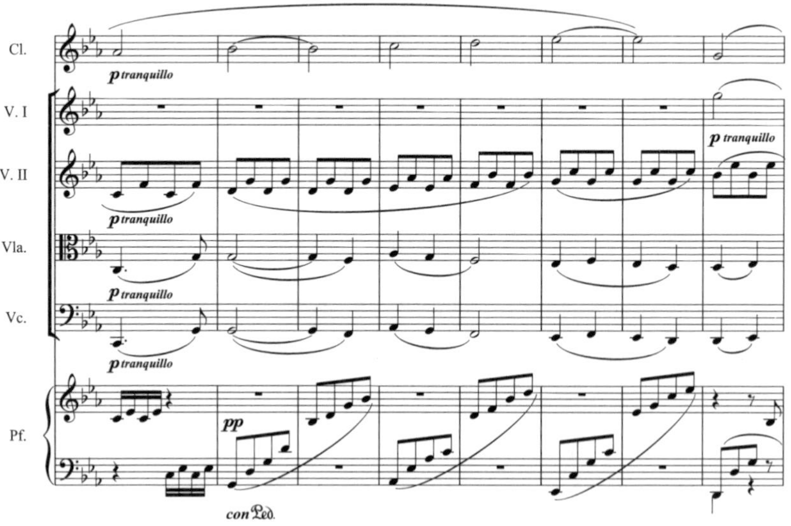

Ex.40 *White Snow*, folk song harmonized by Prokofiev

position of the opera'.[72] This, understandably, Swan took to be *The Love for Three Oranges*. But by then, with that score already lying dormant, Prokofiev was working on something completely different, with a heart of darkness far more real than the threat of the castle housing the three oranges.

8
Devil's work
1919–22

A creative demon of opposition seized hold of Prokofiev shortly after he learnt that the Chicago premiere of *The Love for Three Oranges* had been postponed. Its source was a curious novel by a Russian symbolist set in 16th-century Germany and, Prokofiev later told Nestyev, 'one of the few really artistic Russian books'[1] he had been able to lay his hands on in America (in the original language, of course; the first English translation did not appear until the end of the 1920s). He decided to turn it into an opera which he must have known at the time would be fit neither for American consumption nor for Diaghilev's short, sharp shock treament in Europe.

Ognenny angel ('The Fiery Angel') is a fascinating case of rich and ambiguous transmutation from life to fiction. Its author, Valery Bryusov, drew on his own unfortunate relationship with the kind of woman the leading lights of Russian fiction liked to project as part angel and part devil. Nina Petrovskaya, the literary muse, had lost her sexual hold on another charismatic literary figure, Andrey Bely, when she met Bryusov in 1904, precipitating a duel of verses between the two poets. In a dream, Bryusov was wounded by his opponent and reconciled to him; in reality, fisticuffs in a Moscow backstreet were pre-empted by a peacemaking mutual friend. Bryusov was still in the tormenting thrall of Nina when in 1907 he began to publish *The Fiery Angel* in his pioneering journal of the Russian symbolist movement *Vesy* ('The Scales').

With an erudition almost equal to that of his contemporary, Konstantin Balmont, Bryusov seems to have no trouble inhabiting the world of the 16th century, with its crucial conflicts between superstition and enlightenment, or in casting the novel as the memoirs of a self-taught individualist, Ruprecht, a *Landsknecht*, sailor and gold-digger steeped in the achievements of the Italian Renaissance. The novel's subtitle is faithful to the romance it seeks to emulate and gives a reasoned summary of the nightmare to come: 'a True Story in which is related of the Devil, not once but often appearing in the Image of a Spirit of Light to a Maiden and seducing her to Various and Many Sinful Deeds, of Ungodly Practices of Magic, Alchymy, Astrology, the Cabbalistical Sciences and Necromancy, of the Trial of the Said

Maiden under the Presidency of His Eminence the Archbishop of Trier, as well as of Encounters and Discourses with the Knight and thrice Doctor Agrippa of Nettesheim, and with Doctor Faustus, composed by an Eyewitness'.[2] The maiden is Renata, a woman of irregular features whose Cleopatra-like charm is a matter of mystery. Ruprecht first encounters her in the frighteningly distorted throes of one possessed; her obsession with the godlike, blond Count Heinrich (Bely's fictional-historical incarnation) equates him with her childhood vision of a fiery angel from heaven or from hell.

The picaresque flavour of the narrative was bound to pose problems even for the experienced librettist Prokofiev had already proved himself to be. Ruprecht's omniscient narration had to go – though his is the first theme in the opera – while incidents spread across various chapters were condensed into several scenes, starting with Renata's possession in the inn and an encounter with a fortune-teller which in the novel takes place the next day. Curiously for the composer of the half-comic, half-sinister 'diabolical intermezzo' in *The Love for Three Oranges*, the most stomach-churning episode in the book, the fourth chapter's vision of a witches' sabbath induced by an evil ointment Renata gives to Ruprecht, found no place in the opera. With the satanic orgy of Vasilenko's *Hircus nocturnus* so fresh in Prokofiev's memory from one of the New York concerts, and Musorgsky's *Night on the Bare Mountain* as well as his own *Suggestion diabolique* providing even better models, it is a surprising omission. It may account for the hair-raising orchestral thrash that serves as the interlude of the completed Act II, though its persistence throughout Ruprecht's questioning of the disingenuous necromancer Agrippa von Nettesheim (a real historical character) becomes one of the opera's most puzzling conjunctions. This scene, too, is a suggestive elision of Ruprecht's first meeting with Agrippa in the novel, a sobering experience which seems to chase away 'like a fresh wind the fog of the mysterious and miraculous'[3] in which Ruprecht has been wandering for three months, and their final encounter towards the end which reveals the dying Agrippa by lightning flash as the 'mysterious sorcerer'[4] of popular rumour.

The manuscript short score for *The Fiery Angel* has survived.[5] It reveals that Act I, starting as it was to end with Ruprecht's swagger and Renata's first fit, was begun on 20 January 1920 and completed on 17 March, and that the original Act II, which followed almost immediately, differed greatly from the final version. It was to have begun in Agrippa's house – the unforgettable first scene in which Renata and Ruprecht summon the spirits came much later – with a scene between Ruprecht and four students (roles that eventually disappeared). The score tails off into the barest of sketches for what was to become the second act's orchestral interlude.

There matters rested for nearly two years. Yet at least this, for the moment, was creativity. It gave Prokofiev new impetus at a time when his recital repertory had become very much what the New World impresarios wanted. It could have been worse: his programmes now included such gems as one of Bach's French Suites, Tchaikovsky's Grand Sonata and Schumann's *Carnaval* (sadly not among the piano rolls Prokofiev left to posterity). Of the Russian items, his Rakhmaninov and Skryabin pieces may have been familiar, but the numbers from Musorgsky's *Pictures at an Exhibition* were not as widely known then as we might think; not until 1923, through Ravel's dazzling orchestration for Koussevitzky, did the piano originals begin to achieve worldwide fame. Prokofiev the composer-pianist at his most abrasive was not to be unleashed outside New York, where the *Sarcasms* had so provoked the critics' scorn; nor could he expect to be treated with honour. Fitzhugh Haensel was a rare paragon of probity, and he gave his artist the good advice to ask for payment in advance – not always easy, as Prokofiev found on a tour to Canada to give concerts in Montreal and Quebec at the beginning of 1920. Before one of these events, when a huge hall was being filled with students for the princely sum of 25 cents a ticket,

> the manager came into the green room with a small suitcase and said: 'Students pay for their tickets in silver; I have to pay you, too, in silver'. He handed me 25 enormous silver dollars, then 100 50-cent pieces and 100 quarter-dollars. I filled all my pockets to the brim and immediately felt as if I had four hundredweight of silver on me. A sudden terrible idea occurred to me: 'What if when I reach the stage, my pockets give way at the seams and a heap of quarter-dollars spill on to the floor? The whole of America would make a laughing-stock of me!' 'I shall try to change the rest of the silver for you before the intermission', said the manager. But neither in the interval nor after the concert did I see him again, and so I returned to New York with only a third of my fee.[6]

Prokofiev's brief disillusionment with the New World attitude to musicians, later exaggerated for the Soviet short autobiography, was about to be brushed aside by reacquaintance with Diaghilev. Through his links with the dancer-choreographers Adolph Bolm and Mikhail Fokine in New York, and his constant efforts at correspondence with Diaghilev during and after the later war years, Prokofiev had done all he could to keep in touch with his best prospects for stage success. In December 1919 he had written Stravinsky a witty and detailed critique of *Pribaoutki*, the elliptical Russian 'song-games' Stravinsky had composed in 1914; they were given their American premiere by Vera Janacopulos, the distinguished soprano for whom it has recently transpired he made an orchestral transcription of Rimsky-Korsakov's *The Nightingale and the Rose* in late 1918.[7] Encouraged by his fellow pianists Benno Moiseiwitsch and Artur Rubinstein, Prokofiev set sail for Paris and London on 27 April, to be warmly greeted on his arrival by Stravinsky and Diaghilev.

He soon became acquainted with Stravinsky's latest offering for Diaghilev. Stravinsky later described his Neapolitan divertissement *Pulcinella*, a loving but highly individual treatment of music by Pergolesi and some of his early 18th-century contemporaries, as 'my discovery of the past, the epiphany through which the whole of my late work became possible'.[8] Prokofiev never claimed any such 'epiphany' for his own, earlier 18th-century pastiche. Proofreading Stravinsky's first number, he found the fact that 'the ballet is written in the old style . . . an amazing coincidence: three years ago I wrote a "Classical" Symphony and Stravinsky, who knew nothing about this, has written a classical ballet'.[9] Diaghilev and Stravinsky, however, must have heard of Prokofiev's Gozzi opera, with which *Pulcinella* has explicit *commedia dell'arte* connections.

Given its premiere in May 1920 at the Paris Opéra, *Pulcinella* would at the very least have signalled to Prokofiev that times had changed at the Ballets Russes. The tone was now more conspicuously international. The designer of *Pulcinella*, Pablo Picasso, had accompanied the clattering typewriters, sirens and pistol-shots of Satie's *Parade* in 1917 with Cubist costumes and a curtain that took the audience's breath away. He collaborated, too, on the company's first fully realized Spanish foray, Falla's *The Three-Cornered Hat*. Henri Matisse worked on the ballet drawn from Stravinsky's *The Nightingale*, while André Derain was the artist for *La Boutique fantasque*, one of Diaghilev's string of ballets with contemporary arrangements of music by earlier Italian composers.

The two Russian casualties of the early war years, Stravinsky's *Les Noces* and Prokofiev's *Chout*, were still on the agenda; and it was a mark of Diaghilev's intention to launch Prokofiev at long last with the Ballets Russes that, following discussions in London, *Chout* was set down for the forthcoming season of 1920–21. Diaghilev had also held on to Natalya Goncharova and Mikhail Larionov, the Russian artists whose colourful designs for the two ballets back in 1915 tell us how much progress had been made at that stage; Larionov's *Chout* was to remain much the same artistic conception, but the palette of Goncharova's original, rainbow-hued inspirations for *Les Noces* would be restricted to an austerity in keeping with Stravinsky's slimmed-down score.[10]

Prokofiev was to see a great deal of both artists in the summer of 1920. He also met again Walter Nouvel, his first link with Diaghilev, who had emigrated the previous year, and accompanied Diaghilev to the station to meet him when Nouvel finally arrived in London. But his real preoccupation was the well-being of another Russian whose escape from a beleaguered Russia was altogether less timely: his mother, one of countless refugees from the worsening situation. In the desperate, hungry aftermath of the First World War, the White Army had found itself pushed further and further south by Bolshevik forces whose ruthlessness had taken even sympathizers by surprise. At a London exhibition of scenes from Russia's pagan past by Nicholas Roerich, designer of *The Rite of Spring*, and the constructivist Georgy Yakulov, Prokofiev heard nightmare stories of starvation and death. He continued to have faith in the victorious regime; his liberal mother had thrown in her lot almost involuntarily with the Whites. From Kislovodsk she was propelled, like so many refugees, to Novorossisk in the Crimea and from there across the Black Sea to Constantinople, where for four months the 65-year-old Marya Grigoryevna found herself drinking soup from pails in a refugee camp on one of the Princes' Islands near the city (distinguished Russians suffering a similar fate included

Vladimir Dukelsky). Leaving London, where he had achieved the promising offer by Thomas Beecham to stage *The Love for Three Oranges* at Covent Garden, Prokofiev arrived in Marseilles that June to find his mother nearly blind and crammed into a cabin with 17 other passengers. The eye specialist he found for her, a Professor Polack, diagnosed glaucoma, and Prokofiev was able to be with his mother on the day of her operation.

The other important person in his life, Lina Codina, arrived in Paris from New York at his insistence shortly after the Prokofievs' journey from Marseilles; 'so in these three or four days, all the questions have been settled', he wrote exultantly in his diary, naming the 'questions' as 'Mama, Linette and Diaghilev'.[11] Lina's redoubtable singing teachers in Paris were Emma Calvé, a celebrated Carmen, and Félia Litvinne, whose Brünnhilde Prokofiev had enjoyed in St Petersburg performances of Wagner's *Ring*. He now arranged a summer idyll for all three of them in a three-storey stone house west of Paris, at Mantes-sur-Seine. Marya Grigoryevna had her own room as far as possible from her son and, according to Lina, her imposing personality more than once earned the threatening retort 'stop asking questions or I won't tell you anything at all and I'll put you in a *pension*'.[12] Lina was now very much part of the family as she took the dowdily dressed Madame Prokofieva on shopping expeditions, began to teach her English and generally 'did more for her than I would have done for my own mother'.[13] She was there when Larionov and Goncharova came to sketch and paint Diaghilev's brightest new light. 'Serge would stick his leg high up in the air, and his mother would walk into the room and declare, "You can't be drawn in such a position. This will remain for posterity, and what will they think of you?"'[14] 'Well, let them look at my backside',[15] came the answer as the impudent son lifted his leg still higher, driving his outraged mother out of the room. In fact, the surviving Larionov drawing from this time and a portrait by Goncharova, which has not been precisely dated and has only recently come to light in a revelatory Moscow exhibition of the two artists,[16] show an eminently respectable, well-dressed and serious young man.

Prokofiev was now hard at work on the changes to *Chout.* Diaghilev had kept his original short score safe and neatly bound; the manuscript is helpfully peppered with the suggestions (and the new figure numbers) of 1920.[17] The essential changes were to make *Chout* 'a more unified symphonic work' with freer opportunities for choreography. Most of the original substance remains, with all the melodies and the gist of their accompaniments dating from 1915 except for the Dance of the Buffoons' Wives in scene 2, the sequel for the Buffoons' Daughters in scene 4 and the second melody of the finale, which retains the solo violin theme with a much more consonant accompaniment and builds to an orgy of scintillating exhilaration. All this, apparently, was to meet Diaghilev's objection that so much was in the minor key. Most of the cuts dispense with excess mime and narrative – the raising of the dead, both times, is altogether more concise – and in several cases are replaced by passages that allow themes and dances to be extended in set-piece fashion (the departure of the merchant from the seven Buffoons' house, for example, and the martial frenzy of the seven soldiers in the final scene).

Prokofiev's other alterations were more of a concession to Diaghilev, who wanted extended orchestral interludes to allow for scene changes. The last, between the fifth and final scenes, is a little masterpiece of elegiac lyricism, taking sincerely for once the grief of the merchant over his dead goat-wife; the others are merely padding – lengthy, more or less direct reprises of ideas already developed in the scenes themselves. With the exception of the ritual repetition of the opening whistles, Prokofiev did not in these instances make a virtue out of necessity, as Debussy so strikingly had in *Pelléas et Mélisande.* The interludes may explain why the full score remained unpublished until 1978 and was only then championed complete in the concert hall by Rozhdestvensky. Cutting them from a performance of the entire ballet score is surely the solution and sidesteps the awkward question of what to do with the 1922 suite, which is far too long for all its numbers to be heard.[18]

Chout nearly met another fate on the boat back to New York that October. 'A suitcase was stolen from my cabin', Prokofiev wrote to his mother, 'and in it were a red-brown suit, a smoking jacket, silk pyjamas, a pair of boots, a shirt and some of Larionov's sketches. It's just as well the other suitcase which was standing nearby wasn't stolen – that contained all the manuscripts for the ballet and *The Love for Three Oranges.*'[19] That would have been a blow at a time when his Russian scores were undergoing various fortunes; Marya Grigoryevna had managed with difficulty to bring sketches and scores including *Semero ikh* and the Violin Concerto, but in Mantes they had learnt that their Petrograd home had been plundered and papers destroyed.

On board the liner *Savoie,* Prokofiev continued in his letter to his mother, was one of the répétiteurs from Chicago, who throughout the summer had been playing through the score of *The Love for Three Oranges* to the conductor Gino Marinuzzi and now went round singing the melody of its March. It must have seemed like a pleasing premonition of the opera's success, but that was not as close as Prokofiev imagined. With characteristic stubbornness he demanded compensation from the director of the Chicago Opera for a year's delay in the staging of the opera; the result was its withdrawal from the current season. The collapse of Beecham's finances led to the Covent Garden production also falling through. It is untrue to claim, as did Nestyev, that Prokofiev was 'obliged to begin an extensive tour as pianist'[20] to fill the Chicago gap; he had already negotiated a visit to California with Jessica Colbert in May, and the original autumn dates had simply been moved to the end of the year. It was not, in any case, a treadmill; this second half of his American visit, in contrast to the 'very unpleasant' first half, turned out to be 'completely sunny'.[21] He made a quick visit to Mexico, sending a postcard to Stravinsky from Tijuana, before his engagements began.

Prokofiev's first concert, in San Diego on 22 December, opened serenely with Beethoven's A major Sonata op.101 and proceeded with what the programme described simply as a selection of Schubert waltzes. The arrangement of this suite, in fact, was Prokofiev's own, prepared in Europe at Stravinsky's instigation, along with an even more sober transcription of Buxtehude's Organ Prelude and Fugue in D minor – a delightfully chaste alternative to Bach with a last-minute benediction in D major. His introduction to Buxtehude with the A minor Fugue in his conservatory days had not been forgotten. As for the Schubert, one wonders how many of his dashed-off sequences Prokofiev sifted before alighting on his choice, a pretty rainbow of the capricious, the precipitous and the melancholy connected by a rondo of rustic robustness.

The Californian repertory, which continued with Russian miniatures, the lightest of Prokofiev's op.12 numbers and the Gavotte from op.32 followed by encores which included a Beethoven country dance, offered nothing that would be 'incomprehensible from an American viewpoint',[22] as one paper had lamented in the spring of 1919, and was a conscious contrast to the last New York recital which had included the *Sarcasms* and the Toccata. 'I had to do such a programme for California', Prokofiev later wrote to the polymath Pyotr Souvchinsky, a friend who had recently arrived in the West from Russia.[23] It was also a chance to confound stereotypes of steel-fisted 'Bolshevist' playing. 'Contrary to our expectations, Serge Prokofieff did not exhibit those eccentric and bizarre traits which we had fortified ourselves against', wrote the *Pacific Coast Musical Review*, adding that the Beethoven was 'repressed', the Schubert all Chopinesque poetic calm and sentiment, and the rest subdued.[24] 'If the highest art is simplicity', declared the *San Diego Union*, 'Prokofiev can be said to embody the simplicity of art.'[25]

Moving on to Los Angeles, where he spent Christmas with the promoter of his appearances there, he found himself pleasingly under siege by Californian women. It was a novelty, he told the *Los Angeles Evening Express*, to experience this time of year in a land where 'the sun shines like June and the flowers bloom as in April'.[26] He was profoundly impressed with the Tournament of Roses, contrasting it more or less emotionally with 'the majestic iciness and cold of Petrograd on New Year's Day'.[27] This pleasant tour full of 'marvellous weather and smiling people'[28] also saw the completion of a small-scale creative project with the last of the five *Songs without Words* op.35, dated '28 Dec 1920, Los Angeles'.[29] Their recipient, Nina Koshetz, had more to thank Prokofiev for than just these perfumed repertory gems. He might not have succumbed to her entreaties of love back in Russia, and he hardly intended to do so now that Lina was on the scene, but he did help her leave their beleaguered homeland via his mother's route, Constantinople, and arranged for Fitzhugh Haensel to be her agent.

Koshetz was not the easiest of colleagues – 'she vacillates in America between great success and small misfortunes, eternally penniless, full of indignation and generally choking on the sea of temperament', Prokofiev confided to Souvchinsky the following March[30] – and her 'usual hysterics'[31] suggest a remarkable kinship with the heroine of *The Fiery Angel*. Yet she was certainly one of the great sopranos of her time, as her 1922 recording of Tchaikovsky's *None but the lonely heart* demonstrates. Her sense of rubato may have been acquired from her one-time lover Rakhmaninov (who composed his op.38 songs for her), but it could have been instinctive; it is immediately evident from the 78-rpm recording, along with long-breathed phrasing and secure tone, and these are the qualities Prokofiev exploited in the *Songs without Words.* A soprano without the ability to shape the lines exactly as Prokofiev writes them – and that includes most recent contenders – does best to leave these rarefied creations to the violin-solo version Prokofiev made in 1924. The pitching and the irregularity of the melodies, which etch themselves in the mind after a second or a third hearing, are far from easy to negotiate, though the shapes become easier and more identifiably the composer's own in the last two songs as he moves from fugitive visions to the dance-like clarity of his more elegant earlier piano pieces.

Even so, there are unifying features. The piano takes over the wayward melody of the first song on its return, leaving the voice to provide an expressive counterpoint; this happens again in a becalmed return of the third song's passionate undulations and, crucially, after the climax to the fifth song – the biggest moment for pianist and soprano (reflecting the dramatic strength of Koshetz's upper register). All but the playfully brief no.4 have a contrasting central idea, though this takes up the greater part of the first song, where the legato vocal line finds silken cords to throw round the piano's far-flung major and minor triads. Perhaps the most exquisite of the five is no.2 – not so much for its quaintly oriental central theme in C sharp minor as for the main melody's sudden veering from Prokofiev's most limpid A minor/C major diatonicism towards B major, from which it deftly extracts itself via an equally unexpected excursion into C sharp minor (Ex.41).

Koshetz gave the premiere of one of the songs in her New York recital on 27 March 1921, when it went by the tantalizing title 'Berceuse hébraïque'; this must have been the second song, which was also orchestrated towards the end of 1920. Her benefactor was not there to accompany her, as has often been claimed;[32] he had already gone back to Europe with a spring in his step, delighted at the unexpected news that his enemy at the Chicago Opera had 'gone to blazes'[33] and been replaced by the Scottish soprano Mary Garden, Debussy's first Mélisande as well as Strauss's first Paris Salome and a great enthusiast for contemporary opera. She undertook to stage *The Love for Three Oranges* at the end of the year, offering 'a new contract and such excellent conditions for work that I could wish for nothing better – as many rehearsals as I want and all under my observation'.[34] The greatest honour of all – the request that he conduct his own premiere – was to come later in the year. As he sailed for France in March 1921, Prokofiev was apparently unaware that Diaghilev's abrupt dismissal of Léonide Massine from the company – along lines similar to the Nijinsky crisis, and for the same reason (the threat of feminine rivalry) – still jeopardized the new ballet; only by the time of his arrival was *Chout* scheduled for Paris later that spring. Diaghilev put Larionov in charge of the production, and the relatively inexperienced dancer Taddeus Slavinsky to choreograph his ideas, before travelling to Madrid.

Ex.41 *Songs without Words*, op.35 – II. Lento, ma non troppo

Rehearsals took place in Monte-Carlo, which Prokofiev found 'rather boring and at first glance . . . merely a collection of hotels clustered around the casino and the theatre. The sea is a dark blue, like nowhere else, the mountains enchanting, the climate a delight, but nobody's interested in any of that. We, i.e. the company, are up to our necks in the ballet'.[35] Prokofiev was sketched by Matisse for the new programme booklet, and Goncharova supervised the execution of the decor and costumes in Paris. Larionov had sacrificed nothing of the Russian folk-inspired floral patterns he had used in his original designs; adding a degree of Cubist fantasy to the heavy and elaborate costumes and inventing afresh a drop-cloth which hurled together French and Russian motifs in vibrant shades of red and orange with cheerful disregard for the ballet's subject, he nevertheless caught to perfection the music's brilliant colours.

The problem, as everyone was to agree, was the 'disconnected'[36] choreography. No doubt a greater creative spirit than Slavinsky would have found a way to turn the quaintly cumbersome costumes to inventive use; but there was only infirmity of purpose, and Diaghilev knew it the minute he set foot in Monte-Carlo. 'We must think of other new things. *Chout* won't be enough by itself', he told his régisseur Sergey Grigoriev;[37] the answer was the flamenco dance troupe he had discovered in Madrid. The Ballets Russes had already flirted with Spanish zest, but had never gone for the real thing in the shape of authentically raucous singers and flamboyant folk dancers; both London and Paris were in the mood for genuine Iberiana. So *Chout* had the misfortune to be overshadowed by *Cuadro flamenco*, designed by Picasso, on the first night of the one-week Paris season, held in the unglamorously situated Gaîté-Lyrique, and to slip into the London repertory on 9 June, two weeks after the launch event at the Prince's Theatre. The Paris opening night was a four-course Diaghilev banquet of old and new, with the two new events spotlit between *The Firebird* and the Polovtsian Dances. Comparisons between Prokofiev and the creator of Diaghilev's first truly Russian commissioned score were inevitable. *L'Avenir* understood that the 'big, pale, blond young man' could be mentioned in the same breath as Stravinsky, adding cuttingly 'It seems as if he's his pupil'.[38]

Prokofiev conducted his ballet on both occasions, an honour in the light of the young Swiss *maestro* Ernest Ansermet's excellent work with the company. It was not his Paris debut as composer; Koussevitzky, newly established in Paris, had pipped Diaghilev to the post with a concert in the Salle Gaveau two weeks earlier, on 29 April, when a performance of Prokofiev's *Scythian Suite* 'ignited enthusiasm and also anger'.[39] Louis Schneider, noting that exciting premiere, was reporting on a rehearsal for *Chout*, and he was Prokofiev's warmest advocate so far: 'As soon as the musicians are seated at their desks, M. Prokofiev appears on the scene like an elemental force', he enthused. 'He moulds them, explains his idea and his aesthetic, and they work with joy, for the musicians recognize a master.' As for the score, 'Prokofiev has written music which calls to us directly and in concrete form: it is the sonic embodiment of the action. Above all it is clear, it is music in perfect health; it never drowns in affected details; it is, above all, extremely danceable . . . Tuesday will be a date to remember in the history of Russian music'.[40]

That it was not quite the success Schneider had expected could be blamed roundly on the choreography. But the French critics, having to deal with so much more than the music, were fair to both Prokofiev and Larionov. The same could hardly be said of their British counterparts. '114 reviews have been written, but out of them 113 were abusive',[41] Prokofiev was to reflect; though as he pointed out elsewhere they could do 'little harm to the production, and it was given over a dozen times, always with a sold-out house'.[42] The general tone, it is true, was far from friendly and shot through with that peculiar English parochialism. *The Musical Times*, wishing instead for 'a new ballet composed by an Englishman', began with the none-too-witty dictum 'Don't "Chout"' and decided that 'the whole thing is best looked on as a joke'[43] while the *Morning Post* was even more dismissive, describing 'this season's novelty' as 'no more than brisk stupidity, something to be wiped up without a word said'.[44] *Musical Opinion* generously granted that Prokofiev was at least a musician, but that 'in striving at the heights of the fantastic he too often shows how ugly a really good orchestra can be made to sound'.[45]

The one review Prokofiev regarded as unabusive must have been that of the eulogistic 'Arkay' in the *Tatler*, who decided that the 'most amusing' story could stand as a farce – only then 'we should not have Serge Prokofieff's attractive and quaintly appropriate music'.[46] Most balanced was *The Times*, which reflected the best of the French reviews in deciding that 'in spite of the brilliant Cubist scenery and dresses with which M. Larionov has provided it and the equally brilliant and equally Cubist music of M. Prokofiev, [*Chout*] had the effect of a loosely improvised charade, for lack of any consistent design in the choreography'.[47]

Prokofiev was perhaps unaware of how favourably this same paper had looked on the most important British premieres of his works before *Chout*. In November, some months after an unhelpfully lacklustre Proms performance of the First Piano Concerto by Ellen M. Jensen, conducted by Henry Wood, the irrepressible Albert Coates was back in England at the helm of the London Symphony Orchestra, opening its Queen's Hall season with a sell-out event offering, in the *Times* critic's words, 'a great programme, a very great soloist [Alfred Cortot in Rakhmaninov's Third Piano Concerto], as fine orchestral playing as it is possible to obtain, and conducting of the very highest order'.[48] Elgar's *Cockaigne* Overture and Schubert's 'Unfinished' Symphony were also given, but the critic had no doubt that 'what mattered' were Cortot's playing and Prokofiev's *Scythian Suite*, to which he devoted the bulk of his review. Comparing it to Schoenberg's Five Orchestral Pieces, if only to point out its greater 'definiteness', the review ended with a broadside aimed at the musical conservatives:

> Naturally enough the so-called cacophony, which is another way of saying the modern or rather Prokofiev system of harmony, is not likely to be to the taste of everyone until we have had many more opportunities of growing accustomed to it . . . But under Coates it seemed simple enough even in its most rigorous form, while often when Coates obtained his characteristic *ppp* effects, there was an ethereal atmosphere that was exquisite.[49]

Now, seven months later, London was treated to the latest ballet score which stood, so Schneider thought, in the same relation to the *Scythian Suite* as Musorgsky did to Glinka. It also heard a surprising missing link, the *Classical* Symphony, which Prokofiev conducted several times during the season as one of Diaghilev's newly enterprising concert *entr'actes* (the list makes fascinating reading, ranging from plums by Rimsky-Korsakov and Musorgsky to novelties by Bax, Poulenc, Auric and Satie). *Chout*, as the *Tatler* pointed out, was the 'novelty of the season';[50] but Diaghilev had been banking on Stravinsky's *Renard* to be the real sensation – promising as much in an interview with the *Observer* in which he pointed out that 'the only resemblance between Prokofieff and Stravinsky is that both are Russian, and both are living in the same century!'[51] But *Renard* did not materialize as one of the *entr'actes* any more than the promised Symphonies of Wind Instruments – entrusted instead, and disastrously, to the rival Koussevitzky – which gives a good idea of how improvisatory Diaghilev's programmes so often were.

London would have to wait nearly a year for the next major Prokofiev work, the Third Piano Concerto, begun after the London season when the composer retreated to the west coast of France. In March he had established his base at the Villa des Cytises, St Brévin-les-Pins, 'a spacious house amidst pines and cypresses right on the Atlantic coast, at the point where the Loire meets the sea',[52] installing his dependent mother there before he left for London and Paris. Boris Bashkirov, whose New York-based brother had been such a tower of strength to Prokofiev when he arrived in America and who with his American wife had welcomed him to their influential salon, had finally followed the rest of his family and left Russia for the West. He arrived in Paris on the eve of *Chout* and joined Prokofiev in St Brévin. There he slept late, as usual, while his old friend worked in the morning and joined him for afternoon chess games before a swim off the beach of Les Rochelets. The routine continued more or less as before with the arrival of Lina, who soon grasped the dynamics of the friendship between generous Sergey and the 'chivalrous, good for nothing loafer' Bashkirov.[53] There was one disruption, Prokofiev wrote to an influential Chicago friend, the music-loving insurance agent Ephraim Gottlieb, in painstaking English: 'my quiet work was disturbed by a cycle accident and I had to stay several days in bed, my face being like Carpantier's [*sic*] after the fight ['Gorgeous Georges' Carpentier was in the middle of his three-year run as world light-heavyweight boxing champion]. A tooth is broken and a lip sewn, but now I feel better'.[54] His relationship with wheels, two soon to be followed by four, was not to be a happy one.

An altogether more distinguished poet than the dilettante Bashkirov, the 54-year-old Konstantin Balmont, happened to be staying in one of the few nearby houses with his wife, whom Lina summed up as 'tormented, skinny, chain-smoking',[55] both of them already consumed with longing for the homeland they had recently left. Like many of his compatriots, Balmont had 'arrived [in France] with a clever mind and an empty pocket, and stayed that way',[56] as Prokofiev wrote to another struggling friend, Souvchinsky, from St Brévin. When he returned to America he would do his best to raise funds for Balmont. Now he had the chance to know better the venerable elder whose verses he had set in his two choruses, three of his songs and *Semero ikh*. They went swimming together, and Lina joined in appreciation of this well-travelled polymath's amusing conversation. Almost as a diversion from the hard labour of the concerto, and owing Lina a set of songs to calm her suspicions about Koshetz, muse of the *Songs without Words*, Prokofiev now set five Balmont poems, several of them newly minted, for voice and piano, which became op.36.

Since Balmont soon 'turned his pen against his "suffering homeland" (as he expressed it)',[57] as Prokofiev was under some pressure to write in his short autobiography, his Soviet biographer is obliged to describe the five songs as 'gloomy and despondent in mood' and criticizes Prokofiev for using 'elements of the over-refined chromatic style of French impressionism'.[58] In fact the verse is simple and direct, far from the decadence with which Balmont was unfairly branded, and the music's 'French' harmonies are selectively engaged within clean, uncluttered textures, usually with a firm rhythmic background and sense of forward movement. Only the last song, *Stolby* ('The Pillars'), an echo of the dark, accursed world of *Semero ikh* with a heavy, stalking bass line, offers any sustained gloom. The airy nature that intrudes on this oppressive seashore scene is the subject of the second and third songs, with their crystalline, treble-light accompaniment. The mysteries of the first and fourth songs are hauntingly suggested by the verbal refrain, musically varied, of 'tread softly' in *Zaklinaniye vody i ognya* ('An Incantation of Fire and Water') and the ostinato figure first stated in a single right-hand line at the beginning of *Pomni menya* ('Remember Me: A Malayan Incantation'). The varied harmonies that appear beneath it throughout the song look forward to such great moments as Lyubka's ostinato lament in *Semyon Kotko*, and the veering away from a diatonic C major early on mirrors the same device in the second of the *Songs without Words* (Ex.42).

None of these poems, from the chattery folklore of *Golos ptits* ('Birdsong') to the ritual repetition of *Remember Me*, could have meant more to Prokofiev than Balmont's homage to a special preview of the Third Piano Concerto: echoing Pasternak's poetic response to the inspiring creative work of Skryabin when they were once neighbours in the Russian countryside, Balmont composed a sonnet:

Exultant leaping flame of crimson flower
A keyboard of words plays with sparkling fires
That suddenly dart out with flaming tongues.
A river leaping forth of molten ore.
The moments dance a waltz, ages gavotte,
Suddenly a wild bull, ensnared by foes,
Has burst his chains and stands with threatening horns
But tender sounds again call from afar

Ex.42 *Remember Me: A Malayan Incantation*, op.36 no.4

And children fashion castles from small shells,
An opal balcony, subtle and fair.
Then, gushing fierce, a flood dispels it all.
Prokofiev! Music and youth in bloom,
In you the orchestra craves bright summer
And mighty Scythian strikes the sun's great drum.[59]

Balmont's kaleidoscopic images constitute a just poetic response to the work's compendium of styles. The First Piano Concerto may have toyed daringly with rapid changes of mood, but there a capricious Robin Goodfellow was in control; here a master virtuoso wields his material to show his Western audiences every facet of his performing personality. No work of Prokofiev, at least as far as he was willing to reveal, draws so widely on past sketches. One idea, he tells us, dates back to 1911, the year of the First Concerto, when he also planned a larger-scale work – a passage with 'parallel triads running from the bottom of the register upwards' which he now 'inserted at the end of the first movement':[60] this can only be the brilliant, toccata-like semiquaver charge which is first heard on the strings just after the introduction but, on its two other appearances, reverts to where it belongs – on the piano. The theme of the second movement dates from 1913: this is Balmont's 'gavotte of ages' with its piquant harmonies reminiscent of so many of the early piano dances.

Towards the end of Prokofiev's first Russian years he had thought more seriously about his next concerto; the first two themes were born on home ground, along with the stalking 3/4 which begins the finale and its lopsided waltz sequel. But these last two were originally intended for the second and last movement of the 'white-note quartet' he had resumed on the voyage to America. Only now, in 1921, did he give up this potentially monotonous subject: the opening idea would find a home as the agent of cloistered calm of the fifth act of *The Fiery Angel*, while its even more memorable lyric successor became the leitmotif of the opera's heroine. Its peculiar quality, like several of its more wayward relatives in *Chout*, was to be embedded in dense and dissonant textures that would preserve the ambiguity of Renata (Ex.43*a*), victim or manipulator; but on its own, the contours of its melody link it with the equally diatonic opening of the concerto (Ex.43*b*).

At the opposite end of the spectrum are the new inventions of 1921. One is the wayward monster that dances in the dark after the pastoral sunshine of the opening; the other is the central section of the finale, a keening C sharp rhapsody worthy of Rakhmaninov – 'doesn't this give the impression of a man with a fat belly and short arms and legs?' Myaskovsky was to ask[61] – and undercut by the piano alone as it vacillates on whether to succumb. Inevitably this seems the most synthetic of the three movements. The central variations have a compelling logic, progressively extracting the theme's demonic aspect before the atmospheric night-picture of the fourth variation, which in turn yields to the Scythian cavalcade of the fifth. And the first movement, while substituting another moody study on the opening theme for any

Ex.43*a* *The Fiery Angel*, op.37 – Act V

Ex.43*b* Piano Concerto no.3, op.26 – I. Andante

substantial development, shows at its most brilliant Prokofiev's avoidance of straightforward recapitulation: the apogee of the grotesque dance theme is a virtual development in itself.

All this flashes past in racy performances like Prokofiev's own, recorded a little too hastily with Piero Coppola and the London Symphony Orchestra in 1932, and those of pianists who follow most closely in his footsteps, like William Kapell and Martha Argerich; in a less than scintillating interpretation, the joins begin to show. The scoring is often simple but cleanly effective – strings *divisi* and muted in moderation, telling woodwind solos, interesting filigree piano writing – while the solo role encompasses every effect Prokofiev had learnt to muster. 'No-one apart from you will be able to play it',[62] noted Myaskovsky, when relations were resumed in

1923, observing especially the iron fingers needed for the later stages of the finale; and this obstacle was to give Prokofiev a great deal of extra work in the days leading up to the Chicago premiere.

Before that there was orchestration to complete, proofs to read and *The Love for Three Oranges* to learn as conductor, a task that Mary Garden sprang on him in late August before they both travelled back to America on the *Aquitania*. 'I didn't reckon with this', he told Natalya Koussevitzky, 'and wrote something frightfully difficult; now I'm lamenting the fact several times over.'[63] But not so much as to make him forgo a drive north from St Brévin to Mont St Michel with Lina and Vera Janacopulos, or to be prevented from enjoying a chess tournament on board the *Aquitania* in October. Despite plans to obtain an American visa for his mother (in which McCormick again came to the fore), she remained in Paris for the winter. Other ties were drawn more closely. He would soon meet Bashkirov again, and he had a good colleague in Gottlieb, acting as his unofficial Chicago representative now that his agent seemed to be inactive – a fault he was not slow to point out. 'I note with pleasure that the composer of *Sarcasms* is still on the job',[64] parried Haensel to one of Prokofiev's many sharp, reproachful letters. But his composer had good reason to be upset; only a Pittsburgh engagement, squeezed in before his Chicago duties, resulted from the Haensel & Jones arrangement, and matters were to deteriorate over the next year.

He found time to joke with Haensel, though, writing to him in spirited English from one of the 18 Chicago rehearsals Mary Garden had granted him for *The Love for Three Oranges*: 'showing to the artists how to sing my opera I am singing to myself a great deal the soprano parts too. So that after the failure of the *Oranges* I have good chance to be engaged in the chorus, as a soprano, indeed'.[65] Haensel was ready with a more naturally idiomatic turn of phrase: 'I note that you are singing now, but sincerely trust that the opera may be a great success in order that I may be spared the ordeal of ever hearing you sing'.[66] (By all accounts, not least one concerning his disastrous vocal attempt to preview his *Cantata for the 20th Anniversary of the October Revolution* before a stern committee in 1936, that was an ordeal indeed.)

During the early rehearsals, Prokofiev was confident that the production was in good enough hands – 'it lacks only a Meyerhold',[67] he told Souvchinsky – but disagreements with the 'uninteresting'[68] director Jacques Coini culminated in a spat. '"Properly speaking, which of us is in charge of the staging, you or I?" he asked. I replied: "You are – for the purpose of carrying out my wishes".'[69] Excitement over the promised spectacle ran high. The *Chicago Examiner*, claiming that 200–300 rehearsals would precede the performances, expected 'a stunt that will make Florenz Ziegfeld sick with envy'. (It also missed the point about the monster-oranges in the desert revealing the thirsty princesses, fretting over whether 'three small enough young ladies of the chorus can be found'.)[70] That master of well-scripted wit Ben Hecht was at the dress rehearsal to observe Coini making a spectacle of himself: 'M.

Coini is the greatest opera I have ever seen', he quipped. 'All he needed was M. Prokofiev's music and the superbly childish visions of the medieval Boris [Anisfeld] for a background.'[71] For Hecht, a cosmopolitan observer among provincials, the music was anything but incidental, and it would have done Prokofiev good to have read his supportive words:

> Music like this has never come from the orchestra pit of the Auditorium. Strange combinations of sounds that seem to come from street pianos, New Year's eve horns, harmonicas and old-fashioned musical beer-steins that play when you lift them up. Mr. Prokofiev waves his shirt-sleeved arms and the sounds increase.
>
> There is nothing difficult about this music – that is, unless you are unfortunate enough to be a music critic.[72]

Which Hecht, of course, was not. He ended: 'I would rather see and listen to his opera than to the entire repertoire of the company put together. This is not criticism, but a prejudice in favour of fantastic lollypops'.[73]

The designs of 'medieval Boris', who had taken his inspiration directly from the music, stole the show for rather too many critics when the first of the two Chicago performances opened on 30 December. Duly noting Prokofiev's key role in devising the libretto (translated into French with Vera Janacopulos's help), as well as rehearsing and conducting, Edward Moore of the *Chicago Daily Tribune* went on to enlarge on Anisfeld's designs. 'Never was paint applied to scene cloth any more lavishly or gorgeously. All the "Follies" and "Kismets" and "Chu-Chin-Chows" and "Meccas" rolled into one would hardly equal what you may see in the two hours and thirty-five minutes of this performance.'[74] Unfortunately Moore was a less discriminating and enlightening guide to the music, detecting only 'the beginnings of two tunes' (the March and 'a wee bit of a male chorus sung just before the final scene' – presumably the Eccentrics' jaunty luring of Fata Morgana, which a better student of the score might have detected earlier in the opera).[75]

The quibbles of a provincial press turned into donkey-brays and wolf-pack yelps when the Chicago production, after postponements through sickness in the cast, finally opened in the Manhattan Theatre, New York, on 14 February 1922. One paper generously worked out that the hugely expensive production cost roughly $43,000 per orange. The ubiquitous Aldrich in the *New York Times* trumped Moore's philistine bewilderment over the music. He, too, looked set to commend what he called 'a wild phantasmagoria of sight and sound and sense' before twisting his knife in the 'disagreeable noise' of the music, in which, he granted, 'there are a few, but only a very few, passages that bear recognisable kinship with what has hitherto been recognized as music'.[76] Aldrich gave no credit, or mention, to Prokofiev for conducting the score straight after an afternoon's piano recital at the Aeolian Hall which included his recent transcription of the opera's March and Scherzo; the *Musical Courier*, though, noted that Prokofiev the conductor 'seemed to have difficulty looking away from his own score'.[77] This is one of the few reviews to give us any details about an activity that Prokofiev now dropped as quickly as he had started; he was not to take up the baton again for many years. At least the same journal hit on a truth with which Prokofiev's operatic ideals would probably have concurred: that the music 'seemed provided more to underscore the action and the humour than for its own sake'.[78]

A typical charge levelled against the use of the voice throughout the opera as a 'tangential instrument'[79] was to have an interesting sequel. In a strange correspondence with Prokofiev after his departure from America, Deborah Beirne of the National Irish Theatre Company in New York negotiated for a revised performing version of the opera to include 'a very beautiful and very sensuous ballet'[80] as a dream of the sleeping prince in Act III, an aria for Fata Morgana, a love duet for the prince and princess in Act III and an extended general ensemble: all the trappings, in short, of conventional opera. It looked as if the romantic spectators were to get their way. But Prokofiev drew the line at Fata Morgana's aria in a concise critique of his operatic approach. 'Fata is an angry, turbulent witch. How can she sing a lyric aria?! Other [*sic*] aria than a declamatory one won't fit for this character, but such an aria cannot aim the hearts [*sic*] of the crowd . . . I will compose it should you insist, but my scenic feeling is strongly against.'[81] The contract appears to have been signed in April 1922, with Boris Bashkirov as witness, but no more has been heard of this strange hybrid fruit.

Prokofiev, too, was angry and turbulent, not inclined to burst into lyric gratitude for the reception of his latest works in America. *The Love for Three Oranges* played to full houses of distinguished personages – the *Chicago Daily Tribune* devoted a column half the length of its review to listing the cream of Chicago society present at the premiere – but it could not compete with Chaliapin's overwhelming success as Boris Godunov at the Metropolitan Opera, which Prokofiev duly learnt about from the Chicago papers. The world premiere of his Third Piano Concerto in a Chicago Symphony concert conducted by Stock on 16 December was overshadowed by the visit of Richard Strauss to take charge of the orchestra; and New York did not take it to its heart the following January when the loyal Albert Coates featured the composer-pianist in a New York Symphony programme.

'I had to look the truth in the eyes', writes the autobiographer, this time not exaggerating his American failure for the benefit of his Soviet readership: 'the American season, which had begun so brilliantly, had brought me a nil result. I still had one last hope that Mary Garden would put on *The Fiery Angel* the following season and assign to herself the leading role' – she could probably have managed it, as she was still singing Salome in Chicago – 'but Garden retired from her post. I had a thousand dollars in my pocket, but also an aching head from all the fuss and the desire to go off to work in some quiet place'.[82] That quiet place was to be in Germany, high in the Bavarian alps, close to the country home of the great

German composer whose appearances had dwarfed him in Chicago and somewhat further from the cosmopolitan Mecca of Berlin. There an artistic Russian émigré community was rapidly burgeoning. Its direct lines of communication to the new Soviet Union were to encourage Prokofiev in picking up old ties as his spiritual heart-strings were pulled a little tighter to his homeland.

9
Passion play
1922–3

In July 1922, well installed in his Bavarian mountain retreat, Prokofiev wrote to his old chess-champion friend José Capablanca, with whom he had recently played several fiercely contested games in New York, recommending the 'low cost of living for those who have dollars'.[1] This was the most pragmatic reason for his retreat far east of Paris and its playground of musical opportunity. He had left America in debt to Haensel & Jones as well as to one Doctor Hussa of New York, who was evidently a dentist, for when at the end of the year Prokofiev wrote begging his patience over settlement of costs, he could not resist a characteristic conceit: 'your teeth are serving me admirably, giving me great comfort, so it annoys me to cause you financial discomfort'.[2] Dr Hussa was to remain anxious about the bill for his client's dental work for many years to come. Prokofiev's own financial discomfort was mitigated a little in a land exhausted by the war and entering a period of great inflation, where the 'high *valuta*'[3] of dollars was treasured and genteel folk found themselves reduced to the level of domestic service, like the lady-turned-chambermaid eager to wait on Prokofiev, his ailing mother and the indolent Bashkirov for a handful of dollars.

There was no question of being immersed in the thriving cultural scene of Berlin, where on his early visits Prokofiev met Bely, his old conservatory friend Zakharov and Souvchinsky. Berlin in the early 1920s seethed with Russians, many of whom like Souvchinsky had found themselves penniless in Paris and discovered it was easier to live in this alternative centre of artistic innovation. Prokofiev's aim, however, was to carry out sustained creative work in surroundings which could evoke in general terms the dacha life necessary for the inspiration of the Russian creative artist. Bashkirov had been sent ahead to find the right sort of place, but, not for the first time, squandered the money provided for the purpose, giving Prokofiev no choice, on his arrival in Munich on 25 March, but to search the Bavarian alps himself. The 'dacha' he chose was the Villa Christophorus in Ettal, rented from a cultured German family for at least a year. The locale went some way to imitating the grandeur of Prokofiev's beloved Caucasus, though with a colder climate. 'Our dacha is guarded by mountains to the north and south, the wind blows either from the west or from the east', he wrote to Souvchinsky. 'The former brings rain, the latter fine weather.'[4]

The hub of Ettal life was the Benedictine monastery and its famous grammar school, where Richard Strauss had sent his son Franz during the First World War and for which he was to compose music for a school play, *Des Esels Schatten*, when his grandsons studied there 30 years later. We learn a little about the more characterful monks from Lina, who arrived in Ettal that summer on her first break from singing studies in Italy to find a bed of forget-me-nots shaped in the letter 'L' by her surprisingly romantic suitor. She remembered Father Joseph, who broke the rules by kissing her hand and later became a parish priest, and Father Isadore, who spent long hours discussing church music with Prokofiev. The far from unworldly brotherhood had a chauffeur, whom they put at Prokofiev's disposal to drive a hired open-top car, and tennis courts within the monastery walls to which ladies were not supposed to be admitted. Vera Janacopulos, who paid a visit, was allowed in, much to Prokofiev's surprise, and he commemorated the event with a plea for her to translate the Akhmatova songs: 'Oh diva, I wish that your translation might be as accurate as your serves, your serves as strong as your voice, and your voice as gentle as your husband. All this so you will translate the Akhmatova songs'.[5]

In addition to the obvious remembrance of these far from ascetic monks many years later in the carousing scene of *Betrothal in a Monastery*, something of the community's medieval atmosphere must have coloured the quieter, cloistered moments of *The Fiery Angel*. There were also the passion plays at nearby Oberammergau, which took place every ten years. Prokofiev and Lina were lucky enough to be in Ettal for one of them, attending a performance in which the crucifixion was accompanied by a violent storm. On the walk to it, Prokofiev looked across to a distinctive mountain-top plateau and said: 'I suppose it could be around that low mountain where the witches mentioned in *The Fiery Angel* gave vent to their wild orgies, riding on broomsticks'.[6] With no place found for the hideous witches' sabbath scene in Bryusov's novel, the opera moves straight to the urban surroundings of Cologne after the first act, set in a country inn.

Yet it was in Ettal that Prokofiev completed his first draft of *The Fiery Angel*.[7] There are two remarkable differences from the final version. The first is that Prokofiev originally gave a voice to Count Heinrich, the supernaturally handsome knight believed by Renata to be the human incarnation of her 'fiery angel' Madiel. Ruprecht, baritone, meets his match in the glamorous tenor, encountered vocally repelling Renata at the beginning of the draft of the third act. By making Heinrich a silent role, Prokofiev would return to him the ambiguity Bryusov seems determined to strip away as he tells us about Heinrich's background (he is a member of a secret society sworn to chastity who sees Renata as the devil) and Renata's changed attitude to him (she admits she only imagined him to be her angel, and regrets that she has asked Ruprecht to challenge him to a duel because of his human beauty, not because he has become her 'fiery angel' again). The tension inherent in Heinrich's arrival is ultimately delayed until the invented tableau of his appearance at the window, which has to stand in place of Ruprecht's hallucinatory vision of him as Madiel in the novel's duel (illustrated by the climactic symphonic interlude so clearly delineated in the original draft). From Ruprecht's worst squabble with Renata and his falling in with Faust and Mephistopheles to the havoc created by Renata in the nunnery, with the Inquisitor's sentence of death as its culmination, Prokofiev kaleidoscopes Bryusov's tale with the effectiveness of the born opera librettist. In the Ettal draft, however, he follows him beyond the opera's ending as we know it to Renata's death in a prison cell before Ruprecht and Mephistopheles can rescue her. Perhaps this came too close to the conventional situation surrounding Gounod's mad Marguerite, just as Bryusov seems to be following Gretchen's end in Goethe's original *Faust*; but that is how Prokofiev chose to conclude *The Fiery Angel* in January 1923.

The completed task, as it then stood, was a testament to creative tenacity and, with no hope of performance, nothing more. Prokofiev mentions his work on it to remarkably few correspondents. He knew that Stravinsky followed Diaghilev in his belief that 'opera, as an art form, can go to the devil', even if he did not 'really mean it'.[8] Prokofiev was still taken aback by Stravinsky's refusal to listen to more than an act of *The Love for Three Oranges* when Diaghilev asked him to play it to them both in Paris, during work on the second and only revival of *Chout* in the late spring of 1922. Clearly the rejection hurt, as the space devoted to it in his short autobiography reveals; though Prokofiev, for all his disapproval of Stravinsky's 'Bachism with wrong notes',[9] remained a perceptive critic ready to examine each of Stravinsky's new works in thoughtful detail. The surprise is that Diaghilev, it seems, was ready to change his mind about backing a Prokofiev opera. Boris Kochno, the impresario's latest protégé and eager secretary, was proposed as a librettist, though Prokofiev had nothing but disdain for him as man and artist. Neither the Kochno project nor plans for operatic treatment of stories by Lermontov and Jules Verne knocked *The Fiery Angel* off Prokofiev's private pedestal. But that playthrough of *The Love for Three Oranges* made Diaghilev think again: by the end of the year he was still interested in mounting a production. At the same time there were extended negotiations for a staging in Mannheim after the house's enterprising chief conductor, Erich Kleiber, had paid a visit to Ettal to discuss it.

Again, both schemes failed. But at least by then there was a published vocal score to disseminate interest. Work on it was Prokofiev's first main task in Ettal, and while he tended to keep quiet about his parallel adventures in the world of *The Fiery Angel*, he referred regularly in his letters to his labours over the 'constant abomination' of this lithograph of *The Love for Three Oranges*.[10] 'I've been working for a whole week till 6 o'clock each evening', he told Souvchinsky in May 1922, 'and that's just the whole of the first act!'[11] Further Herculean labours over recent material followed at the end of the year, which found him correcting '700 pages'[12] of proofs for the

Scythian Suite, the Third Piano Concerto and a 12-movement suite from *Chout*. This last was his easiest exercise in extracting music from a stage work for concert performance: apart from extending the 'Dance of the Buffoons' Daughters' by rounding it off with its reprise in the following interlude, all he had to do was to give the necessary manuscript score numbers to his publishers with indications for gaps at the ends of items where he would add new cadences. Yet it was a curious compromise: not a great deal shorter than the full ballet and too long to be performed in its entirety, as Prokofiev acknowledged in advising conductors to choose their own set of numbers from the 12.

The suite and all the other proofs resulted from the efflorescence of Koussevitzky's Édition Russe de Musique, which now had outposts in Berlin, Brussels, Leipzig, London and New York as well as Paris. Koussevitzky had begun by acquiring Prokofiev's most recent piano compositions in 1921. The risk of undertaking to publish larger-scale works coincided with the appointment later that year of Ernest Eberg as managing head of the house – 'a Russian Estonian, and, it seems, a very efficient fellow', Prokofiev told Souvchinsky, 'who rushes about between London, Paris and Berlin, and expands the business in every possible way'.[13] The correspondence between Eberg and Prokofiev now became detailed and fruitful, and after Eberg's death in December 1925 Prokofiev enjoyed an even closer relationship with his successor, Gavriil Paichadze.

Much as he was anxious to seek out more concert engagements as a pianist, Prokofiev had few enough European engagements in 1922 to allow him to concentrate on work in Ettal, but they still brought pleasing recognition. Following the European premiere of the Third Piano Concerto with Koussevitzky in Paris that spring, he travelled to London for a performance with Albert Coates and the London Symphony Orchestra on 24 April. He was to have given two recitals with Vera Janacopulos on his return to Paris, but the capricious diva found the Canary Islands beckoning before the second could be given, and 'my only consolation is that I am earlier back to [Villa] Christophorus and can again enjoy this charming place'.[14] He reiterated this delight to Gottlieb: 'I am so glad to be back in Ettal, this charming quiet place. It is quite high in the mountains, and spring over here is very late, but how wonderful!'[15] His spare time was passed with Bashkirov in chess games and competitive translations into Russian of sonnets by the relatively obscure Cuban-born French poet José-Maria de Heredia (1842–1905).

The success of the concerto in London, he told Gottlieb, was 'much greater than in Chicago, and the critics called me "genius"'.[16] Once again, *The Times* in London showed itself superior to the mean-minded American papers and more able to supply musical chapter and verse. While the *Chicago Daily Tribune* had dismissed the work the previous December as 'neither conventional enough to win the affections nor modernist enough to be annoying'[17] and the *New York Times* had found both work and performance 'everything . . . but musically beguiling',[18] the *Times* critic boldly declared that after the ill-fated British premiere of Roger-Ducasse's *Orphée* 'music entered the room with Mr. Prokofiev'[19] and the 'absorbing interest' of his new work. While the *New York Times* refused even to hear that the work was in the advertised C major – surely impossible to miss in the first-movement Allegro's initial six bars, where cellos and the second group of basses play nothing but C to underpin the argument – *The Times* at least admitted that 'the thing must look very weird on paper, but it was all put before us with complete clarity and proportion'. Above all, it noticed that the piano role was 'a real orchestral part, not *concertante*' and that the orchestral colours reinforced it rather than contrasted with it.

It was hardly surprising if this improvement on his recent American fortunes helped plant Prokofiev's feet more firmly in western Europe. By November Fitzhugh Haensel had come up with only one American engagement for the season, in Indianapolis, and Prokofiev told Gottlieb he was 'not at all sorry that I am not going to US – in Europe my music is much more loved and appreciated than in America, which is still too backward for me. It is true, one cannot earn so much money overhear [*sic*] as in America, and I really feel much better in Europe than among those conceited fools who are directing the musical life of Chicago and New York. I am not rich, but I think it will do for this winter'.[20] He was happy, too, 'that I will not breathe this winter the smoky air of the big cities',[21] and was delighted that Lina and Bashkirov, despite recent sponging which had begun to assail the generous Prokofiev's nerves, were able to join him and his mother for Christmas in Ettal.

An impresario in Spain had arranged several concerts for Prokofiev in February 1923, which allowed him to escape the northern cold, spend time with Lina in Milan and Genoa and then head to Barcelona via the Riviera, where the idle rich irritated the born hard worker. A two-day border interrogation was followed by two noisily received recitals and a tour of the glittering Spanish port with the composer Federico Mompou, two years his junior. In May he made his Italian debut in Milan, where for the first time he partnered Lina (who had already appeared in the city as Gilda in *Rigoletto*) in a difficult programme featuring several of the recent Balmont songs. 'I had little hope of Verdi's descendants having a taste for my music',[22] he confided afterwards; but in fact the couple enjoyed a warm reception. His biggest breakthrough that spring, though, came between his Spanish and Italian debuts with triumphs in Belgium. Brussels had already hailed him, in his absence, for a performance of the *Scythian Suite* conducted by Franz Ruhlmann. A Belgian colleague told him how a 'vibrant general approbation' had smothered the 'timid protestations'[23] heard after the first movement, and he penned a gracious reply: 'Belgium has always been charming to Russian music. It received Borodin before Moscow and Petrograd';[24] and it received Prokofiev the pianist with predictable enthusiasm.

Moscow and Petrograd, despite increasing reports of the hard life there, were much on his mind. This had partly to do with the homeward-looking community of Berlin, where he spent an interesting time with Stravinsky, Diaghilev and the visiting Mayakovsky in the autumn of 1922. He subscribed to the handful of issues published in Berlin of the contemporary Russian arts magazine *Veshch*. ('I am not entirely in agreement with its programme', he told Souvchinsky, 'but it has a freshness about it.'[25]) Correspondence with the motherland was easier, too: 'most, if not all, letters to Germany from Russia manage to hop over here double-quick',[26] he wrote from Ettal to his old harpist friend Eleonora Damskaya, with whom he had already managed to conduct a brief exchange from France. Failing replies from Asafyev, Damskaya became the likeliest person as far as Prokofiev was concerned to reveal what had happened to the manuscripts and possessions left in his Petrograd flat on Pervaya Rota, chief among them the score of the Second Piano Concerto. She led him to believe that 'the new inhabitants evidently used my manuscript as fuel to fry their eggs'[27] – for which he blamed 'the Bolshevik decree which allows the settling of irresponsible personages in flats'[28] as well as 'that scoundrel' the composer Arthur Lourié's part in refusing to allow the extraction of vital material. He was in need of another major work to use as his concert visiting-card in the West and resolved to set about the concerto afresh. There was one saving grace: the full score of *The Gambler*, which he was already considering revising, remained lodged in the Maryinsky Library.

Prokofiev was now having to weigh up seriously the possibility of what it might mean to make even a single appearance in his homeland. Perhaps he was afraid that a brief visit might trap him in a country which he knew still to be in a state of flux. Just how much this question occupied him is revealed in a letter of philosophical advice to Souvchinsky, who was offered a position back in Russia; that advice is all the more valuable since it clearly applies to Prokofiev himself:

> It seems to me that the question needs to be discussed on two planes: one is the matter itself – the other is you yourself. That is, to put it differently, to consider it from the 1) practical and 2) emotional points of view.
>
> From the practical point of view, it is necessary to decide whether you should throw yourself into this business quickly or whether it would be better to save yourself and throw yourself into it a few years later, when it will be possible to work under more favourable conditions. If you find that they can manage now without you, then it would be better to hold yourself in reserve. You'll be able to begin your work afresh when there are circumstances in which your opportunities become clear. To drive in the foundations is good, but if on the striking of the hammer you are going to hit the lintel, then the benefit will be small.
>
> From the emotional point of view, you must decide: are you going to become apathetic out of idleness (or, to be precise, from the lack of full activity) – or do you feel yourself fresh, in good working order and ready to work. If the first, then you have to go to Yavorsky [a renowned theorist then on the board of the newly founded State Institute for Musical Science, GIMN, in Moscow] and risk meeting with the local shortcomings, otherwise you may go off the rails and lose your way forward. If you feel that on the contrary your powers are increasing,

> or if not increasing then at least being preserved without dissipation, or, finally, simply that you can overcome the vortex of emigration after several years, then you don't need to go, for fresh powers prove useful not only for the driving in of foundations, but also for raising walls.[29]

He had, he knew, enough energy to raise his own walls in the West; but the foundations were soon being laid for him back in Russia, when the conductor Alexander Gauk negotiated with the Maryinsky Theatre for performances of *The Gambler* and *Chout*, the first of many unsuccessful attempts on his behalf. But less than a year after the breakthrough of the Leningrad *Love for Three Oranges* in 1926, Prokofiev would be back to capitalize on the last fling of the liberal 1920s in the new Soviet Union.

One crucial tie was resumed at the beginning of 1923: correspondence with Myaskovsky, his closest musical friend at home. After countless inquiries over his old colleague's health and address, the letter writing was back on course, as if there had been no five-year interval; each began by asking the other's advice on whatever of their works they could lay their hands on, and then gave it in characteristically blunt and detailed terms. Myaskovsky had completed his powerfully structured Sixth Symphony and was working on the more compact Seventh – 'very impetuous and discordant to the point of repulsiveness',[30] as he later described it to Prokofiev – but had only the series of piano miniatures *Prichudi* ('Caprices') to show him. Prokofiev noted, as usual, which he liked and disliked of these 'puppies' – so nicknamed by Myaskovsky in honour of Prokofiev's old 'doggies', whose bite they could not hope to rival – and Myaskovsky responded by asking for further advice 'since, apart from your undoubtedly practical experience, I trust you greatly, especially after your opinion about my infants, in which respect it seemed to me that you, as usual, understand even music that is not very close to you and persistently grasp the heart of the matter'.[31]

Dismissing this sort of endearment in his own brusque manner as written in a 'slightly artificial, lovingly complimentary tone that reminded me of Tchaikovsky's letters to Nápravník',[32] Prokofiev nevertheless plunged into doing what he could, as usual, for his friend's offspring, with the result that six of the *Prichudi* were printed by Koussevitzky's firm (and Prokofiev eventually recorded two of them under the German title of *Grillen* as his last contribution to the Aeolian Duo-Art system). He found himself reluctantly having to turn down an opportunity to play Myaskovsky's Third Sonata at the first official festival of the International Society for Contemporary Music (ISCM) at Salzburg, where his *Overture on Hebrew Themes* made an unexpected appearance as a result of its success in Berlin the previous spring. But he was at least able to press the claims of the Fifth Symphony and *Alastor* on the ever-curious Henry Wood, who conducted them both in London. Myaskovsky's judgments on the scores he received of *Chout*, the *Overture on Hebrew Themes*, the Third Piano Concerto and *The Love for Three Oranges* were those of the perceptive critic. Of the new opera he enthused: '"Love" is . . . broad, sweeping and brilliantly effective, picturesquely distinct, in it you've come more distinctly into contact with the effective strength of a Musorgskian approach – an excellent internationalism. What a pity that we can't put it on here – one might think it had been written specially for us. It's put together in so clearly contemporary a fashion – unfortunately not in the style of our opera theatres, which all live in the past, but more suitable for our drama theatres (Kamerny Theatre, Meyerhold, the Studios)'.[33]

Mention of the progressive drama was, of course, the cue Prokofiev had been wanting: to ask whether Meyerhold had seen the piano score. Myaskovsky had nothing to say, mentioning only one new champion of Prokofiev's music in the pianist Samuil Feinberg. He had reason to be more cautious about the attitude of the state-controlled publishing house in Moscow, respectably guided by Pavel Lamm. It might be less than well intentioned to its prodigal son in the West, he hinted, when he told Prokofiev that the suitcase of other precious manuscripts he had lodged with Koussevitzky's firm in Petrograd for safe-keeping was still there at Muzsektor,

> and might, if you please, be extracted from there, since in the publishing firm there are now other people who, perhaps, will not always wish to stand upon ceremony as far as your best interests are concerned. Do you know the precise contents? It has been entrusted to myself and Serg[ey] Serg[eyevich] Popov to make a list of its contents at our leisure, so that we might look carefully to your more intimate concerns. In other words, your letters and diaries were described and listed only externally, but the music has been given a full tally of pages and so on. Might it not be prudent if you were to send me a confidential letter about this suitcase – in case of any eventuality?[34]

The remains of Koussevitzky's publishing enterprise in Russia, now taken over by the state, still brought forth the odd fruit. Prokofiev was happy enough to find that the score of *Semero ikh* had been printed there, which saved him the worry of searching out the sketches his mother had brought with her; his 'incantation' would certainly provide a strong bouquet for Paris, and since Koussevitzky already knew and admired it, a performance should be forthcoming. He urgently needed the Second Piano Concerto as a vehicle, since he had only his First and Third as well as the Rimsky-Korsakov concerto to offer to Western concert managements, but there was no alternative but to work from the two-piano reduction, which was all he had. At least this would allow for the generous application of everything he had learnt since the concerto's premiere.

In the meantime, Prokofiev set about the first of his works in the West to have no roots in his homeland. 'Now I'm writing a Fifth Sonata', he told Myaskovsky at the beginning of June.[35] The 'sweetness and diatonicism'[36] he had pointed out as coming to the very late rescue of his *Overture on Hebrew Themes* are the qualities that the opening bars of the Fifth Piano Sonata seem to proclaim. A neo-classical flourish in marked contrast to the lugubrious plunge at the start of the Fourth heralds a translucent C major theme high in the treble against a Mozartian accompaniment. But within seconds the piling-up of harmonic sideslips almost seems to be parodying the fun and games of the music of a fashionably light French style. With a rootless second theme framed by characteristic chromatic meanders and a development that heaps up the dissonances as textures thicken, the diatonicism is lost in Prokofiev's most consciously intellectual approach to sonata form so far. The procedure is even more marked in the finale, where instead of returning to his C major Allegretto theme in a recognizable recapitulation, Prokofiev gives it the Scythian treatment in the sonata's most dissonant climax. The initial theme springs accidentals off the right-hand material (Ex.44) while the pounding climax has the treble moving at first in parallel 4ths, jamming its C major against the F sharps and A flats of the bass (Ex.45).

Ex.44 Piano Sonata no.5, op.38 – III. Un poco allegretto

All this is a far cry from the inescapable tonics round which the earlier piano pieces frolic and skip; in neither outer movement do the final C major bars make a convincing return to base. Reflecting on his work to Myaskovsky, Prokofiev ascribed the slower tempos to 'my poor state of health . . . when I was planning out the sonata; my heart was in poor condition as a result of the scarlet fever I contracted five years ago'.[37] Only the scherzo is a throwback to the composer in familiar 'wrong-note' vein; but the monotonous insistence of its repeated chords is new and more than a little disconcerting. Nestyev, of course, labelled it as the first product of Prokofiev's contamination by the bourgeois West; but there is some truth in his charge of 'cold, formal speculation'[38] and artificial complexity. It is curious, then, that when Prokofiev revised the sonata shortly before his death and gave it a new opus number, he clarified the outlines of the first-movement exposition's closing stage and the third-movement development but ironed out very little of the sonata's harmonic waywardness.

Ex.45 Piano Sonata no.5 – III. Un poco allegretto

Before he had finished the sonata, Prokofiev also set about his substantial reworking of the lost Second Piano Concerto, having most of the first movement ready by the end of August with a gap for what would turn out to be the mightiest cadenza in the concerto repertoire. By mid-September he was already well aware of its difficulty: 'only I am able to play it',[39] he told Coates as he reproached the genial Englishman with characteristic bluntness for not championing his latest works.[40] The concerto's finale was ready by October, after which Prokofiev returned to the Fifth Sonata at the end of the year; by then, in Sèvres, half an hour from Paris, having worked in 'fits and starts, but with love',[41] he had only the shape of the first-movement development and the composition of its recapitulation to resolve. The scherzo and finale were already to his liking; 'the sonata as a whole seems to be successful, the finale unquestionably so'.[42]

Curiously, the work hardly hints at the special charm of Prokofiev's second Ettal summer. Lina, chickens and chess, in order of importance, were the reasons for his contentment. A gentleman in Algeria sent a postcard with chess moves addressed to 'Prof. Baschprok and son';[43] the respectful correspondent had no idea that he was addressing a major composer and a not so major poet. Having shown some talent for the game, Lina failed to rise to championship level and the couple turned instead to Debussy, Prokofiev's songs and Renata's music from *The Fiery Angel* (it appears from the manuscript that Prokofiev was thinking of extracting a 'vocal suite' from the opera, perhaps for Lina's benefit; the manuscript survives in the Prokofiev Archive of London's Goldsmiths College). The couple were inseparable. Banished now was the threat of other contenders – chiefly, at least from Lina's perspective,

Marya Baranovskaya, a highly sophisticated close friend who had studied with Meyerhold. 'Frou-Frou', as Prokofiev called her, had been a constant presence on his 1921–2 American visit; clearly he looked forward to her company in New York. Yet if she, apparently, treasured thoughts of being the first Mrs Prokofiev, he thought otherwise. Lina was brought closer all the while to Prokofiev through her care for the mother he adored. When Lina asked him why he resisted Marya in favour of her, he answered, 'you were such a nice innocent girl and she was so blasé'.[44] In the autumn of 1922 'Frou-Frou' married Alexander Borovsky, a contemporary of Prokofiev at the conservatory who was now making a name for himself as a pianist. The two couples were to come into proximity in Paris; in the meantime, the seclusion of Ettal gave Lina and Prokofiev time and space for their own relationship to develop.

In the third week of June a new toy arrived in Ettal: an electric incubator for chicken eggs attached to a hen coop. Prokofiev wrote proudly to Natalya Koussevitzky, 'out of 22 [eggs] all 22 were fertilized by our cock. We are awfully proud of our 100 per cent cockerel and at a general meeting we granted him eternal life plus a pound of oats'.[45] The sequel was less heroic, and amusingly recounted by Lina. The contraption sat on a glass-enclosed balcony and stank while the supposedly successfully fertilized eggs took much longer than expected to hatch:

> Sergey was like a little boy: he would go on to the balcony at night to see whether anything was happening. Finally the eggs hatched but the chicks were sickly, miserable things. One egg refused to hatch for the longest time, and in the end a little duckling emerged. Eventually we gave all the chicks and the duckling away.[46]

Lina had good reason to be nauseated by the stench: she was expecting a child. This, it seems, hastened a civil wedding, which took place (in Villa Christophorus, because the pregnant bride was so unwell) on 29 September 1923. The witnesses, of course, were Bashkirov and Marya Grigoryevna who, according to Lina, disliked the idea of becoming a grandmother and insisted on knocking 25 years off her age (a 43-year-old mother with a son of 32 was an especially preposterous notion to the affectionate but critical daughter-in-law). In this way a 'romantic period'[47] of their lives, a time of 'small quarrels and music-making',[48] moved towards its natural conclusion.

10
Three steps of steel
1923–5

Life as a Russian artist based in Paris began officially for Prokofiev with the premiere of the First Violin Concerto on 18 October 1923, shortly after his move there. The soloist, Marcel Darrieux, was, perhaps surprisingly, the brilliant 18-year-old leader of Koussevitzky's orchestra, since better-known luminaries had refused to touch the score brought by Paweł Kokhański from Russia. The occasion, however, was showy enough to establish Darrieux's reputation: among the audience in the glittering auditorium of the Paris Opéra were Picasso, Benois, Anna Pavlova, Artur Rubinstein and Josef Szigeti, whose subsequent championship of the concerto helped to accelerate its reputation in the West. Yet despite its successful reception, it may have been the critical accusation of 'Mendelssohnisms'[1] and outmodedness which led Prokofiev to examine the work's curious status: 'I don't especially like a lot of it', he told Souvchinsky, after noting that the concerto had been well received, 'although I'm happy enough with the second movement [the Scherzo]. But the first movement and the finale were conceived in 1913 and executed in 1916 and now, to be sure, I'd do a lot of it very differently. It's so unpleasant when you write something and it waits seven years for the favour of a performance!'[2]

Nor did it bring Prokofiev immediately closer to establishing either a secure reputation or a permanent home in Paris rather than the temporary accommodation the newlyweds were sharing in Sèvres. He started by looking for somewhere two hours' journey from the city, but the search was interrupted by a brief trip to London, where a second performance of the Third Piano Concerto was less enthusiastically greeted than the first, and by a return to Germany to try and sort out living arrangements for his mother and Bashkirov. The house in Ettal had been sold by the owner, forcing the ménage to move to less salubrious quarters in expensive Oberammergau; since his mother's heart condition prevented her from leaving Germany, he would have to make regular visits from Paris which, 'taking into account that there are nine changes and almost three days' travelling isn't very funny',[3] he wrote to Souvchinsky in December. He was, he pointed out, like some 'comedy traveller, rushing up and down Europe along the lines London–Paris–Bavaria–Geneva–Sèvres';[4] the situation, hardly new for the touring concert pianist, must have been aggravated by a feeling of rootlessness.

By the early spring of 1924, he and Lina had moved from Sèvres to 5 Rue Charles Dickens, in the Passy district of Paris, close to the little house where Balzac wrote his *Comédie Humaine*. The circumstances were not ideal: they were sharing with Borovsky and his pregnant wife 'Frou-Frou', who still looked at Prokofiev, so his new wife thought, 'with such eyes'.[5] There was now a new addition to the household – Sviatoslav Prokofiev, delivered on 27 February in a Paris maternity hospital. Prokofiev's response was less positive than Diaghilev's, who later told Lina on the birth of her second child that she was 'a two-star general; a woman who has no children is nothing'.[6] The father's reaction at first, so Lina observed, was a strange mixture of jealousy and indifference: 'he's not a human being yet, nothing registers . . . I'm sure he will be more interesting when he passes the oyster stage'.[7] Still, Prokofiev would soon be studying an English handbook on 'Wise Parenthood'[8] and reporting the baby's first words to Russian relatives. Lina's horrified mother carried Sviatoslav to the room in the apartment furthest from the piano while Prokofiev hammered away at his 'devil of a cadenza'[9] for the Second Piano Concerto, composed afresh to even more gargantuan specifications. The neighbours, too, were dismayed; he conquered their objections by hammering on a box to prove there were worse noises that might be endured.

Prokofiev's second piano recital of the season was on the afternoon of 9 March 1924 at the Opéra Comique. Like the first, given the previous November, it included several of Myaskovsky's *Prichudi*, which he had campaigned so hard for Koussevitzky to publish, and Musorgsky's *Pictures at an Exhibition*, now much more popular than when Prokofiev had aired them in America owing to Ravel's new orchestration for Koussevitzky. The recital's novelty was his Fifth Piano Sonata, received by the audience with the same 'reserved approval'[10] it showed to the *Prichudy*, and indifferently covered by the patchy, always overdue Parisian reviews; one paper heralded it as 'so long awaited'[11] and then referred at the end of the next day's concert column to 'the grand virtuoso who is M. Prokofieff'[12] with not a word more. He repeated the sonata in the middle of the mighty Olympiad festival in Paris in May, overshadowed by such spectaculars as an opening production of Aeschylus' *Agamemnon*, a performance of Honegger's *Le Roi David*, Walter Damrosch's cycle of Beethoven symphonies and the grand finale of a visit from the Vienna Opera under Busch. Parallel with this, though, were the enterprise and ambition of Koussevitzky's four May concerts at the Opéra in which Prokofiev had more of the limelight than he had expected. Olin Downes, who reviewed the events at length in an article for the *New York Times*, praised the 'conductor of the hour' and 'storm centre of friends and enemies', describing the audience at the sell-out events as possessed of 'that peculiar theatrical flare and glitter which still distinguishes it at the height of the season'.[13]

A falling-out, it seems, had been averted with Koussevitzky, in whose hands Prokofiev's Paris reputation rested now that Diaghilev had temporarily lost interest. The previous September, Prokofiev had had an argument with Koussevitzky and his agent Zederbaum over the conductor's cancelling of the November premiere of *Semero ikh*, the printed score of which he had now received from Russia, and Koussevitzky had furiously accused the impetuous composer of 'propagandist zeal'[14] (Prokofiev's response was more coolly pre-empted by Coates, who had told the 'naughty' composer to 'be a good boy' and 'keep me informed a bit more' instead of 'making foolish reproaches'[15]). A profuse written apology for his 'sharp words',[16] however, brought Prokofiev back into Koussevitzky's indispensable orbit, and *Semero ikh* was scheduled for the last of the four Paris Opéra concerts on 29 May; the logistics of bringing in a large choir and tenor soloist for the seven-minute 'Incantation' were solved, at least for the time being, by including Stravinsky's early Balmont setting *Zvezdoliki* ('The Star-Faced One') and Borodin's Polovtsian Dances from *Prince Igor*, with chorus.

The series opened on 8 May with Prokofiev playing the new version of the Second Piano Concerto in an 'ultra-modern'[17] programme of the kind that Downes admitted would not be tolerated when Koussevitzky came to take up his post as the principal conductor of the Boston Symphony Orchestra the following season. Coming as it did after the rhythmic charge of Alexandre Tansman's *Légende* and the new 'style mécanique' of Honegger's *Pacific 231* (or *Pacific*, as it was called for this premiere), a massive evocation of heavy locomotion, Prokofiev, with his monster concerto conceived a decade earlier, was bound to be included among the 'bruiteurs', 'those musicians who substitute noise for musical thought'.[18] So thought *Le Gaulois*, while thanking heaven for a little real music in the shape of Falla's *El amor brujo* and the one-year-old Musorgsky–Ravel *Pictures at an Exhibition*; it did point out, though, that few interpreters would be able to measure themselves against Prokofiev's personal virtuosity in the finale's 'avalanche of notes'[19] and managed to convey a sense of excitement in the competition between pianist and orchestra.

The real tournament, as Prokofiev had perceived it in February, was to be between himself and Stravinsky, who was due to play the solo part in his new Concerto for Piano and Wind in the same series of Koussevitzky concerts. 'The battle isn't especially advantageous to me', he told Souvchinsky, 'since my old, though rehabilitated, Rosinante has to fight against an angry tank in its latest construction. I have to cram well, and win back on technique.'[20] Whether Stravinsky triumphed was open to debate. Perhaps Prokofiev thought they would be mounting their steeds, as he put it, in the same programme. In fact Stravinsky made his concerto debut on 22 May, suffering a memory lapse in the last movement, and another battle – between the primitive monsters of each composer's Balmont-derived incantations – failed to happen at the end of the month when Stravinsky's *Zvezdoliki* was replaced by another performance of the concerto. For Downes, *Semero ikh* was very much *sui generis*, the 'huge and rather horrible and primitive' creation of a 'bold and bad young man', while Stravinsky, redeeming his first performance of the Concerto with 'finger technique as clean as a steel blade', had 'done a new thing, and this by means of a style that is essentially classic'.[21]

Prokofiev viewed this classicism with suspicion, but as a thinking critic not a jealous rival. He had loved the 'entertaining'[22] *Soldier's Tale* and hated the new Octet when it shared a Koussevitzky concert in October 1922, and he would later confide in Asafyev that he disliked Stravinsky's Concerto as

> a continuation of the course he took in the finale of the Octet, that's to say a stylization of Bach – which I don't approve of, since although I love Bach, and believe that to compose according to his principles isn't a bad thing, it doesn't follow that one should produce a stylized version of Bach. So I don't rate this Concerto as highly as a work such as, for example, *Les Noces* or *The Rite of Spring*, just as I don't rate as highly as those works things like *Pulcinella* or even my own *Classical* Symphony . . . unfortunately Stravinsky thinks differently. . . . He even thinks that this will establish a new epoch.[23]

This in itself was suspect to Prokofiev, who believed – as he repeatedly stated in newspaper interviews – that self-classification was anathema to a composer's creativity. He took issue with Souvchinsky, who paired creativity and modernity all too glibly for his taste. 'Stravinsky . . . frightfully desires his creativity to adhere to modernity', he responded. 'If I want anything, it's that modernity should adhere to my creativity.'[24] And in another, crucial letter to his most aesthetically conscious friend, he enlarged on the definition of the word 'modernity':

> Do you know what kind of attitude Shakespeare had to being modern? I myself don't know, but when I consider his sonnets, I couldn't care less. Perhaps you know what kind of literary-aesthetic influence governed Buxtehude, whose organ fugue I have just arranged for f[orte]p[iano]? It's possible that he was passionate about Shakespeare, but in the meantime Shakespeare had already been dead for 80 years, and in his place was born another 'modernity', totally at odds with Shakespeare, which was antipathetic to Buxtehude's taste, and of which not a trace now survives.[25]

Going on to defend the theme of *The Fiery Angel*, on which Souvchinsky had cast doubt as a suitably contemporary subject, and to praise supposedly outdated Balmont as 'a pillar, standing outside time', he homed in on one final, specific preoccupation:

> I understand when Stravinsky yells at me that opera as a form should go to the devil, for I know that he doesn't really mean it. I would willingly listen to some ultra-Stravinsky who says that now, in place of an orchestra with eight horns, heckelphone and piccolo-oboe and music with twice augmented chords of the 12th, we have knocking at the door dynamos, whirring propellers and x-ray machines [the apparatus of Marinetti's futurists], and so for that reason it is

> necessary to jettison the old and discover a new form of art. But when they say to me that *The Fiery Angel* and *Semero ikh* don't sufficiently acknowledge 'modernity', then my reply is that I don't understand when you say, let's go to the doctor, because for one of us a very important brain cell has atrophied![26]

Here, again, Prokofiev moves to the broader picture after brushing aside Stravinsky's 'yelling', presumably a throwback to the *The Love for Three Oranges* audition when Stravinsky responded less positively than Diaghilev. Stravinsky the man was beginning to worry him. In another crucial letter to Souvchinsky, he wants to unravel the enigma of his fellow composer:

> What is Stravinsky's taste? What, devil take it, does he consider important? [We know that] on his desk he has a portrait of Verdi, that in the newspapers he steps forward in defence of Tchaikovsky, that he tells me (repeatedly and persistently) that in terms of contemporary music he can listen only to me.
>
> When I played through for him my *Visions fugitives* (pieces which for me are all more or less of equal worth), he was enraptured by one, disgusted by another, and expressing himself so emphatically that at around the tenth *Vision*, before the beginning of each piece, I began to wonder what he was going to say; and I could never anticipate what was in his head. As for his and Diaghilev's attacks . . . what's it all about? Both say that they love my music, and how sincerely isn't so important; what's important is that they say it with such aggressive insistence . . . When they yell, sometimes for two hours at a time, I understand nothing, I snap back, so as to add fuel to the fire, I take delight in the scene from the point of view of its picturesqueness, but within my head is aching – what sort of spring is unwinding inside them, why is there so much energy in this spring and where is this spring aiming?[27]

It was not aiming, imminently, at another Prokofiev work for the Ballets Russes. There Stravinsky's *Les Noces*, with Bronislava Nijinskaya's astonishing choreography, was still pre-eminent despite the inroads made by the two new ballet scores of the season: Poulenc's *Les Biches*, which Prokofiev found himself alone in disliking, and Auric's *Les Fâcheux*. A new, brittle kind of French *musiquette*, as it became known, was fast developing as one emblem of 1920s Paris alongside the *style mécanique*. *Chout* had appeared during the new season in quite the wrong place, at the Neighborhood Playhouse in New York, in an arrangement for two pianos, violin, flute and oboe taken from the piano score. Prokofiev objected that this presentation to which he had not given his consent would simply 'not sound right',[28] and Eberg helped him to extract $250 from the well-intentioned company for the 'deformed orchestration'.[29] His choreographic opportunities lay outside the realms of the Ballets Russes: with Diaghilev's new rival Ida Rubinstein, who was dallying with the long-term possibility of incidental music for the drama *Judith* through the mediations of the author, Paul Demasy, and with a new small-scale company led by the former Maryinsky ballet master Boris Romanov. Only the second of these two projects was to bear fruit.

Prokofiev had nothing but a characteristically blunt form of critical encouragement for Diaghilev's new musical protégé, the 20-year-old Russian Vladimir Dukelsky (later Vernon Duke), who had arrived in Paris via Constantinople. An elegant young man with a taste for fashionable clothes when Diaghilev first met him, Dukelsky was briefly to flourish as the impresario's third adoptive son among composers, though his good looks put him in the line of succession to Nijinsky, Massine and Kochno rather than Prokofiev or Stravinsky – neither of whom, as Diaghilev was quick to remark, 'ever won any beauty prizes'.[30] Duke's autobiography *Passport to Paris*, always entertaining and running Prokofiev's own writings close for strong literary style, captures the flavour of the two composers' meeting at Rue Charles Dickens; like many of its details, however, the date he declares seared into his memory, 17 June, must be out by a month because by then Prokofiev had left Paris for the summer. Accompanied by Souvchinsky, Dukelsky took along his punchy and deliberately Prokofievian Piano Concerto:

> Prokofiev, looking like a cross between a Scandinavian minister and a soccer player . . . thought the concerto a good, solid job, convincingly melodious. His lips were unusually thick, explaining to some degree the 'white negro' sobriquet [also adopted in an unflattering description from about this time by the artist Anna Ostroumova-Lebedeva, who made a portrait of Prokofiev in 1926], and they gave his face an oddly naughty look, rather like that of a boy about to embark on some punishable and therefore tempting prank. His pretty wife, Lina Ivanovna . . . sang well, and was a good housekeeper and mother . . . which didn't prevent Serge from picking fights with her hourly and throwing her out of the room at the slightest provocation. Prokofiev pumped my hand energetically, asked me whether I played chess (I did, badly), and suggested I write him in Brittany, where he was going for the summer, to report my progress or lack of same.[31]

So Dukelsky went off to the Chevreuse valley to work with Boris Kochno on *Zéphyre et Flore*, an odd fusion of Greek myth and Russian early 19th-century classicism, and Prokofiev took up residence in his latest summer retreat, the Villa Béthanie in the Atlantic resort of St Gilles-Croix-de-Vie. In addition to the Romanov project, he had a commission from Koussevitzky: a second symphony, which was to take its cue from the mechanistic excesses of the first May concert and specifically from the new sensation of Honegger's *Pacific*: this would be a real, up-to-the-minute manifestation of the new *style mécanique*, not that ten-year-old riveting of metals the Second Piano Concerto, which had been taken as fit company for Honegger's steely audacity.

Yet, as Prokofiev told Myaskovsky, it was the 'sound technique',[32] and not the content or the concept, of *Pacific* which fascinated him. He was especially preoccupied with knowing how to produce the right sonorities within complexity, and Honegger's 'allegory of speed'[33] did just that. 'This summer I want to buy primers on bassoons, oboes and so on, so as to learn to write easily for each instrument', he wrote to Myaskovsky at the beginning of June:

> For difficult figurations in nine performances out of ten sound platonic, muddied and feeble. We recently heard performed here Honegger's *Pacific*, a work insignificant in content but very tough and brilliantly orchestrated, from which resulted such a stunning impression that each instrument played naturally and 'pleasingly' . . . According to Koussevitzky, who conducted this piece, he needed only a minimal amount of time for rehearsal.[34]

He knew, too, what he did not want from a symphony which, out of respect to the status of the *Classical*, would become no.2. Myaskovsky had already learnt to take one of his friend's most intemperate tirades against his own Fifth Symphony, composed in Polish Galicia during the war and heavily reliant on the folk songs from that region. Having upbraided him for the 'dead hand' of Glazunov, now labelled as a tasteless rehasher of old recipes, Prokofiev proffers the advice he was to attempt to take himself:

> concentrate on creating new methods, and a new technique, new orchestration; rack your brains in this direction, sharpen your inventiveness, no matter what it takes, strive for a good, fresh sound; renounce the St Petersburg and Moscow schools as you would a morose devil – and you will immediately feel not only the earth beneath your feet but even wings on your back, and mainly – a goal straight ahead . . . these Medtner-like fragments hang on you like stones and pull you invisibly into a warm, cosy swamp. For those who live in the swamp, the swamp is a paradise, but you, an unspoilt person, let out an involuntary scream on submersion: 'Save me, there is no solid ground underfoot!' And where in a swamp is there solid ground? Only on the bottom.[35]

'Newly styled [*novofakturalno*]':[36] this was what Prokofiev told Myaskovsky he expected from his future symphonies, and a sign of how he was going about his own Second appears in a letter from St-Gilles to Pierre Blois of Pleyel pianos, a good-humoured colleague over the years Prokofiev dealt with the company: 'In composing my symphony, I broke three low strings of your piano . . . I beg you to be very kind and send me replacements as soon as possible'.[37] If the essence of the symphony was to be complicated and noisy, its structure was to have a precedent in Beethoven's op.111 Sonata – a powerful first movement followed by a set of theme and variations. But this was not always the case: at the end of September, with the first movement and five variations of the Second sketched out, Prokofiev was still planning a third-movement finale. His solution was to settle for a sixth variation to pit his theme against the return of the hard-hitting devils from the first movement. Yet the 'most cruel effort'[38] on the draft did not allow him to proclaim it to Myaskovsky until early November, and the entire process, including the harder task of orchestration that lay ahead, was to take him nine agonizing months.

Much simpler, though it trod new ground, was the short chamber work commissioned by Romanov, who had worked with Prokofiev and Gorodetsky on the outlines of *Ala and Lolly* and who was now commanding the choreographic wing of the ambitious little Russian Romantic Theatre founded in Berlin during the autumn of 1922. Its 'romantic' brief had initially been projected to include operas and ballets by Gluck and Mozart, but when the ballet company's attention turned to touring Romanov needed an up-to-the-minute score which could make the most of small instrumental forces. This happily coincided with Prokofiev's own wish to follow the fashion. 'Most recently we've had here the mode for an ensemble of wind instruments', he had told Myaskovsky back in March, 'for example six winds, two brass instruments, plus sometimes a double bass and percussion. Stravinsky and the young composers are all writing for this combination; I also want to, but I can't find the time.'[39] Romanov's commission soon bought that time. It seems Prokofiev's original ambitions were to use a quintet unusually composed of oboe, clarinet, violin, viola and double bass in which the players could double with diverse instruments. By July, though, he was able to confirm to Souvchinsky from St-Gilles, 'the double-bassist won't take up the trombone, nor the viola player the bass drum'.[40]

In any case, the instrumental combination was piquant enough, and there was a blueprint in the slightly larger portable ensemble of Stravinsky's *Soldier's Tale*, with the pioneering abrasive sonorities of clarinet and violin setting an especially bold example. Romanov's scenario, resuscitated from the farcical marionette-like ballet he had choreographed in 1913–14, *What happened to the ballerina, the Chinaman and the tumblers*, did not require too rigid a correspondence in the music, and the six movements of the original 1924 work could easily be located in the chamber halls of western Europe and Russia. In this respect the composer surely had one eye on the International Society for Contemporary Music, now established following its successful first season (which had featured his *Overture on Hebrew Themes*) and providing an audience for such outstanding young figures as Krenek, Hindemith and Weill.

The Quintet op.39, as the 1924 score of the ballet (to be called *Trapèze*) usually appears, makes no compromises for the sake of dance. There are oddities in every movement. The first is a wayward G minor theme led by the oboe with just two variations (in his correspondence Prokofiev placed an exclamation mark after the number), only the second of which vivaciously hints at the sprightly acrobatics of the subject. The ensuing Andante energico begins with a pointedly cumbersome double-bass solo, the melody later embroidered with a rushing figuration for muted violin anticipating Hindemith or the early Weill (Ex.46). Prokofiev knew that the third movement would pose problems for Romanov's troupe. He told Romanov in early August that it was 'most difficult for musicians and dancers, for it is written in the form of a quick, rushing fugato in 5/4 time'[41] (in fact, 10/8 was the metre on which he settled). Yet the cleverest movement is also the most entertaining, with the shrieking ricochets of clarinet and oboe providing the most joyous circus turns in

Ex.46 Quintet, op.39 – II. Andante energico

Ex.46 *cont.*

the ballet. After this, the experimental dirge of the Adagio pesante and the acerbic modernisms of the last two movements strike as lesser inspirations, though the promising pizzicato bass of the fifth momentarily suggests a jam session and the second, 6/8 idea of the finale is the most danceable stretch of the entire score.

Cerebral it may appear at times, but the Quintet cost Prokofiev little effort. The sketches were accomplished in the first month at St Gilles-Croix-de-Vie, and completing the score in August proved no problem since, as Prokofiev told Souvchinsky, 'the instrumentation, it stands to reason, was planned before the composition'.[42] He need not have been so quick; the premiere, planned for the autumn, was postponed to the following summer, by which time Romanov would have more demands for his composer-in-residence. Summer at St-Gilles, in the meantime, passed well enough – 'the beach is splendid, but weather cold',[43] he told Gottlieb in August – and Lina appears to have been suffering poor health after the birth of Sviatoslav. She was visited by Caroline Getty of the Christian Science Committee on Publication, who subsequently advised 'little mother' to 'turn thought away from the body . . . mind is not mortal, it is immortal, it is God'.[44] We find similar sentiments, beginning 'Depression is a lie of the mortal mind, consequently it cannot have power over me, for I am the expression of Life, i.e. of divine activity',[45] written out in immaculate English in Prokofiev's hand, undated but certainly from some time in the 1920s. Quite when the couple developed an interest in Christian Science is uncertain, though Prokofiev's interview with the *Christian Science Monitor* at the beginning of 1922 may have been the starting-point, and we know that Getty came to the Paris apartment several times in the early summer of 1924. The following year Prokofiev wanted to send Christian Science literature to his beloved aunt Katya, widowed since 1914, and her daughter Katyechka, now living south-east of

Moscow in Penza. Having been located, they were regular recipients of concern and money orders, though the solicitous nephew and cousin was anxious that in connection with this particular parcel his name was not to be mentioned 'as according to my experience it will be likely to be confiscated'.[46]

These close family ties were to become more intense in the face of personal loss. Marya Grigoryevna, accompanied by Bashkirov, had finally gathered the strength to leave Ettal and join her son and daughter-in-law on the French Atlantic coast. By early October Bashkirov had found them all a house in Bellevue, half an hour from Paris by train from the Gare St Lazare. 54 Route des Gardes, rented from a Russian-born head of an art-printing firm, was in fact two houses joined by an annexe – a necessity for the growing household, which included Janet Cobbe from California, another diligent Christian Scientist who had replaced a Norwegian as Sviatoslav's nurse. The reappearance of Prokofiev's own childhood governess, Louise Roblin, must have pleased his mother. Madame Roblin had seen her former charge's name in the papers, and begged 'a little audience in the first interval at the artist's entrance'[47] during one of his May concerts. Clearly there was an affectionate reunion, for in her next letter Roblin looked forward to meeting 'your little boy [*marmotte*]'.[48]

There was a communal garden behind the Bellevue residence, where one of the last photographs of Marya Grigoryevna was taken. A still handsome and substantial-looking woman, she sits between her relaxed, white-clad daughter-in-law and son holding Sviatoslav on her knees. On 13 December she had a heart attack and died. Prokofiev's immediate response was a letter to his landlord, assuring him that there was no possibility of contagion. His undemonstrative behaviour on this occasion, as on the death of his father 14 years earlier, should not, however, be construed as any lack of feeling. His mother had been seriously ill for the last few years and he had always been the most solicitous of sons, in deed perhaps more than in word.

Yet Prokofiev showed a marked reluctance to break the news to friends and relatives. Several times the following year Gottlieb passed on his best wishes to wife, mother and child; Prokofiev could have informed him of his mother's death in his replies but failed to do so. The situation with his mother's sister Katya in Penza was clearly more delicate. Perhaps he felt there was no point burdening another frail old woman with bad news when there was no imminent possibility of their establishing face-to-face contact. A letter written in August 1925, eight months after his mother's death, makes for strange reading: 'Dear Auntie, It's very difficult for me to tell you something positive about Mamochka's state of health. This condition has happened before: great weakness and full loss of memory. There was a similar occurrence in the winter of 1923–4, but she was on the mend by the spring; then no change was noticeable'.[49]

Another letter at the end of 1925, to Anna Uvarova, a close family friend, suggests that the request not to break the news came from sources closer to Penza:

> Dear Anna Petrovna,
>
> Is it possible that Aunt Katya still knows nothing of the death of my mama? Don't you think that all the same one ought to speak to her about it? I write to you about it because in a few days' time it will be a year since mama died. It's very difficult in each letter to Aunt Katya to think up something to write about mama's health: it comes out too strained, curt and dry. I'm sure that Aunt Katya very much detects that I have escaped in some general places discussing mama's health and give no details, when in fact to compose such details is simply beyond my strength . . . I would very much like to send Aunt Katya the clothes and linen left behind after mother's death, which are as good as new, but how can I do this when Aunt Katya doesn't know? Write to me to tell me, please, what you think.[50]

Within a few months the constraint had been removed and the warmly affectionate letters from Prokofiev to his aunt that follow are testimony to how much he valued the closest living link with the mother he adored.

Just over a week before his mother's death Prokofiev gave his toughest recital in Paris: a survey of all his major sonatas, from the Second to the Fifth. The programme he had ready for his Polish debut the following month was less taxing and could have been given anything up to four years earlier, but it was still a showcase: the Second and Fourth sonatas opened each half of the programme, with the complete set of *Visions fugitives* concluding the first part and nine shorter pieces culminating in the Toccata ending the second. In Warsaw he gave an interview in which he was able to reply diplomatically that he rated highly the country's leading composer, Karel Szymanowski, for they had become well acquainted in Paris through Kokhański, the violinist who was originally to have given the premiere of the First Violin Concerto. In describing Szymanowski as 'a cultured composer and an enchanting person',[51] Prokofiev answered with succinct sincerity. The qualifications were to come later, when he had a chance to write critically about Szymanowski's First Violin Concerto: 'it is complicated, iridescent, enormous . . . There is in Szymanowski's tendency to languish in 6/4 chords, and to be reconciled to mutes and flageolets (harmonics), a hint of provincialism. This is a cultured gentleman from a god-forsaken place'.[52]

The interviewer from that god-forsaken place, in the meantime, had to abandon trying to draw Prokofiev on his own music – 'I can't talk of it . . . it's my job to write it, yours to discuss it'[53] – but elicited some interesting remarks on the current musical situation in his adoptive France and his homeland (which had recently opened to performers from the West after the signing of the 1922 Rapallo Agreement, with its 'normalization' of relations between Germany and Russia). In the new Soviet Russia, he thought, 'the isolation of Moscow and Petrograd from the latest achievements of the West makes itself felt in Russian music. In this music there is some backwardness of receptivity. If one speaks of the audiences of this music, they are still there in Russia. One quarter of these listeners are old, the best listeners, one quarter students, as always. One quarter is the new intelligentsia and the other quarter, as always, people who understand nothing in music'.[54] His chance to return home and find out for himself would have to wait; an invitation for 1925 from Alexander Ossovsky, director of the Leningrad Conservatory, had to be turned down in the light of uncertainty over an American tour, much to Myaskovsky's disappointment.

As far as the French music of the last quarter of a century was concerned, Prokofiev continued to his interviewer, 'its *maître* is Ravel. Then Debussy – original but watery. Then Honegger and Auric. I don't like Poulenc – I had had such hopes for him'.[55] Of Poulenc the man and musician he was to modify his opinion over the next few years. In the immediate future he had a chance to expand on the contemporary music he heard in an article for Asafyev, 'The Spring Season of 1925', including that chance to assess Szymanowski and embracing events he heard on his trip to Monte Carlo (where so many stage works, including Diaghilev's, were 'tried out' before reaching the capital). His crisp, direct literary style, shorn of diplomatic periphrasis, was an indication that he was currying no favours (or perhaps he thought no-one in the West would read the piece). Writing off as 'soporific' a cluster of works by minor French composers, including André Caplet, Charles Koechlin and Roland-Manuel, a musician better known as a writer, he had more to say about Honegger's Concertino – 'clear, sharp, piquant, but for the pianist there's absolutely nothing to do' – and Germaine Tailleferre's Piano Concerto. He found the latter 'pleasant, lively, written in the style of Mozart, not too difficult for the pianist' but took the composer's remarks on classicism as a response to 'the excessive influence of the East' risible in the light of a 'blatant theft' from *Petrushka*. A real discovery was the young Italian composer Vittorio Rieti, though this was immediately followed by a swipe at Rieti's teacher (a colleague of Prokofiev) Alfredo Casella, and his *Elegia eroica*, which brought forth the most characteristic bluntness of all: 'reading that it was composed on the death of a war hero, I immediately felt hostile towards it. Reading further that in Rome at the first celebratory performance it was booed, I became interested. But when I heard it, I understood why it was booed'.[56]

Daring to judge closer to home, Prokofiev also wrote about the major Diaghilev events of the spring season. Auric's music for *Les Matelots* was like the show itself – jolly but rather hastily thrown together: 'the themes are very sailorish, some of them very likable, others intolerable; the orchestration is clear, although unrefined; generally the whole thing's been composed with broad strokes, quickly, without detailed trimmings'.[57] His prediction for a more lasting success was the ballet score for *Zéphyre et Flore* by Dukelsky, the young man in whom he had shown so much interest and the first composer whose music Prokofiev was aware showed his own influence. It is hardly surprising that Prokofiev had wanted to help him with the orchestration, which as yet he found 'insufficiently clear' – just as the overall contours were, he felt, not yet bold enough; or that he liked best the theme and variations for the muses which form the core of the ballet. Prokofiev loved the virginal candour of the theme, wrote it out for Myaskovsky and carried it round among his personal possessions. But he was wrong, at least in the long term, in naming *Zéphyre et Flore* as the outstanding event of the season. The one work to achieve success in the eyes of posterity was Ravel's *L'Enfant et les sortilèges*, which Prokofiev saw in Monte-Carlo. It says more about his own perspective than Ravel's bewitching one-act opera that, having granted a 'complete mastery of stunning orchestration', Prokofiev preferred the livelier, sharper-focus numbers of the objects that berate the naughty child to 'whole slices of colourless, watery, outdated, unnecessary material'.[58] Among these we would surely include the most enchanting moment in the score, when a duet of wailing cats yields to a depiction of the garden at night. Far from returning to 'outdated' ideas, the masterly Ravel had the courage to return to a softer-edged 'impressionism' when it suited the drama, at a time when Prokofiev and everyone else were aiming at stark, acerbic effects.

Prokofiev's own fairy-tale opera finally reached the German stage in Cologne on 14 March 1925, several years after the unfulfilled promises of a Berlin theatrical agent to have *The Love for Three Oranges* placed in six new productions within a year, and 18 months after his lament to Souvchinsky that no-one in Germany knew or cared about his music (he gave his first recital in Berlin in January 1925 but was never paid for it). The advocate on this occasion was Jenő (Eugen) Szenkar, a Hungarian conductor on the staff of the Cologne Opera soon to make his name in the Soviet Union, and the Prokofievs struck up a warm alliance with Szenkar and his wife. In the first of many letters to Lina after the performance, Margot Szenkar sent a list of reviews – 'good and bad and rather foolish'[59] – but the good, marked with a cross, were in the majority, led by the influential Berlin papers, and the production was 'much more integrated, though less sumptuous, than the one in America',[60] Prokofiev thought. He wrote to the theatre's director to express 'my sincere thanks and to beg you to transmit them to M. Szenkar, who conducted the performance with so much talent, to all the soloists who not only sang well but also acquitted themselves as fine actors, to the excellent orchestra, chorus and technical personnel who all came out victorious from a labour the difficulty of which I hold myself perfectly responsible'.[61]

Clearly this second staging confirmed the problematic corners in the work, for later in the year Prokofiev had detailed advice for the conductor Vladimir Dranishnikov, who was preparing the Soviet premiere in Leningrad (as Petrograd had now become following Lenin's death). He insisted that the chorus should know the prologue by heart to bring out the proper characteristics of the various theatrical groups, 'for in previous productions they gawped at the conductor and waved their arms in time to the music', and that the doctors' difficult 5/4 chorus should be left to a group of soloists. His subsequent points give a rare insight into his sense of theatre:

> In I.ii in the Cologne production the chorus of little devils sat in the orchestra and howled through megaphones. It didn't sound bad.

In III.ii, when the Prince and Truffaldino creep towards the oranges, they don't hear the chattering of the violins, so it's necessary for them to learn their part by rote, but even then they mustn't take their eyes off the conductor.

In III.iii the scene needs to be such that the oranges don't make a noise when they're dragged on to the stage. So ask Radlov [the director] to take this into consideration, and also to rehearse in advance the running-about towards the end of the opera [the flight of the villains pursued by the court]. Usually directors have postponed this until the penultimate rehearsal, and instead of a lively scene what we get is an ill-prepared scrum with a log-jam in the wings.[62]

While *The Love for Three Oranges* suddenly found itself lined up for Leningrad, Moscow and Berlin, Szenkar now had his theatre anxious and waiting not only for 'the Dostoyevsky opera' (*The Gambler*) but also for first refusal on 'the opera about Cologne'.[63] This, of course, was *The Fiery Angel*, work on which had been held up by Prokofiev's anxious concern to consult his literary friend in the Soviet Union, Boris Demchinsky, over the libretto. It may have been difficulty in dealing with the subject matter that caused Demchinsky to stall until 1926; since the death of Lenin at the beginning of 1924, Myaskovsky noted that 'a strict attitude has come into fashion here',[64] that the 'mystical-religious content' of the Balmont settings had caused censorship difficulties and that the 'mystical text'[65] of *Semero ikh* had militated against its performance there. In the meantime Prokofiev had moved on a little further with his 'vocal suite' from *The Fiery Angel*; three of the five movements were to feature Renata's music with soprano solo. No doubt this was to benefit from a collaboration between Koussevitzky and Koshetz; but when that happened, much of the opera would be rewritten and very different elements would come into play. In the meantime, Margot Szenkar was informed that *The Fiery Angel* would not be ready for several seasons, and her husband ploughed on instead with an ingenious ballet double bill in which the comic-strip violence of *Chout* met its match in *The Miraculous Mandarin*, Bartók's blistering mix of orientalism and urban brutality. Prokofiev was to make a great mistake in passing over Cologne in favour of the more prestigious Berlin Städtische Oper for the long-overdue premiere of *The Fiery Angel*.

Returning from Cologne via Liège, Prokofiev and Lina gave their first joint recital since Lina's temporary retirement during her pregnancy and Sviatoslav's early months (Prokofiev had even put his wife forward to the Cologne management to sing Ninetta, the surviving princess of the three oranges – a more substantial role than the short-lived Linetta, named after her – but the part had already been taken). This was one of the composer's few concerts at a time when he was still refusing offers so long as work was needed on the Second Symphony. The married duo's next stop was Monte Carlo, where they saw Ravel's new opera and Prokofiev again cast his objective eye on the Dostoyevskian characters gathered round the roulette tables; after this distraction it was time to resume serious business. He managed to complete the symphony's complicated orchestration only just in time for the premiere on 8 May, giving Koussevitzky a dangerously short period for rehearsal. Prokofiev's fears about his monster symphony had been growing throughout the spring, and in the aftermath he expressed his anxiety to Myaskovsky:

> When I heard it, I couldn't even figure out myself what sort of thing it had turned out to be, so in my embarrassment I kept silent until it was all over. And the symphony elicited nothing but bewilderment among everyone else who heard it: I had complicated the piece to such an extent that as I listened, even I couldn't always find the essence – so how could I expect more of anyone else? So – *Schluss* – it will be a long while before I tackle another complicated work. I'm postponing the publication until next spring, when I'll have another chance to hear it. Still, somewhere in the depths of my soul, there is the hope that a few years from now it will suddenly turn out that the symphony is actually a respectable and even a well-made thing. Can it be that now I'm in my prime, and at the height of my technical powers, I have fallen flat on my face, and after nine months of feverish work?[66]

The answer, from our perspective, even at a time when the Second is the least often performed of the seven symphonies, has to be a stunned 'no'; there is too much energy in the thematic material and its working-out to suggest failure or sterility, as presumably the composer himself recognized when he planned a thorough reworking of it at the end of his life. The first movement reflects his fascination with Honegger's clearly defined 'sound technique'[67] combined with a ferocity to be found previously only in Ornstein's most aggressive piano pieces. His own 'sound technique' suggests that the instruments should be able to make their mark even with extremely difficult figurations and at a high dynamic level (*ff* is preferred throughout). The constant injunctions – 'energico', 'ben articulato', 'ben marcato', 'ben tenuto' – indicate the sort of projection he was hoping to achieve; at first he does so, with the snarling fanfare of the trombones and horns which becomes the first subject proper after nine bars of uproar, leaping and plunging exultantly in intervals of 11ths. Here there is volume and a disconcerting blend of the diatonic with the dissonant, but no over-complexity in the scoring. The second-subject group begins with jabbing wind, piano and pizzicato strings, an attempt to capture the modish sonority Prokofiev had mentioned to Myaskovsky; it is perhaps when the lower woodwind and brass enter below with a sustained chant making much of jazz's 'blue' flattened 3rd that difficulties arise. This is the old *enfant terrible* Prokofiev of the *Scythian Suite*, and he caps the thrilling congestion with the processional climax of the exposition, where another of those diatonic themes linked to the discarded 'white-note' quartet of 1918 sings its heart out on violins, piccolo and trumpets while the rest of the orchestra batters brutally against it. This theme would surely have been a prime candidate for disentanglement from the steel framework of the Second in the planned revision of 1953. It plays little part in the development, which is most impressive in the low sonorities of its early stages (the first of Prokofiev's several homages to Koussevitzky the double-bass player) but somewhat self-defeating when it continues with the mass of counterpoint that has already characterized the movement; only the dynamic levels can go higher. A recapitulation to which Prokofiev skilfully applies his now-familiar truncating technique is capped by a whirlwind coda ending in a percussion tattoo and a surprise wind and brass unison.

The quiet theme of the second movement is the coup that justifies its predecessor's sound and fury, a wistfully supported oboe solo of earlier, 'white-note' provenance which evades its A minor destiny (Ex.47). When the first violins take it up, we are made even more aware of the romantic singing line earlier absent in the frenzy of the first movement. The variations offer richer food for thought than their counterparts in the Third Piano Concerto, seeming to prefigure not just the music of other composers on the Parisian scene, such as Martinů, but also the elaborations of Bartók and early Lutosławski. The tension, of course, rests in the contrast between the innocent quality of the theme and the increasingly complex textures in which it becomes ensnared. A certain good-humoured fantasy offsets the occasional flare-ups of the first two variations, while the third is reminiscent of Prokofiev in *Trapèze* mode. In the fourth variation, though, a child's bad dreams develop into the close-string mesh

Ex.47 Symphony no.2, op.40 – II. Tema

of Renata's hallucinations in *The Fiery Angel*, and the monster fairground barrel-organ of *Petrushka* lends a nightmarish insistency to the syncopated treatment of the theme in the fifth variation. Then comes the climax, the justification for ending the symphony with these variations. Koussevitzky's beloved double basses, divided into three parts, set the ominous scene for the return of the first movement's 'blues' chant; the upper strings lead back their leaping dance and the Scythian climax sets the diatonic theme and the 'blues' at odds with each other. But as this is a set of variations, the grim finality of the climax shatters into a sequence of hammering rhythms and the opening theme returns in its original guise, with the calm insistence of A minor undermined by the final 13-part string chord.

Unease, then, remains the keynote, and Prokofiev wanted no more of it for a while. So he was surely sincere when he turned down a Berlin director's offer to work on a ballet score, *Don Morte*, first because all his time was taken up with the orchestral work and later because the 'fine subject' of *Don Morte* failed to match his mood: 'it's sombre – and I've just finished a great symphony, sombre and austere, on which I have worked for one year. So I'd like to compose something a little more gay'.[68] One response was his transcription for violin and piano of the *Songs without Words* – 'it came out better than it did for solo voice',[69] he told Myaskovsky, and he recast many of the lyric lines here to encompass a specifically violinistic virtuosity. A bigger answer to his prayers came in unexpected form; Diaghilev turned back to him at last for a jolly ballet on the new energy of the Soviet empire neither of them had visited. With the opening up of Russia's brave new world after the Rapallo Agreement, France's recognition of the Soviet regime and the current success of the constructivist artists in Paris, Bolshevism was now the vogue for modish French society. It may have been another desperate bid for centre stage on Diaghilev's part, but he was as curious as Prokofiev to see the latest steps of steel taken by his homeland (and turned down an invitation to visit it only because he feared he might not be let out again).

It was Nouvel, deeply impressed by the premiere of the Second Symphony, who again brought Diaghilev and Prokofiev together; the results effectively closed the protracted negotiations over *Judith* with Ida Rubinstein, whose bad timing in being unavailable when Prokofiev most needed her cooperation led him to tell Demasy that 'regardless of the admiration which I have for your work I have lost all desire to collaborate with this lady'.[70] Until recently, credit for the scenario of what eventually became *Le Pas d'acier* has gone to Diaghilev and the artist Georgy Yakulov, the eventual choice of designer-librettist. But, as yet another crucial letter from Prokofiev to Souvchinsky at the end of June reveals, the composer was a driving force behind the concept. Diaghilev simply commanded 'a subject from contemporary life; this is to put it delicately. Crudely translated, it means that I have to write a Bolshevik ballet'.[71] And since Prokofiev remained antipathetic to the ubiquitous Kochno and was doing all he could to avoid having the immaculate young scribe with his flowery handwriting thrust upon him, who better than Souvchinsky with whom to collaborate:

> Your golden qualities for the given case are the following: you are the most knowledgable of all of us about what's happening today in Russia; you know the scene – and you are possessed of unusual tact so as exactly to take the subject on to such a plane as not to infuriate people either here or there, and entirely to reflect contemporary Bolshevik life. For this one needs not only tact but also sharp vision. It seems to me that if we carry out this ballet in a cheerful and mild fashion, and portray in it not the Bolsheviks but the Russian people under the rule of the Bolsheviks, that will be the best basis for the subject. As concerns the subject itself, in essence, the less of it there is, the better; the simpler it is, the bigger a role the music will play.[72]

The curious thing was that the Soviet regime, for all its cultural celebration of the Revolution and commandeering of such scores as Auber's *La Muette de Portici* and Puccini's *Tosca* for propagandist purposes, had not yet come up with a successful stage work reflecting 'contemporary Bolshevik life'. Only one Soviet opera in 1925 attempted to get to grips with the recent upheavals, Gladkovsky and Prussak's *For Red October*; two more dealt with significant events from the past: Andrey Pashchenko's *Eagles in Revolt* with the Pugachev rebellion against Catherine the Great and Vasily Zolotarev's *The Decembrists* with the doomed uprising against Nicholas I. Asafyev had written a score for a ballet about the French Revolution, *Carmagnole*; when he rewrote it as *The Flames of Paris* in 1932, he would ask his French-based colleague's advice. In 1924 there was also a naive 'synthesized theatrical performance'[73] with music by Vladimir Deshevov called *Red Hurricane*. *Le Pas d'acier* (or *Stalnoy skok*, 'The Steel Step') paved the way for Alexander Mosolov's *Steel*, a ballet score in search of choreography of which only the famous three-minute *Zavod* ('Foundry') movement is still occasionally heard in the concert hall, and Shostakovich's *The Bolt*, his ill-fated, second full-length ballet about factory saboteurs.

Prokofiev's working title was set down on his typewriter as *Ursignol*, Yakulov's idea, an obstinately uncatchy combination of the French initializing of 'USSR' (URS) and *Le Rossignol*, the title of Stravinsky's first opera, familiar to Paris audiences through two Ballets Russes choreographies. The draft and the greater part of the work were thrashed out in the calm surroundings of Bourron-Marlotte, Prokofiev's latest summer retreat not too far from Paris – 'a small, very tranquil place whose inhabitants don't go into town to whoop it up [*faire la bombe*]',[74] he told Szigeti as he offered him the dedication of the fifth *Song without Words* transcription.

The first tasks of the summer outside Paris were at the latest behest of Boris Romanov. He had two substantial demands. There had to be two more numbers for the touring ballet, *Trapèze*: the Overture and *Matelote*, which were to have no place in the Quintet but which eventually became the first and third movements of the orchestral Divertimento cobbled together in 1929 (they have recently been reconstructed in their original chamber form by Noëlle Mann, curator of the Prokofiev Archive in London). The second undertaking was an adaptation of the Schubert waltzes Prokofiev had selected and transcribed for piano in 1919. Romanov wanted an arrangement for small orchestra, but the composer told him they would 'sound better' on two pianos, and amused himself throwing in 'all sorts of cute little counterpoint and ornamentations'.[75] The least documented project of the summer was his instrumentation of *The Ugly Duckling*, usually attributed exclusively to the early 1930s when Lina began to sing it. The performance for which it was made, in the autumn of 1925, 'given in haste, almost without rehearsals, in the Russian language and without translation in the programme, passed unnoticed'.[76] It deserved better, he told the conductor Walter Straram a year later, 'for the orchestration is amusing enough'.[77]

Soon his collaborator for *Ursignol* appeared in Bourron-Marlotte – not Souvchinsky (alas) or Kochno (thankfully) but the Armenian-born Georgy Yakulov, prominent in Paris that year as a jury member for the Exposition Nationale des Arts Décoratifs. Well known from exhibitions throughout Europe, Yakulov also provided an exciting link with contemporary Soviet art and theatre. He had collaborated with Tatlin and Alexander Rodchenko on the astonishing design of the Café Pittoresque in Moscow in 1917 before going on to achieve notable success as a stage designer: although his sketches for Meyerhold's production of Mayakovsky's *Mystère-Bouffe* were not what the director wanted, the production team used him for a revolutionary staging of Wagner's *Rienzi* at the Theatre of Soviet Workers' Deputies in 1923 and he collaborated with another progressive director, Alexander Tairov, on a series of classics.

On 11 August Prokofiev and Yakulov sent Diaghilev their first draft for plot, musical numbers and three sketches for the second part of the ballet, which, as it turned out, was to be very much influenced by the design. The first scene provided a panorama of the new Soviet life before policy and order had a chance to gain control. Sailors, traders, commissars and thieves all parade before us in silhouette before the 'action' begins. A train packed with free-traders pulls into the city station; the three commissars pursue the two robbers; a book-wielding orator pontificates. At last the prima ballerina and male dancer come into focus, she a factory worker harassed by the orator, he a smart, happy-go-lucky sailor who comes to her rescue. They dance, but do not come into contact. Following an *entr'acte* which remained to be clarified in the original scenario, the scene changes to the factory where the young woman works. The sailor has joined the labouring masses, and this is where Yakulov's ambitious stage picture comes into play. Prokofiev and his designer envisaged the sailor-turned-worker starting to labour on one machine, downstage left with four colleagues, while the woman is one of five dancers operating another machine. The sailor finds himself separated from his woman by a work-space, which is immediately occupied by 'five new workers with hammers large and small'. The woman, by this stage having noticed her suitor from another machine, rushes down to meet him. Prokofiev's typescript envisages a vivid finale:

> The main hero and heroine dance together on the pedalling apparatus, and at the same time the whole factory swings into action. The pedal apparatus is constructed

> on the principle of a grinding machine or a treadle sewing machine . . . The first stroke of the pedals serves to set the whole factory in motion; work begins again on the first machine at the left set of wings; at the same time on the upper space, further back, the rolling action and the work on the machine at the right set of wings continues. In the middle space, where the noiseless work with the hammers took place, two workers lower themselves with enormous hammers, wooden, hollow within, and begin to strike them loudly simultaneously with the indications in the score; other workers with smaller hammers remain in the middle space and also strike them rhythmically. From above descends a complex pulley, joining in the action. For the length of the whole finale, which lasts from three to four minutes, brightly coloured lights play on the decor in each of the places.[78]

It all appears immensely complicated, almost geometric in its precision. The result managed to convey the gist with brevity and relative clarity. By 24 August Prokofiev wrote to his first choice of collaborator, Souvchinsky, that he had composed 'more than half' the score and it had 'come out very C-majorish [*domazhorno*]'.[79] This is true of the work as a whole: each of its 11 movements either begins precisely in C major/A minor or works round to the 'C-majorishness' through more complex textures. The steely unisons of the opening (Ex.48*b*) are an up-to-the-minute echo of *Chout*'s closing bars, which in themselves celebrate Prokofiev's most recent tune for Diaghilev – the second theme of the final dance so extensively reworked in 1920 (Ex.48*a*). The passing discords are to become a familiar hallmark of Prokofiev's Soviet era ambiguity. But as the large cast of minor figures peopling the first scene

Ex.48*a* Chout, op.21 – Final dance

Ex.48*b* *Le Pas d'acier*, op. 41 – Scene I, no.1, Entry of the workers

take centre stage, we notice a certain paucity of invention in the determined 'C-majorishness' of the diatonic themes. The fashionable preoccupation with wind and brass results, of course, in the strings rarely playing cantabile; and much is made of the interplay between shrill, high woodwind – the small-fry of contemporary street-life – and bassoons, eventually giving way to brass as the authority figures in the third number (a blueprint for the police and the warring clans in *Romeo and Juliet*). The lyric relief is carefully kept under control, for the sailor and the young woman can hardly be said to dance a *pas de deux*, but the interplay between his arpeggiating clarinets and her flutes is lightly and graciously done – prophetic of the Nurse, rather than Romeo, and Juliet (Ex.49).

This is more openly lyrical than the parodies of love-play in *Chout*, but equally short-lived; and just as the diatonic material of the buffoon disguised as his own sister in *Chout* finds itself distorted as he feigns weeping before the gang of seven, so the factory-girl's winsomeness makes an odd companion for the spinning-jenny chromatics of the machine she is operating – halfway between the worlds of *Chout* and Renata's ensnarement in *The Fiery Angel*. Prokofiev's factory is remarkably light of touch, too, until the hammerers leap on stage; then the entire working ensemble merely plays a scintillating variation on the ballet's cheerful opening music.

Ex.49 *Le Pas d'acier* – Scene I, no.4, Sailor and girl worker

It is all a long way from the relentless battering of Mosolov's *Steel*, less far from the cartoon characters of Shostakovich's *The Age of Gold*, just round the corner. Shostakovich, shortly to make his mark as the 19-year-old composer of a symphony, derived much of his spikiest early satire from his work as an accompanist of silent films; but less has been made of *Le Pas d'acier* as an even more powerful influence.

This third of Prokofiev's ballet scores for Diaghilev (counting *Ala and Lolly* as the first) was the last of his attempts to make something absolutely new out of his time in the West. Although the language was consciously simpler than that of *Trapèze*, unobtrusively premiered in Gotha on 6 November 1925, or the Second Symphony, his two other 'steps of steel', it remained influenced by the wind and brass domination of the new aesthetic led by Stravinsky and Les Six. When, in the year of the ballet's premiere (1927), Prokofiev eventually put the finishing touches to *The Fiery Angel*, the opera would fuse the extremes of recent stylization with an older, lusher idiom. Symbolically, its birth – in manuscript, if not on stage – was to take place only after he had made vital new tours of the New World, which had been so slow to accept his music, and the country he knew best, which had never forgotten him.

11
From America to Bolshevizia
1925–7

Prokofiev orchestrated 60 pages of his Soviet ballet, to be called *Le Pas d'acier*, not in the transfigured land of his birth (which was to welcome him back soon enough) but along the steel tracks of America, travelling between cities in early 1926 on an exhausting but hard-won tour. Earlier, he had decided that the open-minded citizens of Stockholm were ready for his Second Piano Concerto, which he insisted on playing there in both his November appearances with orchestra: 'because of the extreme difficulty of this concerto it's perfectly impossible for me to play two different programmes',[1] he told the management, but he demanded a piano with an easy action to lighten the burden. In between he gave a punishing recital with the Third and Second Sonatas respectively opening each half of the concert. In addition to his own piano pieces – the three gavottes he liked to place side by side, the op.12 Prelude and the Toccata – he played three of Myaskovsky's *Prichudi*, pieces by Taneyev and Medtner and four movements from Musorgsky's *Pictures at an Exhibition.* Lina sang four of his songs, three from op.36 and *In my Garden* from op.23 as well as one of Musorgsky's songs from *The Nursery* and arias from Rimsky-Korsakov's *Snow Maiden* and *The Tsar's Bride.* In December Dutch audiences heard much the same, with modifications (not least the replacement of the Second Sonata by popular miniatures).

In late 1925 Prokofiev was besieged with demands that made recalcitrant America an attractive proposition again. In addition to the Boston tour Koussevitzky had promised him, Fitzhugh Haensel was now active again, having very nearly been ousted at the beginning of the year by Koussevitzky's Boston manager. At first his offer was characteristically meagre and brought a typical response: 'is it possible that after five years you have finally secured me an engagement? Please, the next one before 1930'.[2] The tally did improve: by early November Haensel had secured a clutch of recitals under the aegis of the society Pro Musica, which had 'chapters' in St Paul, Denver, Portland, San Francisco and Kansas eager to welcome the composer. It seems that Prokofiev was ever more willing to compromise; having agreed to the Dutch request that he replace his Second Sonata with his *Love for Three Oranges* transcriptions, the March and Scherzo, he was now happy to propose performing the opening movement of the Third Piano Concerto as a self-contained number, 'perfectly "an und für sich"',[3] as he called it, in place of the short First Concerto, though this proved unnecessary. What he would not consent to were requests from several of the chapters for lectures, for the usual reason ('I've composed – it's for others to discuss'[4]) or for a wider repertory to satisfy, for example, the Kansans' preference for Bach (Kansas wanted a simple programme). As he had already told a Strasbourg organization who wanted him to dilute his own music with a piano performance of Stravinsky's *Petrushka*, 'I am a composer who *par excellence* plays his own compositions. If I can offer you a few pieces by Myaskovsky, it's only by pure chance'.[5] In any case, Lina's presence, to be covered only by travelling expenses, would add variety and glamour to the 'chapter' evenings.

The Prokofievs travelled to America together for the first time on the French liner *De Grasse*, leaving Le Havre just before Christmas and arriving in New York on 1 January 1926. The *New York City World* was proud to report them among arrivals who included the violinist Jacques Thibaud and '12 Venetian gondoliers, imported to propel the gondolas of the Miami-Biltmore Hotel'.[6] Whether this could be said to mark a step forward in American sophistication, musical life in the USA had certainly begun to expand its horizons since Prokofiev's last visit. The radical International Composers' Guild in New York, founded by Edgard Varèse in 1921, now had a more moderate offshoot, the League of Composers, which aimed 'to bring the entire range of modern tendencies before the public'.[7] Prokofiev had long been acquainted through McCormick and friends with the composer of the latest sensation, the Chicago-based John Alden Carpenter, whose 'ballet of modern American life' *Skyscrapers*, a New World anticipation of *Le Pas d'acier*, was given its premiere at the Metropolitan Opera in February after its rejection by Diaghilev. (Writing to Asafyev in April 1927 Prokofiev recommended the score, which includes banjo, saxophones and red traffic lights controlled by keyboard, with reservations: 'I cannot say that it is a first-rate composition, but from the perspective of what's being written in America, it's interesting enough'.[8]) Stokowski's enterprise with the Philadelphia Orchestra, which he had now transformed into a glowing instrument much admired by Prokofiev and other leading musicians, knew no bounds: in April they were to give the premiere of the mighty masses of Varèse's *Amériques*, and a year later they dabbled in the microtonal experiment of the Mexican composer Julián Carrillo's Concertino. Shortly after Prokofiev's arrival in New York, Stokowski and his Philadelphians were airing an altogether less adventurous work which nevertheless gave the new visitor enormous pleasure: the very Myaskovsky symphony he had railed against for its 'Glazunovism', the Fifth.[9] But, loyal as ever, Prokofiev managed to mention the performance in most of his newspaper interviews. He told Myaskovsky about this 'real holiday' of a concert: the Philadelphia Orchestra was 'undoubtedly one of the best in the world'; the performance, conducted by Stokowski from memory, was 'superb' with the exception of a long-drawn-out conclusion to the first movement; and the hall was so full that he, Szigeti and Ziloti had to stand.[10]

In less than a month it seemed as if 'all the most famous conductors'[11] were assembled in New York; in addition to Stokowski, Toscanini, Mengelberg, Klemperer and Furtwängler were offering competition which Koussevitzky, Prokofiev's own conductor, would prove able to match. Although his concerts with 'Kousi' were not scheduled to start until early February, Prokofiev had serious business in New York shortly after his arrival. For Duo-Art he recorded four of Myaskovsky's *Prichudi* (under their German title of *Grillen*) and his own transcription of the key themes from Rimsky-Korsakov's *Sheherazade*, which he had mooted as a possibility with the Aeolian Company as early as January 1923; the disappointingly basic end product was a result of the Aeolian philosophy – 'our people want . . . to hear all with which they are familiar in a condensed form'.[12] A final, more substantial proposal, the Third Sonata, appears to have been dropped from the schedule. The mechanical-piano procedure was neatly outlined to Myaskovsky; it entailed a return visit in February to make corrections to the 'recording', an indication of how much direct contact most of the company's artists had with the editing process. After the initial recording and reunions with old friends like Gottlieb, who wrote to Prokofiev that he had felt like 'a sweetheart who calls upon a girl he has not seen for a long time',[13] Prokofiev and Lina embarked on their demanding Pro Musica recital tour.

Lina recalled the punishing routines all too well: arrival, usually by overnight train (and the occasional station breakfast, attended by brightly painted waitresses), reception by a member of the ladies' committee, a drive round the town, lunch, installation in a hotel or the private house of a Pro Musica luminary, practice (usually in the form of testing out the new venue's acoustics), then the concert. An enthusiastic reception was by no means the end of it; as Lina remembered, 'in one of the clauses of the contract, [it stipulated] we must shake hands with all the members of the society',[14] an exhausting round of commonplaces during which, it seems, the usually short-tempered Prokofiev held his sarcastic instincts in check. Prokofiev continues amusingly in his short autobiography: 'the ritual proceeded thus: a member of the society would come up to the secretary and say, "I am Mr Smith". The chairman would say to me, "Allow me to introduce you to Mr Smith". I would shake his hand and say, "Happy to meet you, Mr Smith!" Then Mr Smith would say, "Happy to meet you, Mr Prokofiev!" and move on to my wife. In the meantime Mr Jones would be approaching in the same manner, and so on, 300 times'.[15]

In spite of less than ideal venues (in the Pythian Hall, Portland, an Ivesian *mélange* ensued when dance music from elsewhere in the building joined the recital) Prokofiev was being received as a modern classic, and the regional newspaper articles tended to range from the surprisingly well informed to the overwhelmingly enthusiastic. The *Morning Oregonian* decided that 'Prokofieff can pack into a single brief piece much of the emotion, contrast and some of the beauty that Schumann and Beethoven could inject into a whole sonata'.[16] The *Kansas City Star* found his honesty about the new Stravinsky Piano Sonata, which he conceded might have to bide its time to be understood despite its awkward pastiche-Bach finale, a refreshing example to other contemporary musicians in interview, while the *St Paul Pioneer Press* concentrated on Prokofiev's attitude to Soviet musical life. His response is interesting in view of the step he would shortly be taking: 'visitors who are Russian by birth do well to exercise caution in returning to their native land – unless they wish to stay there. For human resources of all kinds are at present so necessary to the situation in Russia that every effort is made to detain and utilize the services of each visitor. My opera *The Love for Three Oranges* . . . is to be given in Leningrad, in the former Imperial Theatre, and I am invited for the occasion. I do not expect to go. It is too difficult and complicated as yet'.[17]

The best from the newspaper world was yet to come, in New York. His first debt was a response to Olga Samaroff, the first Mrs Stokowski and a concert pianist turned columnist, who had asked for corrections to her article to be printed in the *New York Evening Post* and apologized for 'the infantile interest of my compatriots in the personal'.[18] Prokofiev had little to add other than to 'thank you for the first *serious interview* that I have had in America. So it goes without saying that your article is written with a great deal of *address* and talent'.[19] In it, Samaroff compared Prokofiev's former rejection at the hands of the Americans with Mahler returning to Europe 'disappointed and disheartened',[20] giving a fair sketch of his career to date and advertising plans for *The Fiery Angel* as well as the still-unnamed Soviet ballet. She then elicited one of his most detailed reflections on the nature of new music:

> 'One can compose', continued Mr. Prokofieff, 'emotional music and absolute music. The former will more excite the passion of contemporaries, but the latter will be more lasting even if first accepted with less enthusiasm, for the emotional expression of a given age can become incomprehensible and sometimes ridiculous to succeeding generations.' Mr. Prokofieff advanced the thought that the manner of making love was a good case in point. The vision of a lass of 1926 being wooed with a Mozartian serenade, or verses à la Cyrano de Bergerac, not to speak of the type of remote and respectful offer of hand and heart that would have reduced a Jane Austen heroine to tears, forced me to admit that there is a good deal in Mr. Prokofieff's argument. He considers Bach as the highest example of the lasting vitality of absolute music.
>
> I then turned to a more technical question of composition and asked Mr. Prokofieff how he felt about quarter-tones (of which we shall soon have a demonstration coming from the unexpected direction of Mexico [Carrillo's Concertino]), and whether he was using them. He said he felt that the field bounded by the semi-tone was still so rich in unused possibilities that he was not tempted in the direction of quarter-tones. He added that quarter-tones are used in India in music of a totally different type wherein it is much more possible to train the ear to the acceptance of infinite gradations of tone than in our music with its complex mass of counterpoint.[21]

Then, in response to Samaroff's question about the use of Tchaikovskian melody in the music of Myaskovsky and other Russian composers, the interviewee made the first of many statements in which he would increasingly hone his thoughts on a pressing subject. Samaroff's ensuing comment already reflects the message behind his own:

> 'The most novel harmonic discoveries can be imitated and adopted by others, whereas a melody is a personal creation and stands as such without possibility of imitation except through obvious plagiarism.' It seems to me this utterance by one of the leaders among modern composers is very significant.
>
> It looks as though the experimentation with harmonic idiom which has been going on feverishly for the last ten or fifteen years has for the time being almost run its course.[22]

The move towards a 'new simplicity' voiced in interviews Prokofiev was to give throughout the early 1930s has its origins here. At any rate, he had no intention of unleashing his 'most novel harmonic discoveries' on American audiences; the other half of his tour schedule, eight concerts with Koussevitzky and the Boston Symphony, featured nothing more adventurous than the Third Piano Concerto, which Chicago and New York had already heard on his previous visit. Clearly Koussevitzky, who had taken up his post in Boston at the beginning of the 1924–5 season, at the age of 50, intended to tread more carefully in the New World than he had in Paris. Hailed at the onset as 'Master of Line, Color, Tone, and Characterization in Music',[23] Koussevitzky maintained the full houses of his first concerts in America; and by the end of 1926, when movements of the *Chout* Suite were heard in Boston, one newspaper noted that 'at his hands Prokofiev has become a favourite composer with the public of the symphony concerts, best loved of the newer moderns'.[24] So Koussevitzky was already achieving with his orchestra what Prokofiev managed in his most recent American recitals; and before the decade was out, he would be taking gambles equal to the new-music banquets he had served up in Paris.

The income from Prokofiev's American tour, registering $107.82 profit on his tax return once all allowances had been taken into account, enabled him to pay some of his outstanding debts, including the money he owed *Musical America* for advertising and small amounts to the long-suffering dentist Dr Hussa. After their return to the Old World, he and Lina stopped briefly in Paris, where he was able to report to Dukelsky on an affectionate meeting with Dukelsky's mother and brother in Boston. (Duke's claim that he introduced William Walton to Prokofiev at this time is contradicted by a letter of eight months later, singing Walton's praises and asking if he can bring him to meet Prokofiev; so the introduction probably took place in December 1926.) The couple then embarked on another tour, this time to Italy – more sightseeing pleasure than money-making business (though negotiations had been protracted and financial squabbles were to ensue). Five concerts were scheduled, only one with orchestra – a performance of the Third Piano Concerto – on Prokofiev's arrival in Rome. There he also had an audience with the Pope on

8 April, described in detail and with more than a little irony in his Diary; presumably it satisfied his intellectual curiosity and gave extra flavour to the Inquisitor's presence in *The Fiery Angel*. After their joint recital in the capital, husband and wife repeated their programmes of Prokofiev and Myaskovsky in Siena, Genoa and Florence. 'I tried in every way to be simple and easily digestible, but even this programme turned out to be too heavy on the Italian stomach', he told Myaskovsky, 'and both your works and mine met with extreme reserve.'[25] The Florentines, at least, asked for an encore of Myaskovsky's song *Circles*, though Prokofiev was horrified by the critical accusation that he composed 'musiquette'[26] and had to be soothed by his wry host in a subsequent letter.

There was one bonus that brought with it a livelier crowd: the belated offer of an appearance in Naples on 20 April. Not only did this allow Prokofiev to go with Lina to many of the sites Diaghilev had shown him on his first visit in 1915 – notably Pompeii and Vesuvius, where they performed the tourist ritual of throwing a coin into molten lava for a souvenir cast – but it also brought a chance meeting with a distinguished old friend. Just before the Naples recital, Lina peered out between the stage curtains and saw 'this very special figure of a man with long hanging moustaches';[27] it was Maxim Gorky, who had acted as such a sympathetic intermediary between Prokofiev and the authorities during his last days in Russia. Gorky's relations with the Soviet regime had soured following his criticism of numerous post-Revolutionary purges, which prompted an infuriated Lenin in 1921 to suggest that he move to the West for health and political reasons; but he was no less a fish out of water in Italy, where his accolades for certain individuals in the party at home led him to be labelled a subversive Bolshevik. Before the Revolution he had held court in exile in Capri; now he was back, but as the authorities refused him permission to resettle on the island he lived in Sorrento, and it was to his residence there that Prokofiev was invited after his recital. 'The big palazzo-type house in which Gorky lived at the time', he wrote in 1936, 'struck me as being chill and uncomfortable in spite of the Italian climate, and hardly fitting for Gorky, who when I asked after his health, replied, "One of my lungs is gone altogether, and only half of the other one is left".'[28] They discussed the Soviet Union's rehabilitation of countless homeless children, the so-called *bezprizorni*, feral after years of war and revolution; and presumably the question of a new commitment to the motherland arose. Gorky went back in May 1928 and died under circumstances still presumed suspicious in June 1936, only months after Prokofiev's own return.

The Prokofievs had returned to Paris before a major musical event in Italy: the world premiere on 25 April of Puccini's *Turandot* at La Scala, Milan, conducted by Toscanini two and a half years after the composer's death. The curious link here is that Toscanini had been suggested by Margot Szenkar, wife of the opera's excellent Cologne interpreter, as another suitable champion of *The Love for Three Oranges*, which shares a source with Puccini's opera in Gozzi's collection of *fiabe*. Prokofiev's opera was now at last reaching the Soviet stage, in Leningrad, and had been scheduled for the Berlin Städtische Oper in October. Prokofiev was 'not entirely satisfied' with the Berlin production, he told Tanya Rayevskaya, now living in Germany; 'they staged it heavily, in the German style. The tempos were not all what I would have wished; a lot of director's tricks came off coarsely. They told us this was necessary for the Berlin public'.[29] Thanking Szenkar for a goodwill telegram which had arrived 'between the second and third acts' of the Berlin opening, Prokofiev announced that during the evening 'I often – very often – was thinking of Cologne, where it was indeed much more *love* to the three Oranges'.[30] Soon enough he would be wishing he had chosen the loyalty of Szenkar over the prestige of Berlin for his next opera.

This second German production was a belated substitute for *The Fiery Angel*, which Prokofiev had hoped to orchestrate the previous summer. He had been held up because he felt he needed extra help with the subject matter from Boris Demchinsky, the literary friend from St Petersburg days who had already assisted him over a crucial impasse in *The Gambler*. Asafyev, his less than satisfactory intermediary throughout, was first approached with a plea back in February 1925:

> Remembering what outstanding service Demchinsky provided in putting together the libretto for the roulette scene in *The Gambler*, I sent my libretto for *The Fiery Angel* for him to look over. Demchinsky swore and promised 'with delight' to make a few changes, the more appropriate since he had in his possession a great deal of material on things medieval. But a year and a half has gone by, I've bombarded him with letters and I still haven't received anything, so I haven't begun the orchestration. Demchinsky is a complex fellow: his undoubtedly Christian soul is hardly free of Mephistophelian flourishes. It seems he can't forgive me my successes, believing that they don't correspond with the rather shallow little soul which I possess. Perhaps you don't entirely agree with this, in which case I beg you, go to Demchinsky, talk to him and clarify whether he intends to make the changes he promised and why he hasn't replied to my questions.[31]

Prokofiev's constant imprecations to Asafyev, based on his own insecurity, continually failed to take into account the possibility that both his Soviet colleagues might be finding it awkward to deal with the subject matter under circumstances at which Myaskovsky had already hinted. With Berlin poised to stage *The Love for Three Oranges* and banking on its success to take up *The Fiery Angel* for the following season, Demchinsky did at last write in the early summer of 1926.

In the end, 'the mountain gave birth to a mouse', Prokofiev told Asafyev, 'and I barely used his suggestions for the libretto'.[32] But it did leave him free to orchestrate *The Fiery Angel* at last, and the document in which he responded in detail to Demchinsky's suggestion is invaluable both in shedding light on his understanding of Bryusov's novel and in revealing his sure theatrical instinct. He plays the role of that master of stagecraft Richard Strauss to the literary unworldliness of Demchinsky's Hofmannsthal, admiring Demchinsky's faithful condensation of

Bryusov but considering that it often lacked theatrical detail. He also emphasizes a dimension that his orchestra would be especially well equipped to serve:

> You've completely removed from the relationship of Ruprecht and Renata the element of magic and the role which it has played in their lives: magic is the pivot on which the whole story turns. It's well known that Bryusov studied magic and made experiments. When he was asked whether *The Fiery Angel* was the result of his studies of magic, or rather whether he studied magic so as to be better able to write *Angel*, Bryusov replied: 'I studied magic for the sake of magic, but *The Fiery Angel* is to some extent the result of my studies'. So it strikes me that this element must be introduced, and most of all into the second act, taking the form of conversations, portents, weighty leather-bound tomes, the forms of Glock and Agrippa – but not, it goes without saying, in the form of experiments and incantations.[33]

This was to be the first of Prokofiev's most radical alterations to his original piano score. We would surely consider the eerie knockings on the wall, and the unusual musical textures that accompany them, the result of 'experiments and incantations', but they turn the supernatural screw significantly. Glock, the purveyor of alchemical books, now makes a brief appearance; but much more important is the entire rewriting of the scene at Agrippa's, which dispenses with most of the discourse, the apprentices and the mysterious dogs of Bryusov's narrative. Demchinsky had recommended the complete removal of this, Prokofiev's original Act II scene 2, but the composer countered with the belief that 'in my opinion Agrippa is the unseen pivot round which *The Fiery Angel* revolves', a symbol of 'the empty and terrifying dead end to which in the end magic leads'.[34] Ruprecht's questioning of the sage now meets with brief aphorisms in a five-minute episode against an 'irrepressible musical and theatrical rhythm which will ensure that this scene is terrifying and compelling'.[35] Prokofiev's most regular steel thrash yet would underpin it and be channelled into the hair-raising finale of the Third Symphony.

In Act III Prokofiev had now adopted Demchinsky's suggestion and removed the tenor role of Heinrich, the incarnation of Renata's 'fiery angel', having him appear instead 'for a minute . . . handsome, dazzling but silent'.[36] As before, the duel between the two men at Renata's instigation is depicted in a climactic musical interlude, after which the scene with the wounded, delirious Ruprecht has a new anticlimax, delivered (as at the end of the new Act I) by minor characters: a Musorgskian device. The fourth act, where Ruprecht falls in with Mephistopheles and a non-Goethean depiction of Faust, is much as before. Prokofiev decided that his final scene, of Renata's death in prison (on which Demchinsky insisted), was clumsy and untheatrical; why not simply conclude the opera in the convent with 'the possession and the sentence pronounced by the Inquisitor on Renata, when he condemns her to fire and torture . . . I am also in favour of my ending of the opera because the scene of general possession is without question daring and will be something new for the operatic stage'.[37] What remained to be achieved was a more effective appearance for the the Inquisitor; Prokofiev wanted him to be 'imposing and showy like an archbishop',[38] a title he hesitated to use because of possible trouble in Catholic countries. One scholar with a profound knowledge of the Russian symbolist movement sees this ending as 'problematic . . . the blunt cessation of the action leaves the religious and philosophical issues raised in the score unresolved'.[39] On an intellectual plane, that is true; but Prokofiev placed his sense of theatre first so that the end would crown the work, and in the stunning, steady crescendo of mass hysteria in the convent he would achieve his aim.

For the moment, haste was of the essence: the Berlin contract stipulated delivery of the manuscript on a fixed date; 'at the beginning of June', Prokofiev told Ernest Blois, 'I went to an isolated dacha in order to devote myself entirely to work on *The Fiery Angel*'.[40] This latest of Prokofiev's summer retreats was a happy compromise after an unsuccessful search for somewhere in the Dordogne, and he wrote about it in the next of his loving letters to Aunt Katya: 'we have rented a dacha in the small and quiet place of Samoreau, 3 kms from Fontainebleau – and Fontainebleau is one hour from Paris. It's very beautiful here – a forest, fields and the river'.[41] Within weeks he would be wrangling, as he so often did, with the owner, a Mme Langlois, who had not provided all the necessities and who responded that he was failing to meet his financial obligations. At least the outcome was settled more swiftly than his contretemps with M. Lapina of Bellevue, which had nearly reached court action over an unsettled payment. Otherwise, life in the Villa Langlois was quiet enough at first with Lina, her mother and Sviatoslav, now nearly two, who was speaking 'in Russian and French, in both languages with a slight accent. He translated from Russian into French for our cook. He knows his name, patronymic and surname'.[42] The departure of Madame Codina for New York in September returned Lina to the role of full-time mother, interrupting her singing studies with her husband (they were now preparing more of his own songs and the role of Rimsky-Korsakov's Snow Maiden).

Prokofiev's own work load was lightened by a secretary, Georgy Gorchakov. On his American rail journeys Prokofiev had discovered a labour-saving method of scoring (occasionally misinterpreted as a way of leaving his orchestration to others), simply a precise indication on the short score of the finest details, down to chord instrumentation, accents and bowing, which could be clearly read by his copyist. Light relief in Samoreau was provided by a host of visitors. Among them were Warren Klein, an American Christian Scientist whom Prokofiev had met as an Aeolian Company representative and whose conversation he had enjoyed in Paris, and Bashkirov, who had again turned up in France. 'Now it seems he's successful enough working as a chauffeur, so he's begun to write verses again', he wrote to Bashkirov's brother in New York, 'and from time to time he's even placed articles about Russia in French newspapers.'[43] Occasional 'Verin' poems on musical themes such as Skryabin and Beethoven surface among Prokofiev's papers of this time.

By mid-August he had orchestrated over 100 pages of *The Fiery Angel*: 'it'll run to 400 pages at least', he told his publisher.[44] He was excited to receive from the artist Anna Ostroumova-Lebedeva in Leningrad background material on the Bely–Petrovskaya–Bryusov triangle, which was 'not only interesting but completely exciting, because it arrived just at the height of my work on *The Fiery Angel*', he told her.[45] The project was interrupted by the instrumentation of an overture for small orchestra (to become known as the *American* Overture op.42), commissioned by his loyal friends in the Aeolian Company to inaugurate a new building with a 250-seat concert hall in New York. The player-piano craze had passed its heyday with the advent of radio broadcasts, and the company was hoping to capitalize on live performance; the commission was its consolation prize for the halt in roll-making. 'The tempo is: "allegro brioso e fastoso"', he told the Aeolian Company representative, Hermann Schaad, 'which can give you the idea of its character – gay and brilliant. In composing it I tried to be simple, and I hope that it can be understood from the very first hearing.'[46]

This was a manifesto of a 'new simplicity' *avant la lettre* and for American consumption rather than Soviet (though the constructivist ballet of Soviet life had already reverted to a framework of diatonicism). The description applies to the jauntily festive B flat major theme heard right at the start and repeated no fewer than five times throughout the work's eight-minute duration, and to its simple form in which two more relaxed and lyrical sequences are heard without prefatory transition between the bright fanfares; in a note for Russian performers, Prokofiev wrote with unusual baldness that 'the form is A–B–A–C–A, and each of these three episodes in turn has the form of A–B–A'.[47] The only development is in the crescendos back to the piece's catchy signature-tune, with the build-up after the first quieter section reminiscent of the startling 'factory at work' sequence from the still-unnamed Soviet ballet, and there is only the briefest counterpoint in the second 'interlude'. Less simple is the usual tension either between the interlacing of diatonic and chromatic material or in their simultaneous presentation, notable in the wind and second piano parts of the second episode (Ex.50).

The group of 17 performers was to suit the new Aeolian Hall's modest auditorium, but its disposition was Prokofiev's choice not the company's – an attempt to show American audiences the new sonorities still welcomed by Parisian audiences. The principle that motivated the Quintet is now fully realized with the absence of violins and violas. Prokofiev explained his unusual forces thus:

> at the centre of motion of this overture are the two pianos; the two harps and celesta employed principally in the highest register serve as a kind of resonator for the piano; for the transaction of the horizontal music the five winds are employed; the two trumpets and trombone which the composer has employed with care, reinforce them and emphasize the rhythmic moments; finally, in the capacity of a bass, now soft, now howling, were conceived the three contrabasses, of which the upper one is substituted by a cello; the seventeenth player plays a few percussion instruments.[48]

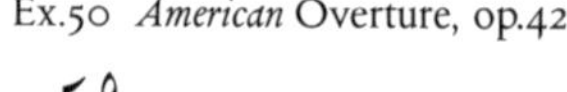
Ex.50 *American* Overture, op.42

The overture's chief attraction would be lost in the arrangement for large orchestra of two years later, with upper strings now softening the brazen timbre of the fanfares.

In late September Schaad wrote to say that the opening of the new Aeolian building had been delayed following a fire; Prokofiev lost no time in asking whether the overture might therefore be given its premiere in Russia. By then he knew exactly the institution willing to play it, and he knew he could be there to hear it. In April he had received news of vital performances by the Moscow orchestra Persimfans, which had played his *Scythian Suite* twice 'with unwavering and great success',[49] adding it to a repertoire that included the First Violin Concerto, the Third Piano Concerto and the March from *The Love for Three Oranges* as the perfect encore. Such information from the motherland was arriving with increasing frequency, especially now that Western colleagues were touring the Soviet Union with unprecedented freedom; in May, for instance, Pierre Monteux reported triumphs with *Chout* in Moscow and Leningrad. 'I'm a well-loved composer there',[50] Prokofiev told Nina Koshetz in September 1926, announcing his plans for concerts there.

The Persimfans was certainly a special case. Its acronym was derived from a lengthy title which provides the key to its originality: 'Pervyi Symphonicheskyi Ansambl bez dirizhora' ('first symphonic ensemble without conductor'). It was part of Moscow's drive to rebuild its culture in a new and democratic form after four years of civil war; at the beginning of 1922, the Moscow State Philharmonic Society, with which Prokofiev would conduct many of his negotiations for his first Soviet tour, came into being, establishing alongside Persimfans a string quartet and a folk orchestra. In its first year, 210 concerts took place not just in the Grand Hall of the Moscow Conservatory but in workers' clubs and factories. The driving force behind Persimfans was Lev Tseitlin, a violin professor at the Moscow Conservatory and former leader of Koussevitzky's orchestra, who took on the responsibility of making it a fusion of professors and students from his institution with outstanding players from the Bolshoy Theatre Orchestra. These players would take part in discussing their roles in the work in hand, sending a representative out into the hall to listen to the ensemble. It was the perfect symbol of true communism, functioning effectively, educationally and influentially for a decade; just how well will be apparent from Prokofiev's comments on his arrival in the Soviet Union.

The invitation for his tour arrived in May from Arnold Tsukker, Tseitlin's co-manager of Persimfans. Unlike Tseitlin, Tsukker had no performing role and appears as a party activist to have served as intermediary between the orchestra and various government departments. Expressing regret and surprise that there had not been a single monograph on Prokofiev written in Russia, Tsukker in his letter of 26 May wanted to know 'in principle your opinion of the possibility of coming to SSSR for a string of concerts'.[51] With Derzhanovsky also acting as friendly prompt from the rival Association of New Music, negotiations were soon well underway with both parties. Lunacharsky, that well-wisher of old, gave an extra fillip to the likelihood of the visit during a lecture on Prokofiev and Beethoven; soon an invitation arrived from the sister Philharmonic organization in Leningrad offering Prokofiev, in addition to two piano recitals, the conducting of one concert and two performances of the Leningrad *Love for Three Oranges* which had been such a success since its premiere in the spring. 'I refused this', he wrote to his aunt and cousin in Penza, 'because it's now four years since I took up a baton'[52] (for the Chicago and New York performances of his opera).

When the crucial exchange of his awkward Nansen passport for a Soviet entry visa and the guarantee of an exit visa had been promised by the Moscow Philharmonic, the visit began to take shape. Surprising links reforged with the past coincided with late stages of the planning towards the end of 1926. Prokofiev heard from Marya Kilschtedt, and reminded her fondly of their collaboration on *Undine*; he also had a letter, at long last, from Morolev, the veterinary surgeon he had befriended in Sontsovka, and had no difficulty in slipping into the familiar tone of jocular reproach: 'As you see, I had strained every effort to find out what had happened to you, and you only decided to write to me after ten years – that's unquestionably swinish! You dedicate sonatas and popular marches to a chap and for a decade he can't be bothered to take up a pen!'[53] Mock indignation notwithstanding, Prokofiev wrote that he would still be delighted to see the liveliest companion of his youth and hoped to make up for Morolev's loss of his old piano, which had 'died an heroic death under shrapnel'[54] by being played to him in his Moscow hotel room. Most eagerly awaited was the chance of meeting Aunt Katya and Katyechka, who had been suffering under the onslaught of a vicious neighbour in Penza. In his last letter to them before his departure, the loving nephew offered to pay for a move 'if it means your escaping from that lovely lady' and to provide return tickets on the sleeper from Penza to Moscow for both of them, 'which would cost the same if we came to Penza',[55] an option that was looking increasingly unlikely as the shower of concert dates increased.

Last-minute musical matters remained to be resolved. Schaad wrote to give his permission for the Soviet premiere of the *American* Overture, and hoped to hear 'good results of its baptism'.[56] Prokofiev also dispatched another 198 pages of the piano score of *The Fiery Angel*, with full details of the orchestration, to the trusty copyist Monsieur Jasmin, adding that 'the fifth act is already advanced, and I'll finish it as soon as possible after my return';[57] the pressure from Berlin had eased, and the premiere was moved from March to October. On 13 January the Prokofievs vacated the shortest of their tenancies, an apartment in Rue Troyon (obtained with extraordinary difficulty for the period following the Samoreau summer), left Sviatoslav with Lina's mother, and the capable secretary Gorchakov in charge of business and administrative matters, and set out for 'Bolshevizia', as Prokofiev now called it, by way of Berlin and Riga.

Prokofiev fully recognized the significance of this return; two years earlier he had told Myaskovsky how such a visit would distract him from important work 'for a long time, if only for emotional reasons'.[58] He now kept his usual shorthand diary up to mid-February but subsequently collated it with Lina's detailed notes and other documents into a polished account, to be typed by Gorchakov. Prokofiev never took this invaluable piece of writing back to Russia; it passed into Lina's hands when she returned to western Europe long after Prokofiev's death and was the first of his most personal writings to be translated in its entirety into English, by his second son Oleg, who also published the Russian original in Paris.[59] Unlike the long and short autobiographies, both remarkable works of literature, it has the impact of immediate impression, and when it was published in 1991 astonished readers who had previously been fed only one-dimensional portraits of the composer. Rude to the importunate and the unduly bureaucratic, infinitely kind to the young and enthusiastic, often ironic but capable of deep emotion, Prokofiev emerges as a rounded and ultimately lovable human being as well as an objective diarist of the first order.

Nostalgia struck Prokofiev even before they had crossed the border – in Riga, where the 'combined smell' of snow and the manure from the horses drawing the sleighs 'pleasantly recalls the Petersburg winters of the old days. I have a special memory for smells and I can sometimes recreate whole pictures from them'.[60] After a happy intimation of the past, a token of the immediate future occurred in the first recital of the tour, in the Riga Opera House: 'I played rather nervously. Where was my American serenity, which I considered a permanent acquisition?'[61] Prokofiev was to refer many times over the next two months to the poise he thought he had acquired on his tour a year earlier. Memory lapses occurred frequently in the middle of pieces; the nervousness refused to go. A feeling of permanent fatigue stayed with the couple. Lina sang with him only in Riga, including in her programme several of the Balmont settings in the presence of the poet, and felt too weak to appear before Russian audiences.

Prokofiev did not formulate in his diary the crucial importance of his return. He told the journalist of Riga's Russian newspaper *Sevodnya*: 'a musician cannot for long lose touch with his native strains. It's possible to be abroad for a pleasant length of time, but it's absolutely essential to return from time to time to the homeland to catch the feeling of contemporary Russian life'.[62] On the way to the station for the two-night train journey to Moscow, doubts surfaced: 'should we not just shrug it all off and stay here? We couldn't be sure whether we would return or whether we might be prevented from leaving. The trip to Latvia would hardly have been a waste of time since we had a number of concert engagements proposed to us'.[63] The fears returned in the early hours of the morning at the Latvian border: 'again the thought occurred to us: "This is the last point at which it's still not too late to turn back. Very well, perhaps it's shameful, but when all's said and done we could go through with it, if it's virtually a matter of life and death"'.[64]

Their arrival in Moscow a day later, however, swept them up immediately in the tide of Russian musical life. The familiar face of Derzhanovsky was there to meet them at the station with Tseitlin and Tsukker, whom Prokofiev immediately nicknamed 'Tse-Tse'; in their large, comfortable room on the only floor of the central Metropole which was functioning as a hotel, overlooking Theatre Square and the Bolshoy, the Prokofievs received Asafyev, 'fatter and healthier looking',[65] and Myaskovsky, 'as refined as before, and just as charming. Maybe some hardly noticeable wrinkles have appeared – the kind which are accentuated when he becomes tired and disappear when he comes in fresh from the street. Evidently Myaskovsky found many more changes in me than I did in him. At any rate, on our first being reunited he examined me for a long time, smiling all the while, probably wondering at how fat and bald I had become'.[66] A few days later there was a respectful meeting with his first significant teacher, Glière, now nearly 60, 'clean-shaven, a somewhat glossy, well-fed cat'.[67] Lunacharsky, a constant presence and yet to be toppled from his sphere of influence, began by reading him Mayakovsky's poetic request to Gorky to return from Italy, suggesting Prokofiev should do the same; the printed copy he gave him remained among the composer's papers.

A first impression of Soviet Moscow was one surely shared by any visitor who has been there at a time of crisis: 'the crowd is quiet, good-natured. Are these the wild beasts who have appalled the whole world?'[68] Creature comforts, meals especially, were excellent, but Prokofiev was on his guard against the Bolshevik reputation for impressing foreigners. It was only over the next few days that vaguer intimations of change began to be felt. When Prokofiev compared the Moscow mansions favourably with Parisian apartments and New York skyscrapers, Myaskovsky's brother-in-law reminded him of life behind those elegant façades – anything up to 18 families sharing a single kitchen. His musical colleague Boleslav Yavorsky, who had been shadowed during his visit to Prokofiev in Paris, described 'the kind of noise which can be heard on the telephone when an official listening device is attached. In fact we have already noticed this kind of noise. Although we have said nothing prejudicial over the phone, we must bear that noise in mind'.[69] There was, besides, one crucial mission which was to give Prokofiev some insight into the difficulties of helping a friend in trouble: the attempted liberation of his cousin Shurik, Aunt Katya's son, who had been imprisoned for his aristocratic connections. Prokofiev's first line of approach was Tsukker, but as the days passed he began to notice a strange reluctance to help on Tsukker's part and a growing irritation with his persistence. Characteristically, he was not to stint in his effort, later introducing Shurik's wife Nadya to Meyerhold, for what little influence he could exert, and to Gorky's ex-wife, a sympathetic woman in charge of the Political Red Cross, but ultimately to no avail. As Oleg Prokofiev points out in the extended notes to his translation of Prokofiev's Soviet diary, 'the quest for help for his cousin keeps coming back like a sinister leitmotif'.[70]

In his musical world-within-a-world, though, his reception offered overwhelming promise for long-term ties; even Lina, impressed by the approach of Stanislavsky's bracing new Opera Studio to Rimsky-Korsakov's *Tsar's Bride* and informing Tsukker that she would be happy to work in such an artistic environment, was 'prepared for this reason to move from Paris to Moscow'.[71] In some respects they were fish out of water, abstaining from alcohol at every reception in a way that their fellow Russians found incomprehensible; the reporter for the theatre programmes, arriving late in true Russian style, was taken aback by Prokofiev's partitioning of visitors into half-hour slots, his stern belief in punctuality and the 'American trait'[72] of his insistence on hard work and practice. Within a day of his arrival, Prokofiev had been able to grasp that Persimfans shared his approach and realized he was home in style. He was welcomed into the Great Hall of the Moscow Conservatory where the concerts were to take place with a 'too slow'[73] rendition of the March from *The Love for Three Oranges* before rehearsing the Third Piano Concerto, which the ensemble had already played with the 'neurotic and unbalanced'[74] Samuil Feinberg and Lev Oborin, the 19-year-old winner of the Warsaw International Piano Competition. Prokofiev's first impression gives the most lucid criticism of this 'institution so essentially communistic in spirit'.[75]

> Without a conductor the orchestra took much more trouble and worked harder than it would with one; a conductor would have to battle with passages of technical difficulty and ask for important voices to be brought out. Here the players are very conscientious, play by nature musically and with great concentration; all dynamics and nuances are precisely observed. No question of learning their parts at rehearsal; they prepare the most difficult passages at home beforehand. On the other hand, problems arise: a ritardando, for example, which with a conductor will come about quite unproblematically, may take them a good twenty minutes to straighten out, because every player slows down in his own way.[76]

He maintained his favourable impression of their conscientiousness, however, comparing it the following day to the attitude of ad hoc orchestral musicians who 'pretend to be playing . . . but in fact leave out half the notes'[77] except in exposed passages; with Persimfans the composer was in the unique position of being able to hear a work in its entirety.

Their first programme together, on 24 January, began with a display of Tseitlin's ambitious scheduling in the shape of no fewer than ten from the 12 movements of the *Chout* Suite – too many, in Prokofiev's opinion, but even so the performance was 'excellent, very precise, clear, given with expression and animation'.[78] The lengthy ovation which then greeted the composer as he came on to the platform to play his Third Piano Concerto turned him into a bashful youth, recorded in prose that is all the more moving for its power of crystal-clear description: 'I stand for a long time, bow to all sides and really don't know what to do, sit down, but since the applause continues, again stand up, again bow and again do not know what to do. I have not been in Moscow for ten years, I want to concentrate so as to play properly, but these emotional displays are not conducive to intense concentration'.[79] After three minutes' pause for composure, the interpretation went 'quite well' but 'I got into something of a muddle in the third variation [of the second movement]'.[80] Steering safely back to the end, Prokofiev met with the most tumultuous reception he thought he had ever received (though the Persimfans accompaniment was, as Myaskovsky later observed, poor because three of their leading players were missing owing to illness). The usual brilliant encores and the orchestral performance of the *Love for Three Oranges* Suite, with the March inevitably repeated, are then dispatched in the diary with a matter-of-factness quite unlike the earlier display of intense emotion.

Four days later, in the first of his three recitals also given in the Great Hall under the banner of Persimfans, Prokofiev gave his last performance of piano music by another composer, and only as an encore: this was one of Myaskovsky's *Prichudi* in the presence of the old friend he had been championing so diligently and whose critical attitude gave him another bout of nerves. By the repeat programme his confidence was beginning to return; the public howled louder than ever at the tour de force of the Toccata. The second recital programme, on 4 February, exchanged the ever-problematic Fifth Sonata and the Third – a favourite 'opener', Prokofiev notes, on Souvchinsky's recommendation – with the Second and Fourth. Another alarming memory lapse came, of all places, in the third of the *Tales of an Old Grandmother*, though the public adored them and Tsukker took this as the cue to advise Prokofiev on the kind of music for the masses he ought to be producing. In a surprising double act, Prokofiev joined the suspicious and wilful Feinberg for the two-piano arrangement of the Schubert waltzes made for Romanov's dance troupe. The final concert with Persimfans, three days later, repeated more 'people's favourites' – the March and Scherzo from *The Love for Three Oranges* – and the *Chout* Suite, but the first half tested its audience with the *American* Overture, sounding 'undernourished'[81] in a hall much larger than its original intended venue in New York, and the Second Piano Concerto in the new form Russia had never heard; the response far surpassed that to the Third Concerto and the scherzo had to be repeated.

On 14 February the Persimfans was due to celebrate its fifth anniversary with a short but potent showcase for its singular virtues: Skryabin's *Poem of Ecstasy* followed by Prokofiev's *Scythian Suite*, which one of the Moscow critics was to hail 'one of the summits of Russian musical art' in its 'colourfulness, power and sweep'.[82] Both works offered great opportunities for one of the orchestra's most outstanding soloists, the trumpeter Mikhail Tabakov. Prokofiev noted his 'astounding B flats'[83] for the concluding Sunrise at a rehearsal before he left for an interim reacquaintance with the city he had never experienced as Leningrad. A first glimpse of Nevsky Prospect covered in snow on a clear, bright day filled him with 'happiness and excitement';[84] later, leaving Lina to take an afternoon nap in the first-class, if slightly run-down, surroundings of the Europa Hotel, he was able to drink in the beauty of Palace Square and the frozen Neva, pink in the sunset. 'Throughout the long years of travelling abroad', he reflected, 'I had somehow forgotten St Petersburg; it began to seem to me that the concept of its beauty was foisted upon it by the patriotism of its citizens, and that, essentially, Moscow was the heart of Russia.'[85] Continuing with reference to Souvchinsky's definition of Russia, and Moscow especially, as a rich meeting of Europe and Asia, he describes how 'I began to think that the European charm of St Petersburg would pale in comparison with the West and that, on the contrary, the Eurasian beauty of certain Moscow lanes was something unique. In my present disposition, however, I was completely overwhelmed by the grandeur of St Petersburg: how much more elegant and magnificent it seemed than Moscow'.[86]

Here Prokofiev had enough free time to enjoy an exhausting tour of the Hermitage Museum, now occupying swathes of the Winter Palace, and to spend a day with Asafyev at Tsarskoye Selo, renamed Detskoye Selo. Again, though, his musical obligations were immediate. He was impressed with the conducting of Vladimir Dranishnikov, the conservatory colleague who had played the orchestral role on a second piano in his examination performance of the First Concerto and who was now poised to give distinguished performances of numbers from *Chout*, the *Scythian Suite* and the Third Piano Concerto with the Leningrad Philharmonic Orchestra in addition to conducting *The Love for Three Oranges*. The Philharmonic, a transformation of the Court Orchestra and officially inaugurated in 1920, was yet to aspire to first-class status. It had inherited many of its former incarnation's superannuated players and their stubborn resistance to new music; but it did at least enjoy the beautiful surroundings of the neo-classical Hall of Columns. Here the concert on 12 February confirmed that 'the orchestra is much poorer than the Persimfans',[87] but the audience was no less vociferous than it had been in Moscow and the composer thought he must have returned to the platform 'probably fifteen times'.[88]

Greater satisfaction came from the production of *The Love for Three Oranges* at the Maryinsky Theatre (as Prokofiev still knew it), or the Leningrad Academic Opera and Ballet Theatre (as it was now officially called, with the acronym 'Akopera'). The director was Sergey Radlov, a former chess partner of Prokofiev and an outstanding protégé of Meyerhold's studio, whose closeness to the world of the

Gozzi fantasy had been brilliantly demonstrated in the 'Popular Comedy' company he ran from 1920 to 1922. His first steps in opera had been successfully taken with an iconoclastic staging of Franz Schreker's *Der ferne Klang* in 1925; *The Love for Three Oranges*, opening the following year, was to be followed by Berg's *Wozzeck* in 1927 and Strauss's *Der Rosenkavalier* in 1928. Prokofiev's opera was best suited to Radlov's Meyerholdian box of tricks. Radlov's aim was to avoid technically complex and cumbersome stage machinery; everything was 'to create a certain fairy-tale mood and lightness . . . I tried to make the whole scenic action dynamic'.[89] He seems to have succeeded, and Dranishnikov was an admirable musical guide. Most of the points Prokofiev had outlined in his letter to the conductor had been well observed – the little devils yelling through megaphones, Dranishnikov's daringly fast handling of the technically difficult exchange between the Prince and Truffaldino in Creonta's castle – and there were plenty of inventive touches, including antiphonal choruses of the various factions from different boxes in the theatre, Truffaldino's entrance as a lifesize doll flying down from the top of the stage, and trapezes filled with actors for the Act II festivities.

On the other hand, neither the battle of monsters nor the final chase met Prokofiev's as yet unattained ideal, and the 'unimpressive' sets by Vladimir Dmitriev were 'the weakest part of the production'.[90] In this respect he had higher hopes for the work of Isaak Rabinovich, one of Diaghilev's preferred choices for the Soviet ballet and now engaged on the designs for a Bolshoy production to be unleashed as a fierce rival to Leningrad at the end of the season. Otherwise, though, Prokofiev was genuinely impressed, and said as much to the Odessa *Vecherneye izvestiya* a month later: 'I can with complete sincerity give my opinion that the Leningrad production surpasses in many respects the productions of my work in America and Germany'.[91] Hopes ran high for a Leningrad production of *The Gambler* in its rightful home, and there was talk of a triple bill of *Chout*, a new choreography for the *Scythian Suite* and the Soviet ballet he had just completed for Diaghilev, but that was scuppered when the impresario insisted on a three-year exclusivity clause.

Meeting old acquaintances was often more fraught than it had been in Moscow. Katya Schmidthof, thrice married and having lost an arm as a result of a tram accident, perhaps touched an affectionate nerve in reminding Seryozha of her long-dead, importunate brother Maximilian by asking for financial help. Vera Alpers is rather cruelly dismissed in the diary as 'still more faded than before',[92] while a now plump and less attractive Eleonora Damskaya met with a chilly reception, no doubt because Prokofiev felt she had done little to salvage what remained of his goods from the apartment in Pervaya Rota. A friendship was resumed with the still-glamorous Karneyev sisters, Lidya and Zoya, however, with whom he had spent several happy summers in Terioki, all the more so since Lina enjoyed their company. One distinguished elderly figure from the past deserved a respectful visit: this was Glazunov, glimpsed in Paris several years earlier, who to Prokofiev's amazement had acquired a partner and now lived with her and her mother in his old apartment. Only the women were there to receive the former *enfant terrible* when he called; the meeting of the two composers had to wait until Prokofiev's second visit to Leningrad, when Glazunov slipped into his familiar role of a reactionary professor, now having to swallow his distaste as the former student returned to his old stamping-ground as hero.

21 February was the day fixed for the Prokofiev festivities at the Leningrad Conservatory. On arrival, 'I peered with sharp curiosity at the institution which, for ten years, from the age of thirteen to 23, was the centre of my life. It was a strange sensation to find the same building, where every corridor and each step are so familiar, entirely full of different people from the ones I had known'.[93] For old times' sake he chose the Small Hall over the Large as the venue; if there were too many students, they could huddle together – 'I remember how that happened more than once during my time at the conservatory, and how very cheerful a squash it was'.[94] The student orchestra under Nikolay Malko, his efficient but not especially vital conductor in one of the Philharmonic concerts, gave a 'highly animated'[95] performance of two movements of the *Classical* Symphony and the first movement of Beethoven's Seventh Symphony which both he and Malko had studied in Tcherepnin's class. His own more youthful music was amusingly prefaced by a speech from Glazunov, who stumbled over the *mot juste* to describe exactly what this former student had brought them all in the old days before settling on a laughably inappropriate 'joy'.

After the recital Prokofiev paid a visit to his old Rubinstein prize, the Shreder piano salvaged by Damskaya and now under lock and key in Asafyev's classroom, and to his surprise found it in good health. An evening chamber recital by the students was followed by supper in the same hall where he had been awarded that prize, countless speeches including an invitation to become the leader of the student communists and a gracious departure at two in the morning, 12 hours after he had arrived. 'The conservatory is both the same, and not the same. Much is old and characteristic: the familiar faces of professors, the same corridors, the seats by the windows, the Small Hall with the organ and the mirrors. But what a lot of changes there have been in those 13 years!'[96]

Did Prokofiev hear descriptions of the freezing rooms, students and staff close to starvation, which were rife during the young Shostakovich's years of study at the conservatory? No doubt Asafyev had touched on such things during their walks in Detskoye Selo. At any rate the 20-year-old Shostakovich, who had weathered the hardships and taken the Leningrad musical world by storm with the premiere of his First Symphony eight months before the start of Prokofiev's visit, was to make a firm impression on the older composer at another musical event organized by Vladimir Shcherbachev, Prokofiev's fellow student at the conservatory, where he was now a professor. In the wake of a 'complicated and not very interesting piece' by Josef Shillinger, Shostakovich's Piano Sonata, performed from memory by the composer, struck Prokofiev as 'so much more lively and interesting'.[97] Yet he was

1. The Prokofiev family in the orchard at Sontsovka: the one-year old Sergey Sergeyevich with his mother, Marya Grigoryevna, and his father, Sergey Alexeyevich.

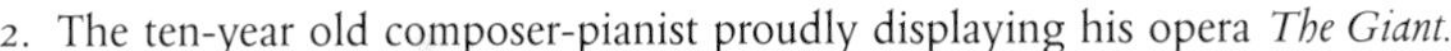

2. The ten-year old composer-pianist proudly displaying his opera *The Giant*.

3. Prokofiev as the youngest student (right) in the St Petersburg Conservatory class of Lyadov (centre, at the piano).

4. Playing chess with former neighbour Morolev at Nikopol, 1909.

5. The young traveller, 1915.

6. Cosmopolitan composer: Prokofiev walking down a Chicago street, 1919.

7. Artists in three spheres: Prokofiev with Boris Anisfeld, set designer for the Chicago premiere of *The Love for Three Oranges,* and dancer Adolph Bolm, 1919.

8. Larionov's impression of rehearsals for *Chout,* 1921: from left to right, Diaghilev, Stravinsky, Prokofiev at the piano, Massine and Goncharova.

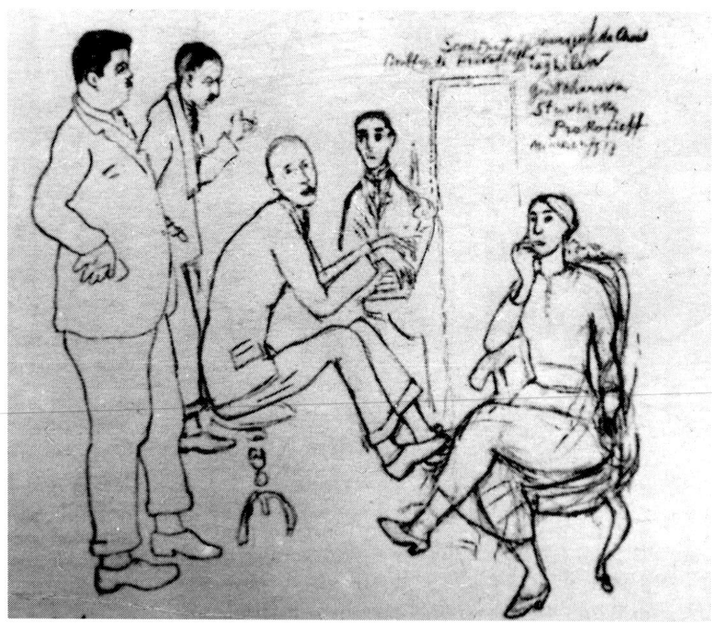

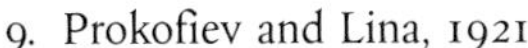
9. Prokofiev and Lina, 1921.

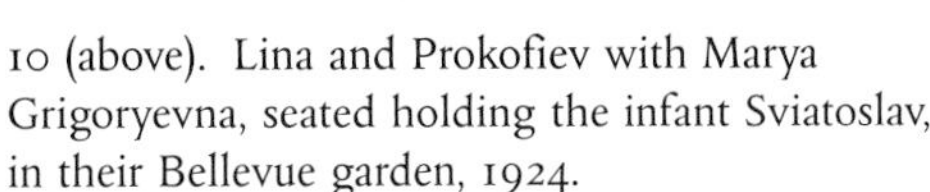
10 (above). Lina and Prokofiev with Marya Grigoryevna, seated holding the infant Sviatoslav, in their Bellevue garden, 1924.

11. Prokofiev and the two-year-old Sviatoslav, France, 1926.

12. Interval in a momentous Leningrad performance of *The Love for Three Oranges*, 10 February 1927 – the first seen by the composer in his native country. Prokofiev, surrounded by courtiers, princesses and infernal villains, is seated at the centre with the director, Sergey Radlov, on his left and the conductor, Vladimir Dranishnikov, on his right.

13. Friends reunited: Prokofiev with Boris Asafyev (left) and Nikolay Myaskovsky (centre) in Asafyev's home at Detskoye Selo outside Leningrad, 1927.

14. Lyubov Tchernicheva as the Girl Worker and Leonide Massine as the Sailor turned Factory Worker in *Le Pas d'acier*, 1927.

15. Serge Lifar's prodigal returns home on his knees in the final scene of *L'Enfant prodigue*, 1929.

16. A *tour gastronomique* in the Ballot, 1929: from left to right Vladimir Sofronitzky, Prokofiev at the wheel, Vladimir Dukelsky (Vernon Duke) and Lina.

17. Prokofiev with sons Oleg (aged four) and Sviatoslav (aged eight) on the terrace of Jacques Sadoul's Villa Les Pins Parasols, south of France, 1932.

by no means uncritical: 'His sonata starts with lively two-part counterpoint, rather Bachian in style. The second movement, which follows the first without a break, is composed with gentle harmonies and there is a melody in the middle. This is pleasant, but diffuse and lengthy. The Andante leads to a fast finale, disproportionately short compared with the preceding movements'.[98] Prokofiev might have appreciated an elaborately contrapuntal chamber piece by Gavriil Popov just as much 'if it hadn't been for the oppressive throbbing in my head brought on by all that I had already heard of the day's music-making'.[99]

He was never at his happiest listening to the music of others, least of all speechifying about his own. The theatre, on the other hand, was an environment in which he could breathe more easily. Not only had he told the Riga *Sevodnya* that stagecraft fascinated him just as much as music, but he had no hesitation in declaring to *Muzyka i revolyutsiya* that 'Russian theatre leaves far behind it the French and American'.[100] His experience of the new Soviet theatre began in Moscow with a visit to Zamyatin's adaptation of Leskov's *The Flea* at MKHAT (Moscow Artistic Academy Theatre), bafflingly caricatural at first but with plenty of vivid touches from the beginning of the second act to the end. 'All things considered, a very pleasant and affectionate reception', he reflected on the cast gathering afterwards, 'the more so in that this was not the musical world but the theatrical one.'[101] Sampling Meyerhold's latest innovations had to wait until his third spell in Moscow, where he saw two very different productions of Gogol's *The Government Inspector* (now one of Meyerhold's most documented achievements) and Crommelynck's *The Magnificent Cuckold,* already five years old. The first involved shifting platforms and mysterious candlelight casting huge silhouettes, the second 'conventional constructivist sets [by Lyubov Popova] and conventional gymnastic movements';[102] but in each case, Prokofiev felt, Meyerhold's fascination with clever detail 'slowed down the tempo of the play'.[103] He was to observe the same in Meyerhold's production of Ostrovsky's *The Forest* during his last days in Moscow. This, however, was of no concern for the future of the Akopera *Gambler*, which Meyerhold had agreed to take on once more: 'an opera can last only as long as the music composed for it, which means that the master of timing will be not Meyerhold but me'.[104] Before the performance of *The Magnificent Cuckold*, Prokofiev and Lina went to dine at Meyerhold's apartment, where details of the forthcoming production were discussed over slices of the same first-class melon served, with Meyerhold's characteristic concern for detail, in his celebrated production of *The Government Inspector*.

Prokofiev's third stay in Moscow was enriched not only by meetings with the great man of the theatre but also by the arrival of Aunt Katya and Katyechka from Penza, described with characteristic restraint. 'Our meeting was very moving. Aunt Katya has become an old lady [as well she might at 69] but in spite of her paralysed leg she was unusually cheerful and had lost none of her charm. Cousin Katya has gone grey. Her deafness hindered much spontaneous conversation. Ptashka [which Prokofiev had informed them was Lina's name 'in domestic life'[105]] liked them very much and they her.'[106] The diary records their frequent meetings, but not what they spoke about, though certainly Christian Science and Mary Baker Eddy's *Science and Health* would have surfaced if Prokofiev's promise of the previous year to 'talk [about it] in detail' and to tell them 'amazing things'[107] (presumably about his own path to enlightenment) had met with the relatives' approval.

Prokofiev was about to take further steps back into the terrain of his childhood. There were two slight departures from the familiar repertoire, both under the auspices of Derzhanovsky's Association for Contemporary Music: a concert conducted by Saradzhev on 27 February, which included a resurrection of the long-buried *Dreams*, and a chamber recital on 6 March in which the Quintet met with unexpected public acclaim and 'quite incredible rapture'[108] from Myaskovsky. Then Prokofiev and Lina left Moscow for Kharkov, along the same railway track between Sontsovka and the capital that he had travelled so often in his youth. Prokofiev had now entered the flexible extension of his Soviet visit and, though he had entertained vague hopes of touring beyond Moscow and Leningrad, the contract for six appearances – in Kharkov, Kiev, Odessa, Rostov-on-Don, Baku and Tiflis – did not materialize until mid-February. In the end he gave six recitals in the first three cities only. Kharkov was 'big, dirty and ugly',[109] redeemed by German buildings near the centre but not by their hotel, which gave them their first taste of Soviet service outside the luxurious cities. Here he met the widow of Dr Reberg from Sontsovka days and one of his daughters, Vera; he played with warmth and enthusiasm for the conservatory students, listened to some 'rather pointless, provincial'[110] Ukrainian quartet music and gave a recital beginning with 'the Fifth and Fourth Sonatas, which was very stupid since no-one understands the Fifth and the Fourth is too slow to generate enthusiasm'.[111] The shorter pieces, however, generated 'the usual great excitement'.[112]

Kiev, which he had not seen for 12 years, seemed much more beautiful, but palpably ravaged by the civil war. Here the more generous side of Prokofiev's character had free rein – charity for southern supplicants, a reluctant visit to the conservatory under pressure from an insistent teacher which turned into 'one of the brightest memories of my Soviet trip'.[113] He listened with interest to his own music played as examination pieces by ten- to 15-year-olds and even succumbed to giving an unscheduled mini-recital. 'But it was actually a pleasure. Children surrounded the piano and screamed with pleasure. It is very good that there are establishments where young people can be trained in this way. If during the Revolutionary era, after a part of the intelligentsia had perished, concert audiences suffered depletion, then through such ways of educating younger people the supplies will quickly be replenished.'[114] He also made sure that the management at his second Kiev recital did not obstruct these willing listeners, whom he had issued with passes; their special enthusiasm contributed to a remarkable success overshadowing a Malko concert given the same evening. Prokofiev's assistance to the young and aspiring would be a regular part of his commitment to the new Russia;

and his concern for the country's thousands of homeless children, first mooted with Gorky in Italy, should not be underrated. Another of those sudden rays of sympathy which illuminate the 1927 diary shines through in his response to the thanks of an elderly lady from the Committee for Homeless Children at the end of the one charity recital he agreed to give in Moscow: 'I replied, "An end to homelessness is our common cause. I have worked towards it for one hour, but you dedicate all your time to it, so it's not you who should thank me, but we who should be thanking you".'[115]

In Odessa, too, Prokofiev played spontaneously to the 'frightful bellowing' of students, which he attributed to their 'southern temperament'.[116] He had never been to the handsome old Black Sea port before. It was a place of special memories for Lina: she had spent time there with her distinguished grandfather in early childhood. There was one young musician of promise Prokofiev did not record in his diary – the 19-year-old violinist David Oistrakh, who later recalled playing the scherzo from the First Violin Concerto at a banquet in the Scientists' Club after Prokofiev's second recital. The composer warmed to a local tenor's performance of *The Ugly Duckling* so much that – again, with unexpected spontaneity – he accompanied him in several of his songs. But he did not mention correcting the humiliated Oistrakh with his own rendition of how the concerto's scherzo should sound. Oistrakh, at any rate, described Prokofiev's playing as 'like nothing I had ever experienced . . . Not a single superfluous gesture, not a single exaggerated expression of emotion, no striving for effect . . . There was a sort of inner purity of purpose behind the whole performance that made an unforgettable experience'.[117]

Travelling back to Moscow in the company of the guitarist Andrés Segovia, who shared a chicken with him at a station buffet, Prokofiev had only one more concert to give, with the Persimfans: a repeat of the Second Piano Concerto, their first performance of the *Classical* Symphony, with the ensemble 'cleaner' than under Saradzhev but occasionally 'rhythmically insecure',[118] and their tour de force, the *Scythian Suite*. Touring the Kremlin and searching for squirrel furs for Lina still took second place to the impact of Moscow's astonishing artistic life. While he refused to put on a concert to celebrate the Chinese Communists' capture of Shanghai, Prokofiev willingly played *gratis* for the luminaries of the Moscow Arts Theatre, among them its founding father Konstantin Stanislavsky and Chekhov's widow Olga Knipper. Quite apart from his fond memories of the Arts Theatre's past triumphs, he had a recent prompt to pay homage: a memorable visit to Stanislavsky's opera workshop and its production of Tchaikovsky's *Eugene Onegin*, 'which I absorbed with exceptional pleasure'.[119] Prokofiev admiringly describes the modest scale of the party at the Larin household, with the dancing glimpsed in the hall at the back of the stage, and the quarrel between Onegin and Lensky by the table at the front, the duel with only Lensky visible, and the stiff court etiquette of the St Petersburg ball. At the time of writing, this production is still in the repertory of the Stanislavsky Arts Theatre, with all the details Prokofiev noted in place; in the year 2000 it passed its 2000th performance. The incredible vitality of this tradition gives more of a clue to Prokofiev's long-term commitment to the motherland than the allure of secure commissions and a guaranteed public. Of such high-quality artistic strands were his dreams of a future in Bolshevizia truly woven.

12
Stage and symphony
1927–9

After the flurry of concerts and recitals in the Soviet Union, Prokofiev's performing career came to a sudden and, in the long run, damaging standstill; with the single exception of a recital in Magdeburg, he would not play again to his satisfaction for more than a year. It was a conscious decision: as the prospect loomed of *The Fiery Angel* in Berlin, the opera had to be finished by the summer, and the emancipation of the original *Gambler* score from the Maryinsky and the theatre's undertaking to stage the work the following season set another deadline for what Prokofiev had decided would be a thorough revision.

Even so, the tempo of his life back in the West was hardly leisurely. After a brief reunion with the three-year-old Sviatoslav in Paris, and preparations for a new lodging at 5 Avenue Frémiet, just round the corner from their first home in the Rue Charles Dickens in the Passy district, he obeyed Diaghilev's command and travelled to Monte-Carlo for rehearsals of the ballet. Much was still provisional, not least the title – 'there is a plan afoot to call it *The Steel Step* [*Stalnoy skok*], but for now that's just between ourselves',[1] he wrote to Asafyev – and the choreography, by Léonide Massine, already involved radical changes to the original Prokofiev–Yakulov scenario which would have dancer, artist and composer disputing percentage rights in the royalties for some time to come. The factory spectacular which was to be the ballet's most memorable feature was never in doubt, but the first part underwent some unlikely metamorphoses. In the programme for the June premiere the set pieces have changed their identity: echoing Diaghilev's 1917 ballet to music by Lyadov, *Contes russes,* the opening number is 'battle of Baba-Yaga with the Crocodile', the third dance involves the sailor with 'three devils', followed by 'the cat, his mate and the mice' and 'the legend of the drinkers'.[2] The outlines of the first part remained hazy to spectators by the time the ballet reached London, when the general synopsis promised 'two aspects of Russian life: the stories and legends of the countryside, and the mechanism of the factories'.[3] Only one alteration was made in Monte-Carlo with Prokofiev's wholehearted participation: an extra musical number which he hoped would make Diaghilev reconsider the prospect of a Soviet production the following year.

If compromise was unwelcome, there was no need to fear from Diaghilev the interference that hampered two other new stagings. In May Prokofiev arrived in Berlin incognito after his Magdeburg recital to see 'a very stupid production of a Dante-style ballet using my *Scythian Suite* (oh, those dear Germans!)',[4] and he appreciated a detailed report from Myaskovsky on the Bolshoy's attempt to compete with Leningrad in its new *Love for Three Oranges.* The verdict: ingenious but somewhat overloaded production and designs, generally poor singing and 'worst of all – the music: a more or less continual din, with the words drowned out, tastelessly accentuated, frequently exaggerated tempos, so that the chorus can't articulate a word, frightful pressure from the percussion'.[5] Responsibility for this rested with a bright new star in the conducting firmament, Nikolay Golovanov, who despite having impressed Prokofiev on his Soviet visit by coming up with the exact metronomic equivalents of the speeds the composer indicated as he played the opera through, evidently now pursued his own wilful path.

Paris, meanwhile, was gearing itself up for the busiest and most glamorous time of the season. Koussevitzky's performance of the new *American* Overture on 28 May offered a kind of festival fanfare. Louis Schneider, in *Le Gaulois,* was in the minority when he declared that 'the small ensemble does not prevent the orchestra from producing a brilliant dynamism',[6] Prokofiev wrote to the work's benefactor, Hermann Schaad of the Aeolian Company, noting that the conductor had advised him 'to orchestrate it also for a standard symphony orchestra'.[7] He followed this with another letter enclosing the reviews in which he noted that 'Koussevitzky's performance in a big hall was one of the reasons for the attacks of the critics, for a piece of music destined for a small hall sounds somewhat thin in a large one';[8] the same had been true of the Soviet premiere. With an opportunism not entirely alien to his character, he would find a way to make Schaad pay for an enlarged version by the end of the year.

La Volonté's conclusion, drawn from the overture's unusual scoring, that 'the violin is no longer king of the modern orchestra',[9] was also applicable to a much grander new work about to be crowned in Paris: Stravinsky's *Oedipus rex.* This opera-oratorio would certainly have been advertised as the jewel of the Diaghilev season, had Stravinsky and colleagues not wished to keep it a secret and make it a present for the impresario's 20th anniversary. The Princesse de Polignac put up the money for all the rehearsals. Otto Klemperer's memory seems to have played him false when he recalled Stravinsky and Prokofiev giving a four-hand preview of the score in the Polignac salon,[10] though Prokofiev was there on the evening of 29 May, having accepted her invitation in pursuit of an imminent private audition of the Quintet; La Polignac's caprices played havoc, as ever, with the dates, and the performance did not take place. Prokofiev certainly knew of Stravinsky's progress with *Oedipus rex,* describing it as 'the height of internationalism': 'the librettist is French [Jean

Cocteau], the text is Latin, the language is Greek, the music is Anglo-German (in imitation of Handel) [and Italian, in imitation of Verdi, he might have spotted had he been more perceptive], and its presentation is built on Monegasque foundations, with American money'.[11]

The official unveiling of *Oedipus rex* at the Théâtre Sarah Bernhardt a day after the Polignac soirée, in concert performance, must have seemed all too sober after a fully staged revival of *The Firebird*. It could be eclipsed in the eyes of Parisian society only by the glamorous premiere of *Le Pas d'acier* on 7 June, when the full force of Yakulov's factory aesthetics combined with fashionably camp costume designs and Prokofiev's climactic motor rhythms to drive audiences to a rare pitch of enthusiasm. Diaghilev was hoping for a White Russian protest, but the only controversial note was a heated scuffle between those two rival dandies Cocteau and Dukelsky. Cocteau, already inflamed by the way Massine had 'turned something as great as the Russian Revolution into a cotillion-like spectacle within the intellectual grasp of ladies who pay six thousand francs for a box',[12] took it personally when he heard Dukelsky talking to Prokofiev about his 'great admiration for the massive, sinewy music of his ballet, which in my opinion would deliver a crushing blow to the decadent Parisian *musiquette*'.[13] Jumping to conclusions from the words 'Paris' and 'musiquette' in the Russian conversation, Cocteau challenged Dukelsky to a duel and a crisis was only narrowly avoided.

Prokofiev would reveal nothing about the premiere of *Le Pas d'acier* to his Soviet correspondents other than its impact on Parisian musical circles and the intriguing news that as a result 'the director of the Grand Opéra invited me to write an opera based on one of Rostand's dramas; but I still have to finish two old ones – *The Fiery Angel* and *The Gambler*'.[14] He was certainly far from delighted with Diaghilev's and Massine's changes to the original scenario, though he did not want to say so; and he was not in the audience when the ballet triumphed in London, where, on 4 July, *Le Pas d'acier* shone in a real Diaghilev banquet of internationalism. The London speciality of orchestral intermezzos included Glinka's *Ruslan and Lyudmila* Overture (to proclaim the tradition of which the ballet was still, after all, a part), Chabrier's *Valses romantiques* orchestrated by Auric and Poulenc, Weber's *Turandot* Overture and a *Rhythmic Dance* by Eugene Goossens; the ballets that followed were *La Chatte*, with music by Sauguet and stylized kitchen decor by Naum Gabo, *Les Matelots* and the Polovtsian Dances from *Prince Igor*. Despite *La Chatte*'s novelty, the *Observer*'s critic bracketed it with the other successors as 'applause-proud favourites . . . simple treats indeed' after the '*méchante* novelties' of *Le Pas d'acier*, which he found 'anything but dull'.[15] Prokofiev's music had clearly inspired Massine's

> remarkably good steps and figures . . . It is noisy, but the scoring, though very thick, is yet balanced, and the final effect is not so much one of noise as of continual deep sound. The climax at the end of the second and last act is finely done, so gradually built up that the listener is carried onward with no sense of effort.

> The stage action helps here, and this moment is one of the best examples of close interplay between dance steps and orchestral sounds.[16]

Here was a rare example indeed of a London critic of the Diaghilev season having anything intelligent to say about the music.

By this time Prokofiev and Lina had headed south-west from Paris for their latest summer dacha: the Villa Les Phares on the coast at St Palais-sur-Mer near the Atlantic resort of Royan. Choosing a west-coast beach holiday was always risky; the weather proved wretchedly wet and remained so for the rest of July. 'In England one woman even took poison because they had so much rain there',[17] Prokofiev gossiped to Aunt Katya. At least the social scene provided pleasures. Regular visitors to the household, which included Lina's parents, were Prokofiev's old friend Zakharov and his wife Cecilia Hansen, an outstanding violinist who was shortly to play the First Violin Concerto in America. They were on holiday nearby, so 'we see them twice a week and have a pleasant time together',[18] Prokofiev told his aunt. Later the Borovskys took their place, putting Lina once more in the position of trying to ignore the sheep's eyes 'Frou-Frou' made at her husband.

Neither rain nor good company was an obstacle, however, to the task in hand: the completion of *The Fiery Angel*. The schedule was tight. On 30 May Prokofiev passed on to Bruno Walter the news that 'at the end of June we can deliver the piano score with German text of the first, third and fourth acts; the fifth we can deliver in July – which I will finish in a few days – and the second act around the first of September'.[19] By early July he was arguing that 'the hold-up with the second act cannot play a significant part in the progress of the opera, since this act is very simple and scenically adds little to the one before'.[20] This was as disingenuous as Agrippa's equivocations at the end of the act, surely, for while the thoroughgoing revisions included the scene in which Renata's seance with Ruprecht encourages hair-raising knockings and bangings – of greater auditory than visual complexity – the new Act II finale, with the overwhelming orchestra and three jangling skeletons contradicting the necromancer's disavowal of the supernatural, poses big scenic problems. Prokofiev was right, though, to point out that rehearsals had to start with the convent mayhem of Act V's complex ensemble. He was still not too worried about Walter's 'faltering'[21] position because Dresden, followed by Clemens Krauss in Frankfurt and his supporter Szenkar in Cologne, to whom the opera should have been entrusted in the first place, were all interested. There were slight adjustments to the schedule. The anticlimactic curtain of Act I and the very end of its successor followed the rest of Act II on 29 August and 13 September respectively. Ten days later Prokofiev wrote exultantly to Myaskovsky: 'I've finished – this time conclusively . . . both the full and the piano scores. Conclusively! But that's only an illusion – one can't escape corrections, checking the foreign translations and other such trains dragging behind, as it were, the finished dress of the composition'.[22]

Through all the vicissitudes that beset the unleashing of his 'animal',[23] as Prokofiev called *The Fiery Angel*, Myaskovsky's response was to prove the most valuable of tonics. Receiving the full score the following year, Myaskovsky told his friend that 'it is worth living in this world while such music is being composed'[24] – words not to be taken lightly from a man prone to suicidal depression. Subsequently he set out in detail his causes for rapture. After the impact of the most immediately striking parts of the score, like the final scene of possession culminating in Renata's screaming to a top C which he thought 'like the sun', there remained the indelible 'humanity' in the creation of Renata and Ruprecht: 'this is not theatre, still less opera; these are two completely living individuals'.[25] Myaskovsky went on to make a distinction between 'lapidary themes like . . . (that of) Renata's hysteria' (Ex.51*a*) and 'plastic' ones, 'rich and boundlessly expressive, like the theme (of love – isn't it?)' (Ex.51*b*).[26] This is a valuable distinction, the starting-point for making sense of the two most important levels on which the opera functions. The 'plastic' themes guide us, leitmotif-like, through the human complexities of Renata's divided soul and Ruprecht's gradual entanglement in her bizarre spiritual life; their transformations help to explain why a pupil of Myaskovsky frowned on the 'Wagnerism'[27] of the opera and why Diaghilev and company found it outmoded.

For Prokofiev, the modification of motifs was something new, only briefly developed in *The Gambler* and not at all in the spirit of *The Love for Three Oranges*. We understand through the metamorphosis of these 'plastic' melodies, for example, that Ruprecht's theme of wayward soldiery has become utterly degraded by the time he meets Mephistopheles and Faust in Act IV, where the once-sprightly figure takes on a tragic cast with violins playing on the sonorous G string. The famous 'white-note' theme which dominates the opera (see Chapter 8, Ex.43*a*) first appears in Renata's lengthy Act I explanation of how she came to meet her 'angel from heaven or hell' against the words 'and he called himself Madiel'. Here the soprano strains to join the high-flying *espressivo* violins, but simply cannot reach up the octave – a

Ex.51*a* *The Fiery Angel*, op.37 – Act I

Ex.51*b* *The Fiery Angel* – Act II

perfect expression of painful yearning. As the narrative continues, the rapturous theme is treated to darker orchestral colours and clashing harmonies, the voice merely touching on it in rapid, recitative-like chatter (the setting of the text often sounds like Musorgskian declamation at speed, rattling away in barely decipherable triplets; and it can be even harder to catch significant lines in Prokofiev's intricately wrought libretto when two voices sing at once, as in the antithesis to a love duet at the start of Act IV). As Renata's mania for tracking down the 'angel on earth' increases (throughout the second and third acts), the theme becomes yet more tortured, despite moments of tender lucidity. Its climactic statement is at the height of the Act III interlude which Prokofiev was usefully to identify as the most symphonic moment of the score, a clash of Renata's latest perversity against Ruprecht's knightliness and love; since this orchestral passage takes the place of Ruprecht's near-fatal duel with the Count at Renata's instigation, the flame tones of the Madiel theme reinforce the ambiguity of the angel–Count in a way the mere text of Bryusov's novel could not.

In Act V, which begins with the cloistered calm of another melody from the discarded white-note quartet, beautifully distributed between divided violas, cellos and basses, the 'Madiel' theme returns to its pristine source. Renata uses it to plead her innocence before an unmistakably malign, bass-heavy Inquisitor, drawing it back into her vocal orbit with the calm assistance of the lower strings. The final, simple transformation is a uniquely poignant moment in the opera: against the six-part nuns' chant 'welcoming' the advent of the fiery angel with staccato anticipation, a solo violin intones the theme an octave above the rest, *dolcissimo*. Prokofiev knew, as did Strauss with his Salome and Elektra, that there must be moments of respite and beauty in the psychopathology of his heroine, and at times such as this our sympathy is vitally enlisted.

Nevertheless the love that Renata and Ruprecht briefly enjoy in the novel has no place in the opera, and Bryusov's background of early Renaissance rationalism, which occasionally triumphs over superstition, is kept on the tightest of reins. Prokofiev's genius is most evident when he engages the themes Myaskovsky describes as 'lapidary' to project a new horror or two in each act. The possession scene into which we are so swiftly and deftly plunged several minutes into Act I is the first and, although its ostinato makes many spine-chilling reappearances, the warding-off of the incantation returns, with masterly dramatic timing, only in the middle of the final convent mayhem. Chromatics stand for the malign spread of the supernatural in its many shapes and forms throughout the opera, magically recast into memorable themes, for example that of the keening, muted first violins accompanying the Fortune-Teller later in Act I (Ex.52) or the purposefully strenuous tessitura of Renata's declaration of love for the wounded, delirious Ruprecht in Act III, mockingly echoed by distant female voices (Ex.53).

Act II is haunted by the skeeterings and susurrations of 13-part strings for the spirit-knockings and by the thickest scoring of the opera as Ruprecht goes off to consult

Ex.52 *The Fiery Angel* – Act I

Ex.53 *The Fiery Angel* – Act III

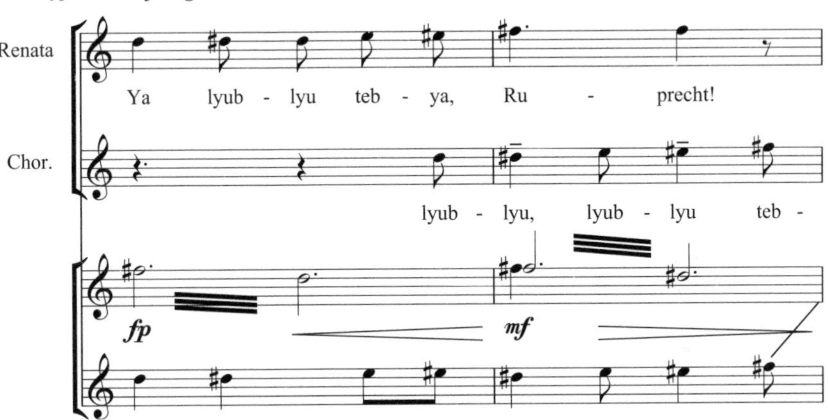

the disingenuous Agrippa – an inferno that contradicts in the most strenuous manner possible the heroic-tenor necromancer's denial of sorcery and returns as the invisible force that guides the ultimate obscenity of the convent possession. In Act IV's macabre intermezzo, Renata's violent self-wounding is followed by the pantomime of Mephistopheles swallowing and regurgitating the pot-boy of a Cologne inn, musically illustrated with comic-grotesque panache. Even here Prokofiev manages to inject a little humanity by giving the disillusioned Faust a striking theme of lyric breadth. Myaskovsky was impressed by the strong images projected by the minor characters. As in *The Gambler* and to a certain extent *The Love for Three Oranges*, Prokofiev's model was Musorgsky's art of the thumbnail sketch and, notably, the inn scene of *Boris Godunov*, which surely informs the pedestrian anticlimaxes of the curtains to the first, third and fourth acts.

They provide yet another dimension to an opera of highly unconventional stagecraft, uncompromising in the toughness of its vocal and dramatic demands. Like *Boris*, *The Fiery Angel* has a life beyond the enclosed world of its chosen scenes, and it is hardly surprising that Prokofiev would soon feel inclined to add to it when yet another illusory chance of a staging emerged. In the autumn of 1927, though, matters came to a standstill with the late delivery of the parts to the Berlin Städtische Oper. 'In my opinion', Prokofiev later reflected to Myaskovsky, 'this is swinish behaviour on Bruno Walter's part: if he couldn't put it on in the autumn, then he could have done it in the spring'.[28] It was surely a case of backing the wrong horse in Berlin; both Klemperer at the Kroll Opera and Erich Kleiber at the Staatsoper were men of a younger generation more amenable to a work that was modern, whatever the Diaghilev set might think of it, and more inclined to risk-taking on the complexity of the orchestral and vocal parts.

So far more reliable, and closer to Prokofiev's heart, was the promise of Dranishnikov and company to mount *The Gambler* at the Akopera, in a production to be co-directed by Meyerhold and Radlov, his former pupil. In the autumn of 1927 there was much work to be done, and the deadline worries which had beset Prokofiev over *The Fiery Angel* began again. His next visit to the Soviet Union, he wrote to one of his most important contacts there at the end of October, 'depends . . . on the production of *The Gambler* in Leningrad, and the production in its turn depends on the time it takes me to finish the revisions . . . so it will probably be at the end of the season'.[29] Exchanging the roar of the Atlantic's autumn storms for the Avenue Frémiet, then, caused little change to the tempo of life, he informed Aunt Katya; *The Gambler* still dictated the pattern of his days. He was anxious to underline to many of his Russian friends and acquaintances how much more mature he had become since beginning the first version of the opera in 1915, and as we have seen in Chapter 6, a great deal was indeed changed, above all in the last act; Leningrad would have to bear in mind, for instance, the extra roles in the extended roulette scene, the opera's *pièce de résistance* which Prokofiev was anxious should go into rehearsal first, and it would have to allow for additional voices (though not a full chorus) for the new interlude underlining Alexey's obsession.

There was one potentially pleasant diversion: 'on 2 December Ptashka and I are going to London for a week for two radio concerts', Prokofiev wrote to Aunt Katya, 'on the 5th a chamber evening when I'm going to play my compositions [the Third Sonata and many of the usual miniatures, ending with the Toccata] and Ptashka will sing in English romances by myself and other Russian composers, among them Myaskovsky, and on the 9th I'm going to play my [Second] concerto with orchestra'.[30] The only pleasures, as it turned out, were the incidental ones: seven nights at Albemarle Court, on Stravinsky's recommendation, and a return trip by plane from Croydon to Le Bourget, where a canny photographic service captured the Prokofievs beaming after their first flight. Lina, however, contracted a virus and was unable to sing, so all the work she had put into studying the correct enunciation, reflecting the even harder time Prokofiev had given the English translator over the text, had gone to waste. As for the Second Concerto, Prokofiev's performance of his most fiendishly difficult work for piano and orchestra with Ansermet conducting was not a happy experience and determined his decision not to play at all on his impending return to Russia; Derzhanovsky and Persimfans were in for an unpleasant surprise. 'I tried to play the Second Concerto for the radio', Prokofiev told Tseitlin, 'and it turned out to be a complete scandal, for it's such a difficult piece that since last March it has completely dropped out of my fingers. To put it bluntly, I'm not on form at the moment and not in a mood for concert-giving, and fearfully overtaxed from composing'.[31] The tape has not so far materialized in the BBC archives; that is a pity for, however unsatisfactory the performance, it would at least give us a chance to hear in outline how Prokofiev approached his most taxing vehicle.

News from Russia was worrying on several fronts. The 'quibbling evasiveness'[32] of Akopera (or the Maryinsky, as Prokofiev still liked to call it) continued even after *The Gambler*'s 730 pages of full score, six months in the making, were ready and waiting. In fact the die was cast; on 18 February Radlov informed Meyerhold that the project was postponed because 'an unexpected delay in receiving the currency' had held up the dispatch of the new score.[33] Directorial struggles, Derzhanovsky told Prokofiev some time after the opera's cancellation, were making for 'troubled times in our opera theatres',[34] and the temporary eclipse of Radlov's reputation hardly made it any easier; even so, the musicologist Viktor Belyayev, proudly announcing a Leningrad resurrection for Musorgsky's own orchestration of *Boris Godunov* in a new performing edition by Pavel Lamm, promised results for *The Gambler* at the Bolshoy if Leningrad failed. Of much more concern was the unavoidable interpretation of two cards from Aunt Katya referring to her daughter's 'sickness', which prompted a volley of letters to other relatives in the West. 'You probably know', wrote Prokofiev to his aunt Mari Rein, 'that when someone in Russia is arrested, they write as if that person has fallen ill.'[35] Cousin Katyechka, on her return to Penza from travels in

Tashkent, had been imprisoned, sharing the fate of her brother Shurik. To his relatives in Germany, at least, Prokofiev could expand on the darker side of Soviet life:

> I cannot understand how this has happened. It's possibly the result of an intrigue, since Katyechka ran her school for the deaf and dumb near Penza very energetically, and in conjunction with her feverish activity could have attracted ill-wishers and enemies. But since on the other hand she is sometimes unconstrained with her tongue in her appraisal of Soviet authority [and to Aunt Tanya he expands on Katyechka's deafness as a further reason for the volume with which Katyechka might speak her mind] and besides which her brother has already spent several years in jail on suspicion of counter-Revolutionary activity, all these might be conjectured as reasons for her arrest. I only hope it won't last long and that mindful of her useful work they will release her soon.
>
> In any case be very careful in your correspondence with Auntie Katya, so as not to let slip a thoughtless word. If you're going to write about Katyechka, then refer to her as sick and not in prison.[36]

And this, of course, was how Prokofiev himself raised the question in his next letters to Aunt Katya ('we are deeply distressed to learn of the illnesses which have beset your family'[37]) though his concern as ever was to make sure that the extra funds he had asked various cultural organizations to send her were reaching their destination. Things were to take a turn for the better in the summer.

In marked contrast to the privations of his Russian relatives, Prokofiev decided to make the most of the sybaritic pleasures available in France after his hard work on *The Gambler*. Having obtained his 'carte rose', a French driving licence, at the beginning of 1927, he was now the proud owner of a second-hand Ballot and ready to take it further afield than the environs of Paris. In early April Lina for once did not join him on a leisurely drive to the south, carefully planned to take in the gastronomic pleasures of every small town on the way. According to Dukelsky (writing as Duke in *Passport to Paris*), only he, a chess set and a collection of books on the food and drink of the region shared Prokofiev's company; but in fact Fatima Samoilenko was also with them when, at the height of a fierce thunderstorm on route 133 between Seyches and Marmande, Prokofiev failed to see two cyclists coming out of a track and, hitting one of them, damaged his beloved car but fortunately injured nobody. It was the second slight accident within a year (the first Prokofiev had reported as occurring at the Place Victor Hugo at the end of the previous April) and gives us some idea why Lina lived in fear of her husband's driving. She was not alone: the poet Marina Tsvetayeva, invited for a visit earlier in the year, was advised to travel by train as she suffered from 'car panic . . . though it's by no means certain why it should be any less frightful by train than by car. To be consistent, you ought to come to us on a white horse',[38] an option that one could interpret as increasingly attractive. Prokofiev the driver did not go much faster – a constant 20 miles an hour, according to Nicolas Nabokov, who noted how on a later tour he 'computed every particle of our time at this average rate of speed and planned all our stops in advance'.[39] (His son Sviatoslav has defended his driving as cautious rather than accomplished, but not life-threatening.)

Undaunted, the company proceeded to Biarritz and Toulon before arriving in Monte-Carlo to meet Diaghilev, who was rehearsing for the new season. *Le Pas d'acier* was being revived but Prokofiev had nothing new in prospect. He did act as godfather to a play-through of Dukelsky's new symphony, a work he was to urge his Soviet contacts to perform after hearing its orchestral premiere, and observed Diaghilev's latest protégé, Nicolas Nabokov, whose *Ode* to a text by the 18th-century scientist poet Mikhail Lomonosov was now enjoying the Ballets Russes treatment. The other new work was Stravinsky's *Apollon musagète*, which Prokofiev had hesitated to judge when he played through the piano score in January; when he finally saw the ballet, he decided that the music was 'absolutely pitiful, and what's more stolen from the most disgraceful pockets: Gounod and Delibes and Wagner; even Minkus',[40] though he did find the string sonorities in the apotheosis impressive.

Barcelona was the next destination after a short period back in Paris. Lina again stayed at home; but on this occasion illness prevented her joint recital appearance with Prokofiev (she was in the early stages of a second pregnancy). Manuel Clausells, the impresario who had arranged the trip, was annoyed and asked Prokofiev to provide another singer. He replied that it was impossible, with the stern rejoinder, 'I trust the Barcelona public has come to see me as a composer and not as a pianist'.[41] One potentially useful new acquaintance was made as a result: the baritone Maxim de Rysikoff, whom Clausells asked Prokofiev to accompany in several of the Akhmatova songs and who become an intermediary in discussions for a Barcelona production of one of the operas. On his return to Paris, Prokofiev sent Rysikoff the Russian libretto of *The Gambler*, adding that 'if a full translation seems too burdensome, then you can put across the general sentiment [to the director of the opera, Raphael Moragas] – only so as not to lose the feverish tempo of the libretto, which is one of the most stageworthy merits of this opera'.[42] As it was now abundantly clear that Leningrad had postponed *The Gambler* at least until the autumn, the Barcelona link offered some hope. Otherwise, Prokofiev's visit was a great success, and he wrote to Aunt Katya that his appearance as soloist with Pablo Casals conducting had gone down best.

Then it was time for the Paris musical scene to reveal its splendours, as usual when other cultural centres were winding down for the summer. Among the 'foreign visitors and expensive concerts'[43] Prokofiev described as adorning the season was Dimitri Tiomkin, the future composer of Rakhmaninov-style film scores for Hollywood, playing Gershwin's two-and-a-half-year-old Piano Concerto under Vladimir Golschmann at the Paris Opéra. Prokofiev was there with Dukelsky and Diaghilev, and while the impresario pronounced upon 'good jazz and bad Liszt',[44] the older composer was intrigued enough to invite Gershwin through their intermediary, Dukelsky, to 5 Avenue Frémiet the following day. One wonders especially what impact the big tune that finally emerges out of the blues in Gershwin's slow movement must have had on Prokofiev's own evolving ideas about 'new melody'. Certainly, according to Dukelsky, he liked the tunes and the embellishments which Gershwin, happy to sit and play for hours at a stretch, rattled off, but he criticized the construction of the concerto 'which, he said later, consisted of 32-bar choruses ineptly bridged together. He thought highly of Gershwin's gifts, both as composer and pianist, however, and predicted that he would go far should he leave "dollars and dinners" alone'.[45] Prokofiev's loathing of Broadway commercialism surfaced again (and he was to give it even more aggressive voice when Dukelsky become irrevocably the Vernon Duke of *April in Paris*).

For now, though, he was very much the Dukelsky who had just composed a symphony. This relatively uncomplicated piece had the honour of sharing a Koussevitzky concert on 14 June with the suite from Rimsky-Korsakov's *The Maid of Pskov* and a preview of music from *The Fiery Angel*. By now Prokofiev had discarded his plans for a 'vocal suite' featuring soprano and orchestra, leaving his heroine still at the centre of the new 'taster'. Nina Koshetz, in a far cry from her Constantinople nightclub appearances with Dukelsky en route to the West, sang Renata, though she had by no means the most difficult slices of this highly taxing role. Prokofiev and Koussevitzky had decided on Act II, in which the tension between Ruprecht and Renata hardly reaches its zenith, but removed the scene with the book purveyor Jakob Glock (understandably, since it saved on an extra singer) and the spirit-raising (a puzzling decision, as the skeetering strings in this seance would have struck Parisians as the most modernistic effect they had yet heard from their *enfant terrible*). There was still the extraordinary bludgeoning of the orchestra which tells us of Agrippa's supernatural status and continues to seethe during his exchange with Ruprecht, a crucial late revision. Prokofiev learnt from the experience to reduce its dynamic level when the singers enter, but he might have predicted that this, of all things, would displease the Diaghilev clique. After his decisive parrying with Souvchinsky back in 1922, he had nothing to lose, since Diaghilev still appeared to need him for his ballet spectaculars, though their respective views on opera as an art form could only become more firmly entrenched. It did not help to have the disapproval of the ultra-moderns offset by the warm acclaim of Sabaneyev, his arch-enemy back in Petrograd days when he had famously denounced the performance of the *Scythian Suite* which never took place. In any case, he told Myaskovsky, the general success was unquestionable 'although the reaction of the audience here was of course rather superficial'.[46]

The obsessive spirit of *The Fiery Angel* hovered over Prokofiev's latest summer retreat, the Château de Vetraz, near Annemasse, in Haute Savoie, which he and Lina reached in early July; it was 'very spacious and simple, though it's called a château'[47] and provided the necessary peace and quiet. Back in April, Prokofiev had raised with Derzhanovsky the question of drawing a concert-hall work from *The Fiery Angel*: time permitting, it would be 'a symphonic paraphrase in the manner of those operatic paraphrases like the one Liszt wrote on *Rigoletto*'.[48] Settling down to work at the château, he told Myaskovsky that 'the material I drew from [the opera] has completely unexpectedly taken the form of a four-movement symphony!'[49] Hesitating over whether to call this 'medley' a symphony, he received the answer he wanted from his confidant: 'As concerns "Fiery Suite", I am certainly on the side of "Symphony". . . 'What does it matter if, strictly speaking, it's a "concoction"? If you do not shout very loudly about it and emphasize it, then perhaps no-one will remark upon it . . . If one were to be candid, is it even the case that the little "Sadko" [Rimsky-Korsakov's early tone-poem of 1867] is worse than the big "Sadko" [the much-enlarged opera of 1898]? I am enraptured by the fulfilment of a Third Symphony, all the more so with such outstanding material . . . You are a staggering fellow!'[50]

Yet despite the fact that Prokofiev believed Myaskovsky's encouragement to have played a vital part in the birth of a Third Symphony rather than 'some modest little suite from the opera',[51] and dedicated the work to him as a result, his initial outlining of the symphonic structure in early August shows that he had already made up his mind. His kernel was the white heat of the Act III interlude when Ruprecht goes off to fight Renata's 'fiery angel' incarnate in Count Heinrich; with its climactic counterpoint of the 'angel' theme versus Ruprecht's two principal motifs, and the triplet figures of Renata's latest perversity hopping around frenziedly in between, it is symphonic development par excellence. Preceding it in the symphony's first movement are clear expositions of all three leading themes, prefaced by an alarm-bell treatment of the possession ostinato and the religious chant that attempts to keep it at bay. The recapitulation is ingeniously sustained at an eerily low dynamic level throughout; it begins with the purified angel theme as the nuns hail it in the convent scene and proceeds, quietly but devastatingly, to smother Ruprecht's music in a coda unique to this purely orchestral work.

After the finest symphonic movement in Prokofiev's output to date, the rest comes closer to the notion of a suite, though in fascinating proportion to what has gone before. In the note he supplied for early performances, Prokofiev was to describe the slow movement as 'a calm and contemplative andante' of 'an abstract and metaphysical character'[52] – it fuses the convent prelude with Faust's disquisition – omitting to explain either the supernatural glissandos and thuddings or the weird intrusion of the macabre keening that first accompanies the fortune-teller. This is all atmospheric expectation, awaiting the eruption of the Scherzo – a new relationship specific to the symphony. The atonal terror of the seance is heightened by another expectant trio drawn from Renata's cradling of the wounded Ruprecht and an elaboration of the spirit world with thematic fragments from her inner life. The opera's final grim tattoo crowns it, begging the question of where the finale can possibly go.

Prokofiev's answer is the 'great blocks'[53] that precede and accompany the Agrippa scene, sandwiching between them another calm before counterpoint accumulates towards the apocalypse. 'Grandiose masses gape and topple over – "the end of the universe"',[54] wrote Sviatoslav Richter of a performance he heard in 1939. This is the best response to the careful declaration Prokofiev made in his short Soviet autobiography, claiming half-truthfully that 'the principal thematic material was composed independently of *The Fiery Angel*' and surely untruthfully that in the Third Symphony 'in my opinion it shed afresh the colouring' it had taken on in the opera.[55] Had that been the case, he would have attempted to free his material from the opera's dense malignant textures; in the symphony, the oppressive aura of catastrophe is, if anything, even more concentrated.

At least one of the two other projects for that summer was more straightforward: the arrangement for larger forces of the op.42 Overture, cannily playing on the twin factors of Koussevitzky's interest in an occasional piece for full orchestra and the Aeolian Company's willingness to pay for it. Hermann Schaad's suggestion that Prokofiev might follow the examples of Stravinsky and Siegfried Wagner in a new, educational Duo-Art scheme could have been followed up during his London visit, but Schaad was unable to cross the Atlantic and eventually accepted the bait of 'their' overture reorchestrated. It would at least sound better in a standard-sized concert hall, but much of the original's piquancy is inevitably lost in op.42*bis*: violins, not trumpet and piano, now double the garish woodwind fanfare, and only the unchanged openings of the two quiet sequences gain from the contrast with a much fuller orchestra.

It was also high time for some new piano pieces. Myaskovsky rejoiced at the news, 'for the repertoire of our pianists is too stereotyped',[56] and Prokofiev had not added anything of this kind to his own recital programmes for a decade. The new seriousness with which he undertook the task was reflected both in his confidence to Myaskovsky that he was working on the two new pieces 'very slowly, since I don't want to dash them off on the spur of the moment'[57] and in the title, *Chose en soi*. Although the plural has been used for this curious diptych, only the singular appeared on the score since each piece was printed separately (as A and B respectively); and although Prokofiev gave translations in both French and Russian (*Veshchi v sebye*), it is the German that signifies. The *Ding an sich* ('thing in itself') was the early 19th-century German philosopher Immanuel Kant's term for the unknowable something that lies behind the world we perceive and understand. Kant's successor Schopenhauer, who agreed with the *Ding an sich* in principle, had some valuable qualifications to make; and in classing the realm of music as the nearest we can reach in the arts to perceiving the unknowable – in this case what lies behind the notes, which we can talk about only in vague terms – he was bound to appeal to composers, Wagner and Prokofiev among them.

We know that Prokofiev studied both philosophers in the summer of 1916, jotting down their thoughts in his private notebook, even if the only palpable result was *A Bad Dog*, that bizarre short story focussing on the interference of Schopenhauer and his poodle in a Florentine love-triangle. Yet clearly his quest for a hidden meaning beyond the phenomenal world, manifest otherwise only in his adoption of Christian Science, had pursued its own course. In musical terms it signalled a change of direction from the extrovert dissonances and complications of works like *The Fiery Angel* and the Second Symphony towards greater self-communing. Even so, the two pieces that constitute *Chose en soi* are not as introspective as the title might suggest. Like the Fifth Piano Sonata, both take a now familiar C major diatonicism as their springboard, though the moods are very different: a robust bass-clef *étude* with the opening pattern two octaves apart in the first piece, a treble-clef two-part invention in the second.

The form of the Allegro moderato is fairly clear cut, given the abundance of material: an expressive theme as counterpart to the *étude*, two dolorous chromatic pauses for thought framing a songful middle sequence in B flat major which gathers surprising weight: but the accumulation of more elaborate textures comes as a surprise, especially in the exciting closing stages. Prokofiev's second piece, Moderato scherzando, a kind of feminine response to the masculine energy of the first, is perhaps the more spellbinding. Here the playful and the lyrical sides of his nature act out a drama unique in his music: the *scherzando* idea continually tries in vain to waylay a wistful Andante theme, which returns each time a semitone higher – from C major to an even more rarefied *dolcissimo* D flat major and on to a D major treatment where the writing on three staves gives an immense feeling of space. The final wriggling round an emphatic C does not convince us that the transcendental singer of the piece has been banished for long (and *The Prodigal Son* will witness her return). This, if anything, is the essence of the *Ding an sich* for Prokofiev.

There were several breaks that summer from working in the heat. On 8 August Prokofiev announced to Nina Koshetz that the following day he was 'going walking in the mountains to lose some weight'.[58] With him went Koussevitzky and Gavriil Paichadze, Eberg's successor as the Paris-based manager of Édition Russe de Musique and the most regular of his chess correspondents. Their four-day excursion took them to Chamonix, 'which reminds me of Kislovodsk', wrote Prokofiev in his diary, 'but smaller, and the air in Kislovodsk is incomparably better'.[59] Stravinsky, an object of fascination to the five-year-old Sviatoslav as his name was on everyone's lips, paid a visit; presumably the subject of *Apollon musagète* was avoided.

Prokofiev was also reunited with another old friend, Boris Asafyev, for whom he had persevered in obtaining a visa through the mediation of Milhaud and others; Asafyev was visiting the Salzburg Festival and wanted the visa so that he could come to Annemasse in mid-September. Together with Pavel Lamm and Lina, Prokofiev showed Asafyev part of the route he had walked with Koussevitzky and Paichadze. This time, however, he drove them in the Ballot to Chamonix, where they took a cable-car to Planpraz and proceeded on foot, leaving the pregnant Lina in a chalet, to the Col de Brévent. A second visit at the end of the month seems to have been achieved without a visa, since it ended in Asafyev's furtive return to Austria by motorcycle in the dead of night. They drove round the Swiss lakes and across the St Gotthard Pass to Lugano, returning via the Rhône Valley. 'Both the automobile and Ptashka emerged from these excursions quite well', Prokofiev reported to Natalya Koussevitzky, 'while Lamm and Asafyev were just ecstatic over the trip.'[60] A journey of a quite different sort, it transpired, had been taken by his aunt and cousin in Russia – 'about 20 hours by train and three on a horse'[61] – from Moscow to Katyechka's compulsory new residence in Kadnikov, north-east of Leningrad in the Vologda region, after her release from prison. Katyechka's situation, Prokofiev wrote to Tanya Rayevskaya, 'must be like a convict deported and left in freedom'.[62] But the relatively spacious new surroundings seemed to suit the troubled Rayevsky women well enough and 'everything's better than we thought when Aunt Katya decided to leave Moscow'.[63]

Prokofiev and Lina returned to Paris on 4 October without a new flat to rent and finding nowhere to stay until early evening (an automobile show was in progress). Their flat-hunting was harder than ever, he told Aunt Katya, since there was less to rent and more to pay; but by early November they had a new address at 1 Rue Obligado. Only the happy chance that his October trip to Russia had been cancelled, because in the current exchange crisis 'Persimfans did not have the means to engage artists from abroad this season',[64] prevented Lina, due to give birth in less than three months' time, from having to search on her own. Prokofiev does not seem to have been too demoralized by the latest postponement. He was worried that the Soviet premiere of the orchestral suite from *Le Pas d'acier* (as *Stalnoy skok*) earlier in the summer had not gone well – largely, it seems, because of the clumsy conducting of his 'second-rate'[65] American-based compatriot Vladimir Savich (or Shavich, as he was sometimes known), but he was hoping to compensate for his falling stock by conducting the newly completed Third Symphony for the ASM in the new year. *The Fiery Angel* was still alive and kicking: it even looked as if the new directorate at Akopera would take it on, and he still hoped to play it through for Erich Kleiber in Berlin, planning for a December meeting that never took place.

There were also two major stagings on the horizon. Work on the new version of *The Gambler* had not gone to waste: it was to be given its premiere in March at the Théâtre Royal de la Monnaie in Brussels. Unexpectedly, too, Diaghilev had commissioned another ballet for the 1929 spring season in Paris and London. Following the new fashion for biblical subjects, he suggested the parable of the Prodigal Son from the New Testament (*St Luke*, chapter 15, verses 11–32). 'In proposing it', Prokofiev later wrote, 'he anticipated very well my wish to turn from external effects to interior lyricism.'[66] Boris Kochno took credit for the scenario, later suing Prokofiev and Paichadze at Édition Russe for publishing the score as *L'Enfant prodigue* rather than *Le Fils prodigue* and omitting his name from the score; Prokofiev's defence was that 'the idea for the libretto (that's to say the adaptation of the biblical parable) was explained to me for the first time by M. de Diaghileff, verbally, in the presence of M. Kochno and a witness (Mr. Igor Glebov) . . . later, when nearly all the music had already been composed, M. Kochno sent me a very brief sketch, in Russian'.[67] Diaghilev, then, was presumably responsible for changes in the parable's *dramatis personae*, substituting two tender servant-sisters for Luke's depiction of the self-righteous elder brother and adding two 'confidants' who help the Prodigal go astray. The proportions, too, were dictated by choreographic necessity: the central part of the ballet takes the hint of verse 13's 'riotous living' in a 'far country' to show the Prodigal seduced by false friends and a siren. This is the divertissement; the drama rests with the Prodigal's departure and the tragic humility of his return in the outer scenes.

By the end of November, Diaghilev was able to tell Serge Lifar, his intended Prodigal, that 'Prokofiev has already composed a good half of his ballet. A lot of it is very good. As yet he hasn't got the female part quite right, but is quite prepared to rewrite it'.[68] The second half seems to have flowed as rapidly from the composer's pen as the first: on 19 November Prokofiev told Vernon Duke that he had 'decided to set a record and write the ballet in two weeks, which seems to have succeeded if I hold the course on the second week at the rate of the first'.[69] He was as good as his word: Diaghilev's second report followed a full audition on 1 December. 'Much of it is very good', he wrote to Lifar about the score. 'The last scene, the Prodigal's return, is beautiful. Your variation, the awakening after the orgy, is, for Prokofiev, quite new stuff. A sort of profound and majestic nocturne. Good, too, is the tender theme of the sisters, and very good, in the genuine "Prokofiev" manner, the pilfering scene: three clarinets performing miracles of agility.'[70]

Diaghilev had certainly selected some of the best themes (and the *pièces de résistance* of the orchestration; clearly, even though the scoring was yet to come, Prokofiev had envisaged his plunder tarantella for the clarinet family). Later, on the eve of the ballet's premiere in London, he would express his opinion that 'the composer has never been more clear, more simple, more melodious, and more tender than in "The Prodigal Son"'.[71] The simplicity belongs to the protagonist and to the brief appearances of his sisters and father in the first and final scenes. A feeble flower among thorns, the Prodigal's music is easily manipulated. Out of the discordant thrash which launches his career away from home comes an easy-going melody in Prokofiev's best diatonic manner (Ex.54). It makes its way through a variety of orchestrations (much as the theme of Renata's fascination with her fiery angel had done in the first movement of the Third Symphony), losing its way as it passes through several keys and from clarinet to tuba, *dolce* on strings, unashamedly brassy in the denouement of no.2; it returns to suggest the Prodigal's naivety in his encounter with the Siren and at later points, the last – in 'division of the spoils' – not, in fact, attributable to the character it has so far accompanied. There is a poise between the personable woodwind of the humanizing touches, the dissonant caricature of the revellers and the bravura set pieces (especially for the Siren) which anticipates the larger-scale proportions of *Romeo and Juliet*. The exuberance of much of the material makes up for occasional hints of cut-and-paste; the 'drunkenness' movement's repetitions of the second number have a certain symmetry but also raise a suspicion that Prokofiev could have invented something new.

For the first time in his ballet music, though, he saves the trump-card until the end. The Prodigal's return to his father's arms calls for the most emotional music in the

Ex.54 *The Prodigal Son*, op.46 – Scene I no.2, Meeting friends

score; Prokofiev must have known Rembrandt's famous picture hanging in the Hermitage, which was also to inspire Britten to write his operatic parable in 1966. But while Britten's 'homecoming' chord strikes a placid, even rather depressing note, Prokofiev dignifies the moment with the simplest of flute melodies, stirring itself briefly from C into B flat major in a way that seems utterly natural and enjoying a gentle peroration on the strings before it subsides without a hint of false pathos to the work's quiet close. 'It is seldom that I have worked with such pleasure as I did on this piece!'[72] Prokofiev told his Christian Scientist friend Warren Klein, and the score bears noble witness.

Another son joined the Prodigal of Prokofiev's musical imagination, ten days later than expected, on 14 December, 'at 5 in the morning, Ptashka brought into the light . . . a very healthy boy called Oleg',[73] Prokofiev wrote to Aunt Katya. The child's progress was noted early in the New Year:

> Oleg is in excellent shape – he looks better and stronger than Sviatoslav did at his age, and what probably helps more than a little in his case is that he was born naturally, whereas at the time of Sviatoslav's birth Ptashka was given chloroform at the last minute . . . You ask what we would have called a girl? I would have preferred a more archaic name – Lyudmila or Svetlana; Ptashka a more generally

> recognized one like Natalya or Lidya. Ptashka feels a little weak, not getting her full night's sleep; in the evening she can't get to sleep for a long time, then the crying of the hungry little glutton starts up at five in the morning. She has enough milk for two feedings a day; for the rest of the time she has special sterilized milk.[74]

The spectacle of Prokofiev playing the concerned father for the sake of his beloved aunt is a strange one, but he seems to have brought a customary objectivity to bear on his dutiful reportage. Something of his delight in childlike things comes across in a description, also to Aunt Katya, of Sviatoslav's fifth-birthday party on 9 March, which involved ten children aged three to 11 (the eldest was the daughter of Boris and Cecilia Zakharov) of 'all nationalities: American, English and even a four-year-old Egyptian Jew . . . They set going an electric train, given by grandma . . . then they drank chocolate; moreover in the American manner there was a cake with five candles, lit and extinguished by electricity'.[75]

Sviatoslav's party was the last divertissement for some time. Prokofiev was to spend his own birthday travelling to Brussels for the premiere of *The Gambler*. It was a project tackled by the Théâtre de la Monnaie with the utmost seriousness. At the beginning of January 1929, the intendant Paul Spaak wrote to Prokofiev asking him how he saw his work so that the company could decide whether to create a stylized production or 'give it in the spirit of exact realism';[76] his answer was to 'stylize it, but a little'.[77] Meyerhold would no doubt go further in Leningrad, if he was ever to have the chance, but that was to be a special case. 'Although Brussels won't do it as in Leningrad', Prokofiev wrote to Derzhanovsky in February, 'nevertheless this is an advanced and cultured theatre, much rated in Europe, and thus very important as a springboard for further productions'.[78]

He managed to weave in visits to rehearsals with several recitals, starting on 18 March with a programme that served up the two pieces of *Chose en soi* for the first time and a piano transcription of the *American* Overture to an appreciative audience. As for *The Gambler*, he heard at his own request 'singers who have already learnt a little of their roles'[79] (the General and Polina) and was impressed by the 'painstaking'[80] nature of the production. The premiere on 29 April, he told Aunt Katya, was 'a great success – the theatre was full of a brilliant public, the papers furnished long articles'.[81] There were the inevitable critical blunders, with one paper referring to a *Suite mythe*, and Prokofiev raged to the conductor, Corneil de Thoran, that 'when they say there are no melodies in *The Gambler*, this isn't amusing but stupid, for I think that even the antimusical ears of these gentlemen will end by finding them'.[82] But of the 20 articles, most were complimentary and several dealt with the opera in a serious manner. Prokofiev planned to go to Brussels for one of the later performances scheduled, by popular demand, for May and June; but the directorship gravely informed him that 'we have had nothing but trouble caused by Mme Leblanc [the Polina, who apparently kept falling sick] and have suspended performances'.[83]

By then, the glamorous Parisian musical season was in full swing and Prokofiev had two important premieres to supervise. The first was Pierre Monteux's preparation of the Third Symphony for a concert on 17 May. 'We were very worried', Prokofiev told the symphony's greatest admirer Myaskovsky,

> because Monteux commanded two extra rehearsals in addition to the three already scheduled, especially for the symphony, and besides, we didn't know if the parts would be ready for these rehearsals. Happily they turned up in time. Monteux was conscientious but *terre-à-terre* in the manner of Malko. Between rehearsals I kept fiddling about in every way with the Scherzo (thank God you haven't yet made the piano arrangement), but then it went and had the greatest success in performance – with Diaghilev and Stravinsky among the admirers. But you know that doesn't stop me considering the first movement as the most important.[84]

The second premiere was to be that of *The Prodigal Son.* A now ailing and newly wistful Diaghilev was pleased to have its emotional subject as a new flag to wave alongside Rieti's score for the élite, syncopated steps of *Le Bal* and a revival of Stravinsky's *Renard.* Stravinsky was now back on board the Diaghilev train after his flirtation with Ida Rubinstein's rival company, for whom he had composed *Le Baiser de la fée* on themes by Tchaikovsky. Though it is light of touch compared to Diaghilev's fulminations over the choreography, Prokofiev's comment to Paichadze hits its target: 'I'm very glad you liked Stravinsky's new ballet; I've always said that Tchaikovsky was an excellent composer'.[85]

Happy as the omens for Prokofiev's new Diaghilev ballet may have seemed, the designer and choreographer were to cause numerous headaches; though this had no long-term effect in making *Le Fils prodigue,* as the ballet now became – dropping the initial mention of the 'parable' – one of the Ballets Russes' most durable and timeless successes. Failing to lure a disillusioned Matisse back to the theatre, Diaghilev chose the experienced hand of the Parisian-born Georges Rouault for the sets and costumes because he knew of the artist's work restoring medieval stained glass and his preference for religious subjects. Much thought and little progress, however, was achieved during the creative gestation period in Monte Carlo that spring. According to Lifar, Diaghilev broke into Rouault's hotel room, plundered his sketches and chose the design he wanted for the first scene; according to Kochno, he 'returned from this trespass empty handed and wild-eyed', having 'not even found drawing paper, brushes and paint'.[86] That same evening, continues Kochno, he booked Rouault a seat on the train to Paris the next day. Rouault disappeared, supposedly to pack his meagre luggage, and 'the following morning, before boarding the train, Rouault brought Diaghilev a stack of sketches – admirable gouaches and pastels which he had executed in one night'.[87] These include several memorable images of an eastern harbour and lighthouse for the opening scene and the tent of the second, outlined in the now familiar thick black strokes. Much, however, was left to the imagination of the costume designer Vera

Soudeikine, the future Mrs Stravinsky, and to Prince Shervashidze, who executed the sets.

Another Georgian, Georgi Balanchivadze, who had become George Balanchin (with an optional final 'e' for the French, the spelling most familiar) in his first season with the Ballets Russes in 1925, was engaged to choreograph his fifth work for Diaghilev. He had recently enjoyed great success with *Apollon musagète*, perfectly mirroring Stravinsky's musical alexandrines. *Le Fils prodigue* was an altogether more emotionally charged subject; Balanchine rose to the challenge with crablike movements for the Prodigal's companions, a contortedly erotic *pas de deux* for the Prodigal and the Siren, and – after much deliberation in Monte Carlo – a return by the Prodigal, made on his knees across the stage to reach his father's embrace.

Prokofiev, however, made no secret of the fact that he was 'not especially happy with the choreography'.[88] In later life Balanchine would maintain that the composer knew nothing about the subject and only wanted a realistic staging: 'bearded men sitting and drinking real wine out of real goblets, the dancers dressed with "historical accuracy". In a word, Prokofiev imagined *The Prodigal Son* somewhat like *Rigoletto*. And, of course, he was horrified by my staging'.[89] In the light of Prokofiev's fondness for Meyerhold and, in particular, his remarks on stylization in the Brussels production of *The Gambler*, it is difficult to take Balanchine's assertion at face value. Nor does it seem entirely plausible that when Balanchine went to ask Prokofiev for money, he would have shouted, as the choreographer recalled, 'What did you ever do? It's all nonsense, what you did! *The Prodigal Son* is mine! Why should you be paid? Who are you? Get out of here! I won't give you anything!'[90] Nevertheless it is true that Balanchine's wages were barely enough to live on, that the royalty agreement established in May gave one-third to Kochno for the libretto and two-thirds to Prokofiev for the music; there was no mention of Balanchine as there had been of Massine in the contract for *Le Pas d'acier*. His name did not feature in Prokofiev's own résumé of the ballet's history, written in January 1931, despite praise for the scene of the Prodigal's return.

Testy as Prokofiev often was when performances failed to meet his expectations, he was always careful in citing chapter and verse to support his dissatisfaction, as two occasions in 1929 attest. The first was a performance of the Quintet in January, with the players assembled for the Paris Pro Musica organization by Marcel Darrieux, the violinist who had given the premiere of the First Violin Concerto. Prokofiev, who had not been invited to the rehearsals, fired off an angry letter bringing down his wrath on the concert. 'The sonorities were badly balanced', he wrote to the president of Pro Musica, 'with oboe and double bass weaker than the rest. All the tempos were wrong; all the *poco rit*s became *rallentando*s verging on the grotesque. The *pochissimo più mosso*s were taken at twice the speed.'[91] And he continued with a list of further details, ending with a general swipe at the 'carnage' and asking for artistic justification. The second object of his wrath, at the end of May, was a performance of *The Prodigal Son* conducted by Désormière; the following day

Prokofiev gave the conductor his opinion in no uncertain terms: 'I don't need to tell you that the playing of our orchestra let me down terribly yesterday. You probably noticed yourself that in the number in 5/4 nothing was together, and the double basses were a half-beat in front. And the solo for the three clarinets? What did they play? It was unbelievable!'[92] His distinguished American guests, he added, had heard better in café-concerts; 'I had to defend our musicians as best I could, but they looked at me pityingly as if to say, poor devil, he has no ear!'[93]

Désormière seems to have been something of a scapegoat; as Prokofiev wrote to Myaskovsky, the orchestra was substandard and his own grasp of the difficult numbers less than proficient when he himself conducted the first performance on 21 May. This opening of the last Ballets Russes season in the Théâtre Sarah Bernhardt included a revival of Stravinsky's *Renard*, also conducted by the composer with new choreography by Lifar and designs by his old friend Larionov. Prokofiev was happy to report to a Brussels colleague that this sequel to his success with *The Gambler* and the premiere of the Third Symphony had gone off equally well: 'now I feel like a schoolboy who has passed his exams'.[94] Lifar's Prodigal, especially his homecoming, was the sensation of the evening, though whether it happened in quite the way Lifar remembered is open to question. 'When the curtain went down, pandemonium broke loose', he recalled. 'Numbers of people were crying, though no-one had realized it was my self, my life, that had been enacted.'[95] When the ballet arrived in London in early July, following a Berlin season conducted by Ernest Ansermet, it was the Siren of Doubrovska who created the greatest impression. 'Was there ever a woman more strangely serpentine?' asked one critic. 'The Prodigal was fascinated by the siren's inhuman contortions, and he joined her in those strange acrobatical feats which characterize Mr. Balanchin's choreography.'[96]

As a composer whose stock had increased in England over the previous few years, Prokofiev attracted far more considered criticism than he had enjoyed at the time of *Chout*. There were the usual insulting generalities – 'Prokofieff's music in this case is neither bizarre nor stimulating; it is thematically jejune, quite inoffensive and rather obviously the work of a tired man';[97] but many critics took the bait of Diaghilev's observations and one pointed out, prophetically for the composer, that 'the new manifesto . . . opens the door wide for sentiment and tradition'.[98] Herbert Hughes of the *Daily Telegraph* even took the trouble to look at the piano score and outlined what has since become an apt summary of Prokofiev's melodic construction: 'a tune must not be allowed to proceed more than a few steps in the same key without side-tracking into one of an entirely different colour . . . It is an old trick of the comic-man-at-the-piano, developed very successfully by Richard Strauss . . . Generally speaking, the music gives an impression of being diatonic but perverse in its treatment of tonalities, the whole mad scheme kept alive by immensely varied and vigorous rhythms'.[99]

Prokofiev did not join the company in London, where Rieti conducted his symphonic suite *Noah's Ark*, where Rieti's new ballet (designed by Giorgio de Chirico) enjoyed success and the 16-year-old Igor Markevitch, Diaghilev's last love who scoffed at the older generation of Russian composers, took the solo role in his Piano Concerto. At the end of the season the company dispersed, never to meet again. But the career of Prokofiev's *Prodigal Son* was far from over. Earlier in the year he had received a $1000 commission from Koussevitzky in Boston to write a new symphony for the orchestra's 1930–31 season. In June he explained to M. Cuvelier of the Société Philharmonique that he had 'expounded to you evasively on the question of fragments from *The Prodigal Son* because at present I'm working on my Fourth Symphony in which there are several themes from the ballet. For this reason I haven't yet thought of a suite'.[100]

The suite would take even longer than the symphony to appear; but, when it did, it was clear that Prokofiev had divided the spoils of his latest stage work altogether more artfully than he had done when making a symphony out of material from *The Fiery Angel*. As two of the ballet's undisputed highlights, the Siren's dance and the Prodigal's homecoming, already belonged to the symphony, this was the first time he had concocted a suite and left out the sugar-plums. The remains include several tasty morsels, though, and perhaps it was only the Siren's ready-made scherzo-and-trio form which prevented the clarinets' plunder scene becoming the symphony's third movement; instead it provided, with no changes, the suite's central number. Other movements had a more synthetic basis; the first featured most of the ballet's opening with the jagged unisons replaced by the lachrymose bassoons of the fifth number. It is perhaps worth mentioning that Kurt Weill might have got to know in this form the passage for woodwind and strings in 3rds which so strongly foreshadows much of his simpler music in the 1930s, including the Second Symphony and *Die sieben Todsünden der Kleinbürger* (Ex.55). The dissonance of the revellers then bursts in, but as Prokofiev is saving the diatonic melody of the Prodigal's credulous

Ex.55 *The Prodigal Son* – Scene I, no. 1, The departure

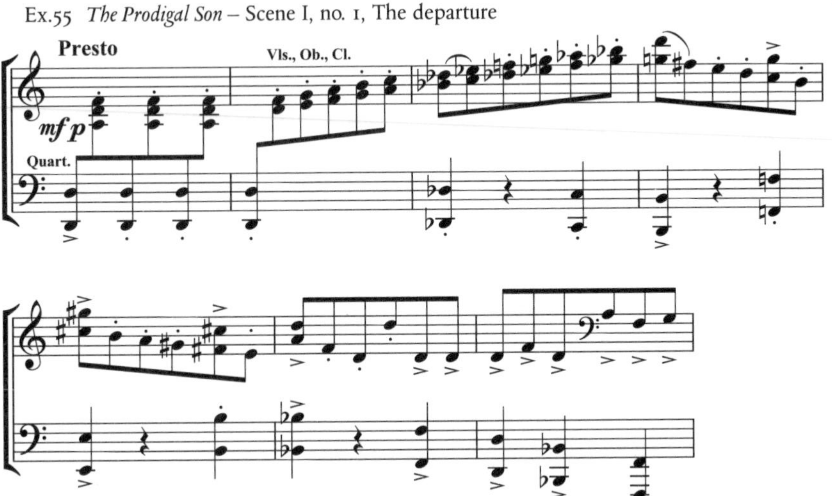

good nature for his symphony, this is the ballet's sixth number with its strutting trumpet tune. After the plunder scene, Prokofiev makes a misjudgment with his suite's slow movement, since the plaintive clarinet theme of the Prodigal's remorse as well as the main event of the return were already earmarked for Koussevitzky's commission; brooding atmosphere misses its resolution. The suite's finale is also unsatisfying in its attempt to graft the *valse lente* of the Prodigal's sense of sin on to 'Les Danseurs' (no.4 of the ballet). A noisy concert ending brings the curtain down abruptly.

The symphony, completed in the spring of 1930, is much more successful on its own terms, though it remains a convenient solution to the problem that Prokofiev's busy performing schedule left little time to work on a major score. It is a manifesto of the 'new simplicity', at least as far as compactness if not the occasional dissonance is concerned; the first movement's lyrical counter-theme, for instance, drawn from discarded music for the ballet, makes its point in an eight-bar sequence for flute and is repeated in an extended 12-bar sequence (in the same G major dominant) before a short, loud *tutti* brings the exposition to a full stop. Of the other music not heard in the ballet, the new introduction is a gentle miracle and shares with the lyrical episode of the finale chaste perfection of orchestral colour; the latter, given here in its final manifestation, also looks forward to the themes of Prokofiev's Soviet period (Ex.56).

As in the case of the Third Symphony's relationship to *The Fiery Angel*, Prokofiev told only a half-truth about the Fourth in his short autobiography when he wrote that 'music that had been intended for *The Prodigal Son* but did not in fact go in to it proved perfectly suitable for the first movement'.[101] Granted, most of its ideas are unfamiliar, and the dissonant development makes a surprising excursion to the territory of the Second Symphony; but the theme of the oddly titled Allegro eroico has already been heard at fig.82 of 'Les Danseurs', albeit without its exciting ostinato support. The two classically brief statements announcing the Prodigal's final state of grace, on flute and then violins, lose much of their impact when they become not a gentle dramatic apotheosis but substance for a slow movement. Here in the symphony they are kept apart by a stalking intruder in the contrasting sonority of

Ex.56 Symphony no.4, op.47 – IV. Allegro risoluto

tuba, contrabassoon and cellos and an emotional reprise of the introduction, with a doleful trumpet pendant that gives the climactic reappearance of the melody a healing role. The movement then subsides with kindly swiftness as in the ballet's closing bars.

The Scherzo is Prokofiev's only movement in his Third and Fourth Symphonies to be taken over in outline bar for bar from its parent work; at least, the music of *The Prodigal Son*'s no.3 is mirrored up to the last four bars when we switch to its reprise at the upbeat to fig.111 of the ballet's no.5. Here Prokofiev indulges in new delicacies of orchestration, giving the sinuous dance to the strings at the start and embroidering it on its return. The angular unisons framing the trio section benefit from a touch of counterpoint in the trumpet and horn parts, and the dance's form lends itself ideally to a classically proportioned scherzo. As for the finale, here at last the opening of the ballet makes its mark in conjunction with the breezy theme quoted in Ex.54; its transformations in the 'changing-background' technique beloved of the 19th-century Russian nationalists make it a good companion. This, of course, was not the last of the Prodigal, who would live on to serve Prokofiev's piano music, or even of the Fourth Symphony. 'The symphony has not met with success, but I love it for its absence of noise and the substantial amount of superior material it contains',[102] he wrote in his short autobiography; and many years later he revised it with so much new music that he gave it the alternative number of op.111. Yet the ballet marked the end of an era, and of all he felt he had to say in his music to Diaghilev. That, at least, is what he told Asafyev at the end of August 1929. By then, though, he was writing with hindsight, shocked by the news that the great impresario was dead.

13
Outlines of a real face
1929–32

'We've been here for the last three weeks', wrote Prokofiev to his Paris friend Pierre Blois at the end of July 1929, 'making war on the dust of the 14th century, cockroaches of the 17th century and the absence of a 20th-century cooker etc., conquering our enemies little by little.'[1] The summer residence which furnished such formidable obstacles was another castle more worthy of the name than the Château de Vetraz, which had served as the previous year's dacha. Culoz, he told Warren Klein, 'lies about 60 kilometres south of Geneva . . . the castle is not quite comfortable but picturesque and very old'.[2]

The most serious drawback, as it turned out, was the delayed arrival of the hired piano: 15 days passed with Prokofiev working neither on the concert programmes scheduled for the end of the year nor on that summer's compositional plans. These, however, posed no great challenges; orchestras, especially in America where plans were fast taking shape for another tour at the beginning of 1930, needed fresh repertoire that was straightforward for both players and audiences, though Prokofiev had his own ideas about what that might involve. He now had a full-time secretary to decode his piano-score annotations as well as to deal with an increasingly voluminous correspondence. This was Mikhail Astrov, encountered at Édition Russe de Musique and a faithful scribe with a mind of his own for the rest of Prokofiev's Paris-based existence. The first project entailed turning the youthful and already once-revised Sinfonietta 'completely inside out', he informed Myaskovsky, 'and the result is a very sweet and utterly well-proportioned old-new piece'.[3] Strictly speaking, there was no new material – the novelty lay in the restructuring and a certain amount of rescoring – but that was no obstacle to giving the revision a special category as 'op.5/48'. It was a pleasant return to the past, a reminder of one of his closest periods of creative exchange with Myaskovsky. Prokofiev had hoped to give his old friend a taste of his new life, as he had succeeded in doing with Asafyev the previous year. Yet no amount of furious pressure on Prokofiev's part could lure the cautious homebody to France that summer.

After finishing the Sinfonietta in mid-September, Prokofiev turned his full attention to orchestrating what we now know as the Divertimento, advertised to his American agent in early July as a 'Suite for orchestra, not very difficult to play or listen to'.[4] In the latter respect, he was surely being disingenuous. The Divertimento's selective and relatively small-scale orchestration – including double woodwind and four horns though retaining the now indispensable tuba beneath three trombones – changes timbre every few bars, making it more difficult to listen to, as it passes round unconventional thematic material, than a determinedly discordant and noisy work like the first movement of the Second Symphony. It stands as a modestly wrought gateway to a new era of melodic experimentation in Prokofiev's music, leading to the First String Quartet, the Fourth and Fifth Piano Concertos and the ballet score *Sur le Borysthène.* The composer as autobiographer, marking the start of this phase a little earlier than we might choose today, with the *American* Overture, neatly encapsulates the problems many listeners have with these works and suggests how they might try harder. He does so by outlining his own reactions from a distance of several years, starting with amazed incomprehension: 'I played them through once, twice, three times – and suddenly through the darkness loomed the outlines of a real face'.[5] It is the perfect image for the kind of unconventional thematic shapes towards which he was now moving.

The composite nature of the Divertimento, too, suggests a perplexing hybrid. The first and third movements are reworked leftovers from the world of the Quintet – the Overture and *Matelote* which Prokofiev had added to *Trapèze* in 1926 at Romanov's request. Yet there are connections beneath the jagged surface. Just as the key scheme of the second *Chose en soi* had moved upwards in semitonal steps before returning to its C major base, the overall 'plan' of the Divertissement takes us down from the opening E minor Moderato, molto ritmato and a limpid D minor Larghetto to the jerky games round a tonic C in the last two movements, with the finale bringing back the wistful melody at the heart of the first movement. This Allegro non troppo (subsequently called 'Epilogue') features themes that never found their way into *The Prodigal Son,* and its lively rhythmic engagement of the C major scale, with characteristic excursions into C sharp minor and F major, would certainly have made it a good companion there (Ex.57). The Larghetto, which Prokofiev acknowledged as 'a continuation of the atmosphere and lyricism of *The Prodigal Son*'[6] is the still, limpid core of the Divertimento. Its special quality is even more pronounced in the piano transcription of 1938, where Prokofiev revised the B minor return of his beautiful theme to calm it down still further; indeed the whole work sounds happier, more centred on the keyboard (Prokofiev even played one of the movements, entitled 'Fragment from the Divertimento', as early as a Brussels recital of December 1930). If the piano version provides another link between the early and later sonatas, the *divisi* then muted strings of the orchestral Larghetto forge a rainbow bridge between the world of *The Prodigal Son* and the love music of *Romeo and Juliet.*

Ex.57 Divertimento, op.43 – I. Moderato, molto ritmato

Was it pure coincidence that a near neighbour that summer at Les Écharvines, Talloires, also happened to be working on a divertissement? Stravinsky, however, changed the title of his piece to *Capriccio*. It was, in essence, another vehicle for his solo appearances with orchestras to follow the Concerto for Piano and Wind, and when he played it through to his colleague at Les Écharvines, Prokofiev 'liked it better than the first one'.[7] Stravinsky's commiserations and fellow-suffering were presumably a help when news arrived of Diaghilev's death in Venice on 19 August. Prokofiev's immediate reaction was to try to understand 'the disappearance of a colossal and without question a unique figure, whose range increases in proportion to his retreat from us',[8] and to wonder about the consequences of the fragmentation of the Ballets Russes' talents; he would hear from Lifar on that count within the year. Less than a decade later he was willing to fight Diaghilev's corner in Soviet Russia, combating the negative image of 'an impresario pure and simple who sucked the creative life-blood of his artists' by asserting that 'his influence on art and his services in popularizing Russian art were tremendous'.[9] His conjecture that had Diaghilev lived he 'would probably be working with us now'[10] was not just wishful thinking; this ever-flexible figure had made moves to forge ties with the artistic forces of Soviet Russia shortly before his death.

The autumn of 1929 brought near-fatality and a loss much closer to home. After enjoying the unseasonably warm days of early October in Haute Savoie, Prokofiev set off with Lina, their sons and their nurse in the Ballot for Paris. He told Aunt Katya what happened next: 'we lost a wheel at high speed, as a result of which the car turned over. Happily we came out of it with minor injuries and the children were completely unharmed. This is a miracle, because the car was going at about 80 kilometres an hour and was completely smashed up. We all had to lie up for about a week. Up to now, Ptashka has had bruises around her eyes and I've lost a tooth, not to mention all the bruises on both our bodies'.[11] They were driven back to Paris by some Americans who were among the many kind onlookers who assisted at the scene, Lina told Haensel, adding that 'accounts of this accident appeared in the French, Russian and English press, but in different distorted variations, making the story more tragic'.[12] There was, however, one further consequence which Prokofiev revealed to Myaskovsky, who must have been thankful to escape that summer's tour of France with this ill-fated driver: 'when I fell, I pulled some muscles in my left hand, which means that for the moment I can play everything on the piano except for an octave in the left hand'.[13]

Newly settled in another temporary Paris residence, 6 Rue Bassano, Prokofiev sent his letter about the accident to Aunt Katya on 23 October. The following day a telegram arrived from Anna Uvarova in Moscow: 'Tanta Catherine Motre [*recte* morte] Mardi 22 Euterrement [*recte* enterrement] jeudi'.[14] His reaction to this bombshell was practical: a return telegram expressing deep grief and the assurance that he would cover all expenses. As he later wrote to another relative, Sonya Brichan in Liège, 'Aunt Katya died from [the consequences of] a simple oedema. She died quite remarkably in full consciousness . . . reading a prayer'.[15] So his last ties with a mother-figure had been severed; there was still bereaved Katyechka left behind in the Kadnikov exile to consider, however, and while her brother Shurik remained in prison, his wife Nadya and their three daughters needed Prokofiev's love and support. Fortunately Katyechka was allowed to visit him during this brief visit to Russia in late October and early November – his first since 1927 – and he later sent to Moscow amusing snapshots of his time with Nadya and the children on the city streets.

Prokofiev was well aware of the changed Soviet musical scene he was about to face. The Russian Association of Proletarian Musicians (RAPM), founded in 1924, was now in the ascendant, wielding its new journal *Proletarsky muzykant* to attack Western, jazz and modernist tendencies. In its first issue of January 1929 the manifesto was to 'oppose the influence of decadent bourgeois music among young Soviet musicians . . . impress on them the necessity of absorbing the best, the healthiest and the most acceptable ideological elements of the musical legacy of the past [by extreme casuistry this included Tchaikovsky and his Sixth Symphony as well as Musorgsky] [and] prepare the ground for the creation of a new, specifically proletarian type of music'.[16] At the same time, the Association for Contemporary Music sank to an all-time low and its mouthpiece, the invaluable *Sovremennaya muzyka*, ceased publication in March 1929. RAPM's influence on the conservatory curriculum was strong, and Prokofiev knew that many of his works had been removed from the programmes.

Had he bargained, one wonders, for the meeting of 14 November at which RAPM brought him into the picture as it tried to remove *Stalnoy skok* from the repertory of the Bolshoy, and as it rejected Meyerhold's special pleading? There was already an ominous ring to the interrogation which would return to haunt Prokofiev – even though it affected only the subject matter and not the (primarily diatonic) musical material. Was the second scene supposed to represent 'a capitalist factory, where the worker is slave, or a Soviet factory, where the worker is boss, and if this is a Soviet factory being depicted, when and where did Prokofiev observe such a thing, as he has lived abroad since 1918 and returned for the first time in 1927 for two weeks [*sic*]?' *Proletarsky muzykant* wrote up the question and Prokofiev's terse answer: 'that is the realm of politics, not music, and therefore I shall not reply'.[17]

His musical concerns during his three-week stay were few but pleasurable. The Bolshoy production of *The Love for Three Oranges*, the opening of which he had narrowly missed on his 1927 tour but which Myaskovsky reported with mixed feelings shortly afterwards, was revived in his honour on 13 November after an interval of a year. Concerned as ever about how it should be staged, he wrote a detailed letter to the theatre the following September to spare a further planned revival in November 1930 the 'infelicities', which he considered to be 'the immobile chorus and the long intermissions (40 minutes)'[18] necessitated by the difficulties of changing Rabinovich's complicated sets; these had already led to the show being dubbed 'The Love for Three Intervals'.[19] Prokofiev's detailed points followed:

> Prologue: the different groups should actively fall upon each other, and not sing looking at the conductor.
>
> Act I scene 1 went a little sluggishly. Try to liven it up like scene 3.
>
> Scene 2. The whole stage must *swarm* with little devils, who creep on their stomachs and run around on all fours.
>
> Act II scene 2. The battle of monsters must be a battle, not a ballet scene. Make sure the quarrel between Truffaldino and Fata Morgana in front of the laughing Prince goes spiritedly. The Prince must laugh sincerely, merrily and contagiously. Last year the singer playing him laughed artificially and unspontaneously, so it came across boringly and did not match the intention of the composer.
>
> Act III scene 3. The scene with the Princesses must flow along in the spirit of a light, supple lyricism, with Truffaldino contributing a degree of humour. The latter does not have to play about or act the fool, just as the Princesses do not have to incline either to tragedy or caricature. The Prince can fool about only at the end of this scene, like a capricious child, when he has to marry the Moor [Smeraldina]. A few exaggerations here are even good.
>
> Act IV scene 2. Pay careful attention to the staging of the traitors' pursuit. I consider that this chase must be staged very entertainingly and, most important, in a lively fashion. Because rehearsal on it is usually left too late, the crowd crams into the wings, then what happens is a stupid obstruction, and then they run from the wings in confused motion. This chase must be staged seriously, like a contemporary police raid, very lively. If the way of thinking behind it is one of clowning, then it will come out quite the opposite: absurd and not amusing.[20]

Golovanov in the pit cannot have impressed him; writing to Alexander Smallens some time later about the production, he hinted at 'a dearth of good conductors in

Moscow'.[21] He himself conducted at a radio concert on 17 November, sharing the podium with the ever-dependable Saradzhev, still going strong under the new regime, who had to repeat the premiere performance of the revised Sinfonietta. One hope for the future, with the Bolshoy staging of *Stalnoy skok* looking increasingly unlikely, was his appointment as 'honorary adviser for foreign music'[22] to Moscow State Radio, an organization capable of influencing millions which he found to be full of enthusiastic and competent people. A key discussion turned out to be about the commissioning of a new opera that might also be staged in the West, and he took the trouble of sending music by Honegger and Milhaud on his return. The subsequent worsening of relations with musical Russia, however, left his position with the Radio uncertain.

Returning to Lina with a new fur coat and presents from the lavishly hospitable Meyerholds, he took off almost immediately for a solo recital in Turin; he was in Amsterdam less than a fortnight later for a concert with Monteux, who also shared a prestigious Prokofiev 'festival' in Paris (such was then the name for a concert devoted to a single figure) in which the composer conducted the world premiere of the Divertimento and kept his hand in as soloist with the Third Piano Concerto. On the same day, 22 December, the Prokofievs relinquished their two-month lease on the flat in Rue Bassano, arranged for their sons to spend the immediate future with 'Meme' and 'Avi', Lina's parents, in Le Cannet, just east of Cannes, and prepared for their own trip to America on board the *Berengaria*, sailing on Christmas eve. As Prokofiev told Fitzhugh Haensel, this was 'a musical boat'[23] – Rakhmaninov, Mischa Elman and Myra Hess were among their distinguished fellow-travellers. The shipboard hours allowed time to rekindle the cautious friendship of Rakhmaninov, who reminisced nostalgically with Lina about his Russian past and played patience with her husband – 'what an idyll', Prokofiev remarked in a letter to Myaskovsky.[24] He was also requested by the ship's purser to sing for the seasonal charity concert, being promised an 'excellent accompanist'[25] – surely a case of mistaken identity.

Several of Prokofiev's most glittering engagements were social: a 'Greek Orthodox New Year's party at the very rich Mrs. Loomis's house',[26] according to Duke, and the premiere of Gershwin's *Strike Up the Band* in its toned-down, revised version followed by a late-night gathering where the star composer played with his usual energy. For the first date in Prokofiev's own American schedule, he served as accompanist as well as soloist; although Lina had just come out of semi-retirement to join her husband in several song programmes, Nina Koshetz was the prima donna in a New York recital on 6 January, giving the premiere of the two folk-song arrangements which Alfred Swan had suggested to Prokofiev a decade earlier, the lament *White Snow* and *The Snowball Tree on the Hill*, advertised as *The Mulberry Tree*. Lina sang them too, but Prokofiev was cynically dismissive: 'they're extremely insignificant little turds', he told Myaskovsky.[27] If this was what he had to say about such winsome raw material, it gives us some idea of what he would later be thinking about Soviet doggerel like *Songs of our Days*, served up without any such commentary permissible.

The experiment continued more daringly with the first American performance of *Chose en soi*. Amazingly, this was well received; a Los Angeles review of the first of the two pieces reveals a changed American attitude to the latest Prokofiev, according the work the 'magnitude of a Beethoven composition' and granting that for all the piquant harmonies it was 'not without a deep emotional appeal'.[28] The only other novelties of the tour were divided between Cleveland, Prokofiev's second port of call on 9 and 11 January (a skyscraper colossus which symbolized the continent's amazing potency for him and a fit setting for his performance of movements from *Le Pas d'acier*), and Chicago, which shared Cleveland's ambition by allowing Prokofiev to conduct both this and the Divertimento (on 25 February; he also played the First Piano Concerto, with which he had made his debut in 1918 under the same conductor, Eric DeLamarter).

Advertised as op.43, the version of *Le Pas d'acier* which America heard was merely a selection yet to be knocked into shape as an official suite. Stokowski would be keen enough to try for a complete performance with new choreography in his association with the League of Composers, following earlier efforts with Stravinsky's *Les Noces* and *The Rite of Spring*. Having dared to give America Prokofiev's Second Symphony the previous October with his magnificent Philadelphia Orchestra – and rewarded for his pains as the audience left in droves – this was the champion Prokofiev should have cultivated assiduously; but he had doubts about the man, though not his orchestra. Then there was Toscanini, whose temperamental rehearsals with the New York Philharmonic he witnessed with amusement towards the end of his trip and who promised to conduct the Sinfonietta the following season.

Yet while 'Sinfonini prepares to conduct the Toscanetta',[29] as Prokofiev told Koussevitzky, his once most ardent champion in Boston now seemed to be cooling. Back in November, the tone of Prokofiev's high-handed remarks about his Bostonians offering $1000 dollars for the 'commission' of the Fourth Symphony, earmarked for its first performance in the orchestra's 50th anniversary season of 1930–31, was hardly diplomatic: 'Prokofiev is paid three to five thousand dollars for a commissioned symphony, or simply for the right to explain "we commissioned this from him"'.[30] Now he urged 'a whole programme of my compositions' on the grounds that Glazunov hardly deserved the festival Koussevitzky was putting on: 'you know that if you devote so much time to Glazunov, then, devil take it, you could give a bit of thought to me'.[31] His complaints, though expressed with the usual tactless petulance that won him many enemies, had some justification. He was giving five concerts in Boston and New York with Koussevitzky and the Boston Symphony Orchestra; but the only work new to American audiences was an 'old piece',[32] the Second Piano Concerto. Koussevitzky did not share Cleveland's or Chicago's enthusiasm for the new works. Yet his performance of the *Scythian Suite* was still something to be reckoned with; 'it is doubtful', wrote *Musical America*, 'if there has ever been a more stunning and tonally resplendent evocation of the Sunrise . . . than Mr. Koussevitzky gave it'.[33]

Prokofiev reiterated thanks for 'the wonderful performance of my Scythian old lady'[34] via Natalya Koussevitzky as he and Lina took a leisurely four-day journey from New York to California on the *Sunset Limited*, travelling through New Orleans and crossing the alligator-filled Mississippi with the train transferred on to a ferry. Artistic America was still interrupting the tourists' peace. An 'important message'[35] from Gloria Swanson was relayed to him on board, and two days later he heard from Paul Nelson of the newly inaugurated Gloria Productions: 'Miss Swanson is very much interested in music of the modern trend and is desirous of discussing it with you in connection with a new motion picture, being prepared for production'.[36] The star of Stroheim's *Queen Kelly* was looking for new avenues now that the silent film era was at an end, and the most likely candidate for the new venture was the comedy *What a Woman*, with music eventually provided by the same Vincent Youmans whose *Tea for Two* had seduced the Soviet public as *Tahiti Trot*. Such a frivolous project, even if it was the first advance made to Prokofiev after the birth of the talkies, could only have been abhorrent to a composer whose admonitions of Dukelsky-as-Duke's popular-song 'whoring'[37] were to become a good deal stronger.

In Los Angeles, where he played the Third Piano Concerto with Artur Rodzinski conducting and gave a recital at the Biltmore Hotel, Prokofiev found that one of his fellow guests was Elisabeth Sprague Coolidge, generous sponsor of a series of commissions for performance in Washington's Library of Congress which already included Stravinsky's *Apollon musagète*. Her description of how a 'siege at the dentist'[38] had left her unable to appear in public brought a candid expression of sympathy from Prokofiev, who always responded well to the personal touch in correspondence; to her declaring 'how pleased I should be if the next "Coolidge Commission" of a chamber composition is distinguished by your name',[39] he replied that 'it will give me great pleasure to compose a quartet for the Washington Library'.[40] On 20 February he formally accepted a fee of $1000 dollars for this chamber work, which was to outstrip in importance his earlier essays in the genre.

The endless round of social functions demanded by the American concert scene bored him, as before, though this was one area in which he exercised tact. Looking forward to a few quiet hours with John Alden Carpenter and his wife in Chicago, he told him how 'that would please me infinitely more than all these official lunches during which (just between ourselves) I lose my appetite'.[41] He remained courteous to autograph-hunters and requests from the young, eventually picking up a short correspondence with a 19-year-old composer (and future novelist) Paul Bowles, who wanted to carry on writing music in New York after a short period of study in France and who mentioned Varèse, Antheil and Virgil Thomson as Parisian mentors; 'only Henry Cowell is here. I'd like to study with you'.[42] Back in Paris, Prokofiev asked Bowles to send him some compositions, adding: 'don't regret not being able to study with the few people you mentioned in your letter – it isn't with them that music will move forward'.[43] This was in tune with the observations on the current musical scene he had given to Olin Downes in the *New York Times*: 'I think we have gone as far as we are likely to go in the direction of size, or dissonance, or complexity in music'.[44] Varèse's vast canvases, in his opinion, were behind the new spirit of the age – or rather, his own, for he had not reckoned with such efflorescences as Shostakovich's *The Nose*, recently given its premiere in Leningrad, or Weill's *Aufstieg und Fall der Stadt Mahagonny*. His views were only on what was best for his own work, and they happened to coincide with the kind of music the Soviet Union wanted. He must have known the cultural commissars in his homeland would hear him, or rather read him, when he told Downes he had become 'simpler and more melodic. We want a simpler and more melodic style for music, a simple, less complicated emotional state, and dissonance once again relegated to its proper place as one element in music'.[45]

The debate continued in his association with the highly cultured music society in Cuba, where he travelled with Lina for recitals on 10 and 13 March. For Maria Muñoz de Cuevedo, who published a journal for the society under the title *Musicalia*, he subsequently provided an article in the form of a letter on the current Russian musical scene. In it he placed the spotlight on Myaskovsky and devoted several sentences to Shostakovich, declaring it a pity that the early First Symphony was so popular since in it 'the composer has not yet found his true voice'.[46] He ended with the émigrés Dukelsky, Nabokov and Markevitch, about whom he would say no more than that there were 'some interesting moments here and there in his work'.[47] Cuba itself, which he was experiencing for the first time (unlike Lina), he described as 'astoundingly beautiful, but all the same I have a northern soul, and wouldn't want to live here for long'.[48] His northern soul was presumably better attuned to Montreal, where he gave a cut-price recital with Lina on 20 March as a special favour to his acquaintances there before hurrying back to Chicago (Horowitz had just been in Montreal, playing the Gavotte and the *Suggestion diabolique* to an ecstatic reception).

By the end of his tour Prokofiev had given 24 concerts in ten far-flung cities. It was a very different story from previous trips, and the critics behaved as if their now-distinguished visitor had always been a 'Russian classic'. Although the *Chicago Daily News* wrote that 'nobody is doing what he is doing, and he is doing it consistently, with all his might and main',[49] both his playing and his music were labelled conservative or 'conservative modern'[50] more than once. 'Virility is the chief characteristic', stated the *Detroit News*, 'never is there a neurotic hint; it is sane, straightforward stuff, the product of an orderly mind, which knows exactly the effect it desires, and how to produce it'; this was 'the spirit of today . . . materialistic, vigorous, humorous, cynical, somewhat lacking in poesy, but very refined in its mechanics'.[51] Those less sure of what they were talking about declared his pianism 'of a pronounced modernistic trend without being of the actually ultra phase'[52] and found him 'sympathetic to the modern movement, though not a musical Bolshevist'[53] (the frequently used phrase had all but dropped from the armoury of Prokofiev-labelling). The consensus was best summed up by Karleton Hackett of the *Chicago Evening Post*, who like most critics found Lina's soprano 'of good natural quality . . . used with discretion' and went on to guess about the composer-pianist's preparation: 'he never seems to bother about the technique and one doubts whether he now sits down seriously to practice, or if he ever has. But he has the fingers which will do what he wishes and his desires are not much confined by academic traditions'.[54]

The financial rewards, though they allowed Prokofiev to settle outstanding accounts over a decade old, were not great: of a total income of $10,500 only $2040.39 remained once he had deducted agents' fees along with travel and hotel expenses. One major hope for the future came to nothing: he negotiated with opera companies all over America, including the Metropolitan, for a premiere of *The Fiery Angel* but the Metropolitan director, Giulio Gatti-Casazza, had an aversion to the subject matter. The most promising discussions were with the American Opera Company based at the Eastman School of Music in Rochester. To this end Prokofiev even made crucial changes to the opera's structure on the advice of the artist Sergey Sudeikin: while the first, fourth and fifth acts remained more or less unchanged, the second and the third were to coalesce as a single act in seven short scenes, the first to be composed afresh. The project foundered for lack of commitment among several wealthy sponsors.

Le Pas d'acier was now definitely off the cards at the Bolshoy, as RAPM hostility had suggested, and Prokofiev postponed a return visit to the Soviet Union with Lina planned for late spring. But his concert schedule was far from slowing down. He travelled back to Europe on rough seas aboard the *Île de France*, in the distinguished company of the composer Alexander Grechaninov, having timed the sailing to allow him to be in Brussels for rehearsals within a day of arrival. One of his six European appearances taking him from Italy to Poland was a recital in Monte Carlo, which reunited him and Lina with their two sons in the south of France. Oleg, his father wrote to cousin Katya, 'didn't want to meet his parents again. Sviatoslav, on the other hand, was very kind and when I played at Monte Carlo participated for the first time in a concert of mine. He was afraid that when I stepped up on to the platform he would cry out "Papa!" but this passed without incident'.[55] Despite this meeting, it was only in early June that Prokofiev could tell his Russian relatives that 'the children have returned from their grandmother to the bosom of their parents'.[56]

One reason for their delayed homecoming was that Prokofiev and Lina were busy in Paris moving into a new apartment, the first they had taken unfurnished, so a great deal of work was required before they took up residence on 28 April; after years of wanderings in the city, 5 Rue Valentin Haüy would be somewhere for the family to call home for the next six years. The street was named, as Prokofiev made it his business to find out, after the inventor of a writing system for the blind, a precursor of Braille, whose 18th-century school was just round the corner; the second-floor apartment was in an elegant 1905 building on one of the impressive streets that grace the Invalides and Eiffel Tower quarter. Its situation allowed Prokofiev, as his recently acquired friend Nicolas Nabokov discovered, to make a pre-lunch circuit round the golden dome of Napoleon's tomb in anything from 'twenty-six minutes seventeen seconds to twenty-six minutes thirty-five seconds'.[57]

During their first days in the Rue Valentin Haüy, Lina was left to choose and arrange the furniture while Prokofiev finished the Fourth Symphony and began the quartet for Elisabeth Sprague Coolidge. A new commission came from an unexpected quarter when at the end of May he received a letter from a concert agent in a city with which he had no previous dealings: Georg Kügel in Vienna. Kügel asked him if he would 'feel prepared to compose for the one-armed pianist Paul Wittgenstein a concerto for the left hand and orchestra and what would be your fee'.[58] Paul, brother of the philosopher Ludwig Wittgenstein, had lost an arm as an officer on the Russian front in the First World War (Prokofiev was fascinated to think how near he must have been to Myaskovsky, serving on the opposite side) and had salvaged his career as a pianist by commissioning a number of composers to write works that would make the most of his left hand. The first was the fellow Austrian Franz Schmidt, whose *Konzertante Variationen über ein Thema von Beethoven* Wittgenstein performed in 1924, following it a year later with the premiere of Richard Strauss's *Parergon zur Symphonia domestica.* A second Strauss work, *Panathenäenzug* (1927), was sent by Kügel for Prokofiev's perusal. At this stage more successful left-hand works by Ravel and Britten lay in the future and Prokofiev, accepting the commission for a handsome $5000, was soon expressing the hope that he would be able 'to find something clearer than Strauss [whose thick orchestration featured quadruple woodwind] and less immature (from the point of view of technique) than Franz Schmidt'.[59] A summer spent for the first time in and around Paris allowed him to meet Wittgenstein, who wanted to play to him with his 'special technique'.[60] Clearly they discussed Prokofiev's Buxtehude transcription, for Wittgenstein subsequently sent him more of that composer's music, adding that 'your kind invitation left me with such an agreeable impression that I hope, with or without music, officially or unofficially, to see you in Paris or Vienna soon'.[61] Prokofiev undertook to complete the concerto by the end of July 1931, making the unprecedented request that after four years he might re-use the material for other works. He told Asafyev that his ultimate intention was to turn it into a concerto for two hands, but that Wittgenstein should remain in the dark about this.

The want of a dacha at a distance from Paris was not for lack of trying. In late June Prokofiev wrote to an agent in Dieppe, telling him 'I seek above all tranquillity and wish to avoid music or noise in the neighbourhood'.[62] A fortnight later he was asking the owner of Stravinsky's former summer residence at Talloires in Haute Savoie whether the Chalet des Écharvines was available as 'I hear my friend Stravinsky doesn't intend to return to you this summer'.[63] By the end of July he was envying Meyerhold's situation in the sunny south, telling him 'we are hopelessly stuck in the city'[64] but that they had decided to settle on somewhere in the vicinity.

This was the Villa Stevens in Le Naze, in the Seine-et-Oise region, 30 kilometres from Paris, for which an agreement was signed on 9 August.

Prokofiev gave all manner of excuses to different correspondents as to why the family had ventured no further, but one at least contained an element of truth. Jacques Rouché, the director of the Paris Opéra and a staunch supporter of Diaghilev's Ballets Russes, had appointed Lifar as the house's *maître de ballet*, and the two of them summoned Prokofiev to discuss the possibility of a new ballet. The *pourparlers* resulted in a signed contract on 18 August for a work to be staged early the following year with designs by Larionov and choreography by Lifar. On the same day Prokofiev sent a telegram to Lifar, who was staying at the Danieli Hotel in Venice, reflecting on Diaghilev's death there exactly a year earlier: 'on this sad day we are with you to remember the irreparable departure of a great artist and friend'.[65]

Without a Diaghilev-style impresario to give an inspired *donnée* for a theme, the project began in abstraction; Prokofiev's plan for 11 short musical numbers – only the ninth and tenth were to exceed a couple of minutes – suggests little more than a divertissement as a vehicle for Lifar's talents, with roles for two leading ladies (one of them Olga Spesivtseva, the other a ballerina from the Opéra) and several scenes for the *corps de ballet*. He told Myaskovsky that 'the Grand Opéra, fortunately, did not specify a subject; it will be soft and gently lyrical'.[66] A plot outline was not to evolve until early 1931, but the ballet was completed in piano score by 20 October.

Before that, Prokofiev finished the development and recapitulation of the String Quartet's first movement, the last work to add to the two he had proudly announced to Meyerhold in late July. He played it through on the piano to Carl Engel, who had officially made the commission, one rainy September day in Paris; Engel, as Prokofiev told Haensel, 'said it was the best composition of all written for this library'.[67] He rated it highest of his chamber compositions, noting to would-be interpreters that it was moderately difficult, somewhere between the simple *Overture on Hebrew Themes* and the dauntingly complicated Quintet. Borodin's and Tchaikovsky's outstanding precedents, rooted in a special form of classical romanticism, were of little use to him, and contemporary Russian examples were thin on the ground: Myaskovsky was working for the first time on his own set of quartets, and Shostakovich's First Quartet was eight years in the future, while Taneyev's intriguing specimens were highly idiosyncratic. The best examples, Prokofiev decided, were the Mozart and Beethoven quartets, ordered from Grandes Éditions Musiques on 9 May.

Prokofiev later admitted that Beethoven's quartet technique was a vital influence, adding that 'probably the somewhat "classical" idiom of my quartet's first movement comes from there'.[68] Yet neither of his chosen composers had written a quartet in B minor – an odd key, he noted to Myaskovsky, because 'its tonic lies just below the big string of the cello and viola',[69] and the whole work had to be composed with this 'absent' note in mind, an interesting puzzle for his complicated mind. The first, sonata-form movement is typically unpredictable once the clear melody of its opening violin line has been established (even this is not always as straightforward as it sounds, being approached by a subtly different sequence of notes in the development). The lyrical second subject is the first of many to slip into the fabric obliquely; by the time we are aware of its E minor presence on the viola, the melody has already begun. In a typically elliptical recapitulation, Prokofiev moves straight to its elaboration when he restores it to the tonic, only bringing back the tune proper later and capping the whole truncated parade with a superbly abrupt five-bar coda.

Slow-movement lyricism appears at first to be the territory of the next movement. Its introduction seems to have been Engel's idea, because when he sent payment for the finished work the following February, he noted 'with much interest the charming beginning of the 2nd movement, which seems to have resulted from our meeting in Paris last summer, when I carried away with me such a strong and deep impression of your work'.[70] Prokofiev replied that he was 'very happy you loved the introduction to the second movement – and thanks for the excellent idea you gave me'.[71] The Russian folk inflections of these opening bars are strikingly akin to the first traditional song arrangement he had entrusted to American audiences earlier in the year, as becomes clear when the two are placed side by side (Exx.58*a* and *b*). Yet Prokofiev deliberately steps on the throat of his own song for reasons which will become apparent in the final movement, launching into a scherzo in which melody's desperate bid to assert itself is captured with great originality in the violin's wayward answer to the initial Vivace (Ex.59), briefly reminiscent of the folk-song finale in Tchaikovsky's Serenade for Strings. There are two trios to embrace Prokofiev's now irrepressible lyric gift; but the first, beginning so promisingly on the cello in its highest register, implodes under the weight of its constant key changes; and something similar happens to its initially bucolic 6/8 sequel.

Clearly, melody is waiting to spread its wings, and it comes to the fore in a final Andante which Prokofiev knew was the 'centre of gravity',[72] perhaps his most sustained movement yet. The oblique approach echoes the introduction of the viola melody in the first movement – weaving its B minor/D major theme into an E minor texture of gently rocking quavers. This time, however, the Russian folk contours of the viola theme seem oddly familiar: we have already heard them in the slow

Ex.58*a* String Quartet no.1, op.50 – Andante molto – Vivace

Ex.58*b* *White Snow*, op.104 no.4

Ex.59 String Quartet no. 1 – II. Andante molto – Vivace

introduction of the Scherzo. From this point on, the argument never loses its way, despite a variation in 9/8 and an anguished outburst of semitonal clashes – one of the few truly discordant passages in the work, briefly suggesting acquaintance with Bartók's middle-period quartets – before a final peacemaking as classically swift as the end of *The Prodigal Son*. It is hardly surprising if this predominantly introspective piece appealed so much to Myaskovsky, who extolled to Asafyev the absence of effects, 'something quite surprising for Prokofiev', and the 'true profundity in the sweeping melodic line and intensity of the Finale . . . How marvellous it would be if this tendency in him were to become firmly fixed'.[73]

Summer and early autumn followed an unusual pattern of meetings with eminent people in town and a holiday mood at the Villa Stevens. The only interlude was a *tour gastronomique* of Alsace and the Vosges mountains with Lina and Nicolas Nabokov, a not entirely happy experience if Nabokov's memoirs are to be trusted; he recalls a clash of interests between wife and husband, whose mania for precise scheduling could easily be derailed by the slightest spontaneity in Lina's sightseeing plans. The necessary peace of the house on the Seine provided a welcome escape from neighbours in the Rue Valentin Hauy who tortured the composer with 'Ravel's *Boléro*, endlessly turning on the gramophone'.[74] (Prokofiev would have been amused to learn of Ravel's debt to *Le Pas d'acier*.) A quieter mechanical invention kept the family amused. 'We've bought a cinematograph – Pathé-Bébé', Prokofiev told his cousin Katya, 'and when friends and acquaintances came to the dacha we acted out detective dramas with them – they came out very amusingly; we also captured the children in the act of gobbling sweets, and other similar little scenes. In the evenings we demonstrated our films. From these reels, you can choose the best moments and then enlarge them, so I'm sending you a collection of lively snapshots.'[75] It was worth recording the progress of the children, who were growing up fast. Two-year-old Oleg had started 'to chatter in English',[76] while that autumn Sviatoslav started attending a private half-board school, the École Tannenberg, where the clever boy was stretched to the limits. 'Besides this, he reads in English and Russian', Prokofiev told Katya, 'but in all three languages he speaks approximately the same. He plays with his little brother as if there were a difference not of four and a half years but merely of one. In any case, the company of his elder brother very much entertains the little one.'[77]

There was one addition to the household: Kolya Sidorov, the nephew of Boris and Vladimir Bashkirov. Vladimir wanted to do the best he could financially for the young man and worried about the 'bad effect'[78] his mother, Vladimir's sister Tatyana, might be having. He and his wife had come closer to the Prokofievs on a visit to Paris the previous year, and he relied on his composer friend to handle both the economic and moral questions surrounding the youngster. Prokofiev could answer back only that the 'good-for-nothing kid' had 'knocked around my place all summer, but when he went to school, he didn't write me a single letter'.[79] Young Kolya seemed to be taking after the more feckless of his uncles, who had had appeared on the scene again. 'I would like to tell you not to worry about Boris's attitude', Vladimir wrote to Prokofiev the following month. 'I think you did everything you could for him, and it is his mistake that he cannot do anything for himself.'[80] This worthier brother at the same time washed his hands of the Sidorov affair, telling his friend 'I write all this to you because you are the only person I can really rely upon and trust and I will never forget what you and your charming wife have done for Nicolas Sidorov'.[81]

The dependable, constant side of Prokofiev's personality continued to make itself felt towards his troubled relatives in Russia. Cousin Katya, bearing up under the double blow of bereavement and exile, had a new enterprise to add to market-gardening – poultry-breeding, about which her cousin knew a little from his days with the incubator in Ettal, and he sent her regular supplies of brochures and magazines on the subject. Because of a hard Soviet winter, more in the way of practical help was required, and in addition to his regular sums Prokofiev made every effort to send food parcels to an emaciated Katya from several of the many exporters that had set up in Paris for just that purpose, as well as expensive medical supplies for an ailing friend in Moscow, for which of course he had no intention of being paid. But there was light at the end of the tunnel: both Katya and Shurik were due to be released from their respective exile and prison some time the following year, though the prospect had to be expressed in terms of health and recovery, in the usual code of correspondence.

Again, Prokofiev did not succeed in visiting Russia at the end of 1930 as planned. He was now more in the dark than ever about musical life there and assumed that the proletarian musicians' campaign had gathered weight to keep his works off the concert programmes. In the meantime he resumed his own tour schedule in the West with further appearances in Berlin as well as ever-receptive Belgium and Poland. New to an otherwise unchanged recital programme were a movement from the Divertimento, paving the way for the complete piano transcription, and some new pieces for his partnership with Lina – Scarlatti, Purcell and an arrangement by Joaquín Nin of an aria from the 18th-century Spanish composer Antonio Literes's *Acis y Galatea*; they also added a song by Nabokov to their Russian repertory. More significant was the Paris premiere of the Fourth Symphony, conducted by Monteux in an all-Prokofiev programme on 18 December, just over a month after Koussevitzky had given the first performance in Boston. 'Both there and here it was received with restraint', Prokofiev told Myaskovsky in some surprise;

> evidently the public has come to love being slapped in the face; when a composer sounds depths, then they lose sight of where he is going. Some of the reviews expressed regret, even going so far as to say: what an example for youth, if both Prokofiev and Stravinsky carry on composing with such pale simplicity! . . . For my part, I'd like to retouch the finale a little, but the rest seems to me so simple and clear that my clients' doubts have astonished me beyond belief.[82]

The younger composers and contemporaries who had come to praise the Fourth Symphony were producing little of substance: earlier in the year Prokofiev had denounced Rieti's and Honegger's violin concertos respectively as 'horrifying' and 'nonsense',[83] and though he praised Nabokov's symphony as a step forward from the *Ode*, he waited in vain for a sequel of substance. Dukelsky came in for a lashing when he turned to writing successful songs for Broadway, and was accused in a colourful letter of acting like those well-born Russian girls who resorted to prostitution to help their mothers and ended up rather enjoying it.[84] Responding to the respected musicologist Mikhail Druskin in Berlin, who wanted his advice on a book he had just written on contemporary music, he praised his knowledge but found it 'unfortunate . . . that you bow and scrape before every empty "one-day butterfly" which we hear today but which tomorrow gets thrown onto the rubbish heap'.[85]

Not that his support for advice-seekers was anything other than carefully considered: he looked over his former secretary Gyorgy Gorchakov's symphony with the attention to detail he had previously reserved for Myaskovsky's latest output, even if he declared that it was 'difficult to see where there's real music and where it's just head-work'.[86] And he had stern advice for Paul Bowles, who had finally sent him a 24-bar minuet with only five bars of music: 'the others are only repeats of these five bars. Suppose I composed a symphony of 24 minutes in which there was only five minutes of music and the rest only repeats of that . . . dear friend, I can't judge a composer after five bars, and a composer has never sent me five bars to let me judge his music!'[87]

Prokofiev's abrupt manner of expression nearly led to a rift with Marcel de Valmalète, the successful but importunate agent he had recently been using for his European engagements, when Valmalète pressed hard for a London engagement in January 1931. Pointing out that he was a composer first and foremost, not a pianist, he explained that 'if I were to be deprived of periods during which I could work calmly, I would write music inferior to that of which I am capable, and this [time to compose] nourishes me more than a concert in a country which has nothing to do with music'.[88] The conflict between the free hours he needed for composition and the increasingly meaningless concert round would be a chief factor in taking up Soviet hospitality.

Prokofiev's opinion of unmusical England shifted a little when he learnt that a performance there in November with Nikolay Orlov as soloist and Hamilton Harty conducting had gone well, noting that 'the English have evidently developed – formerly my music was pointless to them'.[89] Since Lifar's rehearsals had been set back, he crossed the Channel for his first Wigmore Hall recital on 17 January. A London admirer was especially excited about his appearance: 'I am always most grateful to you for your kindness to me over your scherzo from "L'amour des trois oranges", to which I dance the Bogeyman. It is my favourite dance'.[90] A gracious reply followed on Prokofiev's return to Paris: 'it gives me great pleasure to know the success of the dance you made . . . Hoping this success continues'.[91] At the same time he wrote to a helpful London bank clerk asking him to obtain the illustrated souvenir catalogue for the exhibition of Persian art at Burlington House.

The new ballet had now been completed and the time had come to put dramatic flesh, as he later put it to Myaskovsky, on the 'strong choreographic and musical skeleton'.[92] A conscious attempt to try to 'achieve a greater musical and choreographic construction',[93] this was an unfathomable way of working to several generations of Soviet critics: 'could an artist possibly go further in rejecting the natural creative process?' Nestyev was later to ask.[94] The plot as reported by Lifar in *Ma Vie* was a piece of vanity choreography. There was never any doubt that he should dance the principal role, but by naming the hero Sergey and having him return to the scene of his childhood – the banks of the river Dnieper which flows through Kiev, Lifar's birthplace – a strong element of autobiography intruded (the eventual title of the ballet, *Na Dnepre* – 'On the Dnieper' – is shared by one of Musorgsky's last songs, to a patriotic Ukrainian text by Shevchenko).

According to Lifar, there was also a little deliberate cruelty in the naming of the women: the girl who has been Sergey's youthful sweetheart was supposedly called Olga, and was to be danced by Olga Spesivtseva, prima ballerina extraordinary with the Ballets Russes who had long been in love with him, while the girl Sergey now loves went by the name of Natasha, and Lifar's current amour was Nathalie Paley. The significance of Sergey's final reunion with Natasha, leaving Olga alone, dawned on Spessivtzeva and she tried to throw herself out of a rehearsal room 30 feet above the Place Garnier – or so Lifar's *Ma Vie* would have us believe. In fact, at least according to the synopsis drafted in early 1931, Olga is the name of the new love, and this was Spesivtseva's role; the part of the jilted but loyal 'girl in white' was simply assigned to an unnamed 'ballerina from the Opéra'.[95] The plot is simple: Olga and Sergey meet but are separated by the village elders. In the ballet's second scene, Olga is to be married off to a man she does not love. Sergey and his friends come to the rescue, but are defeated by the elders. It is the 'girl in white' who releases her Sergey, only to renounce him to his beloved Olga.

To fit this simple scenario, knocked into shape under the title *Un dimanche soir*,[96] Prokofiev reordered and in some places cut his original score. As violent conflict was hardly part of the abstract sequence, where 'sudden bursts of energy' merely served to punctuate the 'softly lyrical mood',[97] the scenes in which the lovers are threatened or separated lack the cut and thrust of *The Prodigal Son*'s bad company. The strongest contrasts lie in the prevailing 'pale simplicity',[98] announced in the gentle strings and pastoral woodwind of the prelude, and a more complicated, densely scored lyricism. The 'girl in white' is the most distinguished representative of the former; her music alone makes a significant reappearance. In no.2 of the final score, she comes across 'Sergey alone with his thoughts', and 'expresses timid and hopeless love for him';[99] a diatonic flute melody underpinned by bare 4ths and 5ths meets cloudier harmonies (Ex.60). This is as close to the Stravinsky of the 1920s and 30s as Prokofiev ever came; it is even possible that Stravinsky took his friend's cue when he came to compose *Perséphone*, his 'whitest' score, in 1934. Yet the extended treatment of this theme in the ballet's no.10, where the 'girl in white' unties Sergey and executes a 'short happy dance, in the hope that Sergey will at last notice her',[100] is far more characteristic of Prokofiev's move towards

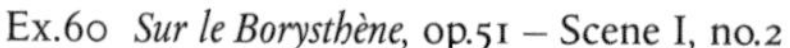
Ex.60 *Sur le Borysthène*, op.51 – Scene I, no.2

a new expressivity; and although she was created after the music had been composed, the 'girl in white' is the true predecessor of Prokofiev's Juliet, Tatyana and Natasha rather than the temptress of *The Prodigal Son*, as Nestyev rather bizarrely asserts.

Deliberately bolder in its thick orchestration, consistently high dynamics and harmonic unfolding is the second of the two *pas de deux*, no.5 (finally entitled 'Fiançailles'). The fact that its *molto cantando* melody illustrates Olga's forced betrothal does not seem to have bothered Prokofiev and Lifar, who brought it back for her happy reunion with Sergey in the short Epilogue; in any case, its throbbing horn accompaniment and the angular turns suit the drama's sudden intensity (Ex.61). The forceful doubling of violins and trumpets and the increasingly fraught orchestration of the theme on its two reappearances look forward to the more powerful of the slow movements Prokofiev was to write in the Soviet Union, culminating in the hysterical opulence of the Sixth Symphony's Largo. Such was the most striking strand in the compendium of *Sur le Borysthène*, to give the ballet its final title with the more French-friendly rendering of 'Dnieper' ('Borysthenus' was the classical name for the Dnieper). Another is the strident edge of a military march in the first scene's final number which sounds like a blueprint for Shostakovich's Fourth Symphony – and that, of course, is indebted to the full-length ballet scores which the younger composer was writing at about the same time, *The Age of Gold* and *The Bolt*. Any cross-reference would appear to be coincidental.

Having established the finished scenario, Lifar was in no hurry to put it into production; the main priority was Roussel's *Bacchus et Ariane*, which took longer than expected to stage. Prokofiev was unimpressed by what he heard of the music,

Ex.61 *Sur le Borysthène* – Scene II, no.5, Betrothal

which he dismissed to Myaskovsky as 'feeble': 'one place reminded me of nothing so much as the "Flight of the Bumblebee"',[101] he added, though Roussel's model was probably the orgiastic buzz of Ravel's *Daphnis et Chloé. Bacchus et Ariane* was given its premiere at the end of May, pushing the Dnieper project off the schedule. There was some compensation in a rival Parisian company's new ballet to the music of the *Classical* Symphony, a move which Prokofiev had done nothing to oppose and with which he seems to have been surprisingly pleased.

Less positive news came from America, where Lee Simonson had drawn up his own scenario for the League of Composers' production of *Le Pas d'acier*. Its theme was the inexorable progress of 'the rhythm of steel'[102] as the emblem of revolution. At one stage 'the bourgeoisie are bound, gagged and trampled on by the human belt . . . the steel rollers send down bales of red cheese cloth'.[103] 'Horrified' to have had his suggestions for the *mise en scène* 'contradicted' by Simonson, Prokofiev wrote to the organization's founder Claire Reis in February insisting on the original 1920 setting and praying her to '*eliminate* all *political elements*, like revolutions, counter-revolution, soldiers, three-colour flags etc'.[104] Despite a reassurance from the League that 'Mr. Simonson's outlook is purely social not political',[105] the Metropolitan premiere in May evidently left much to be desired – and not just by a composer nervous of Americans misinterpreting a work that was still causing him trouble in the Soviet Union. One Richard Hammond, who had clearly expected to take on the director's role and had explained to Reis that 'Mr Prokofieff wanted to be especially careful . . . owing to the relationship with Russia',[106] wrote to Prokofiev that Simonson's appointment had been a matter of 'not too clean' musical politics.[107] The result, in his opinion, was 'out of harmony with the music – vulgar, obvious and ineffective . . . only Stokowski's very fine reading did the score in any way justice'.[108]

Just how anxious Prokofiev was to distance himself from machine-age ethics is apparent in his opinion of a factory evocation contemporary with *Le Pas d'acier*, Mosolov's *The Iron Foundry*, which was performed in Paris that April. 'Here they've become interested in this piece and it's been performed twice', he told Myaskovsky. 'I can't say that the score was uninteresting, it sounds well. But it seemed to me that there was a pitifully small amount of material in it, and besides its constantly repeated bars annoy me – though I did the same at the time of the *Scythian Suite*.'[109] He was in no doubt of how far he had come since then, and dictated to Astrov a letter correcting the view of his music given by Lucilio Nediani in the Italian musical journal *Ambrosiano*. Nediani, it was noted, had made no mention of such recent works as *The Prodigal Son, Chose en soi* or the Third and Fourth Symphonies. 'And yet in all these works', Astrov remonstrated, 'the physiognomy of Prokofiev has changed, turning away from external effects towards melody and intrinsic values.'[110] The same criticism was levelled at Nicolas Slonimsky in Boston, who had similarly 'maintained a silence over the most recent period, which I consider to be the most significant'.[111]

There was, then, in Prokofiev's mind no consciousness of creativity running dry, the image so strongly projected in Soviet accounts of this period (above all Nestyev's). It was all the more frustrating for him that he no longer knew what Russia was making of him; the only thing to do was to let the proletarian musicians 'run mad'[112] and bide his time. One compensation for the postponement of a significant visit was an early spring concert tour with Lina to Bucharest, Budapest and Vienna. 'For us these were new places, and the journey was interesting', he told Tanya Rayevskaya, 'all the more so because we met with such a kind reception.'[113] The children left behind received an enthusiastic postcard from Lina's mother, who had heard one of their recitals on the radio: 'only think: Hungary, the city of Budapest, so far from us, but it was so clear! Mama sang so beautifully and Papa played excellently'.[114]

The programmes were much as Lina and Prokofiev had honed them in recent months, though the Bucharest recital also included eight of the *Visions fugitives* which had been out of Prokofiev's repertoire for some time. In Vienna the Second Piano Concerto created a great impression, and Prokofiev wrote anxiously to Fyodor

Weber, Koussevitzky's manager of the Berlin branch of Édition Russe, complaining that it was not among the scores prominently displayed there for sale. One of the many new acquaintances he made was Artur Holz, an expert graphologist who subsequently furnished him with a psychological portrait deduced from the handwriting sample he had given him after the concert. It was an accurate enough summary, though Holz may well have obtained background information elsewhere: 'his character could be considered from two points of view. On the one hand, he is pensive, critical, logical, exact in his manner of thought without being sentimental. On the other, he is fantastically wrought by virtuous and varied thoughts and by the sensual development which goes on in his subconscious . . . he is a courageous man, regarding life from a clear point of view without being a realist'.[115]

A more important link was forged with the conductor Clemens Krauss, who was anxious to see the scores of *The Gambler*, *The Fiery Angel* and the Third Symphony; Prokofiev furnished him with the changes proposed the previous year for the American production of *The Fiery Angel*, but to no more avail. Crucially, too, he was able to meet Wittgenstein again, an assiduous host. 'I'm about to order a volume containing all the chamber-music works of Schubert', Prokofiev wrote on his return to Paris, 'and I am delighted with the prospect of going through them: you see, it's your good influence. My mind returns to your concerto – I've already sketched some ideas I could use in it. I'm also thinking of the nature of the technique.'[116]

Clearly the question of technique vexed him, for by July, when he finished the sketches, he told Myaskovsky he felt 'annoyance instead of pleasure because of a whole lot of places which still need to be smoothed over'.[117] Now, though, he not only knew that he wanted a clear but intriguing soundworld halfway between Strauss and Schmidt; there was also the grand manner of Ravel's newly completed concerto for Wittgenstein to be avoided. This he told Myaskovsky he found 'perhaps well written and conscientious, but without spark'.[118] His judgment may seem questionable to us now, but there is certainly an enormous difference between Ravel's slow-burn introduction, stirring like the kraken in the depths, and Prokofiev's sparkling opening Vivace, introducing the piano as a mid-range toccata player of lighter spirit than the manic propeller of the Second Concerto's Scherzo. Although the semiquavers soon give way to more capricious play, the outlines of the melodies belong to the violins and clarinet; the only one that comes to prominence is the A flat major countersubject marked 'con eleganza', neatly restated by the flute in a typically truncated recapitulation. In a surprisingly dissonant development, the soloist has a chance to emerge as a more formidable opponent, pounding chromatic scales in overlapping semitones and indulging in low-register growling before the movement returns to the ether.

Prokofiev's penchant for original melody is evident in what remains his most underrated – because so rarely heard – slow movement. The arching lilt of its 6/8 principal theme is the more remarkable for avoiding the tonic of A flat until its fourth bar, a stroke finely reinforced when the woodwind take it over from strings

(Ex.62). Prokofiev taxes the pianist's left-hand technique to the limit with powerfully elaborate writing that spreads to both clefs; it is difficult, though, to pinpoint the 18 bars of solo he told Wittgenstein he had provided at his request (the nearest thing to a cadenza comes in the middle of the next movement). A second, more forceful theme is introduced by the soloist, only to be subjected to some of the most exposed and original effects in Prokofiev's orchestration: violas and double basses two octaves apart, with sonorous underpinning by the pianist, and high wind meshing with rapid figurations from first violins. The later stages of the movement seem to anticipate the central idyll of Ravel's G major Concerto, with the piano providing limpid accompaniment, but the effect remains altogether stranger. If Prokofiev had difficulties shaping this singular work, it shows only in the third movement, blessed with a plethora of striking and well-defined ideas which can be convincingly coherent only when played by the most compelling interpreter. The finale is a masterstroke: a quiet reprise of the opening toccata, this time 'veloce' rather than 'con brio', with melodies flitting across the score in the shadowiest form and the piano dissolving into thin air after a mere minute and a half – again, the antithesis of Ravel's uproarious grandeur.

Ex.62 Piano Concerto no.4, op.53 – II. Andante

At the same time Prokofiev worked on 'six transcriptions for piano from some of my orchestral and chamber works'.[119] 'Of course it would have been better to write six new ones!' he confided to Myaskovsky. 'But my justification rests in the fact that I made these arrangements in between other things, parallel with work on the armless concerto, or more precisely – taking a rest from one-handed technique. I didn't do new ones in between, since this would have taken away vital gunpowder from the concerto.'[120] The possible capriciousness of Wittgenstein's response may have been lurking in Prokofiev's mind – and with reason, as it turned out – for he decided his publishers should send these pieces out to the leading pianists of the day. Top of the list were interpreters who might 'warm up relations' with the Soviet Union at a time when 'sympathy towards me runs less deep'[121] – the names he cited to Myaskovsky were Samuil Feinberg, Lev Oborin, Heinrich Neuhaus and Vladimir Sofronitzky. He settled instead for émigré interpreters in the West: his friend Alexander Borovsky, who was still championing him in Berlin, Artur Rubinstein, Nikolay Orlov and Vladimir Horowitz, who merited the most difficult numbers (the rapid toccata in which the Prodigal Son's spoils had originally been divided between three clarinets and the Scherzo of the Sinfonietta).

Yet though the first of the six pieces was the only one to involve stitching together the original material, transforming music from the first and second numbers of *The Prodigal Son* into a well-contrasted rondo, these were not mere arrangements for piano. The melodies are refracted through a texture that favours extremes of register with either bare or splintered inner lines. The Temptress's dance from the ballet, further refined from its elaborated appearance as the Scherzo of the Fourth Symphony, sounds especially effective, and the fourth of the *Songs without Words* gives little hint of its soloist-and-piano origins. Only the Andante from the String Quartet, the fifth piece, offers anything like a richness of sonority as the movement builds towards its several powerful climaxes; these are more striking, if less fluid, than they sound on the four stringed instruments as the pianist strains to encompass their daunting range. Curious, however, is the break in the continuum of the rocking patterns several bars after the start, serving to announce the great theme altogether less subtly than in the quartet.

The nature of the original material in this, the heart of the six pieces, makes the end result something more than just a diversion from work on the concerto, as Prokofiev had described it to Myaskovsky. Even so, the Wittgenstein project detained him in Paris until late July, by which stage he had finished the first two movements in piano score; perhaps the completion of the rest in the summer holiday accounts for the less concentrated mood of the concerto's third movement. As in 1930, a dacha was not organized until the last minute, though this time it was not for want of trying; Prokofiev had motored down to St-Jean-de-Luz, near Biarritz and the Spanish border, in late May but failed to find a suitable house. 'At the end of July', he wrote to Tanya Rayevskaya, 'we all went our separate ways – the children to their grandparents in Cannes, Ptashka to friends in Savoie'[122] – though husband and wife spent several days together in Divonne-les-Bains and Culoz before Prokofiev drove alone across the Massif Central to look for a house near St-Jean-de-Luz. 'I saw a lot of interesting things', he told his musical friend Alexander Winkler, with whom he had recently spent valuable time in St Cloud, 'especially the department of Ardèche, bleak and unlike the rest of France, the beautiful Tarn gorges and the uniquely fascinating caves of Aven-Armand, with their fantastical woods of stalagmites.'[123] It was after leaving Aven-Armand for Toulouse that the hapless driver encountered another accident, not too serious but needing to be reported to his insurance company. He was now a skilled interpreter of his motoring mishaps, making neat diagrams of both this event and an incident in Paris the previous month when a car smashed into his on the Avenue Wagram in order to avoid an oncoming tram.

None the worse for wear, he established himself in St-Jean-de-Luz, renting a Gaveau piano from a firm in Biarritz which pleased him enormously and taking on the Villa La Croiz Basque in Ciboure from 15 August to 5 October. Lina and the children joined him there immediately, and although the weather brought sunny and rainy days in variable succession, an idyllic seaside holiday to rival the 'Balmont summer' of 1921 ensued. 'This is a lovely place where the Pyrenees meet the ocean', he told Tanya,[124] and he tried to encourage Paichadze to come and stay in their 'spacious' villa, 'to dip in the sea and go into the mountains . . . Sviatoslav's learning to swim but notwithstanding the warm water shivers so much that he comes out again immediately. I think he shivers from fear'.[125] There was good publicity to be had in the USA from a photograph of the seven-year-old as first prizewinner of a St-Jean-de-Luz competition for 'the most beautiful child in bathing suit',[126] as the proud father wrote to Gottlieb.

Prokofiev too went swimming when he could, trying the crawl for the first time: but 'this way I swallow more water than move forward'.[127] There was a good chess companion in Mischa Elman, though it would have been better still to have had the company of Capablanca, whose participation in the Paris congress he had been following with interest – 'congratulations for the games you won, but you're too lazy and you must win more'.[128] Capablanca duly obliged by losing not a single match. Bridge, a recent obsession, was well catered for, prompting thoughts of organizing a big tournament in Paris in the autumn (he had already studied various systems allowing for grand combinations of players). Fellow bridge enthusiasts in Ciboure were the 'inscrutable'[129] Chaliapin and the violinist Jacques Thibaud. 'There are a lot of artistic folk of all nations here', he told Tanya on 1 September, adding that 'tomorrow we dine with Charlie Chaplin. I never met him in my life before, it will be interesting to see him.'[130]

As always with Prokofiev's summers, there was much creative work to be done. In addition to finishing the concerto, he grappled with the problem of forging a concert work from the orchestral music in *The Gambler*. This time it was to be no mere suite; the first four of the five movements were to be studies of the four leading roles – Alexey, the Grandmother, the General and Polina, with the roulette music dominating the grand finale. 'It wasn't easy to bring together from different stretches of the score the physiognomy of each character', he told Myaskovsky, 'but it seems I've managed to do it without the seams showing.'[131] An additional problem was the fresh instrumentation, allowing freer rein to the kind of heady textures carried over and in several cases intensified from *The Fiery Angel* to the Third Symphony. The *Four Portraits and Dénouement from The Gambler* hardly aspire to the same developmental intensity as the symphony, though the metamorphoses of the opening love theme are more apparent here. It is contrasted in the first 'portrait' with the music of Alexey's agitation, which serves as a kind of second subject, and brazens it out against the drive of the roulette music in the 'dénouement'. There is also a crystallization of the opera's structure, which highlights each of these four characters in turn. Framing the brief scherzo of the General's pathetic-grotesque vein are lyric parades of the Grandmother's themes, fading away in a tritonal question mark, and

Polina's twisted love, powerfully textured. Yet while the physiognomies are unquestionably here, the psychological dynamics and caprices of Dostoyevsky's characters, so powerfully rendered in the opera, go for little in these curiously static snapshot montages. Only the tours de force of the interludes that flank the great roulette scene have a comparable drive in the finale.

The *Four Portraits and Dénouement* were lined up for a Paris premiere in March 1932, the third of the suites receiving their first performances in the new season and certainly the most intricate; Prokofiev underlined to Gabriel Pierné of the Concerts Colonne that it was 'very difficult, and you must only programme it if you can give it enough rehearsals'[132] (in the end he conducted the Divertimento himself, played the solo role in the First Piano Concerto and left the *Portraits* to Franz Ruhlmann). He was pleasantly surprised to find Bruno Walter championing the new *Prodigal Son* suite in Berlin (though the pleasure was mixed as he was aware that he had not put many of the ballet's best movements into the work) and even more taken aback that the German public liked it. Some of the critics found it 'too superficial',[133] however, and for that reason he was all the more determined to push the Third Symphony with both Weber and Walter. He was also remarkably compliant with Walter's advice about ending the suite with a 'cymbal tremolo' rather than the 'four dry chords' he had himself provided: 'I submit myself entirely to your artistic taste and ask you to do it in future. I'll try this experiment at my next performance'.[134]

The composer was conducting at another of the 'Prokofiev festivals' which were becoming a feature of Parisian concert life towards the end of each year, sharing the podium of the Orchestre Symphonique de Paris with Roger Désormière on 25 November. It was not the success it should have been; the players had been touring Germany, found themselves unable to accommodate sufficient rehearsals on their return and 'played abysmally, except in *Le Pas d'acier*'.[135] This was the new suite he had polished up to replace the numbers from the ballet previously performed in concert – the same selection, with a few alterations. The programme also featured a transcription he had just made for full string orchestra of the Andante from the Quartet, which involved some changes to the cello part and the addition of double basses along the lines of Mahler's Beethoven quartet arrangements. The results were not what he had expected, he told Derzhanovsky: 'I thought the Andante . . . would sound richer on a string orchestra, but those in the audience said it was altogether better in quartet performance. I conducted, so it was difficult for me to tell'.[136] This last of the three forms in which the Andante exists is indeed curiously unsatisfying – less successful, certainly, than its counterpart in the op.52 pieces, which deserves an independent existence as Prokofiev's most powerful movement for piano solo between the Andante of the Fourth Sonata and the Valse lento of the Sixth.

The Quartet itself, meanwhile, was enjoying the support of two ensembles. The Brosa Quartet, named after its first violinist Antonio Brosa, had given the triumphant first performance at Washington's Library of Congress on 25 April and played it on a tour of Europe later in the year, again owing to the generosity of the

Coolidge Foundation. The work was even performed in Moscow, thanks to another exchange programme, by the Roth Quartet. News of the interpretation worried Prokofiev, who wrote to Brosa saying that he had heard that the right tempos had not been observed and asking if he could have a 'private audition'[137] with the Brosa Quartet to make sure they were not making the same mistakes. The Roth Quartet were shown the errors of their ways in no uncertain terms, with metronomic accuracy provided for each movement, a rare insight into Prokofiev's views on this crucial element of performance: the first had taken seven minutes ten seconds instead of six minutes 30; the second seven minutes instead of six; and the third nine minutes 30 seconds instead of eight minutes 15 seconds.[138] The Roth Quartet replied to assure him that their later performances were quicker.

Prokofiev was still no nearer to re-establishing links with the Soviet Union, though the Roth ensemble were not the only performers playing his music there. He had been surprised to hear of students at the Moscow Conservatory, now very much in the clutches of the Proletarian Musicians' organization, attempting his most complex chamber work, the Quintet; and though he had lost his allies in the Bolshoy Theatre, now under new management and even less likely to revive *The Love for Three Oranges* which would have helped to increase his allowance to cousin Katya and Shurik's children, he heard in February 1932 that the Malegot company based in the Mikhailovsky (now Maly) Theatre in Leningrad was considering putting on *The Gambler*, once more with the possibility of Meyerhold's direction, and was even interested in the new ballet. Despite various promises by the Paris Opéra – at one point it was even scheduled to share an evening with Strauss's *Elektra* – Lifar's attempts to stage *Sur le Borysthène* were constantly being undermined by the parlous state of the Opéra's finances; Rouché had resigned in disgust at the French government's inadequate subsidy.

These were the bleak days of the Depression; and yet in Paris the musical scene carried on unchanged. It was worse in America, where Haensel was doing what he could to find Prokofiev engagements for the 1932–3 season. 'Strange to say, music is holding its own', his agent told him, 'but we find that all the money is going into the hands of the great stars and box office attractions, while business for those not in that class has suffered considerably.'[139] Prokofiev's attitude was naively optimistic; commiserating over the slump of Gottlieb's insurance business, he asked 'would it not go better after the rise in Wall Street which was reported several days ago?'[140] Berlin seemed to be suffering the worst financial deprivation, but its public was hungrier than ever for culture – perhaps because of the grim situation rather than in spite of it, as the pianist Claudio Arrau who was there at the time has observed. Certainly Prokofiev was surprised by the 'packed house'[141] which greeted his performance of the Third Piano Concerto there in February. It was some consolation for the fact that the Third Symphony had been withdrawn from the programme, which at one stage had prompted him to consider cancelling. Yet he carried on for the sake of Weber and his own reputation in this prestigious musical centre. He also played several piano pieces to illustrate a half-hour radio lecture by the eminent critic Hans Heinz Stuckenschmidt, of whose attitude to his music he had been wary. 'Usually these people know *Oranges, Classical* and the *Suggestion diabolique* and talk of me first and foremost as a grotesque composer',[142] he wrote to Weber. Stuckenschmidt's suggestion that he play one of the *Visions fugitives* or the Andante from op.52 came as reassurance. He was glad that Stuckenschmidt liked op.52 more than the March from *The Love for Three Oranges*, 'which I myself can't bear to hear any more';[143] it had become as much of a millstone round his neck as was the C sharp minor Prelude to Rakhmaninov.

In the end, though, he decided not to play the Andante as it would take up the whole of his eight-minute slot in Stuckenschmidt's programme. He offered instead several movements of a new sonatina, one of two he had 'dashed off'[144] earlier in the month; this would make a nice, modest present of a premiere to Berlin. As it happened, these were simple offerings only in terms of the notes on the printed page, frequently reduced to no more than a two-part invention – the result, Myaskovsky felt, of his friend's pursuing a style which was 'phlegmatically Lenten . . . in the vertical respect'.[145] For all his praise of the sonatina's substance, it was Myaskovsky's passing reproach which Prokofiev seized on at greatest length in his reply: 'That's why they're called sonatinas, so as to be single-storeyed edifices! How strange that Saradzhev, a lively fellow in his heyday, is opposed to my new compositional manner. And Asafyev writes: "the lyricism of your creations of recent date is not valued here". Don't you see the melodic aspect is that which reaches the soul easiest of all, and the form is extremely comprehensible'.[146]

In performance, the form is anything but easily grasped; despite Prokofiev's old trick of clearly defining his key in a firm, final cadence, with many clear full stops to the sonatina-form sections, the themes' harmonic restlessness renders them extremely elusive on first hearing. The E minor Sonatina has tonally complex outer movements, while its brighter successor offers more classically outlined G and C major melodies in the opening movement and deliberately muddies the waters only in the two themes of its central Andante (Myaskovsky thought the second of them, with its doleful song underpinned by restless left-hand arpeggios, could be a portrait of *The Fiery Angel*'s Renata, though there is no thematic link). Both composers thought the slow movements most successful, and the Adagietto of the first Sonatina certainly strikes out for big effects in the elaborate variations on its two memorable subjects – imaginative preparation for the big sonatas to come. But while Myaskovsky doubted the ultimate success of the two very different finales, Prokofiev was anxious to defend the *Prodigal Son*-like activity at the end of the first: 'it is more difficult, but it has the quality of improving on each recurring playthrough'.[147] And that is certainly true of both works.

Also characteristic of his recent fascination with half submerging his original themes, this time in unpredictable structures, was another concerto he had just sketched. It would give him a new vehicle with which to join the leading conductors and orchestras now so interested in his music; but to whom should he entrust it? Wilhelm Furtwängler, who had already conducted movements from *Chout* and *Le Pas d'acier* with his Berlin Philharmonic Orchestra and had so impressed Prokofiev when they came to Paris early in 1931, had first call; but there were also the American-based conductors and his future tour to consider. Koussevitzky would engage him in Boston, but only with the new concerto; and he wanted the rights to the world premiere. 'Really this gentleman is getting too important',[148] exclaimed Prokofiev to Haensel. In the end the 'double doctor',[149] as an increasingly disenchanted Prokofiev now dubbed him, settled for the first performance in America and dates were agreed with Furtwängler in Berlin for the end of October.

The new work was all the more necessary while Wittgenstein hung fire over its predecessor. Far from being 'a reaction from the intense expression and formal complexity of the Fourth Concerto',[150] as one critic has judged it, the Fifth Piano Concerto has many stylistic traits in common with it, even if one senses Prokofiev's liberation at being able to write double octaves and solo passages with the widest possible spread for a two-handed soloist. At first he decided it should be called 'Music for Piano and Orchestra';[151] this would appear to refer not only to the five-movement structure but also to the spate of themes launched in the first movement. To paraphrase Eduard Hanslick on Strauss's *Till Eulenspiegel*, hardly an idea fails to get its neck broken by the speed with which the next one lands on its head. The work begins not in nimble toccata activity like the Fourth Concerto but with a discernible if rather Cubist theme refracted through the piano's extremes. The orchestral sections are at loggerheads: violins try a dreamy melody, only to be rudely brushed aside by a high-wire circus tune starring the first trumpet, so often kept in check throughout the left-hand work, and further cheeky fragments of theme are hurled round the different sections, in various keys. This savage parade is tamed, as in the third movement of the preceding concerto, by a more lyrical middle section idyllically introduced by the clarinet; but this, too, tends to fly off into restless activity. The return of the opening music, as in the Fourth Concerto, is brilliantly elliptical; and it finds its quicksilver reflection, also like the Wittgenstein work, in a fast toccata movement. Here, though, this is the third movement, not the finale, and an angry monster making full use of left and right hands rather than a soufflé.

Mercutio is just round the corner in the spikily accented strut of the second movement. The piano glissandos which Prokofiev had so enjoyed introducing into the Temptress's scherzo in the context of op.52 mark the first of the theme's three appearances; in the last, the 12/8 second subject is heard in the piano counterpointing the now familiar trumpet (one of the concerto's unifying sounds). Hints at another world here are expanded in the slow movement, which follows the lyrical formula of the Fourth's Andante but provides equally striking melodic material. Something of the American spaciousness of Copland's music is suggested by the muted strings and flute which preface the piano's limpid song; the second theme, like its parallel inspiration in the left-hand concerto, stretches the pianist's technique to the limit, but as two hands are involved, Prokofiev is able to go to the dramatic extremes of the Second Concerto and the transcription of the quartet's Andante. This time when unison strings unfold the theme, they enjoy the luxury of 26 impressive bars without taking a single predictable turn. The finale strenuously evades a tonality or refuses to settle in one, though curiously the 'outlines of a real face'[152] in the form of a blithe galop theme anticipates the simple tunes in the finales of the last three symphonies; there, too, subversion will be the order of the day, but only gradually. Here the material seems to implode, reaching a strange vegetative state with the piano in overlapping minor scales and two bassoons singing a wan tune in 3rds and 6ths. The coda takes the madcap premises of so much of the concerto to extremes; the last garish G major chord comes as a complete surprise.

With the Fifth Piano Concerto, Prokofiev for the time being rounded off a string of works in which his search for new melody finds itself embedded in complex frameworks. There is not a hint of the artistic fatigue detected by Soviet commentators, and maintained unthinkingly by many critics in the West; even *Sur le Borysthène* contains much first-rate music, though its experimental structure may not have produced the results composer and choreographer had been ambitious enough to expect. Nor was the West getting tired of Prokofiev, who was successfully reinventing his work while remaining true to himself. Stravinsky's latest music was being received with increasing scepticism, but Prokofiev was compared favourably with his only Russian rival; according to Gottlieb, Mischa Elman had maintained that he was the more important of the two 'because you have always great ideas and you start and finish in a very broad and universal way'.[153] Clarence Lucas of the *Musical Courier*, looking to write a biography, declared him 'the most worthy representative of the Russian school of musical composition now before the public'.[154] Glazunov's day was over, maintained Lucas; Medtner no longer courted the public. A less focussed composer than Prokofiev might have been insecure about the future; but he could well reason along the lines of Goethe in one of his late epigrams, that 'it has gone well so far; so will it continue'. What more could he want? The answer lay closer to home.

14
Sound and vision
1932–4

Two technological advances were to enrich Prokofiev's career as composer and performer in 1932. In February he received an invitation to the premiere screening in Paris of Nikolay Ekk's *Road to Life*, the first major Soviet film in which sound and image were conceived simultaneously (*Alone*, with music by Shostakovich, had started life as a silent film). Certainly Hollywood had been way ahead of the Russian film-makers in its sound experiments, but Eisenstein had not been alone in voicing the opinion that it might be better if the art evolved more slowly. On Prokofiev's part, there could be no regrets that he had turned down Gloria Swanson's proposition when a Soviet-based project of the calibre of *Poruchik Kizhe* ('Lieutenant Kijé') was just round the corner.

Kijé would materialize on his next, long-postponed visit to Russia at the end of the year. In the meantime Prokofiev was at last prepared for another development which had changed the course of recording history: the advent of the electric microphone, which in 1925 put paid to the unsatisfactory arrangement whereby musicians huddled round a giant horn transmitting acoustical impulses to the point of a needle. Prokofiev's correspondence with Charles Leirens of the Association des Arts et Sciences Phoniques (ASPHO) in Brussels shows that he had been following more advanced systems of phonography for his own listening purposes, finally settling on a state-of-the-art machine 'with a marvellous sound; piano and voice, which normally make a very mediocre impact on the phonograph, come across perfectly'.[1] On this Pardo machine, for which he paid 3500 francs, he could hear recordings of Stravinsky's music as well as several of his own, which included Koussevitzky's excellent performance of the *Classical* Symphony. Paichadze, Koussevitzky's kindly Paris manager, was 'very nice'[2] to Prokofiev's boys and sometimes brought records especially for them; one that made a special impression on Sviatoslav featured Saint-Saëns's Third ('Organ') Symphony.

Prokofiev's interpretations as pianist, however, had so far reached a wider audience only through the Aeolian reproducing system, latterly replaced by the combined forces of radio and phonograph; now he was ready to make a major statement through the electrical medium. Perhaps it was encouraged by the new admiration he expressed for the sound reproduction of the piano, but a contract with HMV had been signed the previous year. It was not a hugely profitable venture: ten per cent of all sales was to yield him a mere £49 13*s* over the first six months, though American distribution would bring slightly higher rewards. On 26 June he flew to London to record the Third Piano Concerto over the next two days at HMV's Abbey Road studio; he preceded by less than a month a regular visitor to the studio, the 75-year-old Elgar, who was to record his Violin Concerto with the prodigy Yehudi Menuhin. 'Just think', Prokofiev wrote to Myaskovsky, 'I can't sneeze or make a mess of it!'[3]

Nor did he, even if the end result hardly shines as the only recorded example so far to come to light of Prokofiev playing any of his concertos (though by the composer's own reckoning his earlier BBC broadcast as soloist in the Second Piano Concerto with Ansermet would make painful listening). The best moments are those when he has a chance to let his own capricious pianism take wing, as in the lopsided dance of the first movement and several of the central variations. Twelve years on from creating this multi-faceted hybrid, the composer-pianist now had to be content with giving an approximate rendition of the difficulties that accumulate several minutes into the finale, the one part of the work that comes closest to the problematic Second Concerto. Possibly compelled to speed by the six 78-rpm sides to which he was confined, he also plays an uncomfortable cat-and-mouse game with Piero Coppola and the London Symphony Orchestra. As artistic director of HMV's French branch, Coppola was the obligatory conductor, and Prokofiev would surely have been more comfortable with Nikolay Malko, whom he had recently come to respect, or his old friend Albert Coates.

Coates, however, was not free of recent blame; his liking for white-heat speeds had gone awry in HMV's recording of *Le Pas d'acier*. 'Sides 4 and 5 should not be put on sale', Prokofiev wrote to Fred Gaisberg of HMV in July, 'for they do not represent my work at all . . . it is true that we are obliged to cut out one of the best movements, "The Factory", but it is better to omit it than misrepresent it.'[4] Liable as ever to forget *The Times*'s enthusiastic salute of the 1920 concert in which Coates conducted his *Scythian Suite* and their subsequent, successful partnership with his Third Concerto two years later, he used the response to his most recent performance of the concerto before a London audience, which took place on 13 April in the Queen's Hall with Henry Wood conducting, as a chance to note that 'up to now my music has been too much misrepresented by the English press'.[5] The writer to whom he had entrusted that confidence, Watson Lyle of *The Bookman*, turned out to be no better than most. 'I expected your article to be the first serious study of my music after all the nonsense written up to now in England about it', the disappointed interviewee told Lyle in July, 'but I see you had to limit yourself to a kind of drawing-room chat . . . I did not tell you "Music without emotion? But it is not possible". The very word "emotion" I asked you to use with caution; otherwise you will make your readers believe that a new Puccini is born.'[6]

Cantankerousness certainly had the upper hand at about this time. Chastized recipients of his wrath included Messrs Eade, Peckover & Youdan of Sackville Street, who had made him an ill-fitting suit on his first London visit of the year, and Jacques Rouché, back in command at the Paris Opéra. Rouché's objection to what he saw as the outdatedness of *The Love for Three Oranges*, which Prokofiev still hoped might be staged there, brought a tirade against the tedium of the repertoire – 'sleeping in a corner of the box, I dreamt sweetly that at last M. Rouché could have a lively opera which would bring a bit of life to the poor subscribers'.[7] Conductors also came in for varying degrees of disapproval. Fears that Bruno Seidler-Winkler would 'ruin'[8] a Berlin broadcast of the Third Symphony were not entirely realized, though 'in the finale he took all the tempos incorrectly: the middle too slow, the faster ones too fast';[9] and Derzhanovsky was warned off engaging composer-conductor Vasily Nebolsin to conduct the *Four Portraits and Dénouement from The Gambler* in Moscow later in the year: 'he has an insecure technique and absence of conviction that the piece must be played thus and not otherwise'.[10] Two old acquaintances in the performing world came under attack in a letter to Myaskovsky: Rakhmaninov for his 'dry' delivery of a romantic programme which included the 'education manual'[11] of his new *Variations on a Theme of Corelli*, and Medtner for performing nothing but his own music, much of it new but 'such dried-up stuff, so archaic, so thematically and harmonically mediocre, that it seemed that sitting in front of me was a person who had suddenly gone mad and who, having lost his sense of time, was persisting in writing in the style of Karamzin'.[12] Prokofiev's kinder instincts were reserved for two protégés of the young generation – the Chinese pianist Sing-Hai Sien, who would remember the generosity of the Prokofiev family for years to come, and Sergey Tager, who had 'conquered heroically the difficulties of the Second Concerto'.[13]

Although Paris enjoyed such brief efflorescences as Lina's first performance in May of the latest *Ugly Duckling* transcription – 'very pungent',[14] it involved just a few woodwind elaborations and doublings to add to the little-noticed arrangement for strings of 1925 – the city's musical life was also deemed far from healthy. Prokofiev was able to write with honesty for the Moscow *Muzykalny almanakh* of 'the curious and abnormal status of symphony orchestras here. There are a great many of them, too many in fact, and they function in a rather haphazard fashion'.[15] Clashes of programme, inadequate rehearsals and poor funding contributed to a new chaos – 'all the more regrettable since the standard of performance of orchestral musicians in Paris is high, enabling them to cope with any modern score'.[16] One bright new light among the many Paris musical organizations was *Triton*, founded that spring and dedicated to the performance of new chamber works; Prokofiev's role as a juror soon put him in a responsible position as a musical ambassador between several western European countries and the Soviet Union.

Affairs in Paris kept the Prokofievs there for much of July, but early in the month they undertook some island-hopping in the Channel. Although the fun of manipulating the sailing timetables left them with only a day apiece on each of the 'fabulous'[17] islands, as Prokofiev called them in inverted commas, there was time to send Myaskovsky a postcard from Sark – 'under the protection of England, but having its own queen who rules over 600 subjects and lives in the palace depicted on the other side, guarded by six cannons. So it was in the 16th century, and so it remains to this day thanks to some misunderstanding. The island is picturesque, the climate mild, and the numerous tourists diminish its medieval character'.[18] At the beginning of August, Lina again left the children with her parents in Le Cannet and went to stay with friends in a château while Prokofiev enjoyed another of his solitary motoring tours through France, making the usual excursions into caves and up mountains. Reunited, the family moved on to Ste-Maxime, halfway between Toulon and Cannes in the bay of St-Tropez, where they rented a dacha from Jacques Sadoul, 'the French communist, who is well known in Russia',[19] Prokofiev was able to report to Cousin Katya with one eye on the Soviet censor (letters to home still needed careful phrasing). At the same time he advised Tanya in Berlin not to write to Shurik, whose release had followed Katya's at last: 'I get the impression that he is fearfully afraid of attracting some sort of suspicion in his relations with foreigners, which is completely understandable'.[20]

Responding thankfully to Katya's long-overdue letter, in which she told him that her recovery from a tram accident was now complete, Prokofiev painted an idyllic picture of the Ste-Maxime summer: 'we bathe each day. The weather here is warm, but not too hot. Generally over the last ten years the weather in France has been wild, the summers everywhere rainy. So we chose to come to the shores of the Mediterranean Sea – a unique place, which so far the rains haven't reached . . . The children are running around in bathing costumes, and have been tanned to a deep brown'.[21] The Maison Sadoul stood a few miles from the sea with a big pine tree in front of the house and forests sweeping down to the bay, which the family always reached by car. Sometimes Prokofiev worked through the day, in a spacious room with a sea view, though he preferred the mornings when the heat was less intense. He realized he had created unprecedented challenges to his pianistic skills when he came to practise the solo part of the Fifth Concerto, as the fastidious Myaskovsky's dislike of the original title 'Music for Piano and Orchestra' had compelled him to call it.

He also worked on a Sonata for two violins, motivated by a determination to do something different from another composer who had written for the same unusual combination; 'in spite of the seemingly narrow framework of such a duet, it seemed possible to make it interesting enough for the public to listen for ten or fifteen minutes without any sense of fatigue'.[22] Ravel's words on his own Sonata for violin and cello, composed a decade earlier, spoke a language which Prokofiev could easily comprehend: 'the reduction to essentials is carried to extremes . . . A more and more marked reaction in the direction of melody is apparent'.[23] The Sonata for two violins was destined for the first *Triton* chamber concert in mid-December – though Russia, in fact, was to enjoy the premiere shortly beforehand, on 27 November. 'When they play it . . . you'll have to leave the hall',[24] wrote Prokofiev to Myaskovsky from Ste-Maxime, still harping on his friend's detection of a 'phlegmatically lenten . . . vertical'[25] style in the sonatinas. This, inevitably, was going to be even leaner – and 'there are hardly any double-stoppings or chords'.[26] Strictly speaking, that is true, though quadruple stopping helps to support the most emphatic dance-tunes of the vigorous second and fourth movements. Otherwise, violinistic 'effects' – harmonics, *sul ponticello* or spiccato – are kept to a minimum so that the spotlight shines on pure lyricism, announced by a slow opening movement in which the first violin descends from the stratosphere to collect its companion and they ascend together, dovetailing and overlapping. The distinctively shaped melodies, muted throughout in the pensive third movement, are usually taken by each player in turn, and Prokofiev always finds interest in the embroidery of a repeated theme. It is curious that David Oistrakh, whose memorable recording of the sonata with his son Igor realizes his own description of 'a fine, but not over-refined, execution of each individual intonation',[27] a key element in performing Prokofiev's violin music as this great interpreter saw it, does not mention the work in his brief tribute. Perhaps, like so much else composed in the early 1930s, it was reckoned by the Soviets among the pallid specimens of Prokofiev's last Parisian years; but there is iron strength between the lines.

As Prokofiev put the finishing touches to the sonata in early October, the rain which he had travelled so far south to escape finally fell in torrents on Ste-Maxime and the surrounding area. Luckily their house stood on a hill above the floods, but the nearby bridge was washed away; a detour allowed the return of the locally hired piano and the family's eventual departure. Back in Paris he continued his labours on the Fifth Piano Concerto with Tager partnering him in a reduction of the orchestral parts. His mind was elsewhere when he played the Third Concerto with Malko conducting in Copenhagen; the Berlin premiere of the Fifth three days later, on 31 October, loomed too large. Despite only one rehearsal with Furtwängler and the Berlin Philharmonic Orchestra, it turned out, he told Gottlieb, 'very successful, and Furtwängler re-engaged me to play another concerto'.[28] Political events would outstrip his optimism. A more doubtful outcome of his rising fortunes in Germany was foretold a few days later by his Munich admirer Erik Schaal, who wrote of Jewish artists' increasing difficulties in finding positions and of 'Kulturbolshevismus' as the tag for 'everything not understood'.[29] Hitler's accession to power was only three months away.

Now, though, Prokofiev's thoughts turned homewards, where at last he could expect a very different reception. His chief critics among the proletarian composers were muzzled; on 23 April the Central Committee of the Council of People's Commissars had swiftly decreed the dissolution of RAPM as well as its fellow organizations in art and literature. An all-embracing organization, the Soyuz Sovietskikh Compositorov ('Association of Soviet Composers'), with objectives still to be clarified, was mooted during the summer. The long-term implications of centralized control did not occur to most creative artists; relief at being freed from the strictures of the Jacobin fringe overshadowed all other considerations. 'The time has come to visit more frequently and stay for longer',[30] Prokofiev reflected to Myaskovsky. This latest trip, from late November, had already been shortened and changed from the collaboration he had proposed with the students of the Moscow Conservatory to a round of performances along the lines of his 1927 visit, this time kept to a minimum. For two symphonic programmes, one in Moscow with Golovanov and the other in Leningrad with Dranishnikov, he played the Fifth Concerto and conducted the Suite from *Le Pas d'acier,* and there were two all-Prokofiev chamber concerts featuring the Sonata for two violins (its Moscow premiere was given by Dmitry Tsyganov and Vasily Shirinsky of the Beethoven Quartet). Lina, who had parted company from her husband after two Warsaw concerts and gone to perform *The Ugly Duckling* in a Prague broadcast heard by the Russians, received a telegram informing her that the Moscow events had met with 'success equal to 1927'.[31] Subsequently Nestyev's biography would play its part in creating the myth of widespread alienation among the audience, claiming that only the critics had been divided. By then it simply would not do to suggest that Soviet listeners might have enjoyed the latest products of Prokofiev's decadent Western phase – not even the *Four Portraits and Dénouement from The Gambler,* conducted by Golovanov in Moscow, which, though they originated in an earlier era, had been assembled in France.

While negotiations with the Moscow Conservatory hung fire, educational objectives of a different sort were achieved. Links with the outside musical world, long suspended, had resumed with the dissolution of RAPM and Prokofiev took it upon himself to act as musical ambassador for the exchange of chamber music. *Triton* had asked him to promote French composers, which he did by taking with him songs by Fauré, Debussy and Poulenc. 'It would be one of my greatest joys', he told a French newspaper on his return, 'to serve as a link between the Russian performance of music by French composers and those of my countrymen whose works I have brought back, and which I hope to have performed here.'[32] The cross-fertilization went further; he also chose to represent Nin and Falla from Spain and had contacted Erik Chisholm, the founder of the Active Society for the Propagation of Contemporary Music in Glasgow, who sent him his Double Trio along with several songs by Cyril Scott. Prokofiev began his reciprocal duties in the West by promoting Myaskovsky's Second Quartet; younger composers more in need of exposure would follow. Once he had seen that conditions were 'much more favourable concerning the voluntary return to the USSR of full artistic forces coming from abroad',[33] he also began dedicated lobbying for the re-engagement of conductor friends; Malko, Désormière, Stock and Désiré Defauw of Brussels were among many who benefited from his painstaking negotiations. His thoughts on the new situation were best summed up in a letter to the émigré author Dmitry Krachkovsky in Nice. Telling Krachkovsky that his wife was well back in the Soviet Union and was begging him to return to Moscow, he gave his own cautious opinion: 'it's difficult for me to lend my voice to such crucial questions, but I must say that the attitude to scholars and to people in all walks of artistic life has noticeably improved since former times, and the interest of the masses in literature and music is extraordinary. I personally will be returning to the USSR in the spring with the greatest pleasure'.[34]

It looked as if *The Gambler* might again stand a chance of a Soviet production, this time at the Moscow Radio Theatre at some unspecified time within the next two years. He had not abandoned his search for true Soviet themes. 'What kind of subject am I looking for?' he wrote in an article for *Vechernyaya Moskva* on 6 December. 'Not caricatures of shortcomings, ridiculing the negative features of our life. I am interested in a subject that would assert the positive elements. The heroic aspects of socialist construction. The new man. The struggle to overcome obstacles.'[35] This was a genuine declaration in principle, one stressed in his regular rejections of librettos from Western poets and playwrights, though the brushstrokes would have to be less broad, more subtle on the psychological front, than he had suggested to the newspaper. This qualification was stressed by Shostakovich in an article the following year: 'it is impossible to write an opera about the five-year plan "in general" or about socialist construction "in general"; one must write about living people, about the builders of socialism. Our librettists have not grasped this yet. Their heroes are anaemic and impotent, and evoke neither sympathy nor hatred'.[36] That was why, Shostakovich explained, he had turned to Gogol for *The Nose* and was currently working on *The Lady Macbeth of the Mtsensk District*, based on a tale by the 19th-century writer Nikolay Leskov: 'their characters have the power to make us laugh and to make us weep'.[37] So far, the guidelines for what had yet to be labelled 'socialist realism' did not exclude the classics.

While he waited for the ideal opera libretto, Prokofiev found another way of focussing his attention on half-light, half-serious music for a wider audience. On 3 December a provisional agreement was drawn up with the film company Belgoskino, for which Boris Gusman, one of the artistic colleagues he had been able to trust in the former Bolshoy regime, was now working, 'to write music for the sound picture *Lieutenant Kijé*'.[38] His collaborators would be Yury Tynyanov, who was working on the screenplay of his Gogolian tale about bureaucracy spawning absurd fantasy in the time of Paul I, and Alexander Feinzimmer as director. Feinzimmer had made his first film for Belgoskino, *Hotel Savoy*, a year after its formation in 1927 and, were it not for *Lieutenant Kijé*, would remain the merest footnote in Soviet cinema history.

Still in discussion at the end of 1932, the *Kijé* project would help delay Prokofiev's scrupulous search for his own subjects; and the discipline of a film script could focus his imagination in a way that the music-first, plot-later approach to his most recent ballet had not. The long-postponed production of *Sur le Borysthène* was, in fact, one of Prokofiev's main reasons for returning to Paris in the second week of December. On the 14th he told Asafyev that 'not everything is going well yet',[39] and the Paris Opéra premiere two days later, with delicate costumes by Goncharova bizarrely set against Larionov's contemporary blend of ruralism and industry, was not a success. Hostile reviews saw to its withdrawal after a handful of performances – 'the music is some of the weakest M. Prokofiev has composed', lamented *Le Figaro*[40] – but by then Prokofiev was too far away to worry. He sailed for America, in which he was still placing as many high hopes as he had in the new Russia, the day after the premiere.

Travelling companions on the *Europa* included Bruno and Elsa Walter, photographed with Prokofiev on their arrival in New York (Lina stayed with the children in Paris, at one point joining the Furtwänglers in St Moritz). In their New York appearances together Prokofiev was able to cement 'very friendly relations'[41] with Walter, who conducted the *Four Portraits and Dénouement from The Gambler* 'four times, with middling success; with the Third Concerto on the other hand, the success was enormous'.[42] Boston, where he began his tour of 12 concerts on 30 December after a quiet Christmas with the Koussevitzkys, provided the best performance of the Fifth Concerto yet, outstripping even the finesse it had enjoyed in Paris earlier in the month. Koussevitzky and his orchestra 'accompanied with extraordinary brilliance', Prokofiev told Asafyev,[43] while public and press reception was warm.

In Chicago, where the ever-reliable Stock was his partner for the new concerto, Prokofiev was chaperoned by the persistent Gottlieb – not reliably enough, apparently, for Gottlieb's innocent suggestion that a young female friend should join them for an evening's entertainment met with a prim rebuff. It was for this reason that Gottlieb decided he was going 'to write a letter to your charming wife and will tell her of your beautiful behaviour while in Chicago. Unfortunately very few married men, especially geniuses, remember that they are married while travelling'.[44] Lina's response was understandable: after several exchanges, Prokofiev told Gottlieb with jocularity that she had begun to 'believe that my conduct in Chicago has been very bad if in every letter you are obliged to persuade her what an excellent husband I am'.[45] Eve Crain of Cleveland, at any rate, found him a pure upholder of 'the allness of mind'[46] in one of his broadcast concerts, and he confirmed for her the continuing role of Christian Science in his life: it was 'helping me enormously in my music. To say more exactly – I do not see any more my work outside of Science'.[47]

A punishing schedule (with, as ever, a small profit margin) merited a more leisurely return journey. Prokofiev decided to return to Europe on the *Conte di Savoia* – 'a big Italian steamship of 50,000 tons', he told Cousin Katya, 'going via the Azores and Gibraltar and setting us down in Nice; this way the whole journey was through warm waters. There is a big pool on board with sea water, in which I swam'.[48] The sight of Gibraltar in moonlight, with European and African coastlines outlined on either side, provided a romantic postlude to a visit he could look back on with some satisfaction. Americans, it seemed, were taking him more seriously: 'until now, when they didn't understand something', he told the French critic Serge Moreux, 'they thought I was composing to mock them. Now, there is a tendency to admit that I write music for the good'.[49]

Soviet musicologists, led by Nestyev, have constantly asserted that from the end of 1932 Prokofiev saw his fate as inextricably linked with his homeland. His reflections on the American scene, however, and his insecurities once back in Paris over a protracted silence from certain Soviet institutions reveal that this was far from being the case. The worries he expressed to Myaskovsky did not have long to fester as his next return to the Soviet Union was due in mid-April. His self-apppointed ambassadorial duties for exchanging the latest scores had expanded. From his American acquaintances he took with him Copland's *Music for the Theatre* as well as pieces by Hill and Piston recommended by the Boston Flute Players' Club. From Italy came his colleague Rieti's Serenade and Sinfonietta, while new relations established with André Mangeot, founder of the Westminster Music Society for the promotion of contemporary music in London, furnished chamber works by Bax, Bliss, Eugene Goossens and Moeran as well as Mangeot's own performing edition of Purcell's fantasias. Moscow accepted all these for performance except Bax's Quintet, 'which they already know'.[50] In return he recommended Lev Schwarz's *Suite orientale*, Popov's Septet and Shcherbachev's Nonet. He also placed a larger work, Vissarion Shebalin's Second Symphony, with Defauw in Brussels. Shostakovich's latest symphony, the Third, was in no need of such special pleading. Prokofiev had heard Stokowski conduct it in New York. 'It disappointed me to a certain extent', he told Myaskovsky: 'it's fragmentary and the melodic line is not interesting enough for the insistent two-part counterpoint.'[51]

The 26-year-old Shostakovich was currently riding the crest of a wave: in April a Moscow concert devoted to his music was described by *Sovietskoye iskusstvo* as the highlight of the season. But all-Prokofiev concerts were still in demand, despite the doubts about their effectiveness he expressed to Levon Atovmyan before his April visit; alongside the ubiquitous Third Piano Concerto in the senior composer's latest Moscow and Leningrad appearances came not only the *Scythian Suite* but also for the first time the Third Symphony, a work on which he was placing ever stronger emphasis. The execution left a lot to be desired, and to Stock he made unfavourable comparisons with the healthier American orchestras. Safer programmes were reserved for his extended tour in the Caucasus that May. Lina joined him, and they 'travelled as far as the Persian border and the plains of Ararat'.[52] She had not been to the Soviet Union since 1927, and their return to Moscow gave her a chance not only to see the three nieces, who had grown up in the intervening six years, but to meet their father, who had been in prison during her last visit and was now unsuccessful in obtaining a permit to live in Moscow; with his wife Nadya he was bound for the Urals. 'Shurik stayed with us for a few days', Prokofiev told Tanya on his return, 'and got to know Linette; they approved of each other.'[53]

Cousin Katya, meanwhile, had been sponsored by Prokofiev to visit for the whole of May: 'she went back for the summer but in the autumn is looking for somewhere else to live. Shurik doesn't especially want her settling with him, nor do his daughters; Katya Ignatyeva is very lovable, but her character is not easy and her deafness cuts her off from daily life'.[54]

The last, slightly less hectic days back on familiar territory allowed Prokofiev to see his way clear to work on *Lieutenant Kijé*, which he had promised Gusman to consider once his concert tours were over. Rehearsals at the Belgoskino studios enabled him to plan the kind of music which would best suit this singular comedy (a charming photograph shows him seated at the harp, 'played' in the film by the lady who briefly sings the Romance). The film's setting, centred on the court of irascible, pug-nosed Tsar Paul at the very end of the 18th century, required period-flavour military and celebratory numbers with a fantastical tinge; perhaps for this reason Prokofiev declared he had 'absolutely no doubts about the musical language for the film'.[55] The crux of Tynyanov's tale, however, was topical. The Shostakovich of Solomon Volkov's *Testimony* declares with reference to Tynyanov's original tale, 'I have no idea what things were like in Paul's reign . . . but for our day this story was a reality. It tells how a nonexistent man becomes an existent one, and an existent one becomes nonexistent. No one is surprised by this – because it is usual and typical and could happen to anyone'.[56] Or rather, in 1933 it was about to happen to anyone; and when it did, Tynyanov's homage to Gogol could only seem more topical.

In the film, the clerical error that creates 'Poruchik ['Lieutenant'] Kizhe' from 'poruchiki-zhe' ('and the lieutenants') coincides with an absurd scandal. The tsar wants to sleep, but is woken when a courtier, surprised by a flirt pinching his backside, screams blue murder ('karaul'). Who is to blame for this atrocious disruption? To save the real culprits, punishment falls on the newly invented Kijé – an invisible figure flogged over a cannon, transported to Siberia (where the governor comically inspects the thin air), recalled by sleigh when the true miscreant is forced to own up, raised to the rank of general and married to the bottom-pincher. No sooner has he enjoyed his wedding night than another scandal in the bedroom involving the real bride's lover causes him to be taken ill and to die in hospital. It is an ideal scenario for a film in which many of the participants had learnt their craft in the circus and mime routines of FEKS ('Factory of the Eccentric Actor'). There are especially fine performances from Mikhail Yanshin, a Moscow Arts Theatre regular, as the capricious tsar, and Sophie Magarill as the moon-faced minx who becomes Kijé's bride. Anger, bewilderment, shock and amusement are all paraded round the invisible protagonist; and the wedding is perhaps the funniest scene, the holding of the crown traditional to the Russian ceremony quirkily parodied as the bearer tries to judge the newly ennobled general's height.

Yet the tempo of the film is undeniably too slow for so satirical a theme, as Prokofiev's secretary Astrov made bold to note when he first saw it in Paris, and though the dialogue is kept to a minimum, the music does not play as significant a role as anyone who has enjoyed *Alexander Nevsky* might expect. This has partly to do with the dim recording facilities in 1933; but with the exceptions of the opening parade-ground sequence and the drunken song on the troika-ride back from Siberia, the numbers are decidedly incidental, however memorable their clear-cut tunes. This did not prevent Prokofiev working with the utmost precision back in Paris once he had noted down at the Belgoskino studios the music he needed to provide. Not only did every snippet need to be calculated down to the second (a letter to Feinzimmer of 13 July allows for the most minuscule of optional cuts) but the sonorities, spare as they were, had to capture the mood exactly. For the famous fanfare which begins and ends the suite, only a *cornet à pistons*, 'softer' in effect than a trumpet, would do; its role was to play 'very *piano* and from afar, but without a mute'.[57] Five seconds could be shorn off its closing bar if necessary, 'but it would be better for this bar to be lengthened, so that it can die down thoroughly'.[58] In Kijé's return from Siberia, which along with the wedding and burial music was completed later in the summer, the types of baritone and high tenor were stipulated in detail, 'the two horns need to sit very close to the microphone, so they sound powerful' and 'the whole number must go dashingly and be performed with ringing, whooping and drunken but not exaggerated voices'.[59]

Poruchik Kizhe enjoyed wide distribution shortly after its Soviet release; it was screened in London (as *The Tsar Wants to Sleep*) and Paris (as *Le Lieutenant Nantes*), where the spectators included young Sviatoslav Prokofiev, who loved the burlesque surrounding the sleeping tsar. The film has disappeared from the classic repertoire, its title famous only by virtue of the five-movement suite Prokofiev arranged in 1934 at the instigation of Moscow Radio (which has since taken on a new life in more recent films including an Alec Guinness vehicle, *The Horse's Mouth*, and Woody Allen's *Love and Death*). In creating the suite the question was not what to leave out, as had been the case in the simple adaptation of music from *Sur le Borysthène* for a suite in April 1933, but what to extend, and how. The first movement contrasts the parade-ground world of the opening scene and later, more pompous fanfares with the Russian soulfulness of Kijé, lightly sketched by the first oboe, proposing him as a true patriot. This is the only leitmotif of the film, but the suite reveals a surprising unity in the constant conflict of D major and B flat major; as examples of a new simplicity, the melodies rarely stray far from their harmonic base.

Of the seven tunes that dominate the film's soundtrack, the Romance required the most imaginative reworking from the original for soprano and harp; the radio orchestra's resident tenor saxophonist would dominate its colouring, and a new flute counterpoint could be pressed into service as a contrasting theme (Ex.63). Here and in 'The Burial of Kijé', Prokofiev was able to extend the simple, two-part musical language he had used in the film. There is even a bizarre sense of the whole fiction spinning out of control as Kijé refuses to lie down in his coffin and the wedding song persists in F major against the G minor of the Romance – a subtly disconcerting *mésalliance* in a finale that can only self-destruct (Ex.64). Much of the

Ex.63 *Lieutenant Kijé* Suite, op.60 – II. Romance

Ex.64 *Lieutenant Kijé* Suite – V. Kijé's burial

suite leaves the simple melodies free to breathe. But the brilliant use of a larger orchestra is hardly wasted in the glittering 'Troika', where with pizzicato upper strings, piano and percussion Prokofiev follows a tradition of balalaika imitation initiated by Rimsky-Korsakov in *The Invisible City of Kitezh*, along with a dash of *Petrushka* in the trombone solo; if the original baritone is to be engaged here, he should be able to project through the vibrant but never thick textures. The popularity of the song, with or without the vocal part, needs no apology.

Just as Prokofiev had by no means committed himself to the Soviet cause in 1933, so his more complex experimentation of recent years had not quite disappeared. 'You must bring a large-scale piece written specially for us', Myaskovsky commanded in June, as he looked forward to his friend's autumn visit, adding that the piece in question should be 'symphonic, monumental, clear and – don't be angry, o horror! – cheerful! How you can combine these things, I don't know, but you can do it. "Chanson symphonique" isn't quite for us . . . it lacks that which we mean by monumentalism – a familiar simplicity and broad contours, of which you are extremely capable, but temporarily are carefully avoiding.'[60] From this we learn that Myaskovsky had already seen Prokofiev's latest major orchestral work, the *Symphonic Song* (op.57); and he later qualified his opinion by adding that although this could hardly be received as a major statement, Prokofiev should still bring it as he personally longed to hear it.

This underrated missing link between the far less grandly symphonic Fourth Symphony of 1930 and the Fifth of 1945 has a paradox at its heart. Though it is complex at the start, its tripartite form, which Prokofiev later labelled 'darkness – conflict – achievement',[61] progresses towards the light of a 'new simplicity' which presumably comes too late for listeners expecting something straightforward. The supple opening melody is clothed in the powerful textures of the 'Betrothal' scene from *Sur le Borysthène*, but woodwind and trumpet have different, more angular questions. The increasingly embattled song gives way to a leaner conflict, with shrill scoring for piccolo and clarinet more reminiscent of the young Shostakovich. If Prokofiev intended briefly to emulate the good fight of Shostakovich's Third Symphony, he had no wish to celebrate his victory with the kind of Soviet hymn that crowns Shostakovich's example. The triumph is a personal one, a free and easy C major theme for violins on the G string, 'dolce e molto cantando' (Ex.65), which is finally led by a cheerful march to its final assertion in D major. Both keys have been mooted towards the beginning, but their resolution is presented in clearer melodic terms. It is a neatly expressed paradigm of the composer's own journey in the early 1930s, reinforced by the difficult question of whether to give the *Symphonic Song* its first outing in Paris, where the orchestras were by now in too poor and under-rehearsed a state to do it justice, or Moscow, which would hardly welcome its thornier components.

A different route is traced by the piano solo *Mysli* ('Pensées' or 'Thoughts') op.62, which Prokofiev described as 'similar in character'[62] to the *Symphonic Song*.

Ex.65 *Symphonic Song*, op.57

The opening Adagio penseroso wanders in heavily chorded mazes of thought; it is not until the mid-point of the second piece that a grand theme surfaces (Prokofiev thought this 'one of my greatest successes'[63]). But the final number does not offer the *Symphonic Song*'s optimistic resolution; here, the parade of cantabile themes is crushed by the juggernaut of its framework. In total contrast are the clear textures, simple forms and succession of major keys in the Three Pieces op.59, completed alongside *Thoughts* the following summer. These begin with a brief flavour of the much-derided French *musiquette* before reverting to a fantasy familiar from the *Visions fugitives* and a nostalgic Sonatina. A purer aspirant to the title than its predecessors of the same name, the *Pastoral Sonatina* is rounded off by a perfect coda which sidesteps with swift elegance to the final cadence (Ex.66). The shining path to the *Music for Children* op.65 of 1935, though powerfully threatened by the *Thoughts*, is clearly delineated here.

There was still time for leisure in this most rigorous of working years, but much of it involved the complicated thought processes of his favourite games. At the end of March Prokofiev expounded for *La Revue de bridge* his thoughts about a game played simultaneously on several tables, and why he preferred it:

> I often played chess long before learning bridge. This is the reason why in this last case I love the element of combination and deplore that of chance in cards. In short, is there anything more lamentable than one excellent player who loses to three weak ones purely due to the fact that for the whole evening he had nothing but bad cards?[64]

Combination bridge for 12 players at three tables soon became a popular pastime at the Rue Valentin Haüy. As for chess, which he was still enjoying regularly at

Ex.66 *Pastoral Sonatina*, op.59 no.3

Napoleon's old haunt of the Café de la Régence, he played two games with the famous Saviely Tartakower, winning the first and drawing the second. There seemed no reason why he should not exploit his triumph for publicity purposes in America. 'Tartakower is one of the strongest players in the world', he told Gottlieb in an extended version of the news he had already passed on to Haensel, 'and has the title of "Grossmeister" – so you can imagine how proud I was to win. When, after the game was over, I asked Tartakower to show me what mistake he made to lose it, he answered: "I made no mistake; simply you played well".'[65]

An extended summer holiday was out of the question after the late-spring combination of touring and sightseeing in the Caucasus. On 8 July Lina left alone to recuperate with the Szigetis in Divonne-les-Bains, and shortly afterwards her restless husband took another of his solitary motoring trips. 'I travelled (through Savoie, the Alps and Switzerland) completely alone', he told Sonya Brichan's husband Andryusha, 'with a briefcase in which were books, music and corrections.'[66] Arriving back in Paris on 1 August, he spent most of the time on *Kijé* and negotiations for the autumn return to Russia, joining the rest of the family for a short spell of bathing in the south in early September.

The scheduling of his route east that October was complicated. He wanted to stop in Berlin between trains to go shopping with Weber for a camelhair waistcoat and another special pullover; but he had misread the connection time and found that he had only 35 minutes rather than an hour and nine minutes. After successful, if unprofitable, concerts in Riga and Kaunas he could not go directly to Poland for his next engagements since, he told his agent, 'Lithuania has been at war with Poland for 12 years. The border is closed so one has to go via Latvia or Germany'.[67] On 21 October he telegraphed Lina to tell her he had arrived safely in Moscow: 'all friends reunited in the Hotel National and thinking of you and send sincere greetings'.[68] The main novelties of his Moscow and Leningrad concerts were the Fourth Symphony and the Divertimento; the opinion of the critic writing for *Sovietskaya muzyka* is evidence that Prokofiev's latest scores were still being assessed intelligently in his home country. Both works, the journal maintained, were 'of the character of suites, constructed with unusual clarity with short . . . abruptly concluded episodes, more reminiscent of balletic-theatrical music than symphonic. The orchestral sound of these pieces is steely in character, one could say metallic, polished. There is nothing here of *Chout*'s noisy roustabout or of the *Scythian Suite*'s piercing finale'.[69]

The long-awaited revival of *The Love for Three Oranges*, which had been the chief motivation for Prokofiev's latest Soviet trip, did not take place, but the visit was remarkable for his decisive steps towards a new theatrical initiative – his first incidental music. The offer came not, as might have been expected, from Meyerhold, whose forthcoming production of Dumas' *La Dame aux camélias* was to be graced by Shebalin's attentive score, but from Alexander Tairov, the director of the Moscow Chamber Theatre frequently chastized by Meyerhold for mannered theatricality. This was not a company that felt a strong obligation to serve the cause of socialist realism. One of its first new stagings after the Revolution had been of Wilde's *Salome*, and exoticism with a cutting edge was back in favour at the end of 1933. Tairov had the bright idea of a Cleopatra compendium, a showcase for the lithe talents of Alisa Koonen, the Moscow Chamber Theatre's co-founder and leading lady. It was to begin with the high spirits of George Bernard Shaw's *Caesar and Cleopatra*, establishing the power and love play between Rome and Egypt with a light touch, before moving on to Shakespeare's *Antony and Cleopatra*. Between the selective adaptations of the two dramas, in the final scene of the first act, Tairov wanted a dramatic declamation of Pushkin's poem *Yegipetskiye nochi* ('Egyptian Nights'), shorn of its prose context but losing nothing of its power in the unusual depiction of Cleopatra as a vampire claiming the life of her suitors in exchange for a night of love. Pushkin's title was to provide an umbrella for the Tairov project as a whole.

For the recitation of the poem, Prokofiev provided his most extended single number in the shape of a melodrama precisely tailored to the rhythms of the text. But he placed no less store by the 43 other numbers, which his work on *Kijé* had led him to to undertake with confidence and a great deal of careful preparation. He later gave his thoughts on this new departure to *Izvestiya*:

> In the art of writing music for the stage the following point of view can serve as a criterion: if the presence of music in the given scene strengthens its drama or lyricism, then the music is in place here, that is, it is the kind of music needed. If the given theme can be dramatically performed, without the music, with no less effect, then either the music is poor or the scene does not require any music at all, as is the case with various 'naturalistic' moments from contemporary operatic literature . . . Above all this music should not be intrusive and should not

stand out as an independent element in the dramatic action. This kind of music can promote a more complete perception of the characters in the play, especially Cleopatra and Antony, who are the most dramatic and fascinating personages in *Egyptian Nights.*[70]

According to Tairov, Cleopatra's theme, which makes its first appearance in Caesar's meeting with the sphinx (no.7), was Prokofiev's earliest inspiration; the might of imperial Rome came next. These contrasts, as well as the atmosphere of the Eastern night conjured by flutes and muted strings and the quirky characterization of Mark Antony, appear to fit their context well enough (as no-one, at the time of writing, has attempted to recreate Tairov's extravaganza, we can only guess at their aptness). Prokofiev was diligent in capturing the special effects he wanted, checking with Tairov that the theatre orchestra could run to a tam-tam – 'very necessary, especially in those places where I need to represent the menace of Caesar's forces'[71] – a small E flat cornet and a five-string double bass. He also introduced an archaic *corno da caccia* for extra flavour, a modest reflection perhaps of Respighi's six Roman *buccine* in the resplendent procession concluding *Pini di Roma.*

As well as insisting on a 'full number of rehearsals for the music', Prokofiev made it clear from the start that the conductor should 'make a painstaking study of the whole score' and 'pay attention to the metronome marks'.[72] Alexander Medtner, brother of the composer and music director of the Moscow Chamber Theatre, had conducted the premiere of *Autumnal* back in 1911, so Prokofiev had every faith in his abilities; but he still wanted an intermediary to report on whether his wishes were carried out in his absence, and he asked Tairov to cajole the reluctant Myaskovsky into visiting the theatre during the rehearsal period. All this effort proved in vain as rehearsals were postponed to the end of 1934.

It was in fact the later version of the concert suite that was heard first, in a broadcast by its Moscow Radio commissioners. Telling Boris Gusman that he was about to send the score, in October 1934, Prokofiev said it would be 'of "logarithmic" character owing to all the references'.[73] The few recent attempts to revive the *Egyptian Nights* Suite suggest a sequence badly in need of context. The *Kijé* Suite also lacks a core, but its elusiveness is part of its charm and fits the subject of the invisible officer admirably. There are a few unforgettable ideas in *Egyptian Nights,* not least Antony's wayward refrain which brings much-needed focus at a crucial point (Ex.67). Cleopatra's restrained decline, though, needs more preparation, and the sudden might of empire which rounds off the suite serves only to provide a rousing conclusion with little regard to the context. Place the Pushkin poem with its musical support at the centre and the problem is solved; its narrator could also be pressed into service to provide concert-goers with a dash of Shavian rhetoric and the rather more frequent rustle of Shakespearean silk.

The potential glitter of *Egyptian Nights* seemed to be matched by Prokofiev's impressions of a brighter Soviet Union. 'Moscow and Leningrad are better lit', he

Ex.67 *Egyptian Nights* Suite, op.61 – IV. Antony

wrote to Tanya Rayevskaya, 'the roads are asphalted, cafés have opened, there is a sufficiency of shops for all citizens, though at a higher price.'[74] The changed attitude to artistic visitors from abroad was also having its effect: 'generally there is a tendency, and this is a tendency in life', he told Malko, 'to absorb back by chance those who have left for foreign countries, but to do it in a manner pleasant for those who have left, so that they feel an advantage in the return'.[75]

Prokofiev was not so easily seduced by Russian orchestral standards, especially when he soon had a yardstick of excellence with which to compare them. On his return to the West he travelled to Rome to play the Fifth Concerto with the champion of his youthful genius back in 1915, Bernardino Molinari, and to hear him prepare the Augusteo Orchestra in Myaskovsky's Sinfonietta along with his own Third Symphony. 'They rehearsed for five days, at 12 and 8 each day', came the report back to Myaskovsky, 'amounting to ten rehearsals lasting two and a quarter hours apiece – you don't come across such luxury anywhere else these days.'[76] The Third Symphony was a special triumph: 'it came across as a completely different piece from the one performed in Moscow! And that's why the public understood it'.[77] A return to Rome in the New Year of 1934 brought the brightest in a spate of European concert engagements, a recital at the Soviet Embassy on 5 January. Lina appeared with him; their repertory now featured two new folk-song arrangements, Azmaiparashvili's *Georgian Shepherd's Song* and Schwarz's *Bashkirian Lullaby*. At the end of the month Prokofiev learnt that he had been voted an honorary member of the city's Accademia di S. Cecilia, and responded graciously that the honour was 'all the dearer to me since my first concert outside Russia was at the Accademia – always held close as one of my most agreeable memories'.[78]

Parisian musical life, by contrast, was the usual jumble of competing, under-rehearsed orchestras, though there was an entertaining divertissement in the shape of Glazunov's B flat major Quartet for four saxophones. 'The venture was successful', Prokofiev told Winkler, 'but I was amazed that in the piece a harmonic cast prevailed, since the assemblage of a great number of contrapuntal elements would undoubtedly have been more conducive to a variety of figures and colours.'[79] Several of Prokofiev's own chamber works were performed at this conservatory concert, devaluing the worthy master Glazunov in the opinion of the institution's honorary professor Medtner; but Paris was deprived of a large-scale Prokofiev premiere when the composer decided that the *Symphonic Song* would not receive a fair or properly prepared hearing there.

He had no hopes either that this 'complicated piece of music'[80] would be understood in America, but he was surely taking a risk of a different sort by entrusting it to the Soviet mainstream. The Moscow premiere, which took place on 14 April during his next extended return to Russia, turned out to be his only serious miscalculation. Myaskovsky told Nestyev, whose view of Prokofiev's decadent errors the failure very much suited, 'there were literally three claps in the hall',[81] and *Sovietskaya muzyka* struck a warning note when it declared that it regarded the *Symphonic Song* as 'a symphonic monologue for the few, a sad tale of the decline of the fading culture of individualism'.[82] More positive was the bond Prokofiev had forged with the work's interpreters, the Moscow Radio Orchestra and Alexander Gauk. This suited him at a time when the administrative fortunes of the less impressive Moscow Philharmonic Orchestra happened to be in a state of flux, the more so as that 'very decent man'[83] Boris Gusman was his main point of contact at the Radio.

Even Gusman's generous hand could not bring all their plans to fruition. The projected *Gambler* never materialized; nor did the inclusion in the April concert of a recently completed orchestration of the Andante from the Fourth Piano Sonata, bringing this serpentine inspiration full circle to its orchestral origins as the slow movement in his youthful symphony. After the concert, in which he played his First Concerto, Prokofiev also worked on a fuller orchestration of the *Overture on Hebrew Themes*, an even less valuable exercise than the second version of the *American* Overture. Much of this he did in the garden of his friend the artist Pyotr Konchalovsky, outside Moscow, sitting in an armchair while Konchalovsky worked on his full-length portrait. The short autobiography provides its own accompanying sketch:

> 'Well, how are the Jews coming along?' Konchalovsky would ask me from time to time. 'They're making their way gradually, thanks. How about you?' 'Don't move! That's phenomenal!' Konchalovsky would suddenly shout and rapidly begin to paint. I'd sit still, trying to give my face an intelligent expression. For a while Konchalovsky would continue to concentrate on his work, and then lean back. 'What's phenomenal?' I finally decided to ask. 'The boot', replied Konchalovsky.[84]

The official stretch of Prokofiev's visit included a tour of Kharkov, Kiev and Odessa, where he told Myaskovsky he was 'enjoying the sun and the sea . . . and . . . spending my time beating the manager of the local Philharmonic at chess'.[85] He noted a 'rather low standard' throughout the Soviet musical spectrum, was disappointed at the standard of upright and grand pianos being manufactured there ('to order them from abroad is impossible for reasons of *valuta*') and noting that the Moscow orchestras were suffering from the 'poor quality of string teachers'.[86] In Moscow he saw the operatic talk of the town, Shostakovich's *The Lady Macbeth of the Mtsensk District*, which had opened at the Maly Theatre in Leningrad at the end of January and at the Nemirovich-Danchenko Theatre in Moscow only two days later. Shostakovich's musical retelling of Leskov's story, set in provincial 19th-century Russia, about a bored merchant's wife driven to passion and murder, was almost over-stocked with a prodigious range of musical ideas and styles from 1920s propagandist farce to Musorgskian tragedy and could hardly please all the people all the time. To Felix Labinsky Prokofiev was equivocal: 'in Shostakovich's opera there are a lot of interesting things, but a great deal of unpleasantness. It's good, however, that there are new methods of theatrical drama. Rodzinski and Rubinstein were, it seems, in raptures'.[87] Artur Rodzinski was to give the American premiere in Cleveland the following January; performances in Argentina, Czechoslovakia and Sweden were staged before 1935 was out. Not even *The Love for Three Oranges* was taken up so quickly. When, at the beginning of 1936, *The Lady Macbeth of the Mtsensk District* went down at the hands of Stalin in the most famous of all *Pravda* articles, the repercussions on Prokofiev and the Soviet musical establishment were to be unprecedented.

In the meantime, Prokofiev took advantage of his liberty in the new Russia with a July river trip, rekindling memories of the summer of 1917 – though the sketches for the Cello Concerto he had begun, with the skills of Gregor Piatigorsky in mind, hardly blossomed like his holiday work on the First Violin Concerto nearly two decades earlier. The piece would not take shape for another four years. Prokofiev travelled alone, as Gusman and Asafyev had changed their plans to join him. 'I made a very interesting journey', he wrote to Winkler, 'from Moscow to Ufa along five rivers: the Moscow Canal, the Oka, Volga, Kama and Bela. The steamer leaves from Moscow itself and arrives without changes at Ufa.'[88] The food served on board, which the connoisseur of the French *tour gastronomique* found excellent, seemed to have left a greater impression than the natural wonders along the way. From France there was a hint of reproach from Lina's mother that, wonderful as the effects of the Altai region must be on his health and his art, family life was suffering from the father's protracted absence and Lina's different holiday plans. In this letter to her son-in-law, written in English, 'Mémé' announced that the Meudon hosts to whom Sviatoslav and Oleg had been entrusted told her that they were 'such good bright kids . . . we know that . . . but is it not too fatal that they are left to themselves too much and no wonder "they are out of discipline". How can you expect some when at this age they are left nearly alone?'[89] It was becoming apparent that Prokofiev's ever-strengthening ties with his homeland could not continue in the form they were taking, which led to him spending longer away from Lina and the children.

Prokofiev was not to join the rest of the family at Ste-Maxime, where a second dacha in the shape of the Villa Floriana awaited, until September. In the meantime he needed the free days of July and August in Paris to finish work on the piano pieces of opp.59 and 62. The Cello Concerto, he told the expectant Myaskovsky, was 'as before, in a state of somnolence',[90] though there was tantalizing promise of a 'Dance Suite in four movements'.[91] Yet another Gusman commission, this would hang fire for even longer; of the four original movements Prokofiev planned – two Polonaises, a Mazurka and 'Dance' – three were replaced in 1950 by dance movements from the opera *Betrothal in a Monastery.*

Prokofiev had a chance to absorb the substantial latest offering of another colleague when Stravinsky played through *Perséphone,* his second, more pastel-shaded 'Rite of Spring' with the ritual this time drawn from Greek mythology and retold by André Gide. Evidently the performance, complete with Stravinsky's singing of the choruses and tenor part, was convincing, and Myaskovsky was rebuked for judging it unfavourably merely from the score. Prokofiev also paid Stravinsky a visit on his way to Ste-Maxime and found him working on his Concerto for two pianos. It was time to rekindle the question of Prokofiev's own most unusual piano concerto, the left-handed Fourth. In October he wrote to Wittgenstein, who had not come to grips with the style, reminding him of his promise to allow the material to be re-used. 'You must understand', he wrote candidly, 'how a composer suffers when a work has been buried since its birth. Although this piece didn't have the opportunity of pleasing you, I am persuaded that it has a legitimate musical value.'[92] Wittgenstein's reply goes some way to qualifying the earlier rejection ('I don't understand a single note of it and I shall not play it',[93] which Prokofiev later attributed to him in his short autobiography):

> Your concerto, or at least a considerable part of it, is not understood by me. I insist on this word. There is an enormous difference between a poem I don't like and a poem the sense of which I don't understand.
>
> In adapting it mention its source. Should in several years' time, after the version for two hands has taken place, my ears adjust themselves to your music, and should I have the desire to play this concerto in public, I should not like the public thinking it's an arrangement that I play.[94]

The pianist's parting words were, as ever, warm and friendly: 'your room here is always ready'.[95] Yet Vienna, Prokofiev reminded his colleague, 'remains indifferent for the time being to engaging me'.[96] In fact he would be there the following March, fulfilling Wittgenstein's plea to play through the concerto with him in a further attempt at understanding. Meanwhile that October Prokofiev travelled instead to Amsterdam and to London, where he was sufficiently anxious to shed his reputation as an *enfant terrible* and to be embraced as a 'composer of music that is lyrical, dramatic, human'[97] by risking his own interpretation of the Third Symphony. Proving that England was as behind the times as ever, perhaps, the *Times* critic preferred the movements from *Chout* which shared the programme: 'the witty trifler is to be preferred to the full-fledged symphonist . . . M. Prokofiev thrives on irresponsibility'.[98] Yet at least the BBC had shown enterprise in launching a new season of contemporary music invitation concerts with this all-Prokofiev event. There was still no shortage of adventurous concert engagements in the West. All Prokofiev missed was the bigger picture, and that, it seemed, only the Soviet Union could provide.

15
The path to happiness
1934–5

The Soviet Union to which Prokofiev returned via the Baltic in the late autumn of 1934 had taken one step further towards artistic regimentation. In August the Union of Soviet Writers had held its first conference, and to prove that the proletarian puppies were no longer barking, its members had appointed the newly returned elder statesman Maxim Gorky as chairman. The drive towards what would soon take shape as 'socialist realism' now entered a curiously conservative phase: the greater glories of contemporary Soviet writing were supposed to be rooted in a truly international people's literature. Dickens, Stendhal and Twain were high on the list of admissible recent classics; Shakespeare and Molière led the way. At the same time, experimental writers such as Proust and Joyce were denounced. Falling into the latter category was *1919*, a novel by an American of the so-called 'Lost Generation', John Dos Passos. Curiously Asafyev was still recommending it to Prokofiev on his latest visit as the theme of a possible opera. 'It's interesting', came the response, 'but there's not quite enough material. I'll have to return to the subject in the autumn, when I'll be going to America and can discuss the subject with the author.'[1] Because his trip was postponed to a time when the Soviet attitude to such themes would be all too clear, the subject was never raised again.

Composers now had literary guidelines which would affect their choice of subjects for the theatre but which could hardly be applied specifically to the way they composed. With the dissolution of RAPM, as one wag put it, they could write in metres other than march time; but new rules had to appear. The climate offered Prokofiev a good opportunity for making a pre-emptive strike and expounding on what he thought – and quite genuinely, as the echoes of his earlier words to Olin Downes suggest – was necessary. This seminal article, which appeared in *Izvestiya* shortly after Prokofiev's arrival, is worth quoting at length:

> What is needed above all is *great* music, in other words music that would correspond both in form and content to the grandeur of the epoch. Such music would

be a stimulus to our own musical development, and abroad too it would reveal our true selves. The danger of becoming provincial is unfortunately a very real one for modern Soviet composers.

At the same time in turning his attention to serious, significant music, the composer must bear in mind that in the Soviet Union music is addressed to millions of people who formerly had little or no contact with music. It is this new mass audience that the modern Soviet composer must attempt to reach.

I believe the type of music needed is what one might call 'light-serious' or 'serious-light' music. It is by no means easy to find the right idiom for such music. It should be primarily melodious, and the melody should be clear and simple without however becoming repetitive or trivial. Many composers find it difficult enough to compose any sort of melody, let alone a melody having some definite function to perform. The same applies to the technique, the form – it too must be clear and simple, but not stereotyped. It is not the old simplicity that is needed, but a new kind of simplicity. And this can be achieved only after the composer has mastered the art of composing serious, significant music, thereby acquiring the technique of expressing himself in simple, yet original terms.[2]

The application of this to Prokofiev's own music becomes explicit when he mentions the ill-favoured offerings of his previous visit, the *Symphonic Song* and the suite from *Sur le Borysthène*, as the 'serious, significant music' which had made the 'light-serious' development possible. Prokofiev certainly had no intention of denouncing as cerebral the works he had recently completed in the West, and in correcting the facile views of a writer for the Boston *Christian Science Monitor* the following March, he reiterated the stance he had always held on the shock of the new:

The difficulty to be understood right away by the public is the cross which everyone who wants to speak new things must bear. And the consolation is that most of the composers who are recognised now as classical ones had to meet the same obstacle. This barrier grows when the composer, instead of the external pageantry of effect or orchestration, looks for a deeper expression of thought; when a stone immerges in the deep, the eye follows it with difficulty.[3]

Some kind of broad apology also had to be implied in the *Izvestiya* article for the earlier Second Symphony and even the Second Piano Concerto, both conducted by Alexander Gauk with the composer as soloist in the first radio concert of his visit, on 30 November (the programme also included the fully orchestrated version of the *Overture on Hebrew Themes*). His hors d'oeuvres in the new vein, the *Egyptian Nights* and *Lieutenant Kijé* suites, followed on 21 December when he conducted their first broadcast performances. Yet their subjects hardly permitted '*great* music' in the article's sense, and still less could this be said of Tairov's decadent entertainment prompted by the high style of Alisa Koonen's Cleopatra, which finally reached the stage a week before the radio premiere of the suite. It was an enormous success with artistic Moscow, and over a month later Tairov was to send a telegram to Prokofiev with news of its continuing triumph – 'ovation 20 minutes. Much personal applause to you'.[4]

This would not be enough, as it turned out, to satisfy the cultural commissars (the show's excellent run was soon to be wiped from the records) and it was probably just as well that in his article Prokofiev promised music that would be understood in the Soviet Union to 'correspond . . . to the grandeur of the epoch', mentioning the 'collective farm songs I am now working on for the Moscow Radio Committee'.[5] One of these, added as part of op.66 to the four 'mass songs' he would compose for a *Pravda* competition the following summer, was *Za goroyu* ('Beyond the Hill'). Its setting is effective enough: a simple alternation of a sprightly polka, introduced by a characteristically elliptical harmonic sideslip, and a more reflective minor passage with the piano doubling the vocal part in soulful octaves. The Belorussian text, though, inevitably leads one to wonder what Prokofiev knew of the many millions who died in the terror-famine inflicted by Stalin's policies in the early 1930s. 'In the past there was no freedom, no joy', sings the rosy-cheeked girl in the song's sudden change of mood. The piano pauses to meditate, but the cheerful dance song returns: 'Now all that has changed. Now that I am a collective farm worker, I am treated as a human being'.

When it came to his first major work for the Soviet stage, however, Prokofiev was still not ready for a contemporary theme – or perhaps it was a matter of the kind of audience the major theatres wanted to attract. At the beginning of 1934 he freed Malko's wife, Berta Israelevich, from her commitment to *Telescope*, a contemporary story about a professor working on a meteorological station in the middle of Russia, since he had come to the conclusion 'that a ballet for the Bolshoy has to be written "resplendently", with velvet costumes. Otherwise the public won't come'.[6] Moscow's chief opera house had always been the bastion of conservatism; but even in Leningrad the time of Shostakovich's *The Age of Gold* and *The Bolt* had long since passed. Two period-piece ballets had come to nothing. The prospect of a Prokofiev *Till Eulenspiegel* interpreted from the Soviet point of view at Akopera 'turned out interesting', the composer told Malko in the summer of 1933, 'but I didn't want to get down to a ballet';[7] and another possibility of exploiting the *Kijé* era with Paul I as its subject could, he wrote to Gusman, 'either be very pleasing or rather displeasing; it depends on what angle you take'.[8] His angle tended to be the latter. The bait he finally swallowed for a velvet-clad drama came on his latest visit when a new friend, the theatre critic and classicist Adrian Pyotrovsky, suggested Shakespeare's *Romeo and Juliet*.

The ideal director to help them create a full-length ballet, it seemed, would be Sergey Radlov, whose Leningrad production of *The Love for Three Oranges* Prokofiev had so admired in 1927. It had recently returned to the repertory with new dances staged by Radlov's former student Rostislav Zakharov, which suggests that although Meyerhold had not been able to lay his hands on Diky's Moscow production and to add interludes bringing it more into line with the modern theatre, as he had intended, his star pupil Radlov had borne in mind some of his advice. As a director of spoken drama, Radlov had been way ahead of officially approved Shakespeare with a 1927 production of *Othello* at the State Drama (formerly Alexandrinsky) Theatre – Meyerhold declared that in Radlov's 1935 Maly Theatre version he had 'absolutely ruined the original text'[9] – and Prokofiev saw the *Romeo and Juliet* he directed for his own Studio Theatre in 1934. He also knew of his diligent work on Asafyev's two ballets *The Flames of Paris*, for which he had himself spent much time in research on old French tunes in Paris libraries, and the Pushkin-based *Fountain of Bakhchisaray*. Unfortunately the director who had been so free with Shakespeare's Moor of Venice wanted rather too much scrupulous faithfulness to the original *Romeo and Juliet*. An early draft for the ballet scenario calls for 24 scene changes, culminating in the presences of Paris, Laurence and Balthazar at the tomb scene as well as an eminently undanceable final benediction from the Friar (embraced wholeheartedly by Berlioz at the end of his 'dramatic symphony' *Roméo et Juliette*, which became so popular in 19th-century Russia). It would take a great deal of literary collaboration between Radlov and Prokofiev over the next five months before a structure to both their likings could be created.

Political events also overshadowed the partnership. On 1 December the party's first secretary for Leningrad, Sergey Kirov, was murdered inside its Smolny headquarters. His assassin was a member of a terrorist group in opposition to Stalin; it now appears, however, that Soviet security had been complicit in allowing the attack to go ahead. In the long term it signalled an advertised campaign against terrorism which would itself become the 'Terror', a purging of all the major institutions on an unprecedented scale. The immediate consequence of Kirov's assassination was to cripple the relative independence of Leningrad's administrative and artistic life from the Moscow power base. Kirov's replacement was the plenipotentiary Andrey Zhdanov, a leading architect of the terror to come and a name inseparable from the awful events of 1948. The State Academic Theatre, which had been the proposed home for *Romeo and Juliet* and which Prokofiev had continued to call by its imperial title of the Maryinsky, now took the name of Kirov; at the end of 1934 Radlov, who had recently worked there on works as diverse as Wagner's *Das Rheingold*, Verdi's *Il trovatore* and Tchaikovsky's *Swan Lake*, was announced in the press as having been 'relieved of his post as artistic director . . . on his request'.[10]

Prokofiev clearly worried about the implications for his relationships in the city once he had left Russia at the end of the year, and in January Myaskovsky relayed news from Asafyev that 'in the circles of the Leningrad [Composers'] Association (and wherever it – the association – can exert influence: the Philharmonia and above all the theatres) they fear you terribly and will do everything they possibly can to exclude you'.[11] Asafyev's belief, Myaskovsky continued, was that 'your projects for productions at the Mar[yinsky] Theatre are built on sand, and that you're still spoiling your chances all the more in trying for productions of your other former compositions (for example, *St[alnoy] skok*)'.[12] Although Prokofiev advanced no further with his next contact, the 'decent'[13] Vladimir Yokhelson of Malegot, he pinned his hopes on the Bolshoy to step into the breach. Intelligence of such unexpected animosity, though, did not bode well.

There was still no time to stop. A whirlwind European tour in the bitter cold of early January took Prokofiev to Budapest, where it was 'pleasing to conduct a real orchestra, which responds to each stroke of the baton as a good piano does to the application of a finger'.[14] His good fortunes in Prague, where he appeared on 11 January, were soon to be underlined by a concert in his absence, when the 26-year-old Karel Ančerl wrote to him about the 'big success'[15] of the Third Symphony and told him he would gladly conduct the Second; Prokofiev's reply discouraged him from tackling this 'even more complicated'[16] work and suggested that he look first at the *Symphonic Song* or the Sinfonietta. The January tour also took him for the first time to Yugoslavia, where a 13-hour delay in the snow resulted in a madcap dash from train to concert hall.

Prokofiev had to pay even more attention to some of his shorter pieces back in Paris than he had on the road. Another proposal from Coppola led him to submit once more to the inflexible discipline of the gramophone; and, he wrote to Myaskovsky in an expanded echo of his previous apprehension of 1932, 'during the four minutes that the disc is being made you can't afford to hit one wrong note'.[17] During negotiations he had told Fred Gaisberg of HMV that the pieces most popular with the public were 'very short . . . Shall I play two or three for each face? And would it not be wise to put on the opposite face a more serious piece, in order to popularize it by the attraction of the first face?'[18]

Although this procedure was not adopted consistently, the eight recorded sides struck a fine balance between light and serious, with emphasis on a delicacy of touch which had not been easily represented by the Duo-Art system; nor had it been much in evidence for the London recording of the Third Concerto. Prokofiev's selection of *Visions fugitives*, recorded at the initial session on 12 February for the first of the four 78s, emphasizes the evanescent, with harp-like filigree at the heart of no.9, easy rubato that lends a vital quality of improvisation and surprisingly liberal use of the sustaining pedal for poetic chiaroscuro. The four visions that flank the plangently chromatic no.16 on the second side focus more on the drier wit of the series, but even these disappear into thin air with the quick-witted epigrams of the sixth and (to conclude) fifth pieces. Refined poetry resurfaces in the second *Grandmother's Tale* and two of Prokofiev's most recent and transparent works, the *Pastoral Sonatina* and *Landscape* from op.59. The more complex numbers seem to bother the composer-pianist less than a slightly precipitate Gavotte from the *Classical* Symphony; the op.52 *Étude* adapted from the plunder scene in *The Prodigal Son*, which he told Myaskovsky the day before the recording 'would be hot labour',[19] suggests quite the opposite in its effortless, even toccata flow. He saved his most extended effort for the last session on 5 March, the Andante from the Fourth Sonata split over two sides with the op.32 Gavotte to conclude; as with his recording of the *Suggestion diabolique*, the most demanding passages of the Andante are propelled at an alarming rate towards climaxes where the tempo is then more broadly articulated.

These were good performances and he knew it. 'I did my work with much attention and perseverance', he wrote to Gaisberg, 'and I hope that the result from the standpoint of playing will be satisfactory.'[20] But, he continued, the sound left a certain amount to be desired:

> When, after these records, I heard those of Rachmaninoff playing with Stokowski, or of Horowitz, made in London – almost as good, I found that the piano in my records sounds 'comme une casserole'. I do not know to what it should be attributed, for the Steinway piano on which I recorded was bad (dry) only in the upper octaves, but I think your Paris recording department should earnestly work to attain for the piano the same acceptable quality of sound which was already, and several years ago, obtained in other cities.
>
> I hope you will accept these friendly remarks in the same friendly way, for they are encompassing our mutual interests.[21]

Indeed, Gaisberg did, though he assured Prokofiev that Paris had 'the same technical equipment as our Abbey Road studio';[22] and to our ears the sound is good for its time, in transparency if inevitably not in the weighty sonorities necessary for the *Suggestion diabolique*.

Travelling to Moscow in March with Albert Wolff's recording of movements from *Chout* as one of his gifts (a shortage of gramophone needles would be remedied by Lina's arrival in April) he had asked Gusman to solve the continuing problem of the inadequate pianos he had been playing recently and to meet him at the station. During his week in the capital he was delighted as ever to watch his old colleagues Capablanca and Lasker in action at the Second International Chess Tournament. He also spent time, as usual, with Myaskovsky, and drafted a grateful letter in English on his friend's behalf, asking the trusty Stock to accept the dedication of the Thirteenth Symphony – Myaskovsky's best to date, Prokofiev thought – accompanied by 'the gratitude that we Russian composers owe to you for the frequent performances of our compositions'.[23] Stock, who had recently conducted Prokofiev's Third Symphony in Chicago to hostile reviews, now represented a dwindling band of conductors in America whose Russian interests extended beyond Stravinsky. Haensel had already reported 'deplorable results' in trying to fix Prokofiev's next American tour: 'we have four men on the road and they report absolutely no interest in you whatsoever and they seem unable to stir any up'.[24] His loyal artist was not about to give in: 'the affairs are not brilliant indeed, but bad is the soldier who does not defend his position. And, although your proposition to give me up for excess of love and respect on my behalf is certainly very laudable, I will be insistent in asking you to continue your feeble efforts to do something for me, at least for the next season'.[25] He eventually shrugged off his American prospects for 1935 when his New York dates hung fire: Walter was slow in signing a contract and Koussevitzky's usual offer did not on this occasion extend beyond his Boston base.

In the meantime there was further evidence of just how appreciative a wider audience might be. He saw for himself the educational benefits still fostered by the communists when he travelled beyond the Urals to the newly developed industrial towns of Sverdlovsk and Chelyabinsk. His appearances included a lecture-recital at the University of Musical Culture attached to the Uralmash tractor assembly plant; and in a special morning programme he had his first taste of the possibilities for children's music. 'Seven concerts in eight days is a little too much', he wrote to the man who had been guiding him in his latest Christian Science studies, Lawrence Creath Ammons, 'but there were many interesting things to be seen. Cities in this region consist of one or two stories [*sic*] houses, squat and squalid, but now they are building entirely new blocks with large buildings trying to scrape the skies'.[26] Prokofiev's interest in these manifestations of Soviet progress was characteristic and, again, there was no need to manufacture his sentiments in his article 'On Soviet Music and the Worker Audience' for *Vechernaya Moskva*. 'I must say', he wrote, 'that the workers of Chelyabinsk have shown much more interest in the programme than some sophisticated audiences in western Europe and American cities.'[27]

This was evidence that the increased time he was spending in the Soviet Union brought personal rewards not to be expected elsewhere; another was the confirmation of the *Romeo and Juliet* project, which now settled under the wing of the Bolshoy (though it seems throughout the year that Prokofiev still had hopes for the Kirov's involvement). Once he had steered Radlov's diffuse scenario in the direction he wanted that May, the urgent nature of the commission demanded an extended spell of quiet, persistent work. At the beginning of June he told Gottlieb that 'in order to finish this ballet in time I will not go to Paris'.[28] At first this prospect seemed to leave the family in the lurch. Lina's brief visit to Russia in April had been preceded by poignant communications from the children. Sviatoslav wrote of how desolate he had been when he went to the wrong station platform to see his father on his way to Russia; Oleg, who was now an eager correspondent, added his own distinctive voice: 'I write this to tell you how I always think of you. When we went to the station my brother came to say goodbye but the train had already left. My brother started to crie [*sic*] I embraced him'.[29] The summers had always been a time for family holidays as well as hard work. Matters were complicated in June by the death of Lina's father, leaving needy 'Mémé' understandably distraught.

Nevertheless a crucial decision had to be taken. It was decided that Lina would take the boys to Russia at the end of July. Thanks to the ever more attentive care of the state for its artists, the natural beauties the family had always enjoyed would be provided. 'I will stay at the estate of the Bolshoy Theatre', Prokofiev told Gottlieb, 'where artists and people connected with the theatre are having their vacations. It is a beautiful place on the river Oka. I will have there a tiny bungalow (a kind of *izba*) with a piano, so that nobody will disturb me there.'[30] The centre of the estate was the house of the artist Vasily Polenov, with a museum administered by his son and accommodation big and small for the visiting artists. It was an exciting prospect for the Prokofiev boys, and they were not to be disappointed. 'I'll be so glad to come and see you in Russia', wrote Sviatoslav a week before the journey. 'We'll swim together, play volley-ball and tennis.'[31] He remembers well the circumstances of his first trip to the Soviet Union:

> The train was half-empty, so we ran across the wagons. When we arrived in Moscow, we stayed in the Hotel National. It was interesting to me because at that time they were destroying the old houses between the hotel and the Kremlin. I remember meeting my father's relatives, because the youngest of Shurik and Nadya's three daughters was my age, and we could understand each other quite well . . . Then we went to Polenovo in an old open-top car with a chauffeur, and the road was very bad; it had been raining heavily and the car kept lurching sideways through the mud. But once we reached Polenovo all was well. I made special friends with Polenov's grandson Fedya – Fyodor – who has recently become the administrator.[32]

It is amazing, under circumstances which also included a flying visit to sweltering Baku in August after he had been reunited with the family, that Prokofiev managed to compose the entire piano score of *Romeo and Juliet*, and so much more besides, that summer; but with his usual clockwork precision he achieved his objectives: the first two acts by 22 July, the rest by 8 September well in time for an audition at the Bolshoy in early October. The orchestration followed at the incredible speed of 20 pages a day: 'It is difficult', he admitted to Myaskovsky, 'and the main thing is to avoid falling into "Asafyevism", the path of least resistance'.[33]

The scenario from which he worked at Polenovo, marking the numbers with a black cross for 'conceived in principle' and a red for 'composed and copied down', had been much modified from the choreographic nightmare proposed by Radlov at the beginning of the year.[34] Prokofiev's handwritten draft of 16 May contains all the numbers and scene divisions we know today with the exception of half a dozen set pieces added for the Kirov production in 1939 (these include the lively dance skirmish, no.4, in Act I scene 1, and Juliet's variation in Act I scene 2). The structure of the May groundplan was now much simplified: a street scene and ballroom for Act I (with optional extra decor for Juliet's bedroom and the garden at night), a lively civic divertissement and the fatal fight flanking the marriage in the friar's cell for Act II, the chamber music of Juliet's bedroom broken only by her visit to the friar in Act III, and a greatly clarified dénouement in the Capulet vault for Act IV (or 'Epilogue'). It is astonishing to think that this still included a happy ending along the lines of Nahum Tate's *King Lear*, in which Cordelia lives to spare her old father's heartbreak, or the first Russian performance in 1750 of *Hamlet*, where everything ends in Hamlet's marriage to Ophelia. In what is, sadly, the last entertaining digression of his short autobiography, Prokofiev explained:

> In the last act Romeo was to arrive a minute earlier and find Juliet alive, so all ended well. The reason for this barbarism being perpetrated was purely choreographic: living people can dance, the dying can't do it so easily prone . . . It is interesting that, while in London the fact that Prokofiev was writing a ballet on *Romeo and Juliet* with a 'happy ending' [he uses the English phrase] was received with simple verification, our own Shakespeare scholars proved more holy than the Pope and rushed to the defence of Shakespeare. I was, however, influenced in a different way. It was when someone said: 'essentially, in your music there's no real happiness at the end' – and this was true.[35]

It is difficult to imagine how there could have been any real happiness when the complex of themes Prokofiev gives his star-crossed lovers, undergoing a development he had not brought into play since the retrospective framework of *The Fiery Angel*, conveys a sense of tragedy from the start. In a score which in some ways reflects the new spirit of Stalin's era by referring backwards in the Russian tradition, the lyric model of Tchaikovsky's fantasy overture *Romeo and Juliet* is subtly suggested. The love-sigh which goes straight to the heart in Prokofiev's introduction (Ex.68*a*) lands on an interval familiar from Tchaikovsky (Ex.68*b*). Later, when love blossoms (Ex.69*a*), Prokofiev evokes another inescapable example, the hyper-poetical love scene from Berlioz's dramatic symphony and the poetic turn of its central phrase (Ex.69*b*), with a more clearly defined triplet figure the equivalent of Berlioz's romantic appoggiatura. Letting fresh air into the romantic portraits at the heart of the ballet are two of Juliet's

Ex.68*a* *Romeo and Juliet*, op.64 – no.1. Introduction

Ex.68*b* Tchaikovsky, *Romeo and Juliet*

themes, both showing that Prokofiev has by no means exhausted the diatonic vein of the 'girl in white' from *Sur le Borysthène.* The first immediately offsets the lovesickness at the start of the prelude; the second, its essence luminously outlined by the two flutes at the heart of 'Juliet the young girl', is implicated in a minor-key version with the potential danger of her taking poison in Act III.

Ex.69*a* *Romeo and Juliet* – Act I no.21. Love dance

Ex.69*b* Berlioz, *Roméo et Juliette* – III. Love scene

Inevitably the love music and its tragic outcome are the heart and soul of *Romeo and Juliet.* Prokofiev serves them with all the increased sophistication of his orchestral palette, using muted and *divisi* strings more carefully than ever in the balcony scene and running to a poetic sequence of instrumental solos in the fragile mood of Act III; it is hardly surprising that the dancers were taken aback several years later in 1938 when Kirov rehearsals moved from piano accompaniment to a not-so-full orchestra. Yet Shakespeare's dramatic world calls for so much more. Tchaikovsky reduced the contrasts to a doomy Russian Orthodox Friar Laurence and rhythmically charged swashbuckling for the main Allegro of his sonata-form movement; Prokofiev's equivalents are the cowled, more noble contours of his restrained friar and the string toccata when the fight blazes. He was also able to bring into play the dissonances of his earlier years with the licence of a more recent example: the blaring discords as the Duke of Verona outlaws civic uproar, heard again as the fateful introduction to the third act, surely owe something to the shattering blast that launches the Passacaglia at the dark heart of Shostakovich's *Lady Macbeth of the Mtsensk District*; to that example, too, can be ascribed the onstage band which bolsters the pomposity of the duke's processional and which marches across the stage in Act II. Mercutio brings with him not the featherlight fantasy of Berlioz's scherzo on the speech 'Mab, queen of dreams' but Truffaldino's somersaults in *The Love for Three Oranges* and the angular trumpet solos of the Fifth Piano Concerto. The vivid physical gestures of earlier stage works live again in the Nurse's purposeful bustle, the formal steps of Juliet's dance with Paris and the striding violence of the knights at the Capulets' ball. There is also the sheer pleasure of piquant orchestral combinations in the more incidental dances, continuing the novelties of scoring in Tchaikovsky's *Sleeping Beauty* and *Nutcracker*: who but Prokofiev could have combined trumpet and violin solos with mandolin ensemble so effectively?

From a showcase score with no lapses of invention in its three-hour span, selecting music for an orchestral suite was going to be especially difficult. Prokofiev decided to make two (a third was assembled much later) and brought his usual creativity to the task, a particularly important one as a work on this scale was even less likely to tread the worldwide stage over the next few years than the one-act ballets for Diaghilev (and by September 1935 Eugene Ormandy in Philadelphia was already inquiring about a concert version). It was not simply a matter of new orchestration and different juxtapositions, such as the chords of the duke's command placed before the knights' dance to give a composite picture of the violence between Montagues and Capulets. Some symphonic shaping was also desirable: 'Romeo and Juliet before parting', for instance, fuses five of the Act III numbers to make a powerful Adagio. Prokofiev's ordering can seem random, and those conductors who have been most successful in their choice of a concert sequence have tended to juggle the suites with the complete score.

The suites, at any rate, were to spread the ballet's fame during the late 1930s while the Bolshoy hung fire. The audition of the complete score on 4 October 1935, in the

Beethoven Hall of the Bolshoy Theatre, seemed an auspicious affair; many of the leading cultural figures in Moscow were there to hear the composer's full-length preview of his score. 'Prokofiev plays like a real virtuoso', wrote the great writer Mikhail Bulgakov's third wife Yelena in her diary. 'There are marvellous sections in the music'.[36] Unfortunately many of the theatre's dancers and music staff did not agree; with the inherent conservativism maintained by most figurehead ballet companies throughout the world, they doubted if this bold and various score was innately danceable. The events of 1936 would decisively bolster their doubts.

Much other work from the incredibly fertile Polenovo summer of 1935 was destined for more immediate exposure. Prokofiev needed to show willing on the populist front he was supposed to be supporting – not least to further the ballet's chances with the now hostile organizations in Leningrad – and he duly composed his latest 'mass songs' for a competition arranged by *Pravda*. With the poets he had set in so many of his earlier songs now frowned upon by the authorities, there was an added incentive to provide more acceptable examples. The new texts by Alexander Afinogenov and Mikhail Golodny inevitably called for songlines that were more square and solid than any Prokofiev had composed to date; but the masculine dotted rhythms of the marches *Partizan Zheleznyak* and the more varied, narrative *Skvoz snega i tumany* ('Through Snow and Fog') are at least strongly contrasted with the feminine polka of *Anyutka*, which sits more honourably in the Musorgsky tradition. Inevitably Prokofiev was most attracted to the sentiments of *Rastyot strana* ('My Country is Growing'), where a tender meditation on the passing of time provides a tolling minor refrain to the cheerful prospects of Sovet progress; the decisive farewell to 'comrade youth' is marked by reversing the procedure in the third verse, allowing the song to end optimistically with the thought that 'we'll be young even with grey temples'. Although this number later entered the song repertory, chiefly through the wife–husband partnership of Nina Dorliak and Sviatoslav Richter, it was to receive no more than an honorary mention in the admonitory *Pravda* prize-giving of 1936. By then, of course, the paper had already done its worst to music through the famous attack on *The Lady Macbeth of the Mtsensk District*. *Anyutka* won second prize; there was no first. Nestyev tells us that there were no fewer than 400 settings of *Partizan Zheleznyak* alone. The next time Prokofiev returned to approved texts, in the anniversary cantata commissioned by the ever-reliable Moscow Radio as early as the autumn of 1935, there would be more between the lines, and much less to please the all-powerful Committee for Artistic Affairs.

Far less tailored to official specifications than the competition songs were his other modest offerings of the summer. His first brass-band piece, the *March for the Spartakiad*, is a reminder both of the vigorous physical disciplines he had undertaken at the St Petersburg Sokol and the lively marches of his youth which the late, lamented Mayakovsky, who had committed suicide in 1930, once welcomed as the progressive spirit of the times. The *March for the Spartakiad* brings to life the athleticism it serves with an energy that is never bland. Prokofiev stamps his own insolent personality in the opening measures, rounding off the phrase with an individuality that only Shostakovich among his Soviet colleagues could equal (Ex.70). Nestyev, of course, implies a criticism when he remarks that 'save for some harsh chords in the cadences, the harmonies are bright and firm throughout';[37] the unexpected harsh cadence is what will give so many of Prokofiev's Soviet scores their special flavour.

Ex.70 *March for the Spartakiad*, op.69 no.1

Cheerfulness and energy were the qualities Prokofiev told Gorky he thought a national music needed at this time. 'But we also need a sincere and tender music', came the elder statesman's famous reply.[38] That is the prevailing tone of Prokofiev's next commission, from the Soviet publishing house Muzgiz. The 12 pieces that make up his *Detskaya muzyka* ('Music for Children') are, as their most poetic interpreter Frederic Chiu has pointed out, 'the final volume of his "little dogs"'.[39] Inevitably the same forms are invoked – tarantella, march, waltz – though the challenge now is to convey the maximum musical thought with the minimum notes. The models are Schumann's *Kinderszenen* and Tchaikovsky's *Album for the Young*; the piquancy is Prokofiev's own, co-existing with what was for him a new vein of impressionistic tenderness. Bright reflections of a summer's day at Polenovo help the music flow more easily: fun and games with Sviatoslav, pensive Oleg watching his father at work, the moon rising over the water-meadows of the Oka in the evening (the composer's avowed model for the simple sonatina epilogue) all find a limpid reflection here. Major triads and arpeggios at the extreme ends of the piano provide the framework; single lines in both hands govern the main themes of *Promenade, Little Story, The Moon Strolls in the Meadows* and the whole of the Tarantella up to the last two chords. But young pianists will also be able to enjoy the characteristics of Prokofiev's mature style; apart from the unexpected clusters of the odd-man-out *Rain and the Rainbow*, an errant *Vision fugitive*, there is a modicum of deft harmonic sideslips, melodies played in unison doublings two octaves apart (in the surprisingly bleak *Repentance*) and occasional 'wrong' notes as in the clashes of

G/flat F and A sharp/B in the otherwise serene melody of *Evening* (Ex.71). One can well imagine teachers reaching across to correct a pupil, only to find the 'mistake' written into the music. Above all *Music for Children* sounds good on the piano, even in its sparest numbers; Prokofiev's orchestration of seven numbers in 1946 as *Letny den* ('Summer Day') can only muddy clear waters.

Ex.71 *Music for Children*, op.65 – XI. Evening

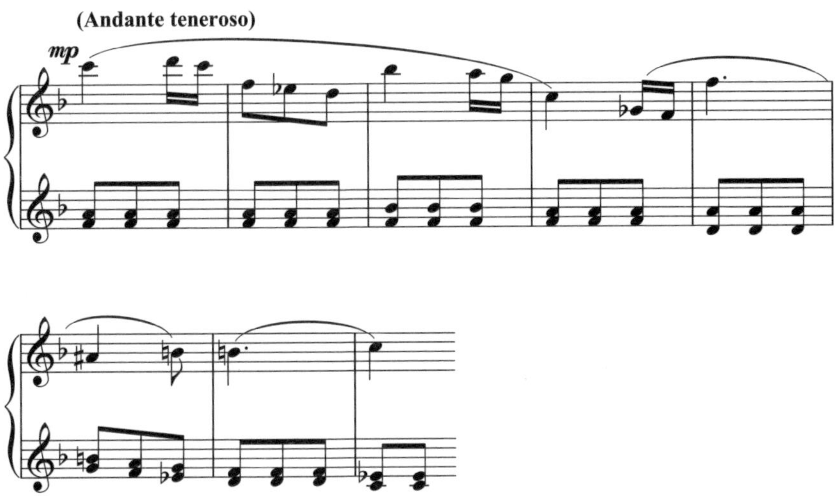

One final, major score of 1935 has frequently been classified as a straightforward product of Prokofiev's new Soviet-style tunefulness when in many ways it is last in the line of the ambiguous works belonging to the later Paris period. The Second Violin Concerto was commissioned, earlier in the year, by admirers of the French-Belgian violinist Robert Soetens who, along with Samuel Dushkin, had played the Sonata for two violins in the *Triton* inaugural concert and who was happy to oblige Prokofiev by championing the Sonata elsewhere, including London, during 1933. In return Prokofiev had been his usual diligent self in arranging Soetens concert dates and visas for Soviet appearances. Dushkin now had his own, distinctive concerto from Stravinsky, and Soetens was to own a year's exclusivity on Prokofiev's new work – which freed the composer from having to think of any immediate impact on Soviet audiences. It is true that the principal themes of the first and second movements, jotted down in Paris and Voronezh respectively before an obvious home could be found for them, offer fine examples of the distinctive melodies Prokofiev had written about in his *Izvestia* article; but they were to take surprising shape, and austere orchestral clothing, by the concerto's completion. Prokofiev had originally planned a more modest scale for his second work for violin and orchestra; on 23 May 1935 he had written to Soetens to tell him that the 'sketches for the concertino are finished, but I'd prefer to put off a private execution until the autumn'.[40] He completed the orchestration in Baku that summer and begged Soetens, who was due to follow in his footsteps there, to come and visit him in Polenovo: 'it's a charming place and we could work in peace'.[41] There was some urgency: the premiere, intended for Paris, was fixed instead for Madrid at the beginning of December.

Prokofiev had two priorities for the character of the new concerto. One had served him well for its predecessor, the essence of which he had recently outlined to Alexander Moskovsky: 'lyrical thoughts preceded virtuosity'.[42] The other was that he wanted to 'make it completely different from no.1 in terms of both music and style'.[43] This goes some way to accounting for the spare and wintry opening: no radiant soloistic dream against ethereal string tremolos, as in the first concerto, but a sombre, unaccompanied G minor song starting in the violin's lower register. Both the irregular metre – a repeated five-beat phrase at the start – and the contours of the meditative descent from the peak of the phrase give it a Russian cast (Ex.72). The lean, dark quality is intensified by muted violas and basses taking up the theme in B minor. The orchestration is spare throughout: apart from strings and double woodwind, Prokofiev calls only for two horns, two trumpets and a selective array of percussion which can be played by one musician. There are occasional reminders of the Stravinsky concerto and its unorthodox ensembles: some time after the lower instruments have taken up the opening theme at a sinister jog-trot in the development, with eggshell-treading violin elaboration, flutes and bassoons weave stark unisons (at fig.13 of the score) reminiscent of a passage in Stravinsky's third movement, and a pompous brass ensemble in the Andante assai briefly evokes the opening of Stravinsky's work.

Prokofiev's own brand of lyricism is hardly in short supply, but usually goes hand in hand with some undermining agent. The pure E flat major second subject of the opening Allegro assai has often been likened to the *Romeo and Juliet* love music; but the first horn foreshadows it with a rather baleful version, and leads this variant to briefly tragic heights in the development. Even the singing slow movement is surprisingly disingenuous. The tension here lies between the coolly beautiful violin melody in 4/4 and its 12/8 pizzicato accompaniment, given an empty, mechanical twist by the hollow intervals of the two staccato clarinets. Distant thunder on the bass drum, unusually exposed throughout the concerto, dogs the violin's ecstatic elaboration at the end of the movement, and the theme dies out abruptly on first clarinet and double basses. Most curious of the intervening episodes is another tense

Ex.72 Violin Concerto no.2, op.63 – I. Allegro moderato

Allegro moderato

mp

idea stuck in semitonal grooves, with nagging passage-work from the soloist. There is plenty of dark fantasy in the finale, too, held together for as long as possible by the stamping dance with which the violinist launches the movement. Castanets grace the refrains, perhaps a late concession to the Madrid premiere; but the dogged determination of this ritual brings to mind the darker side of the Spanish temperament and the opening lines of Federico García Lorca's *Malagueña*, one of the poems set many years after Prokofiev's concerto by Shostakovich in his Symphony no.14 of 1969: 'Death/Moves in and out/Of the tavern'. Certainly the way in which it is undermined and whirled to its tumultuous close by a virtuoso display provides a grim kind of comedy – more dance of death than soloistic extravagance.

Storm clouds were gathering over Spain as Prokofiev attended the premiere on 1 December, and when the Spanish Civil War finally broke the following year, he would be happy to bolster Soviet support for the Republicans with an enthusiastic retrospective article, praising widespread Spanish curiosity in Soviet institutions. His immediate concern, however, was for the fate of his latest progeny in the hands of Soetens and the distinguished conductor Enrique Arbós. 'It gave me complete satisfaction', he told Myaskovsky, 'since it all sounded even better than I'd thought it would when I was orchestrating it, wilting from the heat in stifling Baku. The outward success of the performance was also great – the music somehow or other came across.'[44] Arbós, who in his 70s still showed a keen interest in the music of such younger-generation compatriots as Falla and Turina, later sent him reviews with his own heartfelt footnote: 'I can tell you it was a great joy to get to know your magnificent concerto which is very much the expression of a sincere and elevated art'.[45]

The premiere was preceded by Prokofiev's recitals in Madrid, Barcelona, San Sebastian and sunny Lisbon, where he was surprised to find that 'they aren't even too afraid of new music'.[46] Then he plunged into a hectic three-week tour of North Africa with Soetens. The repertoire took him beyond his usual parameters as a performer, since Soetens wanted Prokofiev to partner him in sonatas by Debussy and Beethoven. This led to a demand for two-thirds of the joint fee 'because I never play the works of other composers – and it's already a concession'.[47] In the end he conquered the Debussy sonata and was surprised to find the music-lovers of Algiers already well acquainted with a perfectly good performance of his Quintet. As the schedule also allowed for several sightseeing excursions, there was time to sharpen the perception which Prokofiev usually enjoyed in experiencing unfamiliar places. He liked the area round Marrakesh, visited the old Muslim town of Fez from the new city of the same name where he was performing and travelled to Carthage from Tunis, the duo's last port of call, on 20 December. 'Tunis is not so interesting', he told Myaskovsky, 'but Carthage certainly is – a few kilometres away from it there is a very impressive spot where Hannibal lost his last battle, after which the Romans destroyed Carthage. As a result the ruins to be seen are mostly of Roman origin; of old Carthage all that's left are kitchen utensils and graves.'[48]

There would be a reunion with Soetens in the near future. The next stop, however, was altogether more important. His objective, he wrote to Gottlieb, was 'to join Mrs. Prokofieff in Moscow for the New Year's Eve'.[49] The new year would see the family at last uproot itself from Paris to settle in the Soviet Union, where Prokofiev was to spend more time in 1936 than at any point over the past decade. His concert tours and his successes in the West were far from over, he thought; but it would all come to a swifter end than he could possibly have imagined.

Notes

Principal sources

AAR	Shlifstein, Semyon, ed.: *S. Prokofiev: Autobiography, Articles, Reminiscences*, trans. Rosa Prokofieva (Moscow: Foreign Languages Publishing House, *c*1956)
D27	Prokofiev, Oleg, ed.: *Sergey Prokofiev: Dnevnik – 27* (Paris: Sintaksis, 1990)
IPSMK	Kozlova, Miralda, ed.: 'Pisma S.S. Prokofiev – B.N. Asafyevu (1920–40)', *Iz proshlovo sovietskoy muzykalnoy kultury*, ii (Moscow: Sovietsky Kompozitor, 1976)
MAI	Blok, Vladimir, ed.: *Sergei Prokofiev: Materials, Articles, Interviews* (Moscow: Progress, 1978)
MDV	Shlifstein, Semyon, ed.: *S.S. Prokofiev: Materialy, dokumenty, vospominaniya* (Moscow: Gosudarstvennoye Muzykalnoye Izdatelstvo, 1956, 2/1961)
PA	*Sergey Prokofiev: Avtobiografiya*, ed. Miralda Kozlova (Moscow: Sovietsky Kompozitor, 1973)
PMP	Kozlova, Miralda and Yatsenko, Nina, eds.: *S. S. Prokofiev i N. Ya. Myaskovsky: Perepiska* (Moscow: Sovietsky Kompozitor, 1977)
PSYV	Bretanitskaya, Alla, ed.: *Pyotr Souvchinsky i yevo vremya* (Moscow: Kompozitor, 1999) [includes Yelena Poldyaeva: '"Ya chasto s nim ne soglashalsya …": Iz perepiski S.S. Prokofieva i P.P. Suvchinskovo', which quotes from the extensive correspondence between Prokofiev and Souvchinsky]
SI	Varunts, Viktor, ed.: *Prokofiev o Prokofieve: Staty i intervyu* (Moscow: Sovietsky Kompozitor, 1991)
SLSP	Robinson, Harlow, ed.: *Selected Letters of Sergei Prokofiev* (Boston: Northeastern UP, 1998)
SM	Nestyev, Israel and Edelman, G., eds.: *Sergey Prokofiev 1953–1963: Staty i materialy* (Moscow: Sovietsky Kompozitor, 1962)
SP110	Rakhmanova, Marina, ed.: *Sergei Prokofiev k 110 letiyu s dnya rozhdeniya: Pisma, vospominaniya i staty* (Moscow: Glinka State Central Museum of Musical Culture, 2001)

Principal archives

GM	Archive of the Glinka State Museum of Musical Culture, Moscow
RGALI	Russian State Archive of Literature and Art (Russkiye gosudarstevnniy arkhiv literatury i isskustva), Moscow
SPA	Serge Prokofiev Archive, Goldsmiths College, University of London
TMA	Theatre Museum, Covent Garden, London

Chapter 1: Of giants and battleships, 1891–1904

1 *PA*, 72
2 *PA*, 17
3 ibid., 22
4 ibid., 75
5 ibid., 41
6 list of works reproduced in *PA*, 108–9
7 RGALI, Fund 1929, op.1, no.198
8 Solomon Volkov, ed.: *Testimony: The Memoirs of Dmitri Shostakovich*, trans. Antonina W. Bouis (London: Hamish Hamilton, 1979), 3
9 *PA*, 53
10 ibid., 55
11 ibid., 72
12 Glière's memoirs, *MDV*, 353
13 Yesipova quoted by Glière, ibid., 354
14 *PA*, 47
15 ibid., 62
16 RGALI, F 1929, 1, 199
17 *PA*, 222
18 ibid., 86
19 Glière's memoirs, *MDV*, 355
20 *PA*, 106
21 ibid., 62
22 RGALI, F 1929, 1, 11
23 *PA*, 66
24 ibid., 67
25 ibid., 69
26 ibid., 72
27 ibid., 87
28 RGALI, F 1929, 1, 209 (with the inscription 'For father on his nameday 1901 25 September')
29 Igor Stravinsky and Robert Craft: *Memories and Commentaries* (New York: Doubleday, 1960; London: Faber and Faber, 1960), 32
30 *PA*, 93
31 ibid., 95
32 Taneyev, diary entry for 23 Jan 1902, quoted in *PA*, 613
33 Glière's memoirs, *MDV*, 354
34 ibid., 351
35 ibid., 355
36 ibid., 351–2
37 *PA*, 104
38 ibid., 112
39 ibid., 125
40 ibid.
41 letter from Prokofiev to his father, 17 Dec 1902, quoted in *PA*, 127
42 letter from Prokofiev to his father, 14 Dec 1902, quoted in *PA*, 125–6
43 *PA*, 145
44 ibid., 146
45 diary entry for 3 Aug 1903, quoted in *PA*, 143
46 *PA*, 158
47 ibid., 161
48 ibid., 162
49 ibid., 163
50 ibid., 165
51 ibid., 132
52 Igor Stravinsky and Robert Craft: *Conversations with Igor Stravinsky* (New York: Doubleday, 1959; London: Faber and Faber, 1959), 37
53 *PA*, 169
54 ibid., 169
55 quoted from RGALI, F 1929, 1, 2
56 RGALI, F 1929, 1, 306
57 *PA*, 188

Chapter 2: Prokosha in St Petersburg, 1904–6

1 Igor Stravinsky and Robert Craft: *Expositions and Developments* (New York: Doubleday, 1962; London: Faber and Faber, 1962), 66
2 ibid., 25
3 Igor Grabar: *Moya zhizn: Avtomonografiya* (1937), quoted in *Mir iskusstva': Obedinenie russkikh khudozhinkov nachala XX veka*, ed. Alexander Kamensky (Leningrad: Aurora, 1991; trans. Arthur Shkarovsky-Raffe as *The World of Art Movement in Early 20th-Century Russia*), 46
4 *PA*, 288
5 letter from Prokofiev's mother to his father, 26 Aug 1904, quoted in *PA*, 195
6 letter from Prokofiev's mother to his father, 2 Sept 1904, quoted in *PA*, 197
7 letter from Prokofiev's mother to his father, 9 Sept 1904, quoted in *PA*, 201
8 *PA*, 206
9 ibid., 148
10 ibid., 319–20
11 ibid., 210
12 ibid., 215
13 ibid., 216
14 Nikolay Rimsky-Korsakov: *My Musical Life*, trans. Judah A. Joffe (New York: Alfred A. Knopf, 1923), 202
15 Vladimir Stasov: 'Nash muzyka pered posledniye' [Twenty-Five Years of Russian Art], in *Selected Essays on Music*, trans. Florence Jonas (London: Barrie & Rockliff, 1968), 6
16 Stravinsky and Craft: *Memories and Commentaries*, 62–3
17 *PA*, 217
18 ibid., 218
19 ibid., 299–300
20 Morolev's memoirs, quoted in *PA*, 290
21 ibid.
22 *PA*, 225
23 ibid., 229
24 letter from Prokofiev's mother to his father, 18 Sept 1904, quoted in *PA*, 212

25 letter from Prokofiev to his father, 12 Jan 1905, quoted in *PA*, 239
26 *PA*, 238
27 ibid., 251
28 ibid., 238
29 ibid.
30 ibid., 244
31 letter from Prokofiev to his father, 20 Feb 1905, quoted in *PA*, 257
32 letter from Prokofiev to his father, 19 March 1905, quoted in *PA*, 259
33 letter from Rimsky-Korsakov to August Bernhard, director of the St Petersburg Conservatory, published in *Russkiye vedomosti* and quoted in Vasily Yastrebtsev: *Reminiscences*, ed. and trans. Florence Jonas (New York: Columbia UP, 1985), 355–6
34 diary entry for 23 March 1905, quoted in *PA*, 263
35 diary entry for 27 March 1905, quoted in *PA*, 265
36 diary entry for 30 March 1905, quoted in *PA*, 267
37 Yastrebtsev: *Reminiscences*, 357
38 ibid., 358
39 letter from Prokofiev's mother to his father, 31 March 1905, quoted in *PA*, 268
40 *PA*, 283
41 Vyacheslav Plehve cited in Serge Schmemann: *Echoes of a Native Land* (New York: Alfred A. Knopf, 1997), 188–90
42 *PA*, 283
43 ibid., 294–5
44 ibid., 291
45 Asafyev's list of Prokofiev's early works, with comments, quoted in notes to *PA*, 644
46 *PA*, 295
47 Asafyev's comments, quoted in notes to *PA*, 644
48 *PA*, 246
49 letter from Prokofiev's mother to his father, 3 Feb 1906, quoted in *PA*, 330
50 *PA*, 335
51 ibid., 323
52 ibid., 486
53 ibid.
54 B. Mazing, paraphrased in Rosamund Bartlett: *Wagner and Russia* (Cambridge: CUP, 1985), 86
55 *PA*, 488
56 Frederic Chiu: introduction to vol.i of his recordings of Prokofiev's complete piano music (Harmonia Mundi HMU 907197)
57 text and examples from *PA*, 326–7
58 Asafyev, quoted in notes to *PA*, 642

Chapter 3: A friend for life, 1906–9

1 *PA*, 360
2 quoted in Alexey Ikonnikov: *Miaskowsky: His Life and Work* (New York: Philosophical Library, 1946), 9
3 *PA*, 469
4 ibid., 470
5 quoted in Ikonnikov, *Miaskowsky*, 16
6 *PA*, 458
7 ibid., 361
8 Semyon Shlifstein, ed.: *N.Ya. Myaskovsky: Avtobiografiya, staty, zametki, otzivi*, 2 vols. (Moscow: Sovietsky Kompozitor, 1959–60), ii, 12
9 *PA*, 362
10 ibid., 380
11 ibid., 364
12 ibid., 395
13 ibid.
14 ibid., 377
15 ibid., 386
16 Myaskovsky followed suit in the finale of the second sonata he completed that summer, eventually revised and published as his Fifth Piano Sonata op.64 no.1. It is curious to find the pianist Murray McLachlan, in the notes to his recording of Myaskovsky's piano sonatas for Olympia, objecting to 'the treatment of the second subject in the reprise, where it appears for only ten bars' and inserting more of the theme as it appeared in the exposition to make up for what he sees as the imbalance.
17 *PA*, 397
18 letter from Prokofiev to Myaskovsky, 26 June 1907, *PMP*, 37
19 letter from Prokofiev to Myaskovsky, 22 July 1907, *PMP*, 41
20 letter from Myaskovsky to Prokofiev, 12 July 1907, *PMP*, 39
21 letter from Myaskovsky to Prokofiev, 26 July 1907, *PMP*, 42
22 letter from Myaskovsky to Prokofiev, 12 July 1907, *PMP*, 41
23 letter from Prokofiev to Myaskovsky, 20 May 1908, *PMP*, 51
24 letter from Myaskovsky to Prokofiev, 10 Aug 1907, *PMP*, 46
25 ibid., 48
26 letter from Myaskovsky to Prokofiev, 12 July 1907, *PMP*, 39
27 letter from Prokofiev to Myaskovsky, 22 July 1907, *PMP*, 42
28 *PA*, 402
29 ibid., 430
30 ibid., 464
31 ibid., 453
32 *SM*, 11
33 *PA*, 498
34 ibid., 458
35 ibid., 476
36 ibid., 458
37 ibid., 488

38 ibid., 492
39 ibid., 493
40 ibid., 119
41 ibid., 496
42 letter from Prokofiev to Myaskovsky, 31 May 1908, *PMP*, 52
43 letter from Prokofiev to Myaskovsky, 27 June 1908, *PMP*, 52
44 letter from Prokofiev to Myaskovsky, 11 July 1908, *PMP*, 55
45 RGALI, F 1929, 1, 113
46 letter from Prokofiev to Myaskovsky, 4 Aug 1908, *PMP*, 57
47 ibid.
48 letter from Myaskovsky to Prokofiev, 27 Dec 1915, *PMP*, 139
49 *PA*, 565
50 ibid., 519
51 ibid., 503
52 ibid., 274
53 ibid., 526
54 ibid., 287
55 Alexander Skryabin, preface to the Third Symphony
56 *PA*, 557
57 Stravinsky and Craft: *Memories and Commentaries*, 29
58 *PA*, 482
59 ibid.
60 RGALI, F 1929, 1, 230
61 *PA*, 482
62 letter from Prokofiev to Myaskovsky, 19 Dec 1908, *PMP*, 62
63 *St Petersburg Zeitung* (24 Dec 1908)
64 *PA*, 539
65 *Rech* (22 Dec 1908)
66 *Slovo* (20 Dec 1908)
67 Stravinsky and Craft: *Memories and Commentaries*, 66
68 letter from Prokofiev to Morolev, 3 March 1909, *SM*, 231
69 Vera Alpers's diary, quoted in *PA*, 550–51
70 *PA*, 552
71 letter from Prokofiev to Alpers, 1 June 1909, *SM*, 269
72 letter from Prokofiev to Alpers, 4 July 1909, *SM*, 272
73 letter from Prokofiev to Alpers, 26 July 1909, *SM*, 273
74 letter from Prokofiev to Alpers, 18 Aug 1909, *SM*, 274
75 *PA*, 580
76 ibid.
77 Lina Prokofiev in conversation with Harvey Sachs; transcripts in SPA
78 ibid.
79 Vera Alpers's diary, quoted in *PA*, 580
80 *PA*, 582
81 ibid.

Chapter 4: Classical, symbolical, 1909–13

1 *PA*, 535
2 letter from Prokofiev to Morolev, 1 July 1910, *SM*, 234
3 *PA*, 537
4 ibid., 575
5 ibid., 572
6 ibid.
7 ibid., 522
8 letter from Prokofiev to Myaskovsky, 6 July 1909, *PMP*, 70
9 letter from Myaskovsky to Prokofiev, 8 June 1909, *PMP*, 67
10 letter from Prokofiev to Myaskovsky, 31 July 1909, *PMP*, 75
11 letter from Myaskovsky to Prokofiev, 9 Aug 1909, *PMP*, 76–7
12 letter from Myaskovsky to Prokofiev, 28 July 1909, *PMP*, 74
13 letter from Myaskovsky to Prokofiev, 8 June 1909, *PMP*, 67
14 ibid.
15 letter from Myaskovsky to Prokofiev, 11 July 1909, *PMP*, 71
16 English synopses, including the one for the only recording available at the time of writing (Marco Polo label), claim that it is based on Poe's poem 'The Raven', but the frontispiece to the score, as well as clues in the correspondence between Prokofiev and Myaskovsky, identify the source as *Silence: A Fable* (1837).
17 Victor Terras, ed.: *A Handbook of Russian Literature* (New Haven, CT: Yale UP, 1985), 37
18 Balmont, letter to his daughter under the pseudonym 'Mstislav', Feb 1927, for publication in a Soviet newspaper, SPA
19 ibid.
20 Israel Nestyev: *Prokofiev*, trans. Florence Jonas (Stanford: Stanford UP; Oxford: OUP, 1961), 42
21 letter from Prokofiev to Myaskovsky, 1 March 1909, *PMP*, 64
22 letter from Myaskovsky to Prokofiev, 4 Sept 1910, *PMP*, 87
23 letter from Myaskovsky to Prokofiev, 13 Aug 1910, *PMP*, 84
24 diary entry for 27 Feb 1927, *D27*, 131–2
25 *PA*, 532
26 short autobiography, *MDV*, 143
27 letter from Prokofiev to Morolev, 30 Nov 1910, *SM*, 234
28 letter from Prokofiev to Zakharov, 6 June 1911, *SM*, 235
29 letter from Prokofiev to Myaskovsky, 27 May 1911, *PMP*, 90
30 letter from Prokofiev to his mother, 5 July 1911, *SM*, 236

31 letter from Prokofiev to his mother, 11 July 1911, *SM*, 237
32 letter from Prokofiev to his mother, 18 July 1911, *SM*, 239
33 ibid.
34 *Golos Moskvy* (21 July 1911), quoted in Nestyev: *Prokofiev*, 58
35 short autobiography, *MDV*, 143
36 letter from Prokofiev to Taneyev, 11 Oct 1910, quoted in notes to *AAR*
37 letter from Taneyev to Jurgenson, 29 Nov 1910, *AAR*, 320
38 letter from Prokofiev to Taneyev, 25 Dec 1910, *AAR*, 320
39 letter from Ossovsky to Jurgenson, 5 May 1911, *MDV*, 641–2
40 letter from Prokofiev to his mother, 5 July 1911, *SM*, 236
41 letter from Prokofiev to Morolev, 1 July 1910, *SM*, 234
42 ibid.
43 letter from Prokofiev to Morolev, 6 June 1912, *SM*, 241
44 ibid.
45 letter from Prokofiev to Myaskovsky, 15 June 1912, *PMP*, 101
46 letter from Prokofiev to Schmidthof, 24 July 1912, *SM*, 243
47 letter from Prokofiev to Schmidthof, 26 July 1912, *SM*, 244
48 letter from Prokofiev to Myaskovsky, 15 July 1912, *PMP*, 102
49 *Golos Moskvy* (1912), no.173, quoted in Nestyev: *Prokofiev*, 63
50 *Peterburgsky listok* (5 Aug 1912), quoted in Nestyev: *Prokofiev*, 63
51 letter to Tcherepnin, 19 June 1912, *SM*, 242
52 short autobiography, *MDV*, 144
53 letter from Myaskovsky to Derzhanovsky, 26 Sept 1911, quoted in Nestyev: *Prokofiev*, 59
54 ibid.
55 ibid., quoted in sleeve-note to the Olympia CD issue
56 letter from Derzhanovsky to Stravinsky, 3 Nov 1913, quoted in Igor Stravinsky and Robert Craft, eds.: *Selected Correspondence*, i (New York: Alfred A. Knopf, 1982; London: Faber and Faber, 1982), 61
57 Edward Downes, introduction to the vocal score (London: Boosey & Hawkes, 1990)
58 *Rech* (10 Dec 1912), quoted in Richard Taruskin: *Stravinsky and the Russian Traditions* (Berkeley: University of California Press, 1996; Oxford: OUP, 1996), 825
59 short autobiography, *MDV*, 142
60 examination report of 4 May 1910, quoted in Nestyev: *Prokofiev*, 40
61 letter from Prokofiev to Taneyev, 11 Oct 1910, *MDV*, 640
62 letter from Myaskovsky to Prokofiev, 20 July 1909, *PMP*, 75
63 Asafyev, *Muzyka* (7 Feb 1915), quoted in Nestyev: *Prokofiev*, 78
64 *PA*, 223
65 Nicolas Slonimsky: *Perfect Pitch: A Life Story* (London: OUP, 1988), 35
66 the programmes are lodged in the Glinka Museum archive (GM), F. 4935, 33, 246–59
67 Yury Tyulin: 'On the Path to Recognition', *MAI*, 162–3
68 *Golos Moskvy* (24 Jan 1914), quoted in Nestyev: *Prokofiev*, 82
69 introduction to *Sarcasms* in Composers' Publishing House edition (St Petersburg: Kompozitor, 1993)
70 short autobiography, *MDV*, 148–9

Chapter 5: Sun worship, 1913–16

1 Mikhail Larionov: 'Rayonnists and Futurists: A Manifesto', quoted in Camilla Gray: *The Russian Experiment in Art 1863–1922* (London: Thames and Hudson, 1962), 139
2 What should succeed the poor old sun remained obscure in a production in 1999 that attempted to reconstruct the drama as a walkabout 'happening' in the small Pit Theatre at the Barbican in London; the absence of text and production details for the actors and production team led to a murkier chaos than had perhaps been intended.
3 Sergey Gorodetsky, quoted in Terras, ed.: *A Handbook*, 6
4 The 'sun questionnaire' is in RGALI, but was under embargo at the time of writing; the Rubinstein quotation is pieced together from Slonimsky: *Perfect Pitch*, 230, and Harlow Robinson: *Sergei Prokofiev* (London: Robert Hale, 1987), 124
5 Anatoly Nekludov: *Diplomatic Reminiscences*, quoted by Richard Buckle: *Diaghilev* (London: Weidenfeld & Nicolson, 1979), 267
6 letter from Myaskovsky to Prokofiev, 13 Aug 1910, *PMP*, 84
7 short autobiography, *MDV*, 151
8 ibid.
9 Myaskovsky, article in *Muzyka* (12 Jan 1913), quoted in Taruskin: *Stravinsky and the Russian Traditions*, 763
10 letter from Myaskovsky to Prokofiev, 26 Jan 1913, *PMP*, 104
11 letter from Prokofiev to Tcherepnin, 29 June 1913, *SM*, 245
12 letter from Prokofiev to Myaskovsky, 11 June 1913, *PMP*, 107
13 ibid.
14 letter from Prokofiev to Tcherepnin, 29 June 1913, *SM*, 245

15 letter from Prokofiev to Myaskovsky, 11 June 1913, *PMP*, 107
16 ibid.
17 letter from Prokofiev to Tcherepnin, 29 June 1913, *SM*, 245
18 ibid.
19 ibid., 246
20 ibid.
21 ibid.
22 Nina Krivosheina: *Chetirye treti nashei zhizni* (Paris: YMCA Press, 1984), 56
23 letter from Prokofiev to Myaskovsky, 31 May 1913, *PMP*, 105
24 ibid.
25 ibid.
26 letter from Myaskovsky to Prokofiev, before 3 Aug 1913, *PMP*, 110–11
27 ibid.
28 letter from Prokofiev to Myaskovsky, 15 July 1924, *PMP*, 200
29 Alexander Toradze: 'An Exceptional Human Document', essay with his recording of the five piano concertos (Philips 462 048-2)
30 ibid.
31 letter from Prokofiev to Katya Schmidthof, 15 May 1913, *SM*, 244–5
32 short autobiography, *MDV*, 144
33 letter from Asafyev to Derzhanovsky, 27 Jan 1915, quoted in Nestyev: *Prokofiev*, 98
34 *Peterburgskaya gazeta* (25 Aug 1913), quoted in Nestyev: *Prokofiev*, 76
35 ibid., 77
36 *Rech* (25 Aug 1913), quoted in Nestyev: *Prokofiev*, 77
37 letter from Prokofiev to Myaskovsky, 10 April 1914, *PMP*, 114
38 ibid.
39 letter from Prokofiev to Derzhanovsky, 4 Oct 1913, *SM*, 247
40 letter from Prokofiev to Morolev, 3 April 1914, *SM*, 247
41 Tcherepnin's report, quoted in Nestyev: *Prokofiev*, 84
42 letter from Prokofiev to Morolev, 3 April 1914, *SM*, 247
43 ibid.
44 *Dyen* (9 May 1913), quoted in Natalya Savkina: *Sergey Sergeyevich Prokofiev* (Moscow: Muzyka, 1982); Eng. trans. Catherine Young (Neptune City, NJ: Paganiniana, 1984), 52
45 short autobiography, *MDV*, 148
46 ibid.
47 GM, F 4935, 33, 241
48 letter from Prokofiev to Tcherepnin, 5 April 1914, *SM*, 248
49 letter from Prokofiev to Tcherepnin, 27 June 1914, *SM*, 250
50 Prokofiev, diary entry for 16 May 1914, trans. Edward Morgan in *Three Oranges*, no.2 (2001), 10
51 letter from Prokofiev to Eleonora Damskaya, 12 June 1914, *SLSP*, 15
52 letter from Prokofiev to Myaskovsky, 6 June 1914, *PMP*, 114
53 letter from Jaeger to Elgar, 5 Oct 1903, quoted in Jerrold Northrop Moore, ed.: *Elgar and his Publishers: Letters of a Creative Life* (Oxford: OUP, 1987), 506
54 letter from Prokofiev to his mother, 22 June (5 July) 1914, *SM*, 249–50
55 ibid.
56 Granville Bantock, diary entry for 4 July 1914; reproduced by kind permission of Fiona Bantock
57 letter from Prokofiev to his mother, 22 June 1914, *SM*, 249–50
58 ibid.
59 quoted in short autobiography, *MDV*, 150, where Prokofiev renders the exclamation in Russian 'no eto kakoye-to dikoye zhivotnoye'
60 letter from Prokofiev to Myaskovsky, 12 June (25 June) 1914, *PMP*, 116–17
61 letter from Prokofiev to Tcherepnin, 27 June (10 July) 1914, *SM*, 250
62 letter from Prokofiev to Myaskovsky, 13 Aug 1914, *PMP*, 118–19
63 letter from Prokofiev to Myaskovsky, 12 June (25 June) 1914, *PMP*, 116–17
64 letter from Prokofiev to Myaskovsky, 13 Aug 1914, *PMP*, 118–19
65 ibid.
66 ibid.
67 letter from Prokofiev to his mother, 1 July (14 July) 1914, *SM*, 251
68 ibid.
69 letter from Myaskovsky to Prokofiev, 6 Aug 1914, *PMP*, 118
70 letter from Myaskovsky to Prokofiev, 17 Aug 1914, *PMP*, 119–20
71 letter from Prokofiev to Damskaya, 3 Sept 1914, quoted in *SLSP*, 19–20
72 letter from Prokofiev to Damskaya, 20 Aug 1914, quoted in *SLSP*, 19
73 letter from Prokofiev to Myaskovsky, 13 Aug 1914, *PMP*, 118–19
74 Krivosheina: *Chetirye treti*, 57
75 ibid., 58
76 ibid.
77 letter from Prokofiev to Damskaya, 3 Sept 1914, quoted in *SLSP*, 19
78 letter from Prokofiev to Myaskovsky, 29 Aug 1914, *PMP*, 120–21
79 Volkov, ed. *Testimony*, 146
80 Mirsky: *History of Russian Literature*, quoted in Taruskin: *Stravinsky and the Russian Traditions*, 859
81 letter from Prokofiev to Myaskovsky, 10 Oct 1914, *PMP*, 122
82 letter from Mikhail Astrov to Dr Hedwig Kraus, 5 Dec 1932, SPA

83 letter from Prokofiev to Myaskovsky, 16 Oct 1914, *PMP*, 125
84 letter from Prokofiev to Myaskovsky, 12 Dec 1914, *PMP*, 129
85 letter from Prokofiev to Myaskovsky, 29 Nov 1914, *PMP*, 128–9
86 quoted (without reference) in Nestyev: *Prokofiev*, 92
87 letter from Prokofiev to Myaskovsky, 29 Nov 1914, *PMP*, 128–9
88 letter from Myaskovsky to Prokofiev, 15 Jan 1915, *PMP*, 130–1
89 letter from Prokofiev to Myaskovsky, 25 Jan 1915, *PMP*, 131–2
90 Krivosheina: *Chetirye treti*, 59
91 letter from Prokofiev to his mother, 20 Feb (5 March) 1915, *SM*, 253
92 *Tatler* (15 July 1914)
93 interview with Olin Downes in the *Boston Post* (19 Jan 1919)
94 letter from Prokofiev to his mother, 20 Feb (5 March) 1915, *SM*, 253
95 letter from Prokofiev to his mother, 25 Feb (10 March) 1915, *SM*, 254
96 *Il messaggero* (22 March 1915), quoted in Nestyev: *Prokofiev*, 99
97 letter from Prokofiev to his mother, 20 Feb (5 March) 1915, *SM*, 253
98 letter from Prokofiev to his mother, 25 Feb (10 March) 1915, *SM*, 254
99 letter from Prokofiev to his mother, 1 March (14 March) 1915, *SM*, 254
100 letter from Myaskovsky to Prokofiev, 7 April 1915, *PMP*, 132
101 letter from Prokofiev to his mother, 1 March (14 March) 1915, *SM*, 254
102 Léonide Massine: *My Life in Ballet* (London: Macmillan, 1968), 171
103 letter from Prokofiev to Stravinsky, 3 June 1915, *SM*, 255
104 letter from Prokofiev to Ziloti, 5 July 1915, *SM*, 256
105 letter from Prokofiev to Stravinsky, 3 June 1915, *SM*, 255
106 copy of manuscript in SPA; other changes include the deletion of a flute line to support the piccolo at the start of the first movement, several cuts in the last two movements and a rewriting of the passage just before the beginning of the final sunrise.
107 Savkina: *Prokofiev*, 62
108 letter from Myaskovsky to Prokofiev, 17 May 1915, *PMP*, 134–5
109 letter from Mikhail Astrov to Dr Hedwig Krauss, 5 Dec 1932, SPA
110 short autobiography, *MDV*, 151
111 short autobiography, *MDV*, 167
112 *Rech* (31 Jan 1916), quoted in Nestyev: *Prokofiev*, 121
113 short autobiography, *MDV*, 153–4
114 Tyulin: 'On the Path to Recognition', *MAI*, 163–4
115 ibid.

Chapter 6: A game of chance, 1915–18

1 short autobiography, *MDV*, 151
2 article in *Birzhivie vedomost* (12 May 1916), *SM*, 297
3 ibid.
4 Prokofiev, diary entry for 19 June–17 July 1913, trans. Edward Morgan in *Three Oranges*, no.2 (2001), 4
5 ibid.
6 letter from Musorgsky to Lyudmila Shestakova, 30 July 1868, quoted in Caryl Emerson and Robert Oldani: *Modest Musorgsky and* Boris Godunov*: Myths, Realities, Reconsiderations* (Cambridge: CUP, 1994), 71
7 ibid.
8 the surviving manuscript is a copy made in 1952, when Prokofiev recalled it for Zakharov 'in memory of 38 years [of friendship]', RGALI, F.1929, 1, 270
9 *Teatr i isskustvo*, no.6 (1915), quoted in *SM*, 338–9
10 ibid.
11 ibid.
12 letter from Prokofiev to Derzhanovsky, 25 July 1915, *SM*, 258
13 Nestyev: *Prokofiev*, 109
14 ibid.
15 ibid.
16 letter from Prokofiev to Tatyana Ruzskaya, 18 March 1916, *SM*, 260
17 letter from Prokofiev to Derzhanovsky, 12 Jan 1915, *SM*, 252–3
18 short autobiography, *MDV*, 153
19 letter from Myaskovsky to Prokofiev, 4 Nov 1915, *PMP*, 138
20 letter from Prokofiev to Ruzskaya, 2 Feb 1916, *SM*, 259–60
21 letter from Prokofiev to Ruzskaya, 18 March 1916, *SM*, 260
22 copies of manuscripts in the SPA
23 Prokofiev, poem dated 18 July 1916, SPA
24 *Musical Times*, lvii (1916), 465–6
25 ibid.
26 letter from Prokofiev to Myaskovsky, 29 May 1915, *PMP*, 135–6
27 short autobiography, *MDV*, 153
28 ibid.
29 short autobiography, *MDV*, 155
30 Asafyev, quoted in Nestyev: *Prokofiev*, 94–5
31 text of a radio speech broadcast on 19 June 1936, reproduced in *MAI*, 42–3
32 ibid.

33 Nikolay Gumilyov in *Apollon*, no.1 (1913), quoted (trans. Robert Whittaker) in Roberta Reeder: *Anna Akhmatova: Poet and Prophet* (New York: St Martin's Press, 1994), 43
34 Vasily Gippius in *Novaya zhizn*, quoted in Reeder: *Akhmatova*, 54
35 *Russkiye vedomosti* (10 Feb 1917), *SM*, 341–2
36 ibid.
37 Karatygin in *Nash vek* (3 May 1918), quoted in Nestyev, 133
38 Konstantin Balmont: *Stichotvoreniya* (Moscow: Khudozhestvennaya Literatura, 1990), 151
39 David Oistrakh: 'In Memoriam', *AAR*, 239
40 short autobiography, *MDV*, 158
41 ibid.
42 ibid.
43 Nestyev, 135
44 short autobiography, *MDV*, 158
45 quoted by Nestyev, 145
46 letter from Prokofiev to Damskaya, 21 May 1917, *SLSP*, 28
47 letter from Prokofiev to Damskaya, 28 May 1917, *SLSP*, 28
48 letter from Prokofiev to Myaskovsky, 29 May 1917, *PMP*, 147
49 ibid.
50 In a letter to Pyotr Souvchinsky (23 Nov 1923), however, Prokofiev says that 'the first movement and finale were conceived in 1913'; see Chapter 10 note 1.
51 letter from Prokofiev to Myaskovsky, 10 Nov 1924, *PMP*, 206
52 The exemption from General Shtab, dated 22 June 1917, is among the photocopied documents in the SPA.
53 letter from Prokofiev to Damskaya, 23 July 1917, *SLSP*, 29
54 Full manuscript of *Tanya and the Mushroom Kingdom* in Oleg Prokofiev's translation; the closing section is in *Sergei Prokofiev: Soviet Diary 1927 and Other Writings* (London: Faber and Faber, 1991)
55 ibid.
56 manuscript in the National Library of Congress, Washington, DC
57 letter from Chaliapin to his daughter Irina, 7 Sept 1917, in *Chaliapin: An Autobiography as told to Maxim Gorky*, trans. Nina Froud and James Hanley (London: Macdonald, 1968), 213
58 *New York Times* (15 June 1924)
59 On 3 November 1991 Mstislav Rostropovich conducted a performance at the Royal Festival Hall, London, with the tenor Gegam Grigorian and the London Symphony Orchestra and Chorus, as the preface to a cumbersome new 'performing version' of the music to *Ivan the Terrible*.
60 copy of the manuscript in the SPA
61 letter from Prokofiev to Damskaya, 5 Dec 1917, *SLSP*, 34
62 letter from Prokofiev to Damskaya, 30 Dec 1917, *SLSP*, 35
63 ibid.
64 letter from Prokofiev to Damskaya, 14 Nov 1917, *SLSP*, 33
65 letter from Prokofiev to Damskaya, 11 Jan 1918, *SLSP*, 35
66 letter from Prokofiev to Asafyev, 14 Sept 1931, *SLSP*, 120–21
67 Vasily Kamensky, quoted in *AAR*, 324
68 ibid.
69 ibid.
70 recalled by Prokofiev in the short autobiography, *MDV*, 161
71 'sun-questionnaire' catalogued (but under embargo) in RGALI
72 Balmont as 'Mstislav', unpublished article of Feb 1927, SPA
73 Isaac Deutscher: introduction to Anatoly Lunacharsky: *Revolutionary Silhouettes*, trans. Michael Glenny (Harmondsworth: Allen Lane, 1967), 17
74 quoted in the exhibition catalogue *Mayakovsky: Three Views* (Edinburgh: Scorpion, 1992), 21
75 Cyrus McCormick, diary entry for 9 July 1917, McCormick Collection, State History of Wisconsin Archives
76 correspondence, 12 Dec and 16 June 1918, McCormick Collection
77 short autobiography, *MDV*, 161
78 permission signed by Lunacharsky, SPA
79 Meyerhold to Solovyov, quoted in Taruskin: 'From Fairy-Tale to Opera in Four Not So Simple Moves', English National Opera programme for *The Love for Three Oranges*, 1989–90 season. Taruskin's assumption that Meyerhold was disappointed presumes that Prokofiev was emigrating, not travelling abroad before returning to settle down to collaborate on the opera. The source, at least, is surely closer to the truth than Asafyev's assertion, in his study of Prokofiev, that the subject had already been decided in early 1917 (reproduced in Nestyev, *Prokofiev*, 131).

Chapter 7: In quest of three oranges, 1918–19

1 author's own translation of a Russian text in *Anna Akhmatova: Selected Poems* (New York: Little, Brown, 1973), 74
2 letter from Prokofiev to Damskaya, 13 May 1918, *SLSP*, 36
3 letter from Prokofiev to Damskaya, 16 and 22 May 1918, *SLSP*, 36–7
4 letter from Prokofiev to Myaskovsky, 20 May 1918, *PMP*, 148

5 Both stories have been translated by David McDuff and appear in *Sergei Prokofiev: Soviet Diary 1927 and Other Writings*, 199–219.
6 postcard from Prokofiev to Stravinsky, 23 June 1918, SPA
7 letter from Prokofiev to Ohtaguro, 8 Sept 1923, SPA
8 programme cover reproduced in *Prokofiev: Albom* (Moscow: Muzyka, 1965), 51
9 short autobiography, *MDV*, 162
10 notes for Lina Prokofiev's memoirs, SPA
11 letter from Prokofiev to McCormick, 12 July 1918, McCormick Collection
12 short autobiography, *MDV*, 162
13 cited in Edward Braun: *Meyerhold: A Revolution in Theatre* (London: Methuen, 1995), 127
14 'The Love for Three Oranges. Divertissement. Twelve scenes, prologue, epilogue and three intermezzi. Authors: K. A. Vogak, Vs. E. Meyerhold and Vl. N. Solovyov', in *Lyubov k tryom apelsinam*, no.1 (1913), 18–47
15 short autobiography, *MDV*, 164
16 files in the National Archives and Records Administration, Pacific Region, USA
17 short autobiography, *MDV*, 162
18 *Los Angeles Daily Record* (25 Dec 1920)
19 short autobiography, *MDV*, 162
20 Sachs transcript, SPA
21 letter from Ossip Gabrilovich to McCormick, 8 June 1918, McCormick Collection
22 letter from Prokofiev to Diaghilev, 1 Oct 1918, *SLSP*, 67
23 *New York Times* (19 Sept 1918)
24 ibid.
25 ibid.
26 Sachs transcript, SPA
27 short autobiography, *MDV*, 163
28 Nicolas Slonimsky: *Music Since 1900* (New York: Charles Scribner, 4/1971), 408. Since his death in February 2002 (at a much debated age, possibly even 109), Ornstein has enjoyed a renaissance of interest, with two recordings of his piano music, including *Suicide in an Airplane* and *Danse sauvage*, released in a month.
29 advertisement in the *New York Times* (19 Oct 1918)
30 *Brooklyn Daily Eagle* (30 Oct 1918)
31 *New York Times* (14 Nov 1909)
32 *New York Times* (21 Nov 1918)
33 *New York Herald* (21 Nov 1918)
34 *New York Times* (21 Nov 1918)
35 short autobiography, *MDV*, 163
36 *New York Times* (11 Dec 1918)
37 ibid.
38 *New York Times* (12 Dec 1918)
39 *New York Tribune* (12 Dec 1918)
40 ibid.
41 *New York Times* (11 Dec 1918)
42 This and other details are from various interviews, principally the major one with Harvey Sachs, lodged by Lina in cassette and transcript form at the SPA.
43 Sachs transcript, SPA
44 ibid.
45 ibid.
46 ibid.
47 ibid.
48 ibid.
49 ibid.
50 *Chicago Herald Examiner* (7 Dec 1918)
51 *Current Opinion* (Dec 1918)
52 short autobiography, *MDV*, 164
53 *Lyubov k tryom apelsinam*, no.1 (1913), 21
54 Sachs transcript, SPA
55 copy of the contract between the Aeolian Company and Prokofiev, 25 Feb 1919, SPA
56 in the introduction to 'The Composer Plays' (Nimbus 'Grand Piano' series, NI 8813)
57 Busoni, quoted in Welte-Mignon brochure of famous artists (New York, 1927)
58 Stravinsky, in *Stravinsky: An Autobiography* (New York: Simon & Schuster, 1937), 101
59 *New York Times* (31 March 1919)
60 Most of the performances on the LP transfer of many of the rolls in the 'Keyboard Immortals Series' (Superscope 4 A103-S), using Welte's 'vorsetzer' or player piano, are a good deal faster than those on the Nimbus 'Grand Piano' series (NI 8813), using a 'robot decoder' completed in 1973. The 'vorsetzer' versions, though featuring more or less unvarying dynamics and presumably less 'correct', have greater spirit – or rather they sound much more like a real pianist at the keyboard – than the curiously mechanical Nimbus performances.
61 short autobiography, *MDV*, 165
62 ibid.
63 *Lyubov k tryom apelsinam*, no.1 (1913), 19
64 short autobiography, *MDV*, 165
65 ibid.
66 Giora Feidman, the soloist in a Sony recording made in 1994 (SK 58966), plays with the wide vibrato and the added inflections of true *klezmer* style.
67 letter from Prokofiev to Myaskovsky, 4 June 1923, *PMP*, 158
68 ibid.
69 letter from Prokofiev to Andrew Fraser, 8 June 1929, SPA
70 letter from Prokofiev to Myaskovsky, 4 June 1923, *PMP*, 158
71 Alfred Swan: *Russian Music* (London: John Barker, 1973), 187
72 letter from Prokofiev to Swan, 26 March 1920, reproduced in Swan: *Russian Music*, 187

Chapter 8: Devil's work, 1919–22

1 Nestyev: *Prokofiev*, 177
2 Valery Bryusov: *The Fiery Angel*, trans. Ivor Montagu and Sergey Nalbandov (1930/*R* London: Neville Spearman, 1975), 14
3 ibid., 170
4 ibid., 390
5 copy of manuscript in SPA
6 short autobiography, *MDV*, 166
7 manuscript in the Janacopulos Collection, Institut de Brasilieras, Rio de Janeiro
8 Stravinsky and Craft: *Expositions and Developments*, 113
9 Prokofiev, diary entry for 10 May 1920, trans. Edward Morgan in *Three Oranges*, no.2 (2001), 4
10 Many of these designs were displayed in the Tretyakov Gallery, Moscow, in 1999 as part of a major exhibition of works by Larionov and Goncharova and catalogued in *M. Larionov, N. Goncharova: Parizhskoye Naslediye v Tretyakovskoi Galeree* (Moscow: Gosudarstvennaya Tretyakovskaya Galereya, 1999).
11 Prokofiev diary entry for June 1920, trans. Edward Morgan in *Three Oranges*, no.2 (2001), 4
12 Sachs transcript, SPA
13 ibid.
14 ibid.
15 ibid.
16 first reproduced in *Mikhail Larionov – Nataliya Goncharova: Chefs d'oeuvres iz Parizhskovo naslediya zhivopis*, catalogue for Tretyakov Gallery exhibition of major paintings by Goncharova and Larionov (Moscow: Gosudarstvennaya Tretyakovskaya Galereya, 1999), 154 (portrait), 178 (text)
17 manuscript in the Pierpont Morgan Library, New York; photocopy in SPA
18 The problem was exacerbated at the London concert premiere of the complete ballet, given by Alexander Lazarev and the London Philharmonic Orchestra on 28 November 1997, because the actor Simon Callow's attempts to narrate the plot between scenes were often thwarted by the high orchestral volume in the interludes.
19 letter from Prokofiev to his mother, 25 Oct 1920, SPA
20 Nestyev: *Prokofiev*, 181
21 letter from Prokofiev to Souvchinsky, 11 March 1921, *PSYV*, 58
22 *World* (31 March 1919)
23 letter from Prokofiev to Souvchinsky, 11 March 1921, *PSYV*, 58
24 *Pacific Coast Musical Review* (25 Dec 1920)
25 *San Diego Union* (23 Dec 1920)
26 *Los Angeles Evening Express* (12 Jan 1921)
27 ibid.
28 letter from Prokofiev to Souvchinsky, 11 March 1921, *PSYV*, 58
29 copy of manuscript in SPA
30 letter from Prokofiev to Souvchinsky, 11 March 1921, *PSYV*, 58
31 ibid.
32 The pianist, according to the *New York Times* review of 28 March 1921, was Frank Bibb; only one song was performed, not the five as is frequently claimed.
33 letter from Prokofiev to Souvchinsky, 11 March 1921, *PSYV*, 58
34 ibid.
35 Prokofiev, diary entry for 1–31 April 1921, trans. Edward Morgan in *Three Oranges*, no.2 (2001), 9
36 Cyril Beaumont: *The Diaghilev Ballet in London* (London: Putnam, 1940), 190
37 Sergey Grigoriev: *The Diaghilev Ballet 1909–1929*, ed. and trans. Vera Bowen (London: Constable, 1953), 164
38 *L'Avenir* (19 April 1921)
39 *Le Gaulois* (14 May 1921)
40 ibid.
41 letter from Prokofiev to Damskaya, 15 July 1921, *SP110*, 21
42 letter from Prokofiev to Gottlieb, 27 July 1921, SPA
43 *Musical Times*, lxii (1921), 499
44 *Morning Post* (1 Aug 1921)
45 *Musical Opinion* (July 1921)
46 *Tatler* (22 June 1921)
47 *The Times* (11 June 1921)
48 *The Times* (3 Nov 1920)
49 ibid.
50 *Tatler* (22 June 1921)
51 *Observer* (5 June 1921)
52 letter from Prokofiev to Damskaya, 15 July 1921, *SP110*, 21
53 Sachs transcript, SPA
54 letter from Prokofiev to Gottlieb, 27 July 1921, SPA
55 Sachs transcript, SPA
56 letter from Prokofiev to Souvchinsky, 8 July 1921, *PSYV*, 60
57 short autobiography, *MDV*, 169
58 Nestyev: *Prokofiev*, 194
59 Sonnet quoted in article by 'Mstislav', SPA; I have rendered a Shakespearean sonnet metre but not the rhymes of the original.
60 short autobiography, *MDV*, 169
61 letter from Myaskovsky to Prokofiev, 25 July 1923, *PMP*, 162
62 ibid.
63 letter from Prokofiev to Natalya Koussevitzky, 30 Aug 1921; ed. Viktor Yuzefovich in *Sovietskaya muzyka* (April 1991), 56
64 letter from Haensel to Prokofiev, 13 Sept 1921, SPA

65 letter from Prokofiev to Haensel, 19 Nov 1921, SPA
66 letter from Haensel to Prokofiev, 21 Nov 1921, SPA
67 letter from Prokofiev to Souvchinsky, 7 Nov 1921, *PSYV*, 64
68 short autobiography, *MDV*, 170
69 ibid.
70 *Chicago Examiner* (2 Nov 1921)
71 Ben Hecht, 'Fantastic Lollypops', *Chicago Daily News*, reprinted from *1001 Afternoons in Chicago* (Covici Friede, 1922) on the website *Ben Hecht Rediscovered*, ed. Whyte Kovan, Florice (http://www.snickersneepress.bigstep.com, 2001-2)
72 ibid.
73 ibid.
74 *Chicago Daily Tribune* (31 Dec 1921)
75 ibid.
76 *New York Times* (15 Feb 1922)
77 *Musical Courier* (23 Feb 1922)
78 ibid.
79 *Musical News* (1922)
80 letter from Deborah Beirne to Prokofiev, 21 March 1922, SPA
81 letter from Prokofiev to Beirne, 10 April 1922, SPA
82 short autobiography, *MDV*, 171

Chapter 9: Passion play, 1922–3

1 letter from Prokofiev to Capablanca, 22 July 1922, SPA
2 letter from Prokofiev to Dr Hussa, 30 Dec 1922, SPA
3 ibid.
4 letter from Prokofiev to Souvchinsky, 11 July 1922, *PSYV*, 73
5 letter from Prokofiev to Vera Janacopulos, undated, SPA
6 Sachs transcript, SPA
7 The third act bears the date 6 June 1922 at the beginning and Sept 1922 at the end; 'October 1922' is inscribed at the end of Act IV and '13 January 1922' at the end of Act V.
8 letter from Prokofiev to Souvchinsky, 12 Dec 1922, *PSYV*, 82
9 short autobiography, *MDV*, 171
10 letter from Prokofiev to Souvchinsky, 13 May 1922, *PSYV*, 69
11 ibid.
12 letter from Prokofiev to Leona Spitzer, 20 Dec 1922, SPA
13 letter from Prokofiev to Souvchinsky, 28 July 1921, *PSYV*, 62
14 letter from Prokofiev to Mme. Ripert, 1 May 1922, SPA
15 letter from Prokofiev to Gottlieb, 14 May 1922, SPA
16 ibid.
17 *Chicago Daily Tribune* (17 Dec 1921)
18 *New York Times* (27 Jan 1922)
19 *The Times* (26 April 1922)
20 letter from Prokofiev to Gottlieb, 5 Nov 1922, SPA
21 letter from Prokofiev to Capablanca, 12 Nov 1922, SPA
22 letter from Prokofiev to Alexey Staal, 28 May 1923, quoted by Sviatoslav Prokofiev, trans. Edward Morgan in *Three Oranges*, no.3 (2002), 5
23 letter from Getteman to Prokofiev, 15 Jan 1923, SPA
24 letter from Prokofiev to Getteman, 18 Jan 1923, SPA
25 letter from Prokofiev to Souvchinsky, 13 May 1922, *PSYV*, 69
26 letter from Prokofiev to Damskaya, 5 May 1922, *SP110*, 27
27 letter from Prokofiev to Asafyev, 7 Nov 1922, *IPSMK*, 6
28 letter from Prokofiev to Damskaya, 7 Jan 1923, *SP110*, 68
29 letter from Prokofiev to Souvchinsky, 30 July 1922, *PSYV*, 74
30 letter from Myaskovsky to Prokofiev, 18 June 1923, *PMP*, 160
31 letter from Myaskovsky to Prokofiev, 15 Jan 1923, *PMP*, 150
32 letter from Prokofiev to Myaskovsky, 6 Feb 1923, *PMP*, 152
33 letter from Myaskovsky to Prokofiev, 25 May 1923, *PMP*, 156
34 letter from Myaskovsky to Prokofiev, 25 July 1923, *PMP*, 163
35 letter from Prokofiev to Myaskovsky, 4 June 1923, *PMP*, 159
36 ibid., 158
37 letter from Prokofiev to Myaskovsky, 15 July 1924, *PMP*, 200
38 Nestyev: *Prokofiev*, 210
39 letter from Prokofiev to Coates, 17 Sept 1923, SPA
40 'You seem – like the geese that saved Rome – to be still proud that many years ago you once or twice engaged me. How long do you intend to remain in passive contemplation of this noble act?': ibid.
41 letter from Prokofiev to Souvchinsky, 10 Dec 1923, *PSYV*, 93
42 ibid.
43 postcard from Soffer in Algiers, undated, SPA
44 Sachs transcript, SPA
45 letter from Prokofiev to Natalya Koussevitzky, 8 July 1923, quoted in *Sovietskaya muzyka* (April 1991), 57
46 Sachs transcript, SPA
47 ibid.
48 ibid.

Chapter 10: Three steps of steel, 1923–5

1 short autobiography, *MDV*, 173
2 letter from Prokofiev to Souvchinsky, 23 Nov 1923, *PSYV*, 93
3 letter from Prokofiev to Souvchinsky, 10 Dec 1923, *PSYV*, 94
4 ibid., 93
5 Sachs transcript, SPA
6 ibid.
7 ibid.
8 title included in an undated list of books and scores to be packed into a special trunk, SPA
9 Sachs transcript, SPA
10 letter from Prokofiev to Myaskovsky, 25 March 1924, *PMP*, 187
11 *Le Gaulois* (9 March 1924)
12 *Le Gaulois* (10 March 1924)
13 *New York Times* (15 June 1924)
14 letter from Prokofiev to Souvchinsky, 23 Nov 1923, *PSYV*, 93
15 letter from Coates to Prokofiev, 22 Aug 1923, SPA
16 letter from Prokofiev to Koussevitzky, 1 Nov 1923, SPA
17 *New York Times* (15 June 1924)
18 *Le Gaulois* (12 May 1924)
19 ibid.
20 letter from Prokofiev to Souvchinsky, 16 Feb 1924, *PSYV*, 95
21 *New York Times* (15 June 1924)
22 letter from Prokofiev to Souvchinsky, 23 Nov 1923, *PSYV*, 92
23 letter from Prokofiev to Asafyev, 8 Feb 1925, *IPSMK*, 8–9
24 letter from Prokofiev to Souvchinsky, 10 Dec 1923, *PSYV*, 94
25 letter from Prokofiev to Souvchinsky, 12 Dec 1922, *PSYV*, 81
26 ibid.
27 letter from Prokofiev to Souvchinsky, 1 Dec 1922, *PSYV*, 80
28 letter from Prokofiev to Miss Curran of the Neighborhood Playhouse, 23 March 1924, SPA
29 letter from Eberg to the Neighborhood Playhouse, 28 March 1924, SPA
30 Vernon Duke: *Passport to Paris* (Boston: Little, Brown, 1955), 114
31 ibid., 120–21
32 letter from Prokofiev to Myaskovsky, 1 June 1924, *PMP*, 195
33 ibid.
34 ibid.
35 letter from Prokofiev to Myaskovsky, 3 Jan 1924, *PMP*, 182
36 letter from Prokofiev to Myaskovsky, 25 March 1924, *PMP*, 188
37 letter from Prokofiev to Pierre Blois, 6 Sept 1924, SPA
38 letter from Prokofiev to Myaskovsky, 9 Nov 1924, *PMP*, 204
39 letter from Prokofiev to Myaskovsky, 25 March 1924, *PMP*, 188
40 letter from Prokofiev to Souvchinsky, 23 July 1924, *PSYV*, 98
41 letter from Prokofiev to Romanov, 6 Aug 1924, SPA
42 letter from Prokofiev to Souvchinsky, 23 July 1924, *PSYV*, 98
43 letter from Prokofiev to Gottlieb, undated, SPA
44 letter from Caroline Getty to Lina Prokofiev, 28 July 1924, SPA
45 undated notes signed 'sprkfv', SPA
46 letter from Prokofiev to Christian Science Committee on Publications, 5 July 1925, SPA
47 letter from Louise Roblin to Prokofiev, 12 May 1924, SPA
48 letter from Roblin to Prokofiev, 28 May 1924, SPA
49 letter from Prokofiev to Katya Rayevskaya, 17 Aug 1925, SPA
50 letter from Prokofiev to Anna Uvarova, 6 Dec 1925, SPA
51 *Za svobodu* (Warsaw, 19 Jan 1925), quoted in *SI*, 44
52 'Paris: The Spring Season 1925', *SI*, 46
53 *Za svobodu* (Warsaw, 19 Jan 1925), quoted in *SI*, 44
54 ibid.
55 ibid.
56 'Paris: The Spring Season 1925', *SI*, 45–6
57 ibid., 45
58 ibid., 46
59 letter from Margot Szenkar to Lina Prokofiev, 2 April 1925, SPA
60 short autobiography, *MDV*, 174
61 letter from Prokofiev to Fritz Remond, 21 March 1925, SPA
62 letter from Prokofiev to Dranishnikov, 19 Oct 1925, SPA
63 letter from Margot Szenkar to Lina Prokofiev, 2 April 1925, SPA
64 letter from Myaskovsky to Prokofiev, 10 June 1924, *PMP*, 197
65 letter from Myaskovsky to Prokofiev, 18 Aug 1924, *PMP*, 202
66 letter from Prokofiev to Myaskovsky, 4 Aug 1925, *PMP*, 216
67 see note 32 above
68 letter from Prokofiev to Max Terpis, 27 June 1925, SPA
69 letter from Prokofiev to Myaskovsky, 4 Aug 1925, *PMP*, 216
70 letter from Prokofiev to Demasy, 8 Sept 1925, SPA

71 letter from Prokofiev to Souvchinsky, 24 June 1925, *PSYV*, 99
72 ibid.
73 description of the first performance quoted (without reference) in Boris Schwarz: *Music and Musical Life in Soviet Russia 1917–70* (London: Barrie & Jenkins, 1972), 73
74 letter from Prokofiev to Szigeti, 22 July 1925, SPA
75 letter from Prokofiev to Myaskovsky, 4 Aug 1925, *PMP*, 216
76 letter from Prokofiev to Straram, 12 Sept 1926, SPA
77 ibid.
78 scenario sent to Diaghilev by Prokofiev, with Yakulov's drawings, 11 Aug 1925, SPA
79 letter from Prokofiev to Souvchinsky, 25 Aug 1925, *PSYV*, 101

Chapter 11: From America to Bolshevizia, 1925–7

1 letter from Prokofiev to the Swedish management, 25 Oct 1925, SPA
2 letter from Prokofiev to Haensel, 6 Oct 1925, SPA
3 letter from Prokofiev to Haensel, 20 Nov 1925, SPA
4 letter from Prokofiev to Madame Schmitz of Pro Musica, 13 Nov 1925, SPA
5 letter from Prokofiev to Groupe de Mai, Strasbourg, 14 Sept 1925, SPA
6 *New York City World* (2 Jan 1926)
7 foreword to the League of Composers' 1923–4 season, quoted in Slonimsky: *Music Since 1900*, 235
8 letter from Prokofiev to Asafyev, 2 May 1927, *IPSMK*, 23
9 letter from Prokofiev to Myaskovsky, 3 Jan 1924, *PMP*, 181
10 letter from Prokofiev to Myaskovsky, 8 Jan 1926, *PMP*, 231
11 letter from Prokofiev to Myaskovsky, 18 Feb 1926, *PMP*, 234
12 letter from the Aeolian Company to Prokofiev, 4 Feb 1924, SPA
13 letter from Gottlieb to Prokofiev, 5 Jan 1926, SPA
14 Sachs transcript, SPA
15 short autobiography, *MDV*, 176
16 *Morning Oregonian* (16 Jan 1926)
17 *St Paul Pioneer Press* (9 Jan 1926)
18 letter from Olga Samaroff to Prokofiev, received 2 March 1926, SPA
19 letter from Prokofiev to Olga Samaroff, 2 March 1926, SPA
20 *New York Evening Post* (31 March 1926)
21 ibid.
22 ibid.
23 *Boston Evening Transcript* (11 Oct 1924)
24 *Boston Evening Transcript* (15 Nov 1926)
25 letter from Prokofiev to Myaskovsky, 21 April 1926, *PMP*, 239
26 quoted in letter from Botta Jaloff to Prokofiev, 25 April 1926, SPA
27 Sachs transcript, SPA
28 'On Gorky', in Prokofiev's notebooks, *AAR*, 102
29 letter from Prokofiev to Tanya Rayevskaya, 16 Nov 1926, SPA
30 letter from Prokofiev to Szenkar, 11 Oct 1926, SPA
31 letter from Prokofiev to Asafyev, 8 Feb 1925, *IPSMK*, 9
32 letter from Prokofiev to Asafyev, 23 Nov 1926, *IPSMK*, 21
33 letter from Prokofiev to Demchinsky with enclosed scenario, 18 June 1926, SPA
34 ibid.
35 ibid.
36 ibid.
37 ibid.
38 ibid.
39 Simon Morrison: 'Prokofiev and Briusov', *Three Oranges*, no.3 (2002), 14
40 letter from Prokofiev to Blois, 10 Aug 1926, SPA
41 letter from Prokofiev to Katya Rayevskaya, 6 July 1926, SPA
42 letter from Prokofiev to Katya Rayevskaya and Katyechka Ignatyeva, 25 Sept 1926, SPA
43 letter from Prokofiev to Vladimir Bashkirov, 15 Sept 1926, SPA
44 letter from Prokofiev to Paichadze, 18 Aug 1926, SPA
45 letter from Prokofiev to Anna Ostroumova-Lebedeva, 6 Dec 1926, SPA
46 letter from Prokofiev to Hermann Schaad, 19 Aug 1926, SPA
47 programme for the *American* Overture op.42, 28 Dec 1926, SPA
48 ibid.
49 letter from Persimfans to Prokofiev, 29 March 1926, SPA
50 letter from Prokofiev to Nina Koshetz, 4 Sept 1926, SPA
51 letter from Tsukker to Prokofiev, 26 May 1926, SPA
52 letter from Prokofiev to Katya Rayevskaya and Katya Ignatyeva, 25 Sept 1926, SPA
53 letter from Prokofiev to Morolev, 5 Dec 1926, SPA
54 ibid.
55 letter from Prokofiev to Katya Rayevskaya, 7 Dec 1926, SPA
56 letter from Schaad to Prokofiev, 10 Jan 1927, SPA
57 letter from Prokofiev to Jasmin, 11 Jan 1927, SPA

58 letter from Prokofiev to Myaskovsky, 15 July 1924, *PMP*, 200
59 The Russian text of the 1927 diary first appeared in an edition published in Paris in 1990, followed by the Russian and English editions in 1991, the centenary of the composer's birth.
60 diary entry for 16 Jan 1927, *D27*, 14
61 diary entry for 17 Jan 1927, *D27*, 15
62 *Sevodnya* (Riga, 17 Jan 1927), *SI*, 62–4
63 diary entry for 18 Jan 1927, *D27*, 16
64 diary entry for 19 Jan 1927, *D27*, 17
65 diary entry for 20 Jan 1927, *D27*, 21
66 ibid.
67 diary entry for 23 Jan 1927, *D27*, 32
68 diary entry for 20 Jan 1927, *D27*, 20
69 diary entry for 30 Jan 1927, *D27*, 51–2
70 Oleg Prokofiev: introduction to *Sergei Prokofiev: Soviet Diary 1927 and Other Writings*, p.xiii
71 diary entry for 2 Feb 1927, *D27*, 55
72 interview in the programme of the Academic Theatres, 15 Feb 1927, *SI*, 68
73 diary entry for 21 Jan 1927, *D27*, 23
74 ibid., 24
75 diary entry for 14 Feb 1927, *D27*, 98
76 diary entry for 21 Jan 1927, *D27*, 24
77 diary entry for 22 Jan 1927, *D27*, 27
78 diary entry for 24 Jan 1927, *D27*, 36
79 ibid., 38
80 ibid.
81 diary entry for 7 Feb 1927, *D27*, 68
82 *Vechernaya Moskva* (18 Feb 1927)
83 diary entry for 8 Feb 1927, *D27*, 71
84 diary entry for 9 Feb 1927, *D27*, 76
85 ibid., 77
86 ibid.
87 diary entry for 12 Feb 1927, *D27*, 92
88 ibid., 93
89 *Rabochy i Teatr* 7 (15 Feb 1926), quoted in David Zolonitsky: *Sergei Radlov: The Shakespearian Fate of a Soviet Director*, trans. Natalya Egunova, Tatyana Ganf and Olga Krasikova (London: Harwood Academic Publishers, 1995), 75
90 diary entry for 10 Feb 1927, *D27*, 87
91 *Vecherneye izvestia* (Odessa, 15 March 1927), *SI*, 75
92 diary entry for 12 Feb 1927, *D27*, 92
93 diary entry for 21 Feb 1927, *D27*, 117–18
94 ibid., 118
95 ibid., 119
96 ibid., 123
97 diary entry for 20 Feb 1927, *D27*, 115–16
98 ibid., 116
99 ibid.
100 *Muzyka i Revolyutsiya* (1 March 1927), *SI*, 72–4
101 diary entry for 29 Jan 1927, *D27*, 49–50
102 diary entry for 5 March 1927, *D27*, 144
103 ibid.
104 diary entry for 26 Feb 1927, *D27*, 131
105 letter from Prokofiev to Katya Rayevskaya, 6 July 1926, SPA
106 diary entry for 25 Feb, *D27*, 130
107 letter from Prokofiev to Katya Rayevskaya and Katya Ignatyeva, 7/9 Dec 1926, SPA
108 diary entry for 6 March 1927, *D27*, 145
109 diary entry for 7 March, *D27*, 147
110 diary entry for 10 March 1927, *D27*, 151
111 diary entry for 9 March 1927, *D27*, 150
112 ibid., 151
113 diary entry for 12 March 1927, *D27*, 155
114 ibid., 154–5
115 diary entry for 15 Feb 1927, *D27*, 102
116 diary entry for 16 March 1927, *D27*, 159
117 Oistrakh: 'In Memoriam', *AAR*, 239
118 diary entry for 20 March 1927, *D27*, 162
119 diary entry for 19 March 1927, *D27*, 161

Chapter 12: Stage and symphony, 1927–9

1 letter from Prokofiev to Asafyev, 15 April 1927, *IPSMK*, 24
2 Paris programme for 8 June 1927, TMA
3 London programme for 4 July 1927, TMA
4 letter from Prokofiev to Myaskovsky, 13 May 1927, *PMP*, 257
5 letter from Myaskovsky to Prokofiev, 27 May 1927, *PMP*, 258
6 *Le Gaulois* (31 May 1927)
7 letter from Prokofiev to Schaad, 8 June 1927, SPA
8 letter from Prokofiev to Schaad, 21 July 1927, SPA
9 *La Volonté* (30 May 1927)
10 Peter Heyworth, ed.: *Conversations with Klemperer* (London: Victor Gollancz, 1973, rev. Faber and Faber, 1985), 72
11 letter from Prokofiev to Myaskovsky, 13 May 1927, *PMP*, 257
12 letter from Cocteau to Kochno, 9 June 1927, quoted in Richard Buckle: *Diaghilev* (London: Weidenfeld & Nicolson, 1979), 490
13 Duke: *Passport to Paris*, 195–6
14 letter from Prokofiev to Katya Rayevskaya, 22 June 1927, SPA
15 *Observer* (10 July 1927)
16 ibid.
17 letter from Prokofiev to Katya Rayevskaya, 11 July 1927, SPA
18 ibid.
19 letter from Prokofiev to Weber, 30 May 1927, SPA
20 letter from Prokofiev to Weber, 12 July 1927, SPA
21 ibid.
22 letter from Prokofiev to Myaskovsky, 23 Sept 1927, *PMP*, 264

23 letter from Prokofiev to Myaskovsky, 1 Aug 1927, *PMP*, 261
24 letter from Prokofiev to Myaskovsky, 18 April 1928, *PMP*, 275
25 letter from Myaskovsky to Prokofiev, 30 May 1928, *PMP*, 278
26 ibid.
27 letter from Myaskovsky to Prokofiev, 18 July 1928, *PMP*, 282
28 letter from Prokofiev to Myaskovsky, 25 Jan 1928, *PMP*, 267
29 letter from Prokofiev to Yavorsky, 27 Oct 1927, SPA
30 letter from Prokofiev to Katya Rayevskaya, 29 Nov 1927, SPA
31 letter from Prokofiev to Tseitlin, 26 Dec 1927, SPA
32 letter from Prokofiev to Belyayev, 4 April 1928, SPA
33 quoted in Zolonitsky: *Sergei Radlov*, 91
34 letter from Derzhanovsky to Prokofiev, 25 June 1928, SPA
35 letter from Prokofiev to Mari Rein, 15 Feb 1928, SPA
36 ibid.
37 letter from Prokofiev to Katya Rayevskaya, 3 May 1928, SPA
38 letter from Prokofiev to Marina Tsvetayeva, 9 Jan 1928, SPA
39 Nicolas Nabokov: *Old Friends and New Music* (London: Little, Brown, 1951), 122
40 letter from Prokofiev to Myaskovsky, 9 July 1928, *PMP*, 281
41 letter from Prokofiev to Clausells, 30 April 1928, SPA
42 letter from Prokofiev to Rysikoff, 19 May 1928, SPA
43 letter from Prokofiev to Katya Rayevskaya, 18 May 1928, SPA
44 Duke: *Passport to Paris*, 209
45 ibid.
46 letter from Prokofiev to Myaskovsky, 9 July 1928, *PMP*, 281
47 letter from Prokofiev to Katya Rayevskaya, 19 July 1928, SPA
48 letter from Prokofiev to Derzhanovsky, 22 April 1928, SPA
49 letter from Prokofiev to Myaskovsky, 3 Aug 1928, *PMP*, 284
50 letter from Myaskovsky to Prokofiev, 10 Aug 1928, *PMP*, 285
51 letter from Prokofiev to Myaskovsky, 21 Jan 1929, *PMP*, 290
52 typescript of Prokofiev's note for the Third Symphony, undated, SPA
53 ibid.
54 Sviatoslav Richter: 'On Prokofiev', *MAI*, 187
55 short autobiography, *MDV*, 182
56 letter from Myaskovsky to Prokofiev, 10 Aug 1928, *PMP*, 285
57 letter from Prokofiev to Myaskovsky, 3 Aug 1928, *PMP*, 284
58 letter from Prokofiev to Nina Koshetz, 8 Aug 1928, SPA
59 diary entry for 12 Aug 1928, trans. Edward Morgan in *Three Oranges*, no.3 (2002), 31
60 letter from Prokofiev to Natalya Koussevitzky, 15 Oct 1928, SPA
61 letter from Prokofiev to Tanya Rayevskaya, 24 Aug 1928, SPA
62 ibid.
63 ibid.
64 letter from Prokofiev to Katya Rayevskaya, 7 Nov 1928, SPA
65 letter from Prokofiev to Katya Rayevskaya, 7 July 1928, SPA
66 Prokofiev, synopsis for Berlin premiere of the Suite (undated), SPA
67 letter from Prokofiev to Maître J. Rauteler, 4 Feb 1930, SPA
68 letter from Diaghilev to Lifar, 25 Nov 1928, quoted in Serge Lifar: *Serge Diaghilev* (London: Putnam, 1940), 475
69 letter from Prokofiev to Duke, 19 Nov 1928, SPA
70 letter from Diaghilev to Lifar, 1 Dec 1928, quoted in Lifar: *Diaghilev*, 480
71 Diaghilev, interview in the *Observer* (30 June 1929)
72 letter from Prokofiev to Klein, 1 Jan 1929, SPA
73 letter from Prokofiev to Katya Rayevskaya, 20 Dec 1928, SPA
74 letter from Prokofiev to Katya Rayevskaya, 9 Jan 1929, SPA
75 letter from Prokofiev to Katya Rayevskaya, 9 March 1929, SPA
76 letter from Spaack to Prokofiev, 2 Jan 1929, SPA
77 letter from Prokofiev to Spaack, 9 Jan 1929, SPA
78 letter from Prokofiev to Derzhanovsky, 12 Feb 1929, SPA
79 letter from Prokofiev to Spaack, 12 March 1929, SPA
80 letter from Prokofiev to Katya Rayevskaya, 16 March 1929, SPA
81 letter from Prokofiev to Katya Rayevskaya, 7 May 1929, SPA
82 letter from Prokofiev to Corneil de Thoran, 7 May 1929, SPA
83 letter from the directorship of the Théâtre de la Monnaie, Brussels, to Prokofiev, 27 May 1929, SPA
84 letter from Prokofiev to Myaskovsky, 30 May 1929, *PMP*, 312–13
85 letter from Prokofiev to Paichadze, 12 Sept 1928, SPA
86 Boris Kochno: *Diaghilev and the Ballets Russes* (New York: Harper & Row, 1970), 275

87 ibid.
88 letter from Prokofiev to Meyerhold, 25 May 1928, SPA
89 Solomon Volkov: *Balanchine's Tchaikovsky*, trans. Antonina W. Bouis (New York: Simon and Schuster, 1985), 159
90 ibid., 160
91 letter from Prokofiev to the director of Pro Musica, 29 Jan 1929, SPA
92 letter from Prokofiev to Désormière, 30 May 1929, SPA
93 ibid.
94 letter from Prokofiev to Collaert, 23 May 1929, SPA
95 Lifar: *Diaghilev*, 502
96 uncredited review (signed 'RC'), 2 July 1929, TMA
97 ibid.
98 *The Times* (2 July 1929)
99 *Daily Telegraph* (29 June 1929)
100 letter from Prokofiev to Cuvelier, 4 June 1929, SPA
101 short autobiography, *MDV*, 185
102 ibid.

Chapter 13: Outlines of a real face, 1929–32

1 letter from Prokofiev to Blois, 29 July 1929, SPA
2 letter from Prokofiev to Klein, 8 July 1929, SPA
3 letter from Prokofiev to Myaskovsky, 11 Sept 1929, *PMP*, 319
4 letter from Prokofiev to Parmalee, 5 July 1929, SPA
5 short autobiography, *MDV*, 178
6 letter from Prokofiev to Asafyev, 8 Oct 1929, *IPSMK*, 26
7 letter from Prokofiev to Myaskovsky, 11 Sept 1929, *PMP*, 319
8 letter from Prokofiev to Asafyev, 29 Aug 1929, *IPSMK*, 24
9 short autobiography, *MDV*, 184
10 ibid.
11 letter from Prokofiev to Katya Rayevskaya, 23 Oct 1929, SPA
12 letter from Lina Prokofiev to Haensel, 29 Oct 1929, SPA
13 letter from Prokofiev to Myaskovsky, 23 Oct 1929, *PMP*, 323
14 telegram from Uvarova to the Prokofievs, 24 Oct 1929, SPA
15 telegram from Prokofiev to Katya Ignatyeva, 24 Oct 1929, SPA
16 *Proletarsky muzykant*, no.1 (1929), quoted in Slonimsky: *Music Since 1900*, 486
17 *Proletarsky muzykant*, no.6 (1929), *SI*, 80
18 letter from Prokofiev to Tserelli, 27 Sept 1930, SPA
19 short autobiography, *MDV*, 185
20 letter from Prokofiev to Tserelli, 27 Sept 1930, SPA
21 letter from Prokofiev to Smallens, 2 Dec 1929, SPA
22 letter from Prokofiev to Haensel, 25 Nov 1929, SPA
23 letter from Prokofiev to Haensel, 4 Dec 1929, SPA
24 letter from Prokofiev to Myaskovsky, 28 Dec 1929, *PMP*, 325
25 request from the purser of the *Berengaria* to Prokofiev, 26 Dec 1929, SPA
26 Duke, *Passport to Paris*, 233
27 letter from Prokofiev to Myaskovsky, 4 May 1930, *PMP*, 330
28 *Los Angeles Record* (20 Feb 1930)
29 letter from Prokofiev to Koussevitzky, 18 March 1930, quoted in *Sovietskaya muzyka* (June 1991), 89
30 letter from Prokofiev to Koussevitzky, 25 Nov 1929, quoted in *Sovietskaya muzyka* (June 1991), 88
31 letter from Prokofiev to Koussevitzky, 15 Jan 1930, quoted in *Sovietskaya muzyka* (June 1991), 88
32 ibid.
33 *Musical America* (25 Feb 1930)
34 letter from Prokofiev to Natalya Koussevitzky, 10 Feb 1930, *SLSP*, 202
35 telegram to Prokofiev on board the *Sunset Limited*, 10 Feb 1930, SPA
36 letter from Nelson to Prokofiev, 12 Feb 1930, SPA
37 Duke: *Passport to Paris*, 248
38 letter from Elisabeth Sprague Coolidge to Prokofiev, 14 Feb 1930, SPA
39 ibid.
40 letter from Prokofiev to Coolidge, 16 Feb 1930, SPA
41 letter from Prokofiev to Carpenter, 19 Jan 1930, SPA
42 letter from Bowles to Prokofiev, 22 Feb 1930, SPA
43 letter from Prokofiev to Paul Bowler [*sic*], 6 May 1930, SPA
44 *New York Times* (2 Feb 1930)
45 ibid.
46 Prokofiev: 'Letter on Contemporary Russian Music', *Musicalia* (5 June 1930), SPA
47 ibid.
48 letter from Prokofiev to Asafyev, 15 March 1930, *IPSMK*, 29
49 *Chicago Daily News* (8 March 1930)
50 *Detroit Evening Times* (2 March 1930)
51 *Detroit News* (3 March 1930)
52 *Los Angeles Evening Herald* (20 Feb 1930)
53 *San Francisco Examiner* (19 Feb 1930)

54 *Chicago Evening Post* (25 March 1930)
55 letter from Prokofiev to Katya Ignatyeva, 3 May 1930, SPA
56 letter from Prokofiev to Uvarova, 10 June 1930, SPA
57 Nabokov: *Old Friends and New Music*, 111
58 letter from Kügel to Prokofiev, 26 May 1930, SPA
59 letter from Prokofiev to Wittgenstein, 22 Oct 1930, SPA
60 letter from Kügel to Prokofiev accompanying the contract for the Fourth Piano Concerto, July 1930, SPA
61 letter from Wittgenstein to Prokofiev, 2 Oct 1930, SP
62 letter from Prokofiev to Hurpin, 20 June 1930, SPA
63 letter from Prokofiev to Madame la Duéchie, 1 July 1930, SPA
64 letter from Prokofiev to Meyerhold, 23 July 1930, SPA
65 telegram from Prokofiev to Lifar, 18 Aug 1930, SPA
66 letter from Prokofiev to Myaskovsky, 25 Sept 1930, *PMP*, 343
67 letter from Prokofiev to Haensel, 12 Sept 1930, SPA
68 short autobiography, *MDV*, 186–7
69 letter from Prokofiev to Myaskovsky, 24 July 1930, *PMP*, 337
70 letter from Engel to Prokofiev, 7 Feb 1930, SPA
71 letter from Prokofiev to Engel, 24 Feb 1930, SPA
72 letter from Prokofiev to Myaskovsky, 24 July 1930, SPA
73 letters from Myaskovsky to Asafyev, 20 Oct 1931 and 6 April 1932, quoted in Nestyev: *Prokofiev*, 235
74 letter from Prokofiev to Myaskovsky, 26 Aug 1930, *PMP*, 341
75 letter from Prokofiev to Katya Ignatyeva, 8 Oct 1930, SPA
76 letter from Prokofiev to Kucheryavy, 18 Oct 1931, SPA
77 letter from Prokofiev to Katya Ignatyeva, 9 Dec 1930, SPA
78 letter from Vladimir Bashkirov to Prokofiev, 13 March 1931, SPA
79 letter from Prokofiev to Vladimir Bashkirov, 9 Dec 1930, SPA
80 letter from Vladimir Bashkirov to Prokofiev, 13 March 1931, SPA
81 ibid.
82 letter from Prokofiev to Myaskovsky, 6 Jan 1931, *PMP*, 349
83 letter from Prokofiev to Asafyev, 18 May 1930, *IPSMK*, 30
84 letter from Prokofiev to Duke, 9 Nov 1930, quoted in Duke: *Passport to Paris*, 246–7
85 letter from Prokofiev to Druskin, 3 Jan 1931, SPA
86 letter from Prokofiev to Gorchakov, 10 July 1930, SPA
87 letter from Prokofiev to Paul Bowler [*sic*], 27 August 1930, SPA
88 letter from Prokofiev to Valmalète, 27 Sept 1930, SPA
89 letter from Prokofiev to Orlov, 11 Nov 1930, SPA
90 letter from Algeranoff to Prokofiev, 16 Jan 1931, SPA
91 letter from Prokofiev to Algeranoff, 21 Jan 1931, SPA
92 letter from Prokofiev to Myaskovsky, 19 Sept 1931, *PMP*, 363
93 letter from Prokofiev to Asafyev, 14 Sept 1931, *IPSMK*, 32
94 Nestyev: *Prokofiev*, 240
95 longer ballet synopsis, Jan 1931, SPA
96 shorter ballet synopsis, Jan 1931, SPA
97 letter from Prokofiev to Myaskovsky, 19 Sept 1931, *PMP*, 363
98 letter from Prokofiev to Myaskovsky, 6 Jan 1931 (referring to the Fourth Symphony), *PMP*, 349
99 longer synopsis, SPA
100 ibid.
101 letter from Prokofiev to Myaskovsky, 22 May 1931, *PMP*, 356
102 Simonson: scenario for *Le Pas d'acier*, SPA
103 ibid.
104 letter from Prokofiev to Reis, 25 Feb 1931, SPA
105 letter from the League of Composers to Prokofiev, 19 March 1931, SPA
106 summarized by Richard Hammond in a letter to Prokofiev, 3 May 1931, SPA
107 ibid.
108 ibid.
109 letter from Prokofiev to Myaskovsky, 15 April 1931, *PMP*, 355
110 letter from Astrov to *Ambrosiano*, 30 April 1931, SPA
111 letter from Prokofiev to Slonimsky, 28 May 1931, SPA
112 letter from Prokofiev to Gusman, 29 May 1931, SPA
113 letter from Prokofiev to Tanya Rayevskaya, 30 April 1931, SPA
114 reported in a letter from Astrov to Prokofiev, 24 March 1931, SPA
115 Artur Holz: 'Essai graphologique', 9 June 1931, SPA
116 letter from Prokofiev to Wittgenstein, 8 April 1931, SPA
117 letter from Prokofiev to Myaskovsky, 7 July 1931, *PMP*, 358
118 ibid.
119 letter from Prokofiev to Asafyev, 14 Sept 1931, *IPSMK*, 31–2

120 letter from Prokofiev to Myaskovsky, 7 July 1931, *PMP*, 358
121 ibid.
122 letter from Prokofiev to Tanya Rayevskaya, 1 Sept 1931, SPA
123 letter from Prokofiev to Winkler, 31 Aug 1931, SPA
124 letter from Prokofiev to Tanya Rayevskaya, 1 Sept 1931, SPA
125 letter from Prokofiev to Paichadze, 28 Aug 1931, SPA
126 letter from Prokofiev to Gottlieb, 16 Nov 1931, SPA
127 letter from Prokofiev to Paichadze, 9 Sept 1931, SPA
128 letter from Prokofiev to Capablanca, 26 July 1931, SPA
129 letter from Prokofiev to Tanya Rayevskaya, 1 Sept 1931, SPA
130 ibid.
131 letter from Prokofiev to Myaskovsky, 7 July 1931, *PMP*, 358
132 letter from Prokofiev to Pierné, 4 Feb 1932, SPA
133 letter from Prokofiev to Weber, 4 Dec 1931, SPA
134 letter from Prokofiev to Walter, 16 Dec 1931, SPA
135 letter from Prokofiev to Derzhanovsky, 5 Dec 1931, SPA
136 ibid.
137 letter from Prokofiev to Brosa, 23 Oct 1931, SPA
138 letter from Prokofiev to the Roth Quartet, 8 Nov 1931, SPA
139 letter from Haensel to Prokofiev, 9 Jan 1932, SPA
140 letter from Prokofiev to Gottlieb, 16 Feb 1932, SPA
141 letter from Prokofiev to Haensel, 29 Feb 1932, SPA
142 letter from Prokofiev to Weber, 13 Feb 1932, SPA
143 letter from Prokofiev to Stuckenschmidt, 19 Feb 1932, SPA
144 letter from Prokofiev to Derzhanovsky, 13 Feb 1932, SPA
145 letter from Myaskovsky to Prokofiev, 19 June 1932, *PMP*, 385
146 letter from Prokofiev to Myaskovsky, 27 July 1932, *PMP*, 389
147 ibid.
148 letter from Prokofiev to Haensel, 21 Jan 1932, SPA
149 letter from Prokofiev to Gottlieb, 16 Nov 1931, SPA
150 Bernard Jacobson: notes for a recording of the five piano concertos (Philips 462 048-2)
151 letter from Prokofiev to Felber, 9 March 1932, SPA
152 short autobiography, *MDV*, 178 (see note 5)
153 letter from Gottlieb to Prokofiev, 17 Feb 1932, SPA
154 letter from Lucas to Prokofiev, 28 Jan 1932, SPA

Chapter 14: Sound and vision, 1932–4

1 letter from Prokofiev to Leirens, 8 Feb 1932, SPA
2 Sviatoslav Prokofiev in conversation with the author, Paris, March 2002
3 letter from Prokofiev to Myaskovsky, 11 June 1932, *PMP*, 384
4 letter from Prokofiev to Gaisberg, 28 July 1932, SPA
5 letter from Prokofiev to Watson Lyle, 30 April 1932, SPA
6 letter from Prokofiev to Lyle, 16 July 1932, SPA
7 letter from Prokofiev to Rouché, 29 July 1932, SPA
8 letter from Prokofiev to Weber, 26 April 1932, SPA
9 letter from Prokofiev to Weber, 9 May 1932, SPA
10 letter from Prokofiev to Derzhanovsky, 21 Oct 1932, SPA
11 letter from Prokofiev to Myaskovsky, 18 March 1932, *PMP*, 376
12 ibid.
13 letter from Prokofiev to Poulet, 3 Oct 1932, SPA
14 letter from Prokofiev to Grzegorz Fitelberg, 4 July 1932, SPA
15 *Muzykalny almanakh* (1932), quoted in *AAR*, 97
16 ibid.
17 letter from Prokofiev to Tanya Rayevskaya, 8 Sept 1932, SPA
18 postcard from Prokofiev to Myaskovsky, 8 July 1932, SPA
19 letter from Prokofiev to Katya Ignatyeva, 31 Aug 1932, SPA
20 letter from Prokofiev to Tanya Rayevskaya, 8 Sept 1932, SPA
21 letter from Prokofiev to Katya Ignatyeva, 31 Aug 1932, SPA
22 short autobiography, *MDV*, 191
23 Ravel, biographical sketch, quoted in Roland-Manuel: *Maurice Ravel*, trans. Cynthia Jolly (London: Dennis Dobson, 1947) [Eng. trans. of *À la gloire de Ravel* (Paris, 1938)], 89
24 letter from Prokofiev to Myaskovsky, 5 Oct 1932, *PMP*, 392
25 letter from Myaskovsky to Prokofiev, 19 June 1932, *PMP*, 385 (see Chapter 13 note 145)

26 letter from Prokofiev to Myaskovsky, 5 Oct 1932, *PMP*, 392
27 Oistrakh: 'In Memoriam', *AAR*, 238
28 letter from Prokofiev to Gottlieb, 7 Nov 1932, SPA
29 letter from Schaal to Prokofiev, 5 Nov 1932, SPA
30 letter from Prokofiev to Myaskovsky, 5 Oct 1932, *PMP*, 393
31 telegram from Prokofiev to Lina, 28 Nov 1932, SPA
32 *Le Petit Marseillais* (26 Dec 1932)
33 letter from Prokofiev to Malko, 11 Dec 1932, SPA
34 letter from Prokofiev to Krachkovsky, 11 Dec 1932, SPA
35 *Vechernaya Moskva* (6 Dec 1932)
36 *Sovietskoye isskustvo* (3 March 1933), quoted in *Dmitry Shostakovich About Himself and his Times* (Moscow: Progress, 1981), 36
37 ibid.
38 contract with Sovietskaya Kino-Fabrik Belorus [Belgoskino], 3 Dec 1932, SPA
39 letter from Prokofiev to Asafyev, 14 Dec 1932, *IPSMK*, 40
40 *Le Figaro* (20 Dec 1932)
41 letter from Prokofiev to Weber, 10 March 1933, SPA
42 ibid.
43 letter from Prokofiev to Asafyev, 2 Jan 1933, *IPSMK*, 40
44 letter from Gottlieb to Prokofiev, 14 April 1933, SPA
45 letter from Prokofiev to Gottlieb, 6 July 1933, SPA
46 letter from Crain to Prokofiev, 23 Jan 1933, SPA
47 letter from Prokofiev to 'Miss Crain', 31 Jan 1933, SPA
48 letter from Prokofiev to Katya Ignatyeva, 23 Feb 1933, SPA
49 letter from Prokofiev to Moreux, 22 February 1933, SPA
50 letter from Prokofiev to Mangeot, 19 June 1933, SPA
51 letter from Prokofiev to Myaskovsky, 18 Feb 1933, *PMP*, 396
52 letter from Prokofiev to Malko, 15 June 1933, SPA
53 letter from Prokofiev to Tanya Rayevskaya, 20 June 1933, SPA
54 ibid.
55 short autobiography, *MDV*, 191
56 Volkov, ed: *Testimony*, 162–3
57 letter from Prokofiev to Feinzimmer, 13 July 1933, SPA
58 ibid.
59 letter from Prokofiev to Feinzimmer, 3 Oct 1933, SPA
60 letter from Myaskovsky to Prokofiev, 17 June 1933, *PMP*, 399
61 short autobiography, *MDV*, 193
62 ibid.
63 ibid.
64 typescript of Prokofiev's article for *La Revue de Bridge* (March 1933), SPA
65 letter from Prokofiev to Gottlieb, 6 July 1933, SPA
66 letter from Prokofiev to Brichan, 5 Aug 1933, SPA
67 letter from Prokofiev to Valmalète, 5 Oct 1933, SPA
68 telegram from Prokofiev to 'Ptashka', 21 Oct 1933, SPA
69 *Sovietskaya muzyka* (26 Dec 1933), quoted in *PMP*, 541
70 *Izvestiya* (30 March 1934), quoted in *MAI*, 32–3
71 letter from Prokofiev to Tairov, 18 Dec 1933, SPA
72 Prokofiev's commentary to the music of *Egyptian Nights*, SPA
73 letter from Prokofiev to Gusman, 3 Oct 1934, SPA
74 letter from Prokofiev to Tanya Rayevskaya, 20 Dec 1933, SPA
75 letter from Prokofiev to Malko, 20 Dec 1933, SPA
76 letter from Prokofiev to Myaskovsky, 23 Dec 1933, *PMP*, 407–8
77 ibid.
78 letter from Prokofiev to Winkler, 23 Dec 1933, SPA
79 letter from Prokofiev to the Accademia di S. Cecilia, 28 Jan 1934, SPA
80 letter from Prokofiev to Gottlieb, 26 June 1934, SPA
81 Myaskovsky, quoted in Nestyev: *Prokofiev*, 255
82 *Sovietskaya muzyka* (1934), no.6, quoted in Nestyev: *Prokofiev*, 255
83 letter from Prokofiev to Malko, 26 June 1934, SPA
84 short autobiography, *MDV*, 193
85 letter from Prokofiev to Myaskovsky, 1 May 1934, *PMP*, 423
86 letter from Prokofiev to Winkler, 20 July 1934, SPA
87 letter from Prokofiev to Labinsky, 20 July 1934, SPA
88 letter from Prokofiev to Winkler, 20 July 1934, SPA
89 letter from 'Mémé' to Prokofiev, 5 June 1934, SPA
90 letter from Prokofiev to Myaskovsky, 15 Aug 1934, *PMP*, 426
91 ibid.
92 letter from Prokofiev to Wittgenstein, 8 Oct 1934, SPA
93 short autobiography, *MDV*, 189
94 letter from Wittgenstein to Prokofiev, 11 Oct 1934, SPA
95 ibid.

96 letter from Prokofiev to Wittgenstein, 25 Oct 1934, SPA
97 letter from Prokofiev to Michel-Dimitri Calvocoressi, 22 Oct 1934, SPA
98 *The Times* (20 Oct 1934)

Chapter 15: The path to happiness, 1934–5

1 letter from Prokofiev to Asafyev, 9 Feb 1935, quoted in *PMP*, 545
2 *Izvestia* (16 Nov 1934), quoted in *AAR*, 99–100
3 letter from Prokofiev to the editorial board of the *Christian Science Monitor*, 6 March 1935, SPA
4 telegram from Tairov to Prokofiev, 1 Feb 1935, SPA
5 *Izvestia* (16 Nov 1934', quoted in *AAR*, 99–100
6 letter from Prokofiev to Malko, 16 Jan 1934, SPA
7 letter from Prokofiev to Malko, 28 Aug 1933, SPA
8 letter from Prokofiev to Gusman, 15 Jan 1934, SPA
9 Meyerhold, 'A Reply to Criticism', *Teatr i dramaturgiya* (1936), no.4, quoted in Edward Braun, ed.: *Meyerhold on Theatre* (London: Methuen, 1969, rev. 1991 and 1998), 291
10 *Vechernaya krasnaya gazeta* (27 Dec 1934), quoted in Zolonitsky: *Radlov*, 112
11 letter from Myaskovsky to Prokofiev, 24 Jan 1935, *PMP*, 424
12 ibid.
13 letter from Prokofiev to Myaskovsky, 23 Feb 1935, *PMP*, 439
14 card from Prokofiev to Myaskovsky, 6 Jan 1935, *PMP*, 434
15 letter from Ančerl to Prokofiev, 1 March 1935, SPA
16 letter from Prokofiev to Ančerl, 5 March 1935, SPA
17 letter from Prokofiev to Myaskovsky, 23 Feb 1935, *PMP*, 439
18 letter from Prokofiev to Gaisberg, 26 July 1934, SPA
19 letter from Prokofiev to Myaskovsky, 23 Feb 1935, *PMP*, 439
20 letter from Prokofiev to Gaisberg, 5 March 1935, SPA
21 ibid.
22 letter from Gaisberg to Prokofiev, 8 March 1935, SPA
23 Prokofiev, handwritten draft of Myaskovsky's dedication to Stock, 21 March 1935, SPA
24 letter from Haensel to Prokofiev, 7 Feb 1935, SPA
25 letter from Prokofiev to Haensel, 28 Feb 1935, SPA
26 letter from Prokofiev to Ammons, 31 March 1935, SPA
27 *Vechernaya Moskva* (23 Jan 1936), *SI*, 131
28 letter from Prokofiev to Gottlieb, 6 June 1935, SPA
29 letter from 'Bébin' (Oleg Prokofiev) to 'Papa', 1 April 1935, SPA
30 letter from Prokofiev to Gottlieb, 6 June 1935, SPA
31 letter from Sviatoslav Prokofiev to his father, 21 July 1935, SPA
32 Sviatoslav Prokofiev in conversation with the author, March 2002
33 letter from Prokofiev to Myaskovsky, 11 Sept 1935, SPA
34 short autobiography, *MDV*, 194
35 Yelena Sergeyevna Bulgakova, diary entry for 4 Oct 1935, in Mikhail Bulgakov: *Manuscripts Don't Burn*, ed. and trans. J.A.E. Curtis (London: Bloomsbury, 1991), 214
36 Nestyev: *Prokofiev*, 260
37 Prokofiev, text of a radio speech for Gorky's funeral, 19 June 1936, quoted in *MAI*, 43
38 Frederic Chiu, note to his recording of Prokofiev's piano music, vol.vii (Harmonia Mundi HMU 907190)
39 letter from Prokofiev to Soetens, 23 May 1935, SPA
40 letter from Prokofiev to Soetens, 1 Aug 1935, SPA
41 ibid.
42 letter from Prokofiev to Moskovsky, 22 Sept 1932, SPA
43 short autobiography, *MDV*, 193
44 letter from Prokofiev to Myaskovsky, 3 Dec 1935, *PMP*, 441
45 letter from Arbós to Prokofiev, 11 Dec 1935, SPA
46 letter from Prokofiev to Myaskovsky, 16 Dec 1935, *PMP*, 445
47 letter from Prokofiev to Soetens, 10 July 1935, SPA
48 letter from Prokofiev to Myaskovsky, 20 Dec 1935, *PMP*, 446
49 letter from Prokofiev to Gottlieb, 14 Nov 1935, SPA

Bibliography

Principal sources for letters and autobiographical writing

Blok, Vladimir, ed.: *Sergei Prokofiev: Materials, Articles, Interviews* (Moscow: Progress, 1978)

Brown, Malcolm Hamrick, ed.: 'Prokofiev's Correspondence with Stravinsky and Shostakovich' in *Slavonic and Western Music: Essays for Gerald Abraham*, ed. Malcolm Hamrick Brown and Roland John Wiley (Ann Arbor: University of Michigan Research Press, 1985; Oxford: OUP, 1985)

Kozlova, Miralda and Yatsenko, Nina, eds.: *S.S. Prokofiev i N. Ya. Myaskovsky: Perepisk* (Moscow: Sovietsky Kompozitor, 1977) [with an introduction by Dmitry Kabalevsky]

Kozlova, Miralda, ed.: 'Pisma S.S. Prokofieva – B. N. Asafyevu (1920–40)', *Iz proshlovo Sovietskoy muzykalnoy kultury*, ii (Moscow: Sovetsky Kompozitor, 1976)

Nestyev, Israel and Edelman, G., eds.: *Sergey Prokofiev 1953–1963: Staty i materialy* (Moscow: Sovietsky Kompozitor, 1962; rev. with additional material Moscow: Muzyka, 1965)

Poldyaeva, Yelena: '"Ya chasto s nim ne soglashalsya . . .": Iz perepiski S.S. Prokofieva i P.P. Suvchinskovo' in *Pyotr Souvchinsky i yevo vremya*, ed. Alla Bretanitskaya (Moscow: Kompozitor, 1999)

Prokofiev, Oleg, ed.: *Sergey Prokofiev: Dnevnik – 27* (Paris: Sintaksis, 1990) [Oleg Prokofiev's Eng. trans. is published with the short autobiography and some of the composer's stories in *Sergei Prokofiev: Soviet Diary 1927 and Other Writings*, ed. Oleg Prokofiev and Christopher Palmer (London: Faber and Faber, 1991).]

Prokofiev, Sergey: *Dnevnik 1907–1933*, diaries, collated by Sviatoslav Prokofiev and Serge Prokofiev Jnr, 2 vols. with supplementary booklet of photographs (Paris: sprkfv, 2002)

Prokofiev, Sergey: *Avtobiografiya*, ed. Miralda Kozlova (Moscow: Sovietsky Kompozitor, 1973; rev. with supplementary chapters, 1982) [there is a much abridged translation, *Prokofiev by Prokofiev: A Composer's Memoir*, ed. David H. Appel, trans. Guy Daniels (New York: Doubleday, 1979); further heavy cuts were made for the English edn, ed. Francis King (London: Macdonald & Jane's, 1979)]

Rakhmanova, Marina, ed.: *Sergey Prokofiev k 110 letiyu s dnya rozhdeniya: Pisma, vospominaniya i staty* (Moscow: Glinka State Central Museum of Musical Culture, 2001)

Robinson, Harlow, ed.: *Selected Letters of Sergei Prokofiev* (Boston: Northeastern UP, 1998)

Shlifstein, Semyon, ed.: *S. S. Prokofiev: Materialy, dokumenty, vospominaniya* (Moscow: Gosudarstvennoye Muzykalnoye Izdatelstvo, 1956, 2/1961) [incl. the first Soviet publication of the short autobiography]

Shlifstein, Semyon: *S. Prokofiev: Autobiography, Articles, Reminiscences*, trans. Rosa Prokofieva (Moscow: Foreign Languages Publishing House, c1956)

Tarakanov, Mikhail, ed.: *Sergey Prokofiev 1891–1953: Dnevnik, pisma, besedy, vospominaniya* (Moscow: Sovietsky Kompozitor, 1991)

Varunts, Viktor, ed: *Prokofiev o Prokofieve: Staty i intervyu* (Moscow: Sovietsky Kompozitor, 1991)

Other publications (excluding journal and newspaper articles)

Bartlett, Rosamund: *Wagner and Russia* (Cambridge: CUP, 1985)

Beaumont, Cyril: *The Diaghilev Ballet in London* (London: Putnam, 1940)

Braun, Edward: *Meyerhold: A Revolution in Theatre* (London: Methuen, 1995)
Braun, Edward ed.: *Meyerhold on Theatre* (London: Methuen, 1969, rev. 1991 and 1998)
Buckle, Richard: *Diaghilev* (London: Weidenfeld & Nicolson, 1979)
Bulgakov, Mikhail: *Manuscripts Don't Burn*, ed. and trans. J.A.E. Curtis (London: Bloomsbury, 1991)
Capablanca, José: *My Chess Career* (New York: Macdonald, 1920)
Chaliapin: An Autobiography as Told to Maxim Gorky, trans. Nina Froud and James Hanley (London: Macdonald, 1968)
Dorigné, Michel: *Serge Prokofiev* (Paris: Foyard, 1994)
Duke, Vernon: *Passport to Paris* (Boston: Little, Brown, 1955)
Garafola, Lynn: *Diaghilev's Ballets Russes* (New York and Oxford: OUP, 1989)
Gray, Camilla: *The Russian Experiment in Art 1863–1922* (London: Thames and Hudson, 1962)
Grigoriev, Sergey: *The Diaghilev Ballet 1909–1929*, ed. and trans. Vera Bowen (London: Constable, 1953)
Gutman, David: *Prokofiev* (London: Omnibus Press, 1990; Alderman Press, 1998)
Hanson, Lawrence and Elisabeth: *Prokofiev: The Prodigal Son* (London: Cassell, 1964)
Hartston, William: *The Kings of Chess* (London: Pavilion/Michael Joseph, 1985)
Heyworth, Peter, ed.: *Conversations with Klemperer* (London: Victor Gollancz, 1973, rev. 1985 [Faber and Faber])
Hosking, Geoffrey: *A History of the Soviet Union, 1917–1991* (London: Fontana, 1985, rev. 1992)
Ikonnikov, Alexey: *Miaskowsky: His Life and Work* (New York: Philosophical Library, 1946)
Jaffé Daniel: Sergey Prokofiev (London: Phaidon Press/Chronicle Books, 1998)
Kamensky, Alexander ed.: *Mir iskusstva: Obedineniye russkikh khudozhinkov nachala XX veka*, trans. Arthur Shkarovsky-Raffe as *The World of Art Movement in Early 20th-Century Russia* (Leningrad: Aurora, 1991)
Kochno, Boris: *Diaghilev and the Ballets Russes* (New York: Harper & Row, 1970)
Krivosheina, Nina: *Chetirye treti nashei zhizni* (Paris: YMCA Press, 1984)
Mikhail Larionov – Natalya Goncharova: Chefs d'oeuvres iz Parizhskovo nslediya zhivopis (Moscow: Gosudarstvennaya Tretyakovskaya Galereya, 1999) [catalogue for Tretyakov Gallery exhibition of major paintings by Goncharova and Larionov]
M. Larionov, N. Goncharova: Parizhskoye naslediye v Tretyakovskoi galereye (Moscow: Gosudarstvennaya Tretyakovskaya Galereya, 1999) [catalogue for Tretyakov Gallery exhibition of theatre designs by Goncharova and Larionov]
Leyda, Jay: *Kino: A History of the Russian and Soviet Film* (London: George Allen & Unwin, 1960, 2/1973; paperback edn with extra text Princeton: Princeton UP, 1983)
Lifar, Serge: *Ma Vie: From Kiev to Kiev*, trans. James Holman Mason (London: Hutchinson, 1970)
Lifar, Serge: *Serge Diaghilev* (London: Putnam, 1940)
Lunacharsky, Anatoly: *Revolutionary Silhouettes*, trans. Michael Glenny (London: Allen Lane, 1967)
Malko, Nikolay: *A Certain Art* (New York: William Morrow, 1966)
Massine, Léonide: *My Life in Ballet* (London: Macmillan, 1968)
Mikhailova, Alla, ed.: *Meyerkhold i khudozhinki* (Moscow: Galart, 1995)
Minturn, Neil: *The Music of Sergei Prokofiev* (New Haven and London: Yale UP, 1997)
Montagu-Nathan, Montagu: *Contemporary Russian Composers* (London: Cecil Palmer & Hayward, 1917)
Nabokov, Nicolas: *Old Friends and New Music* (London: Little, Brown, 1951)
Nabokov, Vladimir: *Speak, Memory* (London: Penguin, 1969) [originally pubd as *Conclusive Evidence* (London: Weidenfeld & Nicolson, 1967)]
Nestyev, Israel: *Zhizn Sergeya Prokofieva* (Moscow: Sovietsky Kompozitor, 1957, enlarged 2/1973; Eng. trans., 1961)
Nestyev, Israel: *Sergei Prokofiev: His Musical Life* (New York: Alfred A. Knopf, 1946)
Nestyev, Israel: *Prokofiev*, trans. Florence Jonas (Stanford: Stanford UP, 1961; Oxford: OUP, 1961)
Pozharskaya, Militsa: *Russkiye sezoni v Parizhe* (Moscow: Iskusstvo, 1988; Eng. trans., as *The Art of the Ballets Russes*, with Tatyana Volodina, London: Aurum, 1990)
Reeder, Roberta: *Anna Akhmatova: Poet and Prophet* (New York: St Martin's Press, 1994)
Rimsky-Korsakov, Nikolay: *My Musical Life*, trans. Judah A. Joffe (New York: Alfred A. Knopf, 1923)
Robinson, Harlow: *Sergei Prokofiev: A Biography* (London: Robert Hale, 1987)
Roland-Manuel, Alexis: *Maurice Ravel* (London: Dennis Dobson, 1947) [Eng. trans. of *À la gloire de Ravel* (Paris, 1938)]
Samuel, Claude: *Prokofiev*, trans. Miriam John (London: Calder & Boyars, 1971)
Savkina, Natalya: *Sergey Sergeyevich Prokofiev* (Moscow: Muzyka, 1982; Eng. trans., Catherine Young, as *Prokofiev* (Neptune City, NJ: Paganiniana, 1984)
Schmemann, Serge: *Echoes of a Native Land* (New York: Alfred A. Knopf, 1997)
Schwarz, Boris: *Music and Musical Life in Soviet Russia 1917–70* (London: Barrie & Jenkins, 1972, enlarged 2/1983)
Shostakovich, Dmitry: *Dmitry Shostakovich: About Himself and his Times, 1926–1975*, ed. G. Pribegina (Moscow: Progress, 1980; Eng. trans., as *Shostakovich about Himself and his Times*, ed. L. Grigoryev and Ya. Platek, Moscow, 1981)

Slonimsky, Nicolas: *Music Since 1900* (New York: Charles Scribner, 4/1971; suppl. 1986, 5/1993)
Slonimsky, Nicolas: *Perfect Pitch: A Life Story* (Oxford: OUP, 1988)
Stasov, Vladimir: *Selected Essays on Music*, trans. Florence Jonas (London: Barrie & Rockliff, 1968)
Stravinsky, Igor, with Nouvel, Walter: *Chroniques de ma vie* (Paris, 1935–6, 2/1962; Eng. trans., 1936; Eng. trans., as *An Autobiography*, London: Victor Gollancz, 1936/*R*1975)
Stravinsky, Igor and Craft, Robert: *Conversations with Igor Stravinsky* (New York: Doubleday, 1959; London: Faber and Faber, 1959)
Stravinsky, Igor: *Selected Correspondence*, ed. Robert Craft, i (New York: Alfred A. Knopf, 1982; London: Faber and Faber, 1982)
Stravinsky, Igor and Craft, Robert: *Expositions and Developments* (New York: Doubleday, 1962; London: Faber and Faber, 1962)
Stravinsky, Igor and Craft, Robert: *Memories and Commentaries* (New York: Doubleday, 1960; London: Faber and Faber, 1960)
Swan, Alfred: *Russian Music* (London: John Barker, 1973)
Taruskin, Richard: *Stravinsky and the Russian Traditions*, 2 vols. (Berkeley: University of California Press, 1996; Oxford: OUP, 1996)
Terras, Viktor, ed.: *A Handbook of Russian Literature* (New Haven: Yale UP, 1985)
Terras, Viktor: *A History of Russian Literature* (New Haven: Yale UP, 1991)
Volkov, Solomon: *Balanchine's Tchaikovsky*, trans. Antonina W. Bouis (New York: Simon & Schuster, 1985)
Volkov, Solomon ed.: *Testimony: The Memoirs of Dmitry Shostakovich*, trans. Antonina W. Bouis (London: Hamish Hamilton, 1979)
Whyte Kovan, Florice, ed.: *Ben Hecht Rediscovered* (*http://www.snickersneepress.bigstep.com*, 2001–2)
Wilson, Elizabeth: *Shostakovich: A Life Remembered* (London: Faber and Faber, 1994)
Yastrebtsev, Vasily: *Reminiscences*, ed. and trans. Florence Jonas (New York: Columbia UP, 1985)
Zolonitsky, David: *Sergei Radlov: The Shakespearian Fate of a Soviet Director*, trans. Natalya Egunova, Tatyana Ganf and Olga Krasikova (London: Harwood, 1995)

English translations of the sources for the stage works

Afanasyev, Alexander: 'The Jester', in *Russian Fairy Tales*, trans. Norbert Guterman (New York: Pantheon, 1945) [from Afanasyev's *Narodniya Russkiya Skazki – 223: Chout* (Moscow, 1897)]
Bryusov, Valery: *The Fiery Angel: A Sixteenth-Century Romance*, trans. Ivor Montagu and Sergey Nalbandov (1930; reprinted London: Neville Spearman, 1975) [Bryusov's *Ognenny angel*, 2 vols. (Moscow, 1908–9) reprinted (Moscow: Izdatelstvo Vyshaya Shkola,1993)]
Dostoyevsky, Fyodor: *The Gambler, Bobok: A Nasty Story*, trans. Jessie Coulson (London: Penguin, 1966)
Gozzi, Carlo: 'A Reflective Analysis of the Fable Entitled "The Love of the Three Oranges"', in *Memoirs*, trans. John Addington Symonds (London: 1862) [Gozzi's *Fiabe teatrali* in Italian (Milan: Garzanti Editore, 1994); Meyerhold's adaptation is in his journal *Lyubov k tryom apelsinam*, i (1913)]

Appendices

Works 1896–1935

Early piano pieces and other works

(quotations are from Prokofiev's notes written alongside the manuscripts in the Russian State Archive of Literature and Art)

1896 Indian Galop, F major (though 'Lydian', originally missing the B flat; five bars with the B flat included in the Catalogue of Childhood Compositions, 1902)

1897 March, C major, Andante (four bars in the catalogue)
Waltz, C major, Moderato (six bars in the catalogue)
Rondo, C major, Allegretto (ten bars in the catalogue)

1898 March, B minor (D major), Allegro (five bars in the catalogue)
March for four hands, C major, Andante
'My Piano Pieces, aged Seven, S. Prokofiev':
1 Polka, G major
2 Waltz, G major, Allegretto
3 March for four hands, C major, Andante, 'op.1'

1899 Waltz, C major (G major), Allegretto
March for four hands, F major, quick (Allegro) ('to my dear beloved mother from Seryozha Prokofiev in 1899'; written down by Louise Roblin)
Piece for four hands, F major, Allegro

1900 *Velikan* ['The Giant'], opera in three acts and seven scenes without opus number (vocal score; in a red folder with gold writing, missing pp.1, 2, 10, 11, 14–17, 20–23, 26, 27)
March
'Two pieces for Papa's nameday':
1 for piano four hands, D minor
2 for piano four hands and zither (unfinished)
Pieces 'probably composed between *Velikan* and *On Desert Islands*':
1 B major
2 E minor, Vivo
3 C major
4 G major, Maestoso

1901 *Na pustynnykh ostrovakh* ['On Desert Islands'], unfinished opera (only a few bars remain in the catalogue)
[Pieces] 'For father on his nameday 25 September' (all themes from *On Desert Islands* except Tarantella):
1 D major
2 C major, Maestoso
3 Tarantella, D minor, Vivo

1902 Bagatelle no.1 for four hands, E minor, Vivo ('probably 1902, written down by my *governantka* Louise Roblin')
Pesenki ['Little Songs'], series 1:
1 E flat major, Allegro

2 A major, Andante
3 F major, Vivo–Presto
4 B major, Vivo
5 C major, Maestoso
6 D major, Tempo di Mazurka
7 C major, Allegro con fuoco
8 D minor/B minor, Lento
9 C major
10 A major, Lento
11 G major, Allegro
12 C minor (seven bars also orchestrated)

Symphony, G major ('First Symphony of Seryozha Prokofiev', dedicated to Glière; the 61 pages of manuscript include a four-hand piano arrangement and an orchestration of the first movement as well as 30 pages of orchestral parts)

Bagatelle no.2, A minor, Presto

1903 *Pesenki*, series 2:
1 C minor
2 A sharp minor, Andante
3 C major, Allegretto
4 B minor, Lento
5 G major, Moderato
6 D major, Grave (also orchestrated as Lento, maestoso)
7 Mélodie, E flat major, Lento
8 C major, Presto
9 A major, Moderato
10 D flat major, Presto
11 F major, Andante ('Written down by L. Roblin')
12 B major for four hands

Violin Sonata, C minor (in three movements; first subject later used in Ballade for cello and orchestra op.15)

Pesenka for violin and piano (no.1), D minor, Lento

Pir vo vremya chumy ['A Feast in Time of Plague'], opera based on the 'little tragedy' by Alexander Pushkin (piano score; only nine bars of the overture have survived); see also 1908

Skazhi mne, vetka Palestina ['Tell me, twig of Palestine'], romance (Lermontov)

O, nyet, nye Figner, nye Yuzhin ['Oh no, not Figner, not Yuzhin'], humorous romance for low voice and piano

Smotri, pushinki ['Look, the down'], sketch for voice and piano to the Prokofiev's own text

Uzh ya nye tot ['I am no longer the same'], romance (Pushkin) ('to beloved mother, 1903, 25 December')

1904 *Pesenki*, series 3:
1 March no.1, G minor, Presto
2 March no.2, E flat major
3 D flat major, Allegro con fuoco ('for Aunt Katyechka and Uncle Sashechka, 20/II/04')
4 C major, Presto ('for Aunt Tanyechka 20/3/04')
5 Romance no.1, E flat minor, Andante ('for Mama 22/3/04')
6 March no.3, E flat major, Allegro ('for Papa 28/3/04'); also arr. for military band)
7 March no.4, F major, Allegro ('for dear Godfather 26/5/04')
8 G minor, Vivo ('for Papochka 8/7/04')
9 March no.5, C minor
10 Romance no.2, F minor, Allegretto ('for Marya Grig. Kipshtett [*sic*]')
11 Waltz, D major, Allegro con brio ('for namedays 24 November 1904')
12 March no.6, F major, Tempo di marcia ('to beloved Papa and Mama 25/12/04')

Pesenka no.2 for violin and piano, C minor, Moderato

Sonata, B major, for piano (third and fourth movements)

Variations on the theme 'Chizhik'

Undina (*Undine*), opera in four acts to a libretto by Marya Kilschtedt (completed 1907; the piano score of the third and fourth acts survives)

1905 *Pesenki*, series 4
1 F sharp minor, Presto con brio ('for dear Mama on her birthday')
2 Romance no.3, D minor, Lento ('for Mama 26/1/05')
3 A minor, Allegretto

4 D minor, Energico ('for dear Aunt Katyechka and Uncle Sashchka 10/2/05')
5 C minor, Allegretto ('for Godfather')
6 A flat major, Allegro ('for Aunt Katya and [her daughter] Katyusha')
7 Romance no.4, B major, Allegro con fuoco ('for Papochka 8/7/04')
8 A minor, Presto ('for Papochka 25 September 1905')
9 D minor, Andante
10 C minor, Presto ('for Mamochka on her birthday')
11 Minuet, F minor, Allegretto
12 E flat major, Moderato ('à la Mendelssohn')

Polka mélancolique, F sharp minor

1906 *Pesenki*, series 5
1 C sharp minor, Moderato ('for [Aunt] Tanyechka 1906 12 January')
2 Scherzo, C major, Allegro ('for dear Mama on her nameday', 26 January 1906)
3 C minor, Presto
4 D minor, Allegro non troppo
5 Waltz, G minor, Allegro
6 March, F minor ('for Vassily Mitrofanovich Morolev'; rev. as March op.12)
7 C major, Prestissimo ('for dear Papa 8 July 1906')
8 A flat major, Allegretto (unfinished)
9 C minor, Allegro con fuoco (unfinished)
[no traces exist of the tenth and 11th *pesenki*]
12 Étude–Scherzo, C major, Vivo

1907 *Mastitiye, vetvistiye dubi* ['Ancient, gnarled oaks'], romance (Maykov)
Upryok ['Reproach'], A minor, Andante
Song without words, D flat major
Intermezzo, A major, Allegretto
Humoresque, F minor, Allegro
Untitled piece, B flat minor, Molto energico
Vostochnaya pesenka ['Eastern Song'], G minor, Andante
Untitled piece, C minor
Sonata for violin (first movement)
Sonata no.2 for piano, F minor, three movements (first movement reworked as official Sonata no.1 op.1)
Sonata no.3 for piano, A minor (rev. as Piano Sonata no.3 op.28)

1907–8 Four pieces for piano (rev. as op.3):
1 *Skazka* ['Fairy Tale']
2 *Shutka* ['Jest']
3 March
4 *Prizrak* ['Phantom']

1908 Examination Fugue, Moderato
Andante, C minor (unfinished)
Two pieces for piano:
1 *Snezhok* ['Snow']
2 *Molby* ['Entreaties']
Four pieces for piano (rev. as op.4):
1 *Vospominaniya* ['Reminisce']
2 *Poryv* ['Elan']
3 *Otchayaniye* ['Despair']
4 *Navazhdeniye* (*Suggestion diabolique*)
Sonata no.5 for piano (rev. as Piano Sonata no.4 op.29)
Sonatas nos.4 and 6 for piano
Operatic scene from Pushkin's *Pir vo vremya chumy* ['A Feast in Time of Plague']; see also 1903
Symphony, E minor, three movements (the second violin part of the complete score survives in the Russian State Archive of Literature and Art)

Mature works, including arrangements

Opus
1 Sonata no.1 for piano, F minor, one movement (rev. from Sonata no.2 of 1907), 1909
2 Four Études for piano, 1909

3 Four Pieces for piano (rev. from the original versions, 1907–8), 1911
  1 *Skazka* ['Fairy Tale']
  2 *Shutka* ['Jest']
  3 March
  4 *Prizrak* ['Phantom']
4 Four Pieces for piano (rev. from the original versions, 1908), 1910–12
  1 *Vospominaniya* ['Reminisce']
  2 *Poryv* ['Elan']
  3 *Otchayaniye* ['Despair']
  4 *Navazhdeniye* (*Suggestion diabolique*)
5 Sinfonietta, A major, five movements, 1909, rev. 1914; rev. 1929 as op.48
6 *Sni* ['Dreams'], symphonic tableau for orchestra, 1910
7 Two Poems for female chorus and orchestra to words by Konstantin Balmont, 1909–10
  1 *Bely lebed* ['The White Swan']
  2 *Volna* ['The Wave']
8 *Osenneye* ['Autumnal'] for small orchestra, 1910; rev. 1915 and 1934
9 *Two Poems* for voice and piano to words by Balmont (no.1) and Alexey Apukhtin (no.2), 1910–11
  1 *Yest drugie planety* ['There are other planets']
  2 *Otchalila lodka* ['The boat pushed off']
10 Concerto no.1 for piano and orchestra, D flat major, one movement, 1911–12 (main Allegro theme, 1907)
11 Toccata for piano, C major, 1912
12 Ten Pieces for piano, 1906–13
  1 March
  2 Gavotte
  3 Rigaudon
  4 Mazurka
  5 Capriccio
  6 *Legenda*
  7 Prelude
  8 Allemande
  9 Humoresque Scherzo
  10 Scherzo
12a *Humoresque Scherzo* from op.12 arr. for four bassoons, 1912
13 *Maddalena*, opera in one act and four scenes to a plot and libretto by Magda Lieven Orlova, 1911–13 (Prokofiev orchestrated only the first scene, 1913; the other three were orchestrated by Edward Downes from the piano score, 1978)
14 Sonata no.2 for piano, D minor, four movements, 1912
15 Ballade for cello and piano, C minor, 1912 (one theme is from the Violin Sonata in C minor, 1903)
— *A Musical Letter to Zakharov* for voice and piano, 1913
16 Concerto no.2 for piano and orchestra, G minor, four movements, 1913 (reconstruction from memory, 1923)
17 *Sarcasms*, five pieces for piano, 1912–14
18 *Gadky utyonok* ['The Ugly Duckling'], fairy tale for voice and piano after Hans Christian Andersen, 1914, rev. 1932 (Prokofiev made two orchestrations, for Nina Koshetz, 1925, and for his wife Lina, 1932)
19 Concerto no.1 for violin and orchestra, D major, three movements, 1917 (incorporating material from the 'concertino' of 1915)
20 *Scythian Suite* (derived from the ballet *Ala i Lolli* ['Ala and Lolly'] (withdrawn) with a scenario by Sergey Gorodetsky), for orchestra, four parts, 1914–15
21 *Chout* ['The Buffoon'] (full title: *Skazka pro shuta, semerikh shutov pereshutivshavo* ['The tale of the buffoon who outwitted seven other buffoons'], ballet in six scenes to a scenario by the composer after the folk-tale in Alexander Afanasyev's collection, 1915, rev. with additional orchestral interludes in 1920)
21a *Chout*, suite from the ballet in 12 movements, 1922
22 *Mimolyotnosti* (*Visions fugitives*), 20 pieces for piano, 1915–17
23 Five Poems for voice and piano to words by Vyacheslev Goryansky (no.1), Zinayda Gippius (no.2), 'Boris Verin' (no.3), Balmont (no.4) and Nikolay Agnitsev (no.5), 1915
  1 *Pod kryshey* ['Under the Roof']
  2 *Seroye platitse* ['The Grey Dress']

3 *Doversya mne* ['Trust me']
4 *V moyem sadu* ['In my Garden']
5 *Kudesnik* ['The Wizard']

24 *Igrok* ['The Gambler'], opera in four acts and six scenes to a libretto by the composer after the novella by Dostoyevsky, 1915–16, rev. 1927–8

25 *Classical* Symphony (no.1), D major, four movements, 1916–17

26 Concerto no.3 for piano and orchestra, C major, three movements, 1917–21 (with ideas from 1911)

27 Five Poems of Anna Akhmatova for voice and piano, 1916
1 *Solntse komnatu napolnilo* ['The sun has filled the room']
2 *Nastoyashchuyu nezhnostu* ['True Tenderness']
3 *Pamyat o solntse* ['Memory of the Sun']
4 *Zdravstvuy!* ['Greetings!']
5 *Seroglazy korol* ['The Grey-Eyed King']

28 Sonata no.3 for piano, A minor, one movement ('from old notebooks'; rev. of Sonata no.3, 1907), 1917

29 Sonata no.4 for piano, C minor, three movements ('from old notebooks'; rev. of Sonata no.5, 1908; the Andante is based on the slow movement of the Symphony in E minor, 1908), 1917

29*a* Andante from Sonata no.4, transcribed for orchestra, 1934

30 *Semero ikh* ['Seven, they are seven'], cantata for tenor, chorus and orchestra to the text of an Akkadian inscription translated by Balmont, 1917–18, rev. 1933

31 *Skazki staroy babushki* ['Tales of an Old Grandmother'], four pieces for piano, 1918

— Rimsky-Korsakov's song *The nightingale enslaved by the rose* arranged for voice and small orchestra
Organ Prelude and Fugue, D minor, by Buxtehude, arr. for piano, 1918
Five Popular Songs of Kazakhstan

32 Four Pieces for piano, 1918
1 Dance
2 Minuet
3 Gavotte
4 Waltz

— Waltzes by Schubert arr. as a suite for piano, 1918, rev. for two pianos, four hands, 1923

33 *Lyubov k tryom apelsinam* ['The Love for Three Oranges'], opera in four acts and ten scenes with prologue to a libretto by the composer after the tale by Carlo Gozzi, 1919

33*a* *The Love for Three Oranges,* symphonic suite, five movements, 1922

33*b* March and Scherzo from *The Love for Three Oranges* arr. for piano, 1918

34 *Overture on Hebrew Themes* for clarinet, two violins, viola, cello and piano, C minor, 1919

34*a* *Overture on Hebrew Themes,* arr. for small orchestra, 1934

35 Five Songs without Words for voice and piano, 1920

35*a* Five Songs without Words arr. for violin and piano, 1925

36 Five Poems of Konstantin Balmont for voice and piano, 1921
1 *Zaklinaniye vodï i ognya* ['An Incantation of Fire and Water']
2 *Golos ptits* ['Birdsong']
3 *Babochka* ['The Butterfly']
4 *Pomni menya* ['Remember me: A Malayan Incantation']
5 *Stolby* ['The Pillars']

37 *Ognenny angel* ['The Fiery Angel'], opera in five acts and seven scenes to a libretto by the composer after the novel by Valery Bryusov, 1919–27

38 Sonata no.5 for piano, C major, three movements, 1923, rev. 1952–3 as op.135

39 Quintet for oboe, clarinet, violin, viola and double bass, G minor, five movements,1924 (score for the ballet *Trapéze,* to which the Overture and *Matelote* were added, 1925)

40 Symphony no.2, D minor, two movements, 1924

41 *Stalnoy skok* (*Le Pas d'acier*) ['The Steel Step'], ballet in two scenes to a scenario by the composer and Georgy Yakulov, 1925–6

41*a* *Le Pas d'acier,* symphonic suite, four movements, 1926

42 Overture (*American* Overture), for flute, oboe, two clarinets, bassoon, two trumpets, trombone, celesta, two harps, two pianos, cello, two double basses and percussion, 1926

42*a* Overture (*American* Overture), for orchestra, 1928

43 Divertimento for orchestra, four movements, 1929 (the first and third movements are rev. versions of the Overture and *Matelote* for *Trapèze,* 1925)

43*a* Divertissement for piano, four movements (arr. of Divertimento op.43), 1928/1938

44 Symphony no.3, C minor, four movements, 1928 (material and most of the orchestration from *The Fiery Angel*)

45 *Veshch v sebye* (*Chose en soi*), two pieces for piano, 1928 [*Chose en soi A, Chose en soi B*]
46 *L'Enfant prodigue* ['The Prodigal Son'], ballet in three scenes to a scenario by Boris Kochno after the New Testament, 1928
46*a* *L'Enfant prodigue*, symphonic suite, five movements, 1929–30
47 Symphony no.4, C major, 1929–30 (material mostly from *L'Enfant prodigue*; second version, with new material, op.112, 1947)
48 Sinfonietta, A major, five movements (rev. version of op.5), 1929
49 *Four Portraits and Dénouement from The Gambler* for orchestra, five movements, 1931
50 String Quartet no.1, B minor, 1930
50*a* Andante from String Quartet no.1 arr. for string orchestra, 1930
51 *Sur le Borysthène* ['On the Dnieper'], ballet in two scenes to a scenario by Serge Lifar and the composer, 1930
51*a* *Sur le Borysthène*, suite for orchestra, six movements, 1933
52 Six Pieces for piano, 1930–31 (each is a transcription of an existing movement, given in parentheses)
  1 Intermezzo (*L'Enfant prodigue*, no.1, 'The Departure')
  2 Rondo (*L'Enfant prodigue*, no.3, 'The Siren')
  3 *Étude* (*L'Enfant prodigue*, no.7, 'Plunder')
  4 Scherzino (Five Songs op.35 no.4)
  5 Andante (String Quartet no.1, third movement)
  6 Scherzo (Sinfonietta, fourth movement)
53 Concerto no.4 for piano (left hand) and orchestra, B flat major, four movements, 1931
54 Two Sonatinas for piano, E minor and G major, each three movements, 1931–2
55 Concerto no.5 for piano and orchestra, G major, five movements, 1932
56 Sonata for two violins, C major, four movements, 1932
57 *Symphonic Song* for orchestra, 1933
58 Concerto for cello and orchestra, E minor, 1933–8
59 Three Pieces for piano, 1933–4
  1 *Progulka* ['Promenade']
  2 *Peyzazh* ['Landscape']
  3 *Pastoral Sonatina*
— *Poruchik Kizhe* ['Lieutenant Kijé], music for the film by Alexander Feinzimmer after the story by Yury Tynyanov, 1933
60 *Lieutenant Kijé*, symphonic suite, five movements, 1934 (optional solo baritone part in the third and fourth movements)
— *Yegipetskiye nochi* ['Egyptian Nights'], incidental music for a play incorporating scenes from Shaw's *Caesar and Cleopatra*, Shakespeare's *Antony and Cleopatra* and Pushkin's poem *Egyptian Nights*, 1934
61 *Egyptian Nights*, symphonic suite, seven movements, 1934
62 *Mysli* (*Pensées*) ['Thoughts'], three pieces for piano, 1933–4
63 Concerto no.2 for violin and orchestra, G minor, three movements, 1935
64 *Romeo i Dzhulyetta* ['Romeo and Juliet'], ballet in four acts and an epilogue to a scenario by the composer, Sergey Radlov, Adrian Pyotrovsky and later Leonid Lavrovsky after the play by Shakespeare, 1935–6
64*a* *Romeo and Juliet*, Suite no.1 for orchestra, seven movements, 1936
64*b* *Romeo and Juliet*, Suite no.2 for orchestra, seven movements, 1936 (a third suite, op.101, followed, 1946; ten pieces arr. for piano, op.75, 1937
65 *Detskaya muzyka* ['Music for Children'], 12 pieces for piano, 1935
65*a* *Letny den* ['Summer Day'], children's suite for small orchestra (arr. of op.65 nos.1, 9, 6, 5, 10–12)
66 Six Mass Songs for voice and piano (1935)
  1 *Partizan Zheleznyak*
  2 *Anyutka*
  1 *Rastyot strana* ['My Country is Growing']
  2 *Skvoz snega i tumani* ['Through Snow and Fog']
  3 *Za goroyu* ['Beyond the Hill']
  4 *Pesnya o Voroshilova* ['Song of Voroshilov']
69 Four Marches for military band: no.1, *March for the Spartakiad*, 1935

Recordings

The Aeolian Duo-Art reproducing piano company (see Chapter 7, pp. 157–8)

Prokofiev's own works

Prelude op.12 no.7 (6153), May 1919
March op.12 no.1 (6160, D299, D737), June 1919
Sarcasms op.17 nos. 1 and 2 (6210, D205), Dec 1919
Gavotte op.12 no.2 (6253), March 1920
Rigaudon op.12 no.3 (6344), Oct 1920
Toccata op.11 (6391), Feb 1921
Intermezzo (Scherzo) from *The Love for Three Oranges* op.33 (6477), Oct 1921
March from *The Love for Three Oranges* op.33 (8018; unpublished), Jan 1922
Scherzo op.12 no.10 (6774), July 1924
Tales of an Old Grandmother op.31 no.3 (6826), Dec 1924

Works by other composers

Rakhmaninov: Prelude op.23 no.5 (6198, A94, D753), Nov 1919
Glazunov: Gavotte op.49 no.3 (6377, D371), Dec 1920
Skryabin: Prelude op.45 no.3 and *Poème ailé* op.51 no.3 (6512, D7), March 1922
Musorgsky: 'Bydlo' and 'Ballet of the Chicks in their Shells' from *Pictures at an Exhibition* (6591), Jan 1923
Rimsky-Korsakov (arr. Prokofiev): *Fantasia on Themes from Sheherazade* (7001), May 1926
Musorgsky: 'Promenade' and 'The Old Castle' from *Pictures at an Exhibition* (7029), mid-1926
Myaskovsky: *Grillen* (*Prichudi*), op.25 nos.1 and 6 (7388), March 1930

His Master's Voice

Prokofiev's own works

Third Piano Concerto in C major op.26: Prokofiev (piano), London Symphony Orchestra/Piero Coppola (HMV DB1725–27), London, 27–8 June 1932
Visions fugitives op.22 nos.9, 3, 17, 18 (side A), 11, 10, 16, 6, 5 (side B) (HMV DB5030), Paris, 12 Feb 1935
Suggestion diabolique op.4 no.4, *Tales of an Old Grandmother* op.31 no.2 (side A), *Pastoral Sonatina* op.59 no.3 (side B) (HMV DB5031), Paris, 12 (Sonatina) and 26 Feb 1935
Tales of an Old Grandmother op.31 no.3, Gavotte from the *Classical* Symphony op.25 (side A), *Étude* op.52 no.3, *Landscape* op.59 no.2 (side B) (HMV DB5032), Paris, 12 (side A) and 25 Feb 1935
Sonata no.4 in C minor op.29, Andante (sides A and B part 1), Gavotte op.32 no.3 (side B part 2) (HMV DB 5033), Paris, 4 March 1935

Recital programmes

Prokofiev's recital repertoire was carefully tailored to his audiences; it ranges from the more conservative programmes of his own and others' music encouraged by American promoters to the uncompromising performances of new works for a more progressive public in Brussels. The following brief selection includes two programmes he gave with his wife and the last of his recitals with the violinist Robert Soetens, for whom he composed the Second Violin Concerto. Works by other composers are given as they appear on the programmes (usually typed out for Prokofiev's reference).

Saratov, 2 February 1917 (all-Prokofiev programme)

First Sonata op.1
Four Études op.2
Suggestion diabolique from Four Pieces op.4
Ten Pieces op.12
Second Sonata op.14
Sarcasms op.17
Encores: *Suggestion diabolique*; Prelude from op.12

San Diego, 22 December 1920

Beethoven: Sonata in A major op.101
Schubert (arr. Prokofiev, though not advertised as such in programme): Waltzes
Rimsky-Korsakov: Novelette
Lyadov: Prelude
Musorgsky: 'Ballet of the Chicks in their Shells' from *Pictures at an Exhibition*
Skryabin: *Poème* op.32
Medtner: *Conte* op.9
Prokofiev: Prelude from Ten Pieces op.12
Gavotte from Four Pieces op.32
Vision fugitive (unspecified)
Scherzo from Ten Pieces op.12
Encores: Beethoven: Country Dance (unspecified); Prokofiev: Gavotte from Ten Pieces op.12; *Étude* no.4 from op.2; *Vision fugitive* (unspecified); Chopin: *Étude* no.3

Two recital programmes with 'Lina Lubera' [*sic*]; the first, planned for the BBC, did not take place owing to Lina's indisposition.

London, 5 December 1927

Prokofiev: Third Sonata op.28
Songs (listed and to be performed in English): Prokofiev: 'Sunlight streaming in the room' from *Five Poems*

of Anna Akhmatova op.27; 'Birdsong', 'The Butterfly' and 'Remember me' from *Five Poems of Konstantin Balmont* op.36

Prokofiev: March and Scherzo from *The Love for Three Oranges* op.33*b*
Tales of an Old Grandmother op.31, nos.2 and 3
Gavotte from the *Classical* Symphony op.25
Gavotte from Four Pieces op.32
Toccata op.11

Songs: Rimsky-Korsakov: Cradle Song from *Boyarinya Vera Sheloga*; Myaskovsky: 'Circles'; Stravinsky: 'A Song of the Dew'

London, 17 January 1932

Prokofiev: Sonatina op.54 no.2

Songs: Musorgsky: Parassia's Song from *Sorochintsy Fair*; Tchaikovsky: 'The Canary'; Taneyev: Minuet op.26; two Russian songs harmonized by Prokofiev: 'Snowflakes' and 'The Snowdrop Tree'; Dukelsky: 'Many Are the Lovely Roses'; Nabokov: 'I Do Not Regret'; Stravinsky: 'A Song of the Dew'

Schubert (arr. Prokofiev): Waltzes
Prokofiev: *Tales of an Old Grandmother* op.31, nos.2 and 3
March and Prelude from Ten Pieces op.12
Suggestion diabolique from Four Pieces op.4

Brussels, 18 March 1929 (all-Prokofiev programme)

Third Sonata op.28
Visions fugitives op.22
Chose en soi op.45 (first performance)
Overture op.43 (opening movement of the Divertissement) (first performance)
March, Rigaudon, Capriccio, *Legenda*, Prelude and Allemande from Ten Pieces op.12
Études op.2, nos.3 and 4

Budapest, 26 February 1936, with Robert Soetens

Prokofiev: Fourth Piano Sonata op.29, Andante
Visions fugitives op.22, ten pieces
Handel: Sonata for violin and piano in A major
Bach: Chaconne (solo for Soetens)
Prokofiev: Third Sonata op.28
Landscape from Three Pieces op.59
Étude from Six Pieces op.52
Tales of an Old Grandmother op.31, no.3
Suggestion diabolique from Four Pieces op.4
Debussy: Sonata for violin and piano

A game of chess

Prokofiev's expertise resulted in momentous chess games with leading players. Among the most remarkable was his defeat of the future world champion José Capablanca in a simultaneous game at the time of the St Petersburg tournament in May 1914. Having lost to Capablanca on previous days, Prokofiev finally achieved victory on the evening of 16 May. The record of that game is reproduced below. The results are given in standard international form, followed in parentheses by what an expert tells me is 'the old schoolboy–familiar intuitive form', which may be 'clearer for the general reader who may, for instance, not have a board marked with the x/y coordinates 1–8 and a–h'. My thanks are due to that expert, Jonathon Brown, for checking and coordinating the following, and to John Saunders of the *British Chess Magazine*.

Capablanca–Prokofiev, 16 May 1914

1 d4 d5 (P–Q4 P–Q4)
2 Nf3 Nf6 (Kt–KB3 Kt–KB3)
3 c4 Bf5 (P–QB4 B–B4)
4 Qb3 Nc6 (Q–Kt3 Kt–B3)
5 Qxb7 Na5 (QxP Kt–QR4)
6 Qa6 Nxc4 (Q–R6 Kt–B5)
7 Nc3 e6 (Kt–B3 P–K3)
8 e4 dxe4 (P–K4 PxP)
9 Bxc4 exf3 (BxKt PxKt)
10 Qc6+ Nd7 (Q–B6 Kt–Q2)
11 g4 Bg6 (P–KKt4 B–Kt3)
12 Bg5 Be7 (B–KKt5 B–K2)
13 Bxe7 Kxe7 (BxB KxB)
14 o–o–o Re8 (o–o–o R–K1)
15 h4 h5 (P–KR4 P–KR4)
16 gxh5 Bxh5 (PxP BxP)
17 Nb5 Kf8 (Kt–Kt5 K–B1)
18 d5 Qf6 (P–Q5 Q–B3)
19 dxe6 Ne5 (PxP Kt–K4)
20 Qc5+ Kg8 (Q–B5+ K–Kt1)
21 exf7+ Bxf7 (PxP+ BxP)
22 Bxf7+ Qxf7 (BxB+ QxB)
23 Kb1 Rab8 (K–Kt1 QR–Kt1)
24 Nxc7 Rbc8 (KtxBP QR–B1)
25 Rc1 Re7 (R–QB1 R–K2)
26 Qd6 Rexc7 (Q–Q6 KR–B2)
27 Rxc7 Qxc7 (RxR QxR)
28 Qe6+ Kh8 (Q–K6+ K–R1)
29 a3 Qc2+ (P–R3 Q–B7+)
30 Ka1 Nd3 (K–R1 Kt–Q6)
31 Rb1 Nxf2 (R–QKt1 Kt–B7)
32 h5 Qc6 (P–R5 Q–B3)
33 Qf5 Ne4 (Q–B5 Kt–K5)
34 Qxf3 Nd2 (QxP Kt–Q7)
35 Qxc6 Rxc6 (QxQ RxQ)
36 Rd1 Rc2 (R–Q1 R–B7)
37 Rg1 Rc5 (R–KKt1 R–B4)
38 Rg6 Rxh5 (R–Kt6 RxP)
39 Ra6 Nb3+ (R–QR6 Kt–Kt6+)
40 Ka2 Ra5 (K–R2 R–R4)
41 Rxa5 Nxa5 (RxR KtxR)
42 b4 g5 (P–Kt4 P–Kt4)
43 Kb2 g4 (K–Kt2 P–Kt5)
44 White resigns (White resigns)

Index

Where composers are mentioned, general references are followed by an alphabetical list of works cited in the text. Items under the heading 'Prokofiev, Sergey' are arranged to provide a chronological outline followed by an alphabetical list of themes and individuals; page numbers in bold type refer to principal discussion of the works.